Isabel Heinemann
Family Values

Isabel Heinemann

Family Values

Divorce, Working Women, and Reproductive Rights
in Twentieth-Century America

Translated by Alex Skinner

The translation of this work was funded by Geisteswissenschaften International – Translation Funding for Work in the Humanities and Social Sciences from Germany, a joint initiative of the Fritz Thyssen Foundation, the German Federal Foreign Office, the collecting society VG WORT and the Bösenverein des Deutschen Buchhandels (German Publishers&Bookseller Asssociation).

ISBN 978-3-11-221494-7
e-ISBN (PDF) 978-3-11-103612-0
e-ISBN (EPUB) 978-3-11-103616-8

Library of Congress Control Number: 2023939395

Bibliographic information published by the Deutsche Nationalbibliothek
The Deutsche Nationalbibliothek lists this publication in the Deutsche Nationalbibliografie; detailed bibliographic data are available on the internet at http://dnb.dnb.de.

© 2025 Walter de Gruyter GmbH, Berlin/Boston
This volume is text- and page-identical with the hardback published in 2023.
First published in German as Heinemann, Isabel. Wert der Familie: Ehescheidung, Frauenarbeit und Reproduktion in den USA des 20. Jahrhunderts. Berlin, Boston: De Gruyter Oldenbourg, 2018.

Cover image: LeoPatrizi/E+/Getty Images
Typesetting: Integra Software Services Pvt. Ltd.
Printing and binding: CPI books GmbH, Leck

www.degruyter.com

Contents

Introduction: family values in a changing society —— 1
1   The American family as the basis of the nation: concepts, key questions, and selection of debates —— 6
2   Norms and values: How can "value change" be studied historically? —— 15
3   Key approaches: gender studies and intersectionality, expert cultures and scientification —— 22
4   The U.S. family in historical research —— 28
5   Period of investigation, sources, and structure —— 33

1   "Race suicide or remedy?" The debates on divorce in the Progressive Era, 1890–1920 —— 40
1.1   Trends in the divorce rate in the United States in the nineteenth and twentieth centuries —— 44
1.2   Divorce as a subject of public debate to the late nineteenth century —— 52
1.3   "Social control and women's place in society": the influence of sociologists on public debates on divorce from the turn of the century onward —— 64
1.4   Religious values versus adaptation to modernity: key groups within the divorce debate and their arguments —— 73
1.5   Interim conclusion: social experts as analysts of social change: the family ideal in the United States at the beginning of the twentieth century —— 92

2   "Scientific motherhood, reproductive morality and fitter families": debates on eugenic family concepts and the government's right to intervene in the 1920s and 1930s —— 95
2.1   Demographic change in the twentieth-century United States: population growth, reproduction rates, and family sizes —— 102
2.2   "Scientific motherhood and reproductive morality" —— 109
2.3   Better Babies and Fitter Families: the popularization of the "healthy family" through competitions —— 117
2.4   Forced eugenic sterilizations for the betterment of the American family —— 129

2.5		Paul B. Popenoe, *The Conservation of the Family* and the American Institute for Family Relations —— **138**
2.6		Interim conclusion: government and family in the 1920s and 1930s —— **151**
3		**"Working women, domesticity, and the expert": public debates and expert discourses on women's employment and motherhood, 1940–1970 —— 154**
3.1		Trends in female employment between 1940 and 1970 —— **159**
3.2		"Career woman or housewife?": the debate on women's employment in the shadow of World War II —— **166**
3.3		"Mom as a social problem": the debate on "momism" and failing mothers in the 1940s —— **174**
3.4		"Women aren't men" or the "return of the new women": motherhood and women's employment in the 1950s —— **178**
3.5		"Modern women's neurosis": the working woman's psyche and reproduction as sites of negotiation of divergent gender role conceptions, 1950–1970 —— **183**
3.6		*The Feminine Mystique* and *Equality between the Sexes*: feminists, women social scientists, and the working woman —— **196**
3.7		"A long and difficult up-hill struggle": African American women, women's work, and motherhood —— **201**
3.8		Interim conclusion: interpretive conflicts over the employment, psyche, and reproduction of the 'modern woman' —— **205**
4		**"Black family pathologies": the limits of the white middle-class family ideal and the debate on the structure and values of the African American family in the 1960s —— 208**
4.1		The changing social structure of African American families in the twentieth century —— **211**
4.2		"The Negro family in America": structure and values of the African American family in the research of black sociologists —— **217**
4.3		From the "American dilemma" to the "tangle of pathology": the black family in the analyses of contemporary social scientists from the 1940s to the 1960s —— **221**
4.4		"To Fulfill these Rights" and the Moynihan Report: June 1965 —— **230**
4.5		Perceptions of the Moynihan Report in the African American community —— **243**

4.6	Plans to improve the African American family as a key example of the "scientification of the social" in the mid-1960s —— **257**	
4.7	"Race genocide?" Black men and white concepts of masculinity in the 1960s —— **263**	
4.8	Interim conclusion: toward an expansion of the national ideal of the family —— **269**	
5	**"From reproductive choice to reproductive rights": abortion, reproduction, and the role of women in family and society in the 1970s and 1980s —— 271**	
5.1	"Sexual revolution" and "women's health": social change in the use of contraceptives and in access to legal abortion since the 1960s —— **276**	
5.2	"From reproductive choice to reproductive rights": the U.S. women's movement and the struggle over access to self-determined reproduction —— **285**	
5.3	Legal framework: *Roe v. Wade* and the implications for the negotiation of gender roles —— **295**	
5.4	The campaign to reduce global population growth, the role of population experts, and the reproduction of the white American woman —— **305**	
5.5	"Race," "class," and "reproductive rights." African American women and their struggle for access to self-determined reproduction —— **317**	
5.6	"Dramatic shift in the American temperament": the debates on divorce and the introduction of no-fault divorce —— **324**	
5.7	Interim conclusion: abortion as a constitutional right —— **328**	
6	**"Culture wars?" Debates on the American family in the 1980s —— 331**	
6.1	"Dual earners and welfare moms": the social history of the family in the 1980s —— **333**	
6.2	Jimmy Carter's White House Conference on families and the U.S. family in the early 1980s —— **345**	
6.3	Ronald Reagan's "traditional family values" campaign and its place in the "culture wars" —— **352**	
6.4	Abortion and adoption as two poles of reproductive decision-making in the 1980s —— **362**	
6.5	Interim conclusion: the family as arena of the "culture wars" —— **386**	

Conclusion: Value of the family—continuity and change in the family ideal in the twentieth-century United States —— 388
1 Debates and expert discourses on divorce, women's employment, and reproduction in the twentieth century—a diachronic overview —— **389**
2 Family values and social change in the modern age —— **392**
3 The family as the basis of the nation and the significance of "race, class, and gender" as categories of inequality —— **398**
4 The value of the family rather than value change —— **403**

Acknowledgments —— 407

Abbreviations —— 411

List of figures —— 413

List of tables —— 417

Bibliography —— 419

Person Index —— 487

Subject Index —— 491

Introduction: family values in a changing society

"I desperately wanted a baby. Life without children was not the future I had imagined. I had so much to give and to teach to my potential children." In November 2022, at the age of eighty-seven, Marjorie Perlman Shafton, a Jewish philanthropist and community activist from Chicago, wrote a letter to the *New York Times*.[1] She related her very personal story of starting a family in the 1960s, a step she had longed to take but that proved extremely difficult. After fertility treatment and the surgical termination of a life-threatening ectopic pregnancy, she finally decided to adopt. "I went on to adopt two children, my daughter and son, and I have seven caring grandchildren. I have lived a wonderful and full life with a loving family, a life I have devoted in service to my community for the greater good." The equation of "family" with "successful life" and "service to the community" that shines through here is a recurring motif in discourses and debates about the public and private spheres, family values, and individual reproductive decision-making in the twentieth and early twenty-first century United States. But why did an educated, upper-middle-class woman of almost ninety decide to make a public statement about her traumatic experience of terminating a pregnancy more than sixty years ago, under her own name, in the largest daily newspaper in the United States?

Unsurprisingly, it was the current controversy over abortion in the United States that prompted Shafton to share some of her life story, a narrative that culminates in an unambiguous plea for choice. "I was fortunate that I lived in a time when the expertise of my doctor took precedence over a politician's ideology [. . .] I write this as someone who survived a traumatic pregnancy, whose baby could not have lived and I might have died at the young age of 26. I fervently hope that generations to come will have the same choice." The proximate trigger for her letter to the editor was a column by a conservative journalist, Ross Douthat. In the previous week's edition of the same paper, he had calculated that one year after legal abortion had ceased to exist in many states in the U.S. (following the controversial Supreme Court ruling of June 2022), some 60,000 babies would be born whose mothers had in fact wanted an abortion, a

---

[1] Marjorie Perlman Shafton, "Letter to the Editor," *New York Times*, November 19, 2022, https://www.nytimes.com/2022/11/19/opinion/letters/abortion-dobbs-midterm-elections.html. For a brief biography of Shafton, see the short article in *Jewish Chicago: The JUF Magazine*, August 23, 2007, https://www.juf.org/news/local.aspx?id=25532. In 2007, Shafton was awarded the Julius Rosenwald Memorial Award for her decades of service to the Jewish community, among other things as president of the Jewish Children's Bureau and Chairman of the Jewish United Fund/Jewish Federation Board of Directors.

development he considered a great success for the "pro-life" movement.[2] Reflecting on her own experience, Shafton asked rhetorically, "Would our world be better if governmental officials had the power to reject my lifesaving surgery because of their personal pro-life beliefs?"

Shafton's abortion was unambiguously necessary from a medical point of view and was performed at a time (1961) when there was no uniform nationwide regulation of legal abortions. Yet her statement leads right into the middle of the current political debate in the U.S. on the legality of abortions, the embryo's right to life, and the woman's right to decide—a debate also bound up with the meaning of family and family values against the backdrop of social change. Her words thus take us right to the heart of this book.

On June 24, 2022, in the case of *Dobbs v. Jackson Women's Health Center*, the majority conservative Supreme Court overturned the epoch-making abortion ruling that had been in force for nearly five decades—the *Roe v. Wade* decision of January 22, 1973.[3] As a result, the states, no longer bound by *Roe*, can enact their own abortion laws, marking a profound shift toward conservative values at the expense of women's decision-making rights. Women across the country vigorously protested the reversal of the constitutional right to abortion, which had been in effect for nearly fifty years, the judges having argued that such a right was in fact inconsistent with the constitution.[4] Numerous states had already passed so-called "heartbeat bills" to effectively restrict legal abortion, including Mississippi, whose 2018 legislation had prompted the Supreme Court to revisit the topic.

The Supreme Court's decision is also the consequence of long-term trends since the 1980s. Both representatives of the religious right and conservative Republicans had placed the fetus's right to life above the mother's right to decide

---

[2] Ross Douthat, "Opinion: What the Pro-Life Movement Lost and Won," *New York Times*, November 12, 2022. https://www.nytimes.com/2022/11/12/opinion/sunday/what-the-pro-life-movement-lost-and-won.html.

[3] Supreme Court ruling in *Dobbs v. Jackson Women's Health Organization*, June 24, 2022 (597 U.S. _ 2022) https://www.supremecourt.gov/docket/docketfiles/html/public/19-1392.html. This ruling, in stating that the U.S. constitution does not include a "right to abortion" under the 14th Amendment, not only overruled the legalization of first-trimester abortion by *Roe v. Wade* (1973), but also overturned other rulings (such as *Planned Parenthood v. Casey*, 1992). See also "Opinion: 'Abortion is Just the Beginning'. Six Experts on the Decision Overturning Roe," *New York Times*, June 24, 2022, https://www.nytimes.com/interactive/2022/06/24/opinion/politics/dobbs-decision-perspectives.html.

[4] "The Dobbs v. Jackson Decision, Annotated," *New York Times*, 24 June, 2022. https://www.nytimes.com/interactive/2022/06/24/us/politics/supreme-court-dobbs-jackson-analysis-roe-wade.html.

and had consistently worked toward overturning *Roe v. Wade,* while advocates of legal abortion warned against the successive erosion of individual rights in the name of conservative moral politics. Many critics were also concerned about a possible domino effect, that is, the gradual abolition of other liberal legal provisions, and highlighted the social costs of the abortion ban. Suddenly, affluence, place of residence, and often minority status once again came into play, as only some women could make expensive trips to states with liberal abortion laws or pay privately for an abortion not covered by health insurance.

The debate over the legality of first-trimester abortions, one that steadily increased in intensity from the 1960s onward and reached an initial peak in the 1970s in the wake of *Roe,* runs like a thread through the history of the United States in the twentieth century.[5] The struggle for self-determined reproduction also exposes the history of systemic racial discrimination in the U.S. like no other issue, and can only be properly narrated from an intersectional perspective. While in the 1960s and 1970s it was predominantly white, middle-class women who battled for the legalization of abortion as an embodiment of "reproductive choice," ethnic minority women began to point out that they were being denied their reproductive rights due to forced sterilizations, still common until the early 1970s, and strict rules on welfare.[6] In response to activist protests and growing public criticism, the states ended their sterilization programs in the early 1970s. Influenced by the Black Feminism of the 1980s, meanwhile, representatives of the white women's movement began to recognize that every woman's right to have and raise children also required protection ("reproductive rights"). In the new millennium, a diverse array of women of color fused their demands for reproductive agency and autonomy into the concept of "reproductive justice" (Solinger and Ross, 2017), which has gained in importance partly in the wake of critiques of the (Western) idea of global population control.[7]

---

[5] Reagan, Leslie, *When Abortion was a Crime. Women, Medicine, and Law in the United States, 1867–1973* (Berkeley and Los Angeles 1997), 173–195. Schoen, Johanna, *Abortion after Roe* (Chapel Hill 2015). Ziegler, Mary Joe, "Roe v. Wade and the Rise of Arguments," in Ziegler, Mary Joe, *Abortion and the Law in America: Roe v. Wade to the Present* (Cambridge 2022), 11–26.

[6] Schoen, Johanna, *Choice and Coercion. Birth Control, Sterilization and Abortion in Public Health and Welfare* (University of North Carolina Press, Chapel Hill 2005). Nelson, Jennifer, "'All this that has happened to me shouldn't happen to nobody else': Loretta Ross and the Women of Color Reproductive Freedom Movement of the 1980s," *Journal of Women's History* 22 (3), Fall 2010, 136–160. Nelson, Jennifer, *More Than Medicine. A History of the Feminist Women's Health Movement* (New York 2015).

[7] Ross, Loretta and Solinger, Rickie, *Reproductive Justice: An Introduction* (Oakland CA 2017), esp. 9–17. On the context of global population policies, see Connelly, Matthew, *Fatal Misconception. The Struggle to Control World Population* (Cambridge and London 2008). Hartmann, Betsy, *Repro-*

At the same time, the #MeToo campaign launched in 2017 exposed gender-based violence as a systemic feature of U.S. and most Western societies, ushering in a societal paradigm shift. Yet in parallel we are now witnessing the hardening of sexist prejudices and the insistence on a "traditional" gender order as propagated by growing right-wing populist and ethno-nationalist movements in the U.S. and Europe.[8] As Alexandra M. Stern has shown, in the United States, members of right-wing and far-right movements as diverse as the Proud Boys, right-wing "trad[itional] wives" such as Sarah Dye and Lacey Lynn, and internationally active female right-wing extremists such as Brittany Pettibone and Lana Lokteff use the family to demonstrate the supposed decline of society. They call for the renewal of society not only through racist exclusion, but also through the revival of biologistic gender roles and a patriarchal order—and in some cases seek to model this themselves.[9] At the same time, verbal and physical attacks on gay people and other members of the LGBTQIA+ community are on the rise in the United States, although the federal government has signaled its embrace of civil equality (for example by enshrining the right to marry in 2015).

Clashes over the American family and its values have always been about more than "just" the private choices of the women, couples, and families concerned. They have always entailed an implicit or explicit commentary on the configuration of the gender order and the significance of present and future families to American society. This is the point of departure for the present book, which traces, over the course of the twentieth century, debates on the family and its role; the relationship between the individual and society; and individual decision-making rights as well as their denial or curtailment. It thus recounts the prehistory of the current conflicts over the family and the gender order while also analyzing the relationship between social change, normative change, and counter-

---

ductive Rights and Wrongs: The Global Politics of Population Control (third edition, Chicago 2016, first published 1987). Bracke, Maud Ann, "Women's Rights, Family Planning, and Population Control: The Emergence of Reproductive Rights in the United Nations (1960s–70s)," *The International History Review*, 2021, DOI: 10.1080/07075332.2021.1985585.

8 Heinemann, Isabel and Stern, Alexandra Minna, "Gender and Far Right Nationalism: Historical and International Dimensions," in "Special Issue: Gender and Far Right Nationalism," *Journal of Modern European History* (JMEH) 3, 20 (2022), 311–321. DOI: 10.1177/16118944221110721. Graff, Agnieska and Korolczuk, Elżbieta, *Anti-Gender Politics in the Populist Moment* (London 2021). DOI: 10.4324/9781003133520.

9 Stern, Alexandra Minna, "Gender and the Far-right in the United States: Female Extremists and the Mainstreaming of Contemporary White Nationalism," *Journal of Modern European History*, 20(3), 322–334. DOI: 10.1177/16118944221110101. Stern, Alexandra Minna, *Proud Boys and the White Ethnostate: How the Alt-Right is Warping the American Imagination* (Boston 2019).

movements, as exemplified in the Dobbs ruling, the activism of Republican pro-lifers, and even the demands of right-wing "trad wives."

The debate on the transformation of the family in the United States of the twentieth and twenty-first centuries was repeatedly framed by its protagonists as a conflict over the "right" family values. The latter term has served as a battle cry for conservatives in the U.S. in recent decades, particularly the religious right.[10] It is currently associated chiefly with traditional and conservative values and is based on the idea that the family plays a key role in strengthening society. For much of the twentieth century, the family was—as it often still is—imagined as a heteronormative nuclear family, consisting of married parents of different sexes and their biological children. This contrasted and continues to contrast with a variety of alternative ways of life and social practices—same-sex couples (and/or parents), single parenthood, families by choice and patchwork families, sexuality without reproduction and cohabitation without a marriage certificate, divorce and remarriage, to name but a few. Around the middle of the last century, commonly misinterpreted as the "golden age of the family," Americans already lived in highly diverse family arrangements, a fact studiously ignored by advocates of supposedly timeless "family values." There is a chasm between family values and the social practices through which the family is lived, a fact that has led to bitter conflicts due to the widespread equation of "family" with "nation."

The intensity of the disputes over the family and its values in past and present is illustrated by the fraught debates in the media conducted since the 1990s in connection with the culture wars. Here, to put it in a nutshell, religion and moral values have replaced politics and economics as indicators of the state—and state of mind—of society and nation and, at the same time, as key fields of social conflict.[11] In this context, "family values" operated and continue to function as conservatives' main counter-concept to an order supposedly threatened by legal abortion, same-sex marriage, gay and transgender rights, feminism, and the teaching of evolution in schools.[12] Right-wing family organizations such as Focus on the Family (FOTF,

---

10 Dowland, Seth, Family Values and the Rise of the Christian Right (Philadelphia 2015). Hoffman, Jana, Sexing Religion: Sexualität, Familie und Geschlecht im amerikanischen Mainline-Protestantismus (Berlin and Boston 2021).
11 On the "culture wars," see chapter 6 of the present book and Hunter, James Davison, *Culture Wars. The Struggle to Define America. Making Sense of the Battles over the Family, Art, Education, Law and Politics* (New York 1991). Browning, Don S. et al., *From Culture Wars to Common Ground. Religion and the American Family Debate* (Louisville KY 1997). Hartman, Andrew, *A War for the Soul of America. A History of the Culture Wars* (Chicago and London 2015). See also the critique by Thomson, Irene Taviss, *Culture Wars and Enduring American Dilemmas* (Ann Arbor 2010).
12 The term "cultural war" was coined by Republican Patrick J. Buchanan, unsuccessful candidate for the presidential nomination, in his Republican National Convention Speech of August 17,

founded by James Dobson in 1977) and the Christian Coalition of America (CCA, founded by Pat Robertson in 1987) began calling for a renewed embrace of the "intact family" in the 1970s, contrasting it with the supposed decline of family values and structures since the 1960s. On the liberal spectrum, meanwhile, People for the American Way (PFAW), founded in 1981 by film producer and journalist Norman Lear, began to monitor the spread of religiously based attacks on civil rights in the U.S., not least with respect to family and reproduction.

Thus, the evocation of supposedly timeless "family values," the family as institution, concept, and set of values—and ultimately the gender order and the social order as a whole—represent a key field of social conflict in the United States that spans the entire twentieth and early twenty-first centuries.

The conflict over the American family and its values provides an ideal field of inquiry if we wish to analyze the relationship between social change and norm change in the twentieth-century United States. That is what this book sets out to do. Through a long-term study covering the period from 1890 to the late 1980s, I examine key social debates—concerning divorce, women's work, and reproduction—in the light of the family values and gender norms with which they grappled. I pay particular attention to discussions in the national press as well as the expert discourses of social scientists and their repercussions. The book's crucial innovation is the lengthy period examined and the analytical linkage of a wide variety of topics related to the family, enabling the integrative yet focused investigation of social change.

1 The American family as the basis of the nation: concepts, key questions, and selection of debates

In the United States—as in all modern Western societies and far beyond them—the family was and is regarded as the basis of the nation, the smallest social unit after the individual. To this day, it is regarded as vitally important to the state of society. By the same token, the polity seems to be changeable and improvable only through intervention in families. This emotional, social, and national imbuing of the concept explains why the "family," its condition, and its well-being have been at the center of heated expert discourses and public debates since the rise of modern industrial society. Since the beginning of the twentieth century at the latest, the dominant model has been that of the white middle-class nuclear

---

1992. The speech can be retrieved at his official website: http://buchanan.org/blog/1992-republican-national-convention-speech-148.

family, consisting of parents and their children. This has either been challenged as a patriarchal symbol of oppression and ethnic-social discrimination or invoked as the sole remedy for social ills. Both the defenders of the associated gender hierarchies, "racial value," and generational relations, and the proponents of normative pluralization, who sought to achieve recognition for extended, matrifocal, single-parent, and patchwork families, those headed by same-sex couples, and other variants, have invoked the nuclear family model—if only to criticize it as outdated.

"Family" is understood in this book as a bigenerational unit, as this most closely reflects the contemporary U.S. conception, which exclusively privileges the parent-child relationship: family is constituted by the presence of children, regardless of whether we are talking about a single-parent family or one in which both parents are present.[13] My focus in the present study, however, is on the conflictual negotiation of family values in the course of the twentieth century.

From the end of the nineteenth century onward, questions such as "What is a family?," "Who are its members?," "What functions does it fulfill?," and "What structures and values underpin the concept?" were the starting point both for public debates and clashing interpretations by social experts in the United States.[14] The topic of the "family" has always been linked to the question of what exactly successful family relationships might be and which families should be considered "at risk" or "failed" from the perspective of the nation. Until the 1960s, it was the white middle-class nuclear family that was widely viewed as the ideal in the United States.[15] Immigrant families, working-class families, families of Mexican descent and African American families, meanwhile, were regarded by most social experts as pathological deviations from the family ideal of the majority society. Due to their language, culture, economic performance, family size, structure and hierarchy, but also their family values, hygiene practices or simply their skin color, scholars and

---

[13] Varenne, Hervé, "Love and Liberty. Die moderne amerikanische Familie," in Burguière, Andre et al. (eds.), *Geschichte der Familie*, vol. 4: *20. Jahrhundert* (Frankfurt a. M. etc. 1998), 59–90, here 59. At the same time, the strict focus on children underlines the dual function of family as a unit that guarantees both biological reproduction and the transmission of values to the next generation. Stephanie Coontz thus describes family as a "socially sanctioned relationship between social and biological reproduction." Coontz, Stephanie, *The Social Origins of Private Life. A History of American Families 1600–1900* (London 1988), 12.

[14] Following Lutz Raphael and others, "social experts" are understood to be academics in the human sciences who sought to reform and shape their own society, here in connection with the family and its values. See also my later remarks in this chapter.

[15] Mead, Margaret and Heyman, Ken, *Family* (New York 1965).

reformers classified them as deficient and made them the object of education, re-education, and social programs.[16]

The conceptual basis for debates on the family in the second half of the twentieth century was laid by U.S. sociologist Talcott Parsons.[17] In 1942, for the first time he identified the "isolation of the individual conjugal family" as the key trait of the contemporary familial structure.[18] Shortly thereafter, he condensed his model into the "modern isolated nuclear family," by which he meant a bigenerational family unit, limited to the heterosexual couple and their children and detached from extended kinship networks or intergenerational relationships.[19] According to Parsons, this model of the isolated nuclear family, based on the division of labor, was best adapted to the requirements of modern industrial society, since it allowed the full mobilization of the man's labor for breadwinning while concentrating responsibility for rearing and educating the children in the woman. Parsons argued that geographical and emotional distance from wider family networks reduced their importance, which concurrently freed the nuclear unit to change its place of residence as often as necessary according to the demands of the labor market, without regard to established social relations. Yet Parsons believed that the nuclear family was ideally suited to providing its members with emotional warmth and social support in an impersonal world, while the school and peer groups took over some of the socialization of offspring previously provided by the family. For Parsons, this

---

16 Ladd-Taylor, Molly and Umansky, Lauri, (eds.), *Bad Mothers. The Politics of Blame in Twentieth-Century America* (New York 1998). Chappell, Marisa, *The War on Welfare. Family, Poverty, and Politics in Modern America* (University of Pennsylvania Press, Philadelphia 2010). Patterson, James T., Freedom is not Enough. The Moynihan Report and America's Struggle over Black Family Life from LBJ to Obama (New York 2010). Overbeck, Anne, At the Heart of It All: Discourses on the Reproductive Rights of African American Women (Berlin and Boston 2019).
17 Talcott Parsons (1902–1979) was a U.S. sociologist and one of the defining figures of U.S. sociology in the twentieth century. He taught sociology at Harvard University from 1930 to 1973. Due to his structural-functionalist and later system-functionalist analyses, he was one of the most influential sociological theorists in the U.S. from the immediate post-World War II period into the 1960s. On Parsons, see esp. the research of Gerhardt, Uta, *Talcott Parsons—An Intellectual Biography* (New York 2002). Gerhardt, Uta, *The Social Thought of Talcott Parsons: Methodology and American Ethos* (Farnham, Surrey 2011).
18 Parsons, Talcott, "Age and Sex in the Social Structure of the United States," *American Sociological Review* 7, 5 (October 1942), 604–616, here 615.
19 Parsons, Talcott, "The Kinship System of the Contemporary United States," *American Anthropologist* 45 (1943), no. 1, 22–38. Parsons, Talcott, "The Social Structure of the Family," in Anshen, Ruth Nanda (ed.), *The Family. Its Function and Destiny* (New York 1949), 173–201, here 179. Parsons, Talcott, "The American Family. Its Relations to Personality and the Social Structure," in Parsons, Talcott and Bales, R.F. (eds.), *Family, Socialization and Interaction Process* (New York and London 1955), 3–33, here 9–11 and 21.

isolation and self-referentiality of the nuclear family was symbolized in ideal-typical fashion by the suburban home, an observation that seemed confirmed by the postwar construction boom in single-family housing developments (such as "Levittown").[20] Parsons' normative family model, however, completely ignored the existence of patchwork families and extended family relationships. It was also based on a supposedly natural division of labor between the sexes and the assumption of a *de facto* separation of male and female spheres of action.[21] Parsons' concept of the "modern isolated nuclear family," then, subtly combined a structural description with the attribution of values. It was to prove immensely consequential in debates on the family in the second half of the twentieth century, both as supposed ideal and as the target of searing critique.

There is a broad consensus among historians that a significant pluralization of the values and gender norms associated with family occurred in the second half of the twentieth century, a phenomenon they view chiefly as the result of the various social movements, especially the civil rights, student, and women's movements. But they have yet to clearly identify the stages of this shift, its pace, and which parts of society it encompassed.[22] Historians are also largely as one in assuming that a conception of "family" tailored to the nuclear unit could emerge in the United States only under the conditions of nascent industrial society, more

---

[20] Baxandall, Rosalyn and Ewen, Elizabeth, *Picture Windows. How the Suburbs Happened* (New York 2000), Jackson, Kenneth, *Crabgrass Frontier. The Suburbanization of the United States* (New York and Oxford 1985).

[21] On the development of the concept of "separate spheres" in modernity, see Rosaldo, Michelle, "The Use and Abuse of Anthropology. Reflections on Feminism and Cross Cultural Understanding," *Signs* 5 (1980), no. 3, 392–416. Rosenberg, Rosalind, *Beyond Separate Spheres. Intellectual Roots of Modern Feminism* (New Haven and London 1982). Hausen, Karin, "Family and Role-Division. The Polarization of Sexual Stereotypes in the Nineteenth Century. An Aspect of Dissociation of Work and Family Life," in Evans, Richard J., and Lee, W. R. (eds.), *Social History of the Family in Nineteenth- and Twentieth-Century Germany* (London 1981), 51–83 (first German edition 1976). Butler, Judith, *Bodies that Matter. On the Discursive Limits of "Sex"* (New York 1993). Bourdieu, Pierre, *La Domination Masculine* (Paris 1998).

[22] Coontz, Stephanie, *The Way We Never Were. American Families and the Nostalgia Trap* (New York 1992). Coontz, Stephanie, *The Way We Really Are. Coming to Terms with America's Changing Families* (New York 1997). Coontz, Stephanie, Parson, Maya, and Raley, Gabrielle (eds.), *American Families. A Multicultural Reader* (New York 1998, revised edition New York 2008). Weiss, Jessica, *To Have and to Hold. Marriage, the Baby Boom and Social Change* (Chicago and London 2000). Zaretsky, Natasha, *No Direction Home. The American Family and the Fear of National Decline, 1968–1980* (Philadelphia 2007). Heinemann, Isabel, "Introduction. Inventing the Modern American Family—Family Values and Social Change in 20th Century United States," in Heinemann, Isabel (ed.), *Inventing the Modern American Family. Family Values and Social Change in 20th Century United States* (Frankfurt a. M. 2012), 7–29. Self, Robert O., *All in the Family. The Realignment of American Democracy since the 1960s* (New York 2012).

precisely in the period encompassing the Civil War, the Industrial Revolution, and the turn of the twentieth century.[23] Previously, nuclear families had coexisted with various extended-family arrangements, which were themselves the outcome of economic and social necessities as well as cultural traditions.[24]

What are the main traits of the "family" at the beginning of the twenty-first century? A virtually ungraspable diversity of family relationships or a surprising constancy of form? U.S. family sociologists give ambivalent answers to this question. In 2008, Andrew J. Cherlin diagnosed an epoch-making change not only in family structure but also in family values. This sociologist argued that whereas fifty years ago the Parsonian nuclear family model had still been widespread, now no particular family structure was dominant: "There is no typical family anymore—at least not in terms of who lives in the household and how they are related."[25] Two years later, social scientists Brian Powell, Catherine Bolzendahl, Claudia Geist and Lala Carr Steelmann found that the majority of Americans now considered same-sex partners and their children to be "families," regardless of whether the parents were married. In contrast, couples living together without a marriage certificate were not considered families as long as they had no children, regardless of their sexual preference.[26]

At first glance, these observations by family sociologists seem to contradict each other. While Cherlin identified a wide spectrum of family forms and relationships, Powell and his colleagues pointed out that most Americans continue to consider bi-generationality, that is, the presence of parents and children, the most important hallmark of a family. Both diagnosed a fundamental liberalization of sexual morality and gender norms in U.S. society over the course of the twentieth century while also highlighting many U.S. citizens' rather traditional

---

[23] The most recent example is Martschukat, Jürgen, *Die Ordnung des Sozialen. Väter und Familien in der amerikanischen Geschichte seit 1770* (Frankfurt a. M. 2013; in English as *American Fatherhood. A History*, [New York 2019]).

[24] Gutman, Herbert G., *The Black Family in Slavery and Freedom 1750–1925* (New York 1976). Mintz, Steven, *A Prison of Expectations. The Family in Victorian Culture* (New York 1983). Mintz, Steven and Kellog, Susan, *Domestic Revolutions. A Social History of American Family Life* (New York 1988). Coontz, *Social Origins of Private Life*. O'Day, Rosemary, *The Family and Family Relationships, 1500–1900. England, France and the United States of America* (Houndmills 1994).

[25] Cherlin, Andrew J., "Public Display. The Picture-Perfect American Family? These Days, It Doesn't Exist," WP, September 7, 2008 <www.washingtonpost.com/wp-dyn/content/article/2008/09/05/AR2008090502652.html>. See also Cherlin, Andrew J., *The Marriage-Go-Round. The State of Marriage and the Family in America Today* (New York 2009). Cherlin, Andrew J., *Public and Private Families. An Introduction* (sixth edition, New York 2010).

[26] Powell, Brian et al. (eds.), *Counted Out. Same Sex Relations and American Definitions of Family* (New York 2010), 204.

understanding of family in the early twenty-first century, especially with regard to structure (parents plus children). How might we explain this tension between the pluralization of norms and the simultaneous insistence on traditional forms?

This is the starting point for the present book, which seeks to investigate whether and if so how the dominant understanding of the family in the United States changed in the twentieth century. In brief, I first ask to what extent the family functioned as an arena of conflict-laden attempts to grapple with the challenges of modernity. Can the ambivalent processes of pluralization and liberalization so typical of modern societies—and the corresponding counter-movements—be discerned in the field of family values? Can these processes explain why family in the twenty-first century is often viewed as a combination of liberal values and traditional forms?[27]

Second, against the background of accelerated social change (industrialization, urbanization, greater social and regional mobility, internal migration, expansion of the middle class), but also profound normative shifts (negotiation of gender norms, pluralization of lifestyles, processes of scientification), I scrutinize to what extent we can discern a connection between social and normative change with reference to the family, and how any such interrelation developed over time. To put it more pointedly: Is it even possible to demonstrate empirically a "change in values" with respect to the family, or do the sources show clear continuities in traditional family models and patriarchal gender norms?

The notion of what "family" can or should be, or must not be, as conveyed by the concept of family values (along with that of "family norms" and the "family ideal"), is a potent means of investigating processes of normative transformation, since the family has been generally accepted as the most important micro-unit of society after the individual. Public debates and expert discourses on the family, its structures, and its values have always reaffirmed its importance as the supposed "basis of the nation." Hence, my third question is how exactly this equation of family and nation came to be, what arguments supported it, and whether we can make out fault lines or realignments over the course of the twentieth century.

---

[27] On the complex processes of liberalization and pluralization in West Germany, see Herbert, Ulrich, "Liberalisierung als Lernprozess. Die Bundesrepublik in der deutschen Geschichte—eine Skizze," in Herbert, Ulrich (ed.), *Wandlungsprozesse in Westdeutschland. Belastung, Integration, Liberalisierung 1945–1980* (Göttingen 2002), 7–49. Doering-Manteuffel, Anselm, *Wie westlich sind die Deutschen? Amerikanisierung und Westernisierung im 20. Jahrhundert* (Göttingen 1999). Chafe, William H., *The Unfinished Journey. America since World War II* (New York and Oxford 2003). Marwick, Arthur, *The Sixties. Cultural Revolution in Britain, France, Italy, and the United States, 1958–1974* (Oxford 1998).

The family ideal of the white "middle class" had a formative effect on all Americans in the twentieth century. Regardless of the specific family arrangements in which people lived, no one could evade the normative ideal of family conveyed by politics and the media, expert advice and advertising. Fourth, then, I examine the extent to which the concept of the white nuclear family served as a projection screen for hopes of integration and advancement (for immigrants and members of ethnic minorities, for example), but also inspired strategies of diversification and demarcation (for instance among members of the new social movements).

Fifth, I scrutinize changes in gender norms within the family and in public discourse. Here, the new laws on divorce, labor, and abortion suggest that female gender norms in particular became more diverse, while women were granted more rights. That these rights could also be rolled back again is illustrated by the Supreme Court decision of June 2022, mentioned at the beginning of this introduction, which overturned the nationwide "right" to legal first-trimester abortion. These developments make it crucial to explore the demands made by various groups of women themselves—in women's movements, as authors of letters to newspapers and magazines, and as recipients of expert advice—and to examine how they used new room for maneuver or sought to oppose the curtailment of their rights. At the same time, it is vital to analyze which norms and roles were ascribed to women by society and in the advisory literature produced by social experts, and how these norms and roles changed over time. We must also shed light on concepts of masculinity and concrete expectations of men ("male breadwinner," "hegemonic masculinity") contained in the family ideal. This allows us to narrate the story of the struggle for appropriate values vis-à-vis the U.S. family and the battle to mold the national family ideal as a story of interwoven concepts of femininity *and* masculinity.

In order to illuminate the "value of the family" and the negotiation of family values in the twentieth century, this book focuses on expert discourses and public debates on divorce, women's work, and reproduction, since these were the major fields of conflict. In addition to mostly male politicians, lawyers, social scientists, journalists and church representatives, the leading actors here were women social reformers, sociologists, and feminists. But the voices of "ordinary" women and men can also be heard, such as writers of readers' letters and activists in local citizens' movements. Still, the statements of male and female experts and their dissemination in the media were of particular importance in these debates. These experts ensured the gradual adaptation of the family ideal to processes of social and cultural change, while also acting as advocates or critics of social change themselves.

I conceptualize public debates as fraught discourses that reach a significant national public and that involve representatives of the following social fields:

media, politics, the justice system, social experts and religion. This definition is of course bound up with the question of the relationship between debates and normative change, and of how debates arise in the first place. I work on the assumption that clashes over norms and values in the media are components of social renegotiation processes in two ways. First, they represent the "catch-up" adaptation of norms to a social practice that has already been modified (the Supreme Court's legalization of abortion in 1973, for example). Second, these media debates constitute the anticipatory and proactive renegotiation of norms (as in the Reagan administration's attempt to return to supposed "traditional family values" in the 1980s). Hence, when analyzing debates, it is always essential to consider the preceding and subsequent transformations of social practice, while relating them to the norms and values that were subject to negotiation.

I use the terms "debate" and "discourse" essentially as synonyms for written and oral negotiations of family values. It is, however, important to note the difference between the term "public debate" as a broad-impact, journalistic discussion (chiefly in the national print media) and that of "expert discourse" as a more specialized confrontation in academic publications and periodicals, though the two may be interrelated. In line with this, my analysis seeks, among other things, to sound out the influence on public debates about family values of specific expert discourses on discrete thematic complexes such as eugenics, women's work, and reproduction.

Debate selection

In deciding which debates to focus on, I attempted to identify topics and controversies of national significance, which were imbricated with the foundations of family concepts and that touched on gender relations as well as the rights of the individual, the duties of the state, and the potential of modern science. Thus, divorce in the Progressive Era, "good" motherhood in the 1920s and 1930s, women's work in the postwar period, the structure of African American families in the 1960s, abortion and reproduction in the 1970s, and finally the call for a return to "traditional family values" in the 1980s were crucial topics of intense controversy within the debate on the relationship between state and individual as well as on the family as the basis of the nation—inflaming the passions of journalists, experts, and the individuals affected.

The focus on women, mothers, and motherhood evident here does in fact reflect the concerns of contemporaries. Well into the twentieth century, the associated debates were primarily about the changing role of women and mothers and its impact on U.S. society or the American nation. Children as historical actors played a subordinate role in discussions on the U.S. family, unless they were focused on child-rearing issues (though even then it was initially mothers and later parents who were the key addressees) or entailed the pathologization of juvenile delinquency, which again was explained mainly in terms of parental failure.[28] Only in the debates and initiatives surrounding the "Americanization" of immigrant families and the imparting to them of "American" family values did children and adolescents sometimes assume a key position as the addressees of the associated programs, as Claudia Roesch has brought out in her study of Mexican American Families.[29] Here children were seen as knowledge brokers within their families and thus as actors. In contrast, in the debates on the "white nuclear family," children were discussed almost exclusively as the passive targets of socialization efforts. This is confirmed by Johanna Brumberg's study, which argues that the socio-statistical observation of the baby boom in the mid-twentieth century was the wellspring of the idea of a need for more births among the "white middle class." Children were once again perceived here as statistical variables rather than acting subjects.[30]

In studying debates on divorce, women's work, and reproduction, then, I focus chiefly on women and mothers, which is consonant with the contemporary sources. Where it seems possible and appropriate, I broaden the perspective to include men and children as actors and subjects within the debates in order to arrive at an integrated treatment of family values as a reflection of gender hierarchies and relations. In addition, the present study builds on productive research on U.S. concepts of masculinity and fatherhood.[31]

---

[28] On the regulation of childrearing, see Grant, Julia, *Raising Baby by the Book. The Education of American Mothers* (New Haven and London 1998). Plant, Rebecca Jo, *Mom. The Transformation of Motherhood in Modern America* (Chicago 2010). Schumann, Dirk (ed.), *Raising Citizens in the "Century of the Child": The United States and German Central Europe in Comparative Perspective* (New York 2010). On the perception of juvenile delinquency as a sociopolitical problem, see Mackert, Nina, *Jugenddelinquenz. Die Produktivität eines Problems in den USA der späten 1940er bis 1960er Jahre* (Konstanz 2014). Mackert, Nina, "'But Recall the Kinds of Parents We Have to Deal With . . . '—Juvenile Delinquency, Interdependent Masculinity and the Government of Families in the Postwar U.S.," in Heinemann, Isabel (ed.), *Inventing the Modern American Family. Family Values and Social Change in 20th Century United States* (Frankfurt a. M. and New York 2012), 196–219.

[29] Roesch, Claudia, *Macho Men and Modern Women. Mexican Immigration, Social Experts and Changing Family Values in the 20th Century United States* (Berlin and Boston 2015), 206–256.

[30] Brumberg, Johanna, *Die Vermessung einer Generation. Die Babyboomer und die Ordnung der Gesellschaft im US-Zensus zwischen 1940 und 1980* (Göttingen 2015).

[31] LaRossa, Ralph, *The Modernization of Fatherhood. A Social and Political History* (London 1997). Martschukat, *American Fatherhood*. Dechert, Andre, *Dad on TV. Sitcoms, Vaterschaft und das Ideal der Kernfamilie in den USA, 1981–1992* (Berlin and Boston 2018). Roesch, Claudia, "Fail-

This is not a book on the social history of the family in the U.S., but a study of the relationship between normative change and social change using family values as an example. Still, to shed light on the basic processes of social change, each chapter begins with a brief social-historical introduction to its central theme, such as rates of divorce and reproduction; the development of women's work and the social structure of African American families; or contraception and abortion. This is intended to facilitate comparative analysis and ultimately furnish us with a more precise grasp of the relationship between social and normative change.

2 Norms and values: How can "value change" be studied historically?

As German research in contemporary history has already recognized, the family is a particularly apt vehicle for the investigation of possible (inter-)relationships between social and normative change in modern societies.[32] Few if any broad-based, long-term studies, however, have analyzed this topic with respect to the United States.[33] This is the point of departure for the present book, which examines whether it is even justified from a historical perspective to refer to a "change in values" vis-à-vis the family or whether it is the continuities that stand out.

The concept of "value change"—and its historiographical differentiation and redefinition—provides us with a unique opportunity to give voice to the experience of acceleration and dynamization undergone by contemporaries in the twentieth-century United States. This perspective also has the potential to cast

---

ure to Provide.' Mexican Immigration, Americanization and Marginalized Masculinities in the Interwar United States,'" in Dominguez Andersen, Pablo and Wendt, Simon (ed.), *Masculinities and the Nation in the Modern World. Between Hegemony and Marginalization* (New York 2015), 149–170.

[32] On Germany from a wide variety of perspectives, see Wirsching, Andreas, *Agrarischer Protest und Krise der Familie. Zwei Versuche zur Geschichte der Moderne* (Wiesbaden 2004). Von Oertzen, Christine, *The Pleasure of a Surplus Income. Part-Time Work, Gender Politics, and Social Change in West Germany, 1955–1960* (New York and Oxford 2007, first German edition 1999). Gebhardt, Miriam, *Die Angst vor dem kindlichen Tyrannen. Eine Geschichte der Erziehung im 20. Jahrhundert* (Munich 2009).

[33] While Coontz provides initial purchase on changing family concepts and gender norms in the post-WWII era, Stacey argues for a broader narrative of postmodern families. Robert Self, meanwhile, addresses the family of the 1960s from a social history angle, while Zaretsky explores family change during the 1970s. Coontz, *The Way We Never Were*. Stacey, Judith, *In the Name of the Family. Rethinking Family Values in the Postmodern Age* (Boston 1996). Self, *All in the Family*. Zaretsky, *No Direction Home*.

much light on the change in attitudes toward the individual and her or his position in society (in terms of sexuality, gender norms, the parent-child relationship, and state-individual relations). By comparing periods of intense change with times of greater social and normative continuity, I seek to bring out the significance and scope of processes of value change using the example of the family.

How exactly can this be done in a historical study? The first key step is to define the core terms "values," "norms," "social change," and "research on value change" before briefly discussing the approaches of both social scientific and historical research on this topic.

With Andreas Rödder, I understand values as "general and fundamental normative conceptions of order [. . .] that provide guidelines for thinking, speaking, and acting on an individual and collective level and that may be explicitly articulated or implicitly assumed."[34] Also important is the definition of Jan van Deth and Elinor Scarbrough, who—following cultural anthropologist Clyde Kluckhohn —consider values to be "conceptions of the desirable," which in turn produce patterns of orientation that guide action.[35] By social norms (in the sense of Emile Durkheim's social facts),[36] meanwhile, I mean supra-individual and specific rules of behavior that structure social interaction: "Norms are made by people, emerging from their shared lives, their beliefs, and their interests."[37] Norms are thus an expression of values and are to a great extent subject to social change. Finally, by "social change" I mean multidimensional shifts in the socio-economic structure of a society, but also in social practices and political-legal structures as well as in the understanding of culture and the public sphere, shifts that may well be heterogeneous and conflictual.[38]

---

[34] Rödder, Andreas, "Wertewandel in historischer Perspektive. Ein Forschungskonzept," in Dietz, Bernhard, Neumaier, Christopher, and Rödder, Andreas (eds.), *Gab es den Wertewandel? Neue Forschungen zum gesellschaftlich-kulturellen Wandel seit den 1960er Jahren* (Oldenbourg Verlag: Munich 2013), 17–39, here 29.

[35] "Values are seen here as conceptions of the desirable which are not directly observable but are evident in moral discourse and relevant to the formulation of attitudes. [. . .] The claim for the empirical relevance of values, we argue, is demonstrated by patterning among attitudes. We call these meaningful patterns value orientations." Deth, Jan W. van and Scarbrough, Elinor (eds.), *The Impact of Values* (Oxford and New York 1995), 46f. See also Kluckhohn, Clyde, "Values and Value Orientations in the Theory of Action. An Exploration in Definition and Classification," in Parsons, Talcott and Shils, Edward A. (eds.), *Toward A General Theory of Action* (Cambridge, MA 1962), 388–433.

[36] Durkheim, Emile, *Die Regeln der soziologischen Methode* (Frankfurt 1984).

[37] Stemmer, Peter, "Die Rechtfertigung moralischer Normen," *Zeitschrift für Philosophische Forschung* 58, 4 (2004), 483–504.

[38] Consequently, the historical analysis of social change should avoid simple teleologies such as "progress" and "modernization."

Finally, the term "research on value change" is commonly used to refer to two quite different strands of inquiry, namely the social scientific and historical variants. What they have in common is their interest in the effects of social change on attitudes in modern societies, but there are major differences in their methodologies and arguments.[39] The present book seeks to contribute to the still young field of historical research on value change, which has developed over the last ten years, especially in Germany. The core aim of this field is to historicize the questions asked and the findings produced by social scientific research on value change and render them fruitful to research in contemporary history. This has not yet been attempted with regard to the contemporary history of the United States.

Yet the key foundational social scientific studies on changing values were produced in the United States, all crucially influenced by the wide-ranging oeuvre of political scientist Ronald Inglehart.[40] His 1977 study *The Silent Revolution* is considered to be the true beginning of social science research on value change.[41] Inglehart discerned a transition from a "materialist" set of values to increasingly "postmaterialist" convictions in Western societies, a shift he located between the late 1960s and the mid-1970s: "The values of Western publics have been shifting from an overwhelming emphasis on material well-being and physical security toward greater emphasis on the quality of life."[42] The majority of people, he contended, are now more focused on their individual self-realization than on securing a livelihood. Inglehart explained this change in values as an element of a broader cultural upheaval deeply bound up with modern industrial society, which, he argued, had provided greater economic and social security for broad segments of the population, making it easier for many people to turn away from traditional religious and cul-

---

[39] For an in-depth discussion of the fruits of historical research on value change in the U.S., see Heinemann, Isabel, "Wertewandel, Version: 1.0," in *Docupedia-Zeitgeschichte*, October 22, 2012 <www.docupedia.de/zg/Wertewandel?oldid=84709> and Heinemann, Isabel, "American Family Values and Social Change. Gab es den Wertewandel in den USA?," in Dietz, Bernhard, Neumaier, Christopher, and Rödder, Andreas (eds.), *Gab es den Wertewandel? Neue Forschungen zum gesellschaftlich-kulturellen Wandel seit den 1960er Jahren* (Oldenbourg Verlag: Munich 2013), 269–284.
[40] Almond, Gabriel A. and Verba, Sidney, *The Civic Culture, Political Attitudes and Democracy in Five Nations* (Princeton 1963). Almond, Gabriel and Verba, Sidney (eds.), *The Civic Culture Revisited. An Analytic Study* (Boston and Toronto 1980).
[41] A first essay focused on Europe had appeared as early as 1971: Inglehart, Ronald, "The Silent Revolution in Europe," *American Political Science Review* 4 (1971), 991–1017.
[42] Inglehart, Ronald, *The Silent Revolution. Changing Values and Political Styles Among Western Publics* (Princeton 1977), 3.

tural norms and embrace pluralistic values.[43] At a more detailed level, he ascertained the value orientation of post-materialists in light of their commitment to aesthetic, intellectual, and social needs. This he contrasted with the materialists' need for security and subsistence. Problematically, however, Inglehart neither contextualizes his categories historically nor discusses to what extent they are comparable in the first place.[44]

Inglehart's sources were exclusively so-called "value surveys," which he justified by claiming that this was the only way to ascertain individuals' values and attitudes.[45] Yet the nature of the questions asked often laid the ground for the answers given, while the selection of attitudes surveyed reduced the range of possible responses. Hence, opinion surveys represent a highly selective source base.[46] Moreover, Inglehart's concept of value change described a linear development that reached its provisional conclusion in postmaterialism. It was based on the notion of "deficiency needs" put forward by Abraham Maslow and on the socialization hypothesis. While the former assumed that the satisfaction of elementary material needs is followed by a greater orientation toward "higher," postmaterial needs and that this process was not reversible, the latter postulated a continuity of the values acquired in youth.[47] The teleological view of value development inherent in both hypotheses is problematic, leaving no room for a change in values in later phases of life or a return to more materialist values, as numerous authors have pointed out.[48]

---

[43] See also his follow-up research, which further elaborates the diagnosis of cultural change on the basis of international value surveys: Inglehart, Ronald, *Kultureller Umbruch. Wertwandel in der westlichen Welt* (Frankfurt a. M. and New York 1989). Inglehart, Ronald and Norris, Pippa, *Rising Tide. Gender Equality and Cultural Change Around the World* (Cambridge, MA 2003). Inglehart, Ronald (ed.), *Human Values and Social Change. Findings from the Values Surveys* (Leiden 2003).

[44] Inglehart, *The Silent Revolution. Changing Values*, 42. The questionnaire on attitudes can be found on 395–430.

[45] Inglehart, *The Silent Revolution. Changing Values*, 4.

[46] This can also be seen in the *World Value Surveys*, which—under the direction of Ronald Inglehart and originating in the *European Value Survey* of 1981 that he coordinated—have been collecting international comparative data on value orientations since 1990. Inglehart, *Human Values and Social Change*. See also the website of the World Values Surveys Association <www.worldvaluessurvey.org/index_html>.

[47] Inglehart, *The Silent Revolution. Changing Values*, 21–24.

[48] Hradil, Stefan, "Vom Wandel des Wertewandels. Die Individualisierung und einer ihrer Gegenbewegungen," in Glatzer, Wolfgang et al. (eds.), *Sozialer Wandel und gesellschaftliche Dauerbeobachtung* (Opladen 2002), 31–47. Rödder, Andreas, "Vom Materialismus zum Postmaterialismus? Ronald Ingleharts Diagnosen des Wertewandels, ihre Grenzen und ihre Perspektiven," *Zeithistori-*

Based on Ingelhart's findings, political scientists and sociologists, particularly in the German-speaking world, have attempted to describe the development of value orientations in the modern industrial societies of the West. They too have identified the period between the mid-1960s and the mid-1970s as one of radical change.[49] Significantly, though, they have generally failed to extend their source base beyond opinion surveys, and many of their studies have perpetuated Inglehart's diagnosis of a linear change in values.[50] In recent years, however, a number of German social scientists have attempted to produce a more nuanced version of Ingelhart's thesis, notably Hans Joas, Norbert Grube, and above all Helmut Thome.[51] Finally, Ulrich Beck's "individualization thesis" foregrounds another key aspect of normative and attitudinal change in modern societies. As early as 1986, in his book *Risk Society*, this sociologist identified the detachment of the individual from traditional contexts of domination and provision (and his or her simultaneous integration into new social structures) along with the loss of security formerly engendered by norms and religious beliefs (the "dimension of disenchantment") as the hallmark of modern society.[52]

---

sche Forschungen/Studies in Contemporary History, online issue, 3 (2006), no. 3, 280–285, online at <www.zeithistorische-forschungen.de/16126041-Roedder-3-2006>.

49 Klages, Helmuth, *Wertorientierungen im Wandel. Rückblick, Gegenwartsanalyse, Prognosen* (Frankfurt a. M. 1984). Klages, Helmuth, *Wertedynamik. Über die Wandelbarkeit des Selbstverständlichen* (Zurich 1988). Klages, Helmuth and Kmieciak, Peter (eds.), *Wertewandel und gesellschaftlicher Wandel* (Frankfurt a. M. and New York 1981). Klages, Helmuth, Hippler, Hans-Jürgen, and Herbert, Willi (eds.), *Werte und Wandel. Ergebnisse und Methoden einer Forschungstradition* (Frankfurt 1992).

50 For example, in addition to a fundamentally pessimistic assessment of value change as a "decline in values," Elisabeth Noelle-Neumann championed the idea of a German "special path [Sonderweg] of value change," contending that this had been particularly extreme due to the confrontation between the younger generation and an older generation burdened by Nazism, finally culminating in the student protests of 1968. Noelle-Neumann, Elisabeth, *Werden wir alle Proletarier? Wertewandel in unserer Gesellschaft* (Zurich 1978). Noelle-Neumann, Elisabeth, "Zeitenwende. Der Wertewandel 30 Jahre später," *Aus Politik und Zeitgeschichte* B 29 (2001), 15–22, esp. 16–18. Deth, Jan van, "Wertewandel im internationalen Vergleich. Ein deutscher Sonderweg?," *Aus Politik und Zeitgeschichte* B 29 (2001), 23–30.

51 Joas, Hans, *Die Entstehung der Werte* (Frankfurt a. M. 1999). Grube, Norbert, "Das Institut für Demoskopie Allensbach und die 'Deutschen Lehrerbriefe' als Instrumente staatsbürgerlicher Erziehung? Ansprüche und Umsetzungen 1947 bis 1969," *Jahrbuch für historische Bildungsforschung* 13 (2007), 267–288. Thome, Helmut, "Soziologische Wertforschung. Ein von Niklas Luhmann inspirierter Vorschlag für die engere Verknüpfung von Theorie und Empirie," *Zeitschrift für Soziologie* 32, 1 (2003), 4–28. Thome, Helmut, "Wandel zu postmaterialistischen Werten? Theoretische und empirische Einwände gegen Ingleharts Theorie-Versuch," *Soziale Welt* 1 (1985), 27–59.

52 Beck, Ulrich, *Risikogesellschaft. Auf dem Weg in eine andere Moderne* (Frankfurt a. M. 1986). For a detailed treatment of the topic of individualization in this context, see Beck-Gernsheim,

So far, research in contemporary history has used the "value change" paradigm mainly to describe modernity in transition to postmodernity, identifying this paradigm narrowly with the period from the mid-1960s to the late 1970s. The assumption of a fundamental change in norms and values also underlies common interpretations of the "Westernization" or liberalization of West Germany after 1945.[53] Yet historians of the contemporary world have often used the term "value change" rather thoughtlessly, which poses a number of problems.[54] First, it is crucial to bear in mind that the interpretive approach centered on "value change" is strongly time-bound, having been produced by the social sciences in the 1960s and 1970s. From today's point of view, this interpretation itself urgently requires historicization in light of its teleology, which is geared toward the ever-advancing modernization of Western societies.[55] Second, the paradigm of a "change in values" is rooted in highly selective opinion surveys in which, as mentioned above, the question prefigures the range of possible answers. What we need to determine, then, is whether this concept of value change has any heuristic value at all when it comes to the historical analysis and description of attitudinal change over the course of the twentieth century. Third, social scientific research has as yet failed to come up with a precise, substantive definition of materialist/traditional versus postmaterialist/progressive values.

Elisabeth and Beck, Ulrich (eds.), *Riskante Freiheiten. Individualisierung in modernen Gesellschaften* (Frankfurt a. M. 1994), esp. 10–39. Beck, Ulrich, "Das Zeitalter des 'eigenen Lebens.' Individualisierung als 'paradoxe Sozialstruktur' und andere offene Fragen," *Aus Politik und Zeitgeschichte* B 29 (2001), 3–6.
53 Doering-Manteuffel, *Wie westlich sind die Deutschen?*, Herbert, "Liberalisierung als Lernprozeß."
54 The following authors, among others, work with an unquestioned notion of value change: Görtemaker, Manfred, *Geschichte der Bundesrepublik Deutschland. Von der Gründung bis zu Gegenwart* (Munich 1999). Kielmannsegg, Peter Graf von, *Nach der Katastrophe. Eine Geschichte des geteilten Deutschlands* (Berlin 2000). Wolfrum, Edgar, *Die geglückte Demokratie. Geschichte der Bundesrepublik Deutschland von ihren Anfängen bis zur Gegenwart* (Stuttgart 2006). For a critical take, see Doering-Manteuffel, Anselm and Raphael, Lutz, *Nach dem Boom. Perspektiven auf die Zeitgeschichte seit 1970* (Göttingen 2010), esp. 151. On Europe, see for example Marwick, *The Sixties*. Kaelble, Hartmut, *Sozialgeschichte Europas 1945 bis zur Gegenwart* (Munich 2007).
55 The critique of the term's use by contemporary historians is particularly pointed in Graf, Rüdiger and Priemel, Kim, "Zeitgeschichte in der Welt der Sozialwissenschaften. Legitimität und Originalität einer Disziplin," *Vierteljahrshefte für Zeitgeschichte* 59 (2011), no. 4, 479–495, esp. 486–488. See the reply by Dietz, Bernhard and Neumaier, Christopher, "Vom Nutzen der Sozialwissenschaften für die Zeitgeschichte. Werte und Wertewandel als Gegenstand historischer Forschung," *Vierteljahrshefte für Zeitgeschichte* 60 (2012), 293–304. Raphael, Lutz and Pleinen, Jenny, "Zeithistoriker in den Archiven der Sozialwissenschaften. Erkenntnispotentiale und Relevanzgewinne für die Disziplin," VfZ 62 (2014), 173–196.

Historical research on value change, meanwhile, though still in its infancy, has produced some promising results.[56] On a broad empirical basis and using a qualitative approach, this field of investigation seeks to find out more about the change in attitudes in modern societies, while concurrently historicizing the categories and theory-building typical of the social scientific study of value change. Outstanding in this regard is the research undertaken by the group around Andreas Rödder at the University of Mainz,[57] though the studies by London-based historian Christina von Hodenberg[58] and the Emmy Noether group in Münster are also important in this context.[59] In contrast to social scientific research on changing values, based primarily on the evaluation of opinion surveys and often adhering to a teleological paradigm of modernization, historical research on value change explores in an open-ended way major shifts in contemporaries' norms and values. To this end, it analyzes, for example, discourses and debates using the methods of discursive, media and mentality history.

Among Anglo-American historians and social scientists, the paradigm of "value change" enjoys much less popularity than among German historians of the contemporary world, just as Inglehart's work has been received primarily in German sociology.[60] American studies on the 1960s and 1970s tend to refer to the

---

[56] Initial findings collated by Dietz, Bernhard, Neumaier, Christopher, and Rödder, Andreas (eds.), *Gab es den Wertewandel? Neue Forschungen zum gesellschaftlich-kulturellen Wandel seit den 1960er Jahren* (Munich 2013).

[57] Dietz and Neumaier, "Vom Nutzen der Sozialwissenschaften," 293–304. Rödder, Andreas, *Wertewandel in der Postmoderne. Gesellschaft und Kultur der Bundesrepublik Deutschland 1965–1990* (Stuttgart 2004), 23. Rödder, Andreas, "Werte und Wertewandel. Historisch-Politische Perspektiven," in Rödder, Andreas and Elz, Wolfgang (eds.), *Alte Werte—Neue Werte. Schlaglichter des Wertewandels* (Göttingen 2008), 9–25.

[58] Hodenberg, Christina von, "Fernsehrezeption, Frauenrolle und Wertewandel in den 1970er Jahren: Das Beispiel 'All in the Family,'" in Dietz, Bernhard, Neumaier, Christopher and Rödder, Andreas (eds.), *Gab es den Wertewandel? Neue Forschungen zum gesellschaftlich-kulturellen Wandel seit den 1960er Jahren* (Munich 2013), 285–306. Hodenberg, Christina von, *Television's Moment: Sitcom Audiences and the Sixties Cultural Revolution* (Oxford and New York 2015). Hodenberg, Christina von, "Television Viewers and Feminism in 1970s North America: How *All in the Family* Drove Value Change," in Vasudevan, Ravi (ed.), *Media and the Constitution of the Political. South Asia and Beyond* (New Delhi 2022), 195–217.

[59] Heinemann, "Wertewandel," Heinemann, "American Family Values." Roesch, *Macho Men*. Dechert, *Dad on TV*. Overbeck, *At the Heart of It All*. Hoffman, *Sexing Religion*.

[60] Kesselman, Mark, "The Silent Revolution. Changing Values and Political Styles Among Western Publics by Ronald Inglehart," *Political Science Review* 72, 1 (1979), 284–286. Miller, Kenneth E., "The Silent Revolution. Changing Values and Political Styles Among Western Publics by Ronald Inglehart," *The Journal of Politics* 40, 3 (1978), 801–803. Newkirk, M. Glenn, "The Silent Revolution. Changing Values and Political Styles Among Western Publics by Ronald Inglehart," *The Public Opinion Quarterly* 42, 4 (1978), 568–569. Wright, James D., "The Political Consciousness of Post-

"great shift" of the 1970s and the "culture wars" of the 1980s.[61] The issue of changing values is discussed less under a blanket label and more in terms of specific case studies (relating to gender norms, the legal system, and political participation). However, since most American studies on the family focus only on short periods of time, they are unable to investigate waves or cycles of value change, let alone ascertain, on a sound empirical basis, whether a long-term change in values occurred at all. The present study is the first to pursue this line of inquiry and it does so from an emphatically diachronic perspective.

3 Key approaches: gender studies and intersectionality, expert cultures and scientification

To probe historically the relationship between social change and normative change using the example of the family, two methodological approaches—in addition to historical research on value change—are of immense importance: gender studies and the investigation of expert cultures and scientification.

Gender studies and intersectionality

Few topics have been so well researched in recent decades as that of changing gender norms since the middle of the twentieth century. This is especially true of U.S. history, with women's and gender studies receiving major impetus from the work of U.S. women historians since the late 1970s. Early women's studies in the wake of the second wave of the women's movement in the 1960s and 1970s had called for women's history to finally receive adequate analysis and for its incorporation into mainstream historiography. The establishment of "gender" (social sex) as a category of historical analysis through the work of Joan Scott in the

---

Industrialism. The Silent Revolution. Changing Values and Political Styles Among Western Publics by Ronald Inglehart," *Contemporary Sociology* 7, 3 (1978), 270–273. For a critique of the tool of opinion surveys, see Igo, Sarah, *The Averaged American: Surveys, Citizens, and the Making of a Mass Public* (Cambridge MA 2007).

61 Schulman, Bruce, The Seventies: The Great Shift in American Culture, Society, and Politics (New York 2001). Hunter, Culture Wars. Bell, Daniel, The Coming of Post-Industrial Society. A Venture in Social Forecasting (New York 1971). Marwick, The Sixties. See also the special issue "Mass Culture as Modernity—European Perceptions, 1890–1980" of the Journal of Modern European History, JMEH 10 (2012), no. 2.

1980s then set new standards.⁶² The new mode of thinking about gender (to which Scott had brought a new systematicity) as an expression of power relations and normative attributions—as distinct from sex (biological gender)—went hand in hand with a rejection of the "public" versus "private" dichotomy, that is, the emphasis on separate spheres of responsibility for men and women. Anthropologist Michelle Rosaldo and historian Karin Hausen demonstrated that the model of "separate spheres," rather than a valid category of historical analysis, must in fact be understood as a self-description rooted in the nineteenth century, one that reflects contemporaries' need to establish clear gender norms.⁶³

Roughly, the conceptual development of gender studies in the 1990s can be divided into three strands: reflection on the significance of the body; inclusion of the categories of race and class (also subsumed under the term "intersectionality"); and an expanded perspective on concepts of masculinity along with men's spheres of action and experience.

The first crucial insight, common to the work of both Judith Butler and Pierre Bourdieu, was that biological sex is first produced or becomes operative through social and cultural constructions, which are always partly an expression of power relations. While Bourdieu mapped out a "gendered habitus," Butler spoke of a "gender-specific matrix." For both authors, the result was always the exclusion or denigration of the feminine.⁶⁴ Going beyond Bourdieu, Butler underlined that the assumption of biological sex is deeply rooted in the assumption of heterosexual norms and the devaluation of the other who fails to conform to the norm

---

62 Scott, Joan W., "Gender. A Useful Category of Historical Analysis," *American Historical Review* 91 (1986), no. 5, 1053–1075. Canning, Kathleen, "Feminist History after the Linguistic Turn. Historicizing Discourse and Experience," *Signs* 19 (1994), no. 2, 368–404. Boydston, Jeanne, "Gender as a Question of Historical Analysis," in Shepard, Alexandra and Garthine, Walker (eds.), *Gender and Change. Agency, Chronology, and Periodization* (Malden, MA 2009), 133–165. Scott, Joan W., "Millennial Fantasies. The Future of 'Gender' in the 21st Century," in Honegger, Claudia and Arni, Caroline (eds.), *Gender. Die Tücken einer Kategorie* (Zürich 2001), 19–38. Scott, Joan W., "Unanswered Questions, Contribution to AHR Forum, Revisiting 'Gender: A Useful Category of Historical Analysis,'" *American Historical Review* 113 (2008), no. 5, 1422–30.
63 Rosaldo, Michelle, "The Use and Abuse." Hausen, Karin, "Öffentlichkeit und Privatheit. Gesellschaftspolitische Konstruktionen und die Geschichte der Geschlechterbeziehungen," in Hausen, Karin and Wunder, Heide (eds.), *Frauengeschichte—Geschlechtergeschichte* (Frankfurt am Main 1992), 81–88. Hausen, "Family and Role-Division."
64 The two were coming from completely different analytical and disciplinary backgrounds: anthropology and sociology in Bourdieu's case, philosophy and poststructuralist discourse analysis in Butler's. Butler, *Bodies that Matter*. Bourdieu, Pierre, *La Domination Masculine* (Paris 1998).

("the abject").⁶⁵ These ideas are highly pertinent to the present book, one of whose key tasks is to lay bare the efficacy and transformation of gender norms.

African American feminists such as Evelyn Brooks Higginbotham, Bonnie Thornton Dill, and Patricia Hill Collins, meanwhile, called for greater inclusion of the category of "race" in gender studies in order to shine a light on the manifold discriminatory mechanisms facing "women of color" by addressing what Higginbotham refers to as the "metalanguage of race."⁶⁶ The same demand reached a new pitch of intensity in research on intersectionality, a term coined by legal scholar Kimberlé Crenshaw.⁶⁷ Intersectionality studies assume that the complex mechanisms of oppression in modern societies can be analyzed adequately only by taking into account the relationality of the factors of "race, class, and gender"—along with other categories of difference.⁶⁸ In a seminal essay, Gudrun-Axeli Knapp thus argued for a concept of intersectionality as an "integral analytical perspective [that enables us to] re-inspect European modernity [. . .]" and to lay bare the interrelatedness of the capitalist economy, bourgeois domination, bourgeois rationality, and the pervasive power of gender norms.⁶⁹ This perspectivization is also a fruitful means of grappling with U.S. society.⁷⁰

---

65 Butler, *Bodies that matter*, 27–45. See also Butler, Judith, *Undoing Gender* (New York, London 2004).
66 Higginbotham, Evelyn Brooks, "African-American Women's History and the Metalanguage of Race," *Signs* 17 (1992), no. 2, 251–274. Dill, Bonnie Thornton, "Race, Class, and Gender. Prospects for an All-Inclusive Sisterhood," *Feminist Studies* 9 (1983), 131–150. Hill Collins, Patricia, "Shifting the Center. Race, Class, and Feminist Theorizing about Motherhood," in Coontz, Stephanie, Parson, Maya, and Raley, Gabrielle (eds.), *American Families. A Multicultural Reader* (New York 2008), 173–187. In this context, see also the research of Elena Gutierrez and Rickie Solinger, which shows how both social experts and the American polity attempted to regulate the reproduction of African American and Mexican American women: Gutiérrez, Elena, *Fertile Matters: The Politics of Mexican Origin Women's Reproduction* (Austin 2008). Solinger, Rickie, *Beggars and Choosers. How the Politics of Choice Shapes Adoption, Abortion, and Welfare in the United States* (New York 2001).
67 Crenshaw, Kimberlé, "Demarginalizing the Intersection of Race and Sex: A Black Feminist Critique of Antidiscrimination Doctrine, Feminist Theory and Antiracist Politics," *University of Chicago Legal Forum* 1989, no. 1, 139–167.
68 Cho, Sumi, Crenshaw, Kimberlé, and McCall, Leslie, "Towards a Field of Intersectionality Studies: Theory, Applications, and Praxis," *Signs* 38 (2013), no. 4, 785–810. Hill Collins, Patricia, "The Difference That Power Makes: Intersectionality and Participatory Democracy," in Hankivsky, Olena and Jordan-Zachery, Julia S. (eds.), *The Palgrave Handbook of Intersectionality in Public Policy* (London 2019, first edition 2017), 167–192.
69 Knapp, Gudrun-Axeli, "'Intersectionality'—Ein neues Paradigma feministischer Theorie? Zur transatlantischen Reise von 'Race, Class, Gender,'" *Feministische Studien* 2005, no. 1, 68–81.
70 On the use of the intersectionality paradigm in U.S. gender studies, in addition to the pioneering work of Kimberlé Crenshaw, see Higginbotham, "African-American Women's History," 251–274, esp. 274. Boydston, "Gender as a Question," esp. 142–147.

Finally, historians and sociologists such as Raewyn Connell, Michael Kimmel, and Jürgen Martschukat have expanded the theoretical foundation of gender studies by scrutinizing concepts of masculinity (or masculinities) as well as male patterns of action and perception, and have provided the first empirical studies in this vein.[71] In particular, the interpretive model of "hegemonic masculinity" established by Raewyn Connell proved discursively productive, although its fixation on the concept of patriarchy and its simplification of the "homosocial dynamic" among men make it an overly blunt tool of historical investigation, as John Tosh has brought out.[72] Still, the concept of "hegemonic masculinity" has great analytical value if we understand it as a normative frame of reference, as "gender norms to which most men subscribe, whether or not they fully enact them."[73] This allows us to describe, from a long-term perspective, both processual shifts in the ideal of masculinity and the ways people have marked their differences from the prevailing norm, deviated from it, and developed strategic alternatives to it.

In recent years, a growing number of gender-historical studies of U.S. society have appeared that are rooted in a postcolonial perspective and a critique of racism. Scrutinizing topics as diverse as reproductive decision-making, police violence, capitalism, and far-right extremism, they reveal that racism and sexism have been inextricably intertwined in recent U.S. history and remain so today.[74]

---

71 Martschukat, Jürgen and Stieglitz, Olaf, *"Es ist ein Junge!" Einführung in die Geschichte der Männlichkeiten in der Neuzeit* (Tübingen 2005). Martschukat, Jürgen and Stieglitz, Olaf, *Väter, Soldaten, Liebhaber. Männer und Männlichkeiten in der Geschichte Nordamerikas. Ein Reader* (Bielefeld 2007). Martschukat, *American Fatherhood*. Kimmel, Michael, *Manhood in America. A Cultural History* (New York 1996). Kimmel, Michael, Hearn, Jeff, and Connell, Robert William (eds.), *Handbook of Studies on Men & Masculinities* (Thousand Oaks 2005). Connell, Robert, *Masculinities* (Cambridge 1995). Dinges, Martin (ed.), *Männer—Macht—Körper. Hegemoniale Männlichkeiten vom Mittelalter bis Heute* (Frankfurt a. M. 2005).
72 Tosh, John, "Hegemonic Masculinity and the History of Gender," in Dudink, Stefan, Hagemann, Karen, and Tosh, John (eds.), *Masculinities and Politics in War. Gendering Modern History* (New York 2004), 41–58. Wickberg, Daniel, "Heterosexual White Male. Some Recent Inversions in American Cultural History," *The Journal of American History* 92 (2005), no. 1, 136–159. Traister, Bryce, "Academic Viagra. The Rise of American Masculinity Studies," *American Quarterly* 52 (2000), no. 2, 274–304. Dinges, Martin, "'Hegemoniale Männlichkeit'—ein Konzept auf dem Prüfstand," in Dinges, Martin (ed.), *Männer—Macht—Körper. Hegemoniale Männlichkeiten vom Mittelalter bis Heute* (Frankfurt a. M. 2005), 7–36.
73 Tosh, "Hegemonic Masculinity," 41–58. See also the further development of this perspective by Connell, R. W. and Messerschmidt, James W., "Hegemonic Masculinity. Rethinking the Concept," *Gender & Society* 19 (2005), 829–859.
74 For an initial impression of the breadth of this research field, see Gurr, Barbara, *Reproductive Justice. The Politics of Health Care for Native American Women* (New Brunswick 2014). Hinton, Elizabeth, *America on Fire. The Untold History of Police Violence and Black Rebellion since the 1960s* (New York, NY 2021). Brückmann, Rebecca, *Massive Resistance and Southern Womanhood*.

Meanwhile, historical research on gender has broadened its perspective to take in the experiences of discrimination and the lived realities of gay, transgender, bisexual, and non-binary people. The field of "queer history" is as diverse and colorful as the associated movements themselves, but what I would like to highlight is its attempt to investigate the ways in which sex/gender difference and power relations interconnect. Recent scholarship has not only elaborated the social and historical situatedness of sexual and gender-related identities, but has also begun to tease out the intersectional linkage of sexuality, race, and gender.[75] Studies of this kind are of signal importance to the present book: the long "success story" of the heteronormative, patriarchal, white and middle-class nuclear family in the twentieth-century United States constitutes the prehistory and point of departure for queer movements, while queer people's room for maneuver was for decades constrained in the name of this vision of the family.

Scientification and expert cultures

Another key jumping-off point for this book is the role played by social experts and scientification in the formation of family-centered norms. In a ground-breaking 1996 essay, German historian Lutz Raphael identified the "scientification of the social" as a core feature of Western modernity. This penetration of all areas of society by the expertise of human scientists reached its apogee between the 1930s and the 1960s.[76] Developing his concept further, some time ago Raphael pointed out that the multifaceted diffusion and implementation of social knowledge ("knowledge about man [sic] in society") associated with this process of scientification must be analyzed from a

---

White Women, Class, and Segregation (Athens 2021). Denise Ferreira da Silva, *Unpayable Debt* (London 2022).

75 Over the last decade, queer history has been a booming yet oscillating field. See the concise overview by Hanhardt, Christina B., "Queer History," https://www.oah.org/tah/issues/2019/may/queer-history/. Hanhardt, Christina B., *Safe Space: Gay Neighborhood History and the Politics of Violence* (Durham 2013). Bronski, Michael, *A Queer History of the United States* (Boston 2011). Romesberg, Don (ed.), *The Routledge History of Queer America* (New York 2019). Stryker, Susan, *Transgender History. The Roots of Today's Revolution* (revised edition, Boston 2017, first edition 2008). Ortiz, Paul, *An African American and Latinx History of the United States* (Boston 2018). Frank, Nathaniel, *Awakening: How Gays and Lesbians Brought Marriage Equality to America* (Cambridge, MA 2017).

76 Raphael, Lutz, "Die Verwissenschaftlichung des Sozialen als methodische und konzeptionelle Herausforderung für eine Sozialgeschichte des 20. Jahrhunderts," *Geschichte und Gesellschaft* 22 (1996), 165–193 (though still with a clear focus on West Germany).

longer chronological perspective, one beginning in the mid-nineteenth century, as well as in light of its transnational interrelations.[77]

Building on Raphael, Thomas Etzemüller has described the practice of "social engineering" as a "specific mode of problematizing modernity." Ideas of order, ordering practices, and concrete orders came together in this engineering of society, with experts functioning as its key agents.[78] Every sphere of social coexistence could be ordered, including urban planning and architecture, the *Volkskörper* or "national body," population policy, and the family—with contemporaries often struggling to adapt themselves to the privileged social order. Borrowing from Michel Foucault, Etzemüller uses the term *dispositif* to convey this.[79]

The family, as the supposed "basis of the nation," furnishes us with an excellent vehicle for examining the *modus operandi* of the "scientification of the social" described by Raphael and the construction of a "new infrastructure of useful knowledge" about the individual in society. Social experts of many different stripes made use of this knowledge, seeking to change and improve the modern family through their interventions. By combining their conceptions of social order with modern social technologies and deriving from them an emphatic "imperative to design" society they acted in pursuit of the "social engineering" outlined by Etzemüller. I thus draw on Raphael's and Etzemüller's theories to illuminate—with reference to the family—the interrelations in the twentieth-century United States between (female and male) social experts and the recipients of expert advice rooted in the human sciences.

In what follows, "social experts" means (predominantly male) academics with a background in the human sciences (especially the social sciences, psychology, medicine, demography, and law) working on a variety of "real-world" projects, who developed their science-led expertise with the goal of reforming their own society. In other words, they were "experts" in the literal sense of the term,

---

77 Raphael, Lutz, "Embedding the Human and Social Sciences in Western Societies, 1880–1980. Reflections on Trends and Methods of Current Research," in Brueckweh, Kerstin et al. (eds.), *Engineering Society. The Role of the Human and Social Sciences in Modern Societies, 1880–1980* (New York 2012), 41–56, 41.
78 Etzemüller, Thomas, "Social Engineering als Verhaltenslehre des kühlen Kopfes. Eine einleitende Skizze," in Etzemüller, Thomas (ed.), *Die Ordnungen der Moderne. Social Engineering im 20. Jahrhundert* (Bielefeld 2009), 36f. Etzemüller, Thomas, "Social Engineering, Version: 1.0," *Docupedia-Zeitgeschichte. Begriffe, Methoden und Debatten der zeithistorischen Forschung* <www.docupedia.de/zg/Social_engineering> (accessed February 11, 2010).
79 On the concept of the *dispositif* in Foucault, see Foucault, Michel, *Der Wille zum Wissen (Sexualität und Wahrheit*, vol. I, Frankfurt 1977), 7–49, esp. 34–35. Foucault, Michel, *Dits et Écrits: Schriften*. Vol. III (Frankfurt a. M. 2003), 392.

namely both theoreticians and practitioners.[80] At the same time, they claimed socially relevant interpretive competence—as consultants, political advisors, members of expert commissions and relevant professional associations—and they entered into interpretive conflicts over family values and the optimal design of society.[81] The debates on concepts of the family, norms, and values show impressively how social scientists first developed concepts of social order (focused on the family in our context), published them, and finally sought to ensure that their diagnoses found expression in social reality, a project in which they often participated themselves.[82]

4 The U.S. family in historical research

At first glance, the U.S. family appears to be a well-researched topic. But a closer look reveals serious research gaps. The social history of the American family,[83] the history of the African American family,[84] and the history of divergent con-

---

[80] On the concept of the social expert, see Raphael, Lutz, "Experten im Sozialstaat," in Hockerts, Hans-Günther (ed.), *Drei Wege deutscher Sozialstaatlichkeit. NS-Diktatur, Bundesrepublik und DDR im Vergleich* (Munich 1998), 231–258. Raphael, Lutz, "Sozialexperten in Deutschland zwischen konservativem Ordnungsdenken und rassistischer Utopie (1918–1945)," in Hardtwig, Wolfgang (ed.), *Utopie und politische Herrschaft im Europa der Zwischenkriegszeit* (Schriften des Historischen Kollegs, Kolloquien 56, Munich 2003), 327–346.

[81] See Raphael, "Sozialexperten," 327–328, Raphael, "Verwissenschaftlichung," 167–169. Raphael, "Embedding," 45–46.

[82] This three-step process of imagining, representing, and producing social reality as pursued by social scientists has been emphasized by Christiane Reinecke and Thomas Mergel. Reinecke, Christiane and Mergel, Thomas, "Das Soziale vorstellen, darstellen, herstellen: Sozialwissenschaften und gesellschaftliche Ungleichheit im 20. Jahrhundert," in Reinecke, Christiane and Mergel, Thomas, *Das Soziale ordnen. Sozialwissenschaften und gesellschaftliche Ungleichheit im 20. Jahrhundert* (Frankfurt a. M. 2012), 7–31.

[83] Smith, Daniel Scott, "Recent Change and the Periodization of American Family History," *Journal of Family History* 20 (1995), no. 4, 329–346. Hawes, Joseph M. (ed.), *The Family in America. An Encyclopedia*, 2 vols. (Santa Barbara, CA 2002). Mintz and Kellog, *Domestic Revolutions*. Hareven, Tamara K., "The History of the Family and the Complexity of Social Change," *American Historical Review* 96 (1991), no. 1, 95–124. Harris, John (ed.), *The Family. A Social History of the Twentieth Century* (New York and Oxford 1991). Skolnick, Arlene, *Embattled Paradise. The American Family in an Age of Uncertainty* (New York 1991).

[84] Billingsley, Andrew, *Black Families in White America* (Englewood Cliffs, NJ 1968). Aschenbrenner, Joyce, *Lifelines. Black Families in Chicago* (New York 1975). Gutman, *The Black Family*. McAdoo, Harriette P., *Black Families* (Thousand Oaks, CA 1997, reprint of 1981 edition). Franklin, Donna L., *Ensuring Inequality. The Structural Transformation of the African-American Family* (New York 1997). Green, Adam, *Selling the Race. Culture, Community, and Black Chicago,*

cepts of motherhood and fatherhood[85] have been the focus of numerous studies. Less investigated, meanwhile, have been changes in family concepts and family values; the same applies to gender norms within families. Here it is striking that over the last twenty years most studies have tended to focus on the period from the end of World War II to the early 1960s.[86] The only major exception is the work of Stephanie Coontz, who asks how notions of the ideal family and its values have changed, but does not subject this to empirical analysis.[87] In contrast, Jürgen Martschukat's study of fathers in American history adopts an explicitly long-term perspective.[88] This German historian examines the (self-)positionings of fathers within their families as an element of a biopolitical *dispositif*, a guiding frame for

---

1940–1955 (Chicago 2007). Glasrud, Bruce and Pitre, Merline (eds.), *Black Women in Texas History* (Texas 2008). Patterson, *Freedom is not Enough*. On Mexican American Families in the United States, see Roesch, *Macho Men*. Griswold del Castillo, Richard, *La Familia. Chicano Families in the Urban South West* (Notre Dame, IN 1984). Sanchéz, George J., *Becoming Mexican American: Ethnicity, Culture, and Identity in Chicano Los Angeles* (New York and Oxford 1993). Rodríguez, Richard T., *Next of Kin: The Family in Chicano/a Cultural Politics* (Durham, NC 2009). Rosas, Ana Elizabeth, *Abrazando El Espiritu. Bracero Families Confront the US-Mexico Border* (Berkeley, CA 2014).

85 Ladd-Taylor, Molly, *Mother-Work. Women, Child Welfare and the State, 1890–1930* (Champaign 1994). Apple, Rima and Golden, Janet (eds.), *Mothers and Motherhood. Readings in American History* (Columbus 1997). Ladd-Taylor and Umanski (eds.), *Bad Mothers*. Roberts, Dorothy, *Killing the Black Body. Race, Reproduction, and the Meaning of Liberty* (New York 1999). Apple, Rima, *Perfect Motherhood: Science and Childrearing in America* (Piscataway, NJ 2006). Sidel, Ruth, *Unsung Heroines. Single Mothers and the American Dream* (Berkeley and Los Angeles 2006). Ruiz, Vicki L. and DuBois, Carol (eds.), *Unequal Sisters. A Multicultural Reader in U.S. Women's History* (New York 2008). Vandenberg-Davis, Jodi, *Modern Motherhood. An American History* (New Brunswick, NJ 2014). Rotundo, E. Anthony, *American Manhood. Transformations in Masculinity from the Revolution to the Modern Era* (New York 1994). Griswold, Robert L., *Fatherhood in America. A History* (New York 1993). Connell, *Masculinities*. Kimmel, *Manhood in America*. LaRossa, *Modernization of Fatherhood*. Martschukat, Jürgen and Stieglitz, Olaf, *Geschichte der Männlichkeiten* (Frankfurt a. M. 2008). Martschukat, *American Fatherhood*.

86 May, Elaine Tyler, *Homeward Bound. American Families in the Cold War Era* (Boston 1988). Weiss, *To Have and to Hold*. Metzl, Jonathan M., "'Mother's Little Helper'. The Crisis of Psychoanalysis and the Miltown Resolution," *Gender & History* 15 (2003), no. 2, 228–255. Gilbert, James Burkhart, *Men in the Middle. Searching for Masculinity in the 1950s* (Chicago and London 2005). Plant, *Mom*. Odland, Sarah Burke, "Unassailable Motherhood, Ambivalent Domesticity. The Construction of Maternal Identity in Ladies' Home Journal in 1946," *Journal of Communication Inquiry* 34 (2010), no. 1, 61–84.

87 Coontz, *The Way We Really Are*. Coontz, *The Way We Never Were*. Coontz, Parson, and Raley, *American Families*.

88 Martschukat, *Ordnung des Sozialen*. Another important exception is Chafe, William H., *The Paradox of Change. American Women in the 20th Century* (New York 1991).

self-management in the sense of Foucault's concept of "governmentality."[89] Through a total of twelve historical vignettes on fathers within their families—from the settler father on the frontier to the African American father as portrayed in film—Martschukat brings out to impressive effect the regulatory significance of the nuclear family ideal across all the fractures and contrasts of U.S. history, while focusing explicitly on men and fathers. But in order to fully appreciate what the changes (notably the reinterpretation of social fatherhood and the growing flexibility of gender norms) and astonishing continuities (above all the breadwinner function and the nuclear family ideal) elaborated by Martschukat meant for U.S. families as a whole, we also have to consider women, mothers, and daughters, which is just what the present book does.

Recently, Sandra M. Sufian has probed the history of adoption in the United States as one centered on family norms and the treatment of disability, and she too examines the entire twentieth century. Her study is also significant to the theme of family values, as it illustrates the extent to which notions of health and "normality" on the one hand and disability and deviance on the other determined the prospects of establishing a family through adoption while also molding the attitudes and actions of adoptive parents, adoption agencies, and social workers.[90] The example of the adoption of disabled children also provides insight into changing concepts of good motherhood and parenthood, desirable children, and "healthy" families.[91]

The important studies by Natasha Zaretsky and Robert O. Self explore the post-1960s U.S. family.[92] Zaretsky analyzes the family as an arena of profound discomfiture for Americans in the 1970s against the backdrop of upheavals within families and fears of national decline triggered by the Vietnam War and economic crisis. Self, meanwhile, scrutinizes how the achievements of the 1960s social protest movements in terms of the family and gender norms paved the way for the conservative revolution of the 1980s. Self comes to the provocative conclusion that the liberalism of the 1960s facilitated the turn toward the neoliberal free-market economy and thus, ultimately, the reaffirmation of the ideal of the "male breadwinner" and the nuclear family as the nation's moral bastion.[93] Both stud-

---

89 Martschukat, *Ordnung des Sozialen*, 22. Cf. Martschukat, Jürgen (ed.), *Geschichte schreiben mit Foucault* (Frankfurt a. M. 2002).
90 Sufian, Sandra M., Familial Fitness: Disability, Adoption, and Family in Modern America (Chicago 2022). On the growing body of adoption stories, see also Briggs, Laura, Somebody's Children. The Politics of Transracial and Transnational Adoption (Durham and London 2012).
91 On this topic, see chapter 6.
92 Zaretsky, *No Direction Home*. Self, *All in the Family*.
93 Self, *All in the Family*, 399–425.

ies, like the monographs by Coontz and Martschukat, are sources of stimulus for the present book. But the diachronic analysis of the struggle over the ideal American family since the turn of the century that I present here is essential if we wish to grasp precisely the background to the conservative restoration of the national family ideal in the 1980s, an understanding that also strips this restorative shift of some of its supposedly "unprecedented" character. Moreover, when attempting to explain the continuities and transformations of the national family ideal, it is crucial to tease out not just the agency of politicians and members of social protest movements, but also to probe the influence of social experts as analysts of social change.

The typical focus on the 1950s as the supposed "golden age of the family," which continues to predominate in numerous studies, can claim some plausibility in light of social statistics (baby boom, marriages, expansion of the "middle class," "suburbia"), the self-perception of contemporaries (the turn to the private sphere during the Cold War), and the subsequent instrumentalization of the family as a locus of safety and security in an increasingly unsettling world. Yet the outcome of this self-imposed analytical limitation tends to be a failure to consider the values and ways of life of ethnic minorities as well as divergent social realities (single parents, working mothers, patchwork families, gays).[94] Overall, the spotlighting of supposed "cold war domesticity" has gravely impeded awareness of countervailing trends in gender relations and longer-term processes of social change. This has already been underscored by Joanne Meyerowitz, whose 1994 volume *Not June Cleaver* laid a key foundation stone for research on the diversity of women's options and identity constructions in the immediate postwar period.[95] With reference to the United States, Meyerowitz recently developed the concept of a "long sexual revolution," which embeds the 1950s—with their supposedly extreme moral conservativism—in the context of a general liberalization of sexual morality extending from the 1920s to the late 1970s.[96]

In general, however, historical research lacks an analysis of gender conceptions and family values from a longer chronological perspective, which is what I

---

[94] May, *Homeward Bound*. Gilbert, *Man in the Middle*. Plant, *Mom*.
[95] Meyerowitz, Joanne (ed.), *Not June Cleaver. Women and Gender in Postwar America, 1945–1960* (Philadelphia 1994). As early as 1984, Eugenia Kaledin had argued that even in the 1950s some women made much more proactive use of their opportunities to shape the private, professional, and political spheres than the dominant view suggests: Kaledin, Eugenia, *Mothers and More. American Women in the 1950s* (Boston 1984).
[96] Hagemann, Karen and Michel, Sonya, *Gender and the Long Postwar: The United States and the Two Germanys, 1945–1989* (Baltimore 2014). On the history of sexuality, see Meyerowitz, Joanne, "Transnational Sex and US History," *American Historical Review* (2009), 1273–1286.

will be providing here with reference to public debates and expert discourses on divorce, women's work, and reproduction. Recent research has already shown that in the vast majority of cases the predominantly male experts sought to propagate the family ideal of the white "middle class" and to motivate other social and ethnic groups (especially African American and Mexican-origin families, but also gay parents and "working-class" families) to accept these values and implement them in practice.[97] Meanwhile, there remains an urgent need to investigate whether and if so how the national family ideal was modified when confronted with divergent family norms, and to what extent the family ideal itself could become a vehicle of integration for immigrant families or a symbol of societal integration and hopes of social advancement.[98] Another important research desideratum is analysis of the production of family values and gender norms through visual and audiovisual media (advertising, film, and television).[99] Likewise, there is a dearth of research on the influence of religious, especially Christian fundamentalist, movements on notions of family and how they impacted the intergenerational transmission of gender norms. Both topics exceed the scope of the present study.[100]

---

[97] Solinger, *Beggars and Choosers*. Sanchéz, George J., "'Go after the Women.' Americanization and the Mexican Immigrant Woman, 1915–1929," in Apple, Rima and Golden, Janet (eds.), *Mothers and Motherhood. Readings in American History* (Columbus 1997), 475–494. Roesch, Claudia, "'Americanization through Homemaking'. Mexican American Mothers as Major Factors in Americanization Programs," in Isabel Heinemann (ed.), *Inventing the Modern American Family. Family Values and Social Change in 20th Century United States* (Campus Verlag: Frankfurt a. M. and New York 2012), 59–81. Roesch, *Macho Men*. Overbeck, Anne, "'The Enemy Within'. African American Motherhood and the Crack Baby Crisis," in Heinemann, Isabel (ed.), *Inventing the Modern American Family. Family Values and Social Change in 20th Century United States* (Frankfurt a. M. and New York 2012), 155–176. Overbeck, *At the Heart of It All*.

[98] In this regard, see for example the contemporary diagnosis put forward by Margaret Mead, which I will be examining. She postulated that all members of a society automatically align themselves with the dominant family ideal, even if they live differently in objective terms. Mead, Margaret, "What is Happening to the American Family? Religion Is the Support of the Family, but the Family is also the Support of Religion," *Pastoral Psychology* 1 (1950), no. 5, 40–50, here 40.

[99] Taylor, Ella, *Prime Time Families. Television Culture in Postwar America* (Berkeley, Los Angeles, and London 1989). Spigel, Lynn, *Make Room for TV. Television and the Family Ideal in Postwar America* (Chicago and London 1992). Dechert, Andre, "Family Man: The Popular Reception of 'Home Improvement,' 1991–1992, and the Debate about Fatherhood," in Heinemann, Isabel (ed.), *Inventing the Modern American Family. Family Values and Social Change in 20th Century United States* (Frankfurt a. M. 2012), 265–288. Hodenberg, *Television's Moment*. Dechert, *Dad on TV*.

[100] Tipton, Steven M. and Witte, John Jr. (eds.), Family Transformed. Religion, Values, and Society in American Life (Washington 2007). Dowland, Family Values. Hoffman, Sexing Religion. Bassimir, Anja-Maria, Evangelical News: Politics, Gender, and Bioethics in Conservative Christian Magazines of the 1970s and 1980s (Tuscaloosa 2022).

This book innovates in four key ways. First, I apply approaches found in the German scholarship on modernity to the United States, test them out on the phenomenon of the "family," so central to the relationship between state and individual, and render them productive to the description of U.S. modernity. Second, scrutinizing the relationship between social and normative change over the entire sweep of the twentieth century allows us to gain a detailed grasp of processes of liberalization and pluralization as well as the associated counter-movements. It is the combination of the findings of U.S. research (which are often highly specific in regional, chronological, and thematic terms) with my own empirical "exploratory drilling" over a lengthy time period (through analysis of six crucial social debates) that allows me to demonstrate trajectories of normative change that have merely been postulated hitherto and to determine their limits. Third, this study identifies the white nuclear family ideal as a key paradigm—or *dispositif* as described by Michel Foucault—to which Americans aligned themselves regardless of all social, ethnic, and cultural disparities; I illustrate, in particular, the significance of expert interventions to the stabilization and actualization of this *dispositif*. Fourth, the book analyzes the complex processes of negotiation between individual rights and community interests in modern U.S. society that culminated in the notion of the family as the "basis of the nation." The study's perhaps most surprising finding is that, at the end of the twentieth century, the focus shifted—at least discursively—from an emphasis on individual rights to divorce, work, and reproduction, back to privileging the interests of the community (as manifest in the prioritizing of the embryo's right to life over the mother's right to decide and in the regulation of families labelled as "deficient").

5 Period of investigation, sources, and structure

"High modernity" under the spotlight

In this book, I have consciously chosen to explore a lengthy period from about 1890 to the late 1980s, that is, one extending from the era in which industrial high modernity came into its own to a time of major structural change in the economy and looming economic crisis. However, it is not socio-economic factors alone, but above all changes in norms and values that determine the choice of period. While the social reform movement emerged in the late nineteenth century and demands for both equal rights for women and improved families were raised on a broader basis than in the preceding decades,[101] the early 1970s saw crucial normative realignments such as the introduction of no-fault divorce in 1970, the passage of the Equal Rights Amendment by both houses of Congress in 1972,[102] and the legalization of abortion by the Supreme Court in 1973. At the same time, counter-movements took off, such as conservative grassroots movements and the New Christian Right, while in 1969 President Richard Nixon coined the term "silent majority" to describe the supposed preponderance of Americans critical of the social movements of the 1960s and the anti-Vietnam War protests.[103] The period under study concludes with the end of Ronald Reagan's term of office at the height of the "culture wars," which were marked by fierce disputes over the family and a revival of alleged "traditional family values." The disputes over the legitimacy of abortion were particularly polarized, with the woman's right to decide being set against the fetus's "right to life" and the interests of the state.

This focus on the long period from 1890 to the 1980s allows for the longitudinal observation of possible normative change, but also dovetails with the current trend toward studying "modernity" as a key phenomenon characteristic of Western societies. Here, the relevant studies usually investigate periods between the late nineteenth century and the 1970s, thus orienting themselves to the concept of "industrial high modernity," as developed among others by Ulrich Herbert, who drew on the work of political scientist and anthropologist James C. Scott.[104] This

---

[101] While the first women's movement had already identified equal rights for women as a social objective in the *Declaration of Sentiments* of 1848, it was not until the formation of the National American Woman Suffrage Association (NAWSA) in 1890 and the adoption of the first amendments guaranteeing women the right to vote by individual states from 1893 onward that the first women's movement achieved national reach. On the women's suffrage movement around 1900, see Matthews, Jean, *The Rise of the New Woman. The Women's Movement in America, 1875–1930* (Chicago 2003). Chafe, *Paradox of Change*.

[102] However, by the end of the (repeatedly extended) ratification period in 1982, the amendment had not been ratified by the requisite thirty-eight states and thus failed to make it into law. Decisive here were the campaigns spearheaded by politician and publicist Phyllis Schlafly, who believed that the amendment violated the rights of the housewife and mother and organized conservative grassroots protests against the ERA. Mathews, Donald G. and De Hart, Jane Sherron, *Sex, Gender, and the Politics of ERA. A State and the Nation* (Oxford 1993). Critchlow, Donald T., *Phillis Schlafly and Grassroots Conservatism. A Woman's Crusade* (Princeton and Oxford 2005).

[103] Richard Nixon, "Address to the Nation on the War in Vietnam," November 3, 1969. <www.vietnamwar50th.com/1969-1971_vietnamization/Nixon-8217-s--8220-Silent-Majority-8221-Speech/>.

[104] Herbert, Ulrich, "Europe in High Modernity. Reflections on a Theory of the 20th Century," *Journal of Modern European History* (2007), no. 5, 5–21. Scott, James C., *Seeing Like a State. How Certain Schemes to Improve the Human Condition Have Failed* (New Haven 1998). Doering-Manteuffel, Anselm, "Nach dem Boom. Brüche und Kontinuitäten der Industriemoderne seit 1970," *Vierteljahrshefte für Zeitgeschichte* 55 (2007), no. 4, 559–581. Raphael, Lutz, "Ordnungsmus-

epochal designation not only reflects processes of economic-technological and political-social modernization, but also takes into account contemporaries' experience of acceleration, individualization, and general changes in lifestyles and norms.[105] Concepts such as the "multiple modernities" described by Shmuel N. Eisenstadt or the "entangled modernities" postulated by Shalinia Raderia have the advantage of foregrounding globally parallel, yet highly diverse forms of cultural modernity without privileging Western patterns of modernization from the outset.[106] This is certainly preferable to contrasting the U.S. and Europe, or even Germany, as "competing modernities," as proposed by Christoph Mauch and Kiran Klaus Patel.[107] What is problematic about the "multiple" or "entangled" modernities approaches, however, is their indeterminacy in terms of both content and chronology.

Recent studies of modernity no longer assume a monolithic, let alone teleological development (as long implied by modernization theory), but instead emphasize the ambivalences of social transformation, together with the limits and costs of modernization processes. Whereas Zygmunt Baumann in his classic *Modernity and Ambivalence* identified the latter as the core characteristic of modernity, Thomas Welskopp and Alan Lessoff examine the United States between 1890 and 1940 as a case of "fractured modernity."[108] By this, they mean a modernity

---

ter der 'Hochmoderne'? Die Theorie der Moderne und die Geschichte der europäischen Gesellschaften im 20. Jahrhundert," in Schneider, Ute and Raphael, Lutz (eds.), *Dimensionen der Moderne. Festschrift für Christof Dipper* (Frankfurt a. M. 2008), 73–91. Doering-Manteuffel and Raphael, *Nach dem Boom*. Doering-Manteuffel, Anselm, Raphael, Lutz, and Schlemmer, Thomas (eds.), *Vorgeschichte der Gegenwart. Dimensionen des Strukturbruchs nach dem Boom* (Göttingen 2016).

105 See Bell, Daniel, "Zur Auflösung der Widersprüche von Modernität und Modernismus: Das Beispiel Amerikas," in Bell, Daniel and Meier, Heinrich (eds.), *Zur Diagnose der Moderne* (Munich 1990), 21–68. Gumbrecht, Hans Ulrich, "Modern, Modernität, Moderne," in *Geschichtliche Grundbegriffe*, vol. IV (Stuttgart 1978), 93–131, esp. 126–127. Herbert, "Liberalisierung als Lernprozeß," esp. 36 and 49. Dipper, Christof, "Die deutsche Geschichtswissenschaft und die Moderne," *Internationales Archiv für die Sozialgeschichte der Literatur*, vol. 37 (2012), 37–62.

106 Eisenstadt, Shmuel N., "Multiple Modernities," *Daedalus* 129 (2000), no. 1, 1–30, 2. Randeria, Shalini, "Geteilte Geschichte und verwobene Moderne," in Rüsen, Jörn et al. (eds.), *Zukunftsentwürfe. Ideen für eine Kultur der Veränderung* (Frankfurt a. M. 2000), 87–96. See also Conrad, Sebastian and Randeria, Shalini (eds.), *Jenseits des Eurozentrismus. Postkoloniale Perspektiven in den Geschichts- und Kulturwissenschaften* (Frankfurt a. M. 2002).

107 Among other things, because this overestimates the importance of Western European developments to the United States. Mauch, Christopher and Patel, Kiran Klaus, *Competing Modernities* (New York 2009).

108 Welskopp, Thomas and Lesssoff, Alan, *Fractured Modernity. America Confronts Modern Times, 1890s to 1940s* (Munich 2013). Baumann, Zygmunt, *Moderne und Ambivalenz: Das Ende der Eindeutigkeit* (Hamburg 2005, first English edition *Modernity and Ambivalence*, 1991).

that has "proven to be an irreversible historical era whose basic mode is permanent change and whose shapeless landscape is dotted with the ruins of ever new ordering schemas that sought—in vain—to achieve permanence."[109]

Against this background, the question naturally arises as to where the United States ought to be placed within the spectrum of current interpretations of modernity. Together with Welskopp and Lessoff, I argue that, contrary to the tendency to evoke "American exceptionalism" or even "Americanism" (Lessoff), the United States should be regarded as part of the "West," but one in which the attempt to get to grips with industrial modernity took a much more radical form than in Western Europe.[110] Such an approach alerts us not only to ambivalences and contingencies, to national and regional specifics, but also allows to analyze how various actors perceived the changing ethnic composition of the American population as a social problem requiring remedy. At the same time, I believe it useful to apply to the United States the concept of "high modernity" developed with a view to Western Europe. First, this allows us to explore a period much longer than that studied by Welskopp and Lessoff, namely one extending from 1890 to the 1980s. Second, it both avoids the problematic concept of the "American Century" that crops up so often in the sources and also enables us to detach the United States from its self-image of "American exceptionalism," examining it as part of Western "high modernity."[111] Crucially, though, against this background the historical investigation of the struggle over the American family and its values in modernity must aggressively scrutinize the blind spots and exclusions associated with the prevailing family ideal in order to avoid telling a "success story of Western values." It is in fact the profoundly consequential linkages of race, class, gender, and sex as core categories of difference that constitute the special focus of this book.

---

109 Welskopp and Lessoff, *Fractured Modernity*, 17.
110 Welskopp and Lessoff, *Fractured Modernity*, 9, 11 and 17. Lessoff, Alan, "American Progressivism. Transnational, Modernization, and Americanist Perspectives," in Welskopp, Thomas and Lessoff, Alan, *Fractured Modernity. America Confronts Modern Times, 1890s to 1940s* (Munich 2013), 61–80. Lipset, Seymour Martin, *American Exceptionalism. A Double-Edged Sword* (New York 1996).
111 Newspaper publisher Henry Luce first proclaimed the "American Century" to broad public effect in a *Life* editorial of February 17, 1941. Luce, Henry, "The American Century," *Life Magazine* 10 (1941), no. 7, February 17, 1941, 61–65.

Sources

The sources I use here to study public debates and expert discourses on divorce, women's work, and reproduction are first and foremost the national daily press (*New York Times, Washington Post*) and numerous magazines,[112] followed by popular guidebooks and contemporary scholarly publications, as well as presidential speeches, presidential conferences, and the reception of landmark Supreme Court decisions. In addition, each chapter takes a close look at a number of social experts and associations that injected themselves into a given debate, shaped it at a programmatic level, and communicated their ideas to the public; I evaluate their writings and papers in particular detail. While chapter 1, on divorce debates, turns the spotlight on a sociologist (Edward E. Ross) and a churchman who drew inspiration from the social sciences (Samuel A. Dike), and analyzes the American Sociological Association's position on the family, chapter 2 examines the initiatives of the American Eugenics Society and the influence of eugenicist and marriage counselor Paul B. Popenoe on the national family ideal. Chapter 3 contrasts the reflections of sociologist Mirra Komarovsky and publicist Betty Friedan on women's work with those of ultraconservative social experts such as Ferdinand Lundberg and David Goodman, while chapter 4 on the African American family draws in particular on the writings and papers of Daniel Patrick Moynihan, Martin Luther King, and the Southern Christian Leadership Conference (SCLC). Chapter 5 examines debates over reproduction, while also taking a close look at population expert Robert C. Cook, anthropologist Margaret Mead, and the various factions of the population control movement and the National Organization for Women (NOW). Chapter 6, meanwhile, evaluates Ronald Reagan's speeches and writings and contrasts them with the rich body of texts produced by social movements, which placed women's reproductive rights at the center of their demands: the National Abortion Rights Action League (NARAL) and its Massachusetts branch (NARAL Mass Choice), NOW, the Boston Women's Health Book Collective, and Concerned United Birthparents (CUB).

---

112 In addition to the *New York Times* and *Washington Post*, other newspapers such as the *Chicago Tribune, Washington Star, New York Herald,* and *Los Angeles Times* were included as needed. The periodicals examined vary according to the subject matter of the debate. Thus, the focus is on the *Atlantic Monthly* and *North American Monthly* when it comes to intellectual debates in the early twentieth century, periodicals of the eugenics movement such as *Eugenical News* and *Family Life* with respect to eugenic concepts of motherhood, women's magazines such as *Ladies' Home Journal* and *Good Housekeeping* with regard to debates on women's work, and finally African American periodicals such as *Ebony* and *Jet* in connection with debates on the values and structure of black families.

Structure of the book

The book follows a largely chronological structure while incorporating a thematic analysis. In chronological order, I examine a total of six national debates that dealt with the topics of divorce, reproduction, and women's work from a variety of perspectives. I evaluate each of the six debates in light of the extent to which we can identify major changes in the normative framework (family values, gender norms) and the practical scope of action enjoyed by families and individuals.

The first chapter analyzes debates on divorce between 1900 and 1920, with a special focus on social scientists' influence on ideas about gender norms and family values, as well as these scholars' impact on the way in which processes of social change were interpreted as a reaction to the "impositions of modernity."[113] Chapter 2 examines how efforts to scientize motherhood and childrearing paved the way for the eugenics booms of the 1920s and 1930s and explores the impact this had on notions of "healthy families." In addition, the chapter examines how eugenic ideas found their way into the mainstream of U.S. society beyond the 1940s through marriage and family counseling informed by hereditary biology. Chapter 3 scrutinizes debates on women's work and maternal employment from 1940 to 1970 and elucidates the consequences of these phenomena for the "substance of the nation" as anticipated by contemporaries and evoked in the debates. There is more at issue here than the social entrenchment of women's part-time work as an economic necessity and an achievement of the liberal women's movement; we can also discern the ongoing centrality of the factors of "race" and "class" despite all efforts at liberalization. Chapter 4 illuminates how, in the second half of the 1960s, with much input from both social experts and the civil rights movement, the U.S. family ideal underwent a major expansion to include non-white families. Yet this chapter also lays bare how social experts, the civil rights movement, and the Black Power movement themselves worked toward the re-biologization of gender norms and, in an attempt to consolidate the family, further narrowed the scope of action for African American women. Chapter 5 analyzes how representatives of the women's movement and population-focused policymakers renegotiated women's roles in the family and society in the 1960s and 1970s. Core aspects of the debates on access to self-determined reproduction included contraception, abortion, the semantic shift from "reproductive choice" to "reproductive rights," national sterilization policies, the movement to curb global population growth (Zero Population Growth), and no-

---

[113] The origin of this concept lies in research on Americanization in the Weimar Republic, but I use it here because it conveys precisely the self-perception of many contemporaries as reflected in the divorce debates. See Saldern, Aldelheid von, Lüdtke, Alf, and Marsolek, Inge (eds.), *Amerikanisierung. Traum und Alptraum im Deutschland des 20. Jahrhunderts* (Stuttgart 1996).

fault divorce. Finally, starting with the Carter administration's first "National Conference on Families," chapter 6 examines the negotiation of family values and reproductive rights in the 1980s. It reveals that the right to individual freedom of choice in matters of reproduction was a core achievement of the 1970s, yet one that fatally undermined any hopes of a nationally binding family policy in the 1980s—so profound were the ideological conflicts in U.S. society. By contrasting the debates over "adoption" and "abortion," the rest of the chapter analyzes the extent to which the symbolic family policies of the Reagan era not only hardened the fronts in the "culture wars" but changed Americans' individual scope of action with regard to their families. In light of its empirical findings, the book then concludes with a fresh look at the question of "change in the value of the family."

1 "Race suicide or remedy?" The debates on divorce in the Progressive Era, 1890–1920

At the beginning of the twentieth century, American sociology discovered the family as a suitable object of research and analysis, one that also served to buttress this still young discipline's scientificity and undergird its status as a source of valid insights. In 1908, the sociologists assembled in Atlantic City, New Jersey, for the third annual meeting of the American Sociological Association—founded just three years before as a national body aiming to promote cohesion and exchange among scholars—already tackled the question of how modern society was changing familial structures.[1] In his opening address, William G. Sumner,[2] then president of the association and one of the founding fathers of U.S. sociology, eloquently expressed many sociologists' great interest in the family. He explained that the American family was undergoing a fundamental process of change, such that traditional gender and generational relationships had in many cases lost their validity:

> Perhaps the family still shows more fluctuation and uncertainty than any other of our great institutions. Different households now differ greatly in the firmness of parental authority and the inflexibility of filial obedience. Many nowadays have abandoned the old standards of proper authority and due obedience. The family has to a great extent lost its position as a conservative institution and has become a field for social change.[3]

At the same time, however, Sumner, although personally a proponent of conservative family values and of stable, patriarchal family structures, warned against excessive concern in view of the process of change he had outlined. Despite all

---

[1] Rhoades, Lawrence J., "A History of the American Sociological Association, 1905–1980" <https://www.asanet.org/wp-content/uploads/rhoades_history_foreward_thru_chap_3.pdf>.
[2] William Graham Sumner (1840–1910), held the Chair of Political and Social Science at Yale University and was one of the founding fathers of U.S. sociology. Sumner, who first studied ancient languages, history, and theology in Geneva, Göttingen, and Oxford, served first as a deacon and then as a priest in the Episcopal Church from 1867 to 1872. In the latter year, he received an appointment as a social scientist at Yale University, where he taught until his death. From 1908 to 1909 he was president of the American Sociological Association, of which he had been vice president since its founding in 1905. Sumner was a staunch supporter of a free market economy, a proponent of laissez-faire economic policies, and a staunch anti-imperialist. In his book *Folkways*, he coined the term "ethnocentrism" to denote national and cultural arrogance. Sumner, William Graham, *Folkways. A Study of the Sociological Importance of Usages, Manners, Customs, Mores, and Morals* (Boston 1906).
[3] Sumner, William G., "The Family and Social Change," in *Publications of the American Sociological Society. Papers and Proceedings*, Volume III: *Third Annual Meeting of the American Sociological Society, held at Atlantic City, N.J., December 28–30, 1908* (Chicago and New York 1909, reprinted New York and London 1971), 1–15, here 15.

the challenges—especially visible in rising divorce figures—the family as an institution, he stated, was not itself at risk.[4]

Sumner's observation of change in the family and the associated discussion among sociologists are key to the subject matter of this book in several different ways. First, the representatives of this young discipline were responding to an important contemporary debate, which had been going on in the United States since about 1890, on the possible effects of divorce on family values, family structure, and the cohesion of society in general.[5] Yet though the theme of the entire event was "The Family," a large proportion of the papers revolved around the problem of divorce.[6] Second, there had indeed been a sharp increase in the number of divorces in the U.S. since the final third of the nineteenth century. Reliable data on this was provided by the first nationwide divorce statistics, the so-called *Wright Report*, which appeared in two parts, published in 1889 and 1909.[7] Third and finally, the social sciences, especially in the shape of the sociologists assembled in Atlantic City, were in the process of staking their claim as a new leading science. This aspiration was underscored by their derivation of socially relevant interpretations from statistical data, as in the case of divorce practices, and the inferences they drew from it about the state of "the American family." Based on statistics, surveys, and models, numerous sociologists published engaged analyses of the impact of

---

[4] Curtis, Bruce, "Victorians Abed. William Graham Sumner on the Family, Women and Sex," *American Studies* 18.1 (1977), 101–122.

[5] William O'Neill was the first to examine this state of affairs. He highlighted the importance of the development of sociology to the renegotiation of gender roles and family values, while also underscoring the significance of the divorce debates to the professionalization of the social sciences. O'Neill, William L., *Divorce in the Progressive Era* (New Haven and London 1967). O'Neill, William L., "Divorce in the Progressive Era," in Gordon, Michael (ed.), *The American Family in Social-Historical Perspective* (New York 1978), 140–151. O'Neill, William L., "Divorce and the Professionalization of the Social Scientist," *Journal of the Behavioral Sciences* 2 (1966), no. 4, 291–302. See also Riley, Glenda, *Divorce. An American Tradition* (New York and Oxford 1991), 108–129.

[6] See, for example, the talk by well-known sociologist George E. Howard and the subsequent heated debate: Howard, George Elliot, "Is the Freer Granting of Divorce an Evil?", *Publications of the American Sociological Society. Papers and Proceedings*, Volume III: *Third Annual Meeting of the American Sociological Society, held at Atlantic City, N.J., December 28–30, 1908* (Chicago and New York 1909, reprinted New York and London 1971), 150–180 (with commentaries on the paper). Howard was the author of the monumental standard work on the history of marriage and an avowed proponent of divorce. Howard, George, *A History of Matrimonial Institutions*, 3 vols. (Chicago 1904).

[7] U.S. Department of Commerce and Labor, *Marriage and Divorce, 1867–1886* (Westport, Conn. 1889); also called the *Wright Report* after its author, Commissioner of Labor Carroll D. Wright. U.S. Department of Commerce and Labor, *Marriage and Divorce, 1867–1906*, 2 vols. (Westport, Conn. 1909, reprinted 1978). Initial figures from the second report were already known to scholars toward the end of 1908.

modernity on the structure and values of modern society, particularly the family, and began to challenge theologians' interpretive authority.[8] This paradigm shift had already been highlighted by Albion Small, chair of sociology at the University of Chicago and, like Sumner, one of the pioneers of U.S. sociology, in a foundational study of 1910: "Our generation is witness that the case MEN VERSUS MEN'S PROBLEMS has taken a change of venue from the theological court to the sociological."[9]

The sociologists' debates on the family must not only be placed within the discourses on science and scientificity in the discipline, but can also be analyzed as a means of negotiating the challenges of "modernity" in the United States and as a contribution to the "scientification of the social" (Lutz Raphael); further, they underscore the relevance of concepts and practices of "social engineering" (Thomas Etzemüller).[10] The rise of sociology to the status of leading science and the formation of a new type, that of social expert, were not, however, the only serious changes that occurred between the last decade of the nineteenth century and the second decade of the twentieth that influenced notions of family in U.S. society. A new understanding of gender roles and especially of women's rights crystallized around the same time. The anchoring of women's suffrage in the constitution in 1920 as the Nineteenth Amendment permanently changed the opportunities open to women. Further, alongside the long-standing women's suffrage movement of the late nineteenth century, the "new women" of the 1920s—a new class of well-educated, professional, independent women—began to formulate broader demands for self-determination and cultural independence than the representatives of the earlier movement had done.[11] In association with social scientists, social reformers, and liberal intellectuals, they began to question rigid Victorian moral concepts as well as the patriarchal model of society based on the subordination of women, a process that engendered long-term

---

[8] For seminal observations on the transfer of interpretive authority over social processes from the church to the social sciences, see Small, Albion W., *The Meaning of the Social Sciences* (Chicago 1910). As analyses of divorce and its consequences for society, see Howard, "Freer Granting of Divorce," 766–796. Lichtenberger, James P., *Divorce: A Study in Social Causation* (New York 1909). Ross, Edward Alsworth, "The Significance of Increasing Divorce," *Century* 78 (1909), 149–152. Spencer, Anna Garlin, "Problems of Marriage and Divorce," *Forum* 48 (1912), 188–204.

[9] Small, *Meaning*, 272. Emphasis in the original. On Small, see the detailed remarks later in this chapter.

[10] Raphael, "Verwissenschaftlichung." Etzemüller (ed.), "Social Engineering als Verhaltenslehre." Etzemüller, "Social Engineering, Version 1.0." See also Reinecke and Mergel, *Das Soziale Ordnen*.

[11] Matthews, *The Rise of the New Woman*. Cott, Nancy, *The Grounding of Modern Feminism* (New Haven 1987).

normative reorientations.[12] These changes were not conflict-free or linear, but thoroughly contradictory and heterogeneous, as especially evident in the case of debates on divorce in the Progressive Era.[13]

At the beginning of the twentieth century, divorce was understood by its opponents not only as a moral problem, but above all as an anti-social phenomenon that threatened the family and thus the foundation of society.[14] In addition, a conflict over the role of women became manifest in the public debate on marriage and divorce. The argument made by the opponents of divorce, that it was primarily the woman who was responsible for maintaining the family and marriage, collided with the postulate privileged by the proponents of divorce, namely that women too had the right to end a relationship that had become intolerable. The debate on divorce crosscut political camps and gender dichotomies. Both sides included conservatives and liberals, women and men, with a slight preponderance of social scientists among supporters of divorce and of churchmen among its opponents. At its core, this was an argument about the right of the individual (often: the woman) versus that of the community. Revealing here is the role of sociologists, who publicly lent "scientific credibility" to the right to divorce, while fueling public fears of its consequences through their analyses.[15] What I seek to clarify is what the debate on the importance of the public versus private spheres, or on the individual versus the community—along with the gradual marginalization of the opponents of divorce—might tell us about the first tentative steps toward modernizing the concept of family at the beginning of the twentieth century.

In the first section, in order to place the journalistic debates on divorce and its moral and social consequences in social historical context, I provide a brief introduction to divorce trends in the United States in the nineteenth and twentieth centuries. In the second section, I then examine divorce debates in the media up to the end of the nineteenth century, scrutinizing what shifts in values we might discern in this discourse with respect to the family. I go on to analyze to what extent the national family ideal in the U.S. changed in the early twentieth

---

[12] Griswold, Robert L., "Law, Sex, Cruelty, and Divorce in Victorian America, 1840–1900," *American Quarterly* 38 (1986), no. 5, 771–745. May, Elaine Tyler, *Great Expectations. Marriage and Divorce in Post-Victorian America* (Chicago 1980).
[13] This was first pointed out by Michael O'Neill. See O'Neill, *Divorce*. O'Neill, "Divorce."
[14] Yamin, Priscilla, *American Marriage. A Political Institution* (Philadelphia 2012). Cott, Nancy F., *Public Vows. A History of Marriage and the Nation* (Cambridge and London 2000). Coontz, Stephanie, *Marriage, A History. From Obedience to Intimacy or How Love Conquered Marriage* (New York 2005). Cherlin, *The Marriage-Go-Round*. Phillips, Roderick, *Untying the Knot. A Short History of Divorce* (New York 1991).
[15] The importance of sociology to the gradual overcoming of restrictive divorce laws in most states receives particular emphasis from Riley, *Divorce*.

century as a result of the divorce debates and what role social experts and their analyses of social change played in this process.

The sources examined in what follows include the writings of American sociologists and exponents of the human sciences such as Edward A. Ross, James P. Lichtenberger, and George Howard. I also consider the work of sociologist Charlotte Perkins Gilman, clergyman and social statistician Samuel W. Dike, and the Divorce Reform League, which he founded. Additional sources are the publications of the American Sociological Association and press organs significant to the contemporary divorce debate, such as the *New-York Tribune* daily newspaper as well as the magazines *Atlantic Monthly* and *North American Review*.

1.1 Trends in the divorce rate in the United States in the nineteenth and twentieth centuries

The first recorded divorce in the New World was granted in Plymouth in 1639.[16] Subsequently, the colonies adopted very different divorce practices, with a clear north-south divide emerging: the northeastern colonies around Massachusetts were characterized by more liberal procedures, while their southern counterparts granted divorces only in exceptional cases. In the wake of the Declaration of Independence and the War of Independence, divorce rates in the various states increased steadily, although different legal bases and forms of divorce make comparison difficult. The spectrum ranged from a strict prohibition of divorce in South Carolina and adultery as the only possible ground for divorce (New York) to the acceptance of a variety of possible grounds (in New Hampshire, no fewer than fourteen such grounds were recognized in the early twentieth century; in Iowa, there were nine)[17] and the use of so-called "omnibus clauses"[18] that left divorce entirely at the discretion of judges. Furthermore, there were three potential forms of sanctioned separation, the most common of which was divorce in court ("juridical divorce"), followed by divorce through an act of the legislature ("legislative divorce"),[19] and the variant of divorce sanctioned by most churches, namely the legally regulated separation of spouses ("divorce of bed and board").

---

16 Riley, *Divorce*, 12.
17 Lichtenberger, *Divorce*, 142. Riley, *Divorce*, 48.
18 Practiced in the nineteenth century in Connecticut, North Dakota, South Dakota, Illinois, Indiana, Maine, Massachusetts, New Jersey, New York, Utah, Ohio, Oklahoma, Pennsylvania, Rhode Island, and Vermont.
19 The practice of "legislative divorce" was abolished in most states between the mid- and late nineteenth century, lastly in Delaware (1897). Riley, *Divorce*, 35–44.

It should be noted, first, that around the middle of the nineteenth century the conviction that divorce was a civil right in a democratic society began to gain ground. Second, the factors underpinning marriage as an institution of provision gradually changed: the emergence of the market economy caused the family to lose some of its importance as a unit of production, while growing mobility and a nascent trend toward individualization were significant too.[20] Contemporary observers had, moreover, identified a divorce boom as early as the 1850s and 1860s, which greatly unsettled them.[21] This was in sharp contrast to developments in Europe, where divorce was completely forbidden in many countries or, as in the United Kingdom, limited to the spatial and economic separation of the spouses. This first discussion of divorce in the U.S. was flanked by a debate on the economic and legal position of women in marriage. From the mid-nineteenth century onward, the early women's movement rebelled against the legal construct of coverture adopted from the U.K., that is, the transfer of a woman's property (and all rights and obligations) to her husband upon marriage. Fierce resistance to this legal form arose in the states as well.[22] Many of them then passed married women's property acts, which granted wives property rights, a move that strengthened their position in potential divorce proceedings.[23]

Throughout the twentieth century, the U.S. had a very high marriage rate as well as the highest divorce rate in the world—despite the fact that divorce was regulated very differently in the different states. Since records began in 1867, the figures for both divorces and marriages increased steadily until the early 1980s, when a gradual decline in both categories set in. Looking at the period from the final third of the nineteenth century to the end of the twentieth, certain phases

---

20 Riley, *Divorce*, 31.
21 Nationwide statistics are only available from 1867 onward, recording 9,937 divorces. In 1887, twenty years later, 483,069 marriages compared with 27,919 divorces. U.S. Department of Commerce and Labor, *Marriage and Divorce, 1867–1906* (Westport, Connecticut 1909, reprinted 1978), vol. I, 7, 12, 22.
22 See the relevant passage in the 1848 Declaration of Sentiments, a key document of the early women's movement: Knight, Denise D., "Declaration of Sentiments," in *American History through Literature 1820–1870*, ed. Janet Gabler-Hover and Robert Sattelmeyer, vol. I (New York 2006), 316–320. For context, see Tetrault, Lisa, *The Myth of Seneca Falls: Memory and the Women's Suffrage Movement* (Chapel Hill 2014). Wellman, Judith, *The Road to Seneca Falls: Elizabeth Cady Stanton and the First Woman's Rights Convention* (Urbana 2004).
23 Speth, Linda E., "The Married Women's Property Acts, 1839–1865: Reform, Reaction, or Revolution?" in Lindgren, J. Ralph et al. (eds.), *The Law of Sex Discrimination* (Wadsworth 2011), 12–15. Boswell, Angela, "Married Women's Property Rights and the Challenge to the Patriarchal Order: Colorado County, Texas," in Coryell, Janet L. (ed.), *Negotiating Boundaries of Southern Womanhood: Dealing With the Powers That Be* (Columbia, MO 2000), 89–109.

stand out: that between the end of the nineteenth century and the close of the Progressive Era, the Great Depression, the "baby boom" era, and the early 1970s. Most importantly, the divorce rate never again grew so dramatically, nor was it perceived in such dramatic terms, as in the period extending from the late nineteenth to the early twentieth century—something I will be returning to in the course of this chapter.[24]

The recording of marriage and divorce rates began in the United States in 1867 with the collection of data by the national Commissioner of Labor, Carroll D. Wright. In 1887, Congress had charged Wright—the forerunner in a sense of the national Secretary of Labor, a bespoke Department of Labor being created only in 1913—with collecting relevant national data, initially retrospectively for the two decades between 1867 and 1886.[25] Wright's report, *Marriage and Divorce*, appeared in 1889 and revealed an unprecedented increase in the absolute number of divorces, from just under 10,000 (1867) to just under 26,000 (1886), an increase of more than 150 percent.[26] To keep track of this trend, in 1905 President Theodore Roosevelt instructed the director of the national statistics authority, the Bureau of the Census, to continue collecting this data.[27] In 1909, the marriage and divorce figures for the years 1887 to 1906 were published.[28] They too showed a considerable increase in national divorce figures from about 26,000 (1886) to 72,000 (1906), or nearly 200 percent. This contrasted with far more moderate increases in the number of marriages, from about 357,000 in 1867 to 534,000 (1886) and 895,000 (1906). However, these statistics were far from complete until 1906 due to the differing legal regulations on marriage in the different states. For instance, by 1886, only fourteen states were reporting their marriage statistics; by 1906, all but South Carolina did so.[29] Even when population growth is factored in, we find a significant increase in the divorce rate from 0.3 to 0.8 divorces per 1,000 people and from 9.6 to 10.5 marriages between 1867 and 1906.

---

[24] Another significant increase occurred between 1965 and 1975 as a direct effect of the abolition of the fault principle with respect to divorce; see chapter 5 of the present book.
[25] Plateris, Alexander A., *100 Years of Marriage and Divorce Statistics. United States, 1867–1967* (U.S. Department of Health, Education and Welfare, National Center for Health Statistics, Rockville MD 1973), 1.
[26] U.S. Department of Commerce and Labor, *Marriage and Divorce, 1867–1886* (Westport, Conn. 1889, reprinted in U.S. Department of Commerce and Labor, *Marriage and Divorce, 1867–1906*, 2 vols. [Westport, Conn. 1909, reprinted 1978], 12).
[27] U.S. Department of Commerce and Labor, *Marriage and Divorce, 1867–1906*, 2 vols. (Westport, Conn. 1909, reprinted 1978, 4). Plateris, *100 Years*, 1.
[28] U.S. Department of Commerce and Labor, *Marriage and Divorce, 1867–1906*, 2 vols. (Westport, Conn. 1909, reprinted 1978).
[29] Plateris, *100 Years*, 2.

Tab. 1.1: Trends in marriage and divorce according to the two national statistical surveys of 1887 and 1909.

Year	Marriages	Rate per 1,000 population	Divorces	Rate per 1,000 population
1867	357,000	9.6	10,000	0.3
1870	352,000	8.8	11,000	0.3
1880	453,000	9.6	20,000	0.4
1890	570,000	9.0	33,000	0.5
1900	709,000	9.3	56,000	0.7
1906	895,000	10.5	72,000	0.8

It is important to note that at this early stage the states not only had very different regulations on divorce, but on marriage as well. Initially, some states had no or only very inadequate "marriage license laws," which hobbled the collection of statistics. Efforts to standardize marriage procedures were, therefore, one reason for the call for the first national statistics in 1887. In 1906, two states, New York and South Carolina, still had no formal marriage procedures.[30] In the field of divorce, the situation was even more chaotic. The comparatively liberal divorce laws of many states in the West and in the American heartland coexisted with restrictive regulations or complete bans on divorce in the states of the Northeast and Southeast.[31] What all had in common, however, was a variety of grounds for divorce, the most important of which were desertion (especially by the husband, who was regarded as the breadwinner), adultery, and (physical or mental) cruelty.

The differences in divorce law were also expressed in a heterogeneous geographical distribution of the frequency of divorce. Thus, the commentary attached to the second national divorce statistics (1887–1906) concluded that "the divorce rate increases as one goes westward." Divorce rates in the western part of the United States in 1906 were in fact about four times higher than those in the Northeast and Southeast.[32] The statisticians were unable to offer any real explanation for this phenomenon—beyond the fact that the communities of the West were still fairly young and thus less likely to abide by traditional rules. The gradually rising divorce rate in the Southern states also seemed to require explanation. The report argued that the African American population, strongly represented in this region, was increasingly resorting to the instrument of divorce. The report

---

30 *Marriage and Divorce*, 1909, reprinted 1978, 4.
31 *Marriage and Divorce*, 1909, reprinted 1978, 14.
32 *Marriage and Divorce*, 1909, reprinted 1978, 14.

found that in these states "divorces granted to colored persons form 50 to as high as 90 percent of all divorces."[33] In contrast, the authors attempted to explain the comparatively low divorce rates in the Northeast as a result of continuous immigration, since continental European immigrants were less familiar with this practice. In addition, they noted a clear divide between urban and rural communities, with divorce rates in the former generally being higher than in the latter.

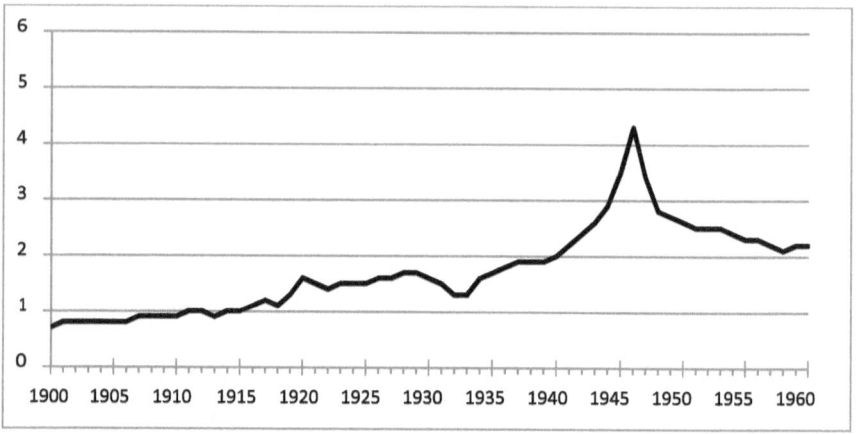

Fig. 1.1: Number of divorces per 1,000 U.S. citizens, 1900–1960.

If we compare divorce statistics over a substantial period, such as the late nineteenth century to the end of the Progressive Era, we find a particularly steep increase in the number of divorces,[34] which quintupled from over 33,000 cases in 1890 (representing a rate of 0.5 divorces per 1,000 inhabitants) to more than 171,000 cases in 1920 (a rate of 1.6 per 1,000 inhabitants). Meanwhile, the number of marriages doubled from about 570,000 to nearly 1.3 million. While World War I and World War II as well had virtually no impact on the general trends in marriage and divorce,[35] the Great Depression triggered a significant decline in both between 1930 and 1932. In 1932, the number of marriages fell below the one million mark (a rate of 7.9); it had been 1.1 million (a rate of 9.2) in 1930. The number of divorces

---

33 *Marriage and Divorce*, 1909, reprinted 1978, 20.
34 Beginning with the second *Wright Report*, both the Bureau of the Census (established in 1902) and the National Center for Health Statistics (founded in 1960; the predecessor organization was the National Office of Vital Statistics, created in 1946, with data collection covering the period from 1890) have collected national marriage and divorce statistics on an annual basis.
35 Unless otherwise noted, these are always indicated through the number of divorces or marriages per 1,000 U.S. residents.

fell from about 200,000 in 1930 (a rate of 1.6) to 164,000 in 1932 (a rate of 1.3). By contrast, immediately after World War II, when many couples had their hastily concluded prewar marriages dissolved, the divorce rate hit a marked high (3.5 in 1945, 4.3 in 1946, and 3.4 in 1947), before levelling off at just over two divorces per 1,000 people by the late 1960s. The marriage rate, meanwhile, declined steadily from its all-time high in 1946 (16.4) until the early 1960s (8.5 in 1962).[36]

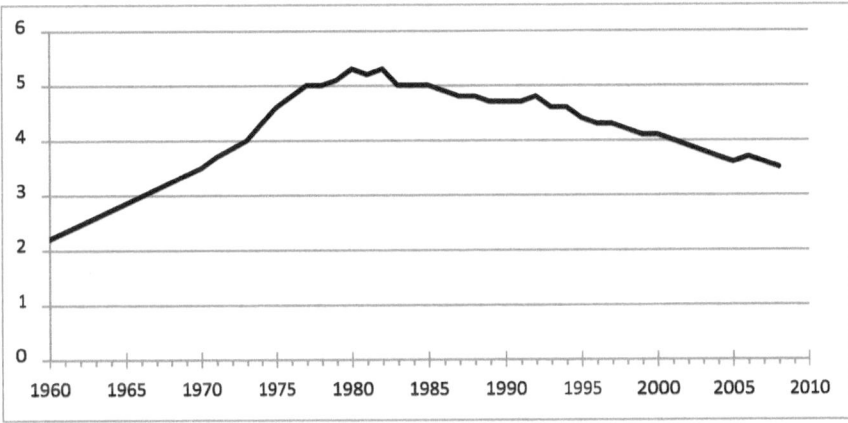

Fig. 1.2: Number of divorces per 1,000 U.S. citizens, 1960–2008.

A second qualitative leap occurred between 1965 and 1975, when divorces climbed from 479,000 to 1.04 million, an increase in the divorce rate from 2.5 (1965) to 3.5 (1970) and 4.9 (1975). In contrast, the marriage rate rose from 9.3 (1965) to 10.6 (in 1970, equating to more than 2 million marriages) and then leveled off at this rate over the next fifteen years. The sharp rise in the divorce rate was due to the nationwide legalization of so-called no-fault divorce, the dissolution of marriage without a court ruling. Starting with the state of California, which introduced this reform in 1969, all states with the exception of New York (until 2010) gradually adopted it from 1970 onward. In 1998, 2.56 million marriages were contracted and 1.3 million divorces occurred, but since the early 1980s the trend in both fields has been slightly downward.[37]

---

36 Plateris, *100 Years*, 22.
37 U.S. Department of Health and Human Services. National Center for Health Statistics. www.cdc.gov/nchs/>. Taylor, Paul, *The Decline of Marriage and the Rise of New Families* (PEW Research Center 2010), 38. Online: <https://www.pewresearch.org/social-trends/wp-content/uploads/sites/3/2010/11/pew-social-trends-2010-families.pdf>.

We can, however, observe major differences by ethnicity and level of education. Susceptibility to divorce has declined since the 1980s for couples with a high level of education and social status; in contrast, the divorce rate among African Americans and, in particular, African American women without a college degree, has increased significantly.[38] At the same time, the marriage rate declined markedly for this group from the middle of the twentieth century onward.[39]

Tab. 1.2: Marriages and divorces, 1900–2009.

Year	Marriage	Rate per 1,000 population	Divorce	Rate per 1,000 population
1900	709,000	9.3	55,751	0.7
1910	948,166	10.3	83,045	0.9
1920	1,274,476	12	170,505	1.6
1930	1,126,856	9.2	195,961	1.6
1940	1,595,879	12.1	264,000	2.0
1950	1,667,231	11.1	385,144	2.6
1960	1,523,000	8.0	393,000	2.2
1965	1,800,000	9.3	479,000	2.5
1970	2,158,802	10.6	708,000	3.5
1975	2,152,662	10.1	1,036,000	4.9
1980	2,406,708	10.6	1,182,000	5.2
1985	2,425,000	10.2	1,187,000	5.0
1990	2,448,000	9.4	1,175,000	4.7
2000	2,329,000	8.5	—	4.2
2009	2,080,000	6.8	840,000	3.5[40]

Other trends apparent over the entire course of the twentieth century were the slightly higher frequency of divorce in urban compared to rural communities and the trend toward shorter marriages. Whereas in the late nineteenth century only five percent of marriages ending in divorce lasted two years or less, by the 1960s this was true of 15 percent.[41] While the average age at marriage for bride and

---

[38] See chapter 4 of the present book. Raley, R. Kelly and Bumpass, Larry, "The Topography of the Divorce Plateau: Levels and Trends in Union Stability in the United States after 1980," *Demographic Research* 8 (2003), 245–260, here 252–253. <www.demographic-research.org/Volumes/Vol8/8/>.
[39] Elliott, Diana B. et al, *Historical Marriage Trends from 1890–2010. A Focus on Race Differences*. SEHSD Working Paper 2012–12, <https://www.census.gov/content/dam/Census/library/working-papers/2012/demo/SEHSD-WP2012-12.pdf>, figure 6.
[40] Without data for California, Georgia, Hawaii, Indiana, Louisiana, and Minnesota.
[41] Plateris, *100 Years*, 15.

groom fell significantly between 1890 and 1920 (from 26.5 to 25.3 years for men and 23.6 to 22.5 years for women), the lowest values were measured in 1950 (24.0 years for men and 20.4 years for women), before rising steadily to a present-day figure of 28.5 years for men and 26.8 years for women (2010).[42] In contrast, the age at marriage for African American males (30.8 years) and females (30 years) is significantly higher than the national average (2010).[43]

Finally, the liberalization of divorce law in the 1970s and the accompanying trend toward remarriage spurred the development of numerous "patchwork families." Between 1970 and 1996, the number of children living exclusively with their biological parents and siblings fell from 85 to 68 percent.[44] But divorce was not the only reason for the new trend towards "families by choice." Since the 1970s, the gay rights movement has fought not only for decriminalization and social acceptance, but also for the right to same-sex marriage. With respect to the latter, they achieved decisive success only from 2004 onward. After the state of Massachusetts introduced civil unions for same-sex couples in 2004 and California accepted same-sex marriages for a period of two years (2008–1010), it was the Supreme Court ruling *Obergefell v. Hodges* in 2015 that granted marriage as a civil right to same-sex couples in all states in the U.S.[45] Far more than the issue of patchwork families, the demand that same-sex couples enjoy the right to marry and to reproduce on their own terms has generated normative and cultural controversy. This plea remains subject to heated debate in large swathes of U.S. society.

Even this brief glimpse into social statistics shows that in the late nineteenth and throughout the twentieth century, a major social change took place in the field of marriage and divorce in the United States. While age at marriage initially declined continuously to an all-time low in the late 1940s and early 1950s and then began to rise again, the total number of marriages increased steadily until 1990. This was due in part to strong population growth through immigration in the early twentieth century. In the 1970s, meanwhile, the baby boomers reached marriageable age, which had a significant impact. The real change, however, was the exponential increase in the divorce rate, especially up to 1920 and also in the

---

[42] *U.S. Decennial Census* (1890). *American Community Survey* (2010) <www.census.gov/acs>.
[43] Elliott, Diana B. et al, *Historical Marriage Trends from 1890–2010. A Focus on Race Differences.* SEHSD Working Paper 2012-12, <https://www.census.gov/content/dam/Census/library/working-papers/2012/demo/SEHSD-WP2012-12.pdf>, figure 4.
[44] Chadwick, Bruce A. and Heaton, Tim B., *Statistical Handbook on the American Family* (Phoenix, AZ 1999), 189.
[45] Powell, et al. (eds.), *Counted Out*. Murray, Heather, *Not in this Family. Gays and the Meaning of Kinship in Postwar North America* (Philadelphia and Oxford 2010). *Obergefell v. Hodges*, 576 U.S. 2015.

period from 1965 to 1975, which triggered a public demand for interpretations and explanations. As will be shown in the following chapters, it was social scientists and especially sociologists who proved to be the group of experts best suited to providing them. By the early twentieth century, they had already ousted church representatives from their hegemonic position when it came to analyzing, negotiating, and interpreting the effects of social change on the normative framework of U.S. society and, in particular, on conceptions of family. To assess this process of adjustment in the twentieth century and its consequences, we must first look at the preceding nineteenth-century divorce debates.

1.2 Divorce as a subject of public debate to the late nineteenth century

As we have seen, neither divorce itself nor the debates about it were an invention of the early twentieth century, although the rise in divorce figures during that period was unprecedented and alarmed many contemporaries. Overall, we can identify four periods in U.S. history in which divorce was discussed in intensive public debates: first, around the middle of the nineteenth century, when the first divorce boom occurred in the wake of the Civil War and industrialization; second, at the end of the nineteenth century, following the publication of the first *Wright Report* in 1889; third, in the first two decades of the twentieth century, when social scientists, churchmen, and lawyers reflected on the perceived threat to the family posed by divorce and discussed proposals for reform, and fourth, during the adoption of no-fault divorce by the states, beginning in 1970. Below, I discuss the first two phases, the mid- and late-nineteenth-century divorce debates, in more detail before examining the early twentieth-century debates on this topic among social scientists in the second part of the chapter. The no-fault divorce debate, meanwhile, I explore as part of my treatment of the debate on abortion in chapter five.

Divorce and divorce debates in the mid-nineteenth century

Alarmed by the pro-divorce legislation adopted by many states and repelled in particular by reports of so-called "divorce mills"[46] in the Midwest, the editor of the

---

46 "Divorce mills" was the name given to cities (and states), particularly in the Midwest, where divorce was relatively easy to obtain due to lax state laws and consequently began to establish itself as a regional business. Couples or individuals who wished to escape their states' partial or total prohibition on divorce (especially in the South and in New York State) traveled to one of

New-York Tribune, Horace Greeley,[47] launched the first major journalistic debates on the subject of divorce in 1852–53 before returning to the topic in 1860.[48] Greeley, himself a strict opponent of divorce, insisted on the biblical view of marriage as a lifelong union that could only be terminated in the event of adultery by one of the partners. He was wholly unimpressed by the arguments of his prominent opponents, theologian and writer Henry James Jr., anarchist Stephen Pearl Andrews, and radical Democrat Robert Dale Owen, all of whom advocated divorce as a means of ending intolerable relationships.[49] In the long run, the "Greeley Debates" had a signaling effect as the first occasion when leading intellectuals reacted to the significant increase in the number of divorces in the mid-nineteenth century, preparing the ground in some measure for the intense discussions that followed.[50] The articles in the New-York Tribune were widely received and commented on, as evident in the case of women's rights activist Elizabeth Cady Stanton;[51] from 1860 onwards, she made several direct references to Horace Greeley and his attempt to lead opinion on divorce, demanding that women in particular be involved in shap-

---

these divorce hubs, met the required minimum residency period, and then obtained their divorce papers. Several economic sectors, including lawyers, hoteliers, real estate agents and the entertainment industry, generated a lucrative side income from divorce tourists.

47 In addition to his work as a newspaper publisher, Horace Greeley (1811–1872) was also a Republican politician and prominent abolitionist. He founded the *New-York Tribune* in 1841, setting standards in American journalism. He ran for the U.S. presidency in 1872 but died during the election campaign. Snay, Mitchell, *Horace Greeley and the Politics of Reform in Nineteenth Century America* (Lanham et. al. 2011).

48 The *New-York Tribune* existed from 1841 until 1924; it was then merged with the *New York Herald* to form the *New York Herald Tribune*, which ceased publication in 1966.

49 Though Andrews flatly rejected any government sanctioning of the relationship between husband and wife. On the two Greeley debates, see Riley, *Divorce*, 72–73. Greeley, Horace, *Recollections of a Busy Life* (New York 1869), 570–618. *New-York Tribune*, December 1, 1852, December 18, 1852, December 24, 1852, January 28, 1853, March 1, 1860, March 5, 1860, March 12, 1860.

50 Previously, criticisms of divorce had been voiced here and there by clergy and intellectuals in treatises but had not taken the form of debates in the press. See the remarks by Glenda Riley, who lists statements critical of divorce by Benjamin Trumbull (1788), Timothy Dwight (1828), and Samuel S. Mahon (1806). Riley, *Divorce*, 53, 59–60.

51 Elisabeth Cady Stanton (1815–1902) was one of the most important American women's rights activists and abolitionists. In 1848, she was one of the main figures behind the Women's Rights Convention in Seneca Falls and wrote the Declaration of Rights and Sentiments adopted there. In 1869 she founded (with Susan B. Anthony) the National American Woman Suffrage Association. Davis, Sue, *The Political Thought of Elizabeth Cady Stanton. Women's Rights and the American Political Traditions* (New York 2010).

ing divorce law.[52] Interestingly, the significance of the "divorce mills" was already subject to controversial debate among contemporaries.

Divorce debates and social statistics in the late nineteenth century

The years 1889 and 1890 saw the first peak in the journalistic debate on the subject of "divorce" and the consequences of skyrocketing divorce figures for the American family. The backdrop was the *Wright Report*, published in 1889, which provided a rational foundation for the concerns of many contemporaries by demonstrating that the number of divorces had increased by 150 percent in just twenty years.[53] The explosive statistical findings and the question of what the consequences might be for American society prompted interventions by opponents and proponents of divorce alike.[54] Not only did a lively debate develop around the pros and cons of current divorce practices in the national daily and weekly press, but calls for national "divorce reform" to harmonize the states' disparate divorce laws gained new momentum. In the years after 1889, opponents of liberal divorce practices in particular campaigned for reform with unprecedented vigor, seeking to reduce the number of divorces by tightening the law.

Of particular importance here was the National Divorce Reform League (later called the League for the Protection of the Family) under Samuel W. Dike, which had advocated Union-wide standardization of divorce legislation since its founding in 1881.[55] Dike, a Protestant, was *the* conservative expert on divorce and di-

---

[52] Cady Stanton, Elizabeth, Anthony, Susan B. and Gage, Mathilda J., *History of Woman Suffrage* (New York 1881), vol. 1, 717, 720, 722. Cady Stanton, Elizabeth, "Are Homogenous Divorce Laws in All the States Desirable?", *North American Review* 170 (1900), 405–409, here 405, 408; Cady Stanton, Elizabeth, "Divorce vs. Domestic Warfare", *Arena* 1 (1890), 560–569; Riley, *Divorce*, 73.

[53] On the *Wright Report*, see section 1.1 of the present book. U.S. Department of Commerce and Labor, *Marriage and Divorce, 1867–1886* (Westport, Conn. 1889). At the instigation of President Theodore Roosevelt, the follow-up appeared in 1909, documenting divorce figures from 1887 to 1906. U.S. Department of Commerce and Labor, *Marriage and Divorce, 1867–1906*, 2 vols. (Westport, Conn. 1909, reprinted 1978).

[54] On the reaction to the *Wright Report*, see for example NYT, February 21, 1889: "Statistics of Divorce." NYT, January 23, 1890: "Divorce Reform League."

[55] Founded by Theodore Woolsey in 1881 as the New England Divorce Reform League, it was led by Samuel Dike from 1884. From 1885 it operated as the National Divorce Reform League and finally, from 1897, as the National League for the Protection of the Family. The League ceased operations in 1915, two years after the death of its longtime chairman and exponent Dike in 1913. It issued regular annual reports; a complete collection from 1880 to 1912 can be found in Dike's literary estate, held at the Library of Congress, Washington D.C: Samuel W. Dike Papers, Call No. O813 J, Box 23.

vorce statistics at the time.⁵⁶ In 1877, as a pastor in Vermont, he had refused to allow a divorcee to remarry and consequently lost his ministry. Subsequently, he devoted himself entirely to the study of divorce and its consequences, first with respect to the New England states and then for the entire United States. In his numerous publications and lectures on the situation of the American family and the threat posed to it by the rising number of divorces, he did not stop at the moral condemnation of those wishing to divorce, in contrast to most of his fellow League members, but tried to approach the problem on the basis of sociological analyses.⁵⁷ Dike was firmly convinced that a revision of the law, for example through a constitutional amendment, was only possible on the basis of accurate social statistics. He thus played a significant role in ensuring that the first *Wright Report* had a solid statistical basis and he contributed to it as co-author.⁵⁸ Contrary to the League's original objective, in the course of his work he realized, in light of the statistics in the *Wright Report*, that the proportion of "migratory divorces," in other words divorce tourism, was very low at less than 20 percent of all divorces and that uniform national legislation on divorce was therefore unlikely to change much in this regard.⁵⁹ He saw the only possible way forward in a combination of stricter laws, punishments for marital offenses, and prohibitions on remarriage. Dike's dilemma, however, was precisely this contradiction between his evident sympathy for the emerging modern social sciences and his moral traditionalism. On the one hand, he failed to establish himself successfully as a social scientist; on the other hand, he alienated his old religiously conservative comrades-in-arms, so that his League for the Protection of the Family became

---

56 Samuel W. Dike (1838–1913) was a Protestant clergyman, divorce opponent, and member of the temperance movement. After studying at Andover Theological Seminary, Massachusetts, he served as a pastor in Connecticut, Vermont, and Massachusetts before assuming leadership of the New England Divorce Reform League and devoting himself to the study of the social sciences. Dike, Samuel W., "Statistics of Divorce in the United States and Europe," *Journal of the American Statistical Association* 1 (1888–89), 206–214.

57 O'Neill, *Divorce*, 50–56. Riley, *Divorce*, 108–112. See also Dike, Samuel W., *Important Features of the Divorce Question* (Royalton, Vt. 1885). Dike, Samuel W., *The Family in the History of Christianity* (New York 1886). Dike, Samuel W., *Perils to the Family* (New York 1888).

58 Dike, "Statistics of Divorce." On the publication of the divorce statistics, see also U.S. Department of Commerce and Labor, *Marriage and Divorce, 1867–1906*, 2 vols. (Westport, Conn. 1909, reprinted 1978), 12. On Dike's contribution to both parts of the *Wright Report*, see the account in the unpublished autobiography in his literary estate: "Draft of an Unfinished Autobiography," Samuel W. Dike Papers, Library of Congress, Washington D. C., Call No. O813 J, Box 22.

59 Recent research also considers it historically verified that the true importance of the "divorce mills" was overestimated by many indignant contemporaries and that in reality only a small number of divorces resulted from interstate divorce tourism. Dike, "Statistics of Divorce," 212. Riley, *Divorce*, 85–107.

increasingly marginal from 1905 onward. The League survived the death of its longtime corresponding secretary in 1913 by just two years before ceasing its work.[60] Dike's transformation from conservative clergyman to social expert striving for scientific credibility is examined later in this chapter.

Also revealing of the state of the public debate on divorce is a series of articles in the liberal *North American Review*, which had a total of ten well-known intellectuals reflect on their attitudes toward divorce between 1889 and 1890 on the basis of a uniform set of questions, before publishing their responses in three tranches.[61] The contributors answered a total of four questions, first about their acceptance or rejection of divorce as a whole, second about their position on the remarriage of divorcees, third on the effects of divorce on the integrity of the family, and fourth concerning their ideas about its consequences for the moral climate of society.[62]

The anti-divorce faction was led by James Cardinal Gibbons,[63] the most prominent Catholic prelate in the United States at the time. For him, divorce was "a monster licensed by the laws of Christian States to break hearts, wreck homes, and ruin souls," one that undermined not only marriage as an institution, but also the entire society, whose foundation was marriage and the family. Divorce, he continued, was "a menace not only to the sacredness of the marriage institution, but even to the fair social fabric reared upon matrimony as its cornerstone."[64] In keeping with the teachings of the Catholic Church, Gibbons considered marriage to be a sacrament, sacred and in principle indissoluble. The only exception the cardinal allowed was "divorce

---

[60] On Dike's importance to the League, see its annual reports from 1896 to 1912: Samuel W. Dike Papers, Library of Congress, Washington D. C., Call No. O813 J, Box 23.

[61] The *North American Review* was the first literary magazine in the United States when it was founded in 1815, and it was also the most important until the *Atlantic Monthly* appeared in 1857. It remained a key information medium and discussion forum for U.S. intellectuals throughout the period covered by this chapter. It appeared quarterly, <www.northamericanreview.org/history>. Peterson gives a circulation of 76,000 for 1891; by 1924, this had declined to 13,000. Peterson, Theodore, *Magazines in the Twentieth Century* (Urbana 1956), 132–133.

[62] Gibbons, Cardinal James, Potter, Bishop Henry C. and Ingersoll, Colonel Robert G., "Is Divorce Wrong?" *North American Review*, 149 (1889), 513–538. Livermore, Mary A., Barr, Amelia E., Cooke, Rose Terry, Phelps, Elizabeth Stuart and June, Jennie, "Women's View of Divorce," *North American Review*, 150, 1 (1890), 110–135. Lee, Margaret and Moxom, Reverend Philip S. D.D., "Final Words on Divorce," *North American Review*, 150, 2 (1890), 263–268.

[63] James Cardinal Gibbons (1834–1921) was a cardinal of the Roman Catholic Church and Archbishop of Baltimore, Maryland, from 1887. He was considered by his contemporaries to be the most important representative of the Catholic Church in the United States. Gibbons' popular religious writings were widely received, and he was also an advisor to several presidents. He was involved in the Catholic trade union movement and the founding of the Catholic University of America in 1887, serving as its first chancellor.

[64] Gibbons et al, "Is Divorce Wrong?", 513–538, 517.

of bed and board," the physical separation of a couple, permissible only in the case of adultery by one of the spouses and tied to a complete prohibition on remarriage by either of them. Even in serious cases of marital conflict, he thus explicitly subordinated the welfare of the individual to that of society. In order to achieve the long-term moral and social ostracism of divorce as well as a reduction in the number of divorces, he proposed a number of immediate measures: fewer grounds for divorce, abolition of simplified divorce proceedings and "secret divorce," prohibition of "migratory divorces," and the total prohibition of remarriage.

Three writers, Rose Terry Cooke,[65] Elizabeth Stuart Phelps,[66] and Margaret Lee[67] reiterated Gibbons' hardline position[68] in their articles. Social reformer Phelps, however, went further, arguing for reform of common divorce practices and for the prohibition of marriages entered into purely for economic reasons, which she called "legalized prostitution."[69]

In contrast, Episcopal Bishop Henry C. Potter,[70] Boston Baptist minister Reverend Philip S. Moxom[71] and writers Mary A. Livermore,[72] Amelia E. Barr,[73] and Jennie June (Jane Cunningham Croly)[74] took a moderate position. Bishop Potter

---

[65] Rose Terry Cooke (1827–1892) was an American writer who made her name primarily through short stories about rural life in New England.

[66] Elizabeth Stuart Phelps, alias Mary Gray Phelps (1844–1911), published, among other things, religious novels and numerous short stories, which were published in magazines such as *Harper's*. In addition to her literary activities, she was a strong advocate of social reform and women's rights.

[67] Margaret Lee published a widely read novel critical of divorce in 1889, using the example of her heroine to present marriage as an indissoluble sacrament. Lee, Margaret, *Divorce. Or Faithful and Unfaithful* (New York 1889).

[68] Livermore et al, "Women's View of Divorce," 123–131. Lee and Moxom, "Final Words on Divorce," 263–264.

[69] Livermore et al, "Women's View of Divorce," 131.

[70] Henry Codman Potter (1835–1908) was a bishop of the Episcopal Church in the Diocese of New York. In addition to pastoral work, his main interest was social reform; he was involved in various reform projects in New York City.

[71] Philip Stafford Moxom was an exponent of the Social Gospel and served as pastor of the First Baptist Church, Boston, and later as pastor of the South Congregational Church in Springfield, MA. NYT, June 6, 1920.

[72] Mary Livermore (1820–1905) was a well-known women's rights activist and journalist. The editor of various periodicals (such as *Agitator* and *Women's Journal*), she fought primarily for women's suffrage, but was also an active supporter of the temperance movement.

[73] Amelia Edith Barr (1831–1919) was a British-American writer who wrote novels as well as religious and historical stories.

[74] Jenny June alias Jane Cunningham Croly (1829–1901) was a journalist and writer who wrote under a pseudonym. She edited several magazines, published fiction, a cookbook and guidebooks, and a history of U.S. women's clubs. June founded the first American women's club, Soro-

clarified that for the Episcopal Church marriage was essentially a civil contract, not a sacrament, and thus divorce was in principle allowable, though it should be avoided if at all possible. Remarriage of divorced persons was not permitted, with the exception of the innocent partner in separations following adultery. Potter rejected an absolute ban on divorce as inefficient, but conceded that a bitter dispute was raging in the Episcopal Church over the interpretation of biblical sources on the subject of divorce, in which he acted as spokesman for the liberal faction.[75] Moxom did not fundamentally oppose the possibility of divorce, but advocated a regulated form of spousal separation (*a mensa et thoro*, of table and bed), which was, he asserted, quite sufficient in most cases. The family in particular, he suggested, would benefit from a strictly prescribed divorce practice: "Rare and difficult divorce may conserve a true family life. Easy divorce promotes a freedom of sexual relations in society in which the family cannot live and thrive."[76]

The protection of the family also enjoyed the highest priority in the texts of writers and social reformers Mary A. Livermore, Amelia E. Barr, and Jenny June. While they accepted divorce as a means of ending intolerable human relationships, they concurrently pleaded for a reform of national divorce law and a strengthening of the family. It is interesting to note that their contributions pursued two lines of argument. The first consisted of a declared belief in women's responsibility for the preservation of marriage and the survival of the family, but this was now coupled with a demand for more rights for women. Exemplary here was Livermore's statement vehemently demanding implementation of the principle of equality: "There should be legal equality established between the husband and the wife, equal ownership of the family property, equal guardianship of the minor children."[77]

The second pattern of argumentation consisted in the coupling of "reform" and "eugenics," for example when Barr and Livermore contended that divorce must be possible in order to protect society from the offspring of failed, socially undesirable unions (Livermore) and that the mentally ill should be excluded from remarriage (Barr).[78] Barr articulated the conviction typical of the era that social ills could be remedied through reform and in this case, if necessary, by di-

---

sis, in 1869 and established the General Federation of Women's Clubs in 1890. Croly, Jane Cunningham, *The History of the Woman's Club Movement in America, Volume 1* (New York 1898).
75 On the intra-episcopal dispute between Potter and the Bishop of Albany, NY, William C. Doane, see O'Neill, *Divorce*, 41–42.
76 Lee and Moxom, "Final Words on Divorce," 264–268, here 267.
77 Livermore et al, "Women's View of Divorce," 116. See also the contribution by Jenny June, ibid., 131–135.
78 Livermore et al, "Women's View of Divorce," 111, 120–121.

vorce: "But when mistakes are made, why give permanency to wrong and finality to suffering? The irrevocable contains no element of reformation."[79]

This point was reinforced by the only unconditional proponent of divorce, lawyer Robert G. Ingersoll.[80] He contrasted the sacramental character of marriage as expounded by Gibbons with the rights of the individual, concluding: "Marriages are made by men and women; not by society; not by the state; not by the church; not by supernatural beings."[81] For him, protecting the family not only meant legally enabling wives to separate from their violent husbands, but also presupposed recognition of the equality of the sexes: "If we wish to preserve the integrity of the family, we must preserve the democracy of the fireside, the republicanism of the home, the absolute and perfect equality of husband and wife."[82]

Although Ingersoll was still largely alone in his call for a "republicanism of the home" in 1889, inspired by this national divorce debate the first upheavals began to occur in the evaluation of gender roles. Jenny June reflected on this development when she asserted that the roots of the progressive decline in the sacramental character of marriage lay in the gradual reassessment of such roles. Women, she underlined, were increasingly questioning the demand for their unconditional obedience:

> That social questions, marriage among the number, have changed their aspects during the past quarter of a century no one will deny. But the tendency is less toward the breaking-up of family life, the disruption of family ties, I think, than appears on the surface. Marriage, as we understand it, is a comparatively recent institution. In the church it has always implied more or less of servitude or unquestioning obedience on the part of the woman. The wisdom of obedience to all men, or to any man under all circumstances, is now doubted by intelligent women; and the sanction of the church has lost much of its sacramental character in the eyes of both men and women.[83]

But the positions put forward by Ingersoll, Livermore, and June were by no means shared by all the discussants. A few months earlier, in the same magazine, five American women writers (including Amelia E. Barr and Rose Terry Cooke), faced with the question "Are Women to Blame?", argued that it was primarily women who caused their marriages to fail through misguided expectations and inappropri-

---

79 Livermore et al, "Women's View of Divorce," 117.
80 Lawyer Robert Green Ingersoll (1833–1899) was a noted Civil War veteran, political orator, and free thinker. After the Civil War, he became attorney general of the state of Illinois. Ingersoll, a member of the Republican Party, chose not to pursue a political career in order to freely expound his often radical, agnostic, and humanist beliefs.
81 Gibbons et al., "Is Divorce Wrong?", 534.
82 Gibbons et al., "Is Divorce Wrong?", 537.
83 Livermore et al., "Women's View of Divorce," 132.

ate behavior.[84] The trend toward divorce could only be reversed through better education, home economics training, and the teaching of religious and moral values to young women. However, in Amelia E. Barr's complaint about "those wives who have what they call 'advanced' ideas—who talk about the animal character of motherhood, the degrading influence of housekeeping, the monotony of home, the slavery of self-sacrifice"[85] and about the fact that many women were no longer willing to be confined to the "domestic sphere," it becomes clear just how much Victorian ideas about the family and the role of women had already been challenged:

> Women are at present in a restless state of transition. They have broken from the citadel of home, where have walked the holy women of all past ages; they are attacking the hoary supremacy of men, and invading the world where men have hitherto toiled and travelled and ruled alone.[86]

This debate makes it clear that in 1889 and 1890, concealed behind the controversy over divorce figures and the effects of the divorce boom on the family, an even more fundamental discussion about gender roles and women's rights was beginning to emerge. Further, we can begin to discern how the first national divorce statistics not only gave new impetus to the divorce debate per se but, in the view of many, demonstrated the need for a "national divorce reform" given the diverging legal bases in the different states.

"Sanctity of the marriage relation": Initiatives by the churches and states toward divorce law reform in the early twentieth century

Subsequently, both church representatives and interstate reform commissions attempted to get to grips with the divorce boom by standardizing (and tightening) divorce law. In addition to Dike's League for the Protection of the Family, other key bodies in this context were the Committee on Marriage and Divorce of the National Conference of Commissioners on Uniform State Laws[87] and the Inter-

---

[84] Harding Davis, Rebecca, Terry Cooke, Rose, Harland, Marion, Owen, Catharine, and Barr, Amelia E, "Are Women to Blame?", *North American Review* 148 (1889), 622–642.
[85] Harding et al, "Are Women to Blame?", 640.
[86] As Barr put it in Harding et al., "Are Women to Blame?", 642.
[87] To this day, the task of the National Conference of Commissioners on Uniform State Laws, composed of representatives of the states, is to standardize the states' legal frameworks. During the period under study, it maintained a Committee on Marriage and Divorce, which put forward numerous proposals for a national standardization of divorce law, which ultimately failed due to resistance from the states. See *Report of the Committee on Marriage and Divorce: With First Tentative Drafts of Acts on the Subjects of Marriages and Licenses to Marry, and Relating to Family Desertion and Non-*

Church Conference on Marriage and Divorce,[88] initiated and led by Episcopal bishop William C. Doane.[89] Doane was less concerned with ostracizing divorce—like the representatives of the Catholic Church, he was only prepared to countenance "scriptural grounds," in other words adultery, as a reason for divorce—than with restricting the remarriage of divorcees. He described the latter as a "foul tide of desecration of marriage, of the degradation of the family, of the deterioration of the home."[90]

While Dike's organization had been steadily losing reach across the United States since the turn of the century, the national working group of the major Protestant denominations under Doane survived for just three years.[91] Doane and his comrades-in-arms at least managed to raise President Theodore Roosevelt's awareness of the issue of divorce. In early 1905, at the annual meeting of the Inter-Church Conference in Washington, D.C., Roosevelt acknowledged the "vital questions of having the unit of our social life, the home, preserved" and warned of the consequences of declining birth rates among "old native American families."[92] Referring to the threat to the "sanctity of the marriage relation" posed by lax and inconsistent laws, which, he emphasized, could only be reformed on the basis of

---

Support (Philadelphia 1909). Digital reprint in *The Making of Modern Law* (Gale 2009). Gale, Cengage Learning. *Report of the Committee on Marriage and Divorce: With Second Tentative Drafts of Acts on the Subjects of Marriages and Licenses to Marry and Family Desertion and Non-Support* (Williamsport, PA. 1910). Digital reprint in *The Making of Modern Law* (Gale 2009). Gale, Cengage Learning. *Report of the Committee on Marriage and Divorce: With Third Tentative Draft of an Act on the Subject of Marriage and Marriage Licenses* (Williamsport, PA 1911). Digital reprint in *The Making of Modern Law* (Gale 2009). Gale, Cengage Learning.

88 The results of the conference were published. See for example *Documents of the Interchurch Conference on Marriage and Divorce* (New York 1903).

89 William Coswell Doane (1832–1913) became a bishop of the Episcopal Church in the Diocese of Albany in New York State in 1869. He initiated and chaired the Inter-Church Conference on Marriage and Divorce from 1903 to 1906, and from 1905 he also served as chairman of the Committee on Family Life of the Federal Council of the Churches of Christ in America, an association of the major Protestant denominations.

90 Doane, William Croswell, "The Question of Divorce and Remarriage," NYT, November 26, 1899. Doane, William Croswell, "Remarriage after Divorce: Catholic Theory and Practice," *North American Review* 180, 4 (1905 April), 513–522.

91 It existed only from 1903 to 1906. Doane continued his reform activities until his death in 1913 as chairman of the Committee on Family Life of the Federal Council of the Churches of Christ in America, together with Samuel Dike, who served as its chairman. Sanford, Elias B., *Origin and History of the Federal Council of Churches of Christ in America* (Hartford, CT 1916), 264–265, 508–510.

92 U.S. Department of Commerce and Labor, Bureau of the Census, Special Reports: *Marriage and Divorce 1867–1906*. Part I: *Summary, Laws, Foreign Statistics* (Washington 1909), 4. See also Riley, *Divorce*, 115. O'Neill, *Divorce*, 245–46.

reliable national statistics, the president urged the Senate and House of Representatives to provide funds for further documentation of divorce figures for the period 1887–1906.[93] Congress proved amenable, and the second *Wright Report* had appeared by 1909.

The National Congress on Uniform Divorce Laws, held in Washington, D.C., in 1906, also came about at the president's instigation, but the model statutes for uniform laws it produced were signed by only three of the then 49 states.[94] The work of the Committee on Marriage and Divorce of the National Conference of Commissioners on Uniform State Laws also achieved little, as one of its leading spokesmen, lawyer Walter George Smith, lamented in retrospect.[95] This, he asserted, was primarily due to the fact that the representatives of the states had failed to recognize the urgency of the problem:

> The fact is that outside the large body of Catholics, the masses of the people do not look upon existing conditions with any real appreciation of the dangers connected with them, being more concerned that the unhappiness arising from the frequent mismatches of married couples shall be cured by what is called "the surgery of divorce," than with the injury entailed upon the morals of the community at large.[96]

There were two key reasons why it proved possible to establish national marriage statistics in the period from 1900 to 1910, but not to standardize divorce law. For one thing, neither declared opponents nor proponents of divorce were willing to compromise; each faction flatly rejected a national middle way. This would have consisted in repealing both extremely restrictive and highly liberal divorce laws in the different states in favor of a regulation acceptable to all, but no agreement

---

[93] President Roosevelt's Message to Congress, January 30, 1905. U.S. Department of Commerce and Labor, Bureau of the Census, Special Reports: *Marriage and Divorce 1867–1906*. Part I: *Summary, Laws, Foreign Statistics* (Washington 1909), 4.

[94] *Proceedings of the National Congress on Uniform Divorce Laws, held at Washington, D.C., February 19, 1906* (Harrisburg, PA 1906). Digital reprint in *The Making of Modern Law* (Gale 2009). Gale, Cengage Learning. For an evaluation of the results of the National Congress and the follow-up meeting in the same year, see Riley, *Divorce*, 115–118.

[95] Walter George Smith (1854–1924) was a lawyer, a professing Catholic and a member of the Philadelphia Bar Association. On behalf of the latter, he participated in the deliberations of the Commission on Uniform State Laws from 1906 and played a major role in standardizing the nation's divorce laws. In 1917 he was elected president of the American Bar Association. On Smith's biography, see Bryson, Thomas A., *Walter George Smith* (Washington 1977).

[96] Smith, Walter George, "Ethics of Divorce," *Case and Comment* 21 (1914), 3–6. Quoted in Johnsen, Julia E. (ed.), *Selected Articles on Marriage and Divorce* (New York 1925), 283. This lawyer and Catholic was an advocate of the strictest possible divorce law and, in contrast to many social scientists, always emphasized the sacramental character of marriage. On his criticism of the position of Howard and other sociologists on divorce, see below.

could be reached. Second, the steadily rising divorce figures told their own story: the majority of Americans did not seem to want divorce to be questioned or even to happen less often. Glenda Riley has made the case, one worth discussing, that the rise of sociologists and sociology and its explanations for the increase in the number of divorces—namely as a result of social upheavals in the wake of industrialization and urbanization—did much to ensure the eventual failure of uniform national divorce laws.[97] Instead of pushing for changes in legislation to curb divorce, most social scientists advocated a shift in emphasis when it came to marriage and the family, highlighting better protection of women's rights in particular.

The task of the second section is to examine whether the social sciences, and sociology in particular, managed to achieve hegemony over the interpretation of social change. The underlying hypothesis here is that at the beginning of the twentieth century there was a shift away from the religious and legal sciences to the social sciences when it came to explaining the change in family values and family structures, as manifest in the unprecedented increase in the number of divorces and the changing role of women. If such a shift toward sociology did in fact occur, did it trigger a process of social transformation, a move away from rigid "Victorian morals" to a greater plurality of lifestyles? Or can it even be viewed as a palpable expression of a change in values that was already underway? Another possible explanation for any shift toward the social sciences, however, could be that only the comparatively young scholarly discipline of sociology had the methodological capacity—by compiling and evaluating statistics and data sets—to offer explanations of social phenomena and make forecasts.[98]

---

[97] Riley, *Divorce*, 123. William O'Neill, on the other hand, assumes that the gradual liberalization of attitudes toward marriage and the family in the course of the overcoming of "Victorian morals" made it impossible to agree on nationally binding divorce laws in the Progressive Era. O'Neill, "Divorce," 142–149.

[98] Although statistical methods for researching social phenomena had existed since the mid-nineteenth century, it took sociology as a full-fledged scientific discipline to apply them to social problems, which it increasingly did over the first half of the twentieth century. According to Jennifer Platt, until the Great Depression, the work of U.S. sociologists was still characterized by great methodological eclecticism and little innovation. It was only through the funding of extensive fieldwork on the social upheavals of the 1930s, she argues, that sociology developed its own quantitative methods of investigation and methodological sensibility. However, it should be kept in mind that Platt does not begin her period of investigation until 1920 and therefore does not take into account the effects of the debate on divorce statistics in the Progressive Era. Platt, Jennifer, *A History of Sociological Research Methods in America, 1920–1960* (Cambridge et al. 1996), 31–32, 271–272.

1.3 "Social control and women's place in society": the influence of sociologists on public debates on divorce from the turn of the century onward

In the first decade of the twentieth century, important works by U.S. sociologists appeared that described divorce as perhaps not desirable but as a rational measure for ending intolerable interpersonal relationships. The first to express an unequivocal view was historian and later president of the American Sociological Association, George E. Howard[99] in his monumental *History of Matrimonial Institutions* of 1904. In view of the disparate divorce laws across the United States, he declared: "Divorce is a remedy and not the disease."[100] It was not divorce per se, he argued, that was immoral, but the lack of uniform marriage and divorce laws throughout the country.[101] Significantly, Howard not only called for liberalization of the practice of divorce and reform of divorce laws, but viewed the proponents of divorce as advocates of social modernization. Attitudes toward divorce were thus no longer a matter of individual moral-religious conviction, but became a subset of the debate on modernity and its consequences:

> The divorce movement is a portentous and almost universal incident of modern civilization. Doubtless it signifies underlying social evils vast and perilous. Yet to the student of history it is perfectly clear that this is but a part of the mighty movement for social liberation which has been gaining in volume and strength ever since the Reformation.[102]

This shift was also evident at the aforementioned conference in 1908, when a section chaired by Howard discussed the question "Is the freer granting of divorce an

---

[99] George Elliott Howard (1849–1928) was actually a historian by training and position, and taught at Nebraska, Stanford, Cornell, and Chicago universities. In the 1870s, he had studied for two years in Europe (in Paris and Munich). As a historian, he was a pioneer of the investigation of social-historical issues and a feminist; as a social scientist, he was interested in the historical dimension of social processes. He served as the seventh president of the American Sociological Association in 1916–1917.

[100] Howard, George Elliott, *A History of Matrimonial Institutions: Chiefly in England and the United States with an Introductory Analysis of the Literature and the Theories of Primitive Marriage and the Family*, 3 vols. (Chicago 1904), 219.

[101] "Divorce is not immoral. It is quite probable, on the contrary, that drastic, like negligent, legislation is sometimes immoral." Howard, *History*, vol. 3, 220. For a broad overview of the group of divorce advocates at the end of the nineteenth and beginning of the twentieth centuries in the social sciences, see O'Neill, *Divorce*, 89–125.

[102] Howard, *History*, vol. 3, 220.

evil?"[103] In his introductory lecture, Howard again criticized the disparate legal bases and shortcomings of divorce practice in the United States, but pointed out that it was "the imperfections of the social systems, notably in false sentiments regarding marriage and the family" that had given rise to the "divorce movement" in the first place. In other words, the divorce trends of the day reflected a process of social transition and development and could chiefly be explained with reference to spouses' unclear expectations of their hastily chosen partners, of marriage and of society in general.[104] Howard regarded rising divorce figures as an expression of a fundamental, far from complete process of individualization and liberalization that, he believed, was changing the patriarchal family forever.[105] It was no coincidence, he claimed, that the majority of those filing for divorce were women, who were thus reflecting their growing independence and demanding equal rights and a fairer division of roles in the family: "The divorce movement [. . .] is in large part an expression of woman's growing independence."[106]

For Howard, this prompted two key conclusions. First, divorce had to be accepted as a necessary social remedy. Second, only by educating American youth more effectively *before* they married could a responsible attitude toward marriage be anchored in society.[107] This would help reduce divorce rates in the long term: "That remedy is proper social control; but adequate social control can be achieved only through the thorough socialization of education."[108] Howard's enthusiasm for "social control" as a means of improving society (in this case, marriage) is symptomatic of the Progressive Era: the call for more (and for more appropriate forms of) education and control pervades the texts of many other authors addressing the issue of rising divorce rates. This is a one of the key findings of the present study.

---

[103] In addition to Howard, the sociologists James P. Lichtenberger and Edward A. Ross gave short presentations, as did Samuel W. Dike and Rabbi Joseph Krauskopf (1858–1923), rabbi of the Reform synagogue Keneseth Israel in Philadelphia from 1887 and a leading exponent of Reform Judaism. Originally from Ostrowo in the Prussian province of Posen, he had emigrated to the U.S. by 1872 and studied at Hebrew Union College in Cincinnati shortly thereafter. Howard, George Elliott, "Freer Granting of Divorce," 150–180.
[104] "The modern divorce movement is an incident of a transition process in social evolution, and hence it is due primarily to social mis-selection and the clash of ideals." Howard, "Freer Granting," 155.
[105] "Through a swift process of individualization for the sake of socialization the corporate unity of the patriarchal family has been broken up or even completely destroyed." Howard, "Freer Granting," 155.
[106] Howard, "Freer Granting," 157.
[107] "In no other way, perhaps, has mis-selection, the failure to develop methods of social control adequate to the new psychic character of the family been so harmful as in dealing with marriage." Howard, "Freer Granting," 159.
[108] Howard, "Freer Granting," 160.

James P. Lichtenberger and Edward Alsworth Ross, also pioneers of sociology in the United States in the early twentieth century, shared Howard's view that rising divorce rates were the product of processes of social upheaval. Lichtenberger,[109] for example, urged sociologists to explore causes rather than fight outcomes. The ideal of the family, he contended, had changed in that Americans were ever less tolerant of grievances within marriage, while women were demanding gender equality and rejecting the moral "double standard"; there was also growing recognition that emotional affection and marital fidelity formed the basis of marriage and family.[110] But in his view, this was no reason to fear the end of the family, since divorces helped families function better in modern society:

> Until the new family finds its equilibrium in the changing economic, social and religious environment a high rate of divorce is inevitable and is an index of progress rather than a sign of social disintegration.[111]

In his study *Divorce. A Study in Social Causation*, published shortly after the conference, Lichtenberger took this argument further, setting out the special role of social scientists. In contrast to the "alarmists, professional reformers, moral and religious dogmatists" who mistakenly interpreted the increase in divorce figures documented in the *Wright Report* as a sign of the decline of the family, sociologists could effectively explain social change,[112] namely by analyzing economic, social, and psychological developments in society:

> What is needed is to bring the subject out into the open, to throw upon it the same white light of scientific criticism and investigation to which we subject the facts of our modern political and industrial life, let the consequences be what they may.[113]

In exemplary fashion, Lichtenberger articulated the optimism and self-image of Progressive-Era sociologists:

---

[109] James Pendleton Lichtenberger (1870–1953) became professor of sociology at the University of Pennsylvania in 1909. Previously, he had served as pastor in the Church of the Disciples of Christ between 1896 and 1908, first in Canton, Illinois, then in Buffalo, New York, and finally in New York City. In 1922, Lichtenberger became president of the American Sociological Society.

[110] Contemporaries referred to the divergent moral standards for men, whose premarital sexual contact was readily accepted, and women, to whom this did not apply, as a "double standard."

[111] "We need to get rid of the fear that the family will disintegrate unless held together by the law. The family always has and probably always will arise and disintegrate as the necessities of life require with scant regard for our laws on the subject." Lichtenberger, James P., "Is the Freer Granting of Divorce an Evil?", AJS, 1908–1909, 789.

[112] "This group seeks to go a little deeper, by the use of inductive methods, into the question of causation. It is making scientific inquiry into the reasons for this seemingly rapid change in human nature which is modified ordinarily only by long-continued processes." Lichtenberger, *Divorce*, 12.

[113] Lichtenberger, *Divorce*, 17.

> We have simply been concerned with the facts as they are. Our effort has been accurately to diagnose the social situation in respect to the subject of divorce, from which we have sought rigidly to exclude all therapeutic treatment.[114]

In the course of his analysis, he diagnosed three epoch-making processes of change as the basis of the divorce boom: first, economic growth on a historically new scale, second, an unprecedented change in the social fabric,[115] and third, relevant shifts in ethical and religious attitudes. Drawing on Herbert Spencer's *Principles of Sociology*,[116] Lichtenberger argued that in view of these upheavals, the high divorce rate was merely a transitional phenomenon. In his view, divorce was one of the costs of progress toward enhanced "industrial efficiency, individual and social freedom, ethical culture," and an eventual improvement of the family:[117]

> Many old restraints have been, and are being, removed and new ideals are in the process of formation. Before external restraints have been thoroughly replaced by internal regulative principles some deterioration is more likely to result, but in the end, a new adjustment will be established and the family will be much improved by the change.[118]

Since voluntariness was the "bulwark of modern marriage," he considered the persistence of marriage—as the key organizing principle of the family—far more likely than its decline.

> Marriage contracted upon the basis of mutual attraction and choice, of companionship, of reciprocal rights and privileges, and of an equal standard of morals, is far more likely to survive than the coercive marriage with its inequality, economic dependence, and dual standard of morals.[119]

Sociologist Edward A. Ross[120] too emphasized the importance of marriage as a "socially approved status", one based on the fact that the two people involved entered

---

114 Lichtenberger, *Divorce*, 20.
115 Lichtenberger spoke of "unparalleled achievements in social progress" and emphasized the connection between democratization, individualization, and divorce rate: "The struggle for social liberation, and the reconstruction of the social order in the interest of the greater freedom of the individual [. . .]—in short, the whole democratic movement of modern times, aside from its purely political aspects—is most significant as to its effect upon the rising divorce rate." Lichtenberger, *Divorce*, 19, 176.
116 Lichtenberger referred to Spencer, *Principles of Sociology*, vol. 1, 764–766: divorce was being facilitated by changing attitudes toward marriage and the individual, thereby making marriage and the family better in the long run. Lichtenberger, *Divorce*, 214–215.
117 Lichtenberger, *Divorce*, 212.
118 Lichtenberger, *Divorce*, 212.
119 Lichtenberger, *Divorce*, 215.
120 Edward Alsworth Ross (1866–1951) was first professor of economics at Cornell University, then professor of sociology at Stanford University, at the University of Nebraska (at times jointly with

into it voluntarily. In his contribution to the debate at the sociological conference of 1908, however, he also made it clear that, in addition to the freedom of choice of the spouses seeking divorce, the welfare of any children and of society in general had to be taken into account.[121] In his early standard work, *Social Control* (1901), which became required reading not only for American sociologists but also for many progressive reformers, Ross had already considered the consequences of social change at the threshold of the transition from pre-modern community to modern society and he had formulated guiding principles vital to achieving a rational social order (what he called "planned social control" to establish a "conscious social order").[122] He also recommended concrete measures to combat the divorce boom, which laid bare his sympathy for greater intervention by the state: education in housekeeping for girls, marriage preparation courses for young people of both sexes, prohibition of marriages between healthy women and men with venereal diseases, marriage only at the place of residence of one of the two partners, official rejection of marriage without a marriage certificate, publication of the intention to marry six weeks before marriage, and the establishment of divorce courts in which women must also be represented.[123] He took this call for more prevention rather than laments over rising divorce numbers further in an article for *Century* magazine, also published in 1909. Since the divorce figures, he believed, did not document a moral decline, but mirrored a development of modern society not amenable to prohibitions or moral ostracism, the goal must be to strengthen the quality of marriages through social reforms.[124] In particular, he contended, the conflict of interests between women, who were now better educated and therefore demanded greater rights, and had also achieved economic in-

---

George E. Howard), and from 1906 at the University of Wisconsin. From 1914 to 1916 he served as president of the American Sociological Association. He lost his chair at Stanford University in 1901 because of his explicit public criticism of the use of Chinese migrant workers in the construction of the Union Pacific Railroad. In protest at Ross's dismissal, his friend and colleague Howard also left Stanford University. Ross's most important works are *Social Control* (1901), *Foundations of Sociology* (1905), and *Principles of Sociology* (1920). On Ross, see McMahon, Sean H., *Social Control & Public Intellect. The Legacy of Edward A. Ross* (New Brunswick and London 1999).

121 Ross, Edward Alsworth, "Is the Freer Granting of Divorce an Evil?", AJS 14 (1908–1909), 793–794.
122 Ross, Edward Alsworth, *Social Control. A Survey of the Foundations of Order* (first edition New York, 1901. Reprint Cleveland and London 1969), esp. 432–438; see also the introduction by Julius Weinberg, Gisela J. Hinkle, and Roscoe C. Hinkle, vii–lv.
123 Ross, "Freer Granting."
124 Ross too spoke of a "transition process in social evolution," referring to the divorce boom as the "product of the modern social situation." Ross, "Significance," reprinted in Johnsen, *Marriage and Divorce*, 59, 61.

dependence, and their husbands, who adhered to traditional ideas of patriarchal authority, led to discord: "The resulting clash of ideals is none the less disastrous because it is only an incident of a transition process in social evolution."[125]

Much like Lichtenberger, Ross predicted a decline in the divorce rate over the long term, because many would recognize the benefits of the family for both society and individual; the first counter-trends, he asserted, were already apparent. Agreeing with Howard and Lichtenberger, Ross acknowledged a leading role for sociologists in analyzing the divorce boom. Anyone seriously interested in reducing the number of divorces "must appeal to sociology rather than to a dogma."[126]

In his concluding statement to the section at the sociological conference, George E. Howard too highlighted the need for regulatory interventions ("social control") to improve society ("social evolution"): "Not individual contract but social control is the key to our problem."[127] An important field here, he emphasized, was the premarital education of young people in order to prevent "sociologically bad marriages."

> Marriages, not legally, but sociologically bad, are meant. They include frivolous, mercenary, ignorant and psychologically vicious unions. They embrace all that would be forbidden by Francis Galton's science of Eugenics; all that might be in part prevented by a right system of education. Indeed, bad marriages are the cause of the clash of ideals referred to.[128]

In addition to the reference to the "science of Eugenics," which relied on "a right system of education," the rationale adduced here is also interesting. This was later to become a permanent feature of the eugenics movement's rhetorical repertoire: "We are far more careful in breeding cattle or fruit trees than in breeding men and women."[129] However, Howard did not (yet) lose sight of the value of the individual: "It is high time to cease the appeal to mere authority and to accept marriage, the home, and the family as purely human social institutions to be freely dealt with by men according to human needs."[130] He had changed his tune just over ten years later in the article "Bad Marriage, Quick Divorce." Now he advocated eugenically motivated intervention in the rights of the individual.[131]

The bottom line of the discussions at the conference of 1908 was that most social scientists agreed with the demand for expert-based, more regulatory interven-

---

125 Ross, "Significance," 59.
126 Ross, "Significance," 60.
127 Howard, George Elliott, "Is the Freer Granting of Divorce an Evil?", AJS 14 (1908–1909), no. 6, 766–796, "Concluding Remarks," 795.
128 Howard, "Concluding Remarks," 795.
129 Howard, "Freer Granting," 159.
130 Howard, "Concluding Remarks," 796.
131 Howard, George Elliott, "Bad Marriage and Quick Divorce," *Journal of Applied Sociology* 6 (1921), 1–10.

tion by the government in the affairs of the family ("social control") for the good of society. At the same time, however, the majority were willing to recognize the rights of the individual within marriage and the family, which included the acceptance of divorce and the emancipation of women. Thus, there was no broad endorsement of either Sumner's concern about the transformation of the family or criticisms expressed here and there of the supposed decline of the family as an institution (through urbanization, the emancipation of women, and the expansion of state educational institutions).[132] A diagnosis of decline in the section entitled "How far should the members of the family be individualized?" was gainsaid by, among others, Albion Woodbury Small, another founding father of U.S. sociology.[133] Small argued that, given the current divorce figures, the U.S. family was not generally in a state of crisis, but that the "demoralizing conditions of surrounding society" and the "undomestic persons who compose it" gave rise to this impression:

> My dictum is that the thing on trial is not the American family, but every condition which interferes with the general realization of the American family in full fruit of its spirit.[134]

While the frequency of divorce was particularly striking in the "upper and lower classes," Small contended, the majority of middle-class families continued to function normally, so that any kind of blanket criticism was quite out of place. Carl E. Parry of the University of Michigan put all this in a nutshell when he argued that divorce was by no means always a consequence of excessive individualism on the part of the woman: "It is no more individual for a woman today to get a divorce under intolerable conditions than it was for the woman of yesterday to throw fla-

---

[132] The full range of the discussion was captured by James E. Hagerty's paper at the 1908 sociological conference and the comments on it. Hagerty, James E., "How Far Should Members of the Family be Individualized," *Papers and Proceedings, Third Annual Meeting, American Sociological Society, held at Atlantic City, N.J., December 28–30, 1908* (Chicago and New York 1909, reprinted 1971), 181–206. Also reprinted in AJS 14 (1908–1909), 797–823. James Edward Hagerty (1869–1946) taught sociology first at Ohio State University and from 1901 at Notre Dame University, Indiana. His literary estate is also located there. University of Notre Dame Archives, Notre Dame Indiana, 46556.

[133] Albion Woodbury Small (1854–1926) founded the first department of sociology in the United States at the University of Chicago in 1892, where he taught until 1925. After studying theology, he studied history, social economics, and politics, with periods of study in Leipzig and Berlin. In 1895, he founded the *American Journal of Sociology* and was president of the American Sociological Society from 1912 to 1913. His most important works are papers on the concept of sociology as a science, Adam Smith, and the meaning of the social sciences; he also examined German sociology. Small, Albion W., *General Sociology* (Chicago 1905). Small, Albion W., *Adam Smith and Modern Sociology* (Chicago 1907). Small, Albion W., *The Cameralists* (Chicago 1909). Small, *The Meaning of the Social Sciences*.

[134] Albion W. Small in his commentary on the paper by James E. Hagerty, "How Far Should Members of the Family be Individualized," 190–194.

tirons under similar provocation." Instead, he pleaded for the "true individualization of members of the family," which would have to include equal rights, access to education, and economic security for all family members.[135]

Although the feminists present diverged on whether men and women should really be considered "equal," they jointly called for the legalization of divorce. Anna Garlin Spencer[136] acknowledged the need for the "democratization of the family," but at the same time, dissenting from Parry, averred that men and women could never stand "on the same plane of competitive professional and manual labor" within society, otherwise the family would lose its social and reproductive role.[137] Elsewhere, she pleaded for the specific "social education of women," that is, education and training for independence combined with household management skills and an emphasis on their social mission as "mothers of the race."[138] She too linked the discussion of divorce to the question of the "just and useful position of women in society," while also underscoring that the common good must take precedence over the spouses' individual needs. The vital "social control" of excessive individual demands could only be exercised by the government: "The modern state is the only adequate and suitable agency for efficient social control of marriage." In this context, she understood "social control" to mean a uniform national marriage law, marriage counseling, and eugenic measures to protect the family from the "marriage of the unfit."[139]

In addition to the fields of "social control" and "reproductive fitness," Spencer's reflections revolved around another important topic that was repeatedly debated at the sociologists' conference in view of the divorce statistics: the position of women in the family. The most prominent advocate of the strengthening of women's rights was Charlotte Perkins Gilman, author of foundational social scientific studies on the position of women in society, such as *Women and Economics* (1898) and *The Home* (1903). She argued that both individual living conditions and society as a whole

---

[135] Carl E. Parry, University of Michigan, in his commentary on the paper by James E. Hagerty, "How Far Should Members of the Family be Individualized," 200–204.
[136] Anna Garlin Spencer (1851–1931) was a feminist, publicist, and priest in the Unitarian Church, at whose Meadville Theological School in Chicago she also taught. She published widely on social issues; see for example Spencer, Anna Garlin, *Woman's Share in Social Culture* (New York 1913). Spencer, Anna Garlin, *The Family and its Members* (Philadelphia and London 1923 [first published 1922]).
[137] As Spencer averred in her commentary on the paper by James E. Hagerty, who had raised the issue; see Hagerty, "How Far Should Members of the Family be Individualized," 196–199.
[138] Spencer, Anna Garlin, "The Social Education of Women," *Publications of the American Sociological Society* 13 (1918), 11–26.
[139] Spencer, "Problems of Marriage and Divorce," quoted in Johnsen, *Marriage and Divorce*, 39–51.

could only be enhanced by improving families.[140] The only way to achieve this was through greater equality between men and women, so that women could develop and educate themselves as independent social beings, while ceasing to see themselves merely as the possessions and servants of their husbands. This would also benefit children, since enlightened, independent mothers would be better able to consider their needs:

> Finally, these same conditions, these limitations in structure and function, this arrested womanhood and low grade child culture do not tend to develop the best individuals nor to promote social progress. [. . .] We need homes in which mother and father will be equally free and equally bound, both resting together in its shelter and privacy, both working together for its interests. [. . .] The woman, no longer any man's property, nor any man's servant, must develop social usefulness, becoming more efficient, intelligent, experienced.[141]

Anthropologist Elsie Clews Parsons, who had produced a study called *The Family* in 1906,[142] made it clear that in view of the "rate of progress or, according to one's point of view, deterioration, in our contemporaneous family type," well-educated women in particular were important to the preservation of the family as an institution. In line with this, as early as 1908 she called for the liberalization of working hours, including those within the domestic sphere, and life stages: "It is then

---

140 Charlotte Perkins Gilman (1860–1935) was a prominent U.S. publicist and feminist. Her best-known work, *Women and Economics*, an analysis of the economic disadvantages of women in U.-S. society, appeared in 1898, followed in 1903 by a study on the sociology of the household (*The Home*, 1903). Subsequently, Gilman became famous for numerous talks and articles in periodicals. From 1909 to 1916 she edited her own journal, the *Forerunner*. Gilman, Charlotte Perkins, "How Home Conditions React Upon the Family," AJS 14 (1908–1909). Cf. Gilman, Charlotte Perkins, *The Home. Its Work and Influence* (Chicago 1972 [reprint of the 1903 Edition, introduction by William L. O'Neill]). Cf. Gilman, Charlotte Perkins, *Women and Economics. A Study of the Economic Relation between Men and Women as a Factor in Social Evolution*. Ed. by Carl N. Degler (New York et al. 1966 [first edition Boston 1898]).
141 Gilman, Charlotte Perkins, "Home Conditions," 592–605. See the *New York Times* report on the sociological conference, which referred in particular to Gilman's paper. "Higher Marriage, Mrs. Gilman's Plea," NYT, December 29, 1908.
142 Elsie Clews Parsons (1875–1941) was a sociologist, feminist, and one of the founding figures of American anthropology. The associate editor of the *Journal of American Folklore* (1918–1941), she also served as president of the American Folklore Society (1919–1920), the American Ethnological Society (1923–1925), and the American Anthropological Society (1941). Her most important research was on Native American culture, but before that she produced several sociological studies, including a handbook on the forms of the family. Parsons, Elsie Clews, *The Family. An Ethnographical and Historical Outline with Descriptive Notes, Planned as a Text-Book for the Use of College Lecturers and of Directors of Home-Reading Clubs* (New York and London 1906).

on the fight of the professional woman to get back into the family that the future of the family will depend."[143]

All in all, the annual meeting of the American Sociological Association in 1908 saw sociologists take two crucial steps. First, they articulated their understanding of the importance of the family in modern society, and second, they constituted themselves as a guild. For the first time, they took stock of the divorce boom in the U.S. on a secure statistical basis thanks to the *Wright Report*, viewing it as an expression of processes of social change unfolding since the end of the nineteenth century: industrialization, mobilization, individualization, and the expansion of the middle class.

Three topics dominated the discussion: first, the demand for greater intervention by the modern state ("social control") to strengthen the family and reduce the divorce rate; second, the development of measures to tighten up marriage regulations (with respect to formal procedures, the education of youth, and ultimately the question of biosocial marriageability); and third, the redefinition of the role and rights of women within the family. Sociologists saw themselves as especially predestined to analyze the supposed crisis of the family in modern society and to develop proposals for resolving it.[144] In so doing, they consciously cast doubt on the interpretive hegemony of church representatives and lawyers. But as the rather meager press response to the conference and its journalistic echo illustrate, the general public was not quite ready for this message.[145] This was to change rapidly in the following years, as the further development of the divorce debate shows.

1.4 Religious values versus adaptation to modernity: key groups within the divorce debate and their arguments

While sociologists and representatives of the major churches have figured as the main actors so far, within U.S. society the divorce debate broadened noticeably during the first two decades of the twentieth century. Feminists, eugenicists, and lawyers joined the fray, each pursuing their own agenda. They formulated goals

---

143 Parsons, Elsie Clews, "Higher Education of Women and the Family," *Publications of the American Sociological Society* 3 (1908), 142–147, here 147.
144 Lichtenberger, *Divorce*, 17.
145 Around the beginning of 1909, only two articles appeared in the national press on the annual meeting of the American Sociological Association. While the *New York Times* essentially covered Charlotte Perkins Gilman's paper, the *Washington Post* devoted itself to the effects of women's work on the family, with the sensationalist headline "Married Woman in Business a Peril, Says Professor," referring to Ulysses B. Weatherly's paper on the effects of women's employment on the family. NYT, December 29, 1908. WP, December 31, 1908.

such as the recognition of women's rights, combating the supposed racial degeneration of society, and standardizing national marriage and divorce laws, which in turn had consequences for the family ideal they evoked. Above all, though, the pluralization and broadening of the divorce debate proved that neither religious values (marriage as a sacrament) nor ethical standards ("Victorian morals") now represented the sole benchmark; increasing emphasis was placed on the implications for society as a whole (women's rights, improvement of the biological foundations of society, and modifications to national law). Within these demands for normative change, which were made from a range of perspectives, the concepts put forward by sociologists, who had of course already reflected on the issues of women's rights, marriage law, and "social control," appeared markedly more adaptable and in keeping with the times than the demands made by Catholic theologians in particular, which were aimed exclusively at preserving the existing situation and thus at prohibiting or impeding divorce.

In what follows, I will look briefly at the other key social groups that, in addition to sociologists and churchmen, intervened explicitly in the divorce debate, namely representatives of the women's movement, eugenicists, and lawyers. Finally, I will assess which argumentational tropes molded the debates on divorce in the 1900–1920 period. This entails probing the extent to which the focus of the debates shifted from reference to "religious values" to interpretations of social change more focused on society as such.

The feminists: Divorce and women's rights

In the shape of Charlotte Perkins Gilman, Anna Garlin Spencer, and Elsie Clews Parsons, leading representatives of the women's movement had already made their voices heard at the sociologists' conference of 1908. But the demand for access to divorce dated back to the women's movement of the late nineteenth century, when it was chiefly viewed as a means of protecting women from abuse and violence in marriage.[146] What is interesting about the debate among feminists at the beginning

---

[146] On this topic, see the Tenth National Women's Rights Convention of 1860 in New York. The majority of the women's rights activists there agreed with the demand articulate by Elisabeth Cady Stanton, Susan B. Anthony, and Ernestine Rose for the expansion of divorce legislation, However, divorce advocates made a point of distancing themselves from the promotion of "free love." Susan Brownwell Anthony (1820–1906) and Elisabeth Cady Stanton (1815–1902) are considered intellectual leaders of the early women's movement. Through the founding of women's organizations such as the National Women's Suffrage Association, the American Equal Rights Association, and *The Revolution* newspaper, as well as through lively sociopolitical and journalis-

of the twentieth century, meanwhile, is that both declared campaigners for equal rights and women's suffrage as well as prominent anti-suffragettes approved of divorce—albeit with differing rationales. In 1901, for example, social reformer and avowed opponent of women's suffrage, Kate Gannett Wells,[147] criticized the Episcopal Church's attempt to impose uniform canonical (and thus restrictive) regulations on divorce nationwide. She declared that marriage and divorce must remain personal decisions, and that the church should not deny a woman the right to end a relationship that had become intolerable. It was legitimate for a woman, she argued, to use divorce to avoid becoming the mother of hereditarily diseased, criminal, or immoral children born to a father with these characteristics.[148] Such proto-eugenic arguments can be found in the work of many authors writing in the early twentieth century, and by no means only among conservatives. A few months earlier, Elizabeth Cady Stanton, a prominent campaigner for women's suffrage, had also spoken out against restrictive, nationally uniform divorce laws in the same magazine. Stanton viewed marriage as a "civil contract" rather than primarily a sacrament, thus contradicting the clerical opponents of divorce. At the same time, she called for women in particular to be involved in drafting a "national divorce statute," which church representatives, lawyers, and politicians all viewed as a provocation.[149]

Within the ranks of the women's movement, opponents of divorce were found chiefly among the "conservative feminists" of the women's clubs, who strove to achieve both the reform of society and a reduction in the number of divorces by improving women's legal status.[150] They argued that women's suffrage, in particular, would reduce the number of divorces in the long term as a

---

tic activities, they did much to shape the struggle for women's suffrage in the United States. Atheist and abolitionist Ernestine Louise Rose (1810–1892) was vehement in her calls for divorce legislation to protect women in the debate at the 1860 Women's Rights Convention. Brown Blackwell, Antoinette, Rose, Ernestine, and Anthony, Susan B., "Debating Marriage and Divorce Laws, at the Tenth National Women Rights Convention" in New York (1860), reprinted in Keetley, Dawn and Pettigrew, John (eds.), *Public Women, Public Words. A Documentary History of American Feminism*, vol. I, *Beginnings to 1900* (Madison 1997), 223–227.

147 Kate Gannett Wells (1838–1911) was an American social reformer, writer, and opponent of women's suffrage.

148 Wells, Kate Gannet, "Some Comments on Divorce," *North American Review* 173.4 (1901), 508–517.

149 Cady Stanton, "Divorce Laws." Cf. Cady Stanton, "Divorce vs. Domestic Warfare," 568.

150 Blair, Karen, *The Clubwoman as Feminist. True Womanhood Redefined, 1868–1914* (New York 1980), 35, 106.

result of women's greater independence and contentment.[151] Some of the most famous clubwomen of the late nineteenth century were themselves divorced, so they were acting against the background of their own experience.[152]

In addition to the right to divorce, the right to work was also discussed intensively in the women's movement. American writer and journalist Marguerite Wilkinson called explicitly for the social acceptance of women's employment, especially that of mothers.[153] Her point of reference was Olive Schreiner's *Women and Labor* (1911),[154] a key text for the women's movement, widely read in the United States as elsewhere, which denounced the "female parasitism" in modern society, a condition characterized by passivity and lack of rights. Drawing on Schreiner's argument, Wilkinson identified the socially sanctioned inactivity of most wives as one of the causes of the divorce boom in the United States. She argued that it was not only better premarital education of youth that would help combat the "divorce evil." It was also crucial, she believed, to raise young people's awareness of the equality of men and women with regard to their privileges, but also their responsibilities, duties, and the opportunities open to them. Married women and mothers must therefore be allowed to engage in wage labor.[155]

The early eugenics movement: Threats to society from "race degeneration"

A significant number of social scientists and physicians considered the dissolution of marriages in which one or both partners seemed to be endowed with undesirable, supposedly hereditary characteristics as a gain. This was true of physician Woods Hutchinson, who viewed marriage not as a religious or civil institution but

---

[151] See, for example, Stone Blackwell, Alice, "The Threefold Menace" (1913). Harper Cooley, Winnifred, "The Younger Suffragists" (1913), both reprinted in Keetley, Dawn and Pettigrew, John (eds.), *Public Women, Public Words*, vol. II, *1900 to 1960* (Lanham et al. 2002), 16–19, 186–189.
[152] As Karen Blair has elaborated with reference to the first club of professional women, Sorosis, founded in New York City in 1868. Blair, *Clubwoman*, 22.
[153] The American Marguerite Wilkinson (1883–1928) published numerous poetry anthologies and worked as a journalist for various magazines. Wilkinson, Marguerite O. B., "Education as a Prevention of Divorce," *The Craftsman* 21 (1912), no. 5, 473–481. Cited in Johnsen, *Selected Articles*, 88–97, 94.
[154] Olive Schreiner (1855–1920) was a South African feminist and writer. In addition to the novel *The Story of an African Farm* (1883), she published *Women and Labor* in 1911. Its plea for equal rights for men and women and for an end to "female parasitism" made it a key text of the women's movement. Schreiner, Olive, *Women and Labor* (Leipzig 1911).
[155] Wilkinson, "Education," 95.

as a biological necessity.¹⁵⁶ He emphasized that monogamous marriage had proven to be the best way to raise healthy offspring.¹⁵⁷ From the point of view of "race loyalty," however, he contended that the church's ban on divorce was a deeply misguided idea. Instead, it should be made easier to dissolve biologically undesirable marriages "upon grave and weighty racial grounds"—this should in fact be the only legitimate reason for divorce. In particular, wives who refused to bear further children by their degenerate, sick, or criminal husbands ought to be freed from moral stigma and all economic hardship, ideally through government support.¹⁵⁸ As early as 1905, by linking social deviance and genetic disposition argumentatively, Hutchinson paved the way intellectually for the eugenics movement of the 1920s and 1930s:

> The existence, for instance, of epilepsy, insanity, moral perversion, incurable viciousness of temper, habitual drunkenness, criminal conduct of any sort, or habitual laziness and shiftlessness, ought to render divorce not merely obtainable, but obligatory, and further persistence in marital relations immoral.¹⁵⁹

Despite this biologistic reasoning, Woods Hutchinson was not among those scholars and publicists who warned of impending "race degeneration" in light of the divorce figures in the U.S.¹⁶⁰ On the contrary, he hailed current divorces as two-thirds biologically desirable and declared that marriage and family were by no means in danger:

> So long as divorces are kept within the limit of from twenty to twenty-five per cent of the marriages, there is no need to shudder for the future either of the race or of the home. To imagine that ease of divorce will cause a general loosening of the marriage tie is pure superstition. [. . .] Eighty per cent of all marriages are a success from a biologic point of view.¹⁶¹

In addition to this proto-eugenic position, which was shared by many divorce advocates (including Marguerite Wilkinson, George E. Howard, Anna G. Spencer,

---

156 Woods Hutchinson (1862–1930), was born in Selby, United Kingdom, and completed his academic training in the United States. He was a professor of anatomy (State University of Iowa) and pathology (University of Buffalo) and of clinical medicine (New York Polyclinic). According to William O'Neill, he was later elected president of the American Academy of Medicine. O'Neill, *Divorce*, 218–219.
157 Hutchinson, Woods, "Evolutionary Ethics of Marriage and Divorce," *Contemporary Review* 88 (1905), 397–410.
158 Hutchinson, "Ethics," 407–409.
159 Hutchinson, "Ethics," 408.
160 Thus, Hutchinson criticized President Roosevelt's postulate of "race suicide" and argued in another article that there was no empirical evidence of impending "race degeneration" in the United States. Hutchinson, "Ethics," 406. Hutchinson, Woods, "Evidences of Race Degeneration in the United States," *Annals of the Academy of Political and Social Science* 34, 1 (1909), 43–47.
161 Hutchinson, "Ethics," 410.

and James H. Hawley), a minority held the view that a high divorce rate, due to the accompanying reduction in the birth rate, harbored the risk of "race degeneration" in the long term. The most important exponent of this view was President Theodore Roosevelt, who already referred explicitly to the threat of "race suicide"—in view of the decline of the American family—in the preface to the *Wright Report* of 1909: "It goes without saying that, for the race as for the individual, no material prosperity, no business growth, no artistic or scientific development will count if the race commits suicide."[162]

Roosevelt drew inspiration, among other things, from the writings of Edward A. Ross, whom he expressly thanked for his elucidations in a letter of 1904.[163] Ross had already coined the term "race suicide" in 1900 and elaborated on it in a programmatic article of 1901.[164] In "The Causes of Race Superiority," Ross underscored that rising immigration (especially from Asia) and declining birthrates posed an internal and external threat to white Americans.[165] In his 1906 State of the Union address, Roosevelt echoed Ross's warning against uncontrolled immigration and the "biological" weakening of the particularly valuable, highly capable rural population of the United States, and called for a tightening of immigration laws in order to avoid the impending "race death" of white America.[166] The 1907 revision of the immigration laws took account of this plea by enacting the first quotas with specific restrictions on immigrants from Asia and increasing the fee for entry into the country.[167] Although this canalized immigration for the time being, Roosevelt remained concerned about the low birth rate among the white middle class and the threat to the family posed by divorce, individualism, and female employment. To further study the pros and cons of immigration restrictions, he appointed a panel of ex-

---

[162] U.S. Department of Commerce and Labor, Bureau of the Census, Special Reports: *Marriage and Divorce 1867–1906. Part I: Summary, Laws, Foreign Statistics* (Washington 1909), 4.

[163] Theodore Roosevelt and Edward A. Ross, November 2, 1904, Edward Alsworth Ross Papers, State Historical Society of Wisconsin, Madison. Quoted in McMahon, *Social Control*, 116.

[164] In a speech on the immigration of Japanese in San Francisco on May 7, 1900. Lovett, Laura L., *Conceiving the Future. Pronatalism, Reproduction and the Family in the United States 1890–1938* (Chapel Hill 2007), 82. Then fleshed out in the written version of his lecture at the fifth annual conference of the American Academy of Political and Social Sciences in 1901: Ross, Edward A., "The Causes of Race Superiority," *Annals of the American Academy of Political and Social Science* 18 (1901), 67–89, 88.

[165] Ross, "Causes," 88. On Ross's theory of race, see McMahon, *Social Control*, 112–118.

[166] Roosevelt, Theodore, "Sixth Annual Message," March 12, 1906, in *State Papers as Governor and President, 1899–1909* (New York 1926, the National Edition of Roosevelt's Works; vol. xv), 377–378.

[167] Lüthi, Barbara, *Invading Bodies. Medizin und Immigration in den USA, 1880–1920* (Frankfurt a.M. and New York 2009), 74–75. McMahon, *Social Control*, 116.

perts, known as the Dillingham Commission.[168] Even after his presidency, he never tired of drawing on expert advice, which brought him into proximity with the early eugenics movement. In a 1913 letter to Charles B. Davenport, a key figure in this movement, the president complained about white Americans' unwillingness to serve their country by bearing a large number of children, which was a threat to society as such.[169] Roosevelt concluded that what was needed were pronatalist policies to increase the number of individuals of 'superior quality' along with restrictions on the reproduction of "degenerates": "Someday we will realize that the prime duty, the inescapable duty of good citizens of the right type is to leave his or her blood behind him in the world and that we have no business to [. . .] perpetuate citizens of the wrong type."[170]

A further development of this position was marked by the initiative for a National Divorce Bill as an amendment to the constitution, which was brought before Congress in 1923 and 1924 by Mrs. Edward Franklin White, president of the General Federation of Women's Clubs and Deputy Attorney General of Indiana, and Senator Arthur Capper of Kansas. The purpose of this divorce bill would have been to provide uniform national regulation of marriage and divorce. By laying down, to binding effect, uniform grounds for divorce (adultery, [physical and mental] cruelty, failure to provide [maintenance payments for the period of one year], mental illness, and violent crime) and a regularized procedure, divorce was to have been made more difficult nationwide. At the same time, the aim was to prevent "hasty and foolish marriages" by, among other things, setting a nationally binding minimum marriage age of sixteen for girls and eighteen for young men, and enshrining a requirement that marriage licenses be obtained in advance.[171] This initiative was characterized both by biologistic-eugenic arguments (marriage bans for the men-

---

168 King, Desmond, *Making Americans: Immigration, Race, and the Origins of Diverse Democracy* (Cambridge, MA and London 2000), 166–228.
169 Letter Theodore Roosevelt to Charles B. Davenport, Jan. 3, 1913. American Philosophical Society, APSSimg4945. On Roosevelt's understanding of nation, see Gerstle, Gary, *American Crucible. Race and Nation in the Twentieth Century* (Princeton 2001), who speaks of a "racial nationalism." On Roosevelt's ideas about family, masculinity, and nation, see Bederman, Gail, *Manliness and Civilization. A Cultural History of Gender and Race in the United States 1880–1917* (Chicago 1995). Hogandon, Kristin L., *Fighting for American Manhood. How Gender Politics Provoked the Spanish-American and Philippine-American Wars* (New Haven 1998). Testi, Arnaldo, "The Gender of Reform Politics. Theodore Roosevelt and the Culture of Masculinity," *Journal of American History* 81, no. 4 (1995), 1509–1533.
170 Letter from Theodore Roosevelt to Charles B. Davenport, January 3, 1913, American Philosophical Society, APSSimg4945.
171 "Uniform Divorce Bill," *Journal of Social Hygiene*, March 1923, 170–173, in Johnsen, *Selected Articles*, 240–43.

tally ill and those with hereditary diseases), and by the desire to protect the family from frivolous divorces.[172] When the amendment ultimately failed in 1924, however, this was not due to its eugenic objectives, but to the unwillingness of the states to accept nationwide marriage and divorce laws.

This initiative, as well as the statements of Ross, Roosevelt, and Wilkinson, reveal the broad appeal of thinking about the family in terms of race and "racial value" at the beginning of the twentieth century. At the same time, it is clear that many scholars and politicians coupled their ideas on the subjects of divorce and family structure with their fear of impending "race degeneration" due to falling birth rates, "less valuable offspring" offspring, and rising immigration.[173]

The lawyers: the decline of the family and the dilemma posed by the absence of national divorce laws

By contrast, in 1909, lawyer Walter George Smith, who played an instrumental role in drafting proposals for national divorce legislation, lamented the "growing tendency towards individualism," echoing a core concern of many conservative churchmen:

> The vigorous attack now being made on the institution of the family is the natural outcome of a gradually weakening religious faith, which has resulted from the loss of the old ideal of duty as the main purpose of life and the frank substitution of individual pleasure in its stead.[174]

This practicing Catholic was particularly concerned about the dissolution of the patriarchal family model and the new legal situation in which women could file for divorce, owned their property within marriage, and were generally no longer considered part of the husband's (fictive) legal person, but viewed as individuals in their own right.[175] A few years later, Smith made it clear that for him only Catholics were in a position to truly recognize the danger to society posed by the frequency of divorce. All advocates of the "surgery of divorce" to improve the lot of unhappily

---

172 White, Mrs. Edward Franklin, "Marriage and Divorce (Amendment to the Constitution. Hearing before a Subcommittee on S.J. Res. 5, 68th Congress, 1st Session. January 11, 1924, p.11–14)," in Johnsen, *Selected Articles*, 250–253.Capper, Arthur, "Proposed Amendment to the Constitution," in Johnsen, *Selected Articles*, 244–250.
173 On the eugenic component of immigration policy, see the study by Lüthi, *Invading Bodies*.
174 Smith, Walter George, "Uniform Marriage and Divorce Laws. Address at the Thirtieth Annual Meeting of the Ohio State Barr Association, Put-In-Bay, July 7th, 1909," 4. For Smith's biography, see footnote 95 of this chapter.
175 Smith, "Uniform Marriage and Divorce Laws," 5. Norris, George W., "Divorce and the Means of Diminishing it," *Editorial Review* 5 (1911), 1081–1084.

married couples were neglecting the "injury entailed upon the morals of the community at large."[176] Smith thus unambiguously placed the welfare of the community above that of the individual (especially the woman).[177] Smith had long championed reform of national marriage and divorce laws as a representative of the American Bar Association (of which he became president in 1917), and as a member of the Commission on Uniform State Laws. Unlike most social scientists, he advocated making divorce as such more difficult and thus reducing divorce rates. Like so many reformers, however, he was defeated by state opposition to federal regulation, which would have required a constitutional amendment. Congressman George W. Norris of Nebraska, another lawyer, expressed himself in even more dramatic terms than Smith in his 1911 proposal for reform of divorce, which would have entailed an interstate reform commission instead of an amendment.[178] His plea, below, reveals the dilemma faced by many opponents of divorce. Although they regarded the practice as a threat to civilization in principle, they concluded that the only way to get it under control was to modify divorce laws since a total ban was unrealistic:

> The marriage relation is at the very foundation of the home. Every time a home is broken up, the onward march of civilization is halted. [. . .] Divorce is the evil influence that retards progress, destroys happiness and ruins morality; yet the history of mankind shows that, at least under the present conditions of society and civilization, it is sometimes necessary. If, therefore, it cannot be entirely eradicated, the people ought to unite in every honest effort to reduce it to a minimum.[179]

Catholics and Protestants: marriage as a sacrament and the ban on the remarriage of divorcees

Smith's critique of individualism and the scenario of civilizational decay evoked by George Norris were core elements in the arguments long put forward by opponents of divorce within the churches. They rejected out of hand the idea of marriage as a potentially terminable "social contract" and highlighted its sacramental character and moral significance. This always entailed an interpretation of the

---

176 Smith, "Ethics of Divorce."
177 For other arguments critical of divorce made by American lawyers concerned with the standardization of divorce laws, see Norris, "Divorce," 1081–1084.
178 George W. Norris (1861–1944) was a lawyer. He served as a Republican in the House of Representatives from 1903 to 1913, and in the Senate from 1913 to 1943, during his last term as an independent senator. He was a committed progressive and later a supporter of the New Deal, which established the Tennessee Valley Authority.
179 Norris, "Divorce," 1081–1084.

effects of modernity and a particular view of the relationship between family, individual, and government, as well as a focus on the supposed threat to the community posed by the loosening of moral ties.

The most consistent position continued to be taken by representatives of the Catholic Church. In 1907, the church reaffirmed its fundamental rejection of divorce in the *Ne Temere* decree. While Catholics were denied divorce as a matter of principle with reference to the sacramental character of marriage and the only conceivable form of separation was "divorce of bed and board,"[180] the decree stated that even Catholics who had divorced Protestants remained united with them in the sacrament of marriage. Therefore, they could not enter into another marriage through the Catholic rite.[181] One of the most prominent spokesmen for Catholics in the U.S., James Cardinal Gibbons, set out this point of view in 1909 in the New York-based magazine *Century*. His reference to "divorce of bed and board" as the only acceptable form of separation in the case of serious misconduct was as time-worn as his affirmation of the ban on remarriage of divorced persons and his call for a "radical cure," namely the abolition of existing divorce laws and a return to a strict reading of Holy Scripture. What was striking, however, was that the cardinal went to some lengths to portray the Catholic Church, and in particular the popes, as protectors of women: the refusal to sanction divorce had shielded them from the "lustful tyranny" of their husbands.[182]

> Christian wives and mothers, what gratitude you owe to the Catholic Church for the honorable position you now hold in society! If you are no longer regarded as the slave but the equal of your husbands; [. . .] you owe your emancipation to the Church![183]

While the position of Catholic churchmen in the United States was essentially determined by the papal decree, in Protestant denominations, especially within the Episcopal Church, a fierce dispute arose between opponents and supporters of divorce, one ignited by the question of the permissibility of remarriage among divorced persons. The leading supporter of a strict ban on remarriage on the Protestant side was Episcopal bishop William Coswell Doane, who played a wide

---

[180] Except for two narrowly circumscribed exceptions, namely dissolution of a non-consummated marriage and dissolution of a non-sacramental marriage "in favor of the faith."

[181] The decree was passed by the Congregation of the Council under Pope Pius X on August 10, 1907, and entered into force on April 19, 1908. Only in 1982 did the *Codex Iuris Canonici* articulate a slightly more liberal understanding of marriage, though this did not deviate from the fundamental prohibition of divorce.

[182] Gibbons, James Cardinal, "Divorce," *Century* 78 (1909), 145–149, cited in Johnsen, *Selected Articles*, 78–84. A similar position is articulated in Caverno, Reverend Charles, "Uniform Divorce Law," *Bibliotheca Sacra* 69 (1912), 242–245. On Gibbons, see footnote 63.

[183] Gibbons, "Divorce," 82–83.

variety of roles within the Protestant movement against divorce.[184] In 1908, together with Samuel Dike, he issued an appeal by the Committee on Family Life to all Protestant churches in the U.S., calling not only for uniform divorce laws but also for marriage bans for morally and physically unfit persons, as well as increased efforts by the churches to combat the "terrible evils of sexual vice" and to strengthen families in general.[185] Protestant theologians, too, thus reaffirmed their view of the family as the basis of society:

> We rest our appeal to you on the proposition that the family and its development into the Home lie at the foundation of human welfare. [. . .] The home is the place were all that builds up or pulls down in the social order does its final work.[186]

But Doane's hardline position on remarriage for divorcees and his general opposition to divorce were by no means uncontroversial among Protestants.[187] First of all, criticism arose at the grassroots, as illustrated by a letter to the editor of the Protestant journal *Homiletic Review* from a pastor in Henderson, North Carolina. In 1912, Pastor Morgan complained that the ban on remarriage for divorcees was disproportionate. Not all divorce was illegitimate, he contended, especially when it came to dissolving marriages that were undesirable from a eugenic standpoint. The best way of preventing divorce, he claimed, was enhanced "social control," marital education, and marriage bans, but the general principle ought to be that "divorce is purer than unholy wedlock."[188]

Indeed, as William O'Neill has shown, liberal Protestant theologians ensured the gradual acceptance of divorce as a social reality and established a link between the interpretation of Scripture and the everyday lives of believers.[189] For example, William Gay Ballantine (1848–1937), former president of Oberlin College, criticized Doane' position by pointing out that the teachings of Jesus could not simply be cast into laws.[190] Ernest DeWitt Burton, one of the country's leading

---

184 On Doane, see footnote 88 in this chapter; on the Inter-Church Conference, see above: Doane, "Question of Divorce." Doane, "Remarriage after Divorce," 513–522. Sanford, *Federal Council*, 264–265.
185 Committee of Family Life of the Federal Council of the Churches of Christ in America, *Appeal to the Church of the United States in Behalf of the Family* (1908). Sanford, *Federal Council*, 508–510.
186 Sanford, *Federal Council*, 508.
187 On the debate concerning the remarriage of divorcees in the Episcopal Church, see O'Neill, *Divorce*, 41–43.
188 Morgan, J. W., "Ministers and Divorce," *Homiletic Review* 63 (1912), 76–77. Cited in Johnsen, *Selected Articles*, 84–87.
189 O'Neill, *Divorce*, 212.
190 Ballantine, William Gay, "The Hyperbolic Teaching of Jesus," *North American Review* 179, 3 (1904), 446–456, esp. 455–456.

theologians and editor of the *American Journal of Theology*, had also joined the discussion early on and, in accord with George E. Howard, called for better premarital education for young people and the official publication of marriage banns before the ceremony was held.[191] This would prevent "rash and unsuitable marriages."[192] With regard to theological foundations, he made it clear that the New Testament texts clearly decreed the indissolubility of marriage and rejected divorce as a matter of principle. While deviations were possible in individual cases, no uniform national divorce law (or ban on divorce) could be derived from this. It did not make sense, he stated, to use Biblical texts as a template for the national regulation of divorce, though this was undoubtedly needed. Since no legislation, no matter how effective, could cure the "evils of divorce," the main focus must be on reducing the number of divorces through preventive measures.

On the same page as Burton, Francis G. Peabody, a moral theologian at Harvard University and progressive reformer, addressed the question of how the teachings of Jesus could be used to counteract "domestic instability" as an "epidemic, social disease."[193] In his treatise *Jesus Christ and the Social Question*, he began by criticizing the marriage and divorce practices of the different states, which he claimed helped ensure that "less care is observed in arranging a contract of marriage than is involved in a contract concerning a horse or a piece of land."[194] More important, however, he asserted, was the underlying conflict over the nature of marriage as a temporary contract or social institution. Underlying this clash, he contended, were two different conceptions of civilization, one placing the individual in the foreground and the other highlighting the centrality of the social order:

> If the individual is the end for which social life exists, [. . .] then the legislation of self-interest, which takes account of nothing more than the happiness or even the whims of individuals, will be set to make and break this contract. If, on the other hand, marriage is an elementary expression of organic social life, a witness of that social continuity, [. . .] if the individual comes to his self-realization only in and through his service of the social order,—

---

[191] Ernest DeWitt Burton (1856–1925) was professor of New Testament theology at the University of Chicago and editor of the *American Journal of Theology*; he was president of the University of Chicago from 1923 to 1925.

[192] Burton, Ernest D., "Some Biblical Teaching Concerning Divorce," *Biblical World* 29 (1907), 121–127. Burton, Ernest D., "The Biblical Teachings Concerning Divorce: II. New Testament Teaching," *Biblical World* 29, 3 (1907), 191–200, here 198–200.

[193] Francis G. Peabody (1847–1936) taught moral theology at Harvard University and became involved in the settlement movement at an early stage. Peabody, Francis, *Jesus Christ and the Social Question* (New York 1903, reprint London 1907), 129. Herbst, Jürgen, "Francis Greenwood Peabody. Harvard's Theologian of the Social Gospel," *Harvard Theological Review* 54 (1961), no. 1, 45–69.

[194] Peabody, "Jesus Christus," 130–131.

then the integrity of the family as the most elementary group of social life, will be reverently guarded and stringently secured.[195]

Peabody himself left no room for doubt that often the subordination of the individual to the welfare of the family as social system was most closely aligned with God's will. This position not only provided points of contact with the ideas of the lawyer Smith in that both criticized the individualism of many of those seeking divorce, especially women, but also opened the door to proto-eugenic objectives and the principle of "social control." Peabody's views exemplify intensified efforts to grapple with a changing society, which brought a wider range of arguments in their wake. Such a broadening of perspective was more common among Protestant theologians, particularly opponents of divorce, which further isolated Catholic hardliners within the debate the longer it went on.

A revealing example of the fusion of sociological expertise and religiously inspired opposition to divorce are the publications of the aforementioned clergyman, social scientist, and founder of the Divorce Reform League, Samuel W. Dike. He too contributed a paper to the 1908 sociological conference in which he identified the process of individualization in modern society as the cause of the scourge of divorce, since it undermined the family:

> The real problem is that of the family, whether we consider divorce, unchastity, lack of offspring, or the more subtle, yet I think more dangerous of its ills, those which come through the disuse of the family in the transfer of its legitimate functions to church, school, and other substitutes for the home.[196]

Reforms aimed at reducing the number of divorces, Dike believed, would have to start with better socialization of the individual in the family. In this remarkably inconsistent line of argument (in favor of the social scientific analysis of the family as an institution but against individualization, in favor of Christian morality but against the churches' intervention in the family), Dike articulated both his sympathies for the modern social sciences and his experiences as a clergyman. After his dismissal as a priest—due to his refusal to remarry a divorced parishioner—Dike had devoted himself to researching the social underpinnings of the "divorce evil." In the process, he made a name for himself not only as a theological publicist, but above all in the field of national marriage statistics.[197] This earned him a role of some responsibility in both *Wright Reports*. Interestingly, his more than three decades of experience researching the family as the "most funda-

---

195 Peabody, "Jesus Christus," 133.
196 Dike, Samuel W., "Is the Freer Granting of Divorce an Evil?", *American Journal of Sociology* 14 (1909), no. 6, 766–796. On Dike, see footnote 56 earlier in this chapter.
197 Dike, "Statistics of Divorce."

mental institution of society" changed his perspective on the problem of divorce. It is true that, when it was founded in 1881, the Divorce Reform League[198] had already set out to replace the "conventional lines of biblical interpretation and the ordinary method of treating the history of divorce" with sociological research and statistics, and to achieve effective reforms of divorce law and practice.[199] But it is Dike's writings of the early twentieth century that show how much the clergyman's thinking had changed as a result of his experiences as social scientist. Some (partly unpublished) manuscripts and an unfinished autobiography from his literary estate shed light on this.[200] In his undated manuscript "Suggestions for the Study of Social Questions" (from around 1909), for example, Dike comments on the importance of social scientific knowledge to the clergyman in particular, as "good methods of study are of supreme importance to ministers if they would make the most of their efforts in dealing with social questions." Only the clergyman who had understood the family as a social institution and had researched its history, as well as its social transformation, should express views on the "divorce question" or on the family.[201] Here, he underlined, statistics was a tool of the social scientist "like the microscope in the hands of the biologist," but the more far-reaching task was "to apply principles and find laws where the statistician can only stop at mathematical conclusions":

> The cure for bad statistics is simply more and better statistics. The remedy for crude opinions on social topics is the cultivation of the scientific method and the development of a keen and true social sense.[202]

In another manuscript of 1911, Dike conceded that such investigative zeal was hard to reconcile with the Protestant doctrine of marriage:

---

[198] From 1885, the organization was known as the National Divorce Reform League, and from 1897 as the National League for the Protection of the Family. See above in this chapter.

[199] See Dike's report on the League's twenty-fifth anniversary, "Report of Corresponding Secretary, Our Twenty-Fifth Anniversary," in *Report of the National League for the Protection of the Family for the Year Ending December 31, 1905* (Boston 1906), 6, 8. Samuel W. Dike Papers, Library of Congress, Washington D. C., Call No. O813 J, Box 22.

[200] "Some Fundamentals of the Divorce Question by the Rev. Samuel W. Dike, Auburndale, Mass." (unpublished manuscript 1909). "Some Suggestions on the Divorce Problem by Rev. Samuel W. Dike," LL.D., 1911. "Draft of an Unfinished Autobiography" (n.d.), Samuel W. Dike Papers, Library of Congress, Washington D. C., Call No. O813 J, Box 22.

[201] "Suggestions for the Study of Social Questions by the Rev. Samuel W. Dike, Auburndale, Mass." (n.d., c. 1909, intended for the journal *Homiletic Review*, according to Dike's handwritten note), 1. Samuel W. Dike Papers, Library of Congress, Washington D. C., Call No. O813 J, Box 22.

[202] Dike, "Suggestions for the Study of Social Questions," 6.

> The Christian teacher has a grave question before him in this matter of divorce. Shall he, believing that Christ taught that divorce should never be granted, or granted for one cause only, insist that He [sic] thus practically <u>legislated</u> for both church and state to this effect? Or shall he, in view of the practical needs of society, turn his back on what seem to be the authoritative words of our Lord?[203]

For Dike, the solution lay in viewing marriage and family as social institutions, which required a joint push for reform by "church, school, and home":

> All this leads to the conclusion that while legal reform should be urged on, the roots of the divorce evil and of all other domestic evils run far and deep in the social soil and must be met with a correspondingly wide and thorough treatment.[204]

This view of the social facts, for Dike, meant that the churches should not impose their moral convictions regarding divorce on the government if, from the latter's point of view, it served the good of the community: "The Church may not insist on the incorporation of its ideals in either the legislation of the state or even the church [. . .]." Instead, Protestants, Catholics, citizens of other faiths, and atheists should work together to reduce divorce rates. Such an argumentational connection between the "divorce problem," "family as a social institution," and "the entire social question" went far beyond traditional scriptural interpretation. Dike's efforts to reconcile his position as a former clergyman with that of a social scientist brought him intense criticism, which sought to discredit either the "minister" as religiously unfaithful or the "social scientist" as influenced by the church.[205] His "dilemma," however, exemplifies the position of many scholars and publicists at the threshold of modern society. It demonstrates that there was no seamless transfer of interpretive hegemony from theologians to social scientists within the divorce debates.

Key tropes in the debates on divorce, 1890–1920

My analysis of divorce debates in the U.S. between 1890 and 1920 has shown that certain core arguments cropped up time and again. Some were used only by supporters or opponents of divorce, while others appeared in the statements of both

---

[203] "Some Suggestions on the Divorce Problem by Rev. Samuel W. Dike," LL.D., 1911, 1. Samuel W. Dike Papers, Library of Congress, Washington D. C., Call No. O813 J, Box 22. Emphasis in the Original.
[204] Dike, "Suggestions on the Divorce Problem," 3.
[205] Numerous examples of this in Dike's "Draft of an Unfinished Autobiography" (n.d.), Samuel W. Dike Papers, Library of Congress, Washington D. C., Call No. O813 J, Box 22.

camps. I will first systematically elaborate the arguments mainly put forward by the supporters of divorce, before discussing the principal assertions of its opponents; I then contrast these perspectives with the positions articulated by both factions. What we will find is that, although there was a major difference in the assessment of the consequences of divorce for the individual, the family, and the nation, representatives of both camps largely agreed on the need for "social control" and the eugenic improvement of families.

Four aspects in particular stand out in the arguments used by divorce advocates. First, sociologists such as Howard, Lichtenberger, Ross, and Small used the argument that the increasing number of divorces was a reaction to the emergence of "modern industrial society." Urbanization, migration, and industrialization, they claimed, had generally changed the family ideal, as clearly reflected in the redefined roles of women. Since many women, they went on, were now employed and thus had a new independence, including in economic terms, the divorce rate reflected not just their discontent, but also the social upheaval provoked by the renegotiation of gender relations.[206]

This is directly related to the second, frequently made argument that a "new morality" was discernable in U.S. society: many women were said to be fed up with the "double standard" of the Victorian era and unwilling to be bound to men with unsound morals or venereal diseases. Further, according to many social scientists and women's rights activists, the possibility of remarriage after divorce was much better for public morality than the extra-marital relationships particularly common in states with a strict ban on divorce, such as New York and Louisiana.[207]

The third and most important argument, which arose from these two assessments, was that the divorce boom was a symptom of a process of social transformation and that divorce itself was an apt remedy for social problems. This was the classic position of many liberals and in particular social scientists, who based themselves on an analysis of the social change spawned by the rise of industrial modernity. Many averred that it was fundamentally better for both the community and the

---

[206] See the positions of Edward A. Ross, George E. Howard, and James P. Lichtenberger as articulated in the relevant section of the 1908 sociological conference in Atlantic City: all in Howard, "Freer Granting." See also Albion W. Small's commentary on James E. Hagerty's paper at the 1908 sociology conference: Hagerty, "How Far Should Members of the Family be Individualized," 190–194. Howard, *History*. Lichtenberger, *Divorce*.

[207] These views usually went hand in hand with calls for gender equality within the family: Gilman, "Home Conditions." Lichtenberger, "Freer Granting," 789. Lichtenberger, *Divorce*, 172–189.

family to end intolerable marriages and allow the partners, especially the blameless ones, to remarry.[208]

Fourth, the proximity of many scholars, publicists, women's rights activists, and social reformers to the emerging eugenics discourse became apparent. They argued that it was irresponsible to promote the reproduction of the "inferior" by refusing divorce or to bind women who could have "high-quality" offspring to "inferior" men. This is an understanding of science and reproduction typical of the time, which we will look at in more detail in the following chapter.[209]

While the proponents of divorce focused more on the transformation of modern society, its opponents, regardless of whether they were churchmen or lawyers, publicists or women's rights activists, mostly referred, first of all, to canon law and the interpretation of the Bible ("scriptural grounds"). Catholics, whether clergy or laity, generally expressed highly consistent views, which also found favor with many representatives of the Episcopal Church: marriage was a sacrament, divorce was possible only in cases of adultery, and no remarriage was permitted during the lifetime of the partners. A modified variant of this strict reading allowed the remarriage of the blameless partner in cases of adultery.[210]

A second argument that was often put forward acknowledged the dynamic of change in modern society but interpreted it as negative. Divorce appeared as the consequence of excessive individualism, while the conduct of those seeking divorce was viewed as both directly and indirectly harmful to the community. It was crucial that individual self-realization be subordinated to the welfare of the community and of the family as its nucleus.[211]

---

208 On this topic, see esp. the perspectives put forward by George E. Howard, James P. Lichtenberger, and Edward E. Ross at the 1908 sociologists' conference and in their monographs: Howard, "Freer Granting." Howard, *History*. Lichtenberger, *Divorce*. Ross, *Social Control*.
209 See the positions advocated by E. A. Ross, George E. Howard, Marguerite Wilkinson, Anna Garlin Spencer, Kate Gannett Wells, and James Hawley. Ross, "Significance." Howard, "Bad Marriage." Wilkinson, "Education." Spencer, "Problems of Marriage and Divorce." Wells, "Some Comments on Divorce." Hawley, James H., "Uniformity of Marriage and Divorce Laws. Proceedings of the Governor's Conference 1912," 162–173, quoted in Johnsen, *Selected Articles*, 160–164. Arguments of an emphatically proto-eugenic character can be found in Hutchinson, "Ethics."
210 Among leading Catholics, this modified view was expounded especially by James Cardinal Gibbons and Reverend Charles Caverno. With respect to Protestants, see the remarks of William C. Doane, as well as the more moderate perspectives of Burton, Ballantine, and Dike. Gibbons, "Divorce." Caverno, "Uniform Divorce Law." Doane, "Question of Divorce." Doane, "Remarriage after Divorce." Burton, "Some Biblical Teaching." Burton, "The Biblical Teachings Concerning Divorce: II." Ballantine, "Hyperbolic Teaching." Dike, "Freer Granting."
211 Peabody, *Jesus Christ*. Smith, "Ethics of Divorce." Smith, "Uniform Marriage and Divorce Laws." Dike, "Freer Granting."

A third argument took this idea further, positing that the phenomenon of divorce itself and, in particular, the liberal divorce laws of certain states, were to blame for the breakdown of the family as a form of organization and as a community of values. On this view, the looming disintegration of the family posed a direct threat to society itself, which faced "degeneracy"—though this was not understood here in a racial-eugenic sense. While this classic argument made by the opponents of divorce could easily be refuted by its advocates, who pointed out that it mixed up cause and effect, it enjoyed great popularity during the entire period considered here.[212]

Fourth and finally, many opponents of divorce addressed the idea of a constitutional amendment to regularize divorce law. Here, a reevaluation took place during the period with which we are concerned. Until about 1910, an amendment was seen by many opponents of divorce as an apt means of tightening up divorce law, among other things by reducing the grounds for divorce in the divorce-friendly states and putting an end to "migratory divorces."[213] In the following years, however, fears grew that the standardization of divorce procedures would curtail the rights of the states and fundamentally liberalize divorce. As a result, most opponents of divorce came to oppose a constitutional amendment.[214]

Despite the two camps' divergent views, a total of four arguments can be identified that were used by both opponents and proponents of divorce. This is particularly interesting, as these positions may indicate an understanding of society that cut across the two groups. First, almost all those involved in the divorce debate highlighted the connection between the increasing frequency of divorce and women's emancipatory aspirations. The discussants discerned a tendency toward women's economic independence, a new lifestyle, the recognition of women's rights, and above all, backing for women's suffrage, whatever their opinion of these developments (what some saw as the overdue renegotiation of gender roles others deprecated as the decline of the family). Further, they almost always referred to the fact revealed by the national divorce statistics that it was mostly women who filed for divorce.[215]

---

[212] See esp. the arguments put forward by Samuel Dike at the sociologists' conference of 1908, but also the texts listed in the bibliography by James Cardinal Gibbons, William C. Doane, and Walter G. Smith.

[213] See the positions expressed by the National Divorce Reform League and Samuel Dike's League for the Protection of the Family between 1880 and 1910. Library of Congress, Washington D.C: Samuel W. Dike Papers, Call No. O813 J, Box 23.

[214] For a critical take on this, see Norris, "Divorce."

[215] For more detail, see the discussion on the topic in the James E. Hagerty section at the 1908 sociological conference: Hagerty, "How Far Should Members of the Family be Individualized," 181–206, also in AJS 14 (1908–1909), 797–823.

Second, almost all those involved in the debate, whether conservative or liberal, called for the formalization and modernization of national and state-level marriage laws. The prerequisite for reducing the number of divorces, they believed, was a clear legal foundation. Marriage should be understood not only as a sacrament, but also as a legal act sanctioned by the government. This, in turn, they underlined, required certain obligatory steps, such as prior publication of the banns, the presence of witnesses and a state official, the issuance of a marriage certificate, and the statistical registration of the marriage.[216]

The third argument was directly related to this endeavor to standardize marriage: divorce, like marriage, should be performed in public ("public divorces"). A divorce should only be granted in the presence of both parties or if the person being divorced had been informed about it in advance, and the latter must be given the opportunity to defend himself or herself. This was intended to prevent divorce proceedings in the absence or without the knowledge of one of the partners. This was an argument put forward both by avowed opponents of divorce, such as James Cardinal Gibbons, who hoped that public proceedings would have a deterrent effect, and by staunch advocates, such as Robert Ingersoll, who argued that a contract should be publicly terminated.[217]

All of the arguments mentioned above culminated in the unanimous call for greater "social control": in order to promote the development of the community and the family as its smallest unit, the argument here was that the government must take adequate measures to limit citizens' potential actions. This included laws that would deny marriage to immoral individuals, those with hereditary defects, and the socially unfit, as well as premarital education of young people to enhance their understanding of the nature of marriage and help prevent hasty, ill-considered unions. The proponents of increased "social control" were above all the sociologists, none more than Edward A. Ross, who had first introduced and elucidated the term in his monograph *Social Control* (1901), but also James Lichtenberger and George Howard.[218] Representatives of the women's movement and social reformers also backed this call.[219] Revealingly, the demand for more efficient, more rational guidelines from the government as a means of improving individual living conditions and helping advance the community included eugenic measures.

Analysis of the sources shows that World War I played no special role in the debates on divorce—in contrast to those on reproduction, as we will see in the

---

[216] See the views of Cady Stanton, "Divorce Laws" and Capper, "Proposed Amendment."
[217] Gibbons and Ingersoll, "Is Divorce Wrong?".
[218] Ross, *Social Control.* Ross, "Freer Granting." Lichtenberger, *Divorce.* Howard, "Freer Granting."
[219] Spencer, "Social Education." Spencer, "Problems of Marriage and Divorce." Wilkinson, "Education."

next chapter. At first glance, this may seem surprising, but on closer inspection the social statistical data reveals, first, that the divorce rate remained nearly constant during the war (1.1 divorces per 1,000 Americans) and did not rise again until the immediate postwar years (1.6 divorces in 1920). Given that the divorce rate remained at this level until the Great Depression, World War I represented no great turning point. Second, as we have seen, the identification of divorce as a national problem occurred within the first decade of the twentieth century. The documentation and discussion of the social transformation associated with the spread of divorce was chiefly inspired by the publication of the second national divorce statistics in 1909, long before the United States entered the war.

1.5 Interim conclusion: social experts as analysts of social change: the family ideal in the United States at the beginning of the twentieth century

My analysis of Progressive-Era divorce debates has shown that a thematic shift occurred between about 1890 and 1920. At the beginning of this period, Victorian family values ("domesticity, chastity, restraint") dominated the discussions and church representatives occupied a fairly strong position within them ("scriptural grounds"). Over time, however, the center of gravity gradually shifted to social scientists and their interpretations, which presented divorce as a necessary measure ("remedy") to end intolerable family discord and social problems ("individual and social ills"). At the same time, divorce became increasingly accepted as a social practice, as evident in the divorce statistics.[220]

> Between 1905, when the magnitude of divorce as a social problem had become fully apparent, and 1917, when the movement to limit or direct the spread of divorce had clearly failed, something of importance for American social history had occurred. This was the recognition by moral conservatives that they could not prevent the revolution in morals represented by mass divorce. Their failure of morale in the immediate prewar period paved the way for spectacular changes which took place after the war.[221]

---

[220] Though, as William O'Neill argued early on, an analysis of divorce discourse in the Progressive Era is more fruitful than examination of the failure to pass unitary laws. O'Neill, *Divorce*, 245. Glenda Riley addresses divorce debates and legislative initiatives in relation to one another, occasionally risking the dilution of argumentative levels. Riley, *Divorce*, chapter 5.
[221] O'Neill, "Divorce," 148–149.

1.5 Interim conclusion: social experts as analysts of social change — 93

However, there was more to this upheaval than a more liberal morality replacing the strict etiquette of the Victorian era, as William O'Neill thought in 1967.[222] Nor did sociologists simply wrest interpretive authority over processes of social change from the churchmen, as Glenda Riley has argued.[223] Rather, with reference to family, marriage, and divorce, those involved—and this is the main argument of this chapter—sought to grapple with the challenges of modernity in the shape of industrialization and urbanization, individualization and pluralization, the codification of women's rights, and the spread of paid employment among women. In this context, the family appeared less as a stronghold of moral values than as a "social institution" that demanded social scientific analysis.

This process produced ambivalent results. Against the background of a widespread perception of accelerated change and social dynamism, social scientists made their mark as representatives of a new guild. Thanks to the methods of statistics and empirical research, this was equipped to provide answers to burning moral questions and put forward proposals for political-legal frameworks with the aid of the "white light of scientific criticism."[224] Exemplary figures here include Edward A. Ross, Albion W. Small, James P. Lichtenberger, and George Howard, along with other participants in the American Sociological Association's "Family Conference" of 1908. A particularly telling example is statistics pioneer and clergyman Samuel Dike, who advocated a reduction in the number of divorces out of conviction but, as a result of his social scientific research on the frequency of divorce, came increasingly into conflict with morally orthodox explanations of the "divorce evil."

Using the example of divorce in the Victorian Era, Robert L. Griswold has argued that lawyers took on a new importance as mediators of marital disputes and as arbitral authority on the threshold of the twentieth century. Something similar may be said of social scientists as analysts of social change.[225] But sociologists, for

---

222 As William O'Neill has suggested. O'Neill, *Divorce*, 257. O'Neill, "Divorce," 148–149. In contrast, Elaine Tyler May argues that there was no "moral revolution" in the field of marriage by 1920; at most, she asserts, modern desires were fused with more traditional notions of marriage, generating greater expectations of married life. May, *Great Expectations*, 158.
223 This, to put it very briefly, is one of the conclusions reached by Glenda Riley in her important study of divorce in the United States, in which she attributes to sociologists and their interpretations a key role in the failure to achieve uniform laws. Riley, *Divorce*, 123.
224 Here, the impact of the groundbreaking texts by Ross, Howard, Lichtenberger and Small in particular can hardly be overstated; the Wright Report also had a formative effect. From today's perspective, conversely, the first social scientific field studies, such as the pioneering work *Middletown* from 1921, seem less analytically impressive. Lynd, Robert S. and Lynd, Hellen Merrell, *Middletown. A Study in Contemporary American Culture* (New York 1929).
225 Griswold, "Law," 738–740. Griswold's notion of an "expanded conception of sexual cruelty" from the second half of the nineteenth century onward, a development rooted in strict "Victorian

example, did not want to simply let the new individuality, especially that of women, run its course, but to contain it through measures that they summarized under the term "social control." Many of those committed to a still widespread, though perhaps no longer dominant, conservative morality agreed with this demand. The plea for increased use of eugenic practices and regulations to protect both individual and community also found favor with a wide variety of political and moral camps. In the following chapter, I explore to what extent sympathies for greater "social control" acted as an intellectual conveyor belt culminating in the biologistic-eugenic conception of family and gender roles at large in the 1920s and 1930s. But it should be borne in mind that at the start of the twentieth century the nascent eugenics movement was just one possible response to the challenges of modernity.

---

morals" (domesticity, sexual restraint, and chastity), and one that he claims made a major impact on the divorce crisis in the early twentieth century, is fascinating—though it was during this period that the focus shifted from domesticity to individual fulfillment and personal autonomy.

2 "Scientific motherhood, reproductive morality and fitter families": debates on eugenic family concepts and the government's right to intervene in the 1920s and 1930s

In 1921, the Bureau of Naturalization in the U.S. Department of Labor published a short pamphlet entitled "Suggestions for Americanization Work Among Foreign-Born Women." The text was intended as a source of information for (mostly female) social workers and offered practical guidelines on educating and training immigrant women. It also provides a revealing snapshot of the prevailing understanding of motherhood, nation, and family among American social experts at the time:

Under the heading "Why Schooling For Foreign-Born Women Is Necessary," the following list appeared:

A. Because America is no better than its homes.
B. Because the mother determines the kind of home and the health and happiness of the family.
C. Because thousands of foreign-born women have or will have the right to vote and they must be able to do this intelligently if a high standard of citizenship is to be maintained.
D. Because the foreign-born mothers have much of the responsibility of determining what kind of citizens their children shall become.
E. Because the schooling of the mother is the only effective way to enable her to take her full responsibility in the home and in the community.[1]

The social experts involved thus centered the responsibility for the future of children, the family and, in a figurative sense, the American nation, on the mother. She became the target of educational efforts and behavioral guidelines, especially if, as in this case, she was not born in the United States. Yet in the 1920s and 1930s, white American women too were called upon by social experts to strengthen the nation by giving birth to and raising "high-quality" offspring, as the following assessment by a well-known representative of the eugenics movement shows: "The healthy and intelligent married woman who could have a normal family and who has only one child or two is, in most cases, pulling back on the wheels of racial progress."[2]

---

[1] U.S. Department of Labor, Bureau of Naturalization, *Suggestions for Americanization Work Among Foreign Born Women* (Washington 1921).
[2] Popenoe, Paul B., *The Conservation of the Family* (Baltimore 1926), 135. On Popenoe, see below.

https://doi.org/10.1515/9783111036120-003

Instead, well-educated, well-off white middle-class women in particular should regain awareness of their "natural" role as mothers and supply numerous offspring in order to strengthen the family and thus also the nation, rather than pursuing careers or self-fulfillment.

It is these demands for eugenics, reproduction of the "desirable" and "healthy motherhood" on the one hand, and for welfare and women's education to enhance their raising of future citizens on the other, that I examine in this chapter. I thus evaluate the debate on motherhood in the national press, the writings of the eugenics movement, texts by a number of social experts and, in particular, the publications of eugenicist and marriage counselor Paul B. Popenoe. My aim is to bring out how social experts from a wide variety of backgrounds conducted a debate on the government's right to intervene in the family, developing their positions with reference to reproduction and motherhood. At the national level, this led to a significant shift in emphasis when it came to clarifying which women were to be considered mothers of "desirable offspring" and therefore deserving of the nation's support and whose reproductive rights were to be restricted on the basis of race, class, or ethnicity. Social experts and their behavioral guidelines played the key role here.

External factors also contributed to the family becoming the preferred object of analysis and therapy for social experts in the 1920s and 1930s and helped ensure the rise to prominence of racial-biological ideas. The key factors were steadily increasing immigration and the world economic crisis of 1929, along with its consequences. Since the nineteenth century, the flow of immigrants had been fueling fears that the country was being "swamped by foreigners," a prospect referred to polemically from 1901 onwards as the threat of "race suicide."[3] The U.S. government had initially sought to curb the influx by introducing the hygienic-medical screening of arrivals at the various immigration stations. Ellis Island in New York Harbor was not only the point of entry for most immigrants from 1892 onward, but developed into a model for the country's other immigration stations, becoming a "laboratory" for the fight against the "threatening diseases and people coming from the outside."[4] As recent studies have emphasized, the debate on immigration restrictions after World War I provided representatives of the young eugenics movement with a platform for popularizing both the idea of biological differences between people and the demand for selection derived from it.[5] At the instigation of prominent eugenicists, the Immigration Act of 1924 added a quota system inspired by

---

[3] For more information, see my remarks in chapter 1.
[4] On the medicalization of the immigration process, see Lüthi, *Invading Bodies*, 148.
[5] King, *Making Americans*. Zolberg, Aristide, *A Nation by Design: Immigration Policy in the Fashioning of America* (Cambridge, MA 2006), 248–267.

ideas about race to the hygienic-medical examination. Harry H. Laughlin, head of the Eugenic Record Office (ERO),[6] the central eugenic research body in the United States, was pioneering in this regard.[7] This institution, located in Cold Spring Harbor, New York, was founded in 1910 by Charles B. Davenport as part of the Station for Experimental Evolution (a subdivision of the Carnegie Institution of Washington Station [CIW] and later renamed the Department of Genetics), which he had headed since 1904. Its primary mission was to collect eugenic data by archiving and analyzing eugenic field research, family trees, and medical records. Davenport hired Harry H. Laughlin as superintendent of the new institution, a post he held it until the institution closed in 1939.

Laughlin, himself a staunch proponent of eugenic sterilization, had been a member of the Committee on Immigration and Naturalization of the House of Representatives since 1921 and had helped initiate modifications to immigration law informed by racial concepts. The quota system now facilitated the rejection of a large portion of would-be immigrants from Eastern and Southeastern Europe

---

6 Today, Cold Spring Harbor Laboratory still exists as one of the most important human genetics research sites in the United States <https://www.cshl.edu/>. Most of the ERO's records are housed in the archives of the American Philosophical Society in Philadelphia.

7 Harry H. Laughlin (1880–1943) was a well-known representative of the American eugenics movement who helped to shape immigration legislation as an expert and, through his expert opinions, played a significant role in the legalization of sterilization practices in the United States. After working as a teacher and school principal, he received his doctorate from Princeton in 1907 on the basis of a study in cytology. In addition to his leadership of the ERO from 1910 and participation in the Immigration Commission from 1921, Laughlin advised the Department of Labor on immigration issues from 1923 to 1924 and served as a consultant on eugenics issues to the Municipal Court of Chicago from 1921 to 1930. His numerous publications on eugenics and eugenic sterilizations were widely received in the United States and served as an inspiration to German racial scientists in particular. An expression of the esteem in which he was held in German academia in the 1930s was his honorary doctorate from the University of Heidelberg in 1936. The Harry H. Laughlin papers, containing files from his time as director of the ERO, are housed in the Pickler Memorial Library at Truman State University, Kirksville, Missouri <https://oldlibrary.truman.edu/manuscripts/laughlinbio.asp>.

His most important publications were Laughlin, Harry H., *The Legal, Legislative and Administrative Aspects of Sterilization* (Eugenics Record Office, Cold Spring Harbor 1914). Laughlin, Harry H., *Eugenical Sterilization in the United States* (Psychopathic Laboratory of the Municipal Court of Chicago) (Chicago 1922). Laughlin, Harry H., *The Legal Status of Eugenical Sterilization. History and Analysis of Litigation under the Virginia Sterilization Statute, which Led to a Decision of the Supreme Court of the United States Upholding the Statute* (Chicago 1930). Laughlin, Harry H., *Immigration and Conquest. A Study of the United States as the Receiver of Old World Emigrants who Became the Parents of Future-Born Americans*, Chamber of Commerce of the State of New York (New York 1939). Laughlin, Harry H., *Official Records in the History of the Eugenics Record Office* (Cold Spring Harbor 1939).

(Asians were completely barred), so that immigration numbers fell sharply.[8] However, unregulated immigration from Mexico in particular provided a new opportunity to link the demand for "protection of family and nation" with that for racial purity and eugenics.[9] As Alexandra Minna Stern has shown with reference to the Border Patrol along the frontier with Mexico, the border states, from Texas to California, attempted to protect American families (and thus the American nation) from "contamination" by illegal immigrants with the aid of paramilitary units.[10] These "patrol men" were tasked with tracking down illegal immigrants from Mexico, arresting them, and expelling them across the border, and thus performed a policing role. The argument used to justify the establishment of the Border Patrol in 1924 was that immigrants posed an economic and health threat to the American nation.[11] Hence, in 1926, a military expert defended its work and warned the U.S. Congress about "undesirable aliens [who] often become public charges and must be cared for by our pauper institutions and insane asylums." He also underscored the supposed risk to the biological substance of society, as the unwanted immigrants constituted "a further menace to the health of the communities in which they settle."[12]

While immigration was seen by many contemporaries as a "biological" threat to the American family, the economic crisis initially appeared as a threat to the socio-economic existence of many families, but also as a normative crisis. Due to the collapse of the U.S. economy, millions of men with families lost their jobs from 1929 onward and could no longer perform their traditional function (at least

---

8 Also known as the National Origins Act or Johnson-Reed Immigration Act. Zolberg, *Nation by Design*. King, *Making Americans*. The law itself was based on the eugenicist literature of the time; in addition to Harry H. Laughlin's own reflections, Madison Grant's and Lothrop Stoddard's diagnoses of the impending racial decline of the United States as a result of immigration were a particularly important source of inspiration for proponents of strict regulations. Grant, Madison, *The Passing of the Great Race or the Racial Basis of European History. Fourth Revised Edition with A Documentary Supplement, with Prefaces by Henry Fairfield Osborn* (New York 1924, first edition 1916). Stoddard, Lothrop, *The Rising Tide of Color against white Supremacy* (Reprinted Brighton 1981, first edition New York 1920).
9 In particular, the California-based Commonwealth Club, a think tank of conservative social experts, called for the adoption of quotas for Mexican Americans as well, in order to canalize their immigration and protect border states such as California from being "swamped." See Roesch, *Macho Men*, 184–186.
10 Stern, Alexandra Minna, *Eugenic Nation: Faults and Frontiers of Better Breeding in Modern America* (Berkeley 2005), 57–81.
11 Stern, *Eugenic Nation*, 74, refers to the unpublished dissertation by Lytle Hernández, Kelly Anne: "Entangling Bodies and Borders: Racial Profiling and the US Border Patrol 1924–1955" (Los Angeles: University of California, 2002).
12 Quoted in Stern, *Eugenic Nation*, 77.

within the middle class) as "sole breadwinner." Married women began working to make ends meet, and large-scale internal migration from rural Midwestern regions to California began.[13] Marriage and birth rates declined, but above all, gender roles in families seemed to shift in the eyes of contemporaries. For example, on the basis of fifty-nine interviews, contemporary sociologist Mirra Komarovsky traced how paternal authority broke down due to the impossibility of providing for the family. She quotes an unemployed former breadwinner:

> There certainly was a change in our family and I can define it in just one word—I relinquished power in the family. I think the man should be the boss in the family. [. . .] But now I even don't try to be the boss. She controls all the money, and I never have a penny in my pocket but that I have to ask her for it. The boarders pay her, the children turn in their money to her, and the relief check is cashed by her or the boy. I toned down a good deal as a result of it. How did it all come about? Very simple. I stopped earning money, and most of the money that was coming in was coming in through her.[14]

Recently, however, alternatives to the simple diagnosis of a crisis of the family and gender roles during the Great Depression have appeared. Ralph LaRossa, for example, has identified a tentative modernization and pluralization of fathers' role in the 1920s and 1930s, since the economic crisis opened up opportunities for their increased theoretical and practical involvement in child-rearing tasks, though by no means all fathers took advantage of this.[15] Jürgen Martschukat, conversely, concludes that the diagnoses of crisis in the wake of the Great Depression always entailed a call for the restabilization of the existing order, in this case for restoration of the male breadwinner role. Drawing on the work of sociologist Mirra Komarovsky, however, he makes the point that this period "at least hinted at the possibility of fundamental shifts in an order of the social in which gender was a mobile, mutable category."[16] Finally, in an edited volume of contemporary letters from children and young people to First Lady Eleanor Roosevelt, Robert Cohen argues that even

---

13 A contemporary overview of the effects of the Great Depression was provided by the journalist Lorena Hickok, who traveled the country at the behest of Harry Hopkins. Lowitt, Richard and Beasly, Maurine (eds.), *One Third of a Nation: Lorina Hickok Reports on the Great Depression* (Urbana 1981). See also the collection of oral history interviews on the Great Depression published by journalist Studs Terkel in 1970. Terkel, Studs, *Hard Times. An Oral History of the Great Depression* (New York 1970).
14 Komarovsky, Mirra, *The Unemployed Man and His Family: The Effect of Unemployment Upon the Status of the Man in Fifty-Nine Families* (New York 1940). Cf. Kennedy, David M., *Freedom from Fear. The American People in Depression and War, 1929–1945* (Oxford 2001), 165–166. The same quote can also be found in Martschukat, *Ordnung des Sozialen*, 249.
15 LaRossa, *Modernization of Fatherhood*, 11–12, 69.
16 Martschukat, *Ordnung des Sozialen*, 261–262.

the "children of the Great Depression" referred predominantly to intact family relationships (and, implicitly, gender hierarchies), despite the economic hardship and their fathers' unemployment.[17]

At the same time, it is evident that within the framework of the New Deal the government intervened in the domestic sphere more than ever before in American history in an attempt to combat the Great Depression and its aftermath, discovering the family as an object of policy for the first time. Previously, it had only intervened in immigrant families to bring them into line with the values, hygiene standards, and productivity of U.S. families.[18] The Social Security Act (1935) contained the first measures laying the foundations of a modern welfare state, and differentiated for the first time between contributory insurance benefits such as pensions, unemployment insurance, and government aid for the needy (welfare for the aged, widows and orphans, and the blind or disabled, as well as government-funded health benefits).[19] In particular, Title IV, Aid to Families with Dependent Children (AFDC), made the family the focus of government welfare by offering widows and single women the prospect of a basic income to sustain them and their children.[20] AFDC, which quickly became the most important government welfare program, openly propagated the traditional family image of the "white middle class" with the man as the sole breadwinner. Only if he died, stopped earning money, or left the family were mothers to receive support so they could continue to devote themselves to their traditional role as housewives and mothers. The states were responsible for awarding benefits, and they were

---

[17] Cohen, Robert (ed.), *Dear Mrs. Roosevelt. Letters from Children of the Great Depression* (Chapel Hill 2002), 18–20. See also: Morgan, Winona, *The Family Meets the Depression. A Study of a Group of Highly Selected Families* (Westport 1939).

[18] Lüthi, *Invading Bodies*. Cf. the special issue "Migration History as a Transcultural History of Societies," ed. by Dirk Hoerder, *Journal of Migration History* 1 (2015), no. 2.

[19] On the Social Security Act and the Second New Deal in general, see Brinkley, Alan, *The End of Reform. New Deal Liberalism in Recession and War* (New York 1995). Kennedy, *Freedom from Fear*, 271–274.

[20] The forerunner of this welfare program was the "Mothers' Pensions" scheme, which was enshrined in law by the states between 1911 and 1933. This was intended to allow single mothers to devote themselves entirely to the upbringing and care of their children rather than engaging in wage labor—which was entirely in line with the maternalistic views of the General Federation of Women's Clubs and the National Congress of Mothers. Receipt of benefits was contingent on proof of the applicant's "worthiness," so that only about 5 to 8 percent of single mothers received assistance. 80 percent of those receiving benefits in 1933 were white widows. Mynk, Gwendolyn, *The Wages of Motherhood: Inequality in the Welfare State, 1917–1942* (Ithaca 1995). *Report of the Children's Bureau on the Mothers' Pensions Program* (1933), reprinted in Nadasen, Premilla, Mittelstadt, Jennifer and Chappell, Marisa, *Welfare in the United States. A History with Documents 1935–1996* (New York and London 2009), 87–99.

then reimbursed for part of their costs by the federal government, which led to major regional differences in the guidelines for granting benefits and in the amount paid out. Before the reform of widows' benefits and their incorporation into the federal pension system in 1939, the bulk of AFDC recipients consisted of white middle-class widows, while in subsequent years the percentage of African American mothers and mothers of illegitimate children increased rapidly. By 1948, 30 percent of families receiving benefits were considered "non-white," leading to a wave of criticism of AFDC in the years that followed.[21] While conservative Republicans in particular questioned the purpose of government benefits and the "welfare state" as such, critics generally argued that by supporting unmarried women and single African American mothers the government was undermining the nuclear family model, while encouraging lax sexual morality and a lack of responsibility.

This chapter therefore focuses on whether and if so how the connection between the individual, the family, and the government was reformulated in the 1920s and 1930s and how biologistic and economic concepts of family and nation were linked. Of particular interest is the extent to which the family values prevalent in this phase were endowed with a biologistic charge, that is, whether the eugenics movement left its mark on the prevailing understanding of the family. To try to determine this, I examine public debates centered on eugenics, sterilizations, and ideas of good motherhood with reference to expert publications, press reports, and political-legal frameworks. Prior to this, the first section scrutinizes demographic change in the United States in the twentieth century and thus provides the background to the debate on eugenics and good motherhood in the 1920s and 1930s.

Specifically, the sources on which my analysis is based include the files of the American Eugenics Society and the Eugenic Record Office, as well as the writings of prominent eugenicists such as Charles B. Davenport, Roswell H. Johnson, and Paul B. Popenoe. Also crucial are the journal of the American Institute for Family Relations (AIFR), *Family Life*, and the reportage of the national press (the *New York Times* and *Washington Post*) on the practice of eugenic sterilization in the United States.

---

21 Nadasen, Mittelstadt, and Chappell, *Welfare*, 20. Katznelson, Ira, *When Affirmative Action was White: The Untold History of Racial Inequality in Twentieth Century America* (New York 2005). Quadagno, Jill, *The Color of Welfare: How Racism Undermined the War on Poverty* (New York 1994).

2.1 Demographic change in the twentieth-century United States: population growth, reproduction rates, and family sizes

Looking at U.S. demographic trends in the twentieth century, we first note a significant population increase from about 76 million U.S. citizens in 1900 to more than 280 million in 2000.[22] The nonwhite share of the population increased from 12.1 percent (1900) to 17.2 percent (1999), but the proportion of African Americans remained relatively constant at 11.6 percent (1900) and 12.4 percent (1999) of the total population. The period studied in this chapter, that from 1920 to 1940, also reflects these trends characteristic of the century: the population grew from just under 106 million (1920) to just under 132 million (1940), but the ethnic composition remained largely unchanged. African Americans accounted for about 10 percent of the population, and "White Americans" for about 90 percent.

Other ethnic groups (such as Native Americans and Mexican Americans) played a major role only at the regional level until 1970.[23] Finally, between 1920 and 1940, the fertility behavior of African Americans, despite contemporary fears, hardly differed from that of the white majority.[24] It is striking that in the 1920s and 1930s, population growth was almost exclusively urban: while the rural population remained almost constant at 69.8 million (1920) and 68.7 million (1940), the population of cities in the same period nearly doubled, from 35.9 to 63 million.[25]

This population growth came about in part as a result of immigration, with the first and final thirds of the twentieth century in particular showing high im-

---

22 Unless otherwise noted, all statistical information refers to data published by the US Bureau of the Census <www.census.gov> or the National Center for Health Statistics <www.cdc.gov/nchs/>.
23 Hobbs, Frank and Nicole Stoops, *U.S. Census Bureau, Census 2000 Special Reports, Series CENSR-4, Demographic Trends in the 20th Century*, (U.S. Government Printing Office, Washington, DC, 2002), 11, 77.
24 While one contemporary statistic indicated that in 1920 there were 71.9 births for every 1,000 American women between the ages of 15 and 54 nationwide, it recorded 71.4 for the white majority and 78.8 for "all other races." This contrasted with 52.0 births overall, 51.0 for White Americans and 60.4 births for "all other races" in 1940. Thus, the decline in births among the White majority was slightly greater (19.1 births per 1,000 female Americans) than among the non-White minority (18.4 births), but the difference was by no means dramatic. Linder, Forest Edward and Grove, Robert D., *Vital Statistics of the United States, 1900–1940*. (United States Government Printing Office, Washington D.C. 1943), 672. More recent statistics arrive at divergent figures as they attempt to compensate for data collection gaps but confirm the tendency for the birth patterns of African Americans to differ little from those of White Americans. Hamilton, Brady E. et al, *National Vital Statistics Reports*, vol. 62, no. 3, September 6, 2013, 2.
25 Hobbs and Stoops, *Demographic Trends*, 32.

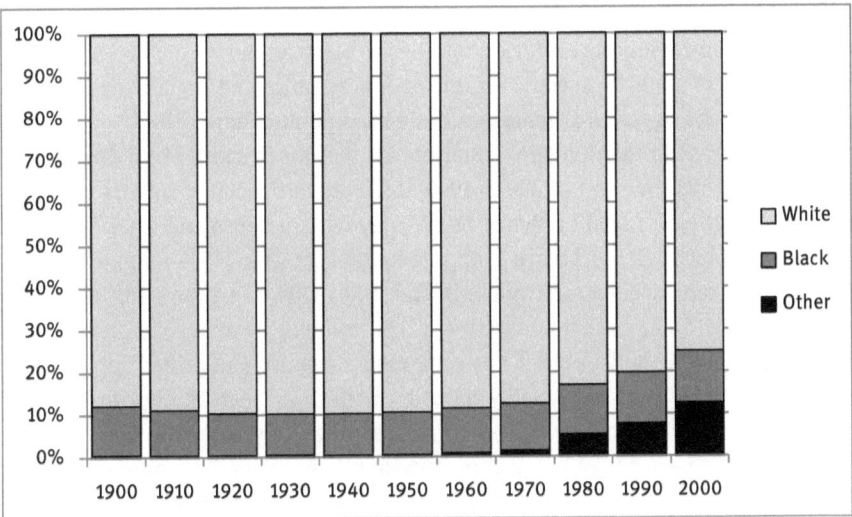

Fig. 2.1: Population distribution 1900–2000 by ethnic group.

migrant numbers. More than 18.6 million immigrants arrived in the U.S. between 1901 and 1930 (including about 14.5 million between 1901 and 1920 and only 4.1 million between 1921 and 1930), compared with nearly 21 million immigrants who reached the country between 1971 and 2000. By contrast, in the four middle decades of the twentieth century, only 7.4 million immigrants entered the U.S. (and just under 530,000 in the decade from 1931 to 1940).[26] This was the result of the racially oriented Immigration Act of 1924, which severely restricted immigration, especially from Eastern and Southeastern Europe, while barring Asians completely. In the course of the twentieth century, meanwhile, the ethnic composition of immigrants also changed radically. Whereas in the first third of the twentieth century it was mainly Europeans who came to the United States, from 1971 onward it was chiefly immigrants from Mexico, Latin America, and Asia. The immigrants brought with them not only their own culture and language, but also family models and values that sometimes differed significantly from those of the white majority society. This is particularly palpable in the case of Mexican Americans, a minority whose family life was strongly influenced by Catholicism and the ideal of the extended family until the 1970s. This was based, at least formally, on the strong position of the male family head and the inclusion in the family of godparents not related by blood (the traditions of *machismo* and *compadrazgo*),

---

[26] U.S. Census Bureau, *Statistical Abstracts of the United States, 2003. Mini Historical Statistics*, 15.

which, from the beginning of the century, gave social experts and social reformers a supposed reason to re-educate families of Mexican descent to make them fit better with the majority society. To this end, academics and social workers took either mothers and wives or male youths as their point of departure.[27]

The increase in the number of households was much more pronounced than population growth (almost 16,000 in 1900 and close to 105,000 in 2000), a result of the fact that the average number of persons living in a household grew from just under five persons (1890), before dropping to four persons (1930), and then breaking through the three-person mark in the mid-1970s (the figure for 2000 was 2.62 persons).[28] Since 1975, the majority of U.S. residents have lived in one- or two-person households, a trend that has remained constant. The proportion of four-person households, the supposedly "classic" modern nuclear family consisting of two parents and two children, has remained relatively constant (16.9 percent [1900] and 14.6 percent [2000]). It thus consistently represented a minority model —despite being conceived and propagated as the dominant family ideal. In the mid-1950s, at the height of the so-called baby boom, just under 19 percent of all households consisted of four people, but even then the majority of Americans lived in two-person households.[29]

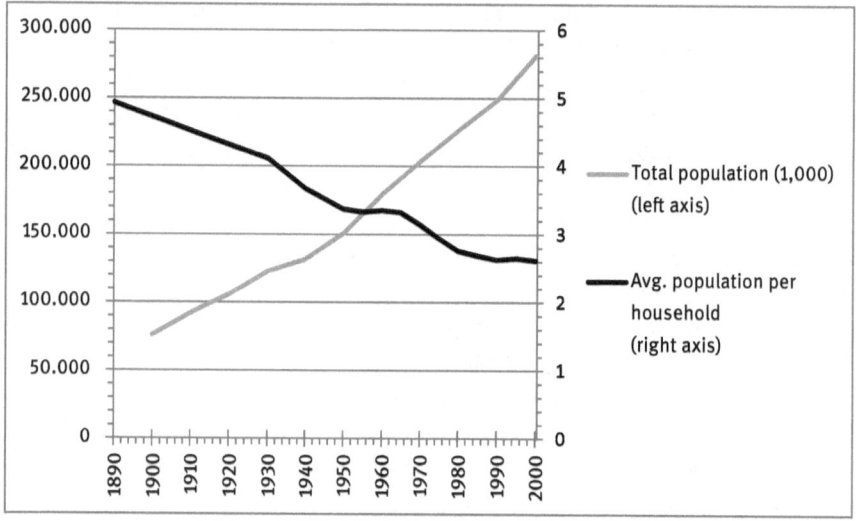

Fig. 2.2: Population trends and average household sizes, 1900–2000.

---

27 Roesch, *Macho Men*. Sanchéz, "'Go after the Women.'" Sanchéz, *Becoming Mexican American*.
28 Hobbs and Stoops, *Demographic Trends*, 143. No figures are available for 1910 and 1920.
29 Hobbs and Stoops, *Demographic Trends*, 143.

The development of the total fertility rate provides another significant indicator of a changing understanding of the family in the twentieth-century United States. While the average American woman still gave birth to 3.8 children at the turn of the century and 3.3 children in 1920, this figure fell to 2.1 children in the 1930s as a result of the Great Depression, rebounding to a rate of 2.2 only in 1940.[30] From the mid-1940s to the mid-1960s, the figure recovered again to more than 3 children, with the birth rate in the second half of the 1950s standing out at 3.7 children per woman. From the mid-1960s onward, a decline in the fertility rate set in that was found in all Western industrialized nations. The average American woman still gave birth to 2.5 children in 1970, 2.1 children in 1994, and 1.9 children in 2012. This means that although the fertility rate in the U.S. is currently below the replacement level, it is still slightly higher than that in Germany, at 1.6 children per woman.[31] The birth rate among African American women was slightly higher than the national average: in 1970, members of this group gave birth to an average of 3.1 children, 2.4 in 1994[32] and 2.0 in 2010.[33]

The sharp rise in the fertility rate in the 1950s and 1960s is particularly characteristic of the United States,[34] the baby boom in Western Europe being far more modest. Even at the height of this boom, German women had an average of only 2.2 children in 1955 and 2.5 in 1965, while their counterparts in the U.S. had well over 3.[35] Another specific feature is the convergence of the fertility rate of the African American population with that of the majority white population at the beginning of the twenty-first century (from 2.5 in 1990 to 2.0 in 2010). A similar trend can be observed for the minority Mexican American population (from 3.0 in 1990 to 2.4 in 2010), while the fertility rate of the Asian American minority is currently slightly below the national replacement rate.[36]

---

30 Haines, Michael R., "American Fertility in Transition: New Estimates of Birth Rates in the United States, 1900–1910," *Demography* 26 (1989), vol. 1, 137–148.
31 Livingston, Gretchen, *In terms of childlessness, U.S. ranks near the top worldwide*, Pew Research Center <www.pewrsr.ch/1bDZfz2>, March 17, 2014.
32 Chadwick and Heaton, *Statistical Handbook*, 68.
33 National Center for Health Statistics, Population Reference Bureau, *World Population Data Sheet 2012, Fact Sheet: The Decline in U.S. Fertility*, figure 1. Figures for 2011 are based on estimates.
34 How the population increase was diagnosed, rationalized, and staged via statistical self-observation in the 1940 and 1950 censuses as a product of the childbearing propensities of the suburban "white middle class" is shown impressively by Brumberg, *Vermessung*, 87–105, 131–151.
35 Human Fertility Database <www.humanfertility.org>.
36 Chadwick and Heaton, *Statistical Handbook*, 84, Livingston, Gretchen and Cohn, D'Vera, "The New Demography of American Motherhood," Pew Research Center. <www.pewsocialtrends.org/2010/05/06/the-new-demography-of-american-motherhood/>, April 7, 2014. 11.

By the beginning of the twentieth century, the understanding of childhood in the United States had already changed substantially, in the sense that this life stage had become more individualized as well as more regulated. After the "invention of childhood" at the beginning of the twentieth century,[37] that is, the widespread recognition of this phase as a special, discrete one that is worthy of protection rather than merely a transitional stage on the way to adulthood, reformers and scientists in the United States engaged intensively with childhood and the welfare of children.[38] Already fiercely contested in the Progressive Era, child labor was finally banned in 1938 by the Fair Labor Standards Act within the framework of the New Deal. From the turn of the century onward, social reform advocates, physicians, and especially mothers' associations such as the National Congress of Mothers launched initiatives to improve health care and education for children and adolescents, while guidebooks such as Benjamin Spock's famous *Commonsense Book of Baby and Child Care* (first published in 1946) homogenized middle-class parenting styles around midcentury.[39] One of the most important legal changes of the twentieth century, ushered in by the Supreme Court's 1954 *Brown versus Board of Education* desegregation ruling, fundamentally changed the lives of America's youth by (at least theoretically) providing African American children with full access to the nation's educational system for the first time. The second half of the twentieth century saw the development of a distinct youth culture (in terms of music, clothing, morals, and lifestyle), fueled in large part by the social protest movements of the 1950s to 1970s and young people's need to distinguish themselves from their parents' generation.[40] At the same time, in the 1950s an intense debate kicked off in the United States about juvenile delinquency, which was seen less as an expression of generational conflict than as an

---

37 Key, Ellen, *The Century of the Child* (New York and London 1909, original edition: *Barnets århundrade*, 1900).
38 Ladd Taylor, *Mother-Work*. Stern, Alexandra Minna and Markel, Howard (eds.), *Formative Years. The History of Children's Health in the United States, 1880–2000* (Ann Arbor 2002). Mintz, Steven, *Huck's Raft. A History of American Childhood* (Cambridge 2004).
39 Spock, Benjamin, *The Commonsense Book of Baby and Child Care* (New York 1946). Engelhardt, Janine, "Konzeptionen von Mutter- und Elternschaft in Benjamin Spocks Ratgeber 'The Common Sense Book of Baby and Child Care'" (Masters thesis University of Münster, 2015–16). Weiss, Nancy Pottishman, "Mother, the Invention of Necessity. Doctor Benjamin Spock's Baby and Child Care" *American Quarterly* 29 (1977), no. 5, 519–546. Grant, *Raising Baby*. Apple, *Perfect Motherhood*. Schumann (ed.), *Raising Citizens*.
40 Mintz, *Huck's Raft*, Bailey, Beth, *Sex in the Heartland* (Cambridge [et al.] 2004).

acute threat to the foundations of society. Experts argued that American parents should be educated in advance in how to raise their offspring to become upright citizens.[41] In addition to genuine generational conflicts and assertions of autonomy on the part of American youth, the last third of the twentieth century saw a proliferation of attempts by many parents to be committed, emotionally devoted partners to their children. This was especially true of fathers ("involved fatherhood"). At the same time, childhood and adolescence were more strongly regulated by the government and the family than ever before (a trend that persists to this day).[42] The entire discussion about juvenile delinquency, however, was based on profound presuppositions about the significance of ethnic, social, and gender-related categories ("race, class, and gender") to the question of what constituted "deviant behavior" and "delinquency" in the first place. These expectations were to some extent forged as early as the first third of the twentieth century.[43]

It was during this period that social scientists articulated their perception that Americans were living through a time of unprecedented social change. They believed it important to analyze this change, especially with regard to the U.S. family. The 1929 study *Middletown* by sociologists Robert S. Lynd and Helen Merrell Lynd is a good example of this. In their pioneering work on the inhabitants of the small town of Muncie, Indiana, the Lynds investigated social and cultural change in "Middletown" over a period of thirty-five years, more precisely between 1890 and 1925. To this end, they carried out anthropological field research and drew on social scientific data (statistics, press reports, documents, surveys, and interviews). Their aim was "to present a dynamic, functional study of the contemporary life of this specific American community in the light of the trends of changing behavior observable in it during the last thirty-five years."[44] A follow-up

---

41 Mackert, Nina, "Danger and Hope. White Middle-Class Juvenile Delinquency and Parental Anxiety in the Postwar U.S.," in Ellis, Heather and Chang, Lily (eds.), *Juvenile Delinquency and Western Modernity, 1800–2000* (New York: Palgrave Macmillan, 2013). Mackert, *Jugenddelinquenz*.
42 LaRossa, *Modernization of Fatherhood*. LaRossa, Ralph, *Of War and Men. World War II in the Lives of Fathers and Their Families* (Chicago 2011). Mintz, Steven, "Regulating the American Family," in Hawes, Joseph M. and Nybakken, Elizabeth I. (eds.), *Family and Society in American History* (Chicago 2001), 9–36. Martschukat, *Ordnung des Sozialen*. Dechert, *Dad on TV*.
43 Mary Odem shows impressively how female delinquency, unlike male delinquency, was primarily defined in terms of sexuality at the beginning of the twentieth century. Odem, Mary E., *Delinquent Daughters: Protecting and Policing Adolescent Female Sexuality in the United States, 1885–1920* (Chapel Hill and London 1995).
44 Lynd and Lynd, *Middletown*, 6.

volume, *Middletown in Transition*, grappled with the impact of the Great Depression on the town.[45]

In their research, the two sociologists deliberately construed the notional "average American" and his average family in positivist terms. For example, in *Middletown* the Lynds completely disregarded the African American minority and thus contributed to the construction of the average family as "white." Nevertheless, they provided some key insights into the social structure of American families in small Northeastern towns in the 1920s. The population was divided strictly into upper and working classes, with class membership strongly determining life chances and life trajectories. 70 percent of the population belonged to the working class and 30 percent to the "business class" (understood here in the broadest sense as those employed in the service sector).[46] Many "working class families" managed to acquire residential property thanks to favorable loans, which was the prerequisite for advancement to middle-class respectability. Middletown's 38,000 inhabitants made up more than 9,200 households. 86 percent of these lived in their own homes, and in keeping with the national trend, household sizes (and thus families) were smaller than they had been in the nineteenth century.[47] The divorce rate rose considerably; while in 1909 there were 25 divorces for every 100 marriages, by 1924 there were 42.[48] Yet women's employment remained the exception, while men had to assume the role of sole breadwinner for their families. In contrast, in Middletown too the responsibility for reproduction and child-rearing continued to lie solely with the woman, being viewed as her "moral obligation."[49] The mixture of secular change (divorce rates, household sizes, and home ownership) and constants (bipolar gender norms, social stratification, and the failure to acknowledge ethnic differences) found in the Lynds' study provides a good starting point for deeper investigation of the debates on family values, eugenics, and "good motherhood" in the 1920s and 1930s, which is the task of the present chapter. Five major processes of social change can serve as our foundation here, the last three of which were particularly significant to these debates.

First, there was strong population growth between 1920 and 1940, but this mainly affected the cities. The proportions of African Americans and "white Americans" remained constant at just under ten percent and almost 90 percent, respec-

---

[45] Lynd and Lynd, *Middletown*, esp. 3–6, 110–131. Lynd, Robert S. and Lynd, Helen Merell, *Middletown in Transition. A Study in Cultural Conflicts* (New York 1937). For a critique, see Igo, *The Averaged American*, 68–102.
[46] Lynd and Lynd, *Middletown*, 511.
[47] Lynd and Lynd, *Middletown*, 93.
[48] Lynd and Lynd, *Middletown*, 121, 521.
[49] Lynd and Lynd, *Middletown*, 131.

tively. Second, this period was characterized by a drastic clampdown on immigration through legislation informed by race-based arguments. Third, the reproduction rate in the U.S. declined steadily. This fueled fears among contemporaries that the white majority was committing "race suicide," although social statistics gave no indication of this. Fourth, contemporaries noted a marked decline in household size, which meant that the number of children per family was falling, while the number of those living alone was rising sharply, partly as a result of the high divorce rate. Fifth and finally, during this period, childhood rose to even greater prominence as a theme informing efforts at social reform and as the subject of advice literature, but the focus here was not on "children as actors" but on maternal responsibility for the upbringing and educating of good citizens.

2.2 "Scientific motherhood and reproductive morality"

With the rise of eugenics as a scientific paradigm, a trend already in evidence at the turn of the century, American families, and mothers in particular, increasingly became the focus of social scientists, physicians, and population planners.[50] On the one hand, guidebooks, press reports, and advertising conveyed to mothers the message that healthy child-rearing depended on heeding expert advice (rather than "unhealthy instincts").[51] The concept of "scientific motherhood" complemented that of "maternal love"—or as an advertisement in *Parents' Magazine* put it in 1938: "Add Science to Love to be a Perfect Mother."[52] Healthy nutrition, rational housekeeping, hygiene, and child-rearing knowledge were to the fore here. However, this scientific turn had no effect on gender roles, as "modern" expert advice was pre-

---

[50] On the eugenics movement in the United States, see Kline, Wendy, *Building a Better Race. Gender, Sexuality, and Eugenics from the Turn of the Century to the Baby Boom* (Berkeley 2001). Kühl, Stefan, *Die Internationale der Rassisten. Aufstieg und Niedergang der internationalen Bewegung für Eugenik und Rassenhygiene im 20. Jahrhundert* (Frankfurt a.M. 1997). Ordover, Nancy, *American Eugenics. Race, Queer Anatomy, and the Science of Nationalism* (Minneapolis 2003). Kevles, Daniel, *In the Name of Eugenics. Genetics and the Use of Human Heredity* (New York 1985). Carlson, Elof Axel, *The Unfit. A History of a Bad Idea* (Cold Spring Harbor 2001). Black, Edwin, *War Against the Weak: Eugenics and America's Campaign to Create a Master Race* (New York and London 2003). Dowbiggin, Ian Robert, *A Merciful End. The Euthanasia Movement in Modern America* (New York 2003).
[51] Apple, Rima D., "Constructing Mothers. Scientific Motherhood in the Nineteenth and Twentieth Centuries," in Apple, Rima D. and Golden, Janet (eds.), *Mothers and Motherhood. Readings in American History* (Columbus 1997), 90–110.
[52] Quoted in Apple, "Constructing Mothers," 101. On this topic, see also the analysis of the reception of expert advice by mothers in Grant, *Raising Baby*.

dominantly supplied by men and child-rearing continued to be regarded as the exclusive domain of women.[53] Men were assigned the role of scientific authorities, while women were regarded at best as practitioners. On the other hand, politicians, social scientists, and intellectuals called for the improvement of modern families by increasing the birth rate, lowering the number of divorces, and strengthening the quality of offspring, which for many scientists (both liberal and conservative) made eugenic measures seem imperative.[54] Recent research rightly emphasizes that social reformers and eugenicists entered into a coalition with respect to the essence of their ideas. Eugenics penetrated deeply into American notions of the freedom of the individual and his or her obligation to society, of individual agency and economic cost. Thus, the eugenics movement in the United States should not be viewed as a short-lived episode that was definitively discredited by the experience of Nazism. In fact, American eugenicists engaged in an intensive exchange with their German colleagues both before and after World War II. Above all, though, as we will see, eugenic considerations were a more or less universal element of demographic discourse in the United States up to the welfare reform of 1996.[55]

The scientification of child-rearing and motherhood in the United States began with the founding of the National Congress of Mothers as a federation of the major American Women's Clubs in 1897.[56] Alice McLellan Birney, the founder and longtime president, focused the organization on two core goals at its founding conference: providing information to mothers by drawing on the latest expert advice (on child-rearing, nutrition, and morality) and raising the status of the child ("child culture") through better knowledge of her or his physical and psy-

---

53 Apple, *Perfect Motherhood*.
54 Ideas of this kind had appeared in social science discourse since the turn of the century and mere had to be revived in the 1920s and 1930s. For instance, at the beginning of the twentieth century, liberal sociologist Edward A. Ross and feminist Anna Garlin Spencer had explicitly argued that there was a link between "social control" and eugenic measures: Ross, "Causes of Race Superiority." Spencer, "Problems of Marriage and Divorce." See also the positioning of the influential Federation of Women's Clubs on this issue, which advocated sterilizations both to promote "healthier and better families" and to relieve the government of high welfare costs for the disabled. "Club Women's Session Urges Birth Control," WP May 12, 1935, 10.
55 Ryan, Patrick J., "'Six Blacks from Home.' Childhood, Motherhood, and Eugenics in America," *Journal of Policy History* 19 (2007), 253–281, here 274. Kline, *Better Race*. Ordover, *American Eugenics*. Stern, *Eugenic Nation*. Dowbiggin, Ian Robert, "'A Rational Coalition': Euthanasia, Eugenics, and Birth Control in America, 1940–1970," *Journal of Policy History* 14 (2002), no. 3, 223–260.
56 The National Congress of Mothers was renamed the National Congress of Parents and Teachers in 1924, then the Parent Teacher Association, PTA, in 1965. The records of the National Congress of Parents and Teachers is housed at the University Library of the University of Illinois at Chicago. <www.uic.edu/depts/lib/specialcoll/services/rjd/findingaids/NCPTf.html>.

chological needs.⁵⁷ At the same time, the "Congress Women" professed their faith both in motherhood as *the* natural role of women and in the principles of the nascent eugenics as a means of improving society. In contrast, their concept of "scientific motherhood" did not include mothers' paid work outside the home or the integration of mothers from the "working class" or ethnic minorities.⁵⁸

Also crucial was the expansion of women's education, especially through the spread of women's colleges and the home economics movement. The latter was based on the idea that how people managed their households and their lives more generally should be based on scientific knowledge, which could be imparted, to women in particular, as part of educational programs.⁵⁹

Further impetus for the spread of "scientific motherhood" came from progressive reformers and the government. After the first White House Children's Conference on the Care of Dependent Children was held in 1909, the Children's Bureau was founded in 1912 as part of the Department of Labor and as the nerve center charged with coordinating support for mothers and their children.⁶⁰ The first director of the Children's Bureau was progressive reformer Julia Lathrop (1912–1921),⁶¹ a graduate of the prestigious Vassar College and a former member

---

57 The WP printed Birney's opening address, which culminated in a call to "make the child the watchword and ward of the day and hour" and an affirmation of "mother love" as the "cornerstone of home." "A Thousand Mothers: Congress Exceeds in Numbers the Highest Estimate," WP, February 18, 1897. See also NYT reports: "The Congress of Mothers will be a Unique Gathering," NYT, February 17, 1897. "The Congress of Mothers: The Second Day's Session," NYT, February 19, 1897.
58 On the National Congress of Mothers, see the seminal work by Ladd-Taylor, *Mother-Work*, 43–73. Grant, *Raising Baby*, 56–57. Ehrenreich, Barbara and English, Deirdre, *For Her Own Good. 150 Years of the Expert's Advice to Women* (London 1979), 175.
59 The founder of the home economics movement was MIT graduate Ellen Swallow Richards (1842–1911), who first presented her notion of healthy and scientifically based nutrition to fairgoers at the Chicago World Fair in 1893 in the shape of the Rumford Kitchen. Richards founded the American Home Economics Association (now American Association of Family and Consumer Sciences) in 1908. Goldstein, Carolyn M, *Creating Consumers. Home Economists in Twentieth-Century America* (Chapel Hill 2012).
60 The Children's Bureau was part of the Department of Commerce and Labor, becoming a subunit of the Department of Labor in 1913. Ladd-Taylor, *Mother-Work*. Gordon, Linda, *Pitied But Not Entitled: Single Mothers and the History of Welfare, 1890–1935* (New York 1994). Grant, *Raising Baby*, 114.
61 Julia Lathrop (1858–1932), social worker and reformer, had first attended Rockford Female Seminary and then studied statistics, institutional history, sociology, and community organization at Vassar College, graduating in 1880. She joined Chicago's Hull House in 1890. Lathrop, "America's first official mother," became the first female head of an agency when she took over the Children's Bureau in 1912. She championed both juvenile justice reforms and the fight for women's suffrage, lastly as president of the Illinois League of Women Voters. Stebner, Eleanor J.,

of Jane Addam's Hull House in Chicago, the focal point of the North American settlement movement.[62] She was followed in 1921 by Grace Abbott, another former resident of Hull House and a social reformer who had studied at the University of Chicago.[63] In addition to providing support for mother and child, the institution's core goals were the abolition of child labor and the battle to reduce infant and child mortality.[64] The latter purpose was also served by the Children's Bureau's best-known publication, Mary Mills West's guidebook *Infant Care*, first published in 1914, which reached large swathes of the U.S. population through numerous reprints.[65] In the work of the Children's Bureau, Lathrop and later Abbot combined a commitment to science and modern child care (in part through their own scientific studies of the situation of children and mothers in the United States) with the promotion of motherhood and domesticity as the primary obligation of women. In the research, the term "progressive maternalism" has come to be used

---

The Women of Hull House: A Study in Spirituality, Vocation, and Friendship (Albany, N.Y. 1997). *Vassar Encyclopedia* <vcencyclopedia.vassar.edu/distinguished-alumni/julia-lathrop>.

62 In 1889, social reformers Jane Addams (1860–1935) and Ellen Gates Starr (1859–1940) had jointly founded Hull House in Chicago as a drop-in center for immigrants, modelling it on London's Toynbee Hall, with which they had become acquainted on a trip to Europe. In Hull House—as in the settlement houses set up along its lines in other cities—predominantly female social reformers combined practical help for immigrants with cultural and political education, applied social research, and, not infrequently, paternalistic Americanization efforts.

63 Grace Abbott (1878–1939), social worker and reformer, was dedicated to eliminating child labor and protecting children and mothers. She headed the Children's Bureau from 1922 to 1934, having previously chaired its Child Labor Division. She too had lived in Hull House for a time and graduated from the University of Chicago in 1909 with a master's degree in political science. In the 1930s, championed the social reforms of the New Deal and was one of the authors of the Social Security Act. Costin, Lela, *Two Sisters for Social Justice: A Biography of Grace and Edith Abbott* (Chicago 1983). Sorensen, John and Sealander, Judith (eds.), *The Grace Abbott Reader* (Lincoln 2008).

64 Meckel, Richard A., *Save the Babies. American Public Health Reform and the Prevention of Infant Mortality, 1850–1929* (Baltimore 1990). Lindenmeyer, Kriste, *A Right to Childhood. The U.S. Children's Bureau and Child Welfare, 1912–1930* (Urbana and Chicago 1997).

65 West, Mary Mills (Mrs. Max West), U.S. Department of Labor, Children's Bureau, *Infant Care* (Washington: Government Printing Office, 1914). 12 million copies had been distributed by 1940, and over 59 million by the 1970s. Apple, Rima, "Physicians and Mothers Construct 'Scientific Motherhood,'" in Warner, John and Tighe, Janet, *Major Problems in the History of American Medicine and Public Health* (Boston and New York 2001), 332–339, 335. On the Children's Bureau and its communication with mothers, among other things through the guidebook *Infant Care*, see Limper, Verena, "Verantwortung für Körper, Kind, Nation. Mutter-Werden in der Kommunikation zwischen dem United States Children's Bureau und amerikanischen Frauen zu Beginn des 20. Jahrhunderts" (Master's thesis University of Bielefeld 2012).

to convey this.[66] It is interesting that Lathrop and Abbot both embodied this contradiction between reformist zeal and the acceptance of biologistic gender roles. Both women had university degrees and lived for their professions without marriage or children, yet flatly rejected gainful employment for mothers. They advocated an orientation toward expert medical advice to curb infant and child mortality and called for welfare policies tailored to the needs of children and mothers, but still postulated motherhood as women's most nationally significant role. While they reached immigrant and working-class women too through the expansion of home economics instruction (marriage preparation, household management, and child-rearing),[67] the work of the Children's Bureau's was initially limited primarily to white mothers and their children. Reformers failed to acknowledge the far higher mortality rate among African American children, a narrowing of focus typical of early twentieth-century progressive reformers.[68] This was also evident in the controversy over the Sheppard-Towner Act (1921–1929), the first law to protect expectant mothers and their children in the United States through federal welfare payments and the nationwide establishment of maternity hospitals. The passing of the act in 1921 was a major lobbying success for the Children's Bureau, which had shown that 80 percent of expectant mothers were not receiving medical care. In 1929, however, opposition from a number of states and especially from the American Medical Association (AMA) ensured that Congress ceased to provide funding. In the years that followed, the children of poor, non-white women again died in large numbers due to a lack of medical care and hygiene, illustrating the extent to which child health was determined by ethnic

---

66 Ladd-Taylor distinguishes emphatically between the "progressive maternalism" expounded by representatives of the Children's Bureau and the "sentimental maternalism" of the National Congress of Mothers. Ladd-Taylor, *Mother Work*, 73–103. For an international comparison, see Koven, Seth and Michel, Sonya (eds.), *Mothers of a New World. Maternalist Policies and the Origins of Welfare States* (New York 1993). Gordon, Linda (ed.), *Women, the State and Welfare* (Madison 1990). Stern, Alexandra Minna, "Making Better Babies: Public Health and Race Betterment in Indiana,1920–1935," *American Journal of Public Health* 92 (2002), no. 5, 742–752. Ladd-Taylor, Molly, "Saving Babies and Sterilizing Mothers. Eugenics and Welfare Politics in the Interwar United States," *Social Politics* 4 (1997), 136–153.
67 For example, the "Little Mothers' Clubs" established by Dr. S. Josephine Baker in New York in 1910 served to Americanize young immigrant women by preparing them for their role as future mothers. Apple, "Physicians and Mothers," 336. Sanchéz, "'Go after the Women.'" Roesch, "'Americanization through Homemaking.'".
68 Bullard, Catherine S., "Children's Future, Nation's Future. Race, Citizenship and the United States Children's Bureau," in Schumann, Dirk (ed.), *Raising Citizens in the "Century of the Child": The United States and German Central Europe in Comparative Perspective* (New York 2010), 53–67. Sealander, Judith, *The Failed Century of the Child. Governing America's Young in the Twentieth Century* (Cambridge 2003).

and social background.⁶⁹ At the same time, however, this development fostered the scientification of pediatrics, which was established as a discipline in its own right. In protest against the actions of the AMA, which had considered the law an attack on physicians' professional autonomy and had lobbied intensively for its revocation, the pediatricians now founded their own American Academy of Pediatrics (AAP) in 1930.⁷⁰

Molly Ladd-Taylor has argued that the Sheppard-Towner Act was an attempt at the "rationalization of reproduction" because it translated expert medical knowledge into federal family policy. In this regard, she compared it to the contemporaneous legalization of forced sterilization. However, she concluded that the reason for the much longer-term success of sterilization policy in the U.S. was that it sought to reduce welfare costs, whereas the Sheppard-Towner Act would have meant a further increase in costs.⁷¹ This indicates that by the late 1920s, eugenics appeared to many white Americans as the more racially and economically appealing alternative to welfare policy.

Another key source of inspiration for the "child culture" for which the Congress Women had called and for the Children's Bureau's fight against infant and child mortality in the white middle class was the book *Barnets åhundrade (The Century of the Child)* by Swedish educator Ellen Key, which first appeared in English in 1909.⁷² In this book, Key argued for a genuinely child-centered approach to pedagogy and the upgrading of motherhood as a socially significant task. For her, "the care of the new generation" was "the great business the mother takes over for society". "During its progress society must guarantee her existence."⁷³ At the same

---

69 Ladd-Tayor, "Saving Babies." Lemons, J. Stanley, "The Sheppard-Towner Act: Progressivism in the 1920s," *Journal of American History* 55, no. 4 (1969), 776–786.
70 Brosco, Jeffrey P., "Weight Charts and Well Child Care: When the Pediatrician Became the Expert in Child Health," in Stern, Alexandra Minna and Markel, Howard (eds.), *Formative Years. The History of Children's Health in the United States, 1880–2000* (Ann Arbor 2002), 91–121.
71 Ladd-Tayor, "Saving Babies," 139–140, 149–150.
72 Ellen Key (1849–1925) was a Swedish feminist, reform educator, and writer. *Barnets åhundrade* is her most important text and was translated into several European languages, including English and German. Key, Ellen, *The Century of the Child* (New York 1909) (German edition: *Das Jahrhundert des Kindes* [Weinheim 2000, first edition in German translation Berlin 1902, original edition: *Barnets åhundrade*, 1900]). Register, Cheri, "Motherhood at Center. Ellen Key's Social Vison," *Women's Studies Int. Forum* 5 (1982), no. 6, 599–610. Allen, Ann Taylor and Baader, Meike Sophie (eds.), *Ellen Keys reformpädagogische Vision. Das"Jahrhundert des Kindes" und seine Wirkung* (Weinheim 2000).
73 Key, Ellen: *The Century of the Child* (New York 1909), 86.

time, Key, like so many reformers in the early twentieth century, incorporated "racial science" and eugenic arguments into her ideas.[74] Thus, referring to the pioneer of "eugenics," Francis Galton,[75] and other authors such as naturalist Alfred Russell Wallace and psychologist Henry Maudsley, she called for "the whole antique love for bodily strength and beauty, the whole antique reverence for the divine character of the continuation of the race, combined with the whole modern consciousness of the soulful happiness of ideal love". To her, the body and genetics were likewise important, as they formed the "basis of natural science".[76] Marriage sanctions for hereditarily burdened or sick people, in order to exclude them from reproduction, met with her approval. At the same time, however, she criticized any anthropological absolutism, such as that expounded by German racial anthropologist Otto Ammon, since she was chiefly concerned with the "formation of a new and higher race of mankind" through the "elevation of sensuousness to love."[77]

However, the debates on "scientific motherhood" were not only about child-rearing, hygiene, and household management, but always also about the position of women and mothers in modern society. The question of the legitimacy of women's employment, especially when the women involved were "mothers," was another area of conflict. It was here especially that the eugenics movement found multiple easy routes into the debate, since it could argue on the basis of suppos-

---

[74] This can be seen, among other things, in the discussion of divorce up to 1920; see chapter 1 of the present book.

[75] British anthropologist and polymath Francis Galton (1822–1911) was the originator of the term eugenics, for a "science of improving stock, which [...] takes cognisance of all influences that tend [...] to give the more suitable races or strains of blood a better chance of prevailing speedily over the less suitable than they otherwise would have had." He established a correlation between the social and genetic "value" of an individual and proposed "negative eugenics" to increase the "quality" of both the human "race" and the British population. Galton became president of the newly founded Eugenics Education Society in London in 1907. Galton, Francis, *Inquiries into Human Faculty and Its Development* (London 1883), 24. Galton, Francis, *The Possible Improvement of the Human Breed under the existing Conditions of Law and Sentiment, Huxley Lecture at the Royal Anthropological Institute 1901, Annual Report of the Board of Regents of the Smithsonian Institution* (Washington 1902), 523–538. Galton, Francis, *Hereditary Genius. An Inquiry into its Laws and Consequences* (London 1869).

[76] Key, *Century*, 12. The reference to contemporary racial science and eugenics in Key's work is also emphasized by Mann, Katja, "Pädagogische, psychologische und kulturanalytische Perspektiven im Werk von Ellen Key" (Dissertation HU-Berlin, 2002), 313–314. <http://edoc.hu-berlin.de/dissertationen/mann-katja-2003-02-12/HTML/>.

[77] Key, *Century*, 5, 42. Implicitly, Key criticized Otto Ammon's racial absolutism in his book *Die natürliche Auslese beim Menschen* (1893). Key, Century, 27, 46. See also Ammon, Otto, *Die natürliche Auslese beim Menschen auf Grund der Ergebnisse der anthropologischen Untersuchungen der Wehrpflichtigen in Baden und anderer Materialien* (Jena 1893).

edly objective findings. As early as 1911, neuropathologist Max G. Schlapp, writing in the *New York Times*, construed women's work as a "racial problem" in the United States, one responsible for a massive "degeneration of the race." The work-related strain on women, who were created exclusively for their reproductive role, irreversibly damaged their nervous system and ultimately even their cells: "When to this stress is added the function of motherhood the child must suffer through life, because it cannot receive the normal amount of 'harmons' [sic] necessary for its perfect development."[78] Schlapp further expanded this reading of cytology and endocrinology, which is highly questionable from today's perspective. In the mid-1920s, he called in the same newspaper for the gradual exclusion of women from the labor market so they could once again fulfill their function as mothers of healthy offspring.[79] Modern industrial work had ensured—as Schlapp sought to prove with reference to European immigrants, among others—that previously healthy women were now giving birth to disabled offspring. They were therefore crucially responsible for the "menacing growth of the unfit and the dependent":

> Woman, both because of her unchangeable physiology and her age-long habitute, is not adapted to the catabolic role in life. Under the stress and strains of business life all her important endocrine glands become quickly disordered and she is, once this has happened, unfit for healthy motherhood.[80]

Schlapp clothed his general critique of the modern lifestyle and women's work in an argument that claimed scientific respectability, one he tried to substantiate with examples from his practice.

This pessimistic assessment was contradicted by a study on *Marriage and Careers* conducted by the Bureau of Vocational Information in New York, which was also re-

---

78 Schlapp, Max G., "Activity of Modern Women a Racial Problem," NYT, August 13, 1911, SM6.
79 Max G. Schlapp (1869–1928) was professor of neuropathology at Cornell University, taught at the New York Post-Graduate Medical School from 1911, and headed the New York Children's Court Clinic. He was considered an expert on the heritability of criminality and mental illness. Schlapp, who had received his doctorate in Berlin, was strongly influenced by German hereditary and racial science. Together with Edward H. Smith, he authored the controversially received study *The New Criminology: A Consideration of the Chemical Causation of Abnormal Behavior* (New York 1928), which attempted to describe criminal behavior as an endocrine pathology. See the review by Karl A. Menninger in the *American Journal of Psychiatry* 85 (1929), 959–961. Obituary for Schlapp, NYT, March 6, 1928.
80 Schlapp, Max G., "Civilization Burdened by Costs of its Unfit," *NYT*, May 16, 1926, XX17. Just a few years earlier, he had argued in the *Journal of Heredity* that many disabilities in children resulted from "glandular disturbances" in mothers who failed to concentrate on their maternal role and instead pursued a professional career. Schlapp, Max G., "Causes of Defective Children. Prenatal Development Affected by Glandular Disturbances in the Mother—Induced by Unfavorable Environment," *Journal of Heredity* 14 (1923), no. 9, 387–398.

ported in the *New York Times* in 1926.[81] The author of the study, Virginia MacMakin Collier, had examined the living situation of 100 college-educated working women from the greater Boston and New York area. She concluded that for well-educated members of the middle class, women's employment did not lead to neglect of their maternal duties. On the contrary, it produced greater contentment, since these mothers had sufficient help with housekeeping and childcare. The preconditions for this were "(1) sympathetic cooperation from the husband, (2) good health, (3) good training and experience before marriage, (4) short or flexible hours of work."[82]

Collier thus raised the problem from the biologistic to the social level: conflicts thrown up by attempts to reconcile work and motherhood now began to seem like a class phenomenon, as a study by the Women's Bureau in the Department of Labor on the situation of working-class women indirectly admitted. The study argued that the double burden of paid work and child-rearing was detrimental to working-class women and thus also to their families, because "the welfare of home and family life is a woman-sized job in itself."[83] Putting the concept of "scientific motherhood" into action required not only education but also social status: only if the man as breadwinner could fully provide for the needs of his family was it possible for the wife to devote herself exclusively to her role as housewife and mother. But it was the biologistic paradigm, the triad of "healthy motherhood," "healthy family," and "healthy nation," that crucially shaped expert discourses and the attempts to popularize them in the 1920s and 1930s.

2.3 Better Babies and Fitter Families: the popularization of the "healthy family" through competitions

The American eugenics movement gained increasing ground from the beginning of the twentieth century onwards through the establishment of the Eugenics Record Office (ERO, 1910) in Cold Spring Harbor and the American Eugenics Society (AES, 1922). The latter was founded as a result of the Second International Confer-

---

[81] The Bureau of Vocational Information was founded by the alumnae associations of the Seven Sisters Colleges in 1911–12. Bearing this name from 1919 to 1926, it researched and propagated female employment. See the organization's papers in the Schlesinger Library at Harvard University, Records of the Bureau of Vocational Information, 1908–1932, B-3; M-118.
[82] "Working Mothers are Studied by Experts," NYT, December 19, 1926, X18.
[83] "Working Mothers are Studied by Experts," NYT, December 19, 1926, X18. Reference was made to a study by the Head of the Women's Bureau, Mary Anderson, of 40,000 working women in the cities of Jacksonville, Wilkes-Barre, Butte, and Passaic, based on 1920 census data published by the Women's Bureau in 1926. United States Women's Bureau, Women Workers and the Federal Government, Washington D.C. 1926.

ence on Eugenics in New York in 1921. In addition to Laughlin and Grant, founding members included Yale political scientist Irving Fisher, who became its first president, Henry Fairfield Osborn, and Henry Crampton. The organization sought to popularize genetics and eugenics for the purpose of improving the 'genetic stock' of the American people.[84] The leading exponents of the eugenics movement in the United States were two biologists, Charles Benedict Davenport, a zoologist at Harvard and founder of the ERO, and Harry H. Laughlin, Davenport's student and later director of the ERO.[85] They found inspiration not only in the writings of British anthropologist Francis Galton, creator of the term eugenics, who related Mendel's findings on heredity to humans and in particular to the question of the heritability of aptitude,[86] but also in texts by contemporary authors such as Madison Grant and Theodore Lothrop Stoddard.[87] In *The Passing of the Great Race* (1916) Grant used an examination of the "racial substance" of the peoples of Eu-

---

[84] Under Frederik Osborn's presidency, the AES increasingly focused on population policy and controlling population growth in the United States and developing countries. In 1972, it changed its name to The Society for the Study of Biology. See Kühl, *Internationale der Rassisten*, 58.

[85] Charles Benedict Davenport (1866–1944) received his doctorate in biology from Harvard University and was one of the most prominent biologists of his time in the United States. A committed advocate of Mendelian genetics, in 1898 he became head of the Cold Spring Harbor Laboratory research center near New York, where he founded the ERO in 1910, appointing his student Laughlin as its director. In 1925, he established the International Federation of Eugenics Organizations (IFEO), cooperating closely with German racial scientists and eugenicists such as Eugen Fischer and Otto Reche. See Kühl, *Internationale der Rassisten*. The estate of Charles Benedict Davenport is in the American Philosophical Society Library in Philadelphia <www.amphilsoc.org/mole/view?docId=ead/Mss.B.D27-ead.xml>. Key texts include Davenport, Charles B., *Eugenics. The Science of Human Improvement by Better Breeding* (New York 1910). Davenport, Charles B., *How to Make a Eugenical Family Study* (Washington 1919). Davenport, Charles B. and Love, Albert G., *Defects Found in Drafted Men* (Washington 1920). Davenport, Charles B. and Steggeerda, Morris, *Race Crossing in Jamaica* (Washington 1929). Davenport, Charles B., *How We Came by Our Bodies* (New York 1936). On Laughlin see footnote 7 in this chapter.

[86] Francis Galton first coined the term in 1883 in his *Inquiries into the Human Faculty and Development* (London 1883), 24. See also Galton, Francis, *Essays in Eugenics* (London 1909). Galton, *Hereditary Genius*.

[87] Madison Grant (1865–1937) was a lawyer, eugenicist, and writer. In his best-known work, *The Passing of the Great Race* (1916), he postulated race as the engine of all civilization and put forward a history of Europe based on his analysis of its variable racial substance. Grant was vice president of the Immigration Restriction League from 1922, and his statistics formed the basis for the Immigration Act of 1924, though this did not go far enough for him. Theodore Lothrop Stoddard (1883–1950) was an American historian, eugenicist, and journalist. He authored numerous texts on the supposed importance of racial difference and warned of the consequences of unrestricted immigration. His book *The Rising Tide of Color Against World Supremacy* (1920) was particularly well known. He served as one of the first directors of the American Birth Control League, founded by Margaret Sanger in 1921.

rope to postulate the superiority of the "Nordic race" and to warn Americans that their society faced degeneration as a result of the immigration of "undesirable races" and through racial mixing. In *The Rising Tide of Color* (1920) Stoddard, meanwhile, described the supposed threat to the "white world" (which for him meant the United States and Europe) in view of the rapid spread of the "colored races," especially Asians.[88] Both books were written against the background of World War I, and they served as a source of inspiration not only for American eugenicists, but also for Adolf Hitler, who owned both books in the 1925 German editions. As Timothy Ryback has shown, Hitler referred to Grant's work as "his bible" and made it one of the foundations of his racial policy after 1933.[89] For example, we can trace direct links to the Law for the Prevention of Hereditarily Diseased Offspring (*Gesetz zur Verhütung erbkranken Nachwuchses*) of 1933, the birth certificate of the Nazi euthanasia program.[90] Hitler was so taken with Stoddard's thinking that he received him in Berlin in 1939.[91]

The program of the eugenics movement entailed demands for both "positive" and "negative" eugenics: the reproduction of "high-quality" individuals and families was to be promoted, while that of the "inferior" was to be prevented.[92] In each case, the mother and her reproductive function were central: while society had to be protected from "unfit mothers," "responsible mothers" ought to be granted social recognition and economic support. First, this objective required coercive measures such as the sterilization of potentially undesirable mothers and the placement of supposedly disabled (but often just poor or socially conspicuous) children in special children's homes or in foster families.[93] Second, the principles of "positive" eugenics had to be popularized in U.S. society. This is illustrated,

---

88 Grant, *Passing of the Great Race*. Stoddard, *Rising Tide*.
89 Ryback, Timothy W., *Hitlers Bücher. Seine Bibliothek—sein Denken* (Cologne 2010), 126–149, esp. 135, 146–149.
90 Kühl, Stefan, *The Nazi Connection: Eugenics, American Racism, and National Socialism* (New York 1994), 42–45. Kühl, Stefan, *Die Internationale der Rassisten. Aufstieg und Niedergang der internationalen Bewegung für Eugenik und Rassenhygiene im 20. Jahrhundert* (Frankfurt a.M. 1997), 130, 133.
91 Stoddard, Lothrop, *Into the Darkness. Nazi Germany Today* (New York 1940), 201. Ryback, *Hitlers Bücher*, 322.
92 Davenport, Charles B., *Eugenics*. Davenport, Charles B., "State Laws Limiting Marriage Selection Examined in the Light of Eugenics" (Cold Spring Harbor, N.Y. 1913), in *The Making of Modern Law* (Gale, 2011). Gale, Cengage Learning. March 22, 2011. Laughlin, Harry H., "The Socially Inadequate. How Shall we Designate and Sort Them?", *American Journal of Sociology* vol. 27, no. 1 (1921), 54–70. Laughlin, *Legal Status of Eugenical Sterilization*.
93 Foster mothers in particular served as intermediaries between eugenicists, psychologists, social reformers, children, and society. See Ryan, "Six Blacks," 263.

Fig. 2.3: Fitter Family Medal, "Yea, I Have a Goodly Heritage." This medal was awarded to outstanding families by the American Eugenics Society.

among other things, by the popular Fitter Family Contests, conducted by the American Eugenics Society in the mid- to late 1920s in numerous states (Kansas, Michigan, Massachusetts, Texas, Georgia, Pennsylvania, Arkansas, and Iowa).[94] Here, the general public was sensitized to eugenics issues and confronted with the demand for a new "reproductive morality" through instructions on drawing up genealogical charts, prizes awarded to the "hereditarily most valuable" families in various categories, and through the visualization and publication of the competition results. One of the prizes was a medal engraved with the words "Yea,

---

[94] The files (photographs, examination forms, reports) on the Fitter Family Contests are in the archives of the American Philosophical Society in Philadelphia (APS). Some photographs are held in the Eugenics Archive at the Dolan DNA Learning Center, Cold Spring Harbor Laboratory (former home of the Eugenic Record Office). See also Boudreau, Erica Bicchieri, "'Yea, I Have a Goodly Heritage.' Health Versus Heredity in the Fitter Family Contests, 1920–1928," *Journal of Family History* 30 (2005), 366–387. Selden, Steven, "Transforming Better Babies into Fitter Families: Archival Resources and the History of American Eugenics Movement, 1908–1930," *Proceedings of the American Philosophical Society* 149 (2005), no. 2, 199–225.

I have a Goodly Heritage."[95] These events intended to promote "race betterment," which were also widely advertised in the local press, were mostly held at agricultural fairs, the so-called State Fairs, and they took place at the same time as the issuing of awards for breeding cattle.[96]

Fig. 2.4: Winners of the "small," "medium," and "large" family categories, Fitter Families Contest, Kansas Free Fair, 1923. Members of the winning families are holding their trophies.

These state-level contests played a major role in disseminating the eugenicist view that only eugenic interpretations of scientific data on physique and psyche could guide responsible decisions about marriage and reproduction.[97] The family

---

95 "Fitter Family Medal," undated, American Eugenics Society Records, American Philosophical Society, Digital Collection, APSimg1539.
96 Examples of advertising for the Fitter Family Contests can be found chiefly in the local press, though the national papers were not immune to the phenomenon. *Chicago Daily Tribune*, January 10, 1925: Doris Blake, "'Fitter Families' Campaign Advises Looking to Heredity." *Washington Post*, March 16, 1926: "Certificates given to 'Fitter Families.'" *New York Times*, October 22, 1927: "Southern Fairs." *Atlanta Constitution*, October 28, 1923: "Fitter Family Slogan of Drive On In Savannah." *Atlanta Constitution*, September 28, 1926: "Annual State Fair Opens At Savannah."
97 Selden, "Transforming Better Babies," 212.

Fig. 2.5: Winner in the "large family" category, Texas State Fair, 1925. This is a good example of the connection evoked between nature, healthy bodies, and family. The message of the image is: this is what a hereditarily healthy family featuring lots of children looks like.

in particular served as a preferred object of study for eugenicists, as it allowed several generations to be anthropologically examined in context. The exhibits and information boards accompanying the Fitter Family Contests made a correlation between intelligence and race, and highlighted the social and economic costs of caring for the "feeble-minded" and "unfit."[98]

A display board at the entrance of the first exhibition pavilion in Topeka, Kansas, in 1923 argued: "Some people are born to be a burden on the rest. Learn about Heredity. You can correct these conditions." One feature of the installation were five blinking lights that lit up at regular intervals. Next to each light was a text intended to inform visitors about the threats to society associated with the uncontrolled reproduction of "undesirables." The caption below the top flashing light read: "Every 15 seconds $100 of your money goes for the care of persons with bad heredity such as the insane, feeble-minded, criminals and other defec-

---

[98] For more information, see the extensive digital photo collection of the American Philosophical Society in Philadelphia, which includes files of both the American Eugenics Society and the Eugenics Record Office. <www.amphilsoc.org>.

Fig. 2.6: Installation with flashing lights, opening exhibit of the eugenics exhibition at the Fitter Families Contests.

tives." This raised the issue of the economic costs of caring for the sick and disabled—a key point in the German debate of the 1930s as well but first raised in Kansas in 1923. The other flashing lights and their accompanying texts, meanwhile, then informed visitors about the reproduction of those "desired" and undesired from the eugenic point of view. The left side of the installation was dedicated to the "mentally ill" and "criminals," under the heading "America needs less of these":

> This light flashes every 48 seconds: Every 48 seconds a person is born in the United States who will never grow up mentally beyond that stage of a normal 8 year old boy or girl.

> This light flashes every 50 seconds: Every 50 seconds a person is committed to jail in the United States. Very few normal persons go to jail.

In contrast, under the heading "America needs more of these," the visitor was informed:

> This light flashes every 16 seconds: Every 16 seconds a person is born in the United States.

> This light flashes every 7 minutes: Every 7 minutes a person is born in the United States who qualifies for creative work and is fit to provide leadership. 4 percent of Americans fall into this class.[99]

---

[99] "Flashing light sign used with first exhibit at Fitter Families Contest, 1926." American Philosophical Society, American Eugenics Society Records, Mss. 575.06.Am3. APSimg1491.

The message was clear: society was to advance not only with the help of a higher reproduction rate, but above all through a greater number of offspring produced by families with "high-quality" genetic material.

Fig. 2.7: Eugenics Building, Fitter Family Contests, Kansas Free Fair. A winning family (center) is shown with various dignitaries, representatives of the eugenics movement, and nurses involved in the contest.

The popular Fitter Family Contests grew out of the Better Babies Contests of the first decades of the twentieth century, which were launched by committed social reformers together with pediatricians and cattlemen's associations at the rural state fairs of the Midwest.[100] The declared aim, by means of appropriate prizes at these events, including monetary rewards, was to encourage the rural population to devote the same care to the rearing of their children as they did to that of their breeding stock—"for the future of the race." As early as 1908, on the initiative of

---

[100] "New York Joins the Big Movement for Better Babies," NYT, April 20, 1913. The best overview is to be found in Vance Dorey, Annette K., *Better Babies Contests: The Scientific Quest for Perfect Childhood Health in the Early Twentieth Century* (Jefferson NC 1999). See also Selden, "Transforming Better Babies."

the president of the Louisiana Congress of Mothers, teacher Mary De Garmo, the first Better Babies Contest was held on the occasion of the Louisiana State Fair.[101] In the years that followed, the movement spread rapidly to encompass the states of Missouri, Iowa, Colorado, South Dakota, North Dakota and Nebraska before the trend reached the West Coast in the shape of Oregon; in 1913, New York became the first metropolitan area on the East Coast to host a Better Babies Contest.[102] That same year, the women's magazine *Women's Home Companion* initiated another such contest in collaboration with the Louisiana State Fair.[103] A year later, according to the magazine, all states except West Virginia, New Hampshire, and Utah had hosted similar contests, and more than 100,000 children had already been examined.[104] In Indiana, the Better Babies Contests reached a particularly high level of organization from 1920 to 1932, as they were held under the aegis of the State Board of Health's Division of Infant and Child Hygiene.[105] During the same period, infant mortality in that state fell from 8.2 percent (1920) to 5.7 percent (1930). According to Alexandra Stern, this was indirectly related to the contests, as they helped popularize hygiene standards and pediatric knowledge.[106]

The close link between the medical examination of—and the awarding of prizes for—babies and the later Fitter Family Contests can also be seen in staffing continuities. For example, Mary Tirell Watts and Dr. Florence Brown Sherbon were the organizers of the first Fitter Family Contest in Kansas in 1920; the two had already

---

101 Mary de Garmo (1865–1953) worked as a schoolteacher in Missouri before marrying Frank de Garmo, and then became involved in a variety of women's organizations, including serving as president of the Louisiana Congress of Mothers. Particularly committed to improving health care for children, she founded the Better Babies movement. Her literary estate is in the University of Tennessee Special Collections Library in Knoxville under call number MS-1879. Online finding aid: <https://embryo.asu.edu/pages/better-babies-contests-united-states-1908-1916>. On the 1908 Louisiana Better Babies Contest, see Vance Dorey, *Better Babies Contests*, 31.
102 "New York Joins the Big Movement for Better Babies," NYT, April 20, 1913.
103 Selden, "Transforming Better Babies," 210.
104 Stern, "Beauty is Not Always Better," 71.
105 The organizer was Dr. Ada E. Schweitzer of the Indiana Board of Health's Division of Infant and Child Hygiene, where she chaired the Division on Infant and Child Hygiene from 1919 to 1933. Stern, "Beauty is Not Always Better," 70. Stern, "Making Better Babies."
106 Stern attributes the termination of the popular Better Babies Contests in Indiana in 1933 not only to the effects of the Great Depression and a change in emphasis by the new Democratic governor, but also to the skepticism of the male medical establishment toward the activism of female social reformers, nurses, and female pediatricians. She makes the plausible case that the "Better Babies" campaigns pursued by Schweitzer and her fellow women campaigners were not only immensely successful, but simultaneously helped consolidate the authority of (predominantly male) pediatricians and experts, thus leading to a further shift in gender roles. Stern, "Making Better Babies," 750.

Fig. 2.8: Eugenic and Health Exhibit, Fitter Family Contests, Kansas Free Fair, 1929.

organized the Better Babies Contests in Iowa since 1911.[107] The two women were social experts closely linked with the eugenics movement. Watts, originally president of the Parent-Teacher Association in Iowa, rose to become chairwoman of the Committee on Popular Education of the American Eugenics Society in 1924.[108] Sherbon, a pediatrician and professor at the University of Kansas, became director of the Division of Child Hygiene of the Kansas State Board of Health.[109] Examining only the most recent descendants of a family seemed to them to provide insufficient insights

---

[107] Lovett, Laura L., "'Fitter Families for Future Firesides?' Florence Sherbon and Popular Eugenics," *The Public Historian*, vol. 29, no. 3 (2007), 69–85. Boudreau, "Fitter Family Contests," 368.

[108] Mary Tirell Watts, member of the Advisory Council of the Eugenics Committee of the United States, died December 12, 1926 in Pocahontas, Iowa. NYT, December 13, 1926.

[109] Johnson, Hildegard Walls, "Fitter Families for Future Firesides. The Kansas Eugenic Contest," *Journal of Heredity* 16.1 (1925), 457–460. Florence Brown Sherbon (1869–1944) studied medicine at the University of Iowa after working as a nurse and educator. From 1915 to 1916, she was commissioned by the Children's Bureau to conduct numerous studies on child health in rural Indiana and Wisconsin until the bureau discontinued her research as too costly. In 1917, she gained a post as

into its ancestry and genetic value, so Watts and Sherbon developed the idea of the medical and hereditary examination of entire families within the context of the Fitter Family Contests.[110] Here they could count on the support of American eugenics pioneer Charles B. Davenport.

The example of Sherbon and Watts, however, also shows clearly that while women often provided the impetus for eugenic studies, in this case family examinations, and themselves functioned as experts and field researchers, the positions of power in the eugenics movement were held exclusively by men. In their studies of female Eugenic Record Office (ERO) workers who collected hereditary data on American families across the country from the turn of the century through the 1920s, Margaret Rossiter and Amy Bix have argued that these women experienced routine discrimination in their capacity as researchers. For example, Davenport and other eugenics pioneers insisted that women were determined solely by their reproductive function. Therefore, they regarded women eugenicists only as research assistants and deliberately limited their academic career options.[111] This also affected the staff of the Fitter Family Contests, who felt this contradiction particularly keenly. On the one hand, they propagated a eugenic family ideal based on a patriarchal and naturalistic distribution of gender roles. On the other hand, they challenged this very ideal through their own professional involvement in the contests.[112]

The Better Babies Contests and the Fitter Family Contests were both the result of the commitment of two women social experts and were developed and realized in conscious analogy to the awards for breeding cattle at agricultural fairs.[113]

Director of Physical Education for Women at the University of Kansas, before becoming Professor of Childcare in its Department of Home Economics in 1920. Lovett, "Fitter Families," 72–75.

110 Johnson, Hildegard Walls, "Fitter Families for Future Firesides. The Kansas Eugenic Contest," *Journal of Heredity* 16.1 (1925), 458.

111 Rossiter, Margaret, *Women Scientists in America: Struggles and Strategies to 1940* (Baltimore, MD 1982). Bix, Amy Sue, "Experiences and Voices of Eugenic Field-Workers: 'Women's Work' in Biology," *Social Studies of Science* 27 (1997), 625–68. Another example is given by Dirk Hoerder: at the end of the nineteenth century, in the Columbia School of Interdisciplinary Research, women collected the data while men formulated the influential theories. Hoerder, Dirk, "'A Genuine Respect for the People': The Columbia University Scholars' Transcultural Approach to Migrants," *Journal of Migration History* 1 (2015), no. 2, 136–170.

112 In contrast, Larson argues that it was the eugenics movement in the Southern states that opened up political participation and public positions to women. Larson, Edward J., "'In the Finest, Most Womanly Way': Women in The Southern Eugenics Movement," *American Journal of Legal History* 39 (1995), no. 2, 19–147, esp. 147. Larson, Edward J., *Sex, Race, and Science. Eugenics in the Deep South* (Baltimore, MD 1995).

113 This was also reflected in scattered press reports on the contests. See for example Doris Blake, "'Fitter Families'—Campaign Advises Looking to Heredity," *Chicago Daily Tribune*, January 10, 1925, 14: "This 'fitter families' idea is merely a practical application of the principles of

After the first five years of the family contests, which were exported from Kansas to other states, the Kansas Bureau of Child Research thus commented:

> The Fitter Families Project is a legitimate outgrowth of scientific agriculture. It is the application of the principles of scientific plant and animal husbandry to the next higher order of creation, the human family, and contemplates the development of a science of practical husbandry.[114]

Further, these events helped popularize and affirm racial elements within notions of what was healthy, normal, and beautiful, thus indirectly propagating the ideal of the "white middle class nuclear family" as the basis of society and the object of "race betterment." The award-winning children and families were invariably of white skin color, had roots in the United States extending back several generations, and were middle class.[115] Ultimately, the competitions served to celebrate traditional family values (valuing the community over the individual, family unity, a large number of children, and an awareness of ancestry and tradition) using the example of the rural family, while helping to further optimize and control them with the help of scientific techniques (better standards of child care, nutrition and healthcare, anthropological and medical examinations, and scientific documentation of examination results).[116]

Yet the number of participants was not especially large: between 1920 and 1926, 126 families (523 persons) in Kansas were eugenically screened and provided with information as participants in contests, or approximately 21 families per contest.[117] In addition to the families' quasi-"official" profession of faith in eugenics, this was certainly due in part to the elaborate procedure, which took several hours and included not just medical examinations but also the collection of data on hereditary biology and social statistics, blood and urine samples, as well as personality and IQ tests.[118] At the same time, the competitions attracted consider-

---

scientific plant and animal husbandry to the highest order of creation, the human family. [...] Now it remains to score families as well as animals, following largely the methods of stock judges, who always take into account inheritance when passing their judgment."

114 Kansas Bureau of Child Research, "Fitter Families for Future Firesides. A Report of the Eugenics Department of the Kansas Free Fair, 1920–1924." Quoted in Boudreau, "Fitter Family Contests," 368.
115 Stern, "Beauty is Not Always Better," 77. Boudreau, "Fitter Family Contests," 368, 379. Selden, "Transforming Better Babies," 210.
116 Lovett, "Fitter Families," comes to a similar conclusion.
117 "Certificates Given to 'Fitter Families'. Kansas Contest Bases All Pride of Lineage upon Eugenic Standing," WP, March 16, 1926, 13.
118 Ladd-Taylor, Molly (2014, April 29). "Fitter Family Contests." Retrieved May 17, 2016, from <www.eugenicsarchive.ca/discover/connections/535eebfb7095aa0000000228>.

able attention both regionally and nationally, as can be seen from the continuous and consistently positive press coverage between 1923 and 1927.[119]

Even the NAACP (National Association for the Advancement of Colored People), the oldest black civil rights organization in the United States, adopted the method of awarding prizes to particularly "high-quality," gifted, and healthy children from this context. The civil rights activists thus sought to demonstrate the capability of the African American minority, revealing the extent to which thinking in categories of rationally verifiable "value" and biological "performance" had infected the whole of U.S. society in the 1920s. Further, the contests served to raise money for the NAACP's anti-lynching campaign.[120]

While the initiators of the Fitter Family Contests regarded making American families aware of heredity and racial science as the "positive" side of measures to improve the genetic makeup of the nation, the same actors viewed forced sterilizations as an equally necessary form of "negative" eugenics. The public discussion of sterilization practices in the 1920s and 1930s is the focus of the following section.

2.4 Forced eugenic sterilizations for the betterment of the American family

Through the handbook *Applied Eugenics*, which appeared in 1918, biologist Roswell H. Johnson[121] and the then little-known Paul B. Popenoe, a young date grower and editor of the *Journal of Heredity*, popularized the call for the introduction of

---

[119] "Fitter Families, Slogan of Drive On in Savannah," *Atlanta Constitution*, October 28, 1923, 7. "Fitter Families' Campaign Advises Looking to Heredity," *Chicago Daily Tribune*, January 10, 1925, 14. "Physical Education Center is Opened," *Atlanta Constitution*, March 1, 1925, 11. "Certificates Given to 'Fitter Families'. Kansas Contest Bases All Pride of Lineage on Eugenic Standing," WP, March 16, 1926, 13. "Annual State Fair Opens at Savannah," *Atlanta Constitution*, September 28, 1926, 16. "Large Families Are Few. So Kansas Fair Drops Awards for Five or More Children," NYT, October 2, 1927, E6. "Southern Fairs," NYT, October 22, 1927, 16.
[120] Dorr, Gregory Michael and Logan, Angela, "'Quality, Not Mere Quantity, Counts': Black Eugenics and the NAACP Baby Contests," in Lombardo, Paul (ed.), *A Century of Eugenics in America: From the Indiana Experiment to the Human Genome Era* (Bloomington, Indiana 2011), 68–92.
[121] Roswell Hill Johnson (1877–1967) was a biologist and geologist who, among other things, studied under E. A. Ross at the University of Wisconsin. He taught as a geologist at the University of Pittsburgh, where he also gave courses in eugenics. In 1931, he became president of the American Eugenics Society, and from 1935 onward he headed the Department of Counseling of the American Institute for Family Relations under Paul B. Popenoe. In 1941, he developed the Johnson Temperament Analysis for personality diagnosis, which the Institute's marriage counselors used to classify clients into standardized personality types, renamed the Taylor-Johnson Temperament Analysis in 1966. See the obituary for Paul Popenoe, *Family Life* xxvii, no. 3 (1967), 1–3.

practical eugenic measures in the United States.¹²² Influenced by World War I, they attempted to apply the fundamentals of genetics and eugenics to the social sphere. Their declared goal was to promote the reproduction of "superior persons" and reduce the number of supposed "inferiors."¹²³ It is revealing, first, how the authors defined "superiority," namely as the ability "to live past maturity, to reproduce adequately, to live happily and to make contributions to the productivity, happiness, and progress of society"—and thus always had the alleged social utility in mind.¹²⁴ Second, it is striking that sociologist Edward A. Ross wrote the preface. His notion of a form of "social control" that would improve society had contributed in no small measure to the popularity of sociology as a leading science of the early twentieth century, while also having a major influence on the reform initiatives of the Progressive Movement.¹²⁵ Ross based his plea for eugenics, among other things, on the effects of World War I, which, he asserted, had deprived the United States (and the "white race" as a whole) of part of its most valuable demographic, so that now special efforts were required to prevent the decline of Western civilization. At the same time, Ross claimed, old prejudices had outlived their usefulness, and new opportunities were thus opening up to transform society, to put the common good before that of the individual:¹²⁶

> But the plowshare of war has turned up the tough sod of custom, and now every sound new idea has a chance. Rooted prejudices have been leveled like the forests of Picardy under gun fire. The fear of racial decline provides the eugenicist with a far stronger leverage than did the hope of accelerating racial progress.¹²⁷

---

122 Johnson, Roswell Hill and Popenoe, Paul B., *Applied Eugenics* (New York 1918). A fully revised new edition was produced by the same publisher in 1933. Paul B. Popenoe was active as a nationally known eugenicist, marriage counselor, and columnist from the 1920s through the 1970s. On Popenoe, see below in this chapter and Ladd-Taylor, Molly, "Eugenics, Sterilization and Modern Marriage in the USA. The Strange Career of Paul Popenoe," *Gender and History* February 13.2 (2001), 298–327. Stern, *Eugenic Nation*.
123 Johnson and Popenoe, *Applied Eugenics*.
124 Johnson and Popenoe, *Applied Eugenics*. Preface, v. An identical definition appears in Popenoe, *Conservation of the Family*, 125.
125 On this point, see the comments in Chapter 1.
126 Recommending the book not only to sociologists but also to physicians, social workers, and settlement workers, as well as to pastors, teachers, youth workers, lawyers, and immigration inspectors, Ross concluded with reflections on marriage and family that clearly sought to subordinate the individual to the interests of the community: "Finally, the thoughtful ought to find in it guidance in their problem of mating. It will inspire the superior to rise above certain worldly ideals of life and to aim at a family success rather than an individual success." Edward A. Ross, "Introduction," in Johnson and Popenoe, *Applied Eugenics*, xi–xii.
127 Edward A. Ross, "Foreword," in Johnson and Popenoe, *Applied Eugenics*, xi.

For Popenoe and Johnson, eugenics meant the combination of the biological and sociological study and improvement of society, and they referred explicitly to British eugenicist Francis Galton. Specifically, the authors called for increasing the marriage and birth rates of the "genetically superior." At the same time, restrictive eugenics was to limit the reproduction of those who appeared to be "of lesser quality" from the hereditary-biological point of view, for example by prohibiting marriage, or they were to be prevented from reproducing entirely through sterilization. The aim of the eugenics movement, through legal, social, and economic measures, was to ensure that

> (1) a larger proportion of superior persons will have children then at present, (2) that the average number of offspring of each superior person will be greater than at present, (3) that the most inferior persons will have no children, and finally that (4) other inferior persons will have fewer children than now.[128]

The handbook enjoyed immense success. It remained the standard work on the subject in the United States for over forty years; publication ceased in 1957.[129] It was Popenoe in particular who formulated the idea of negative eugenics through sterilization of the hereditarily defective in the 1920s. His research was financed by Californian lemon magnate Ezra Seymour Gosney, founder of the Human Betterment Foundation, which had dedicated itself specifically to popularizing eugenic sterilization.[130]

The state of California was one of the first in the U.S. to pass a law in 1909 permitting forced sterilizations of patients in state institutions and clinics to protect society from the spread of "mental illness" and criminality (both considered hereditary).[131] In 1929, Popenoe and Gosney published an eloquent defense of sterilization practices in California that quickly became a standard work (along with

---

128 Johnson and Popenoe, *Applied Eugenics*, v–vi.
129 "Notes from the AIFR," *Family Life* 17 (1957), no. 5, 3.
130 Ezra Seymour Gosney (1855–1942) made a fortune as a lemon farmer in California, some of which he used for philanthropic purposes. The Human Betterment Foundation existed from 1928 to 1942 and was one of the major eugenic organizations of the first half of the twentieth century in the United States, along with the American Eugenics Society and the Eugenic Record Office. During the 1930s, the HBF maintained its own column in the *Los Angeles Times* entitled "Social Eugenics." The files of the Human Betterment Foundation are now held by the California Institute of Technology, Pasadena. <www.oac.cdlib.org/findaid/ark:/13030/tf2 h4n98gb/entire_text>. In 1942, the HBF renamed itself the Association for Voluntary Sterilization; see chapter 5 for details.
131 The first sterilization law was passed in 1907 in the state of Indiana, while Washington, California and Connecticut passed corresponding laws in 1909, followed by Iowa, Nevada, and New Jersey in 1911 and New York in 1912. By the mid-1930s, thirty states had legalized forced sterilizations. See Carlson, *The Unfit*, 247. Reilly, Philip R., *The Surgical Solution. A History of Involuntary Sterilization in the United States* (Baltimore and London 1991).

Laughlin's eugenics handbook and Popenoe's *Applied Eugenics*). This book, "Sterilization for Human Betterment," drew on an evaluation of more than 6,000 sterilization cases and argued that the majority of those affected had welcomed the measure and were now living without health-related or personal limitations.[132] In general terms, Gosney and Popenoe justified their affirmative view by underlining the fundamental goal of "reducing hereditary defects," especially curbing "mental disease" and preventing "the birth of defective offspring" as well as reducing welfare costs:

> Persons should be sterilized if it is to the interests of the commonwealth (or more broadly, of the human race) that they bear no children, or no further children; and if it appears that sterilization is the most effective and satisfactory means of preventing such reproduction.[133]

It can be assumed that this plea for "eugenic sterilization" served as a source of inspiration for many race theorists in Germany when it came to the practical implementation of forced sterilizations. *Applied Eugenics* was one of the first books on the subject that the Nazi government commissioned for translation into German.[134] Popenoe, for his part, publicly praised the German Law for the Prevention of Hereditarily Diseased Offspring as the "first example in modern times of an administration based frankly and determinedly on the principle of eugenics."[135]

Although the 6,255 forced sterilizations in hospitals and state institutions in California were by far the highest number carried out in a U.S. state up to 1929, other states also used this measure in the first half of the twentieth century.[136] Epileptics, the mentally disabled and those suffering psychological problems, were targeted by eugenicists, especially if they lived in government-run asylums and clinics, but in some states alcoholics, girls and women considered "immoral",

---

132 Gosney, Ezra Seymour and Popenoe, Paul B., *Sterilization for Human Betterment. A Summary of Results of 6,000 Operations in California, 1909–1929* (New York 1929). See also Gosney, Ezra Seymour and Popenoe, Paul B., *Collected Papers on Eugenic Sterilization in California. The Human Betterment Foundation* (Pasadena 1930). Gosney, Ezra Seymour and Popenoe, Paul B., *Twenty-Eight Years of Sterilization in California. The Human Betterment Foundation* (Pasadena 1938).
133 Popenoe and Gosney, *Sterilization*, 116.
134 Popenoe, Paul B. and Gosney, Ezra Seymour, *Sterilisierung zur Aufbesserung des Menschengeschlechts* (Berlin 1930).
135 Popenoe, Paul B., "The German Sterilization Law," *Journal of Heredity* 24 (1934), 257–260. Kühl, Stefan, *The Nazi Connection: Eugenics, American Racism, and National Socialism* (New York 1994), 42–45.
136 On California, see Stern, *Eugenic Nation*. On Virginia, see Kevles, *Eugenics*, 168f. On North Carolina, see Schoen, *Choice and Coercion*. Schoen, Johanna, "Choice and Coercion. Women and the Politics of Sterilization in North Carolina, 1929–1975," *Journal of Women's History* 13 (2001), no. 1, 132–156.

convicted criminals, and sex offenders came into their crosshairs as well.[137] The sterilization law passed by the state of Virginia in 1924 with the involvement of ERO director Harry H. Laughlin was considered particularly "progressive" because it was limited exclusively to the supposedly hereditary forms of "insanity, idiocy, imbecility, epilepsy, and crime."[138] Inmates of state hospitals, especially women, were sterilized with the goal transforming them into wholly or partly self-supporting, law abiding, and reasonably happy" citizens—while eliminating their potential to reproduce.[139] Decisions on sterilization were made by a panel of doctors. An officially appointed guardian could appeal on behalf of the sterilization victim—so that his or her constitutional rights were at least *pro forma* preserved. The form used to order sterilization described the person involved as a "potential parent of socially inadequate offsprings," such that the intervention served the "welfare of the inmate and of society."[140] There is no doubt at all that the Virginian law served directly as a model for the Nazi Law for the Prevention of Hereditarily Diseased Offspring of 1933.[141]

In 1927, state sterilization practices were endowed with a federal legal framework: a landmark Supreme Court decision (*Buck v. Bell*) declared forced sterilizations for the "protection of society" constitutional.[142] Carrie Buck, a young woman born in 1906 and the mother of an illegitimate daughter (born in 1925), had been an inmate of the State Colony for the Insane or Feeble-Minded in Amherst County, Virginia, since 1924. Her mother had given birth to her and her three siblings out of wedlock and put them up for adoption. Carrie was said to have initially had an unremarkable childhood with her adoptive parents, but later became a rebellious adolescent and teenage mother, prompting her parents to have her committed to the State Colony. There she was diagnosed as epileptic and mentally retarded, although the true reason for her incarceration was likely her illegitimate pregnancy and thus her supposedly out-of-control sexual conduct.[143]

---

[137] It was this mixture of eugenic and punitive goals in particular that led to the laws of many states being struck down as unconstitutional by the Supreme Court in the 1920s. Nationally, the Supreme Court decision in *Skinner v. Oklahoma* (1942) brought a ban on punitive sterilization but did nothing to curb forced eugenic sterilization. Carlson, *The Unfit*, 248.
[138] Carlson, *The Unfit*, 249.
[139] Popenoe and Gosney, *Sterilization*, 105.
[140] Sterilization Form, State of Virginia. Carlson, *The Unfit*, 252.
[141] See "Gesetz zur Verhütung erbkranken Nachwuchses," July 14, 1933, <www.1000dokumente.de/pdf/dok_0136_ebn_de.pdf>.
[142] Supreme Court decision in *Buck v. Bell*, 74 U.S. 200 (1927). See Reilly, *Surgical Solution*.
[143] This is the plausible argument made by Lombardo, Paul A., "Three Generations, No Imbeciles: New Light on Buck v. Bell," *New York University Law Review* 60 (1985), no. 1, 31–62.

The trial was intended to affirm the legality of the Virginia Sterilization Act, again on Laughlin's initiative and with his massive involvement as an expert witness.[144] The Supreme Court's decision was unequivocal: while eight justices favored Carrie Buck's sterilization, only one opposed it, but authored no written dissent. In his infamous opinion, presiding Judge Oliver Wendell Holmes, Jr., stated:

> It is better for the world, if instead of waiting to execute degenerate offspring for crime, or to let them starve for their imbecility, society can prevent those, who are manifestly unfit from continuing their kind. [. . .] Three generations of imbeciles are enough.[145]

In the light of additional evidence and present-day analyses, the verdict must clearly be seen as erroneous and as an expression of prejudice against Carrie Buck and her family—as convincingly elaborated by lawyer and eugenics expert Paul A. Lombardo.[146]

Press coverage of the ruling in *Buck v. Bell* was comparatively meager. The *Washington Post* contented itself with a brief mention on page two and the *New York Times* devoted a short report to the decision in its back pages.[147] While the former merely informed its readers of the outcome, the latter quoted the remarks of the presiding judge, commenting that those who were already a burden on the country must be prepared to make those "lesser sacrifices, often not felt to be such by those concerned." Only by sterilizing people such as Buck could the flooding of society with "the unwanted" and "the incapable" be prevented. Furthermore, it is striking that the newspaper unquestioningly adopted the assessment that Carrie Buck, as well as her mother and illegitimate daughter, were "feeble-minded."[148] Criticism of sterilization laws and practice was subsequently voiced mainly by representatives of the major women's clubs, though they discussed and condemned the practice not as an encroachment on the personal rights of the sterilized, but as an unwelcome variant of birth control.[149]

---

[144] The case of Carrie Buck crops up in almost every study of the eugenics movement in the United States. See for example Carlson, *The Unfit*, 250–256. Kevles, *In the Name of Eugenics*. Reilly, *Surgical Solution*. Selden, Steven, *Inheriting Shame: The Story of Eugenics and Racism in America* (New York 1999). The best analysis is provided by Lombardo, "Three Generations."
[145] Carlson, *The Unfit*, 255.
[146] Lombardo, "Three Generations."
[147] "Virginia Sterilization Law Upheld by Court," WP May 3, 1927, 2. "Upholds Operating on Feeble-Minded. Supreme Court Majority Find Virginia's Sterilization Law Valid. Right to Protect Society," NYT May 3, 1927. 19.
[148] NYT, May 3, 1927. 19.
[149] As early as 1926, some members of the Union City Women's Club resigned over its acceptance of forced sterilization and birth control; at its seventh annual meeting in Washington, D.C. in 1927, the National Council of Catholic Women then expressed its vehement opposition to

Despite the meager public response, the *Buck v. Bell* case had a major impact on the practice of negative eugenics in the United States. Now that the Supreme Court had legalized forced sterilizations, the states were free to enact their laws without hindrance, citing *Buck v. Bell*. But it did not stop there. Once again, it was the state of Virginia that was out in front, seeking to tighten up its sterilization law as early as 1934. The idea was to extend sterilizations to "sick" people who were not cared for in public institutions.[150] It is interesting to note that the arguments put forward here were dominated by economic factors. For example, the superintendent of the Western State Hospital for the Insane, Dr. J. S. Dejarnette, who had already played a major role in initiating the state's 1924 sterilization law, proclaimed that widening the scope of the law could save the state millions of dollars: "As things now exist [. . .] we're building up a race of defectives. There are a 12.000 people of Virginia who ought to be sterilized. None of you would breed cattle, except from good stock."[151]

That the amendment was not ultimately ratified was due less to the protest of a single senator, who feared that it was analogous to the Nazi state's sterilization policy, than to the governor's legal concerns. In any case, Virginia ranked second in the national statistics, with 1,333 sterilizations since 1924, behind California with 8,504.[152] According to research by United Press, by the end of August 1935 some 20,000 sterilizations had been performed in the eighteen U.S. states that had introduced relevant laws, 10,000 of them in California alone. Those affected were mainly people categorized as "insane and feeble-minded"; only 5 percent of those forcibly sterilized were considered "criminals." The majority of all those subject to forced sterilization were women, as many as 90 percent of all cases in some states.[153]

Sterilizations were the object of heated public debate. While sociologists and criminologists welcomed an expansion of the related laws "to prevent socially dangerous types from reproducing their kind," the Catholic Church took the lead in opposing sterilization. It was above all its opposition that kept many states from enacting their own sterilization laws; this at least was the conclusion reached by the

---

both national and state sterilization laws. "Two Bolt Women's Club. Reset Jersey Federation's Approval of Birth Control Pill," NYT, June 11, 1926. 8. "Catholic Women Plead for Peace," NYT September 29, 1927, 5.
150 "Rigid Bill Due in Sterilization," WP January 17, 1934, 7.
151 Quoted in Dough Warrenfels, "Battle Delays Sterilization Bill in Virginia," WP February 6, 1934, 9. See also "Sterilization Urged For Weak Minded," WP April 25, 1934. "Sterilization and Birth Control Favored to Aid Virginia Group," WP April 24, 1935, 17.
152 The governor evidently wished to avoid jeopardizing the legal certainty established by the *Buck v. Bell* decision. "Sterilization Figures Show Virginia Is 2nd," WP July 18, 1935, 15.
153 Thus, 678 persons had been sterilized in Wisconsin by 1935, including 69 men. In North Carolina, the ratio was 156 to 41. "Total of 20,000 Persons Sterilized in U.S.A," WP September 1, 1935, B5.

Washington Post.[154] However, those state governments convinced of the value of sterilization, led by California, Virginia, Michigan, Oregon, Minnesota, and Wisconsin, did not allow their zeal to be curbed; on the contrary, they stepped up their efforts. By 1939, more than 33,000 people had become victims of forced sterilization, a large proportion of them inmates of state asylums, hospitals and clinics for the mentally ill.[155] By the end of the 1960s, their number had risen to more than 65,000.[156]

Most of the procedures were performed without the consent of the men and women concerned, with a disproportionate number of those forcibly sterilized from the 1940s onward being African Americans, Mexican Americans, and female.[157] Until the 1940s, sterilizations mainly punished the violation of gender roles. Deviation from prevailing sexual norms led to the ascription of "feeble-mindedness" and then to sterilization, as illustrated by the example of Carrie Buck. Subsequently, scientists, physicians, and state eugenics boards were increasingly concerned with reducing supposed burden on the welfare state by sterilizing poor women and allegedly "bad mothers."[158] In line with this, the practice of forced sterilizations represented a "rationalization of reproduction" taken to an extreme and oriented toward the principles of race and nation.[159]

If we consider how biologistic conceptions of "motherhood," the popularization of eugenics through Fitter Family Contests, and the practice of forced sterilizations of mentally ill, socially conspicuous, or non-white people found expression in the national press, a contradictory finding emerges. Despite the scope of these measures and the large number of people affected, it is striking that there was no major public debate in the 1920s and 1930s about the purpose and benefits of sterilization

---

[154] "Total of 20,000 Persons Sterilized in U.S.A.," WP September 1, 1935, B5.

[155] Ladd-Taylor, "Saving Babies," 136–153, 141. Carlson cites the figure of 38,087 sterilizations by the end of 1942. Carlson, *The Unfit*, 257.

[156] Kline, *Building a Better Race*, 95–123. Kevles, *Eugenics*.

[157] See Del Castillo, Adelaida R., "Sterilization: An Overview," in Del Castillo, Adelaida R. and Mora, Magdalena (eds.), *Mexican Women in the United States. Struggles Past and Present* (Los Angeles 1980), 65–70. Velez-I, Carlos G., "Se me Acabó la Canción: An Ethnography of Non-Consenting Sterilizations among Mexican Women in Los Angeles," in ibid, 71–91. Roberts, *Killing the Black Body*. Nelson, Jennifer, *Women of Color and the Reproductive Rights Movement* (New York 2003). Silliman, Jael, Gerber Fried, Marlene, Ross, Loretta, and Gutiérrez, Elena R. (eds.), *Undivided Rights: Women of Color Organizing for Reproductive Justice* (New York 2004). Gutiérrez, *Fertile Matters*.

[158] Carey, Allison C., "Gender and Compulsory Sterilization Programs in America: 1907–1950," *Journal of Historical Sociology* 11 (1998), no. 3, 74–105. Ladd-Taylor, "Saving Babies," 149f. Schoen, *Choice and Coercion*.

[159] See Ladd-Taylor, "Saving Babies."

2.4 Forced eugenic sterilizations for the betterment of the American family — 137

policy or eugenics in general.[160] Although there are press reports about Better Babies Contests and Fitter Families Contests, these are predominantly affirmative.[161] There are also reports here and there on the cases decided by the Supreme Court. However, neither the legalization of the forced sterilization of hospital inmates (in *Buck v. Bell*, 1927) nor the prohibition of sterilization for punitive purposes (in *Skinner v. Oklahoma*, 1942) sparked substantial public interest.[162] This finding requires explanation.

Medical historian Martin S. Pernick's remarks concerning the debate on euthanasia in the first third of the twentieth century can help us here. He identifies a "growing consensus among social, medical and media leaders that the topic itself was unfit to discuss in public."[163] The background to this was the case of Chicago physician Dr. Harry J. Haiselden, who in 1915–1918 allowed malformed children to die without treatment in his clinic, the German-American Hospital in Chicago, with the consent of their parents. This formed the basis for an educational film on euthanasia called *The Black Stork* (1916), which tells the story of a young couple who fear they are afflicted with a hereditary disease. Haiselden played the role of the doctor who refused to treat their hereditarily diseased child. The movie was shown in the U.S. from 1917 to 1927, under the title *Are You Fit to Marry?* from 1918 onward. A revised version, first shown in 1927, ran in theaters until 1942.[164] As Pernick reveals, the cases of euthanasia of malformed newborns popularized by Haiselden and the film sparked a short-lived but nonetheless intensive public debate. The *Chicago Tribune* in particular propagated Haiselden's views until 1918, after which media interest in such cases declined rapidly. In the 1920s, instead of a debate about euthanasia, there was public discussion of the progress and merits of eugenics, but now with a strong orientation toward Germany—as evident, among other things, in the fact that educational eu-

---

160 Findings of a thematic evaluation of the NYT and WP between 1920 and 1940. Ladd-Taylor comes to a similar conclusion: Ladd-Taylor, "Saving Babies," 149.
161 On this point, see the remarks earlier in this chapter.
162 "Virginia Sterilization Law Upheld by Court," WP May 3, 1927, 2. "Upholds Operating on Feeble-Minded. Supreme Court Majority Find Virginia's Sterilization Law Valid. Right to Protect Society," NYT May 3, 1927. 19. The WP did not report on the *Skinner v. Oklahoma* decision, through which the Supreme Court banned sterilization for punitive purposes on June 1, 1942, while the NYT merely noted the ruling: "United States Supreme Court," NYT Special, June 2, 1942, 39.
163 Pernick, Martin S., *The Black Stork. Eugenics and the Death of Defective Babies in American Medicine and Motion Pictures since 1915* (New York 1996), esp. 11.
164 Pernick, *Black Stork*, 6. *The Black Stork* (1917), original source: <www.imdb.com/title/tt0160056/>.

genics films now mostly came from that country.[165] When interest in euthanasia revived in the 1930s, the German example was in the foreground; there was no longer any reference to U.S. cases.[166]

With regard to the legality and social desirability of forced sterilizations of the sick and disabled, as well as those subject to discrimination on a social or racial basis, a similar situation appears to pertain. Although a number of cases occupied U.S. courts here and there in the 1920s and 1930s, the practice of sterilization did not constitute a publicly contentious issue. This indicates a broad consensus among physicians, social experts, social workers, administrative officials, and family members that the procedure represented a modern, humane solution to a human and economic dilemma. From the 1920s to the 1940s, the practice of sterilization promised to protect society from social problems and economic costs by preventing undesirable parenthood, which meant, above all, motherhood.

2.5 Paul B. Popenoe, *The Conservation of the Family* and the American Institute for Family Relations

"Healthy motherhood" in a stable marriage was also the central theme for eugenicist and marriage and family counselor Paul B. Popenoe. Popenoe advised a wide following and readership on family planning and marriage issues from 1920 until the 1970s, contributing quite significantly to the popularization of eugenics in the United States.[167] In the process, he underwent a revealing evolution from a con-

---

[165] Since the founding of the German Society for Racial Hygiene (Deutsche Gesellschaft für Rassenhygiene) in 1905 there had been a strong eugenics movement in Germany, which remained active during the Weimar Republic. In addition, hereditary and racial science was established as a university subject. Schmuhl, Hans Walter, *Rassenkunde, Nationalsozialismus, Euthanasie. Von der Verhütung zur Vernichtung "lebensunwerten Lebens": 1890–1945* (Göttingen 1987). Allen, Garland E., "The Ideology of Elimination: American and German Eugenics, 1900–1945," in Nicosia, Frances and Heuner, Jonathan (eds.), *Medicine and Medical Ethics in Nazi Germany: Origins, Practices, Legacies* (New York 2002), 13–39, esp. 32.
[166] Pernick, *Black Stork*, 160–167.
[167] Paul Bowman Popenoe (1888–1979) began his career as an expert in date palm cultivation, traveling to Asia and Africa to acquire plants for his father's plantation in California. His interest in eugenics brought him into contact with banker and entrepreneur Ezra S. Gosney, whose Human Betterment Foundation funded his collection of data on the significance of California's sterilization laws. During the 1920s and 1930s, numerous publications on eugenics and the policy of forced sterilizations in the United States, of whose benefits Popenoe was firmly convinced, established his reputation as one of the country's foremost eugenics experts. In 1930, Popenoe founded the American Institute for Family Relations (AIFR) and built a highly successful second career as a marriage counselor in the postwar United States. He never abandoned his eugenicist

vinced advocate of eugenically based forced sterilization to a popular marriage counselor, "America's Mr. Marriage", whose guidebooks became bestsellers and under whose name a highly regarded column appeared in the women's magazine *Ladies' Home Journal* from 1953 to the 1970s ("Can This Marriage Be Saved?").[168] As founder of the American Institute of Family Relations (AIFR), headquartered in Los Angeles, he also established a network of marriage and family counseling centers in California, which in turn trained hundreds of family experts, and published **his** own magazine, *Family Life*, from 1940 to 1979.[169]

Popenoe was particularly important to the formulation and popularization of eugenic ideas in the United States—he published the standard textbook on the subject and researched forced sterilizations in California. He also played a key role in integrating eugenics into the booming agenda of marriage and family counseling in the post-World War II period through his marriage counseling institute and his numerous guidebooks and columns. This makes him a revealing example of a social expert whose activities made a broad social impact from the 1920s through the 1970s. His writings and initiatives, which were central to the negotiation of the field of "family" in the United States during this period, will now be examined in three steps.

---

beliefs but formulated them more cautiously, emphasizing the positive effects of his marriage and family counseling. The best work on Popenoe is Ladd-Taylor, Molly, "Eugenics, Sterilization and Modern Marriage in the USA. The Strange Career of Paul Popenoe," *Gender and History* 13 (2001), 298–327. Paul Popenoe's literary estate, which includes the AIFR papers, is held by the American Heritage Center at the University of Wyoming. Paul Popenoe Collection, Accession Number 04681.

168 Popenoe, Paul B., *Modern Marriage: A Handbook* (New York 1925); Popenoe, Paul B., *Marriage Is What You Make It* (New York 1950); Popenoe, Paul B., *Divorce. 17 Ways to Avoid It* (Los Angeles 1959); Disney, Dorothy Cameron and Popenoe, Paul B., *Can this Marriage be Saved?* (New York 1960). The "Can this Marriage be Saved?" column first appeared in *Ladies' Home Journal* in 1953; it was de facto written by journalist Dorothy Cameron Disney, but referred to cases from Popenoe's AIFR. See Ladd-Taylor, "Eugenics," 317.

169 On the history of the American Institute of Family Relations (AIFR), see Stern, *Eugenic Nation*, 150–181. Founded by Popenoe in Los Angeles in 1930 and originally funded by the Human Betterment Foundation, which also supported the ERO, the AIFR saw itself as a eugenically inspired marriage and family counseling institution and achieved considerable popularity. By the time of its founder's death in 1979, it had a total of seven branches in California. That the AIFR's entire existence was tied to the figure of Popenoe is illustrated by the fact that it ceased operations a few years after he died.

Marriage, family, and reproduction in Popenoe's writings from the 1920s to the 1960s

Like so many eugenicists, Popenoe, who was born in 1888, started out as a farmer interested in breeding, in his case in the context of his father's date farm in Coachella, California. Through his work as editor of the *Journal of Heredity*, he quickly achieved some renown as a eugenicist, but it was the publication of the textbook *Applied Eugenics* together with Roswell H. Johnson in 1918—and later of the paper "Sterilization for Human Betterment" on sterilization practices in California—that triggered his meteoric rise to fame. Yet "Dr. Popenoe" had never pursued a scientific career, but merely held an honorary doctorate. His lack of scientific merit did not prevent him from writing numerous books in popular science and guidebooks on marriage, family, and reproduction. In these publications, Popenoe propagated strictly naturalistic gender roles and a biologistic concept of marriage as a reproductive community for the good of the nation. He adapted his rhetoric to his readers' expectations: while in his early publications he vehemently advocated eugenics as an appropriate modern technique for improving the population structure and as the key to achieving "race betterment," later marriage and family counseling to improve the American nation came to the fore. In the latter context, Popenoe continued to assume a naturalistic ordering of the sexes and professed fundamental eugenic principles (the differing value of different human beings and the promotion of the "better") but formulated them in a more restrained manner. We can trace the development of Popenoe's conception of eugenic family planning and policy in three crucial texts that appeared in the mid-1920s, in which Popenoe set out practical measures to improve marriage and the family. In his first marriage guide, *Modern Marriage: A Handbook for Men* (1925), Popenoe explicitly addressed his own gender, since it was the responsibility of the eventual husband "to take the initiative in most matters pertaining to marriage." In addition, the latter was "responsible in a large part for the education of his wife."[170] Popenoe also advocated the exclusion from marriage of men suffering from hereditary diseases (understood at the time to encompass "imbecility," epilepsy, and mental illnesses), as well as men who had syphilis or were sterile.[171] Those afflicted with heart disease, obesity, gonorrhea, or tuberculosis should, Popenoe argued, have recovered completely before mar-

---

[170] Popenoe, Paul, *Modern Marriage: A Handbook for Men* (first edition New York: Macmillan, 1925; reprinted New York: Macmillan, 1929), x. The handbook appeared in a second edition (Macmillan, 1940) as well as various reprints (1944, 1945, 1946 and 1954), and thus attracted great interest into the 1950s.
[171] Popenoe, *Modern Marriage*, 207–231.

riage. This biologistic reasoning marginalized men based on their health status and supposed genetic makeup.

Meanwhile, in the short paper "Problems of Human Reproduction," which appeared in 1926, Popenoe examined this topic from a medical and biological point of view, but without making an explicit plea for eugenic measures.[172] He was particularly interested in the relationship between the sexes, which he described as a primarily biologically based "sex antagonism." In the shape of reproduction, however, this fulfilled a clear social purpose:

> In mankind, sex antagonism is always present. [. . .] But at bottom it seems to be a biological phenomenon, based merely on the dissimilarity of the sexes, but having achieved a utility to the race which has preserved it and perhaps increased it in intensity.[173]

The biological differences between men and women served him as a means of legitimizing strictly biologistic gender roles. Women should concentrate on their reproductive function, while men should support them in this. A high degree of mutual adaptation would guarantee "happiness in marriage."[174]

Meanwhile, in his handbook *Conservation of the Family*, also from 1926, Popenoe argued more sociologically. He described his proposals for improving the American family (better education and dissemination of eugenic knowledge, marriage counseling and family policy, a minimum income for families, and maternity benefits), referring directly to Edward A. Ross, as a "means of social control."[175] In addition, he put forward a comparatively modern concept of the family when he stated: "A normal family must promote the welfare of father, mother, and children. If it does so, it will also benefit society as a whole."[176] However, he remained true to his conviction that the distribution of tasks between the sexes was biologically determined. He thus continued to define women exclusively in light of their contribution to the reproduction of the nation. He felt particular contempt for well-educated women who preferred to pursue a professional career rather than devote themselves to their reproductive duties. For Popenoe, they were doing serious damage to society, prompting him to describe them as "superior single women, who [. . .] under the banner of individualism, are destroying the machinery of society."[177]

---

172 Popenoe, Paul, *Problems of Human Reproduction* (Baltimore 1926).
173 Popenoe, *Problems of Human Reproduction*, 147–148.
174 Popenoe, *Problems of Human Reproduction*, 192–196.
175 Popenoe, *Conservation of the Family*, 157–242. A new edition was published in 1984 by Garland in New York and London.
176 Popenoe, *Conservation of the Family*, 39.
177 Popenoe, *Conservation of the Family*, 135f.

This highly contradictory amalgam of biologistic arguments, demands for greater partnership in marriage and within the family, and for better sex education for young people, which Popenoe set out in *Conservation of the Family*, is especially evident in its final chapter, in which he reflected on the "Changing Family of the Future." For him, this should be characterized by

> 1) much better mate selection, 2) much greater understanding, making for permanence of love, 3) more intelligent consideration of children, 4) greater concern for individual development, particularly of women, 5) more democracy, 6) fuller biological differentiation of function.[178]

It was probably this incongruity of his demands—simultaneous advocacy of better selection of spouses and "more democracy," of individual development opportunities for women and, at the same time, of a biology-based division of roles within the family—that made Popenoe's reflections appealing in so many different ways that the staunch eugenicist could become a nationally sought-after marriage counselor and public speaker, America's "Mr. Marriage."[179]

Education, eugenics, and "happy homes": the American Institute for Family Relations (AIFR)

How this relatability functioned can be brought out by two of Popenoe's texts from 1935 and 1940, in which he linked eugenics, education, and family support and thus conveyed the self-image of his AIFR, founded in 1930. While his 1929 evaluation of forced eugenic sterilization in California was still entirely committed to negative eugenics,[180] in his articles published after the founding of the AIFR Popenoe consciously bridged the gap to "positive eugenics" in the sense of educating youth to embrace "eugenic mate selection" and better manage both

---

[178] Popenoe, *Conservation of the Family*, 253–254. The same quote is chosen by his son, sociologist David Popenoe, in an appreciation of his father, but no mention is made of point 6, Popenoe's insistence on the biological inequality between the sexes. Popenoe, David, "Remembering My Father. An Intellectual Portrait of 'The Man Who Saved Marriages.'" URL: <www.popenoe.com/Paul Popenoe.htm>. The same text can also be found as chapter 14 in Popenoe, David, *War Over the Family* (New Brunswick 2005), 227–244.

[179] To quote the obituary in the journal of the AIFR, *Family Life*: Peacock, Edward, "Goodbye, Mr. and Mrs. Marriage," *Family Life* 39 (1979), 2–8. Quoted in Ladd-Taylor, "Eugenics," 298.

[180] Popenoe, Paul and Gosney, Ezra Seymour, *Sterilization for Human Betterment* (New York 1929). Already translated into German in 1930: *Sterilisierung zur Aufbesserung des Menschengeschlechts* (Berlin 1930).

marriage and family.[181] In the 1935 article "Education and Eugenics," Popenoe argued: "Young people should be educated in eugenics as a matter of citizenship."[182] In particular, colleges that educated young people "eugenically superior to the average of the population" must create the preconditions for them to choose their spouses carefully and raise large families.[183] After all, as he asserted: "The future of America depends largely on whether in the next generation educators can produce citizens who will be eugenically minded."[184]

Five years later, in an article on "Eugenics and Family Relations" (1940), Popenoe declared that the AIFR, as the spearhead of the so-called family relations movement, was based in large measure on the ideas of eugenics and was making an important contribution to "positive eugenics" in the sense of the qualitative improvement of the American nation. As he saw it, in addition to traditional marriage and family counseling based on hereditary biology, the primary role of the AIFR was to train family experts and disseminate eugenic knowledge through training, courses, and talks at colleges, universities, churches, and community organizations. This, as he envisaged it, was to be supplemented by an elaborate program of conferences, publications of all kinds, and radio broadcasts. By emphasizing that modern family policy must always be conceived partly in eugenic terms, Popenoe confidently bridged the gap between eugenics and family support:

> Eugenic progress is slow indeed where family life is deprecated, celibacy exalted, motherhood regarded as a misfortune and children as a nuisance. [. . .] Eugenic advance depends, of course, on having a community which is not merely family-minded, but discriminatingly family-minded.[185]

The history of the AIFR itself attests to its founder's dual approach to strengthening the American nation by means of the American family, on the one hand through effective marriage and family counseling and on the other by promulgating knowledge of hereditary biology and eugenics. On the occasion of the institute's founding in February 1930—it was financed by Ezra S. Gosney's Human Betterment Foundation—Popenoe emphasized that it represented a "scientific attempt to deal with the causes of unhappiness in homes."[186] What he had in mind

---

181 Popenoe, Paul B., "Education and Eugenics," *Journal of Educational Sociology*, vol. 8, no. 8 (1935), 451–458. Popenoe, Paul B., "Eugenics and Family Relations," *Journal of Heredity* 31 (1940), 532–536.
182 Popenoe, "Education," 456.
183 Popenoe, "Education," 455.
184 Popenoe, "Education," 457.
185 Popenoe, Paul B., "Eugenics and Family Relations," 532–536.
186 Ransome Sutton, "What's New in Science: Marriage Clinics," *Los Angeles Times*, September 28, 1930, K11.

here, reflecting the objectives of his main sponsor, was both improving the American family and lowering the divorce rate, especially in California, as well as bolstering Californians' hereditary makeup through genetic counseling and eugenics. The choice of location, however, in the middle of Hollywood at 5287 Sunset Boulevard, shows that Popenoe was not primarily concerned with *all* families but preferred to focus on the Californian upper and middle classes. It was particularly important to him to provide those seeking advice with science-based information furnished by proven experts, "a group of specialists representing the best modern thought and experience."[187] Their task was to confront people with "plain, unvarnished facts" about the state of their marriage and family, and then let them draw their own conclusions: "We shall allay anxiety in some instances and sound warnings in others; we may stop some unwise marriages, and, on the other hand, promote successful ones, where there has been doubt."[188] Aspiring to guide the development of Californian families on the basis of scientific knowledge and objective facts, Popenoe provides us with a revealing definition of what historiography has called "social engineering."[189]

A year later, Popenoe again described the circumstances surrounding the establishment of the AIFR in the *Journal of Home Economics*, highlighting the model of marriage and family counseling in Germany, which had inspired the forty-five "socially-minded men and women" involved in getting the AIFR off the ground in Los Angeles. Its first clients, Popenoe continued, were composed of one-fifth each of the following groups: (1) persons seeking premarital counseling, (2) persons with marital problems, (3) those seeking advice on ancestry issues and inherited diseases, (4) those seeking information, (5) persons with various problems (relating to sexuality, legal issues, and welfare) who could be referred to other sources of help.[190] In 1951, just over twenty years after its founding, the AIFR reported that it had provided about 10,000 one-hour counseling sessions to 4,460 people annually.[191] A total of 37 marriage and family counselors worked for the institute, which

---

[187] Quoted in Constance Chandler, "Marriage Ills Clinic Formed: Family Relations Institute for Wed and Unwed," *Los Angeles Times*, February 9, 1930. A1.
[188] Quoted in Constance Chandler, "Marriage Ills Clinic Formed: Family Relations Institute for Wed and Unwed," *Los Angeles Times*, February 9, 1930. A 1.
[189] On the state of research, see the introduction to the present book. Etzemüller, Thomas (ed.), *Die Ordnungen der Moderne. Social Engineering im 20. Jahrhundert* (Bielefeld 2009). Brückweh, Kerstin, Schumann, Dirk, Wetzell, Richard F., and Ziemann, Benjamin (eds.), *Engineering Society: The Role of the Human and Social Sciences in Modern Societies, 1880–1980* (New York 2012).
[190] Popenoe, Paul B., "The Institute of Family Relations," *Journal of Home Economics* 22, no. 11 (1930), 906–907.
[191] "Notes from the AIFR," *Family Life* 12, no. 2 (1952), 5.

Dr. Popenoe berät Heiratswillige

Fig. 2.9: Paul B. Popenoe explaining the basic principles of heredity to a couple planning to get married. This picture was published in 1930 to mark the foundation of the AIFR, and appeared, for example, in the German journal *Eugenik*.

also broadcast its own television program on the ABC network.[192] The AIFR was able to build on this rapid growth in subsequent years. On the institution's 30th anniversary in 1960, Popenoe proudly reported that it now employed more than 100 people, 70 of whom were marriage counselors specially trained through a one-year course, who provided about 15,000 hours of counseling annually to some 5,000 different individuals.[193] In addition, the AIFR put on numerous courses every year, held workshops at universities and colleges, and organized talks on topics such as motherhood/birth, housework, and "social effectiveness." Popenoe's column in the *Ladies' Home Journal* was based on cases from the institute's counseling practice, as was his daily newspaper column "Your Family and You," which appeared in various

---

[192] Wednesday evenings from 9:30 to 10:00 p.m. "Notes from the AIFR," *Family Life* 12, no. 2 (1952), 5.
[193] "Thirty Years of AFIR," *Family Life* 20, no. 3 (1960), 1–3.

publications. Popenoe and the AIFR counselors also had a regular radio presence, with their own show from 1962 onwards that aired six days a week.[194]

Popenoe and the AIFR received additional publicity thanks to a 1950 movie, *A Modern Marriage*, directed by Paul Landres.[195] The film showed how, with the help of an AIFR marriage counselor, a potentially suicidal young woman recognized the cause of her sexual problems (her relationship with her domineering mother) and learned to come to terms with her marriage and husband.[196] In a second version from 1962, a prologue preceded the film (now titled *Frigid Wife*). In it, a marriage counselor tells two women—whom he is counseling about sexual problems in their marriages—the story of the young wife of 1950 (which constitutes the vast majority of the film). This he does in order to motivate them to keep working on their relationships.[197] It is characteristic of Popenoe's understanding of "natural gender roles" and typical of the counseling practice of the AIFR that in both versions of the movie it is solely the wives who are identified as unwilling to adapt to the marriage and thus as the cause of sexual problems and the resulting need for therapy. Although the AIFR emphasized counseling the couple as a unified entity, the majority of counseling hours were spent with wives, who mostly took the first steps toward counseling:

> Most of our clients are couples who have been married from five to ten years, with a child or two. One fourth of them have failed in previous marriages. In three-quarters of the cases, it is the woman who comes first, but we are usually able to get the husband to come afterward so that, of the total counseling load, 57 percent is devoted to wives and 43 percent to husbands.[198]

Toward the end of the 1960s, the AIFR had four branches in California in addition to the Hollywood headquarters: a branch was opened in Orange County in late 1966 and in Riverside County in October 1967. The South Bay branch began operations in November 1967[199] and the East Side Counseling Center in October 1966,

---

194 The radio show was broadcast on KABC and produced by AIFR executive director Floyd M. Anderson, who answered questions from listeners on aspects of marriage and family counseling with the assistance of guest commentators. *Family Life* 22 (1962), no. 10, 4. See also "Thirty Years of AIFR," *Family Life* 20, no. 3 (1960), 3.
195 Together with Ben Parker. Paul Landres became best known as a director of early TV series, shooting episodes of *The Lone Ranger*, *Maverick*, and *Flipper*.
196 Internet Movie Database, IMDb <www.imdb.com/title/tt0042743/?ref_=ttfc_fc_tt>. See also <www.tcm.com/tcmdb/title/83802/A-Modern-Marriage/>.
197 See plot details at <www.afi.com/members/catalog/DetailView.aspx?s=1&Movie=19752> and <www.fandango.com/amodernmarriage_v133316/plotsummary>.
198 "Thirty Years of AFIR," *Family Life* 20, no. 3 (1960), 2.
199 *Family Life* 26 (1966), no. 11, 3–4. *Family Life* 27 (1967), no. 1, 4. *Family Life* 27 (1967), no. 12, 4.

the latter offering counseling courses in Spanish in an attempt to reach the Spanish-speaking population of East Los Angeles.[200]

Family life: from family to population

From 1940 to 1979, the AIFR published its own journal, *Family Life*. It regularly published reviews of literature on marriage, the family, and eugenics, as well as editorials by Paul B. Popenoe and guest authors, in addition to "Notes from the AIFR" and advertisements for AIFR lecture series, seminars, and publications.[201] An analysis of the volumes available in Germany for the period 1952 to 1969 reveals that the editorials repeatedly addressed the topics of "natural" gender roles, sexuality in marriage, intergenerational and family relations, marriage and divorce, as well as marriage and family counseling in general. Popenoe's belief that the maintenance of "healthy" family structures and the avoidance of divorce depended in substantial part on positive eugenics emerges clearly from his editorials, which bore titles such as "The Case for Eugenics" (1958), "Heredity and Marriage Counseling" (1962, 1963), and "Family Strength and Mental Health" (1969).[202] More significantly, however, the call for the biological improvement of the American population shone through subcutaneously in the treatment of seemingly neutral subjects. Thus, Popenoe packaged his plea for eugenic measures in innocuous titles such as "What is Marriage Counseling? (1955), "Family Life 15 Years From NOW" (1958), "Happiness in Marriage" (1959), "The Role of Men in the

---

200 *Family Life* 29 (1969), no. 10, 6.
201 *Family Life*, 12 (1952) to 29 (1969) in the Münster University Library. The journal was acquired at the behest of anthropologist Otmar Freiherr von Verschuer for his Institute of Human Genetics (Institut für Humangenetik). Verschuer (1896–1969) taught and conducted research in Münster from 1951 until his retirement in 1965, despite his responsibility for human experimentation under Nazism. He was a member of the American Eugenics Society and a corresponding member of the American Society of Human Genetics. Like Verschuer's membership of these American bodies, the fact that he prompted the acquisition of this journal, which was extremely rare in Germany, is indicative of strong contacts between German and U.S. eugenicists even after the caesura of 1945. On Verschuer's second career in West Germany, see Weiss, Sheila Faith, "After the Fall. Political Whitewashing, Professional Posturing, and Personal Refashioning in the Postwar Career of Otmar Freiherr von Verschuer," *Isis*, vol. 101 (2010), no. 4, 722–758.
202 Editorial: "The Case for Eugenics," *Family Life* 18 (1958), no. 2, 1–2. Popenoe, Paul, "A French Eugenic Garden City," *Family Life* 20 (1960), no. 6, 3–4. Popenoe, Paul and Phillips, C. E, "Heredity and Marriage Counseling," *Family Life* 22 (1962), no. 10, 1–4. Popenoe, Paul and Phillips, C. E, "Heredity and Marriage Counseling," *Family Life* 23 (1963), no. 2, 1–5. Popenoe, Paul, "Family Strength and Mental Health," *Family Life* 29 (1969), no. 12, 1–3.

Modern Family" (1961), "Family Crisis" (1963), and "Toward Fewer Divorces" (1969).[203] The journal did not deal in any serious way with the coercive nature of Nazi hereditary health policy (*Erbgesundheitspolitik*) or, most strikingly, with Nazi euthanasia, either before 1945 or after.

In the 1950s, by way of contrast, reviews of writings by German eugenicists, human geneticists, and population scientists still dominated the review section of *Family Life*. For example, the postwar writings of formerly prominent Nazi scientists, such as Hans F. K. Günther, Hermann Werner Siemens, Otmar Freiherr von Verschuer, Hans Harmsen, and Friedrich Wilhelm Burgdörfer, were reviewed with interest and generally favorably in the journal.[204] Popenoe's appraisals of Otmar Freiherr von Verschuer's publications are particularly interesting due to the close connections between the latter and the American eugenics movement. In 1955, a concise but positive review of Verschuer's book *Wirksame Faktoren im Leben des Menschen* ("Effective Factors in Human Life," Wiesbaden 1954) appeared, emphasizing that here the author was presenting the results of twenty-five years of twin research and underlining his status as one of the top experts in the field. His book *Eugenik* (Witten 1966) was presented positively in 1967 as the "first book on eugenics that has appeared in Germany since 1945."[205] In addition, the journal printed advertisements for the publications of the American Eugenics Society, in particular those of Frederik Osborn and Paul Popenoe. When the latter's standard 1918 work *Applied Eugenics* (coauthored by Roswell H. Johnson) ceased to be reprinted in 1957, *Family Life* noted that the number of courses offered on the subject of "eugenics" at colleges and universities had plummeted. This, however, readers were told, should be seen as a success of the eugenics movement, since "the subject has been absorbed into other courses such as social

---

203 Popenoe, Paul, "What is Marriage Counseling?", *Family Life* 15 (1955), no. 7, 5–6. Popenoe, Paul, "Family Life 15 Years From NOW," *Family Life* 18 (1958), no. 8, 1–2. Popenoe, Paul, "Happiness in Marriage," *Family Life* 19 (1959), no. 7, 1–2. Popenoe, Paul, "The Role of Men in the Modern Family," *Family Life* 21 (1961), no. 7, 1–4. Popenoe, Paul, "Family Crisis," *Family Life* 23 (1963), 1–4. Popenoe, Paul, "Toward Fewer Divorces," *Family Life* 29 (1969), no. 11, 1–3.
204 See, for example, the reviews of Hans F. K. Günther's books *Formen und Urgeschichte der Ehe* (Göttingen 1951) and *Gattenwahl* (Munich 1951) in *Family Life* 12 (1952), no. 1, 4; no. 2, 10. Friedrich Burgdörfer was presented in the review of his book *Bevölkerungsdynamik und Bevölkerungsbilanz* (Munich 1951) as "probably the leading expert in population statistics in Germany"; *Family Life* 12 (1952), no. 6, 9. The review of the new edition of Hermann Werner Siemens' handbook *Grundzüge der Vererbungslehre, Rassenhygiene und Bevölkerungspolitik* (Munich 1952, first edition Berlin 1921 under the title *Einführung in die allgemeine Konstitutions- und Vererbungspathologie*) praised it as an indispensable, foundational text; *Family Life* 12 (1952), no. 5, 10.
205 *Family Life* 15 (1955), no. 3, 10. *Family Life* 17 (1967), no. 5, 9.

problems, family relations, and social psychology."[206] In the late 1950s, the focus of the reviews shifted from eugenics to population control techniques, supplemented from the early 1960s onward by examples of the use of genetic counseling. Yet neither the AIFR nor Paul B. Popenoe completely lost sight of eugenics. In 1969, for example, we still find a firm commitment to eugenics in *Family Life*:

> The fundamental position of eugenics was, and is, that important human traits are inherited, and that survival of a nation is possible only if a majority of births are in families that can produce children who are mentally and physically sound rather than defective.[207]

The same year also saw a positive review of Frederik Osborn's new work, *The Future of Human Heredity* (1968), in which the doyen of the postwar American eugenics movement attempted to keep eugenics alive in 1960s U.S. society.[208] It is instructive that to this end Osborn made a connection between genetic quality and both social performance and a commitment to "American" norms and values, as evident in a quote reprinted by *Family Life*:

> The new eugenic policies do not give offense to the habits and customs established in the long experience of mankind; they are compatible with the highest American ideals; they propose to reinforce trends that are already underway and to reinforce them in ways which the public is wholly willing to accept. Everyone wants children to be wanted children, born to parents who will give them homes where they will have the best and most affectionate care and a fine parental example. Achievement in building a home as well as success in other aspects of life constitutes a eugenic criterion today just as it did during the long period of man's evolution when achievement meant survival. Proposals based on such criteria are the best we can be sure of at present. They are fully acceptable to the public.[209]

In the 1950s and 1960s, Popenoe and the experts at AIFR began to fuse the notion of the genetic improvement of the general population through eugenic measures

---

206 "Notes from the AIFR," *Family Life* 17, no. 5 (1957), 3.
207 Quoted in a critical review of the historical analysis of the eugenics movement by Donald K. Pickens, *Eugenics and the Progressives*, Nashville 1968. *Family Life*, 29 (1969), no. 12, 9–10. An example of the ongoingly positive appraisal of texts on eugenics is the review of Otmar Freiherr von Verschuer, *Eugenik* (Witten 1966); *Family Life* 27 (1967), no. 6, 9.
208 Frederic Osborn (1889–1981) was among the prominent proponents of eugenics in the United States after World War II. President of the AES from 1946 to 1952, Osborn shifted the organization's activities toward population policy and control, while replacing negative eugenics with a call for positive eugenics, though without abandoning the goal of improving the genetic makeup of U.S. society. At Princeton University, he founded the Office of Population Research, the oldest such institute in the United States. Osborn co-founded the journal *Eugenics Quarterly*. Osborn, Frederic, *The Future of Human Heredity: An Introduction to Eugenics in Modern Society* (New York 1968).
209 Review of Frederic Osborn, *The Future of Human Heredity: An Introduction to Eugenics in Modern Society*, *Family Life* 29 (1969), no. 5, 7–8.

with the popular demand that population growth be curbed.[210] Instead of focusing on genetic and social defects and their prevention, Popenoe and the AIFR, like Osborn, now identified social performance and the acceptance of familial norms as criteria for a positive eugenics based on the fostering of the supposedly "better," which proved a highly effective means of popularizing eugenics.[211] Until the early 1960s, Popenoe's marriage counselors, as well as the AIFR's counseling service, promised to make modern society compatible with traditional values—and furnished many Americans with a sense of private constancy during a period of political uncertainty.[212] It was not until the emergence of the second phase of the women's movement and its advocacy of the right to abortion that Popenoe's biologistic gender conservatism lost its persuasive force.[213] However, neither eugenic arguments nor the biologistic notion of the family as the basis of the nation disappeared from academic and public discussion. This is illustrated, for example, by the debates on the structure and values of African American families in the 1960s, the zero population growth movement of the 1960s and 1970s, and the welfare policies of the 1980s and 1990s, each of which correlated genetic "value" with social performance. Whenever social experts asserted their fundamental, scientifically legitimized right to intervene in order to curtail the reproductive rights of the poor and non-white population (African Americans, Mexican Americans, and welfare recipients), they indirectly echoed the eugenics movement's codification of the different "values" of individuals and groups.[214] We might note that present-day evolutionary biology is revitalizing the biologistic definition of gender roles, as gender theorist Joan W. Scott pointed out as early as 2001.[215]

---

210 "The Case for Eugenics," *Family Life*, xviii, no. 2 (1958), 1–2. In 1959, *Family Life* referred to a statement by the British population scientist L. N. Jackson in the January 1959 *News of Population and Birth Control*, who emphasized that "Eugenic sterilization should be more widely used in many countries to reduce the excessive birthrate," citing the example of India. *Family Life*, XIX, no. 2 (1958), 4–5. During the same year, the magazine also reported on sterilization experiments in Puerto Rico and quoted the president of the International Planned Parenthood Federation, C.P. Blacker, as stating that eugenics was especially important in the atomic age because of the pressing need for highly intelligent young people. *Family Life*, XIX, nos. 6 & 7 (1959). The genesis of "genetic counseling" as a science, profession, and social practice is analyzed by Stern, *Telling Genes*.
211 Ladd-Taylor, "Eugenics," 318.
212 On the need for family and a sense of security in the first decades of the Cold War, see May, *Homeward Bound*. Ladd-Taylor, "Eugenics," 320.
213 Ladd-Taylor, "Eugenics," 320.
214 On this topic, see chapters 4 and 5 and Heinemann, "Social Experts." Ladd-Taylor, "Eugenics," hints at this development, but pursues it no further.
215 Scott, "Millennial Fantasies."

The astonishing career of eugenicist and marriage counselor Paul B. Popenoe points up the need to analyze the history of eugenics from a long-term perspective. The biologistic conceptions of gender and society that, together with the state's right to intervene, constituted the substantive core of the eugenics movement, had been around far longer than it had.

2.6 Interim conclusion: government and family in the 1920s and 1930s

The debates on eugenics, sterilizations and ideas of "good motherhood" in expert publications and press reports of the 1920s and 1930s show how the government discovered the family—and especially the mother with her reproductive function—as an object of policy. In view of the sociopolitical upheavals after the end of World War I (the women's movement, women's suffrage, and women's employment), the Great Depression (the sense of a "crisis of the family," internal migration, and the New Deal as the first national program of social reform), but also scientific progress (genetics, hygiene, and reproduction) and continuing immigration, scholars, journalists and politicians alike called for the strengthening of the American family, which they regarded as the likeness of the nation.

But it is vital to separate social upheavals from merely "perceived" problems. Given that immigration had been greatly reduced since 1924 and the fertility of the non-white minority was declining at the same rate as that of the white majority, from the mid-1920s on there was no evidence to back claims of "population pressure" emanating from "undesirables." Nevertheless, the protagonists of the eugenics movement successfully mobilized the scenario of white America's impending "race suicide" to establish sterilization laws at the state level. The call for "scientific motherhood," on the other hand, was a response not only to the new valorization of childhood and the child, but also to the reduction in infant mortality achieved through medical advances. At the same time, this call provided a gateway for attempts to control reproduction by eugenic means.

The still relatively young species of the social expert proved particularly well-equipped to deal with these socio-economic and mental contingencies and respond to them with simply formulated practical instructions. In the initiatives put forward by self-styled experts and reformers to improve the American family, a surprisingly clear line can be drawn from "scientific motherhood" to eugenics and ultimately to marriage and family counseling informed by hereditary biology: the call for "scientific motherhood" as a means to improve pregnancy, childbirth, and child-rearing initially expedited the growth of the fledgling eugenics and helped popularize it, among other things through the medium of competitions (Better Babies and Fitter Families Contests). In the face of internal migration and declining birth rates, the Fitter Family Contests idealized the "rural family" and exalted traditional family values, a retrograde approach to the challenges of modernity that simultaneously drew on modern science and eugenics in particular. Finally, the representatives of the eugenics movement presented their creed as a highly modern and effective means of making the right to self-determined reproduction dependent on biologistic parameters. These supposed experts legitimized the fact that "positive eugenics" (the promotion of "high-quality" offspring for the nation) included coercive measures such as sterilizations and marriage bans with reference to economic and health policy benefits. Subsequently, under the impact of Nazi racial policies and the emerging Cold War, eugenics in the United States began to morph into genetically informed marriage and family counseling. This continued to be based on a system of biologistic inequalities, exemplified by the family as a community of descent. Marriage, on the other hand, was reduced mainly to its reproductive function, which was viewed as a vital service to the nation.

The astonishing career of Paul B. Popenoe, who went from date grower and Californian eugenicist in the 1920s to nationally recognized marriage and family counselor, "America's Mr. Marriage," from 1930 onwards, is an ideal-typical case of the continuity of biologistic thinking about family and reproduction in the United States. In his attempt to improve the hereditary substance of the American family, to combat divorce and childlessness, and to present those seeking advice with scientific findings, Popenoe was focused on California's white upper and middle classes, and maintaining traditional, "natural" gender norms (with, at most, moderate adjustments in the form of an understanding of marriage as a partnership). This traditional conception of the categories of race, class, and gender, packaged in the modern garb of an applied science of reproduction, made Popenoe's reflections from the 1930s onward highly appealing far beyond the circle of American eugenicists. The promise that modern civilization could be made compatible with traditional values and socioeconomic performance, as encapsulated in the family as a microcosm of the nation, also made a major contribution here.

With regard to the relationship between the government and the individual as reflected in the family, the Supreme Court ruling legalizing the sterilization of mentally and physically ill people in 1927 and the adoption of corresponding sterilization laws at state level show that the government was prepared to intervene significantly in the family, a step legitimized by eugenically minded social experts. Here, too, the focus was undoubtedly on the woman as the potential mother of hereditarily diseased offspring, represented both in the scientific debates and in sterilization statistic.

With the unprecedented rise in women's employment during World War II and as the second wave of the women's movement began to emerge, the debate over working mothers and their reproduction, as well as on the impact of women's paid work on American families, came into sharper focus. In the process, biologistic arguments gradually took a back seat to social ones. This debate on women's employment and family values is the focus of the following chapter.

3 "Working women, domesticity, and the expert": public debates and expert discourses on women's employment and motherhood, 1940–1970

In a 1947 essay entitled "What Is Happening to the American Family?", anthropologist Margaret Mead reflected on changes in family structure and in the norms and values of the U.S. family after World War II. In a number of research projects, Mead had explored the effects of social and geographic mobility during the war on U.S. society, focusing particularly on the family.[1] In addition to structural changes such as the decline of family networks and the trend toward hastily contracted marriages in the face of war, she also underscored the serious consequences of a new culture of "choice" for American women, especially married women and mothers:

> The only group to whom we have given no choice is married women. [. . .] Women in our society are still a status group; if they marry, certain sorts of behavior are expected from them. I do not think at all that most married women do not want to stay at home, but I do think that most married women would like not to have it taken quite so for granted that they should stay home. If they were given a choice, most of them would stay home.[2]

---

1 Margaret Mead (1901–1978) was a cultural anthropologist whose research on Samoa, particularly the study *Coming of Age in Samoa* (1928), made her world famous in the 1930s. From the 1940s to the 1970s, she was one of the most sought-after experts in the American media, her subjects including the family, gender roles, child-rearing, personality formation, and diagnoses of social change. During World War II, Mead first headed the Committee on Food Habits, a division of the National Research Council, where her priorities were wartime nutrition and attempts to fortify the home front. This work led to *And Keep Your Powder Dry* (1942), not so much a book on wartime economics as a study of U.S. culture and "national character." Later, in collaboration with anthropologist Ruth Benedict, she worked for the Office of War Information, where both researched Japanese culture. While Benedict turned this research into her influential book *The Chrysanthemum and the Sword* (1946) on Japanese society, Mead developed the concept of analyzing foreign cultures in the absence of immersive experience, as set out in *The Study of Culture at a Distance* (1953). In the immediate postwar period, Mead then focused her analyses on the preconditions for social change and the role of anthropology in this context. For Mead's observations on changing gender roles, see her influential book *Male and Female. A Study of Sexes in a Changing World* (London 1949). Mead, Margaret, *And Keep Your Powder Dry: An Anthropologist Looks at America* (New York 1942). Bowman-Kruhm, Mary, *Margaret Mead: A Biography* (Westport and London 2003). Her literary estate is in the Library of Congress, Manuscript Division. On Mead, see also chapter 6 of the present book.
2 Mead, "What is Happening."

The anthropologist was referring to an important debate, conducted with bitter intensity in the United States after the Second World War, on the pros and cons of women's and especially mothers' paid work. At issue here was women's freedom of choice, as addressed by Mead, their opportunity for self-development, but also the possible consequences for children, the relationship between the sexes, and ultimately for the family and its values as the core unit of society.[3] At first glance, the male role model appeared much more homogeneous to contemporaries. This was noted by sociologist Talcott Parsons in a piece published about the same time as Mead's comments:

> The American masculine role does not seem to display a structural ambivalence at all comparable to that of the feminine. Its firm anchorage in the occupational structure seems to be the principle explanation of this. Virtually the only way to be a real man in our society is to have an adequate job and earn a living.[4]

Yet, the fact that men and male family heads in the 1950s also wrestled with ambivalence had already been described by David Riesman and C. Wright Mills in their studies of white middle-class employees. Riesman's *The Lonely Crowd* (1950) and Mills' *White Collar* (1952) argued that modern industrial society reduced (male) white-collar workers to isolated, conforming drones within the great mass of working people, at risk of becoming effeminate and unmanly.[5] In contrast, these scholars were unwilling to grant women the agency and independence they demanded from responsible men and family fathers. The following chapter explores this field of tension spanning social history, male and female role attributions, and family values, analyzing both public debates and expert discourses on motherhood and women's employment from the 1940s to the 1960s.

Generally speaking, the situation of families and women in particular in the immediate postwar period is one of the best researched topics in U.S. history. In the last twenty years, numerous studies have appeared that focus on concepts of

---

[3] Mead, Margaret, "What's the Matter with the Family?", *Harper's Magazine* 190 (1945), April, 393–399.
[4] Parsons, Talcott, "Social Structure of the Family," 199. In contrast, Ralph LaRossa shows how the ideal of fatherhood developed in the 1950s away from a self-image more oriented toward participation in child-rearing toward a stronger privileging of the breadwinner. Jürgen Martschukat and James Gilbert, on the other hand, have examined the ambivalences of the white ideal of masculinity in the 1950s between expectations of self and others, the breadwinner role, and a supposed "crisis of masculinity." LaRossa, Ralph, "The Culture of Fatherhood in the Fifties. A Closer Look," *Journal of Family History* 29 (2004), no. 1, 47–70. Gilbert, *Men in the Middle*. Martschukat, *Ordnung des Sozialen*.
[5] Mills, Charles W., *White Collar. The American Middle Classes* (New York 1952). Riesman, David, *The Lonely Crowd. A Study of the Changing American Character* (Garden City 1954, first edition 1950). See also Martschukat, *Ordnung des Sozialen*, 281.

motherhood, domesticity and the baby boom, the postwar family, and the issue of female employment.[6] Several lines of interpretation can be distinguished here. The older research literature mostly describes the 1950s as a time of the reinstatement of supposedly traditional gender roles after a brief phase of female employment and greater independence during World War II.[7] The emergence of suburban row-house developments in the wake of the GI Bill of Rights became emblematic of a "new domesticity" and a renewed turn to the family, which the baby boom then followed demographically. The longing for privacy and personal happiness in the shadow of the Cold War was simultaneously visualized and iconized by contemporary TV sitcoms (*Leave it to Beaver, Ozzie and Harriet, Father knows Best*), with the nuclear families portrayed always belonging to the white middle class.[8] The power of this ethnically and socially highly selective representation of the 1950s family was demonstrated, for example, in the 1980s, when President Ronald Reagan declared the 1950s the "golden age of the family" and referred explicitly to the ideal world of the sitcoms.[9] Since the 1990s, however, researchers have increasingly foregrounded the ambivalences of the 1950s American family in the form of female employment and gender role conflicts, as evident in new studies on motherhood, housewives, and "cultures of fatherhood."[10] It has become clear that the realities of life for Americans were more complex than the mainly conservative family rheto-

---

[6] Most recently Brumberg, *Vermessung*. Other relevant research projects underway or not yet published include Anna Bostwick Flaming's dissertation at the University of Iowa, "'The Most Important Person in the World': The Changing Political and Cultural Meanings of the Modern American Housewife," and Elizabeth Singer More's dissertation at Harvard University, "Best Interests: Feminism, Social Science, and the Revaluing of Working Mothers in Modern America" (Department of History, Harvard University, 2012).

[7] May, *Homeward Bound*. Evans, Sara M., *Born for Liberty. A History of Women in America* (New York 1991). Anderson, Karen, *Wartime Women. Sex Roles, Family Relations, and the Status of Women During World War II* (Westport 1981). Varenne,"Love and Liberty." A more nuanced account is provided by Coontz, *The Way We Never Were*. Chafe, *Paradox of Change*.

[8] Leibman, Nina C., *Living Room Lectures. The Fifties Family in Film and Television* (Austin 1995). Taylor, *Prime Time Families*. Haralovich, Mary Beth, "Sit-coms and Suburbs. Positioning the 1950s Homemaker," in Cameron, Ardis (ed.), *Looking for America. The Visual Production of Nation and People* (London and Boston 2004), 238–263.

[9] Coontz, *The Way We Never Were*, 23–25.

[10] Meyerowitz (ed.), *Not June Cleaver*. Metzl, "'Mother's Little Helper.'" Weiss, *To Have and to Hold*. Plant, *Mom*. Apple and Golden (eds.), *Mothers and Motherhood*. As early as the 1980s, Eugenia Kaledin had described the diverse range of options open to women in the 1950s. Kaledin, *Mothers and More*. More, Elizabeth Singer, "'The Necessary Factfinding Has Only Just Begun.' Women, Social Science, and the Reinvention of the 'Working Mother' in the 1950s," *Women's Studies* 40 (2011), no. 8, 974–1005. On masculinities see, among others, Kimmel, *Manhood in America*. Gilbert, *Men in the Middle*. LaRossa, *Modernization of Fatherhood*; LaRossa, Ralph, "The Culture of Fatherhood." Martschukat, *Ordnung des Sozialen*.

ric in the media, politics, and expert writing would suggest. Moreover, a number of studies have demonstrated that sociology's invention of the "modern isolated nuclear family" with clearly delineated gender roles did not simply consist in the revival of traditional "Victorian morals," but was itself a new development.[11]

This new perspective on the conflicting options simultaneously open to women in the 1950s is no accident. Women in the United States were the focus of public debates throughout the twentieth century, which reflected on their biological and social function as mothers and as the educators of future citizens, while grappling with challenges to this traditional gender role.[12] After an intense discussion of the supposed consequences of women's suffrage and divorce at the beginning of the century and the call for "reproductive morality" in the 1920s and 1930s, the debate on women's rights and gender roles experienced another peak in the period between the United States' entry into World War II and the height of the social protest movements in the late 1960s. In this context, the relationship between domesticity, women's employment, and reproduction became the focus of public discussion. This was increasingly shaped by experts, such as male and female physicians, social scientists, and psychologists on the one hand, and activists, such as women's rights campaigners, feminists, and engaged journalists on the other.[13] But the voices of "ordinary" women and mothers were also audible, for example as authors of readers' letters or as activists in grass roots movements. However, the statements of male and female social experts were particularly potent, since they ensured the

---

[11] This is one of the findings of our research group. See the contributions in Heinemann, Isabel (ed.), *Inventing the Modern American Family: Family Values and Social Change in 20th Century USA* (Frankfurt a.M. 2012).

[12] This role as guardian of the home and, in particular, educator of future citizens is in the tradition of "republican motherhood" dating back to the days of the early republic, which thus assigned a very specific task to the bourgeois woman that went beyond preserving domestic virtues. This contrasts with the claim that the nineteenth century was typified by a rather static bourgeois ideal of femininity, which Barbara Welter has described as "piety, purity, submissiveness and domesticity." Welter, Barbara, "The Cult of True Womanhood: 1820–1860," *American Quarterly* 18 (1966), no. 2, part 1, 151–174. Kerber, Linda, *Women of the Republic: Intellect and Ideology in Revolutionary America* (Chapel Hill 1980). Boydston, Jeanne, *Home and Work: Housework, Wages, and the Ideology of Labor in the Early Republic* (New York 1994).

[13] See, for example, Komarovsky, *Unemployed Man*; Komarovsky, Mirra, *Women in the Modern World. Their Education and Their Dilemmas* (New York 1932). Farnham, Marynia F. and Lundberg, Ferdinand, *Modern Woman. The Lost Sex* (New York 1947). Wylie, Philip, *A Generation of Vipers* (Champaign and London 2007, first edition 1942). Friedan, Betty, *The Feminine Mystique* (reprinted New York and London 2013, first edition New York 1963). For an innovative take on the role of women social scientists in this debate, see More, "Necessary Factfinding." On "momism," see Plant, *Mom*, and on Friedan's bestseller, see Coontz, Stephanie, *A Strange Stirring. The Feminine Mystique and American Women at the Dawn of the 1960s* (New York 2011).

gradual adaptation of the mother ideal to processes of social and cultural change, while they themselves acted as advocates or critics of such change. Two important points should be noted. First, liberal social and cultural scientists (such as members of the "neo-Freudian culture-and-personality school" examined by Joanne Meyerowitz with reference to Michel Foucault's concept of biopolitics) contributed to the cementing of naturalistic conceptions of gender.[14] As Meyerowitz shows, anthropologists Margaret Mead, Ruth Benedict, and Ashley Montague, as well as psychologists Karen Horney, Erich Fromm, Abraham Kardiner, and Harry Stack Sullivan, advocated overcoming the biologistic determinism of the eugenics movement by pointing out that "race" was a cultural construct. Yet, they also established a new distinction between "pathological" and "healthy," now on the basis of socio-cultural difference. Since, in the eyes of these experts, the upbringing and early childhood imprinting of the individual played the decisive role in explaining neuroses and pathological personality formation (homosexuality being considered an example at the time), they came to demand a re-evaluation of the "natural" role of the mother and to propagate an expert-led "social engineering" aimed at improving society. Their liberal "biopolitics" included a valorization of child-rearing as well as the promotion of white middle-class reproduction for the good of society. Second, a look at social experts and the methods and concepts they promulgated allows us to overcome the hitherto prevailing fixation on the political and economic implementation of reform projects (which is what the term "social engineering" is mostly associated with) and instead to analyze the discourse that foregrounded the improvement of mid-century U.S. society.[15] The debate on reproduction and the associated concepts of gender and family show vividly how the "scientification of the social" described by Lutz Raphael functioned on a discursive level and how actors' motivation and room for maneuver shifted in this context.[16]

What historical research has not yet been able to clarify, however, is how the negotiation of the social model of motherhood affected the dominant family ideal. How did the gradual spread of women's employment and the step-by-step expansion of tolerated women's roles change ideas about the family? How important

---

[14] Meyerowitz, Joanne, "'How Common Culture Shapes the Separate Lives.' Sexuality, Race, and Mid-Twentieth-Century Social Constructionist Thought," *Journal of American History* 96 (2010), no. 4, 1057–1084. Foucault, Michel, *Il faut defender la société. Cours au Collège de France 1976* (Paris 1976).

[15] Etzemüller (ed.), *Die Ordnungen der Moderne*. Etzemüller, "Social Engineering, Version: 1.0." Etzemüller, Thomas, "Auf den Spuren einer gesellschaftspolitisch problematischen Formation: social engineering 1920–1960," *Potsdamer Almanach des Zentrums für Zeithistorische Forschungen* (Göttingen 2008), 39–47. Mindick, Burton, *Social Engineering in Family Matters* (New York 1986).

[16] Raphael, "Verwissenschaftlichung." Raphael, "Embedding."

were factors such as race and class, the expansion of women's education, and the development of a consumer culture? What role did liberal and conservative social experts play in the associated discourses? When was their interpretive power challenged by (married) women wishing to work? And finally, how significant was the postwar period in general to the renegotiation of family values and gender roles in U.S. society, taking a long-term perspective on the entire twentieth century? To answer these questions, for the period from 1940 to 1970 I evaluated popular guidebooks and contemporary scholarly publications in addition to the national daily press (*New York Times, Washington Post, Chicago Tribune*), relevant women's magazines (*Good Housekeeping, Ladies' Home Journal*), an African American journal (*Ebony*, as well as excerpts from *Jet*), and the American Eugenics Society journal *Eugenics Quarterly*. This allows us to compare the debate in the press about "working women and motherhood" with the corresponding expert discourses. This comparison shows, to cite the core thesis of this chapter, that under the growing influence of social experts the focus of debate shifted from the question of the basic legitimacy and economic effects of women's employment to its impact on fertility and women's mental health, though it was solely white American women who were meant. Thus, although women's paid work was recognized by experts in the 1960s as a social reality, its consequences for the women involved, their families, and ultimately U.S. society remained controversial.

3.1 Trends in female employment between 1940 and 1970

In the first instance, the background to the debate on "working women" and "working mothers" was the unprecedented increase in women's employment during the Second World War as a result of the absence of many men due to the conflict and the need for labor in the armaments industry. Whereas in 1940, 27 percent of all employees were women, in April 1944 the figure was no less than 35 percent (approximately 18.4 million women).[17] This trend was to prove irreversible in the further course of the twentieth century, apart from a temporary slump in the immediate post-war period.

During the Second World War, the proportion of married women and mothers over 35 in the female workforce rose particularly sharply: more than 3.7 million women—out of 6.5 million women who took a job for the first time during this period—were in this category.[18] This opened up new opportunities for many women

---

17 See Tab. 3.1; see also Chafe, *Paradox of Change*, 133.
18 Chafe, *Paradox of Change*, 131.

Tab. 3.1: Women's share of the labor force, 1900–1970. (The figures for divorced persons and widows are included in the "single" column.)

Year	Women in the labor force (1,000)				Percentage of women (percent)			
	Total	Single	Married	Other	Total	Single	Married	Other
1900	4,997	3,307	769	920	20.6	43.5	5.6	32.5
1920	8,347	6,427	1,920	(18)	23.7	46.4	9.0	()
1930	10,632	5,735	3,071	1,826	24.8	50.5	11.7	34.4
1940	13,840	6,710	5,040	2,090	27.4	48.1	16.7	32.0
1944	18,449	7,542	8,433	2,474	35.0	58.6	25.6	35.7
1950	17,795	5,621	9,273	2,901	31.4	50.5	24.8	36.0
1955	20,528	5,281	10,809	4,458	35.7	61.1	28.5	40.7
1960	23,240	5,410	12,893	4,937	37.7	58.6	31.9	41.6
1965	26,200	5,410	14,829	5,396	39.3	54.5	34.9	40.7
1970	31,543	7,265	18,475	5,804	43.3	56.8	40.5	40.3
1980	45,487	11,865	24,980	8,643	51.5	64.4	49.9	43.6
1990	56,829	14,612	30,901	11,315	57.5	66.7	58.4	47.2

for the first time despite the multiple burdens of housework, child-rearing, and wage labor: vocational training, financial independence or at least the awareness of helping provide for the family by their own efforts, a new sense of purpose and self-affirmation, and expanded opportunities for consumption. Significant changes occurred for many African American women, who either found work for the first time or were able to leave domestic or agricultural employment for better-paying jobs in industry, a trend flanked by large-scale internal migration from the rural regions of the South to the large urban centers of the Northeast.[19] Ongoing racial discrimination made it difficult for these women to gain vocational qualifications and permanent employment over the long term, prompting historian Karen Anderson to refer to the "myth" that black women enjoyed improved employment opportunities in wartime and in the postwar economy. Other population groups, such as white women and African American men, she states, benefited far more from the wartime boom.[20] Thus, the 600,000 black women who did paid work for the first

---

[19] Anderson, Karen, *Changing Woman. A History of Racial Ethnic Women in Modern America* (New York 1996), 188–195.

[20] Anderson, Karen T., "Last Hired, First Fired. Black Women Workers during World War II," *Journal of American History* 69 (1982), no. 1, 82–97, esp. 92–97. Anderson, Karen, *Changing Women*, 191, 194. In contrast, cf. the position of Freeman, who finds greater economic opportunities for African American women in the postwar period. Freeman, Richard B., "Changes in the Labor Market for Black Americans, 1948–72," *Brooking Papers on Economic Activity* 1 (1973), 67–131, 119.

time during the war were mainly to be found in the lowest wage categories in industry and the service sector. Even after 1945, their opportunities for advancement and qualifications remained slim, and they were the first to lose their jobs to allow for the reemployment of war returnees.[21] Of crucial importance to the context of their labor is Anderson's conclusion that norms change more slowly than economic data:

> By stressing the modification of traditional patters fostered by rapid economic growth, scholars ignore the degree to which prejudices inhibited change and constrained the rate of economic expansion even in the face of strong patriotic, political, and economic incentives favoring expanded output at all costs. For black women, especially, what is significant about the war experience is the extent to which barriers remained intact.[22]

That the rise in gainful employment among African American women in the 1940s and 1950s, at least among married women, was not as revolutionary as long suspected is also illustrated by Fig. 3.1 below. Employment in this group increased, but at a much slower pace than in the case of white American women. These statistics, however, do not convey the expansion of employment among unmarried black women.[23]

Contrary to the popular notion of the classically structured "Cold War family," women's share of the labor force declined only briefly in the mid- to late 1940s. According to data from the U.S. Bureau of the Census, no less than 31.4 percent of all women worked in the civilian sector in 1950 (and thus only slightly fewer than in 1944, when 35 percent did so); by 1955, the figure had risen to 35.7 percent—with an upward trend in subsequent decades.[24] It is also significant that the ratio of single to married female employees began to reverse. In 1940, just under half of all women workers were unmarried and only about 36 percent were married; by 1950, married women (52 percent) outweighed single women (32 percent). By contrast, the share of divorced women and widows in the female labor force remained largely unchanged.[25] Another trend, which continued be-

---

21 Anderson, "Last Hired," 82–83, 96–97.
22 Anderson, "Last Hired," 97.
23 See Landry, Bart, *Black Working Wives. Pioneers of the American Family Revolution* (Berkeley and Los Angeles 2000), 88.
24 No. HS-30: "Marital Status of Women in the Civilian Labor Force: 1900-2002," in U.S. Census Bureau, *Statistical Abstract of the United States: 2003, Mini Historical Statistics*, 52–53. <www.census.gov/compendia/statab/hist_stats.html>. Slightly different figures in Spain, Daphne and Bianchi, Suzanne, *Balancing Act. Motherhood, Marriage, and Employment among American women* (New York 1996), 82. Weiner, Lynn Y., *From Working Girl to Working Mother. The Female Labor Force in the United States, 1820–1980* (Chapel Hill and London 1985), 4–7.
25 WP, June 2, 1949: "Women Workers on Increase." Cf. Weiner, *Working Girl*, 7.

yond 1950, was the rise in employment among older women when the family-raising stage of their lives was over.[26]

Although there was pressure from many quarters after the end of World War II, particularly on white women and middle-class mothers, to give up their gainful employment in favor of war returnees, many women incorporated their jobs into their self-image.[27] A 1945 survey by the Women's Bureau in the Department of Labor documented that nearly 90 percent of African American women and more than 70 percent of all female wartime employees would have liked to keep their jobs, and that women looked with new confidence on their roles as mothers and workers.[28] Frankie Cooper, a female crane operator at American Steel during the war, pithily captured the gradual change in perspective undergone by many women:

> They didn't want to go back home and some of them didn't. And if they did go back home, they never forgot, and they told their daughters, "You don't have to be just a homemaker. You can be anything you want to be." And so we've got this new generation of women.[29]

That the experience of unprecedented independence changed the attitudes of many women has already been elaborated in the research.[30] There is therefore much to be said for Susan M. Hartman's proposal to describe the immediate postwar period and the 1950s as a transitional phase that saw the juxtaposition of the conservative ideal of motherhood and domesticity, as propagated in the majority discourse, and progressive initiatives by individuals and interest groups that, for example, fought for greater equality for women in the workplace.[31]

---

[26] "Labor Force Participation Rates of Older Workers by Sex, 1950–2012," in United States Department of Labor, Women's Bureau, "Facts Over Time. Women in the Labor Force," <https://www.dol.gov/agencies/wb/data/facts-over-time/women-in-the-labor-force>.
[27] May, *Homeward Bound*, ix–xxvi, chapters 1 and 3.
[28] Anderson, *Changing Woman*, 188–191: Survey "Women Workers in Ten War Production Areas and Their Postwar Employment Plans," by the Women's Bureau in the U.S. Department of Labor, 1946. Anderson, *Wartime Women*.
[29] "Interview with Frankie Cooper," in Harris, M. J., Mitchell, Franklin D., and Schechter, Steven J. (eds.), *The Home Front. America during World War II* (New York 1984), 133.
[30] Thus, even before the boom in research on the 1950s, Eugenia Kaledin emphasized the diversity of options open to women in that decade. Kaledin, *Mothers and More*. This is also the finding of the social scientific investigation of paid employment and the role of mother in the 1950s by Miller et al., who established a correlation between role diversity and self-esteem. Miller, Melody, Moon, Phyllis, and Dempster McLain, Donna, "Motherhood, Multiple Roles, and Maternal Well-Being. Women of the 1950s," *Gender and Society* 5 (1991), no. 4, 565–582.
[31] Hartman, Susan M., "Women's Employment and the Domestic Ideal in the Early Cold War Years," in Meyerowitz, Joanne (ed.), *Not June Cleaver. Women and Gender in Postwar America, 1945–1960* (Philadelphia 1994), 84–100.

There was also a financial imperative: the consumer culture of the 1950s and the rise of many families into the middle class were by no means based exclusively on the earnings of the male breadwinner, but to a very substantial degree on wives' and mothers' contribution to the family income. Cars, household appliances, the family home, the children's college education—all these attributes of the middle-class lifestyle could not, in many cases, be financed on a single salary.[32] By the end of the 1950s, more than a third of all women in the United States were employed (37.7 percent, or 23.2 million, in 1960; 31.4 percent, or 17.8 million, in 1950).[33] More than half of working women were married and about a third had part-time jobs, with an upward trend—though a historical study of part-time women's employment in the United States is still a research desideratum.[34] The rise of the "dual earner family" as the dominant social reality in the 1970s and 1980s rested to a significant degree on the expansion of female wage labor in the 1950s and the American desire for the material "good life" in the midst of the Cold War. Finally, beginning in the 1980s, dual-earner couples made up the clear majority of American families featuring children.[35] Apart from economic necessity, this was a manifestation of the improved education of many women and the desire of numerous mothers for independence and careers. In addition, a small group of women began to earn more than their partners, again as a result of better education: while in 1960 only 6.2% of all wives earned more than their spouses, by 1980 this had risen to about 11%.[36]

---

[32] Cohen, Lizabeth, *A Consumers' Republic. The Politics of Mass Consumption in Postwar America* (New York 2003), 282–286. Spain and Bianchi, *Balancing Act*. Hartman, "Women's Employment." Kaledin, *Mothers and More*. Weiner, *Working Girl*, 89–97. On West Germany, see the instructive study by Christine von Oertzen, *Teilzeitarbeit und die Lust am Zuverdienen. Geschlechterpolitik und gesellschaftlicher Wandel in Westdeutschland 1948–1969* (Göttingen 1999). See also Anderson, *Wartime Women*. Kessler-Harris, Alice, *Out to Work. A History of Wage-Earning Women in the United States* (Oxford 1982). Hesse-Biber, Sharlene and Carter, Gregg Lee, *Working Women in America. Split Dreams* (New York 2000). Ladd-Taylor and Umansky (eds.), *Bad Mothers*.

[33] No. HS-30: "Marital Status of Women in the Civilian Labor Force: 1900–2002," in U.S. Census Bureau, *Statistical Abstract of the United States: 2003, Mini Historical Statistics*, 52–53.

[34] Initial attempts to fill this gap can be found in Waite, Linda J. and Nielsen, Mark, "The Rise of the Dual-Earner Family, 1963–1997," in Hertz, Rosanna and Marshall, Namy L. (eds.), *Working Families. The Transformation of the American Home* (Berkeley 2001), 23–41. Blossfeld, Hans-Peter (ed.), *Between Equalization and Marginalization. Women Working Part-time in Europe and the United States of America* (Oxford 1997). Hesse-Biber and Carter, *Working Women*.

[35] Wang, Wendy, Parker, Kim, and Taylor, Paul, "Breadwinner Moms. Mothers Are the Sole or Primary Provider in Four-in-Ten Households with Children; Public Conflicted about the Growing Trend," PEW Research Center, March 29, 2013, 20. www.pewsocialtrends.org. Cf. the discussion in chapter 6 of the present book.

[36] Wang, Parker, and Taylor, "Breadwinner Moms," 23.

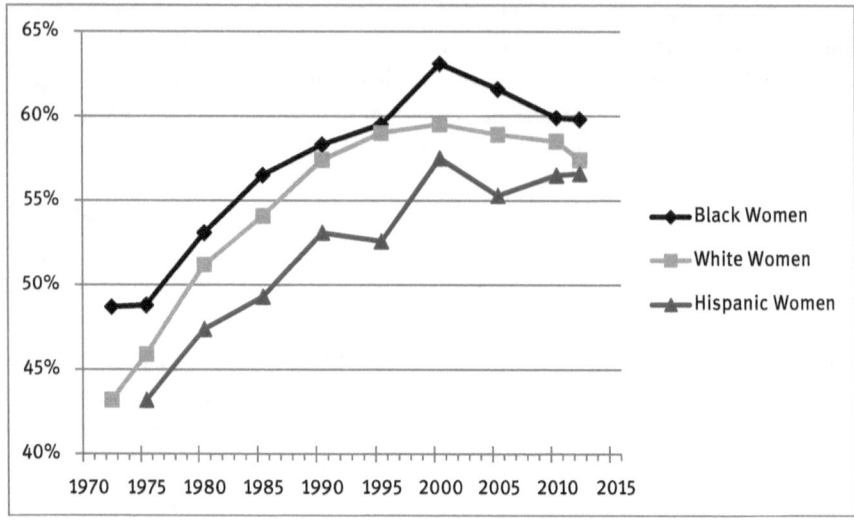

Fig. 3.1: Labor market participation of American women by race, 1972–2012.

The question of the impact on the family of female employment, particularly in the case of mothers of young children, was a bone of contention between women's rights activists, social experts, and representatives of religious movements as early as the 1940s—and it still is today.[37] However, since this debate tends to reflect the debater's ethnicity and social status, it is important to take these factors into account when considering women's labor market participation as well (Fig. 3.1).

Prior to 1970, the statistical basis is decidedly meager when it comes to the employment of African American and Mexican American women, as no employment statistics differentiated by race were collected by the Bureau of the Census.[38] Reliable data exist only from the 1970s onward, and for Mexican Americans only from 1975, but this shows that the employment rate of black women (1970: 48.7%) was generally higher than that of white women (1970: 43.2%) as well as

---

[37] Hertz, Rosanna and Marshall, Namy L. (eds.), *Working Families. The Transformation of the American Home* (Berkeley 2001), 23–41. More, "Necessary Factfinding."

[38] For a useful overview, see United States Department of Labor, Women's Bureau, "Facts Over Time, Women in the Labor Force," https://www.dol.gov/wb/stats/facts_over_time.htm. Recent social scientific studies, moreover, have pointed out that there is no theory or research centered on the labor market participation of African American women as such. However, these studies assert, it is not enough to simply carry over the models developed for African American men or white women. Corcoran, May, "The Economic Progress of African American Women," in Browne, Irene (ed.), *Latinas and African American Woman at Work: Race, Gender, and Economic Inequali.*

higher than the average for all women (1970: 43.9%). In contrast, employment among Mexican-born women has been consistently below average, only gradually approaching the mean over the last decade or so (2012).

Moreover, it has become clear that African American women have always been affected by unemployment to a far greater extent than their white American counterparts. In 1972, for example, nearly 6% of unemployed white American women contrasted with nearly 12% of unemployed black women.[39] Throughout the rest of the twentieth century, the unemployment rate among the latter was consistently twice as high as that for white American women. Possible explanations for this include the tendency for African American women to have poorer educational opportunities and their disproportionate employment as "unskilled labor," that is, without specific training and in the low-wage sector, making them easily replaceable and particularly dependent on the general state of the economy. Meanwhile, if we look at maternal employment, we find that mothers of school-age and older children made up the highest proportion of working mothers.[40]

If we summarize the trends in labor market participation presented here, we see a total of four major processes of change that form the backdrop to the issue of normative transformation to be discussed in a moment.

First, women's labor market participation rose steadily in the twentieth century, and to a particularly marked degree when the United States entered the war. The decline between 1945 and 1950 was only very gradual; from 1947 onward, the number of women in the labor force grew significantly again, and by 1955 the female employment rate had returned to wartime levels.

Second, the wartime economy provided opportunities for many African American women to obtain better-paying jobs in industry instead of domestic and service sector employment. Yet they remained disproportionately employed in the most poorly paid, low-skill jobs and were subject to racial discrimination. Still, throughout the twentieth century, this group's labor market participation consistently exceeded that of white American women.

Third, the employment of mothers of school-age children increased steadily from World War II onward, as did the employment of older women after their families had grown.

Fourth and finally, the rise of the "dual earner family," the family with two working parents, became a clear and irreversible trend from the middle of the twentieth century onward, making the "male breadwinner" an obsolete economic

---

[39] United States Department of Labor, Women's Bureau, "Facts Over Time, Women in the Labor Force," <https://www.dol.gov/agencies/wb/data/facts-over-time/women-in-the-labor-force>.
[40] United States Department of Labor, Women's Bureau, "Facts Over Time, Women in the Labor Force," <https://www.dol.gov/agencies/wb/data/facts-over-time/women-in-the-labor-force>.

model. In 1980, dual-earner families outnumbered those with a breadwinner father for the first time.

These socio-economic trends (women's employment, maternal employment, and the growing presence of dual earners) are important to correctly interpreting the sometimes highly emotional discussions of "career women," "working mothers," and "women's neurosis," and to identifying where we are dealing with future-oriented processes of renegotiation and where we are seeing fears of decline.

3.2 "Career woman or housewife?": the debate on women's employment in the shadow of World War II

> Staying at home with little to do—particularly after children have started school—will make a neurotic woman even more neurotic. It probably won't affect a psychologically healthy woman—but there are very few such women. It is definitely good for the wife and mother to get some training and go to work.[41]

In March 1945, the *New York Times* printed two related articles that explored whether life as a housewife or career woman was more fulfilling and socially important for the American woman and mother.[42] While correspondent Edith Efron argued in favor of careers for women—citing, among other things, psychologist Karen Horney's thoughts on female neurosis—Ann Maulsby, also a journalist, argued that only in her role as a housewife could the American woman become truly happy, because "no happily married woman who is honest with herself could possibly prefer the office to the home."[43] Maulsby countered Efron's call for fundamental equality between men and women with respect to paid work and housework, as well as for adequate childcare, by pointing out that career women evidently did not show their husbands the appreciation they deserved and neglected their children, which ultimately increased the divorce rate and turned children into neurot-

---

[41] To cite German-American psychologist and psychoanalyst Karen Horney, quoted in NYT, March 4, 1945: "Career Woman or Housewife?" Karen Horney (1885–1952) taught in the U.S. from the early 1930s, where she quickly made a name for herself with her work on the relationship between personality and neuroses. After a stint at the Chicago Institute for Psychoanalysis, she founded the Association for the Advancement of Psychoanalysis and finally taught at New York Medical College. She founded the *American Journal of Psychoanalysis* and is considered the founder of feminist psychology. Horney, Karen, *The Neurotic Personality of Our Time* (New York 1937). On Horney's biography, see Peters, Uwe Henrik, *Psychiatrie im Exil: Die Emigration der dynamischen Psychiatrie aus Deutschland 1933–1939* (Düsseldorf 1992), 189–201.
[42] As articulated by the title of an article in the NYT of March 4, 1945, written by Edith Efron. See also the reply by Ann Maulsby, "Housewife or Career Woman?", NYT, March 11, 1945.
[43] NYT, March 11, 1945: "Housewife or Career Woman?" See also Horney, *Neurotic Personality*.

ics who struggled to form solid bonds with others. Furthermore, she went on, the relationship between the sexes was coming apart at the seams:

> What devastation the career woman may ultimately wreak upon the American male if she persists in competing with him in his own field is an awesome subject over which the American woman well may brood.[44]

This war of words in the largest national daily newspaper in the U.S. was no isolated incident in the mid-1940s: it illustrates the fierce debate on women's and mothers' roles that had erupted as a result of female wartime employment and women's access to higher education. As the two articles already suggest, the main controversy was over white middle-class women and mothers, for whom the decision for or against wage labor was not dictated exclusively by economic necessity.[45] Moreover, scholars, journalists, and politicians attributed to them greater importance to the preservation of the American nation than, for example, African American or Latino mothers, due to explicitly or implicitly racist premises.[46]

What is also revealing about Efron's statement is that here a liberal journalist was discussing housework in the context of female neurosis, as something of a critique of the otherwise common way of describing the supposed failure of working mothers. Efron understood the term "neurosis," with Karen Horney and borrowing from Sigmund Freud, as a psychological disorder triggered by an inner conflict. In the further course of the debate, it was mainly conservative social experts who pathologized female gainful employment and, in particular, the wage labor of mothers by applying this term. The question, then, is to what extent social experts struggling for interpretive hegemony initially interpreted a conspic-

---

44 NYT, March 11, 1945: "Housewife or Career Woman?".
45 Maulsby declared that while it was a "melancholy fact" that some mothers had to work, their example should not set a precedent. Further, she asserted, the contented housewife whose life she described usually had additional "household help," a luxury that only women from the (white) middle and upper classes could afford. NYT, March 11, 1945: "Housewife or Career Woman?".
46 On the stigmatization of non-white mothers as "welfare queens" and "hyperfertile breeders," see Finzsch, Norbert, "Gouvernementalität, der Moynihan-Report und die Welfare Queen im Cadillac," in Martschukat, Jürgen (ed.), *Geschichte schreiben mit Foucault* (Frankfurt a. M. 2002), 257–282. Ladd-Taylor and Umanski (eds.), *Bad Mothers*. Gutiérrez, *Fertile Matters*. Chappell, *War on Welfare*. On the employment of African American women, see Landry, *Black Working Wives*. Anderson, *Changing Woman*. On the work of Mexican American Women, see Ruiz, Vicki L., *Cannery Women, Cannery Lives: Mexican Women, Unionization, and California Food Processing Industry, 1930–1950* (Albuquerque, NM 1987). Zavella, Patricia, *Women's Work and Chicano Families. Cannery Workers of the Santa Clara Valley* (Ithaca 1987). For a general account of female employment, see Kessler-Harris, *Out to Work*.

uous social change (increasing gainful employment among women and mothers) as pathological rather than helping modify the family ideal.

A look at the national daily press, namely the *New York Times*, *Washington Post*, and *Chicago Tribune*, however, shows that various roles for women and mothers were already being discussed in the 1940s.[47] After the United States entered World War II, press reports initially focused on women's work as a contribution to the war effort and, in particular, on working mothers and their families. The key topic here was how to organize the necessary childcare, since hardly any of the required structures existed at that point.[48] After the war, there was then an intensive debate on the extent to which women had the right to keep their jobs. Most reports stated that women and mothers worked out of economic necessity in order to secure their family's livelihood.[49] At the same time, there was an increase in the number of those, particularly female journalists, arguing that married women and mothers too should have the right to work.[50] For example, Malvina Lindsay of the *Washington Post* averred that the growing contribution even of married women to the family income was a secular trend, though she assumed a natural difference between men and women that assigned the latter to a "female sphere" of employment:

> The participation of married women in industry has steadily risen throughout the century. [. . .] This war, like all other wars has given more women a taste of economic independence, also opened new working opportunities to them. Yet women today are also showing a tendency to turn to those vocations in which they can best express their special talents.[51]

---

[47] The source basis of this section is an evaluation of reports in the daily newspapers *New York Times* and *Washington Post* for the period 1940 to 1960 in which the keywords "motherhood," "working mothers," "working women," "women's work," and "female labor" appeared. For an overview of the debates in the *Chicago Tribune*, see Hüning, Louisa, "Die Diskussion um Mutterschaft in den 1950er Jahren in den USA am Beispiel von 'Chicago Tribune' und 'Washington Post'" (BA thesis, Münster 2010).

[48] NYT, October 26, 1942: "Quick Action Urged On Day Care of Children of Working Women." NYT, March 15, 1943: "City Centers Help Working Women." WP, March 23, 1944: "Child Care."

[49] WP, October 4, 1944: Malvina Lindsay, "Women's Jobs. Married Workers," 4. NYT, May 10, 1946: "Survey Tells Why Women Take Jobs," 16. WP, March 3, 1947: "From Necessity: 16 Million Women Hold Jobs in US." NYT, January 31, 1949: "16,323,000 Women Work For Wages," 16.

[50] An important exponent of these views was Malvina Lindsay (1883–1972), a WP columnist responsible for women's issues until 1959. In her column "The Gentler Sex," Lindsay reported regularly from the start of the war onwards on the economic and non-material need of many women to work. WP, January 19, 1943: Malvina Lindsay, "The Gentler Sex: Back to the Kitchen?" WP, March 31, 1944: Malvina Lindsay, "The Gentler Sex: Peace Jobs for Women." WP, January 9, 1946: Malvina Lindsay, "The Gentler Sex. Which Women Should Work?", 14. WP, December 19, 1946: Malvina Lindsay, "Dividing the Jobs. Woman Problem," 8. NYT, March 31, 1947: "A Woman Worker Defends Her Kind." NYT, October 10, 1948: Iphigene Bettman, "A Second Career for the Older Woman," SM22.

[51] WP, December 19, 1946: Malvina Lindsay, "Dividing the Jobs. Woman Problem," 8.

At the same time, Lindsay emphasized elsewhere that many modern women also felt a psychological need for paid employment:

> Also, there is a psychic need for women to work. The days of the feminine idler, butterfly debutante, bridge fiend matron, middle-aged or elderly hotel gossip are slowly drawing to a close.[52]

In addition, articles regularly appeared on attempts by trade unionists and the Women's Bureau in the Department of Labor not only to facilitate a fusion of female employment and family responsibilities, but to initiate a longer-term change in gender roles.[53]

Two other topics dominated media coverage of families in the mid- to late 1940s: overcoming the consequences of war (fatherless families and returning fathers)[54] and the dissemination of novel expert advice (newly published guidebooks and training courses for fathers and mothers).[55] In particular, the increased demand for marriage counseling and marriage preparation courses at colleges were subject to intense discussion in the immediate postwar period.[56]

Expert advice was also mobilized to ease the transition from career to homemaking, as can be seen in the column by Mary Haworth, who answered readers' letters for the *Washington Post*.[57] Haworth advised a despairing career woman who was desperately trying to learn how to be a housewife after a twenty-year career that she should consult Mary Davis Gillies' guidebook *How to Keep House*, and encouraged her in her quest to become as perfect a housewife as possible.[58]

---

52 WP, January 9, 1946: Malvina Lindsay, "The Gentler Sex. Which Women Should Work?", 14.
53 WP, October 11, 1944: "Women Told of Hard Fight to Retain Jobs," 5. NYT, January 27, 1946: Margaret Barnard Pickel, "How Come No Jobs For Women?", SM11. NYT, February 19, 1948: Bess Furman, "'Domestic Revolution' Urged To Reduce Toil in the Home," 1.
54 NYT, May 26, 1946, "Parent and Child: Fatherless Boys and Girls." NYT, September 22, 1946: "Mothers-to-Be and Fathers." See also the detailed study: LaRossa, Ralph, *Of War and Men: World War II in the Lives of Fathers and Their Families* (Chicago 2011). Martschukat, *Ordnung des Sozialen*, 263–292.
55 NYT, September 22, 1946: "Mothers-to-Be and Fathers." NYT, April 24, 1946: "Maternity Center Has Perfect Record."
56 WP, January 4, 1947: Malvina Lindsay, "Index to Family Life, Divorce Boom." WP March 6, 1947: Malvina Lindsay, "Strengthening Family Life. Roots for Marriage." For a practical example, namely the American Institute for Family Relations (AIFR), see section 2.5 of the present book.
57 Mary Haworth (alias Elizabeth Young) published her widely read advice column "Mary Haworth's Mail" in the WP beginning in 1933. In it, she answered her readers' questions, usually with wit and irony, occasionally biting sarcasm. See *Time*, November 22, 1943: "The Press: So You Want an Answer?" (about Haworth).
58 WP August 19, 1949: "Mary Haworth's Mail: Former Business Woman, Lately Married, Now Tackling Housework for the First Time, Sends Out SOS," C1. Gillies, Mary Davis, *How to Keep House* (New York 1949).

In addition, reports on motherhood as the "chief role and most glorious career" of American women were part of the standard repertoire of the national daily press in the 1940s.[59] It is revealing, however, that toward the end of the decade, it was no longer representatives of the political and journalistic mainstream who were quoted making such statements, but Catholic clergy and ultra-conservatives.

The major American women's magazines,[60] which were aimed at a predominantly white, middle-class readership, also dealt with "working women," housewives, and mothers in the immediate postwar period, albeit with characteristic differences.[61] Joanne Meyerowitz has already pointed out that the major women's magazines of the 1950s propagated diverse women's roles,[62] but each publication also maintained its own distinct profile. In *Good Housekeeping*, for example, articles and large-format advertisements complemented each other in revealing ways. During the war, working women and their needs occupied a large proportion of its reportage, with matching visual ads promoting practical and elegant work clothes (pants), ready-made products, household appliances, and cosmetics for the working woman.[63] Conversely, when the war was over, reports about re-

---

[59] For example, the *New York Times* quoted from the Mother's Day address by New York priest John Flemming, an associate of the cardinal: "Consequently, no career or profession so completely and uniquely realizes the qualities and gifts and capabilities of woman as that of motherhood." NYT, May 9, 1949: "Role of Motherhood Lauded By Flemming," 18.

[60] The following analysis refers to an evaluation of the magazines *Good Housekeeping* (GH)—for the years 1940, 1941, 1942, 1945, 1948, 1950, 1956, and 1959, and *Ladies Home Journal* (LHJ) for the years 1945 and 1948. Non-fiction articles, columns, and advertisements were examined. For an abridged version of my argument here, see Heinemann, "Concepts of Motherhood," 72–85. For an analysis of the change in mother concepts in the advertisements of the major women's magazines in the 1950s and 1960s (LHJ, GH, McCall's, *Better Homes and Gardens*), see Mester, Anika, *Die Veränderung von Mutterkonzepten in den 1950er und 1960er Jahren in den amerikanischen Women's Magazines: Das Beispiel der Werbung* (Master's thesis, Department of History, University of Münster, 2013).

[61] The current state of research on women's magazines in the Anglo-American world can be described as exceptionally good. Damon-Moore, Helen, *Magazines for the Millions. Gender and Commerce in the Ladies' Home Journal and the Saturday Evening Post 1880–1910* (New York 1994). Scanlon, Jennifer, *Inarticulate Longings. The Ladies' Home Journal, Gender, and the Promises of Consumer Culture* (New York 1995). Walker, Nancy, *Shaping our Mothers' World. American Women's Magazines* (Jackson 2000). Ballaster, Ros et al, *Women's Worlds. Ideology, Femininity and the Woman's Magazine* (Basingstoke [et al.] 1991). On the United Kingdom, see Ferguson, Marjorie, *Forever Feminine. Women's Magazines and the Cult of Femininity* (London 1983).

[62] Meyerowitz, Joanne, "Beyond the Feminine Mystique. A Reassessment of Postwar Mass Culture 1946–1958," *Journal of American History* 79 (1993), no. 4, 1455–1482, esp. 1456–1457. Reprinted in Meyerowitz, *Not June Cleaver*, 229–262.

[63] *Good Housekeeping* (GH) (1942), February: "Housekeeping and War," 19, "What Makes Females so Useless," 46, 187. Advertisement: "Campbell's Chicken Noodle Soup: All-Out Aid for a

turning fathers, starting a family, and a new domesticity dominated. In keeping with this, advertising first showed returning GIs, then couples and nuclear families, in order to tout household appliances, cars, and other consumer goods.[64] Toward the end of the 1940s, the articles no longer talked about women's work or working mothers. The focus was now on marriage-related advice: women college graduates learned how to find a man for life, and wives how to maintain and improve their marriage. Advertising displayed a new luxury in the realms of fashion and home furnishings—once again, it was ads that immediately responded to a change in female consumers' interests.[65] There is something to be said for viewing this reorientation—toward household appliances and ready-made products for the working woman, along with luxury goods and advice columns for the modern wife—as an expression of an initial change in postwar values. Alongside the orientation toward material values and virtues such as thrift and diligence for the good of the nation, we can already discern a little self-realization for female consumers, albeit within the narrow confines of the idealized nuclear family. This, however, already demonstrates that social scientific interpretations of value change were of limited informative value to the historical analysis of norm and attitude change.

In contrast, the *Ladies' Home Journal*, the country's largest-circulation women's magazine with more than 4 million copies sold,[66] focused on the good housewife

---

Hungry Man," 59. GH (1942), March: Maxine Davis, "Women Without Men," 30, 180. "Do You Want to be a Nurse," 42–43. Column: "The Beauty Clinic: Now It's Every Woman's Job to Look Like Good News," 47, 73, 144. "If You Must Wear Slacks," 50–53. "Well Dressed for Work," 136. Advertisement: "Sanforized: Women at Work—for their Uncle Sam," 135. Advertisement: "Servel Refrigerators: I Understand a Lot of Things Since I Joined the Motor Corps," 146. GH (1942), May: "How Do You Feed Your Children in Wartime," 68, 192. GH (1942), June: "I Marry My Soldier Anyway," 33, 74. "I'm Carrying My Share for Victory," 48–49.

64 GH (1945), June: "You Married Him, Now Stick With Him," 17. "I Find Out Why Women Get Married," 26, 149. Advertisement for Ford: "You'll Be 'On the Beam,'" 70. "Singer Sewing Machines: 'Shh! You're Making Me Blush!'", 160. GH (1945), July: "Silly to Try to be Perfect," 43, 138. "Keeping Cool, Keeping House," 92. Advertisement for Norge Refrigerators: "When Your Waiting Days are Over," 15. GH (1945), August: advertisement for Westinghouse Laundromat: "When Too Many Cooks Make Work For Washday," 121. Advertisement for Ford: "There is a Ford in Your Future," back cover. GH (1945), December, advertisement: "Gorham Sterling Silver: Lucky, Lucky Me!", 113.

65 GH (1948), January: "Nothing Personal," 15, 186; "Advice to a Girl on New Year's Eve," 33, 187. GH (1948), February: Advertisement for Coca-Cola: "Hospitality in Your Hands," 137. GH (1948), April: advertisement for Quadriga Cloth: "All Those Clothes . . . On Her Husband's Salary! How Does She Do It?", 226. GH (1948), June: "Most Likely to Succeed," 33, 217.

66 The LHJ increased its circulation from more than 3.8 million (1941) to over 4.8 million (1955). Peterson, *Magazines*, 55. In February 1948, the editors even referred to a readership of 25 million Americans—on the assumption that the entire family read the magazine. See the introduction to John Steinbeck's, "Women and Children in the U.S.S.R" (photos by Robert Capa), LHJ 1948, no. 2, 45–59, here 45.

and attractive wife in its reporting and advice during the war and in the immediate postwar period.[67] When "working women" were mentioned, it was mostly in a negative context, for example with respect to the consequences of mothers' wartime employment for their families and children.[68] Numerous columns aimed to provide advice on and preserve orderly family life, such as the marital advice column "Making Your Marriage Work" (precursor to Paul Popenoe's column "Can This Marriage be Saved?", launched in 1953),[69] the visually rich "How America Lives" reports, the "Ask any Woman" column, and the "Diary of Domesticity", which focused on household issues. In contrast, John Steinbeck's report on "Women and Children in the U.S.S.R." of February 1948 is a singular text that reflects gender norms in the United States *ex negativo*, as it were, discussing them in the context of the Cold-War competition between capitalism and communism.[70] In Steinbeck's article, the accent was quite clearly on underlining how hard women worked in the Soviet Union:

> From the moment our plane landed in Leningrad, our continuing impression was of how hard Soviet women work. The stevedores who loaded the airplane were tough, stringy young women, who carried heavy bundles that would stagger an untrained man. In Kiev and Stalingrad, both destroyed by the Germans, women lifted the great chunks of rubble and iron, cleaning up the mess. Women laid bricks and hoisted timbers, they swung picks and sledge hammers on the rebuilding railroads. They drove trucks, and busses, and streetcars. In the factories we saw them at the lathes and drill presses and pneumatic hammers. On the farms they went into the fields at dawn and stopped work at dusk. They reaped, and bound, and winnowed the grain by hand. They carried sacks of wheat on their shoulders.[71]

---

67 On the other hand, Sarah Burke Odland's thesis that in 1946 the *Ladies' Home Journal* propagated a new concept of motherhood by demanding only that mothers limit themselves to the domestic sphere, while leaving other women the choice between working and being a housewife, falls short. Odland, "Unassailable Motherhood." See also Scanlon, *Inarticulate Longings*. Walker, *Mothers' World*. More generally on women's magazines, see Ballaster et al., *Women's Worlds*.
68 See, for example, the report on "duration orphans" in foster homes, children whose fathers served as soldiers and whose mothers worked in war industries and were thus unable to look after them. *Ladies' Home Journal* (LHJ) 1945, June: "Help the Children NOW!", 6. LHJ 1945, May: "Ladies are Lovely," 8. Jane Barbour, "Housewife in the Dark," 26–27, 80, 82 (about a blind housewife who nonetheless performs her duties in exemplary fashion). LHJ 1946, April: "Evelyn Sager: Profile of Success," 32, 109. LHJ 1948, June: Barbara Benson, "Husbands, Wives and Marriage," 31.
69 On this topic, see section 2.5.
70 Steinbeck, John, "Women and Children in the U.S.S.R" (photos by Robert Capa), LHJ 1948, no. 2, 45–59. The writer and later Nobel Prize winner for literature, John Steinbeck (1902–1968), toured the Soviet Union in 1947 with the photographer Robert Capa as one of the first Western journalists to do so. In 1948, his travel impressions were published as *A Russian Journal*. Steinbeck, who had become world-famous as a result of his novel about the consequences of the Great Depression, *The Grapes of Wrath* (1939), had already worked during the war as a reporter for the *New York Herald Tribune* and the magazines *Time* and *Life*.
71 Steinbeck, "Women," 45.

Steinbeck left no room for doubt that women had to work to rebuild their devastated country and replace the ten million fallen soldiers:

> There is a great shortage of manpower in Russia. Ten million men of working age are gone. Women have taken over their work. They have to, the work must be done.[72]

But he was particularly astonished that Soviet women, despite their extremely hard work and lives full of privation, had retained a certain "femininity" even without elegant fashion, perfume, or makeup—items that were so self-evidently available to American women. His example is the women in Stalingrad, which had been reduced to rubble:

> This Stalingrad housewife, hanging out her laundry in the sun, is one of many we saw who continue to live right on in the caves they have constructed of what once were houses. We were amazed not only that they could survive such conditions, but that they also remained feminine, managing to look neat and fresh.[73]

Joanne Meyerowitz has read this article as a defense of American women and a plea for women's political participation.[74] This is certainly not wrong, but Steinbeck used this account of women's incomparably worse living and working conditions on the other side of the Iron Curtain chiefly to evoke a humanist ideal that transcended the clash of competing political and economic systems: "Russians are people too." Yet, when Steinbeck registers with relief that while women in the Soviet Union worked much harder than their counterparts in the U.S., most of them appeared neat and well-groomed, in other words, "feminine," he is also articulating the dominant image of women in the U.S. during the Cold War. The great extent to which the competition between political-economic concepts during the Cold War was fought out at the level of gender norms and the national image of the family was illustrated a decade later by the so-called "Kitchen Debate." Here, Vice President Richard Nixon tried to convince Soviet Premier Nikita Khrushchev of the merits of the U.S. model of society during the opening of the American National Exhibition in Moscow in July 1959. His example was the ideal American suburban home, with breadwinner father and housewife-mother, the latter residing in a modern fitted kitchen full of electronic appliances. For Nixon, freedom in

---

72 Steinbeck, "Women," 45.
73 "The women we saw do not have the clothes, the ease, the food, the cosmetics that women in America have." Steinbeck, "Women," 57.
74 Meyerowitz, "Feminine Mystique," 241.

the United States was not a matter of political structures or citizenship, but of the housewife's freedom to consume.⁷⁵

3.3 "Mom as a social problem": the debate on "momism" and failing mothers in the 1940s

But it was not only working mothers who drew criticism from experts and concerned contemporaries; the exemplary mother and housewife—"mom"—was also at the center of a heated debate between publicists, journalists, social scientists, and mothers themselves in the 1940s.⁷⁶ The so-called "momism debate" was triggered by the bestsellers *Generation of Vipers* by Philip Wylie (1942) and Edward Strecker's *Their Mother's Sons* (1946), each of which dealt with the experience of World War II from its own perspective.⁷⁷ Philip Wylie declared that the average American mother had turned her sons into dependent, unmanly beings through an excess of control and attention. As a result, and given the universal cult of motherhood, American society was in grave danger:

> Mom is an American creation. [. . .] Mom is everywhere and everything, and damned near everybody, and from her depends all the rest of the US. [. . .] But never before has a great nation of brave and dreaming men absent-mindedly created a huge class of idle middleaged women.⁷⁸ [. . .]

Instead of letting their sons grow into self-determined men, they wrecked their dreams and goals in early childhood, leaving them incapable of leading more than a mediocre existence in the shadow of a quasi-religious mother cult:

> Mom had already shaken him out of the notion of being a surveyor in the Andes which had bloomed in him when he was nine years old, so there was nothing left to do but take a

---

75 See May, *Homeward Bound*, 10–13. The transcript of the "Kitchen Debate" of July 24, 1959, can be found at <https://www.cia.gov/readingroom/docs/1959-07-24.pdf>.
76 See the quote "mom as a social problem" by Edward Strecker, quoted in WP, December 1, 1946: Clip Boutell, "Untie Those Apron Strings: American 'Mom' Is a Menace," S6.
77 Wylie, *Generation of Vipers*. Strecker, Edward, *Their Mothers' Sons: The Psychiatrist Examines an American Problem* (New York 1946). Philip G. Wylie (1902–1971) was already a well-known American author of science fiction novels (among others *When Worlds Collide*, 1933), short stories, and essays before the publication of *A Generation of Vipers*. Edward A. Strecker (1896–1959) was a professor of psychiatry at the University of Pennsylvania Medical College and a recognized consultant in psychiatric matters to public authorities and government agencies. During World War II, he had selected and trained army psychiatrists on behalf of the U.S. Army. In *Their Mother's Sons*, he processed the experiences he had gained through the mass screening of soldiers.
78 Wylie, *Generation*, 197–200.

stockroom job in the hairpin factory and try to work up to the vice-presidency. Thus the women of America raped the men, not sexually, unfortunately, but morally, since neuters come hardly by morals.[79]

Using deliberately overblown, sometimes scathing and hurtful imagery, Wylie set out his view of the "all-American mom" as an uninformed and politically disinterested, consumerist housewife and mother who found a rich field of activity in the countless women's clubs:

> She is a middle-aged puffin with an eye like a hawk that has just seen a rabbit twitch far below. She is about twenty-five pounds over-weight, with no sprint, but sharp heals and a hard backhand, which she does not regard as a foul but a womanly defense. In thousands of her there is not enough sex appeal to budge a hermit ten paces off a rock ledge. She none the less spends several hundred dollars a year on permanents and transformations, pomades, cleansers, rouges, lipsticks, and the like—and fools nobody except herself. [. . .]
>
> Knowing nothing about medicine, art, science, religion, law, sanitation, civics, hygiene, psychology, morals, history, geography, poetry, literature, or any other topic except the all-consuming one of momism, she seldom has any special interest in *what*, exactly, she is doing as a member of any of these endless organizations, so long as it is *something*.[80]

Edward Strecker, meanwhile, drew on his experiences as an army psychologist in World War II, lamenting in *Their Mothers' Sons* that overprotective mothers were responsible for the high rate of mental illness among soldiers and thus indirectly threatened national security.[81] He made a clear distinction between "mom" (the mother who refused to release her children into independent adulthood and was thus to blame for the functional shortcomings described in the recruits) and "mother" (who succeeded in releasing her children from emotional dependency). A questionnaire at the end of the book was supposed to enable the reader to find out whether she too bore within her the predisposition to be a "mom."[82] Unlike Wylie, however, Strecker stated that it would be wrong to blame "mom" alone for her situation: "Mom is not of her own making. . . . Furthermore, momism is the product of a social system veering toward a matriarchy in which each individual mom plays only a small part."[83]

Both authors thus portrayed the "all-American mom" as either ridiculous and superfluous (Wylie) or as a danger to the nation (Strecker). Despite all the exaggeration, their acerbic criticism captured the spirit of the times, as evident in the

---

[79] Wylie, *Generation*, 200.
[80] Emphasis in original. Wylie, *Generation*, 201–204.
[81] Wylie, *Generation*, 194–217. Strecker, *Mothers' Sons*.
[82] Strecker, *Mothers' Sons*, 205–210.
[83] Strecker, *Mothers' Sons*, 30.

intensive reception of their texts.[84] On the basis of their observations, a lively public debate then developed by the end of the 1940s on the causes and effects of "momism."[85] It is important to note that Wylie did not oppose women's work in principle, but rather, as Rebecca Plant has pointed out, criticized women who allowed themselves to be provided for by their husbands and led lives of affluence.[86] His aim was to strip white middle-class mothers of their influence as moral authorities ("moral motherhood") and to denounce as out of keeping with the times the vision of the self-sacrificing mother who was above any factual criticism. But this message was deliberately ignored by most recipients, who used Wylie's *Generation of Vipers* either to undergird their critique of modern women or their call for a return to "Victorian domesticity."

Thus, in *Love in America. An Informal Study of Manners and Morals in American Marriage* (1943), publicist David L. Cohn, citing Wylie, argued that the role of women in U.S. society urgently needed to change through the rediscovery of domestic virtues.[87] The most important task of women was "the continuing mission of humanizing our society, of civilizing it, of keeping it civilized." Otherwise, U.S. society faced ruin: "Unless there is a sweeping revaluation of values in this country after the war, we shall perish. And perish not at the hands of the Axis, but at our own hands."[88]

---

84 WP, June 13, 1943: "Lonely Hearts Dept." NYT, December 8, 1946: E. B. Garside, "The Habit of Momism," 199. WP, December 1, 1946: Clip Boutell, "Untie Those Apron Strings: American 'Mom' Is a Menace," 6. *Washington Post* columnist Mary Haworth also referred to Strecker several times in her column when advising young couples on how to move toward independence in the face of an overly domineering parental home. WP, December 17, 1946: "Mary Haworth's Mail: Married a Year, Girl and Husband Make Home with Her Parents," 14.

85 On the Momism Debate, see Plant, *Mom*, 19–54, who quite rightly points out that Wylie criticizes not only the child-rearing methods of American mothers, but also their wasteful consumption and their claim to moral superiority. On Strecker, see ibid., 101–103. See also Buhle, Mari Jo, *Feminism and its Discontents. A Century of Struggle with Psychoanalysis* (Boston 1998). Feldstein, Ruth, *Motherhood in Black and White. Race and Sex in American Liberalism, 1930–1965* (Ithaca 2000). On the significance of the momism debate to the renegotiation of gender norms and the relationship between the government and the individual in the immediate postwar period, see Stieglitz, Olaf, "Is Mom to Blame? Anti-Communist Law Enforcement and the Representation of Motherhood in Early Cold War U.S. Film," in Heinemann, Isabel (ed.), *Inventing the Modern American Family. Family Values and Social Change in 20th Century United States* (Frankfurt a. M. 2012), 244–264, esp. 250.

86 Plant, *Mom*, 32–33.

87 Cohn, David L., *Love in America. An Informal Study of Manners and Morals in American Marriage* (New York 1943).

88 NYT, May 23, 1943: "American Love Scene," BR8. See also WP, June 13, 1943: "Lonely Hearts Dept.," L5.

In 1949, physician Lester Warren Sontag, director of the Samuel Fels Research Institute for the Study of Human Development in Yellow Springs, Ohio, and leader of a long-term study on child development, went one step further. The majority of American mothers, he asserted, were not living up to their responsibilities. They felt unfulfilled and, as a result, increasingly suffered from mental illness. Since they had been brought up for achievement and competition, they did not regard housework and child-rearing as sufficiently fulfilling activities:

> Marriage poses many problems of a frustrating nature to the woman who has been reared and geared to competition, to freedom and monetary reward. These factors are not inherent in homemaking.[89]

It was not just the president of the otherwise rather conservative New York State Federation of Women's Clubs, Mrs. Illiam H. Golding, and popular writer Mary Ella Roberts Rinehart, who objected to such sweeping criticism of mothers.[90] Ferdinand Lundberg, sociologist and co-author of the bestseller *Modern Women: The Lost Sex* (1947), also conceded that at most one-third of American mothers were failing; the rest were doing their job well. In particular, the "pressures of modern life" and their own contradictory desires for motherhood *and* a career, he emphasized, were making mothers' task more difficult.[91]

By contrast, the aforementioned *Washington Post* columnist Malvina Lindsay recommended that mothers revolt: it was simply unfair to blame them for all of society's ills, from the drastic rise in unfitness for service among young recruits to the mental weakness of the younger generation.[92]

> Nearly everyone is taking a whack at "Mom" these days. She is blamed not only for all the psychoneurotics that the war uncovered, but for the Nation's alarming mental illness and juvenile delinquency, for the boyishness of American men, for virtually all adults who are soft, weak, selfish, maladjusted, incompetent.[93]

Her conclusion was simple: women needed more support both from their spouses and from society in general.

---

89 WP, November 16, 1949: "Expert Finds U.S. Women Poor Mothers," M13. See also WP, November 27, 1949: "Motherhood, 1949 Model," B4.
90 NYT, November 20, 1949: "U.S. Mothers Held Best in the World," 80.
91 NYT, November 20, 1949: "U.S. Mothers Held Best in the World," 80. WP, November 27, 1949: "Motherhood, 1949 Model," B4. Farnham and Lundberg, *Modern Woman*.
92 "In view of what she has faced, it might seem that 'Mom' should be the one to revolt. Too much has been expected of her in the past, and in doing it, she has had too little help from 'Pop' as well as from society." WP, August 30, 1944: Malvina Lindsay, "'Mom' Stirs a Tempest: New Revolt Pattern," 6.
93 WP, January 18, 1947: Malvina Lindsay, "Society's Scapegoat: In Defense of 'Mom'", 4.

> If women, in rearing the next generation of children, get more assistance from schools, churches, public health agencies [. . .] and above all from marriage partners who are educated to a greater sense of responsibility in the home, there will be much less danger of their becoming either matriarchs or maternal vampires.[94]

What all the authors of this debate on "momism" and "deficient mothers" in the 1940s have in common is that they propagated a highly exclusive notion of the American mother as white and middle class–without ever being criticized for it. This underscores once again the "color blindness" that characterized the entire public discourse on motherhood, women's work, and equality in the 1940s and 1950s. It is also revealing that the supposedly lazy middle-aged housewife and mother ("idle homemaker") was the focus of criticism, rather than the working wife and mother. Nevertheless, the momism debate formed an important reference point for the wider public debate on gender norms and women's work in the 1950s and 1960s.

3.4 "Women aren't men" or the "return of the new women": motherhood and women's employment in the 1950s

Given that the consumer culture of the 1950s was largely based on an increase in family income as a result of many wives' employment, it is surprising that at first little changed on the normative level. The U.S. held fast at least to the ideal of the nuclear family with breadwinner-father and housewife-mother. Though almost 25 percent of all married women were working by 1950 and around 32 percent by 1960, the 1950s are still regarded today as the "golden age of the family," one characterized by family stability, a large number of children and rigid gender roles.[95]

Yet contemporaries were already discussing the necessity and social consequences of mothers' wage labor in a nuanced way. The national daily press of the 1950s, for example, featured two lines of argument with respect to maternal work. The first emphasized the socially important reproductive and child-rearing function of women and mothers. The key idea here was that they were the ones looking after the nucleus of society, the family, and rendered an indispensable service to society by raising children. Therefore, they should concentrate on this core competence rather than pursuing wage labor.[96] Journalist Agnes E. Meyer

---

[94] WP, August 30, 1944: Malvina Lindsay, "'Mom' Stirs a Tempest: New Revolt Pattern," 6.
[95] For recent research critical of this notion, see Coontz, *The Way We Never Were*. Meyerowitz, *Not June Cleaver*. Weiss, *To Have and to Hold*.
[96] WP, August 14, 1950: "Women Aren't Men." WP, August 15, 1950: "No Job More Exacting Than Housewife's." WP, May 11, 1957: "Marriage and Motherhood Most Popular Role." CT, May 9, 1954: "Mother's Job Is Important, Too."

took this position to an almost grotesque extreme in her essay "Women Aren't Men," which originally appeared in *Atlantic Monthly* in August 1950 and was immediately reprinted by the *Washington Post* as a series of short articles.[97] Meyer, herself the mother of five children, made an unequivocal plea:

> What a modern woman has to recapture is the wisdom that just being a women is her central task and her greatest honor. [. . .] Wherever women are functioning, whether in the home or in a job, they must remember that their chief function as women is a capacity for warm, understanding, and charitable human relationships. Women are throwing their greatest natural gift out of the window when they cease to function as experts in cooperative living.[98]

In a trenchant reckoning with the ambition and selfishness of "career women," Meyer argued that the modern woman must relearn humility and prove herself as a guardian of moral values, rather than demanding equality and giving her "destructive sexuality" free rein.[99] By ensuring that her marriage lasts, she was also saving society from the "moral suicide" caused by the divorce boom and individualism.[100] What sounds like a reprise of the conservative critique of divorce and the call to restore conservative gender roles from the first decades of the twentieth century[101] was evidently still attractive in the early 1950s, as the piece made the leap from the intellectual *Atlantic Monthly* into the columns of the *Washington Post*.[102] The fact that Meyer, a mother of five, was outraged by working mothers and "career women," but had made a career for herself as a successful journalist and publicist–a fact that went undiscussed and uncriticized–is one of the ironies of this debate.

---

97 Agnes E. Meyer (1887–1970) was a U.S. journalist who worked for the *New York Morning Sun*, among other publications, and who continued to write as the mother of five children. She corresponded with Thomas Mann from the 1930s to the 1950s. Meyer, Agnes E., *Out of These Roots. The Autobiography of an American Woman* (Boston, MA 1953). Meyer, Agnes E., *Education for a New Morality* (New York 1957). Vaget, Hans R. (ed.), *Thomas Mann, Agnes E. Meyer, Briefwechsel 1937–1955* (Frankfurt a. M. 1992).
98 WP, August 15, 1950: "No Job More Exacting Than Housewife's." See also the other articles in the Meyer series: WP, August 14, 1950, beginning: "Women Aren't Men." WP, August 16, 1950: "Too Many Females Emphasize Success." WP, August 17, 1950: "'Sex Freedom' is the Path of Delusion." WP, August 18, 1950: "Womanhood Holds Key to Better Society."
99 WP, August 16, 1950: "Too Many Females Emphasize Success." WP, August 17, 1950: "'Sex Freedom' is the Path of Delusion."
100 August 18, 1950: "Womanhood Holds Key to Better Society."
101 See chapter 1 of the present book.
102 Meyer, Agnes E., "Women Aren't Men," *Atlantic Monthly* 194 (1950), August, 32–36. WP, August 13–17, 1950.

But more interesting than this radically anti-feminist position, which clearly echoed the tone of the "momism debate" of the late 1940s,[103] are readers' letters, which give us an insight into the self-image of staunch housewives who felt challenged by the general trend toward women's work. Longtime *Washington Post* columnist Mary Haworth, for example, kicked off a wave of protest in February 1953. She had described the desire of a mother working against her will to finally be a housewife as "your frustrated longing to be a cherished parasite" and advised her to seek the reason for her dissatisfaction with her husband's lack of economic success in herself.[104] As a result, she was inundated with angry statements from other housewives who felt personally denigrated and lamented a disastrous shift in family values. One mother objected to being forced into the "rat race" of job and family simply because it had become the order of the day:

> I don't object to a woman's being both careerist and homemaker if she has exceptional energy and ability and can afford help. But I do object to wives being pushed into this rat race simply because it is the trend of the times [. . .].[105]

Another letter writer stated:

> The whole pattern of family life is being altered, for the worse, by women working outside the home. It is true that many women work of necessity, to support dependents, but when a woman has a husband making a fair income she should content herself with that, especially if they have children. Social conditions may change but human nature doesn't change—and a married man should support his wife if he expects to be respected in the home.[106]

She expressed satisfaction that none of her sons was married to a working wife, which meant they were "worthy to be called men."[107] Other women asked with concern whether women no longer had the right to support from their husbands, or whether mutual appreciation and support were not in fact the basis of every marriage.[108] This minor episode shows that the mothers concerned perceived the

---

[103] According to Joanne Meyerowitz, in the nearly 500 articles she examined from the monthly and weekly press (1946–1958), only just under 2 percent took a comparably critical position on the subject of women's work. Meyerowitz, "Feminine Mystique," 1475.
[104] WP, December 12, 1953: "Mary Haworth's Mail, Seek Solution in Self-Examination."
[105] WP, March 17, 1953: reader's letter from R.S. in "Mary Haworth's Mail, Housewives Take Up Cudgel," 28.
[106] WP, March 17, 1953: reader's letter from G.E. in "Mary Haworth's Mail, Housewives Take Up Cudgel," 28.
[107] WP, March 17, 1953: reader's letter from G.E., in "Mary Haworth's Mail, Housewives Take Up Cudgel," 28.
[108] Letters from B.N. and J.Y. in WP, March 18, 1953: "Mary Haworth's Mail, What Price the Sturdy Oak?".

discussion on women's work and, in particular, on gainful employment, as a personal challenge and a fundamental threat. It is telling that all the letter writers complained about a change in family values ("trend of the times," "pattern of family life being altered").

A second strand of reporting, meanwhile, discussed the circumstances under which it was possible for women and mothers to combine employment and family duties. While numerous articles underscored that part-time work for mothers was only permissible in cases of absolute economic necessity,[109] by the end of the 1950s a growing number of commentators were advising women to take up employment for the sake of their personal development.[110] For example, a study commissioned by the National Manpower Council argued that American women around the mid-twentieth century had managed to develop "a new system for combining marriage and career." Malvina Lindsay of the *Washington Post* acknowledged that many mothers gained a "sense of personal independence" from employment and the "stimulation of working in an adult environment." The expansion of women's work, she claimed, was the result of societal trends since the turn of the century and was no cause for concern:

> However, every new woman whether of the 1840s, the 1890s or the 1920s, has been regarded as a threat to the home and to society. Whatever critics may say of the mid-century "new woman" she seems to be here to stay.[111]

Others emphasized the professional and social successes of working women—ultimately, they were even the best housewives.[112] One key topic was the question of a possible connection between "working mothers" and juvenile delinquency. Most articles concluded that working mothers could not be held responsible for

---

[109] WP, September 13, 1951: "New Figure of Controversy: The Working Mother." WP, May 31, 1954: "Should Mother Stay at Home?" WP, September 7, 1954: "Why Do They Work? They Have To. Ages of Working Women Reach from 16 to 80."
[110] CT, March 21, 1954: "More Freedom for Housewives?" See also the readers' letters quoted in the following article. The author of the article herself takes the opposite view: CT, July 19, 1955: "Mother Should Have Time for Herself, Says Reader." WP, October 9, 1955: "Mission Work Begins at Home." CT, March 9, 1957: "'Let Wife Earn It' Trend Hit by Professor."
[111] WP, March 14, 1957, Malvina Lindsay, "'New Woman' Seen in Job Revolution."
[112] WP, May 6, 1950: "Less Than Half of U.S. Women Find Housework is a Pleasure." WP, December 29, 1950: "Sweet Briar President Says: Working Wives Are Here to Stay." WP, December 3, 1954: "Better Housekeepers Than Stay-At-Home Sisters. Working Wives Rate Tops." WP, June 17, 1956: "Working Women Amazons in Accomplishments." WP, September 25, 1957: "Important Working Women. She's Mrs. Housewife USA."

its rise, which affected the children of working mothers and housewives alike.[113] This conclusion is rather surprising given that recent research emphasizes the great extent to which the fear of rising juvenile delinquency in the 1950s served to subject families—and the gender norms and generational relationships lived out within them—to expert-backed regulation.[114] These expert interventions also conveyed a very specific image of parents' responsibility for their children, one that was racially encoded and that disregarded economic and social realities. While fathers had to be good role models for their sons, mothers' primary responsibility was to raise their children. Through this propagation of a distinct middle-class lifestyle, members of ethnic minorities and the working class were stigmatized *a priori* as potential criminals.[115]

In the women's magazine *Good Housekeeping*, meanwhile, the focus of the now sparse reports on women's work shifted in the 1950s to the part-time employment of wives and mothers in view of the steady increase in this variant of women's work.[116] Once again, advertising was in tune with the times, showing the part-time working mother with products designed to make her job easier (ready-to-eat meals, household appliances, and Avon cosmetics that could be selected at home after work).[117] A 1956 full-page ad from the Chevrolet company provides a perfect illustration of this. The image shows a woman unloading her groceries from a new Chevrolet convertible in front of a single-family suburban home. The accompanying text states, "You want me to come home from work and fix a six-course dinner? Then I want a Chevrolet of my own!"[118] But rather than signaling a change in gender norms, the ad showed that employment was merely being integrated into household maintenance and childcare—which included the evening

---

[113] WP, May 8, 1954: "Working Wife Gets Boost." WP, April 17, 1957: "Working Mothers Not to Blame." WP, October 26, 1957: "Working Women Make Life Better." Only the report on the scientific findings of two Harvard Law School criminologists, Sheldon Glueck and Eleanor Turoff Glueck, took the opposite position. WP, August 14, 1957: "Job Flitting Mothers Criticized."

[114] Mackert, "Recall the Kinds of Parents." Gilbert, James, *A Cycle of Outrage: America's Reaction to the Juvenile Delinquent in the 1950s* (New York and Oxford: Oxford University Press, 1986).

[115] Gilbert, *A Cycle of Outrage*. Mackert, *Jugenddelinquenz*.

[116] GH, January 1959: "How to Keep House and Get Paid for it," 98–99. GH: February 1959, "How to Get a Job as a Pollster," 123–124. GH, April 1959: "How to Become Officer at the WAC," 165–166.

[117] GH, March 1950, advertisement: "Betty Crocker Enriched Flour," 178. GH, September 1956, advertisement: "Palmolive: You're Prettier Than You Think You Are . . . and Can Prove It with a Palmolive Bar!", 130, advertisement: "KitchenAid: How to Make Your Children Sparkle," 138, advertisement: "Avon: Take Time Out for Beauty When Your Avon Representative Calls," 156–157, advertisement: "Crisco Fried Foods: Afraid You Serve Your Family Fried Foods Too Often? Don't Worry . . .," 179.

[118] GH September 1956, advertisement: "Chevrolet: If He Complains About those Last-Minute Dinners . . . Put This Next to His Napkin," 25.

meal for one's husband. At the same time, advertising from the early 1950s onward increasingly celebrated the family; all products that had previously been advertised through individual beauties or efficient housewives were now presented within the family.[119] Thus, one ad iconized the nuclear family–using the example of a cake mix:

> The love's so thick you can cut it. The light of the candles dances on a face all bright with joy—and from two soft brown eyes glows a radiance strong enough to weld a gay young mother and a strong young father and a small young daughter into a single whole. And time stands still. This is now. This is a family.[120]

The press coverage of the 1950s on the topic of "working mothers" thus initially confirms Joanne Meyerowitz's argument that postwar journalism about women was diverse and did not one-sidedly privilege the role of housewife and mother. There were unquestionably both articles that considered the housewife role and motherhood to be the only valid female activity and reports that evaluated women's and mothers' employment as socially relevant and contributing to women's economic and personal development. The contours of the debate were sharper than in the 1940s, and more and more women expressed their views in readers' letters. But which evaluations of female employment managed to gain traction in the debate over the long term? Which views attained interpretive hegemony and when?

3.5 "Modern women's neurosis": the working woman's psyche and reproduction as sites of negotiation of divergent gender role conceptions, 1950–1970

From the early 1950s onward, the debate on women's work gained a new facet.[121] In the midst of the baby boom, mostly male psychologists, physicians, and demographers began to worry about the mental health of working women and mothers,

---

119 GH, January 1950, advertisement: "Ipana Tooth Paste: This Maryland Family Guards Teeth and Gums Both—With Ipana Care!", 1. Advertisement: "Listerine Antiseptic: When a Cold Threatens to Run Through a Family . . . It's Listerine Antiseptic Quick! . . . For Everybody," 3. GH, June 1950, advertisement: "American Airlines: How to Lower the Cost of Bringing UP Your Family," 45. GH, September 1956, advertisement: "Lux Liquid: For Making Child's Play of Dishwashing, There's No Liquid or Powder Like Lux Liquid. For a Family This Size, You Do About 3,500 Dishes a Month," 68.
120 GH September 1956, advertisement: "Betty Crocker White Cake Mix: Daddy's Cake," 33.
121 This section revisits some ideas I first articulated in the essay "Social Experts and Working Women's Reproduction: from 'Working Women's Neurosis' to the Abortion Debate, 1950–1980,'

their understanding of their roles, their sexuality, and the connection between these aspects and fertility.[122] The focus was exclusively on the white mother and her children; the reproduction of African American women or members of other minorities was to be curbed rather than encouraged.[123] This discussion was no chance occurrence–it reflected alarm over the biological survival of the American nation. Here the findings of modern biology and eugenics breathed new life into an old stereotype of "national decline" and "race suicide," which was updated in the context of the Cold War.[124] Also at play here were the findings of modern statistics and the boom in the new discipline of demography, which was made to serve a targeted population policy.[125] In addition, over the course of the decade the results of long-term empirical studies on the sexual behavior of American women, such as the Kinsey reports, were published, and in the 1970s the research of William Masters and Virginia Johnson on sexuality and sexual dysfunction rose to prominence.[126] Ultimately, the debate on the reproduction and fertility of

---

in Heinemann, Isabel (ed.), *Inventing the Modern American Family. Family Values and Social Change in 20th Century United States* (Frankfurt a. M. 2012), 124–151.

122 On the importance of experts in the early reproduction debate, see D'Emilio, John and Freedman, Estelle, *Intimate Matters. A History of Sexuality in America* (Chicago 1997). Ehrenreich, Barbara and English, Deirdre, *For Her Own Good. 150 Years of the Expert's Advice to Women* (London 1979), 243–281.

123 For a detailed account of attempts at both federal and state level to limit minorities' authority over their own reproduction, see Solinger, *Beggars and Choosers*. Gutiérrez, *Fertile Matters*. Roberts, *Killing the Black Body*.

124 See sections 1.4 and 2.2 of the present book.

125 Between 1946 and 1959, the national birth rate reached an all-time high of more than 24 births per 1,000 people per year; from 1960 onward, this trend declined to a historic all-time low of 14.6 births per 1,000 people in 1975. These statistics provided a rational backdrop to the debate on the reproduction of white American women and the impact on the nation of female employment and changing family concepts. Center for Disease Control and Prevention, "Vital Statistics of the United States: Live Birth, Birth Rates, and Fertility Rates, by Race: United States, 1909–94," <www.cdc.gov/nchs/data/statab/t941x01.pdf>. On the rise of statistics and forecasting in the twentieth century, see Igo, *The Averaged American*. On the intertwining of family planning and population policy, see Unger, Corinna, "Family Planning: A Rational Choice? The Influence of Systems Approaches, Behavioralism, and Rational Choice Thinking on Mid-Twentieth Century Family Planning Programs," in Hartmann, Heinrich and Unger, Corinna (eds.), *A World of Populations: Transnational Perspectives on Demography in the Twentieth Century* (New York 2014), 58–82.

126 Kinsey, Alfred, *Sexual Behavior in the Human Male* (Philadelphia and Bloomington 1948). Kinsey, Alfred, *Sexual Behavior in the Human Female* (Philadelphia and Bloomington 1953). Masters, William and Johnson, Virginia, *Homosexuality in Perspective* (Boston 1979). Masters, William and Johnson, Virginia, *Human Sexual Inadequacy* (Boston 1970). Masters, William and Johnson, Virginia, *Human Sexual Response* (Boston 1966). Masters, William and Johnson, Virginia, *Human Sexuality* (Toronto 1982). Masters, William and Johnson, Virginia, *The Pleasure Bond* (Boston

the white American woman provides a vivid example of how, around the middle of the twentieth century, social experts of various stripes attempted to reshape society in light of the findings of modern science, which ultimately led to the rebiologization of the social.

In the first instance, however, the debate revitalized the 1940s critique of motherhood familiar from the "momism" controversy. Here, an important ultraconservative text of the late 1940s that had construed the modern woman as a risk to the nation, *Modern Woman: The Lost Sex* (1947), proved to be a key point of reference. In their national bestseller, journalist Ferdinand Lundberg and psychiatrist Marynia Farnham had presented the psyche and behavior of the modern woman as "one of modern civilization's major unsolved problems."[127] This, they argued, was as significant as the other social challenges of the time, namely "crime, vice, poverty, epidemic disease, juvenile delinquency, group intolerance, racial hatred, divorce, neurosis and even periodic unemployment, inadequate housing, care in old age, and the like."

> Women are a problem not only as individuals (some are, some are not), but collectively, as a separate group with special functions within the structure of society. As a group, and generally, they are a problem to themselves, their children and families, to each other, to society as a whole.[128]

The authors understood "healthy womanhood" as "motherhood" and criticized modern women for striving for a good education, careers, and personal fulfillment. This, they contended, always occurred at the expense of children: given their mothers' neuroses, they themselves were bound to become attachment-deficient neurotics. Worse yet, modern working women shrank from their biological predisposition and reproductive duty, causing serious damage to the nation. Here, then, the critique of female employment was repeated in the idiom of pathologization; women's work was classified either as female "neurosis" or as the "masculinization of women":

1975). Robinson, Paul, *The Modernization of Sex. Havelock Ellis, Alfred Kinsey, William Masters, and Virginia Johnson* (New York 1976).

127 Farnham and Lundberg, *Modern Woman*. Ferdinand Lundberg (1902–1995) was an investigative journalist who had worked for the *Wall Street Journal*, the *Chicago Daily News*, and the *New York Herald Tribune*, among other publications. He published numerous critical bestsellers exposing the connection between money and power, including a biography of William Randolph Hearst, *Imperial Hearst: A Social Biography* (1936) and *America's Sixty Families* (1937). Marynia F. Farnham was a psychiatrist.

128 Lundberg and Farnham, *Modern Women*, 1.

> Work that entices women out of their homes and provides them with prestige only at the price of feminine relinquishment, involves a response to masculine strivings. The more importance outside work assumes, the more are the masculine components of women's nature enhanced and encouraged. [. . .] The plain fact is that increasingly we are observing the masculinization of women and with it enormously dangerous consequences to the home, the children (if any) dependent on it, and to the ability of the woman, as well as her husband, to obtain sexual gratification.[129]

What was articulated here in the context of a bestseller aimed at a broad audience received scientific backing from modern reproductive medicine in the 1950s.[130] In a highly regarded essay from 1952, for instance, physician and social psychologist Therese Benedek described the connection between infertility and psychological factors, reducing it to a clash between the "biologic needs" and "cultural values" associated with motherhood:

> In other words, women incorporating the value-system of a modern society may develop personalities with rigid ego-defenses against their biological needs. The conflict which arises from this can be observed clinically not only in the office of the psychiatrist, but also in the office of the gynecologist and even of the endocrinologist.[131]

For Benedek, the value system of modern society had crucially influenced the role of mother in two ways: first, through changes in the "aims and aspirations of women" and in the relationship between spouses, and second, through changing "patterns of childcare."[132] Since girls too were increasingly being brought up to be active, extroverted (in effect: masculine) individuals, they struggled consciously

---

129 Farnham and Lundberg, *Modern Women*, 235.

130 See also the reception of the text in the social science discourse of the time: affirmative reviews by Arnold W. Green in, *Annals of the American Academy of Political and Social Science*, vol. 251 (May 1947), 187–188 and Sophie H. Drinker, "Marriage Council of Philadelphia," *Marriage and Family Living*, vol. 9, 3 (August 1947), 75. For a critical take, see for example Donald W. Calhoun, *Social Forces*, vol. 26, 3 (March 1948), 350–351.

131 Therese Benedek (1890–1977) was a Hungarian-American physician, social psychologist, and psychoanalyst who initially worked as the latter in Leipzig. After emigrating from Nazi Germany to the United States in 1936, she conducted research at the Chicago Institute of Psychoanalysis and also maintained a private practice as a psychoanalyst. She broke new ground by collaborating with endocrinologist Boris B. Rubinstein; their studies on the psychoendocrinology of women were considered pioneering. Benedek, Therese, "Infertility as Psychosomatic Disease," *Fertility and Sterility* 3 (1952), 527–541, 529. This study was first published in 1942 as Benedek, Therese and Rubenstein, B. B., *The Sexual Cycle in Women* (Washington 1942). See also Benedek, Therese, *Psychosexual Functions in Women* (New York 1952). For Benedek's biography, see Peters, *Psychiatrie*, 343–351. Weidemann, Doris, *Leben und Werk von Therese Benedek 1892–1977: Weibliche Sexualität und Psychologie des Weiblichen* (Frankfurt a. M. 1988), 115–122.

132 Benedek, 'Infertility,' 528.

or unconsciously as women against their "biologic needs for motherhood." This, Benedek believed, could lead to impaired fertility and unwanted childlessness.[133] Her ideas were positively received and found their way into medical and psychological textbooks.[134] Symptomatic here is the positive comment by one of her colleagues at the annual meeting of the American Society for the Study of Sterility, who emphasized that women were using both the denial of motherhood and their fertility as a mechanism to fend off their husbands' demands.[135] Benedek herself presented variations on the thesis of the "un-motherly modern mother" in a number of publications, interpreting modern women's reluctance to accept their "natural" mothering role as psychopathology. In an essay on the emotional structure of the family from 1949, which was reprinted in 1959, she lamented that the "so-called modern mother" was seriously harming her children. Through her intellectuality as well as her social and professional ambitions, "which lured the woman from her tasks of child care," she was delaying her necessary psychosexual maturation process. As a result, she was unable to develop a balanced and thus natural relationship with her child–quite the opposite. Instead, she was using motherhood as "a continuation of herself, of her personality, and to relive what was her past, her hopes, and her expectations in the future for her child."[136] In light of this, she averred, the child's path into neurosis was in a sense a foregone conclusion.

In his popular 1959 guidebook *A Parents' Guide to the Emotional Needs of Children*—with a foreword by Marynia Farnham—psychologist David Goodman also drew a picture of a woman who, if not reproductively impaired, was at least severely restricted in her function as a mother. She ruled over husband and children and was about to take control of the American economy, but as a result of her pretensions she was psychologically insecure and suffered from "gender pangs," a fundamental malaise with regard to her gender role:

---

[133] Benedek, 'Infertility,' 531.
[134] Benedek, Therese, "The Psychobiology of Pregnancy" and "Motherhood and Nurturing," both articles in: Anthony, Elwyn James (ed.), *Parenthood: Its Psychology and Psychopathology* (Boston 1970), 137–165. Benedek, Therese, 'Die Funktionen des Sexualapparates und ihre Störungen,' in Alexander, Franz (ed.), *Psychosomatische Medizin: Grundlagen und Anwendungsgebiete*, (Berlin 1951), 170–210 (first edition *Psychosomatic Medicine*, New York 1950). Sturgis, Somers H. and Menzer-Benaron, Doris, *The Gynecological Patient: A Psycho-Endocrine Study* (New York and London 1962), 200.
[135] Flanders Dunbar, Helen, "Comment on the Paper of Benedek," *Fertility and Sterility* 3 (1952), 538–541.
[136] Benedek, Therese, "The Emotional Structure of the Family," in Anshen, Ruth Nanda (ed.), *The Family. Its Function and Destiny* (New York 1959 [1949]), 353–380, esp. 373–374.

> The American woman is suffering from gender pangs—psychophysical unfulfillment as a woman. She rules her husband, she rules her children, and to an ever increasing decree she is beginning to own, if not rule, American business. But is she happy? That's a question. Does she exert a wholesome influence on her children? That's another question.[137]

In the chapter "Live Your Gender!", Goodman advised American women (again, of the white middle class) to embrace their "truly feminine qualities" instead of chasing male ideals as professional women:

> Success in a career is not the same as success as a woman. The successful career woman is rarely a success as a woman.[138]

In fact, a focus on the family as "the woman's business" was the prerequisite not only for all successful child-rearing, but also the guarantor of her own content:

> Discontent is the mood mark of the modern woman. Only as she recovers her self-confidence as a woman, will she be happy again.[139]

These two examples from the popular scholarly discourse of the 1950s suggest that, in light of psychoanalysis and reproductive biology, male and female gender roles were once again to be codified—this time with reference to the "biological needs of motherhood." Both Benedek and Goodman thus fused the conservative demand for the re-establishment of the "healthy womanhood" of past generations with the findings of modern natural sciences. Referring to the latest research, they categorized all modern adaptations, such as women's career aspirations, as neuroses, that is, as psychological disorders that endangered the rearing of future generations and society as such.

We can discern an interesting analogy to the change in gender roles discussed so ambivalently here if we look at the consumption of narcotics from the mid-1950s onward. A practice developed of ensuring that insecure or dissatisfied housewives complied with their roles by selectively prescribing to them psychotropic drugs such as Miltown or Valium—popularly known as "mother's little helper."[140] This was not infrequently done at the request of their worried husbands or as an expression of doctors' fear of losing control over their female patients.[141]

---

[137] Goodman, David, *A Parent's Guide to the Emotional Needs of Children. With an Introduction by Marynia Farnham M.D.* (London 1959), 51–52.
[138] Goodman, *Parent's Guide*, 52.
[139] Goodman, *Parent's Guide*, 52.
[140] This is the title of a song by the Rolling Stones from the 1966 album *Aftermath*.
[141] Metzl, "Mother's Little Helper," 228–255. Metzl, *Prozac on the Couch. Prescribing Gender in the Era of Wonder Drugs* (Durham 2003). Tone, Andrea, *The Age of Anxiety. A History of America's Turbulent Affair with Tranquilizers* (New York 2009).

Yet as early as the 1950s, some commentators were already calling for women's employment and motherhood to be recognized as compatible and for women not to be restricted to the domestic sphere. The work of sociologist Mirra Komarovsky and psychologists Lois Meek Stolz and Alberta Siegel from the 1950s is a case in point.[142] In her book *Women in the Modern World*, published at the early date of 1953, Komarovsky analyzed the dilemmas of college-educated housewives and mothers on the basis of interviews and autobiographical material collected from graduates of Barnard—the women's college where she herself taught sociology.[143] Komarovsky compared three groups of college-educated women: confirmed housewives, housewives who wanted to return to work, and women who combined marriage and motherhood with employment. She was able to show that full-time housewives in particular were dissatisfied with their role and suffered due to the contradictions between traditional social role patterns and their own education and career aspirations.

---

[142] Mirra Komarovsky (1905–1999) taught at Barnard College as a professor of sociology from 1938 to 1970. She is considered the founder of the sociology of gender and a dedicated critic of naturalistic conceptions of gender roles, as represented in sociology chiefly by Talcott Parsons. From 1973 to 1974 she was president of the American Sociological Association, the second woman to hold that office. In groundbreaking studies, she analyzed gender norms in post-Great Depression families, the situation of female college students, and the impact of the 1960s on the gender role conceptions of Columbia graduates. Komarovsky, *Modern World*. Komarovsky, *Unemployed Man*. Mirra Komarovsky, *Dilemmas of Masculinity. A Study of College Youth* (New York 1976). Mirra Komarovsky, *Women in College. Shaping New Feminine Identities* (New York 1985). See the brief biography of Komarovsky by Rosalind Rosenberg at <archive.ph/aNpmi>. Alberta Engvall Siegel (1931–2001) was a student of Stolz and taught as a psychologist at Stanford, her specialty being early childhood development. Her mentor, Lois Meek Stolz, had received her PhD from Columbia University and then worked for the American Association of University Women for several years. In 1929, she returned to Columbia University, first as associate director of the Child Development Institute, of which she became director shortly thereafter. She taught as an educationalist at Teacher's College, Columbia University, before eventually moving to Stanford University as a professor of psychology. Stolz, Lois Meek, "Effects of Maternal Employment on Children: Evidence from Research," *Child Development* 31 (1960), 4, 749–782. Siegel, Alberta E. and Stolz, Lois Meek (eds.), *Research Issues Related to the Effects of Maternal Employment on Children. A Symposium. Presented at the Biennial Meeting of the Society for Research in Child Development, March 16, 1961* (University Park, Pennsylvania, University Park Social Research Center, Pennsylvania State University, 1961). Siegel, Alberta Engvall, Stolz, Lois Meek, Hitchcock, Ethel Alice, and Adamson, Jean, "Dependence and Independence in Children," in Nye, F. Ivan and Hoffman, Lois Wladis (eds.), *The Employed Mother in America* (Chicago 1963), 67–81. On this topic, see More, Elizabeth Singer, "Best Interests: Feminism, Social Science, and the Revaluing of Working Mothers in Modern America" (dissertation, Harvard University 2012). More, "Necessary Factfinding."
[143] Komarovsky, *Women in the Modern World*.

Komarovsky argued that a precondition for later role conflicts lay in the fact that biologistic gender concepts were still deeply rooted in the thinking and socialization of young women. Thus, the majority of the female students expected their potential spouses to be more intelligent and better educated than them—and identified with the inferior "feminine role." At the same time, they themselves, by virtue of their more egalitarian upbringing and education, were the best evidence of the socially constructed nature of the supposedly natural difference in intellectual capacity between men and women, and they were thus the living embodiment of a "modern role." This role conflict led to a paradoxical situation in which no less than 40 percent of these "college girls" presented themselves as less intelligent than they actually were to potential husbands ("playing dumb") in order not to diminish their social prospects.[144] Thus, one female student explained how she deliberately downplayed her education to her boyfriend:

> One of the nicest techniques is to spell long words incorrectly once in a while. My boyfriend seems to get a great kick out of it and writes back, "Honey, you certainly don't know how to spell."[145]

According to Komarovsky, this dilemma then reappeared for many women when they gave up their careers and employment to focus on their husbands and children and later, as full-time mothers, asked themselves "What is wrong with me that home and family are not enough?"[146] In the chapter "The Homemaker and Her Problems," Komarovsky describes very precisely the inner turmoil of "discontented housewives" of the educated white middle class on the basis of numerous interviews and case histories. An exemplary case is that of Mrs. Sanders, a 25-year-old mother of two young children (of three-and-a-half years and eighteen months) who had a college degree in art and gave up her career aspirations for her marriage. She described in minute detail her strenuous day and its routines, consisting of housework and child-rearing:

> I wouldn't call myself a contented housewife. I find it hard to be so tied down. [. . .] Besides, I find my life dull. I described my day to you. It isn't just one day, it is every day.[147]

---

[144] As an empirical basis for this argument, Komarovsky used seventy-three autobiographical texts written by college undergraduates over a two-year period (1942 and 1943) and eighty interviews with female students in a social psychology seminar. The monograph then adopted some passages from the article verbatim. Komarovsky, Mirra, "Cultural Contradictions and Sex Roles," AJS, November 1948, 184–189. Komarovsky, *Women in the Modern World*, 67–87.
[145] Komarovsky, *Cultural Contradictions*, 187; Komarovsky, *Women in the Modern World*, 79.
[146] Komarovsky, *Women in the Modern World*, 77, 127.
[147] Komarovsky, *Women in the Modern World*, 109–110.

In view of the foresight with which Komarovsky presented the discontent of countless housewives, some of her analytical conclusions seem surprisingly captive of her era.[148] For example, she favored better preparation of women for marriage and family through special college courses and a social upgrading of housework as potential solutions. Her main focus, however, was on the need for the renegotiation of social values and gender roles. For Komarovsky, there was no contradiction between strengthening the American family and expanding the leeway for intellectual and employed women and mothers, even if this required a new willingness to adapt on the part of husbands and their commitment to "more egalitarian gender roles."[149]

It is interesting to note that Komarovsky had published her study by 1953, ten years before Betty Friedan's bestseller *The Feminine Mystique* (1963) and the discussion it triggered among feminists about housework and the employment of mothers, which I analyze below.[150] Friedan's book, which vividly described the inner emptiness and turmoil of white middle-class housewives as the "problem that has no name," advanced to become a key text of the women's movements. Completely forgotten, however, is the fact that Komarovsky had clearly identified this problem ten years earlier. Rather than referring to the relevant passages of *Women in the Modern World*, Friedan painted an abridged picture of the sociologist Komarovsky as a functionalist who had merely described the "infantilizing" of American women but had proposed no change in the status quo.[151]

In the same year as *The Feminine Mystique*, however, a large-scale interdisciplinary study was published. *The Employed Mother in America* (1963) was the first publication to examine the effects of women's employment on their families and gender norms on the basis of census and survey data as well as interviews. In this study, sociologists, psychologists, economists, and social workers painted a largely optimistic picture. Psychologist Lois Wladis Hoffman, who co-edited the volume with family sociologist Francis Ivan Nye, summarized the study's findings in her conclusion: "The employed mother is a permanent and significant addition to the familial and economic structure of American society."[152] For Hoffman and Nye,

---

148 Although Komarovsky's pioneering work was highly empirical (collecting ego-documents, conducting interviews), from today's perspective scientific analysis took a back seat to the thorough presentation of individual cases. Komarovsky was already criticized for this by contemporaries, who complained that she had relied too much on the interpretations of the people concerned instead of making direct observations herself. Other reviewers took exception to Komarovsky's avid political reformism. More, "Necessary Factfinding," 981.
149 Komarovsky, *Women in the Modern World*, 288–300.
150 See section 3.6.
151 Friedan, *The Feminine Mystique* (New York 1963), 147–150.
152 Nye and Hoffman (eds.), *Employed Mother*, 398.

the large-scale entry of married women and mothers into the labor market since 1940 represented an unprecedented process of social change, but one they did not evaluate negatively—consciously distancing themselves from previous social scientific research—but instead explored empirically.[153] Nye and Hoffman explained the fact that in 1960 nearly 40 percent of all mothers of children between the ages of 6 and 17 and nearly 20 percent of mothers of preschool children were in paid work first with reference to technological developments (pointing out that time-saving household appliances and the food and textile industries had taken over aspects of the mother's economic role), second in light of the trend toward smaller families, and third as a result of the spread of a more egalitarian family ideology (the slow shift away from "male supremacy" when it came to securing the family income and within intrafamily decision-making processes, along with the rise of a person-centered rather than child-centered family philosophy). Yet the gradual change in "family ideology" in particular was proving to be somewhat tentative with regard to society as a whole:

> A modified ideology favoring male dominance still appears to be accepted by most American families. However, this is not entirely inconsistent with the employment of the wife, provided her position is lower than her husband's in the occupational hierarchy and yields a smaller portion of the family income.[154]

At the same time, the authors averred, the wife's and mother's employment often had a relieving function for the husband, who was no longer the sole breadwinner, and it also enabled upward mobility and a higher standard of living. But the change in roles, they underscored, was placing great demands on women, as they now had to balance paid work, housekeeping, and child-rearing.[155] Although many husbands supported their wives' employment in principle, they went on, responsibility for the household and children still lay with the mothers in most cases. Lois W. Hoffman articulated the conflicting self-images and external images of the working woman in a personal conclusion ten years later:

> Not content with being professionals and mothers, we wanted to be gourmet cooks, hostesses, supportive wives, and femme fatales. The major problem reported by the professional

---

[153] F. Ivan Nye (1918–2014) was one of the leading family sociologists in the United States in the 1960s and 1970s. He taught at Washington State University and was president of the National Council on Family Relations (1965–66) and editor of the *Journal of Marriage and the Family* (1960–64). Lois Wladis Hoffman (born 1929) taught psychology at the University of Michigan, Ann Arbor and published extensively on working mothers, their children, and their families. Nye and Hoffman, *Employed Mother*, 3.

[154] Nye and Hoffman, *Employed Mother*, 5.

[155] Nye and Hoffman, *Employed Mother*, 397–398.

women in several studies has been the management of the household. [. . .] And our husbands may have helped more than the husbands of the nonworking women, but by no means was there equal responsibility for housework and child care.[156]

Yet these characteristic multiple stresses did not necessarily lead to psychoses or neuroses. A case study examined 76 working and 76 non-working mothers who suffered from various mental illnesses. The authors demonstrated that—contrary to popular belief among sociologists, psychologists, and physicians—there was no simple correlation between maternal employment and mental illness. On the contrary, the study concluded, "that it may well be that employment contributes to the mental health and well-being of some employed mothers, while it serves the opposite effect for other employed mothers, depending on contingent conditions yet unknown."[157] Moreover, the various chapters of the book showed that working mothers of very young children in particular were more content than housewives, especially if they had a college education. It also emerged that "working mothers" did not develop more feelings of guilt toward their children because of their frequent absences than "homemaker mothers."[158]

But despite such cautious assessments by social experts working with empirical methods, fears of the negative effects of women's and mothers' work were far from allayed. During the 1960s and 1970s, the focus of discussion among experts shifted from the possible connection between women's work and neuroses to the question of its impact on the fertility of white, middle-class working women. As early as 1958, in a study of the "Fertility of American Women" for the Social Science Research Council, three demographers had identified a trend toward declining birth rates among working women of the white, urban middle class: "Fertility rates and ratios were considerably lower for women in the workforce than for those not in it."[159] Thanks to the baby boom between 1946 and 1956, with its all-time high birth rate, and the lower age at marriage, they explained, there was no cause for concern. But, they went on, the connection between education, employment and the number of children was palpable—a phenomenon that also seemed to be confirmed by the Census Report for 1960, which showed that working

---

156 Hoffman, Lois Wladis, "The Professional Woman as Mother. Paper presented at the Conference on Successful Women in the Sciences" (New York, May 1972). "Developmental Program, Report no. 21" (Washington, D.C. 1971), 211–217, 215.
157 Sharp, Lawrence J. and Nye, F. Ivan, "Maternal Mental Health," in Nye and Hoffman, *Employed Mother*, 309–319, 318.
158 Nye and Hoffman, *Employed Mother*. Compare the review by Bernard, Jessie, *Journal of Marriage and the Family*, vol. 16, 1 (1964), 119–121.
159 Grabill, Wilson H., Kiser, Clyde V., and Whelpton, Pascal K., *The Fertility of American Women* (New York and London 1958), 388.

women had fewer children.[160] Almost two decades later, with the national birth rate at an all-time low, the problem had become much more acute in the eyes of the experts.[161] In his overview of "The Fertility of Working Women in the United States," demographer Stanley Kupinski argued in light of recent census data and contemporary research that everything pointed to a correlation between women's reproductive rate and their employment. First, he contended, this was due to the better education of women and to more financially attractive and generally more satisfying career options. Second, it was an expression of a changed social norm: working mothers, even of small children, were becoming ever more accepted.[162] Since, Kupinski stated, there was a clear correlation between "sex-role orientation" and the number of children, policymakers could intervene here if an increase in the birth rate was viewed as desirable:

> The more modern, instrumental, and individualistic her sex-role education, the more likely a married woman is to perceive the economic and psychological benefits of working as greater than the economic and psychological benefits of bearing and rearing children and thus to be more strongly committed to her worker role and to restrict her family size. Conversely, the more traditional, familial-centered her sex-role orientation, [. . .] the greater the likelihood that she would bear more children then modern-oriented, work committed women.[163]

This expert discourse points to a change in social norms in the late 1960s. Not only were there significantly more working mothers of young children than at the end of the war, but female gainful employment and that of mothers in particular generally enjoyed greater acceptance—even if the dispute over the demographic consequences and possible countermeasures among experts continued into the 1970s and 1980s.[164] In the press, too, the employment of mothers was no longer fundamentally questioned. This is implied by headlines such as "Problems or not, Women Work,"[165] "Women Find Wider Roles in a Career,"[166] and "More Women Want Men's Jobs."[167] Even Robert Stein, editor of *Redbook*, one of the country's leading women's magazines, conceded in 1963: "It is wrong to try to con-

---

160 Grabill, Kiser, and Whelpton, *Fertility*, 262–271. *1960 Census of Population and Housing*: <www.census.gov/history/www/reference/publications/demographic_programs_1.html>.
161 See the fertility statistics in Kupinski, Stanley, "The Fertility of Working Women in the United States. Historical Trends and Theoretical Perspectives," in Kupinski, Stanley (ed.), *The Fertility of Working Women. A Synthesis of International Research* (New York 1977), 188–249, 194.
162 Kupinski, *Fertility*, 222–223.
163 Kupinski, *Fertility*, 223.
164 For more on this topic, see chapter 5 of the present book.
165 Ellen Key Blunt, "Problems or Not, Women Work," WP, March 27, 1965.
166 Joan Cook, "Women Find Wider Roles in a Career," NYT, September 9, 1964.
167 Frank Swoboda, "More Women Want Men's Jobs," WP, September 2, 1966.

vince every woman that she will find fulfillment in having babies and baking bread."[168]

Most articles now revolved around the elimination of discrimination when it came to access to jobs and wages, based on the Civil Rights Act of 1964,[169] and underlined the need to strike a balance between housekeeping and maternal duties on the one hand and employment on the other.[170] The Johnson administration in particular made waves by increasing the number of female civil servants and holding several national "conferences on the status of women," which mostly met with a positive response in the national press.[171] In addition, there was increased emphasis on the importance of women's work in raising the standard of living of African American families and more discussion of the special importance of black mothers to the family.[172] Finally, journalists pointed to two characteristic changes in the discussion of women's work in the 1960s. First, the age of the average working woman had increased significantly: in 1963, she was 41 years old (up from 38 in 1920 and 32 in 1940).[173] Second, the social acceptance of the working mother had changed the overall concept of the family. The *Washington Post*, for example, quoted the (female) author of a study on "the changing status of women" from 1964:

> There is a trend among young people to establish a new type of family based on living, learning and loving—not with a division of labor between the sexes but jointly and simultaneously.[174]

---

168 The quote continued: "It's equally wrong to try to convince every woman that she will find fulfillment in practicing a profession." Peter Bart, "Advertising: Benton and Bowles Wins Client," NYT, May 31, 1963.
169 WP, July 3, 1966, "Some Urge Equality, Some Protection for Women." WP, September 15, 1970, "Rights for Working Women."
170 WP, September 5, 1960: "Hardships Keep Women Happy." NYT, November 18, 1960: "Child Day-Care Centers Needed, Kennedy Says." WP, May 27, 1961: "1970: 30 Million Working Women." NYT, July 9, 1962: "Brides Seek to Combine Homes, Jobs." WP, October 20, 1962: "Designed for the Working Woman." WP, October 16, 1963: "Not All Women Are Equal." NYT, January 7, 1968: "Someone to Mind the Baby." NYT, May 15, 1968: "Answers to the Question 'What's a Working Mother to Do?'". NYT, December 15, 1968: "When a Mother Goes Back to Work." WP, January 11, 1970: "She Hired a Housekeeper and Cried Over Boiled Steak."
171 WP, April 12, 1964: "He's Changing Her Image." WP May 25, 1964: "They Make Men Nervous."
172 WP, March 30, 1968: "Wives Help Raise Family Incomes." NYT, August 20, 1968: "Negro Women Explore the Perplexities of Their Family Role." NYT, July 20, 1979: "Lower Middle Class Working Women: What Help Is Needed."
173 NYT, April 2, 1963: "Today's Working Girl is Often a Mature Woman."
174 WP, February 21, 1964: "Stay-at-Home is Out." NYT, September 9, 1964: "Women Find Wider Role in a Career." NYT, January 11, 1965: "Personal Finance: Wives Who Work."

3.6 *The Feminine Mystique* and *Equality between the Sexes*: feminists, women social scientists, and the working woman

When Betty Friedan and a few comrades-in-arms founded the National Organization of Women (NOW) on October 30, 1966, their goal was to change ideas about the family in precisely this way. They sought "to take action to bring women into full partnership in the mainstream of American society NOW, exercising all the privileges and responsibilities thereof in truly equal partnership with men."[175] The legal basis for the struggle against general discrimination on the basis of gender was the Civil Rights Act, signed into law by President Johnson in 1964, with its Title VIII outlawing discrimination on the basis of "race" and "sex." In addition, the activists advocated for an Equal Rights Amendment (ERA) to the constitution.[176] One of the core goals of the new women's movement, in addition to the ERA and the fight for the legalization of abortion, a battle that was to exercise a formative influence on the work of its counterpart movement in the late 1960s and early 1970s, was to eliminate discrimination against women on the labor market, and with respect to appointments, wages, and the educational system. The employment of mothers became a key aspect in this context, since the aim was to show that motherhood and child-rearing had often served to exclude women from professional life and careers:

> With a life span lengthened to nearly 75 years it is no longer either necessary or possible for women to devote the greater part of their lives to childrearing; yet childbearing and rearing which continues to be a most important part of most women's lives—still is used to justify barring women from equal professional and economic participation and advance.[177]

To prove that maternal employment was not detrimental to a child's wellbeing, the feminists of the 1960s drew on the work of liberal social scientists from the 1950s and 1960s such as Komarovsky, Stolz, and Nye and Hoffman. This also enabled them to criticize the prevailing conservative expert discourse, which confined women to domesticity and motherhood, in the light of social scientific knowledge.[178] Two texts by feminists occupied a key position in the discussion of socially prescribed domesticity and the potential for and opportunities of female

---

175 National Organization for Women (NOW), "An Invitation to Join," Nov. 1966. Schlesinger Library, Harvard University (SLHU), MC 496, Box 1, Folder 2.
176 Overview in D'Emilio and Freedman, *Intimate Matters*, 301–325. Mathews and de Hart, *Sex, Gender, and the Politics of ERA*.
177 NOW, "An Invitation to Join," Nov. 1966. SLHU, MC 496, Box 1, Folder 2.
178 More, "Necessary Factfinding," 998–999, 1001–1002.

employment in the 1960s: Betty Friedan's *The Feminine Mystique* (1963) and Alice Rossi's *Equality between the Sexes: An Immodest Proposal* (1964).[179] Friedan and Rossi were both among the founders of NOW. While Friedan became its first president, Rossi, a sociologist, became a member of its board of directors in 1967.[180] Rossi and Friedan were both working mothers of three children who, in calling for women's employment, also spoke to their own history—Friedan as a journalist, Rossi as a sociologist.[181]

In trenchant prose, *The Feminine Mystique* described the situation of college-educated housewives in the 1960s. To gather the relevant evidence, Friedan had interviewed college graduates of her own generation and had evaluated women's magazines and the contemporary press, along with sociological, psychological, and medical literature. Her undoubted achievement was to have evocatively described the feeling of emptiness and insignificance, the sense of lacking one's own personality and intellectual stimulation characteristic of middle-class housewives of white suburbia in baby-boom America. The oft-quoted beginning of her book perfectly expresses her overall theme:

---

[179] In addition to Friedan's *The Feminine Mystique*, see also Rossi, Alice, "Equality Between the Sexes: An Immodest Proposal," *Daedalus* 93 (1964), 2, 607–652.

[180] Betty Friedan (1921–2006) was one of the best-known intellectuals and feminists in the United States. After studying sociology and psychology at Smith College, she spent another year at the University of California, Berkeley, where she studied with psychologist Erik Erikson, among other things. She went on to work as a journalist, writing for union journals and women's magazines. According to Friedan's own account, inspired by a survey of college graduates of her own cohort she began to think about the situation of middle-aged housewives and their unspoken sense of unfulfillment and lack of independence, for which she coined the term "problem that has no name." Friedan worked up her first articles on the subject into her 1963 book *The Feminine Mystique*, which was a key "revivalist text" of the new women's movement before becoming a national and international bestseller. Yet Daniel Horowitz has brought out the extent to which Friedan was already active as a political journalist and freelance publicist in the 1950s, which is hardly consonant with the image of the apolitical housewife she portrayed. Friedan, *The Feminine Mystique*. On the impact of the book, see Coontz, *Strange Stirring*. On Friedan, see Horowitz, Daniel, *Betty Friedan and the Making of the Feminine Mystique. The American Left, the Cold War, and Modern Feminism* (Amherst 1998). Horowitz, Daniel, "Rethinking Betty Friedan and the Feminine Mystique. Labor Union Radicalism and Feminism in Cold War America," *American Quarterly* 48 (1996), 1, 1–42.

[181] Alice S. Rossi (1922–2009) was one of the pioneers of American feminism and co-founder of NOW. Rossi gained a doctorate in sociology and taught at Harvard, the University of Chicago, and Johns Hopkins University, among others. From 1974 until her retirement, she taught as a professor of sociology at the University of Massachusetts, and she was president of the ASA in 1983–84. Her research field was family sociology, especially the formation and legitimization of male and female gender roles. On Rossi, see the obituary in the NYT: Margalit Fox, "Alice S. Rossi, Sociologist and Feminist Scholar, Dies at 87," NYT, November 8, 2009, A34.

> The problem lay buried, unspoken, for many years in the minds of American women. It was a strange stirring, a sense of dissatisfaction, a yearning that women suffered in the middle of the twentieth century in the United States. Each suburban wife struggled with it alone. As she made the beds, shopped for groceries, matched slipcover material, ate peanut butter sandwiches with her children, chauffeured Cub Scouts and Brownies, lay beside her husband at night—she was afraid to ask even of herself the silent question—"Is this all"?[182]

For Friedan, the way to escape the constraints of the "feminine mystique" was first to become aware of the limitations associated with it. As a next step, she advised every woman who could relate to the above description to develop her own personality, ideally through "creative work of her own." By this, Friedan did not mean that dissatisfied housewives should accept any kind of paid work. What she had in mind was self-discovery within the framework of a professional career or related training.[183] Crucially, the education of female students had to change; they had to be instilled with confidence in their own abilities and a sense of the possibilities of meaningful employment, rather than inculcated with the "feminine mystique."

Friedan, who referred to the household provocatively as a "comfortable concentration camp," was not the first publicist to grapple with the problem of the modern housewife. As we have seen, Mirra Komarovsky had explained the dilemma of the "discontented homemaker" a decade earlier with reference to the conflict between the expansion of women's education and societal expectations of the female gender role.[184] Sociologist Alice Rossi, like Friedan one of the founders of NOW, went a step further and derived a subversive demand from a similar analysis. In her essay "Equality between the Sexes: An Immodest Proposal," which stemmed from a 1963 lecture to the American Academy of Arts and Sciences and was published in 1964 in the journal *Daedalus*, she called for nothing less than full equality between women and men. The imbalance between the sexes, which was justified in terms of biological differences and found expression in the breadwinner role and housewife ideal, she argued, was essentially socially produced.[185] What seems self-evident from today's perspective was explosive at the time. To back up her call for women's full participation in society and thus also the possibility of employment, Rossi argued that the social scientific literature provided no substantive evidence that maternal employment had a negative effect on children. Moreover, she contended, full-time motherhood for women,

---

182 Friedan, *Feminine Mystique*, 1.
183 Friedan, *Feminine Mystique*, 407–456.
184 Komarovsky, *Women in the Modern World*. On this topic, see above.
185 Twenty years later, in her inaugural address as president of the ASA, Rossi further developed her gender analyses to take greater account of the biological determinants of gender, citing examples from evolutionary biology and neuroscience. Rossi, Alice S., "Gender and Parenthood," *American Sociological Review* 49 (1984), February, 1–19.

which was extolled as an ideal in the twentieth century, was a relatively novel phenomenon; in U.S. history, women had always had to contribute to the family's livelihood in addition to their family responsibilities and they had still raised their children.[186] But the key to combining maternal employment and child-rearing, Rossi underscored, was the quality of childcare.[187]

In keeping with their own experience, initially Friedan, Rossi, and others deliberately limited their focus to white middle- and upper-class women living in stable families—just as the social scientific studies they cited had done.[188] In doing so, however, these feminists marginalized a large number of working mothers from the outset: African American women, Mexican American women, immigrant women in general, working-class women, single mothers and those living in other family arrangements. At first, then, the multiple real-world burdens borne by many women as a result of wage work, family tasks, and social pressure to conform were entirely absent from the NOW's activists' agenda.[189] This did not change after the election of Aileen C. Hernández, a trade unionist and civil rights activist with Jamaican-American roots, as its second president in 1970.[190] The founding of the National Black Feminist Organization (NBFO) in 1973, based on the NOW model, was intended to give non-white feminists a voice, but the group broke up in 1977. At the same time, there were also efforts within NOW to better represent the concerns of non-white women. Thus, in addition to its traditional engagement for "equal opportunity in employment," a separate NOW task force called "Minority Women and Women's Rights" was formed in 1974.[191]

At the same time, Friedan especially—but indirectly Rossi and the activists of NOW as well—made an essential contribution to propagating a homogenous ideal

---

[186] Rossi, "Equality," 615, 617.
[187] Rossi, "Equality," 619–620.
[188] Recent research has strongly criticized this, especially with reference to Betty Friedan's *The Feminine Mystique*. Meyerowitz, "Feminine Mystique." Horowitz, *Betty Friedan*. Plant, *Mom*. Coontz, *Strange Stirring*, 121–138. More, "Necessary Factfinding."
[189] Benita Roth has elaborated the extent to which NOW focused on the white middle class from its inception until the early 1970s, leaving many working women, African American women and Mexican American women feeling excluded. Roth, Benita, *Separate Roads to Feminism. Black, Chicana, and White Feminist Movements in America's Second Wave* (Cambridge 2004), 105–118.
[190] Aileen C. Hernandez (1926–2017) was one of the co-founders of NOW and its president from 1970 to 1971 but left the organization in 1979 out of frustration with the continued ethnic inequalities within it. An African American labor activist, she had served on Lyndon B. Johnson's Equal Employment Opportunity Commission, co-founded the National Women's Political Caucus, and Black Women Organized For Action. Hernandez served on the board of several civil rights organizations, including the NAACP and ACLU.
[191] Jane Plitt, "NOW National Office: The Inside Story: How NOW Operates," July 1974. SLHU MC 496, Box 1, Folder 10.

of mother and family in the late 1960s and early 1970s. In Friedan's work, the consumerist white middle-class housewife who let her breadwinner husband provide for her and had put aside all career aspirations was supplanted by the working white wife and mother who, thanks to adequate childcare, managed to combine her dual obligation of career and childrearing—though this presupposed education and a fitting income. Although Friedan's new conception of women and the family, formulated as a response to the postwar domesticity ideal, was characterized by more egalitarian gender roles, it was based on preconditions (education, income, social class, and nuclear family) that made it unattainable for many American women.

This was also evident in the text's reception. Almost fifty years after the publication of *The Feminine Mystique*, historian Stephanie Coontz interviewed former readers about their experiences reading it around the time it was published, highlighting how it seemed to express exactly what the majority of white college-educated young housewives felt, but was largely lost, for example, on black women. Two reactions recorded by Coontz provide a good illustration of these very different perspectives. Cam Stivers talked about her reading experience as follows:

> I had the feeling (at 25!) that my life was over, and that nothing interesting would happen to me again. . . . I had everything a woman was supposed to want—marriage to a nice, dependable guy (a good provider), a wonderful little kid, a nice house in the suburbs—and I was miserable.[192]

While Stivers, like thousands of other readers, saw this text as an affirmation that she was not alone in feeling empty, for Lorraine G., an African American woman, it caused nothing but incomprehension. When Stephanie Coontz asked her about her reading experience, Lorraine G. explained that she had deliberately ignored the book at first because she and her friends "were too busy struggling to achieve the American dream to be concerned with women who seemed to have it all." When she did read it years later, she felt that Friedan's text was not addressed to her; it was primarily aimed at "white women [who] had the luxury of being bored with their middle-class, full-time homemaker role, a role that most working women would cherish."[193] This was not an isolated perception, but was to be a key criticism of Friedan's work from the outset. The feminist and historian Gerda Lerner had already argued in a letter to Friedan shortly after the book's publication that

---

[192] Cam Stivers, interviewed by Stephanie Coontz, reprinted without date or location in Coontz, *Strange Stirring*, 83.
[193] Lorraine G., interviewed by Stephanie Coontz, reprinted without date or location in Coontz, *Strange Stirring*, 102.

working women, especially Negro women, labor not only under the disadvantages imposed by the feminine mystique, but under the more pressing disadvantages of economic discrimination.[194]

The discussion of "non-white working women" in the 1950s and 1960s is the focus of the following section.

3.7 "A long and difficult up-hill struggle": African American women, women's work, and motherhood

The liberal social scientists of the 1950s and 1960s ignored the situation of working-class women and members of ethnic minorities in their analyses of women's work, while the fertility discourse of the late 1950s to 1970s among demographers and physicians also had unmistakably racist implications.[195] Even the U.S. eugenics movement discussed the connection between education, employment, and fertility, as revealed for the 1960s by an evaluation of the American Eugenics Society's journal, *Eugenics Quarterly*.[196] Since the statistics showed a consistently high fertility rate among nonwhite mothers (initially, black Americans in particular were the focus of attention, then from the 1980s onward Mexican Americans as well), eugenics experts unabashedly discussed how to control reproduction in these groups. Proposals alternated between improving education and family planning and implementing coercive measures.[197]

In the postwar period, most experts considered employment among African American and other non-white mothers an economically rational development

---

[194] Gerda Lerner to Betty Friedan, 1963, quoted in Coontz, *Strange Stirring*, 101.
[195] See Komarovsky, *Women in the Modern World*. Nye and Hofmann, *Employed Mother*. Stolz, "Effects." On Friedan's selective use of the findings of Stolz and Komarovsky, see More, "Necessary Fact-finding," 998–999. The quote in title, however, "A long and difficult up-hill struggle" originates from an article in Ebony: "The Long Thrust Toward Economic Equality," *Ebony*, August 1966, 38–42, 38.
[196] To this end, I reviewed all volumes of the journal *Eugenics Quarterly* from the 1960s. Bajema, Carl Jay, "Relation of Fertility to Educational Attainment," *Eugenics Quarterly* 13 (1966), 4, 306–315. Mitra, S., "Child-Bearing Pattern of American Woman," *Eugenics Quarterly* 13 (1966), 2, 133–140. Mitra, S., "Occupation and Fertility in the United States," ibid., 141–146. Mitra, S., "Education and Fertility in the United States," *Eugenics Quarterly* 13 (1966), 4, 214–222. Mitra, S., "Income, Socioeconomic Status, and Fertility in the United States," ibid., 223–230. Goldberg, David, "Some Observations on Recent Changes in American Fertility Based on Sample Survey Data," *Eugenics Quarterly* 14 (1967), 4, 255–264. Kiser, Clyde V., "Trends in Fertility Differentials by Color and Socioeconomic Status in the United States," *Eugenics Quarterly* 15 (1968), 4, 221–226. Pohlmann, Edward, "The Timing of First Birth. A Review of Effects," ibid, 252–263.
[197] On African American Women, see Overbeck, *At the Heart of It All*. On Mexican American Families, see Ruesch, *Macho Men*. Solinger, *Beggars and Choosers*. Gutierrez, *Fertile Matters*.

conducive to the well-being of U.S. society, as it reduced the burden on welfare budgets.[198] As explained earlier, most social experts were in any case not interested in increasing the reproduction rate of ethnic minorities. In addition, non-white families were fundamentally associated with notions of deficient values and family structures (chapter 4 of the present book explores the debates on the supposedly dysfunctional black family of the 1960s).[199]

But what did the minority African Americans themselves think about women's work? Did the relevant media and journals present being a housewife to their readers as a normative ideal, a symbol of advancement into the respectability and economic security of the middle class? *Ebony* magazine, for example, which had been published monthly since 1945 and was aimed directly at the black middle class, embodies an interesting change in reporting in the 1960s.[200] Until the mid-1960s, this publication only ever reported on women's work with reference to particularly successful or heroic individuals: the respected gynecologist who cared *pro bono* for Mexican-born migrant workers in a Texas labor camp, the undaunted churchwoman who presided over her congregation despite poor health, the aerospace engineer who solved the physics problems that had stumped her male colleagues, the police officer who followed in her father's footsteps yet remained "ladylike."[201] They all stood for the special achievements of individual non-white middle-class women in the spirit of "uplift ideology," the notion of potential social advancement through self-management.[202] It is telling that

---

[198] On the cliché of the African American "welfare queen" and the fear of bleeding the welfare system dry, see Finzsch, "Welfare Queen." Chappell, *War on Welfare*.

[199] On the so-called Moynihan controversy surrounding the assistant secretary of labor's 1965 report on "The Negro Family," see Rainwater, Lee and Yancey, William (eds.), *The Moynihan Report and the Politics of Controversy. A Trans-Action Social Science and Public Policy Report. Including the Full Text of The Negro Family. The Case for National Action by Daniel P. Moynihan* (Cambridge and London,1967). Patterson, *Freedom is not Enough*.

[200] For the present book, I considered the years 1950 to 1970, reviewing the 1950, 1955, and 1959 volumes of the print edition for the 1950s; I was able to examine the digital edition from 1960 onward. Keywords used were "working women," "women's work," and "women [and] work."

[201] "Lady Doctor to Migrant Workers," *Ebony*, February 1962, 59–68. "Woman On the Go for God," *Ebony*, May 1963, 79–88. "My Daughter—The Policeman," *Ebony*, October 1965, 82–89. Similar "success stories" about individuals appeared in the 1950s, but they were more explicitly focused on their status as the first African American women in the relevant professions. See, for example, "Harlem's Lady Wholesaler," *Ebony*, January 1955, 53–56. "Virginia's First Negro Medical Grad," *Ebony*, July 1955, 77–81. "TWA Hires First Negro Air Hostess," *Ebony*, July 1959, 37–40. "Lady Selectman," *Ebony*, September 1959, 36–38.

[202] On "uplift ideology," see Gaines, Kevin K., *Uplifting the Race. Black Leadership, Politics, and Culture in the Twentieth Century* (Chapel Hill 1996). For an analysis of the desired self-

the women portrayed were also characterized by a distinct femininity, which was every bit the equal of the concept of "feminine mystique" described above as primarily white. For example, the engineer, a university professor, was described as a "teacher-housewife" who possessed specifically feminine skills of accuracy, which in turn guaranteed her professional success.[203] On its twentieth anniversary in 1962, the Women's Army Corps (WAC) wooed non-white recruits in an *Ebony* article by highlighting clothing allowances ("for lingerie and high heeled pumps") and the opportunity to meet the right man when the working day was over ("many dining halls incidentally, like service clubs, are consolidated ... so girl meets boy").[204]

Only in the second half of the 1960s did articles appear that placed work by nonwhite women in a longer continuum of economic exploitation and highlighted the dual oppression of African American women in U.S. society due to their gender and race. "Negro women working in the economy are special victims of limitations, discriminations and disadvantages imposed on all women through outmoded but ingrained prejudiced ideas and practices."[205] At the same time, however, these texts also discerned the great strides being made by black women in particular through better education and legal equality, and they asserted that many had succeeded in making the transition from low-paid work as unskilled laborers in homes, industry, or agriculture to the service sector.[206] They also underscored that the high incidence of family break-ups among African Americans could not be blamed on the fact that many black women worked. Here, the expert discussion on the supposed decline of the African American family since 1965 is clearly palpable, but it was only cautiously rebutted.[207] In general, it is noticeable that the voices or stories of "ordinary" black working women are completely absent from this magazine's reports. This may have been down to its self-imposed educational mission, which meant that it preferred to present its readers with examples of the successful social advancement of black women.[208] One exception, however, was the August 1966 issue, the entirety

---

management of African American men in particular as imagined within this ideology, see Martschukat, *Ordnung des Sozialen*, 293–326.
203 "Tenn. State's Lady Engineer," *Ebony*, July 1964, 75–78.
204 "Women in Uniform," *Ebony*, December 1962, 62–67.
205 "The Long Thrust Toward Economic Equality," *Ebony*, August 1966, 38–42, 40.
206 "The Long Thrust Toward Economic Equality," *Ebony*, August 1966, 38–42. Ross, Arthur M., "The Changing Pattern of Negro Employment," *Ebony*, July 1967, 38–39.
207 For more on this, see chapter 4 of the present book.
208 African American women from the working class, on the other hand, appear as underage single mothers who are to be helped into a stable family life through education and training: Ponsett, Alex, "A Despised Minority. Unwed Mothers are Targets of Abuse from a Harsh Society," *Ebony*, August 1966, 48–54.

of which was devoted to "the Negro woman" and that contained articles not only on the role of African American women in the civil rights movement, but also on their professional advancement and social life, the impact of the sexual revolution, their achievements in the arts and culture, and their opportunities for education and consumption.[209] Enthusiastic readers' letters in subsequent issues praised this edition and, in particular, the publisher's statement by John H. Johnson, which described black women in their historical role as guardians of the family under slavery, but also, quite self-evidently, as modern working mothers and wives: "She is a cab driver, civil rights worker, maid, teacher, preacher, doctor, cook, poet, housewife, fashion designer and novelist. You name it and she is it."[210] In response to Johnson's statement, Mrs. H. L. Mickens of Pomona, California, for example, wrote: "As a colored woman, I have always felt the colored female was not as appreciated, understood, or respected as females of other races. You have changed my conception. To you I am sincerely grateful."[211] Grace Williams of Philadelphia added:

> All my life I have struggled to rise above oppression, and here at last, someone recognizes my plight. [. . .] There was a time in my life when I thought only God in Heaven knew what we Negro women have been going through, and it makes me feel darn good to know that man not only knows, but is beginning to recognize us for it. [. . .] When my girls are grown and married and start feeling the way I have felt, I shall give it to them to read and let them know that they are not alone.[212]

Howard B. Woods, employee of the U.S. Information Agency in Washington, D. C., wrote a letter to the editor criticizing the debate over the supposed matriarchy of African American women as "mass male psychosis" and once again acknowledged their accomplishments as working mothers and homemakers:

> The Negro woman, by any standards, has been through the years, an astute homemaker, economist and cost accountant as she parlayed minimal income to meet her family's needs. This perseverance has paid off. Today her children and grandchildren are taking their rightful places in the total society in ever increasing numbers.[213]

---

209 See, for example, the following articles, all published in the August issue of *Ebony*: Phyl Garland, "Builders of a New South," 27–37. "Young Woman in a 'White World,'" 69–74. "The Long Thrust Toward Economic Equality," 38–42. Allan Morrison, "Women in the Arts," 90–94. "The Negro Woman in Politics," 96–100. Ragni Lantz, "The Pleasures and Problems of the Bachelor Girl," 102–108. C. Eric Lincoln, "A Look Beyond the 'Matriarchy,'" 111–116. Lena Horne, "The Three-Horned 'Dilemma' Facing Negro Women," 118–124. Ponchitta Pierce, "Problems of the Woman Intellectual," 144–149.
210 *Ebony*, August 1966, "Publisher's Statement," 25.
211 *Ebony*, October 1966, 18.
212 *Ebony*, October 1966, 12.
213 *Ebony*, October 1966, 12–14.

In the 1950s, the magazine *Jet*, another publication aimed predominantly at black readers, also still dealt rather marginally with the effects of African American women's employment. Interestingly, when articles addressed whether women and mothers should work, the careers of white women and mothers served as examples.[214] However, when it came to the morality and decency of working women, images and stories about black women were presented.[215] Much like the reportage in *Ebony*, while the successful careers of individuals tended to dominate until the mid-1960s, *Jet* gradually began to scrutinize the impact of women's work on families, a discussion that interfaced with the then-current debate on the structure of the African American family. In December 1965, for example, the magazine reported on a speech by the head of the Women's Bureau at the U.S. Department of Labor, Mary Keyserling, on the connection between women's work and the state of the black family. According to Keyserling, "it is 'simply not true' [sic] that an excessive entry of younger women into the labor force has helped to break down the Negro family."[216] The following chapter is devoted to this shift of discursive emphasis from working mothers to the structure of families.

3.8 Interim conclusion: interpretive conflicts over the employment, psyche, and reproduction of the 'modern woman'

From World War II to the height of the social protest movements in the late 1960s, the role of women and mothers within the idealized conception of the American family was subject to intense debate in the United States. The public discussions and expert discourses revolving around the relationship between domesticity, women's employment, and reproduction provide telling evidence of how, in the face of processes of social change (the expansion of women's paid work, the rise of dual earner families, the collapse of the fertility rate, and the emergence of the new women's movement), ever new elements of the imagined family required discussion. Yet there was certainly no linear process of change

---

[214] See, for example, the article "Do Working Women Make Better Wives?", *Jet*, May 27, 1954, 56–57.
[215] "Are Working Wives Less Moral?", *Jet*, December 3, 1955, 24–26.
[216] *Jet*, December 2, 1965, 46. For the context, namely the debate on the state of the African American family in the wake of the publication of the so-called Moynihan Report, see chapter 4 of this book. The occasion of Keyserling's speech was a conference marking the thirtieth anniversary of the most important black women's organization, the National Council of Negro Women, in Washington, D.C.

encompassing all ethnic groups and classes equally, as evident in the failure to consider, within the overall debate on women's work, the interests and needs of African American women, who traditionally had to combine wage labor and motherhood. Overall, the ideal of the American family as a white, middle-class "nuclear family" went unchallenged; the goal was to balance gender roles within this core unit.

After the relationship between the sexes had already been reworked during the Progressive Era through the discussion of women's suffrage, women's employment, and divorce, the debate on women's work and domesticity reached a new peak of intensity in the 1940s and 1950s in response to wartime employment and the baby boom. Initially, supporters and opponents of women's employment, especially that of mothers, were irreconcilably opposed. Physicians and psychologists in particular contributed to the denunciation either of female gainful employment or the role of housewife as the basis of psychological disorders ("neuroses"). But it was the steady rise in female employment—that is, a clearly identifiable process of social change—that ultimately led to its recognition as a social reality in the course of the 1950s, which included the gradual acceptance of wage labor among mothers. Liberal social scientists of the 1950s and 1960s provided empirical evidence of the compatibility of family and work in their studies. Beginning in the mid-1960s, moreover, the second wave of the women's movement made the elimination of gender discrimination in the workplace one of its core themes—which naturally included the acceptance of mothers' employment. This discourse clearly focused on white, middle-class mothers, both among scholars and in the daily press; good childcare that could be organized privately was seen as a key criterion for reconciling the role of mother and employment, whereas women from the working class and ethnic minorities simply lacked the means to do so in most cases. Consequently, the women's movement of the 1960s implicitly contributed to a racist and class-specific restriction of the family ideal, although it had of course set out to overcome the idea of gender roles as biologically determined.

From the mid-1950s to the early 1970s, moreover, an expert discourse on women's mental health and reproductive function broadened the debates on motherhood and the consequences of women's employment and self-fulfillment. Here the neurosis debate returned, but was now clearly related to the modern woman, who was refusing to perform her natural reproductive duties. Contrary to the demands of the women's movement and radical feminists—and also in contrast to the much more liberal coverage of women's work and reproduction in the national press—psychologists joined with physicians and demographers in calling for an increase in the birth rate of white women after the baby boom. This discourse, consciously discriminatory in social and ethnic terms, again emphasized the biological difference between the sexes and attempted to reassign women to their reproductive roles. It thus not only represented a powerful attempt to redefine gender roles but also provided an important benchmark for the conservative family rhetoric of the 1980s.

Consequently, over a period of almost thirty years, what we find is a shift from rejection to gradual acceptance of (part-time) work among white middle-class women, though over time this was linked to their (declining) reproduction—with the white nuclear family always remaining the key point of reference, despite all the social realities diverging from it. But women's employment was not the only field of conflict in which we can identify a readjustment of family values; the same applied to the development of the divorce debate and reflections on the social structure of the African American family. The latter are the focus of the following chapter.

4 "Black family pathologies": the limits of the white middle-class family ideal and the debate on the structure and values of the African American family in the 1960s

> America has defined the roles to which each individual should subscribe. It has defined "manhood" in terms of its own interests and "femininity" likewise. Therefore, an individual who has a good job, makes a lot of money, and drives a Cadillac is a real "man," and conversely, an individual who is lacking these "qualities" is less of a man. The advertising media in this country continuously informs the American male of his need for indispensable signs of his virility—the brand of cigarettes that cowboys prefer, the whiskey that has a masculine tang, or the jock strap that athletes wear.[1]

This description of the ideal of "hegemonic masculinity" that prevailed in the U.S. in the late 1960s—professional career, breadwinner role, and access to consumer goods widely touted in the media, ranging from automobiles to whiskey brands—was part of an attempt to expose this concept as racist and socially exclusive.[2] In her 1969 pamphlet "Double Jeopardy. To Be Black and Female," one of the key texts of U.S. feminism, black activist Frances Beale not only described the precarious situation of African American women in American society, but also analyzed the contradictory expectations placed on African American men.[3] Beale argued that while black women faced dual discrimination in U.S. society, as women and as blacks, African American men too were denied both socioeconomic and social participation. According to Beale, black males were co-opted by society, media, and advertising to pursue a specific national family ideal entailing

---

1 Beale, Frances M., "Double Jeopardy. To Be Black and Female," Cade, Toni (ed.), *The Black Woman. An Anthology* (New York 1970), 90–100, 91. The text was written as a pamphlet on the status of black women in 1969. It first appeared in print in 1970 in the anthology edited by Cade, but made also part of the document collection Morgan, Robin (et al.) (eds.), *Sisterhood is Powerful. An Anthology of Writings from the Women's Liberation Movement* (New York 1970).
2 On the concept of "hegemonic masculinity," see Connell and Messerschmidt, "Hegemonic Masculinity." Connell, *Masculinities*. Dinges, "'Hegemoniale Männlichkeit.'".
3 Frances Beale (b. 1940) is an African American feminist, publicist, and political activist. "Double Jeopardy" is her most influential text to date. In 1968, Beale co-founded the Black Women's Liberation Committee of the SNCC, which then transformed into the Black Women's Alliance and later the Third World Women's Alliance (TWWA). In the 1970s, Beale campaigned mainly for abortion rights and against forced sterilizations. On Beale, see the biographical note in "Voices of Feminism Oral History Project," Sophia Smith Collection, Smith College, Northampton, MA. Frances Beal interviewed by Loretta J. Ross, March 18, 2005, Oakland, CA.

white middle-class values and gender norms that served to underpin the capitalist system. In Beale's analysis, this contradictory value orientation—that saw African American men internalize a family ideal and gender concept from which they were excluded by socioeconomic deprivation and racial discrimination—helped make life even more difficult for black women, particularly within the Black Power movement:

> Since the advent of Black power, the Black male has exerted a more prominent leadership role in our struggle for justice in this country. He sees the system for what it really is for the most part, but where he rejects its values and mores on many issues, when it comes to women, he seems to take his guidelines from the pages of the *Ladies' Home Journal*.[4]

This chapter analyzes the assumptions about the values, structures, and supposed pathologies of African American families discussed in academia, the media, and the civil rights movement up to the end of the 1960s, when Frances Beale's text was published. Of particular interest here, first, is how the assumption of the black family's deficient structure and value orientation was constructed and explained among social scientists—and what reactions this provoked in the civil rights movement, including the Black Power movement.[5] Why was the notion of "black family pathologies" able to gain a foothold so easily on a broad social basis and even among those affected? Second, we need to ask what effect this had on the debate on the gender norms of the African American family. In short, how did it come about that even the men of the Black Power movement seemed to draw their gender role concepts from white women's magazines—although they themselves were denied access to the white ideal of masculinity centered on the "self-made man" (Michael Kimmel) due to socio-economic discrimination?[6] How

---

4 Beale, "Double Jeopardy," 502.
5 The Black Power movement was the radical response to the moderate civil rights movement around Martin Luther King and his path of nonviolent protest against racial discrimination. Black Power activists such as Malcolm X, Bobby Seale, Eldridge Cleaver, and Stokely Carmichael openly propagated violence as a response to oppression by the white majority society. The most important organization was the Black Panther Party. Carmichael, Stokely, Hamilton, Charles V., and Ture, Kwame, *Black Power. The Politics of Liberation in America* (New York 1967). Ogbar, Jeffrey O. G., *Black Power: Radical Politics and African American Identity* (Baltimore 2004). Estes, Steve, *I am a Man! Race, Manhood, and the Civil Rights Movement* (Chapel Hill 2005). Wendt, Simon, "'They Finally Found Out that We Really Are Men.' Violence, Non-Violence and Black Manhood in the Civil Rights Era," *Gender & History* 19 (2007), 543–564. Murch, Donna Jean, *Living for the City. Migration, Education, and the Rise of the Black Panther Party in Oakland, California* (Chapel Hill 2010).
6 On the "self-made man" as a concept of hegemonic masculinity in the twentieth-century United States, see Kimmel, *Manhood in America*.

did black feminists like Beale attempt to counter this "double jeopardy"?[7] The third key question is to what extent the debate on the values and structure of the black family in the mid-1960s left longer-term traces on the national family ideal. Did this conception become more pluralistic, liberal, and diverse, or did normative processes of enclosure and closure prevail? What role did social experts, but also civil rights activists, play in this?

In order to clarify the socio-economic underpinnings of the discussion of the African American family, the first section sheds light on socio-structural changes in this entity in the twentieth century. Next, I show how social scientific research on the structure and values of the black family developed from the beginning of the twentieth century to the 1960s. To this end, the second section looks at the research conducted by black sociologists in the first half of the twentieth century, given that it was largely they who first constituted the African American family as a research object while white social scientists were still barely addressing it. A third section is devoted to the text *American Dilemma* by Swedish sociologist Gunnar Myrdal, which catapulted the question of how to deal with the black minority to the status of social scientific research object and subject of public debate around the middle of the century. A fourth section examines the impact of the so-called Moynihan Report and its diagnosis of a supposed "pathology" of the African American Family in the mid-1960s. In contrast to previous research on the Moynihan Report, I interpret it as an expression of proactive "social engineering" that took the family as its starting point. The context here was President Johnson's War on Poverty and a broader discourse on population policies in general, in which sociologists and other social experts foregrounded the problems of poor, large families as key target of intervention. Two further sections analyze, first, the perception of the report in the African American community and, second, the extent to which concepts centered on "improving" the black family of the 1960s must be read as examples of the "scientification of the social." A final section compares the concepts of family and masculinity privileged by the various wings of the black civil rights movement. Reflections on the positioning of black feminists within debates on the self-assertion of the African American family conclude the chapter.

---

[7] On the intertwining of racial discrimination against and sexual exploitation of African American women, see also McGuire, Danielle L., *At the Dark End of the Street. Black Women, Rape and Resistance—A New History of the Civil Rights Movement from Rosa Parks to the Rise of Black Power* (New York 2010).

4.1 The changing social structure of African American families in the twentieth century

The history of the social structure of black families is always partly the history of social experts discriminating against and pathologizing them, of their coining of potent stereotypes such as "black hyperfertility," African American "welfare queens," and "black family pathologies." These ideas stand in contrast with the profound processes of social change actually experienced by black families in the twentieth century—though here it is crucial to ask in exactly what ways they developed differently from white families. As the previous chapters have shown, first, the divorce rates of African American couples increased substantially in the first decades of the twentieth century—but this correlated with national trends, regardless of "race." Second, black women's fertility rates were significantly higher than those of white American women, particularly in the first two decades of the twentieth century. In contrast, the last third of the twentieth century saw a decline in births among African American women, again in line with the general national trend. Third, black females have always made up a greater percentage of the labor force than white American women, and this share continued to rise after 1945. Interestingly, however, the proportion of black wives with children among women in employment grew at a much lower rate than among the majority white population—although African American women married younger up to 1950 and were less likely to remain unmarried than their white counterparts until 1970.[8] This observation is important, especially as a foil for the debates on single parents and mothers of children born out of wedlock.

In the mid-twentieth century—culminating in the 1965 Moynihan Report, to be discussed in a moment—white social experts criticized the black population for its higher fertility rate, higher proportion of out-of-wedlock births, and greater presence of single mothers. While these observations are borne out by statistics, they highlight parallel national trends. Hence, the birth rate of "nonwhites" (until 1970, there was no separate data collection for African Americans and "persons of Hispanic origin") was proportionately higher than that of white Americans, but both rates declined consistently from the mid-twentieth century onward. While nonwhite American women had 35.0 children per 1,000 persons in 1920 (whites: 26.9), the figure fell to 26.7 in 1940 (whites: 18.6), before rising to 34.7 births in 1955 (whites: 23.8), and falling back to 27.6 births in 1965 (whites: 18.3), the year

---

8 Elliott, Diana B. (et al.), "Historical Marriage Trends from 1890–2010. A Focus on Race Differences." SEHSD Working Paper 2012–12, https://www.census.gov/hhes/socdemo/marriage/data/acs/ElliottetalPAA2012paper.pdf, figure 4.

the Moynihan Report was published.[9] Thus, after a brief upswing during the baby boom, both birth rates fell once more, so that in 1965 the pre-war level had essentially been reached again.

Fourth, data on the evolution out-of-wedlock births in the United States also points to a secular trend into which African Americans' childbearing behavior neatly fits. Throughout the twentieth century, out-of-wedlock births increased, with black women having more children with this status than their white counterparts. At the beginning of the twenty-first century, however, the proportion of such births among African American women declined. While the proportion of all births out of wedlock in the U.S. was 3.8 percent in 1940, in the last third of the twentieth century it rose from 10.7 percent (1970) to 28 percent (1990) and 41 percent (2008) of total births, then declined to 40.3 percent (2014).[10] Among black mothers, the proportion of out-of-wedlock births rose from 37.6 percent (1970) to 67 percent (1990) and 72 percent (2008), though there was a pronounced fall to 70.9 percent in 2014. Among Hispanic mothers, the proportion who had a child without a marriage certificate climbed in recent years from 37 percent (1990) to 53 percent (2008). In 2015, it then decreased slightly to 52.9 percent. Among white mothers, almost one third currently have children without being married, at 29.2 percent (2014) and 29 percent (2008), compared with only 17 percent in 1990 and just 5.7 percent in 1970.[11]

Fifth, the percentage of single mothers was and is higher among African American mothers than among Mexican Americans and white American women.[12] However, while the percentage of single mothers among the black minority increased from about 18 percent to around 30 percent between 1960 and 1990, the increase among members of the white majority was greater during the same period—from about 2.5 percent to around 7.5 percent; in absolute numbers, in any case, the white majority dominated.[13] At the same time, it should be noted that in 1960 more than 70 percent of all African American families had two parents; in 1990, the figure was still more than half.

---

[9] Grove, Robert D. and Hetzel, Alice, "Vital Statistics Rates in the United States 1940–1960." National Center for Health Statistics (Washington D. C. 1968).

[10] Ventura, Stephanie J. (et al.), "Nonmarital Childbearing in the United States, 1940–99. National Vital Statistics Report from the Center for Disease Control and Prevention," National Center for Health Statistics, National Vital Statistics System, 48, no. 16, October 18, 2000.

[11] Chadwick and Heaton, *Statistical Handbook*, 84, Livingston and Cohn, "New Demography," 11.

[12] For the first third of the twentieth century, see Igra, Anna, *Wives without Husbands. Marriage, Desertion, and Welfare in New York, 1900–1935* (Chapel Hill 2007). On discrimination against African American mothers, see Ladd-Taylor and Umansky (eds.), *Bad Mothers*. Landry, *Black Working Wives*. Chappell, *War on Welfare*.

[13] Landry, *Black Working Wives*, 8.

4.1 The changing social structure of African American families in the twentieth century — 213

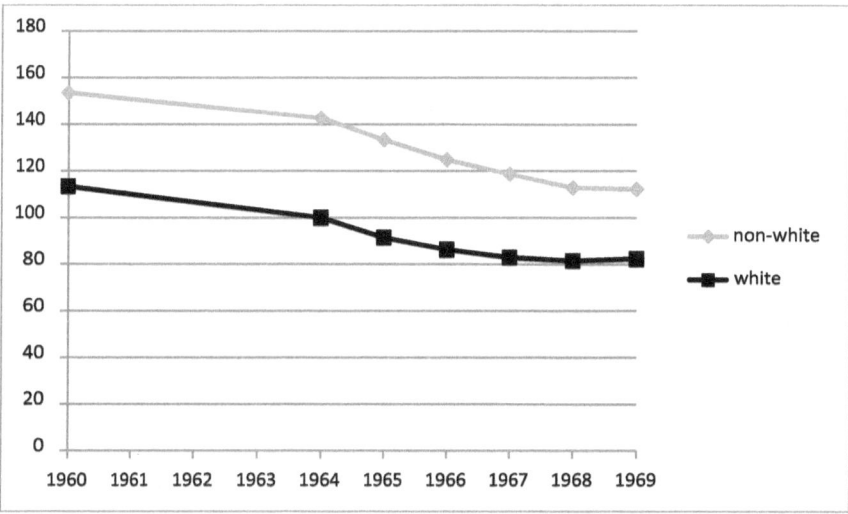

Fig. 4.1: Births per 1,000 women aged 15 to 44, 1960–1969.

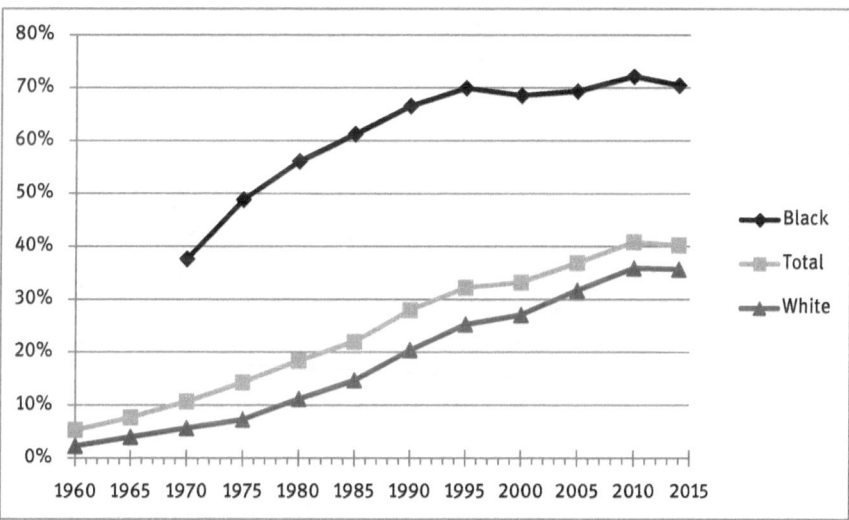

Fig. 4.2: Proportion of out-of-wedlock births by ethnicity, 1960–2014.

This was in line with the secular trend toward a greater number of single mothers, which was particularly pronounced among African American families, but even in the latter group single mothers were by no means the dominant family type.[14] It is also important to note that for all ethnic groups the proportion of married couples fell significantly in the second half of the twentieth century.[15] These figures alone prove that the panic about the "breakdown of the black family" rampant in the mid-1960s was not based on a careful evaluation of social scientific data, but on the extrapolation, which made a major splash in the media, of dramatic findings from deprived inner-city areas.

Despite initial steps toward desegregation since the 1950s (*Brown v. Board of Education*, 1954) and despite the push for equality through the civil rights policies of the 1960s (Civil Rights Act of 1964 and Voting Rights Act of 1965), members of the African American minority, sixth, were subject to severe legal and socioeconomic disadvantages, which translated into significantly lower household incomes, higher unemployment, poorer educational opportunities, and higher infant mortality rates. During the first half of the twentieth century, the mortality of black babies under one year of age was still strikingly higher than that of white infants, but it dropped significantly during the twentieth century, while remaining about twice as high. Whereas in 1935 more than 80 of every 1,000 African American babies born alive died, by 1960 the figure was just over 40, and by 1980 it was slightly more than 20. This compares to just over 50 deaths per 1,000 newborns of white skin color in 1935, just over 20 in 1960, and about 10 infants dying per 1,000 live births in 1980.[16] By contrast, another indicator of unequal health care that has tended to worsen in recent decades is the preterm birth rate. In 1990, for example, 19 percent of the children of black women were born prematurely, compared to just 8.5 percent of those born to white mothers. In 2012, the preterm birth rate was 17.5 percent among the black minority and 10 percent among the majority white population.[17]

Generally, the educational attainment (and thus career opportunities) of African American mothers was also significantly lower than that of white mothers, whereas the rate of teenage pregnancy was markedly higher. Finally, while black mothers were employed in greater numbers, they were also appreciably more likely to be unemployed than white American women. The unemployment rate for African American women was consistently twice as high between 1962 and

---

14 United States Census Bureau, "Current Population Survey," <www.census.gov/hhes/families/files/graphics/CH-1.pdf>.
15 United States Census Bureau, "Current Population Survey," <www.census.gov/hhes/families/files/graphics/FM-2.pdf>.
16 "Seven Decades of Progress and Disparities," U.S. Department of Health and Human Services, Health Resources and Service Administration, Maternal and Child Health Bureau (Rockville, Maryland 2010), <www.mchb.hrsa.gov>.
17 Hamilton, Brady E. (et al.), "Birth: Preliminary Data for 2012," *National Vital Statistics Reports*, vol. 62, 3 (2013), 4.

2012 (around 12 percent, with an outlier of nearly 18 percent in 1982) as that of white females (around 6 percent, with a high of 8 percent in 1982).[18]

Consequently, the affluent American family was essentially white—this was already true in the 1930s but was especially the case during the economic boom of the 1950s and 1960s. Thus, we can observe a steady increase in family incomes since the end of World War II, but this exhibits serious ethnic differences. Whereas in 1947 a family in the U.S. had to get by on an average of $20,402 a year (in 2001 dollars), the figure was $38,954 by 1970 and $52,310 by 2000. The incomes of white families were slightly above the national average, at $21,250 (1947), $40,411 (1970) and $54,742 (2000). In contrast, African American families had to content themselves with a much lower average household income, despite a higher percentage

Fig. 4.3: The affluent American family is white. Victims of the Ohio River flood of 1937 in Louisville, Kentucky, wait for food donations.

---

18 Bureau of Labor Statistics, U.S. Department of Labor, The Economics Daily, "Unemployment Rates by Race and Ethnicity, 2010," <www.bls.gov/opub/ted/2011/ted_20111005.htm>. U.S. Department of Labor, Women's Bureau, "Facts over Time, Women in the Labor Force," (2012).

increase in income, namely an average of $10,864 (1947), then later $24,789 (1970) and $35,146 (2000). The economic situation was particularly difficult for single mothers, whose average family income grew from $14,640 (1947) to $20,107 (1970) and $26,514 (2000).[19]

Although many African American families succeeded in moving up into the middle class, they did so to a much lesser extent than white ones.[20] For example, after World War II, it was above all white ex-soldiers who benefited from the Servicemen's Readjustment Act, the law intended to reintegrate veterans into society, better known as the G. I. Bill of Rights: they received low-cost home loans and business start-up loans, job skills training, and free college tuition. Although non-white G. I.s were formally eligible as well, local officials, banks, housing commissions, and, not least, the large white colleges continued to exclude them. The majority of the approximately 100,000 black veterans who had applied for educational grants by 1946 had to make do with the overcrowded and poorly equipped African American colleges and a return to lower-paying, under-skilled jobs.[21] White veterans' generally superior education and low-cost loans made it easier for them to participate in the economic recovery and achieve an initially modest level of economic prosperity, epitomized in the suburban single-family home produced cheaply and en masse in the 1950s.[22] Its picture windows, like the surrounding lawn, the white picket fence, and the architectural uniformity became a key signifier of U.S. family life in the first two postwar decades. This world was long inaccessible to most African American families or was deliberately denied to them by housing developers and landlords, who demanded inflated rents or purchase prices to keep the residential environment ethnically homogeneous.[23] Also significant was the practice of "redlining," the delimitation of mostly inner-city residential neighborhoods according to ethnic and social criteria—so that in the "ghettos" inhabited by ethnic minorities, services such as healthcare, educational facilities, and even supermarkets were generally costly and of poor quality, help-

---

19 "Money Income of Families—Median Income in Current and Constant (2001) Dollars by Race and Type of Family: 1947 to 2001," U.S. Census Bureau, *Statistical Abstract of the United States 2003, Mini Historical Statistics*, 42–43.
20 Billingsley, *Black Families*. Landry, Bart, *Black Working Wives. Pioneers of the American Family Revolution* (Berkeley and Los Angeles 2000).
21 Katznelson, Ira, *When Affirmative Action was White. The Untold History of Racial Inequality in Twentieth Century America* (New York 2005).
22 Baxandall and Ewen, *Picture Windows*. Jackson, *Crabgrass Frontier*.
23 On the segregation of the suburbs, see Baxandall and Ewen, *Picture Windows*, 171–190. Jackson, *Crabgrass Frontier*.

ing to ensure that these areas steadily worsened compared with the neighborhoods and suburbs inhabited by whites from the middle of the century onward.[24]

Meanwhile, the iconic images of suburbia—such as Levittown near New York—should not obscure the fact that families in the United States were by no means predominantly "ideal" white nuclear families living in the suburban family home, but were also to be found in the city and countryside. This was especially true of African American families, who found themselves disproportionately often in urban neighborhoods and big-city ghettos—this too was a result of the intensive internal migration between the rural regions of the South and the cities of the North and Northeast as well as the practice of "redlining."

The vast majority of all families in the United States now live in cities. Whereas at the beginning of the twentieth century (1900) 60.4 percent of the U.S. population lived in rural areas and only 39.4 percent in cities, the ratio had already reversed by 1950 (64 to 36 percent). From 1920 onward, the urban population already outnumbered the rural populace. By 2000, 79 percent of all Americans lived in urban agglomerations and only 21 percent in rural regions. It was the difficult living conditions of the poor black urban population that were the focus of interest for some of the first African American sociologists.

4.2 "The Negro family in America": structure and values of the African American family in the research of black sociologists

In the first decades of the twentieth century, it was mainly African American sociologists who studied the structure of the black American family; white social scientists, meanwhile, had not yet discovered it as an object of research, but instead focused primarily on immigrants. For example, W. E. B. DuBois, one of the first African American sociologists of national importance, published a study entitled *The Negro Family in America* as early as 1908.[25] It was written at the University of At-

---

[24] On the concentration of African American families in big-city ghettos since the early twentieth century, see Taylor, Henry Louis, *Historical Roots of the Urban Crisis. African Americans in the Industrial City, 1900–1950* (New York and London 2000). Massey, Douglas S. and Denton, Nancy A., *American Apartheid: Segregation and the Making of the Underclass* (Cambridge MA 1993).

[25] William Edward Burghardt DuBois (1868–1963), was a historian, sociologist, and one of the most influential early civil rights activists in the United States. The co-founder of the National Association for the Advancement of Colored People (NAACP), he was also the first African American to earn a doctorate from Harvard University. From 1897 he taught history and economics at Atlanta University, where he established the Atlanta Conference for the Study of Negro Problems.

lanta, where DuBois taught, in the context of the annual Atlanta University Negro Conference, which he had founded. Since the late nineteenth century, this institution had been conducting a large-scale "social study of the Negro American" with the aim of collecting scientific data and promoting "social reform." Although the first available statistics suggested that African Americans had a marriage frequency and family size comparable to that of the U.S. population as a whole, DuBois nevertheless feared a threat to the black family, firstly because of a slightly higher number of "broken families." Second, he noted an increase in the proportion of single women due to later marriage and higher infant mortality.[26] He was particularly concerned about the higher number of out-of-wedlock births among the black minority, explaining the illegitimacy rate of just over 20 percent (1907) with reference to a generally laxer sexual morality:

> Sexual immorality is probably the greatest single plague spot among Negro Americans, and its greatest cause is slavery and the present utter disregard of a black woman's virtue and self-respect, both in law court and custom in the South.[27]

At the same time, however, DuBois also made it clear that through her genuine motherly love, sense of family, and the number of children she typically had, the African American woman was well-placed to provide a positive example for white females and for modern white society in general, whose survival was threatened by "prostitution, divorce and childlessness."[28] DuBois' work was always overshadowed by that of the Chicago School of Sociology, which was run by white sociologists around Robert E. Park and adhered to a gradualist theory of assimilation. Given his groundbreaking and empirically grounded research on the mechanisms of race and social inequality within the interplay between black and white Americans, however, he was leaps and bounds ahead of them in terms

---

He was founder and longtime editor of the NAACP journal *The Crisis* (1910–1933) and published a variety of sociological and historical studies as well as several novels and a total of three autobiographies. Marable, Manning, *W. E. B. Du Bois—Black Radical Democrat* (New York 2005). Zamir, Shamoon (ed.), *The Cambridge Companion to W. E. B. Du Bois* (Cambridge [etc.] 2008).

26 DuBois, William Edward Burghardt, *The Negro Family in the United States* (London and New York 2005, original edition Atlanta 1908), 31.

27 Elsewhere, DuBois emphasized the connection between sexual morality and family even more strongly: "Without doubt the point where the Negro American is furthest behind modern civilization is in his sexual *mores*. [. . .] It does mean that he is more primitive, less civilized, in this respect than his surroundings demand, and that thus his family life is less efficient for its onerous social duties, his womanhood less protected, his children more poorly trained." DuBois, *Negro Family*, 37, 41.

28 DuBois, *Negro Family*, 42.

of content.[29] As Aldon Morris has brought out, DuBois, unlike his contemporaries, opposed both the thesis of the biological or cultural inferiority of African Americans and the demand for unconditional assimilation into the white mainstream as early as the first third of the twentieth century.[30] To shed light on the social problems of many black Americans and their families, meanwhile, he highlighted the importance of the social environment, the interaction between racial prejudice and economic-social repression, and the connection between racial and sexist discrimination—thus laying the argumentative foundation, as early as 1920, for the civil rights movement's demand for full social participation.

Three decades after DuBois' pioneering work, the sociologist E. Franklin Frazier, himself a member of the Chicago School, published his study on *The Negro Family in the United States* (1939).[31] This was based on his 1932 dissertation "The

---

29 The Chicago School of Sociology is a collective term for a school of thought and a body of work on urban sociology that emerged in the 1920s and 1930s at the Department of Sociology of the University of Chicago, one of the most tradition-steeped in the country. Here sociologists combined theoretical approaches from developmental biology, ecology, and evolutionary theory with ethnographic fieldwork, a revolutionary practice at the time that permanently changed sociological research. Members of this so-called First Chicago School included Ernest Burgess, Edward Franklin Frazier, and Robert E. Park. Robert Ezra Park (1864–1944) was one of the most influential first-generation sociologists in the United States. After a period at the Tuskegee Institute in Chicago (1905–1914), where he collaborated with Booker T. Washington, he taught sociology at the University of Chicago from 1914 to 1933 and was one of the key figures in the First Chicago School. His work focused on urban ecology and race relations; he condensed his reflections on the causes of racial discrimination from his time at the Tuskegee Institute into an assimilation theory that he used to examine the integration of immigrants into U.S. society. In addition, through his theoretical work, Park contributed significantly to the development of the Chicago School's approach to urban sociology. He was also an influential academic manager, and president during several periods of the American Sociological Association (ASA) and the Chicago Urban League. Park, Robert E., McKenzie, R. D., and Burgess, Ernest, *The City. Suggestions for the Study of Human Nature in the Urban Environment* (Chicago 1925). Park, Robert E., "Human Migration and the Marginal Man," *American Journal of Sociology* 33 (1928), 881–893. Park, Robert E. and Thompson, Edgar T., *Race Relations and the Race Problem. A Definition and an Analysis* (Durham, NC 1939).
30 Morris, Aldon D., "Sociology of Race and W. E. B. DuBois: The Path Not Taken," in Calhoun, Craig (ed.), *Sociology in America. A History* (Chicago: Chicago University Press, 2007), 503–534.
31 Edward Franklin Frazier (1894–1962) taught as a sociologist at Howard University, Washington, D. C., from 1934 until his death in 1962. After first directing the Atlanta School of Social Work at Atlanta University (W. E. B. DuBois, who also worked at Atlanta University, was among his academic role models) and serving as a lecturer in sociology at the prestigious black Morehouse College, Frazier took up an appointment at the University of Chicago. In Atlanta, he had been dismissed after the publication of his controversial article "The Pathology of Race Prejudice" in the *Forum* journal (1927). At Chicago, he earned his doctorate in 1932 from the Department of Sociology (his teachers and mentors included Burgess and Parks); the Chicago School's ap-

Negro Family in Chicago" and explained the problematic state of the black family with reference to the consequences of slavery.[32] Although Frazier too viewed the political, social, and economic discrimination against African Americans in U.S. society as an explanation for the threats facing the "Negro family" in the shape of illegitimacy, absent fathers, and juvenile delinquency, his conclusions were very different from those of his former mentor DuBois:

> The survival of the Negro in American civilization is a measure, in a sense, of his success in adopting the culture of the whites or an indication of the fact the Negro has found within the white man's culture a satisfying life and a faith in his future.[33]

Unlike DuBois, who had always criticized the demand, especially as put forward by white sociologists, for the total assimilation of African Americans, Frazier foregrounded this very prospect. For him, successful assimilation functioned via the family.

> The gains in civilization which result from participation in the white world will in the future as in the past be transmitted to future generations through the family.[34]

Thanks to better opportunities for education and upward mobility, Frazier averred, a black middle class had gradually emerged in modern society. This social stratum, he contended, formed the backbone of the black community, not only because of its focus on upward social mobility and consumerism, but especially because of its stable families and its orientation toward the values of the white majority society.

> The emergence of a relatively large and influential middle class which has been uprooted from its "racial" traditions has influenced in other ways the form and functioning of the Negro family. The Negro family has been largely oriented to the values of the American culture.[35]

---

proaches to the sociology of the black minority clearly influenced his work. Frazier was the first African American to become president of the ASA.

32 Frazier, Edward Franklin, *The Negro Family in the United States* (New York 1939). See also Frazier's further research: Frazier, Edward Franklin, "Problems and Needs of Negro Children and Youth Resulting from Family Disintegration," *Journal of Negro Education* 19 (1950), 269–277. Frazier, Edward Franklin, *The Negro in the United States* (New York 1949). Frazier, Edward Franklin (ed.), *The Integration of the Negro into American Society* (Washington D. C. 1951). Frazier, Edward Franklin, *Black Bourgeoisie. The Rise of a New Middle Class in the United States* (Glencoe, IL 1957, French first edition 1955). Frazier, Edward Franklin, *On Race Relations. Selected Writings* (Chicago 1968).

33 Frazier, Edward Franklin, "The Negro Family in America," in Frazier, Edward Franklin, *On Race Relations*, 191–209, 209.

34 Frazier, *The Negro Family*, 488.

35 Frazier, "The Negro Family," 207.

In arguing that African American families could decisively improve their social, economic, and ideational situation by adopting the values and moral concepts of the white middle class, Frazier forged a link to the assimilation theory espoused by his academic teacher Robert E. Park of the Chicago School of Sociology.[36] The explosive force of this argument was intensified by the fact that here a renowned African American sociologist was advocating the unconditional adaptation of blacks to white middle-class culture on the basis of empirical findings. Frazier's work, moreover, provided the frame of reference for the reception of the first monumental study by a white researcher on the situation of the black minority in the United States, Gunnar Myrdal's *American Dilemma* of 1944.

4.3 From the "American dilemma" to the "tangle of pathology": the black family in the analyses of contemporary social scientists from the 1940s to the 1960s

The year 1944 saw the publication of *An American Dilemma. The Negro Problem and Modern Democracy*, an examination of the situation of the African American minority and the significance of racism in the United States.[37] This text was to have a decisive influence on thinking about black families, their structure, and their values over the next two decades, partly because it was the first time that an internationally renowned researcher had made clear statements about the causes and effects of racial discrimination in the United States.[38] Hence, in a certain sense, Myrdal—rather than Moynihan in 1965—initiated a change of scholarly direction and induced the white mainstream of social science to gradually discover this minority and its families as a subject of research. Gunnar Myrdal's reflections on the persistence of racism in the United States were based on exten-

---

[36] It is interesting to note that while both Robert E. Park and Ernest Burgess examined the significance of racial discrimination and the structure of the family, they did not make the African American family itself the object of their research. Burgess, Ernest W., "The Family as a Unity of Interacting Personalities," *The Family: Journal of Social Case Work* (1926), 7, 3–9. Park et al., *Race Relations*.

[37] Myrdal, Gunnar with the assistance of Richard Sterner and Arnold Rose, *An American Dilemma. The Negro Problem and Modern Democracy* (New York 1944).

[38] Jackson, Walter A., *Gunnar Myrdal and America's Conscience. Social Engineering and Racial Liberalism, 1938–1987* (Chapel Hill 1990). Southern, David W., *Gunnar Myrdal and Black-White Relations. The Use and Abuse of An American Dilemma, 1944–1969* (Baton Rouge and London 1987).

sive empirical surveys, but they could also build on the work of African American sociologists. This was especially true of their studies on the family.[39]

Myrdal himself was a renowned Swedish social scientist who is regarded by contemporary historians as one of the founding fathers of modern "social engineering."[40] At the behest of the Carnegie Foundation, which had specifically appointed a foreigner and citizen of a neutral country to head the study, Myrdal and his large team of researchers had been collecting material in the U.S. since 1938.[41] In his 1500-page monograph, he examined the living situation of African Americans in the United States, the discrimination they faced and their lack of social and economic integration from various perspectives. The nine empirical chapters dealt with the topics of "race, population and migration, economics, politics, justice, social inequality, social stratification, leadership and concerted action, the Negro community" and thus pursued a broad socio-historical approach. A first section outlines Myrdal's scholarly perspective, a concluding chapter takes stock of ways of solving the "American dilemma," and two appendices elucidate Myrdal's methods. The latter are particularly important because Myrdal took a new approach within sociology by considering values and beliefs in his analysis of relations between majority whites and minority blacks.[42] For him—and here he consciously set himself apart from all his social scientific predecessors—racial discrimination in the U.S. could only be examined as a moral problem, as part of

---

[39] Myrdal himself cited Frazier's research extensively, but also mentioned how much inspiration he had drawn from DuBois's early 1899 study, *The Philadelphia Negro*. Myrdal, *American Dilemma*, 1132. Morris, "Sociology of Race," 531.

[40] Gunnar Myrdal (1898–1987) was an economist, sociologist and social reformer who received the Nobel Prize in economics in 1974. In his early career, he was particularly interested in the connection between politics and economics: in 1927, he gained his doctorate from Stockholm University with a study on the role of expectations in price formation. In 1933 he became a professor at the Stockholm School of Economics. Together with his wife Alva Myrdal, he published a widely acclaimed study on the *Crisis in the Population Question* (*Kris i bevolkningsfrågan*) in 1934, followed by numerous other reflections on how to compensate for the negative consequences of modernity by reorganizing social relations. The Myrdals' ideas found their way into Swedish social policy and the couple became a prime example of Western social engineers. Etzemüller, Thomas, *Die Romantik der Rationalität. Alva & Gunnar Myrdal—Social Engineering in Schweden* (Bielefeld 2010). Etzemüller, Thomas, "Die Romantik des Reißbretts. Social Engineering und demokratische Volksgemeinschaft in Schweden. Das Beispiel Alva und Gunnar Myrdal (1930–1960)," *Geschichte und Gesellschaft* 32 (2006), 445–466.

[41] Myrdal's most important collaborators were the Swede Richard Sterner and the American Arnold M. Rose.

[42] For a critique of this approach, see the discussion below. On *The American Dilemma*, see also Etzemüller, "Romantik des Reißbretts," 273–288.

the American constitution's promise of equality and freedom, and at the same time as fundamentally at variance with the "American Creed."

> The American Negro Problem is a problem in the heart of the American. [. . .] The "American Dilemma," [. . .] is the ever-raging conflict between, on the one hand, the valuations preserved on the general plane which we shall call the "American Creed," where the American thinks, talks and acts under the influence of high national and Christian precepts, and, on the other hand, the valuations on specific planes of individual and group living, where personal and local interests; economic, social, and sexual jealousies; considerations of community prestige and conformity; group prejudice against particular persons or types of people; and all sorts of miscellaneous wants, impulses, and habits dominate his outlook.[43]

Myrdal did not consider the American Creed primarily as a national characteristic, but rather as a value system subject to dynamic change within certain limits, a system that stood symbolically for the basic values of modern, democratic states. Yet for the United States, he averred, the "Negro problem" represented a painful discrepancy with these universal values for both white and black citizens:

> The Negro in America has not yet been given the elemental civil and political rights of formal democracy, including a fair opportunity to earn his living, upon which a general accord was already won when the "American Creed" was first taking form.[44]

Only in the economic sphere, Myrdal argued, was the social value system of the "American Creed" less effective; here, it was the tradition of economic exploitation since slavery that dominated, along with its consequences. Myrdal referred to a "vicious circle" to convey this state of affairs, a downward spiral of constantly worsening living conditions for African Americans as a result of racist discrimination, social depravation, and economic exploitation: "Poverty itself breeds the conditions which perpetuate poverty."[45]

Despite Myrdal's profound decision to clearly identify moral prejudices and traditions of economic oppression, the section on the "Negro community"—as Walter A. Jackson has already pointed out—was surprisingly weak and characterized by cultural prejudices.[46] Myrdal described "Negro culture" and the "Negro community" as deviations from the norm of the majority society, as a "pathology,"

---

43 Myrdal, *American Dilemma*, xlvii. "The American's Creed" is a 1918 affirmation of the contents of the constitution endorsed by the House of Representatives, written by William Tyler Page in 1917. Text at <www.ushistory.org/documents/creed.htm>.
44 Myrdal, *American Dilemma*, 24.
45 Myrdal, *American Dilemma*, 208. See also the abridged version of the book authorized by Myrdal: Rose, Arnold M., *The Negro in America. A Condensation of An American Dilemma, by Gunnar Myrdal with the assistance of Richard Sterner and Arnold Rose* (London 1948), 294–296.
46 Jackson, *Gunnar Myrdal*, 227.

while emphasizing that this was not meant in a pejorative sense.[47] It is important to note here that Myrdal understood "Negro culture" as in principle culturally changeable and not as biologically determined:

> In practically all its divergences, American Negro culture is not something independent of general American culture. It is a distorted development, or a pathological condition, of the general American culture.[48]

Myrdal argued pragmatically that it was desirable for "American Negroes as individuals and as a group to become assimilated into American culture, to acquire the traits held in esteem by the dominant white Americans."[49] At the same time, he qualified this by underscoring that he had no wish to disparage a minority culture, but was merely seeking to highlight this minority's practical life chances. One expression of this alleged "social pathology" was the "instability of the Negro family," and here Myrdal distinguished between direct and indirect signs of "family disorganization."[50] For him, the most important direct characteristics were the comparatively high illegitimacy rate and the proportion of "broken families."[51] Indirect signs of the threatened stability of African American families, meanwhile, were the high number of "lodgers," the cohabitation of several nuclear families in one household, the tendency to live in cramped spaces, and the generally low proportion of property ownership. Drawing on the reflections of E. Franklin Frazier, Myrdal identified slavery as the cause of the specific structure and lower stability of the black family.[52] In addition, and this represents a real achievement of *An American Dilemma*, Myrdal highlighted positive factors, such as the fact that illegitimacy and living together without an official marriage document ("common law marriage") were not stigmatized as morally reprehensible, which had a fundamentally positive effect on those involved. He also considered the generally high esteem in which children were held and the rejection of forced marriages in conjunction with moral standards (rejection of sexual promiscuity and lax sexual

---

47 Myrdal, *American Dilemma*, 928f.
48 Myrdal, *American Dilemma*, 927f.
49 Myrdal, *American Dilemma*, 929.
50 Here, Jackson demonstrates an inconsistency in Myrdal's thinking, since in earlier works he had described the nuclear family as almost pathological and mulled social techniques for overcoming it. Jackson, *Gunnar Myrdal*, 226.
51 Based on the U.S. Bureau of the Census, Myrdal refers to 20.3 illegitimate babies per 1,000 births in 1936 among the white majority population and 162.1 illegitimate births per 1,000 among the members of so-called "other races," which he assumes to be "predominantly Negro." In 1930, we are informed, about 19.5 percent of all white families were "broken families," compared with 29.6 percent of broken "Negro families." Myrdal, *American Dilemma*, 932, 934.
52 Myrdal, *American Dilemma*, 931–935. Frazier, *The Negro Family*.

morals) to be positive. In general, he noted that these practices were often consistent with the wellbeing of the community, even if they lay outside American traditions:

> But the important thing is that the Negro lower classes, especially in the rural South, have built a type of family organization conductive to social health, even though the practices are outside the American tradition. When these practices are brought in closer contact with white norms, as occurs when Negroes go to the cities, they tend to break down partially and to cause the demoralization of some individuals.[53]

This fundamental idea of Myrdal's that the African American minority featured family structures and values that were conducive to the common good is of signal importance. More than twenty years later, in the midst of the debate over the Moynihan Report, only representatives of the civil rights movement were to take this position, whereas social experts merely emphasized the threat to society as a whole posed by the supposed pathologies of the black family.

An American Dilemma was praised shortly after its publication as a monumental social scientific study that analyzed a crucial social problem on the basis of a broad range of material. In her review in the *New York Times*, writer Frances Gaither praised Myrdal for holding up a mirror to Americans and their contradictory interpretation of the "American Creed" through his study. She pointed out that the belief in human rights and the opportunity for upward mobility for all people ("our rational creed") clashed with persistent prejudices and assumptions of biological "inferiority" ("our irrational customs"). Myrdal, she contended, had made it clear that the white majority society was responsible for legal and social discrimination against African Americans—and there could be no justification for this oppression as an aspect of regional customs and traditions of the South.[54] This extremely positive review of the study by the *New York Times* continued to have an effect in the years that followed: whenever equal rights for blacks were discussed in the 1940s, articles referred to the groundbreaking role of *An American Dilemma*.[55] The book's title advanced to the status of fixed expression, which could be invoked at any time in the political-social debate, as evident in sociologist Horace R. Cayton's review of another book:

---

53 Myrdal, *American Dilemma*, 935.
54 Gaither, Frances, "Democracy—the Negro's Hope," NYT, April 2, 1944, BR7.
55 "Education and the Negro," NYT, February 9, 1948, 18. "Race Relations Changes Held Due Soon," WP, June 5, 1948. Patrick Dempsey, "American Dilemma, Army Model: Last of the Conquerors," NYT, September 5, 1948, BR6. Hodding Carter, "The Negro in America, by Arnold Rose," WP, December 5, 1948, B5.

> The American dilemma has been described as our inability to live up to the high moral precepts we have enunciated in such political documents as the Bill of Rights, the Constitution, and even the Four Freedoms—a dilemma documented in "American Dilemma", the monumental work of Gunnar Myrdal.[56]

Myrdal also received overwhelmingly positive reviews in the specialized press of the 1940s, the reaction of African American sociologists being particularly enthusiastic. W. E. B. DuBois, for example, praised Myrdal's focus on the norms and values of U.S. society, since the Swedish scholar understood the American "Negro problem" primarily as a "moral problem." This, DuBois stated, was the only way to adequately explain the persistence of racism—rather than by referring to material categories of discrimination supposedly amenable to precise scientific measurement: "In other words, the sociology of Myrdal emancipates itself from physical and biological and psychological analogies, and openly and frankly takes into account emotions, thoughts, opinions and ideals."[57] In the *American Journal of Sociology*, meanwhile, E. Franklin Frazier praised the book's breadth of empirical research, methodological foundation, and the timing of its publication "during the present critical stage in race relations." At the same time, he claimed that characterizing the "Negro problem" as a "moral problem" did not sufficiently take into account the attitudes of many whites, who were accustomed to considering African Americans as neither part of their social world nor of their moral order:

> One would certainly agree with the author in the sense that all social problems are moral problems. But it might be questioned whether the problem is on the conscience of white people to the extent implied in his statement of the problem.[58]

Myrdal also received positive reviews in other sociological journals,[59] although some white social scientists criticized his assumption of sole white responsibility for the "Negro problem" as too one-sided[60] or, in the style of Frazier, warned that

---

56 Cayton, Horace R., "A Study of Race Relations," NYT, April 17, 1949, BR16. See also Cayton, Horace R. and Drake, St. Clair, *Black Metropolis. A Study of Negro Life in a Northern City* (New York 1945).
57 DuBois, W. E. B., "An American Dilemma," review in *Phylon*, vol. 5, 2 (1944), 118–124, here 122. See also the review by L. D. Reddick in *Journal of Negro Education*, vol. 13, 2 (Spring 1944), 191–194.
58 Frazier, E. Franklin, review of *An American Dilemma* by Gunnar Myrdal with the assistance of Richard Sterner and Arnold Rose, *AJS* vol. 50, 6 (May 1945), 555–557, 556.
59 See, for example, the enthusiastic review by political scientist Harold F. Gosnell in *American Political Science Review*, vol. 38, 5 (October 1944), 995–996.
60 See, for example, the review by the thirty-fifth president of the ASA, Kimball Young, in *American Sociological Review*, vol. 9, 3 (1944), 326–330, here 328.

white society was not yet sufficiently aware of its moral prejudice.[61] Most notable, however, was the review by lawyer and judge of the United States District Court for the District of Massachusetts, Charles Edward Wyzanski Jr., in the *Harvard Law Review*. He argued that the book's true merit lay in its potential use as a tool for the "widespread education of the white man as to the capacities of the Negro":

> Thus, in deciding the rights and liberties which the Negro should have, the people cast their vote when the Negro applies for a job, or he seeks admission to a union, or he asks for equal pay for equal work, or he tries to rent an apartment or buy a house, or he applies for public assistance, or he is in a lawsuit arising out of an automobile accident, or he is arrested on suspicion, or he goes to a town meeting or he seeks to enter an institution of higher education. It is because on these occasions you or I or our neighbor may have a determining voice that we need to know what Myrdal has written.[62]

This largely enthusiastic reception of the book in the 1940s—and of the abridged version produced by Arnold Rose in 1948—contrasts with a somewhat more nuanced as well as more polarized discussion in the 1960s.[63] Against the backdrop of the civil rights movement, the race riots in the Los Angeles neighborhood of Watts and in Chicago, and the debate surrounding the Moynihan Report, Myrdal's analyses were now seen as simplistic and tending to obscure the true backdrop to racial discrimination.[64] Still, Oscar Lewis's notion of a

---

[61] According to Maurice R. Davie in his review for the *Annals of the American Academy of Political and Social Science*, vol. 233 (May 1944), 253–254. Davie specifically criticized Myrdal's marked interest in changing society through "social engineering" and his consequent overestimation of rationalism and morality.

[62] Wyzanski, Charles E. Jr., "An American Dilemma. The Negro Problem and Modern Democracy," *Harvard Law Review*, vol. 58, 2 (December 1944), 285–291, here 291.

[63] When it comes to the 1950s, it is important to note that *An American Dilemma* was among the texts referred to by the Supreme Court in its famous *Brown v. Board of Education* ruling (1954), along with the UNESCO declaration on race (to which E. Franklin Frazier had contributed on behalf of the United States), which assailed attempts to use science to justify racism and the works of Kenneth B. Clark and Mamie Phipps Clark. UNESCO, Publication 791: *The Race Question* (1950). Clark, Kenneth B. and Clark, Mamie Phipps, "Racial Identification and Preference among Negro Children," in Hartley, E. L., *Readings in Social Psychology* (New York 1947), 169–178.

[64] Thomas Etzemüller too states that *An American Dilemma* rapidly lost influence from 1965 on, which he explains as a result of the fact that Myrdal's diagnosis of racism as an irrational phenomenon, chiefly of the South, and his belief in human rationality—while neglecting economic-social conditions—now seemed obsolete. It is interesting that Etzemüller does not mention Moy-

"culture of poverty" (1959, 1969)[65] and Daniel Patrick Moynihan's thesis of the "tangle of pathology" (1965) implicitly interfaced with Myrdal's reflections on the "vicious circle" of racial, social, and economic oppression, though from a different perspective.[66] The so-called Moynihan Report is considered the most conclusive example of the social scientific description of a supposed "culture of poverty" among the black minority. Yet Oscar Lewis had previously emphasized that the thesis of a "culture of poverty" could not be straightforwardly applied to African Americans. Lewis argued that the structures of oppression afflicting black Americans due to centuries of slavery and racist laws were fundamentally different from the treatment of other ethnic minorities. The anthropologist had first developed this thesis with reference to slum-dwellers in Mexico City, before going on to argue that the "culture of poverty" was a characteristic of the lowest social strata in all modern capitalist industrial societies.[67]

In the press of the early 1960s, meanwhile, the discussion was dominated by the extent to which the situation of African Americans in U.S. society had improved. A rather skeptical interjection by historian John Hope Franklin, who—paraphrasing Myrdal's title—referred to the "Negro's Dilemma,"[68] contrasted with Myrdal's own assessment that, after a long period of stagnation following the Civil War, tremendous progress had been made toward equality for the black minority over the preceding twenty years.[69] Myrdal confidently declared to students at Howard University in 1962 that the apt analysis presented in *An Ameri-*

---

nihan or the controversy over the supposed pathology of the African American Family in 1965. Etzemüller, *Romantik der Rationalität*, 287–288.

65 First set out in Lewis, Oscar, *Five Families. Mexican Case Studies in the Culture of Poverty* (1959). Lewis, Oscar, "The Culture of Poverty," in Moynihan, Daniel P., *On Understanding Poverty. Perspectives from the Social Sciences* (New York 1969), 187–220.

66 Moynihan, Daniel Patrick, "The Negro Family. A Case for National Action," in Rainwater, Lee and Yancey, William L. (eds.), *The Moynihan Report and the Politics of Controversy. Including the Full Text of The Negro Family. The Case for National Action by Daniel Patrick Moynihan* (Cambridge and London 1967), 39–124, esp. 75–91.

67 On the Moynihan Report, see below. Lewis, *Five Families*. Lewis, "Culture of Poverty."

68 John Hope Franklin (1915–2009) was a multiply honored, influential American historian of black descent. After stints at Howard University and as head of the History Department at Brooklyn College, he taught at the University of Chicago (1964–1982) and Duke University (1983–1985). His research on nineteenth- and twentieth-century history primarily analyzed the struggle for legal and social equality for African Americans. Franklin, John Hope, "The Negro's Dilemma. The Negro Must Endure Inhospitality in a Land That is His by Right of Birth and Toil," NYT, January 17, 1960, AD5.

69 Baker, Robert E., "'An American Dilemma' Resolved. Myrdal in Howard U. Address Notes Rising Trend of Negro's U.S. Status," WP, June 6, 1962, A1. Myrdal had delivered the commencement address to the graduates of Howard University as early as 1948. See also Myrdal, Gunnar, "Social

can Dilemma had set the stage for this. However, he averred, after the Supreme Court's 1954 desegregation of education through the *Brown v. Board of Education* ruling (which cited *An American Dilemma*), the economic boom, among other things, was now also helping to ease the situation of blacks.[70]

In the second half of the 1960s, the notion of the "American dilemma" had virtually taken on a life of its own in the press. Depending on one's point of view, the economy, racism, or the radicalization of the civil rights movement constituted the "new American dilemma."[71] At the same time, we can identify a growing number of critical voices, such as that of social historian Carl Degler. On the twenty-fifth anniversary of *An American Dilemma* in 1969, he analyzed the current situation of African Americans for the *New York Times*.[72] Under the title "Where Myrdal Went Wrong," Degler criticized the Swedish scholar for overestimating white Americans' willingness to overcome their prejudices and contribute to the integration of blacks. Conversely, he contended, Myrdal had underestimated the importance of the civil rights movement in Southern states and the racism of many whites in the North. Myrdal's conviction that racist prejudices could be overcome through education and "social engineering," he went on, failed completely to grasp the virulence of racism as a social force. Although significant successes in eliminating legal segregation had been achieved since 1944, this had not yet had the desired socio-economic effect. Real equality, he underscored, must not only be invoked as an idea but must also be attained through legal frameworks and federal economic and social programs as well as civil society initiatives.

The reception of Myrdal's classic in the United States thus reveals—in the wake of the civil rights movement and the equal rights legislation of the Johnson era—important changes in perspective on the African American minority and in the parameters of the debate on the social and economic opportunities open to it. The key factor here continued to be the field of the family, as the discussion of

---

Trends in America and Strategic Approaches to the Negro Problem," *Phylon*, vol. 9, 3 (1948), 196–214.

70 Southern, *Gunnar Myrdal*, 127–128. Patterson, James T., *Brown v. Board of Education. A Civil Rights Milestone and Its Troubled Legacy* (New York 2001).

71 Handlin, Oscar, "A Book that Changed American Life. A Revisit to a Classic Work on U.S. Negroes Reminds Us of Progress Made and Yet to Come," NYT, April 21, 1963. Segal, Harvey H., "New 'American Dilemma' is Economic Stagnation," WP, October 15, 1963 (review of Myrdal's new work *Challenge to Affluence*). "The National Commission of Negro Churchmen, Racism and the Elections: The American Dilemma 1966," NYT, November 6, 1966. Glazer, Nathan, "The Negro's Stake in America's Future," NYT, September 22, 1968.

72 Degler, Carl N., "The Negro in America—Where Myrdal Went Wrong," NYT, December 7, 1969.

the events of 1965, especially the racial unrest in major cities[73] and the so-called Moynihan Report, lays bare.[74]

4.4 "To Fulfill these Rights" and the Moynihan Report: June 1965

In the summer of 1965, more than twenty years after Myrdal's study and more than twenty-five years after the publication of Frazier's book, the values and living conditions of black families were once again at the center of a heated public and political debate. This time, the reason for the focus on "black families" was, of all things, a speech by President Lyndon B. Johnson. He had already drafted his program for a Great Society at the beginning of 1964, a project of legal and social reforms that aimed to eliminate racial discrimination and combat poverty in the United States.[75] The two civil rights acts of 1964 and 1965, the War on Poverty[76] waged by means of the Economic Opportunity Act, and the reform of social security through the introduction of health insurance (Medicare) and health benefits for the needy (Medicaid) represented major milestones in this regard.[77]

---

[73] In the second half of the 1960s, there were violent clashes between African American youth and the police in several major U.S. cities. The background was the excessive violence and obvious racism of white police officers, but also the precarious socioeconomic conditions in inner-city slums. In particular, the August 1965 riots in Watts, a suburb of Los Angeles, attracted national attention and underscored the need for sociopolitical solutions. This unrest served as a key reference in the discussion of the Moynihan Report. Cohen, Jerry and Murphy, William S., *Burn, Baby, Burn! The Los Angeles Race Riot, August 1965* (New York 1966). Rustin, Bayard, "The Watts 'Manifesto' & the McCone Report," *Commentary* 41 (1966), 3, 29–35. Horne, Gerald, *Fire This Time. The Watts Uprising and the 1960s* (Charlottesville 1995).

[74] On the connection between Myrdal, Moynihan, and attempts to diagnose the problems of the African American family through the 1980s, see also Southern, *Gunnar Myrdal*, 266–268, 301–303.

[75] For a detailed description of the vision of a "Great Society," see Johnson's speech to students at the University of Michigan at Ann Arbor on May 24, 1964: <www.lbjlib.utexas.edu/johnson/archives.hom/speeches.hom/640522.asp>.

[76] The War on Poverty was the Johnson administration's attempt to combat poverty in the United States through government programs such as the Economic Opportunity Act, the Office of Economic Opportunity (OEO), and the Job Corps. See Orleck, Annelise and Hazirjian, Lisa Gayle (eds.), *The War on Poverty: A New Grassroots History, 1964–1980* (Athens, GA 2011). Bailey, Martha J. and Danziger, Sheldon (eds.), *Legacies of the War on Poverty* (New York 2013).

[77] Gettleman, Marvin E. and Mermelstein, David (eds.), *The Great Society Reader. The Failure of American Liberalism* (New York 1967). Helsing, Jeffrey W., *Johnson's War/Johnson's Great Society. The Guns and Butter Trap* (Westport and London 2000). Dallek, Robert, *Lyndon B. Johnson. Portrait of a President* (Oxford and New York 2004). On Johnson's civil rights policy, see below.

In July 1965, in his commencement address to the graduating class of 1964/1965 at Washington's Howard University—at the time one of the most tradition-steeped members of the category of historically black colleges and universities (HBCUs) in the U.S.—Johnson made the case for his civil rights legislation and announced further measures to combat political, social, and economic discrimination against the black minority. The Civil Rights Act of July 2, 1964, which prohibited any discrimination on the basis of race, skin color, religion, sex, or national origin, was barely a year old.[78] In addition, the Voting Rights Act, which was intended to guarantee African Americans the unimpeded right to vote, was about to be passed.[79] Johnson's famous "To Fulfil These Rights" speech is now considered a landmark in his administration's civil rights policy. It was written by Johnson's personal assistant and speechwriter Richard M. Goodwin, together with Daniel Patrick Moynihan, at the time assistant secretary of labor.[80]

The president stated in no uncertain terms that, despite all the efforts to achieve legal equality, large segments of the black minority still lived as "another nation" in the middle of America—afflicted by poverty, unemployment, inadequate housing, lack of social security and health insurance, poor educational institutions, high infant mortality and low incomes, and penned up in urban ghettos. The president conveyed his promise to help improve the situation of the black minority through further social programs in the famous slogan "freedom is not enough." For him, however, the most important evidence of the precarious situation of African Americans was the lot of the "black family":

---

[78] Loevy, Robert D. (ed.), *The Civil Rights Act of 1964. The Passage of the Law That Ended Racial Segregation* (Albany, NY 1997). Loevy, Robert D., *To End All Segregation. The Politics of the Passage of The Civil Rights Act of 1964* (Lanham, MD 1990). Kotz, Nick, *Judgement Days. Lyndon Baines Johnson, Martin Luther King Jr., and the Laws that Changed America* (New York 2005). On Johnson's civil rights policies in general, see the work of Steven F. Lawson: Lawson, Steven F., *Civil Rights Crossroads: Nation, Community, and the Black Freedom Struggle* (Lexington, KY 2003). Lawson, Steven F., *Running for Freedom. Civil Rights and Black Politics in America Since 1941* (New York 1997).

[79] This then took place on August 6, 1965. Garrow, David J., *Protest at Selma. Martin Luther King, Jr., and the Voting Rights Act of 1965* (New Haven, CT and London 1978). For a good overview of the impact of the act in the individual Southern states, see Davidson, Chandler and Grofman, Bernard (eds.), *Quiet Revolution in the South. The Impact of the Voting Rights Act, 1965–1990* (Princeton, NJ 1994).

[80] Johnson, Lyndon B., "To Fulfill these Rights. Commencement Address at Howard University, June 4, 1965." Reprinted in Rainwater and Yancey, *Moynihan Report*, 125–132. See also the Editor's Note on 125. For the digital version, see <www.lbjlib.utexas.edu/johnson/archives.hom/speeches.hom/650604.asp>.

> Perhaps most important—its influence radiating to every part of life—is the breakdown of the Negro family structure. For this, most of all, white America must accept responsibility. It flows from centuries of oppression and persecution of the Negro man. It flows from the long years of degradation and discrimination, which have attacked his dignity and assaulted his ability to produce for his family.
>
> Only a minority—less than half—of all Negro children reach the age of 18 having lived all their lives with both of their parents. At this moment, tonight, little less than two-thirds are at home with both of their parents. Probably a majority of all Negro children receive federally-aided public assistance sometime during their childhood.
>
> The family is the cornerstone of our society. More than any other force it shapes the attitude, the hopes, the ambitions, and the values of the child. And when the family collapses it is the children that are usually damaged. When it happens on a massive scale the community itself is crippled.
>
> So, unless we work to strengthen the family, to create conditions under which most parents will stay together—all the rest: schools, and playgrounds, and public assistance, and private concern, will never be enough to cut completely the circle of despair and deprivation.[81]

This passage illustrates the extent to which the family, its values and "condition" were believed to indicate the situation of an entire social group (here African Americans). Underlying this is the traditional interpretation of the family as a symbol of the U.S. nation, here employed, interestingly enough, by the nation's leading liberal, the first American president of the twentieth century to pursue a serious civil rights policy. By describing the decline of the black family as a threat to the nation, Johnson inscribed himself in a decades-long discourse of crisis that accompanied the development and transformation of the American family and its values from the beginning of the modern era. Importantly, however, Johnson derived from this diagnosis of crisis an obligation to take political action, announcing a government conference made up of scholars, experts, civil rights activists, and government officials, which would be tasked with drawing up guidelines for social and economic reform.

The main argumentative basis of the speech was provided by Daniel P. Moynihan's reflections on the supposed "pathologies" of African American families. We can also discern traces of Oscar Lewis's work on the "culture of poverty," Michael Harrington's observations on poverty in America, E. Franklin Frazier's comments on the significance of slavery to family structure, and Kenneth B. Clark's analyses of the poor living conditions in urban ghettos.[82] In the weeks following the presidential address, a fierce debate took off among politicians, social scientists,

---

[81] Johnson, Lyndon B., "To Fulfill These Rights. Commencement Address at Howard University," June 4, 1965.
[82] Moynihan, *The Negro Family*. Lewis, "Culture of Poverty." Harrington, Michael, *The Other America. Poverty in the United States* (New York 1962). Clark, Kenneth B., *Dark Ghetto. Dilemmas*

journalists, and civil rights activists about the structure and values of the black family, at the center of which was the so-called Moynihan Report, originally penned as a confidential memorandum.

The report

Under the title *The Negro Family: The Case for National Action*,[83] Daniel Patrick Moynihan, in his capacity as a member of the Department of Labor, had wished to inform the Johnson administration about the problems facing many African American families, while concurrently putting forward arguments for bolstering federal reform programs to help them.[84] The confidential document had been submitted to Johnson and his staff in the spring of 1965, shortly before the presidential address at Howard University.[85] For Moynihan, too, the family represented the central unit of society, a notion he backed up by highlighting its socializing role. A crisis of the family, he contended, was having a particularly

---

of Social Power (New York, Evanston 1967, first edition 1965). Johnson, "To Fulfill these Rights," in Rainwater and Yancey, *Moynihan Report*, 128–129.

83 Some of the other titles Moynihan considered in 1965 were much more offensive: "After the Barriers are Down: The Negro in the US," "The Negro Family: A Strategy for National Action," and "Negro Equality: Dream or Delusion." Daniel P. Moynihan Papers, Library of Congress, Manuscript Division (LOC), Box 66, Folder 4. Original copy of report in Box 66, Folder 7.

84 Daniel Patrick Moynihan (1927–2003) was a Democratic U.S. senator, sociologist, U.S. ambassador, publicist, and collaborator with four U.S. presidents. He served as assistant secretary of labor under Lyndon B. Johnson but left the administration before the end of 1965 to become director of the Harvard-MIT Joint Center for Urban Studies. Beginning in 1968, Moynihan advised Richard Nixon on urban development and social policy issues, particularly supporting his idea of a guaranteed annual income. He served in the U.S. Senate from 1977 to 2001, as a senator from New York State. As ambassador, he represented the U.S. in India and at the United Nations in New York. On Moynihan, see Hodgson, Godfrey, *The Gentleman From New York. Daniel Patrick Moynihan. A Biography* (Boston 2000). Katzmann, Robert A. (ed.), *Daniel Patrick Moynihan. The Intellectual in Public Life* (Baltimore 2004). Weisman, Steven R. (ed.), *Daniel Patrick Moynihan. A Portrait in Letters of an American Visionary* (New York 2010).

85 The text was written by March 1965 in the Department of Labor's Office of Policy Planning and Research. In addition to Moynihan as assistant secretary of labor, authors included his assistants Paul Barton and Ellen Broderick. Moynihan's estate contains all the research material and also various drafts and versions of the report. Daniel P. Moynihan Papers, LOC, Box 66, Folder 4 through 11. The report and the debate about it can be considered well researched. For the best discussion, see Estes, Steve, *I am a Man! Race, Manhood, and the Civil Rights Movement* (Chapel Hill 2005), 107–130. See also Massey, Douglas S. (ed.), *The Moynihan Report Revisited. Lessons and Reflections after four Decades* (Thousand Oaks 2009). Patterson, *Freedom is not Enough.*

deleterious effect on the entire black minority: "At the heart of the deterioration of the fabric of Negro society is the deterioration of the Negro family."[86]

It is interesting to note that in an early draft from the beginning of 1965, Moynihan had still attributed significant responsibility for the problems faced by African American families and the minority in general to the white majority society, a passage that no longer appears in this form in the report itself:

> The Negro family is the fundamental source of the weakness of the Negro community. This has nothing to do with Negro Americans. It has everything to do with White Americans. The present condition of the Negro family is the result of two institutions which the White world has permitted to exist, and from which it has in considerable measure profited. These are slavery and unemployment.[87]

This acknowledgment of the consequences of social and economic exploitation is absent from the text itself, in which Moynihan instead emphasized the dramatic differences in the structures of white and African American families:

> The white family has achieved a high degree of stability and is maintaining that stability. By contrast, the family structure of lower class Negroes is highly unstable, and in many urban centers is approaching complete breakdown.[88]

Three key facts, Moynihan contended, were associated with this decline. First, black families were particularly unstable in their structure. There were far more single mothers, absentee fathers, broken marriages, and illegitimate births than among the white population. This, he went on, was partly due to the particularly weak position of African American men.[89] Second, the decline of the family was the cause of the intolerable conditions ("tangle of pathology") in the big-city ghettos, which was apparent, among other things, in the lack of education among young people, in criminality and drug abuse.[90] Third, these problems were con-

---

[86] Daniel P. Moynihan, "The Negro Family. The Case for National Action," Office of Policy Research, United States Department of Labor, March 1965, 5, Daniel P. Moynihan Papers, LOC, Box 66, Folder 7. The full report is reprinted in Rainwater and Yankey, *The Moynihan Report*, 39–124.

[87] Daniel P. Moynihan, "The Negro American Family" (January 1965), Daniel P. Moynihan Papers, LOC, Box 66, Folder 8.

[88] Moynihan, "The Negro Family," 5, Daniel P. Moynihan Papers, LOC, Box 66, Folder 7.

[89] For example, we are informed, the divorce rate among the African American urban population is nearly 25 percent, and nearly a quarter of all black births are out of wedlock. About 25 percent of all black families are headed by women alone, with fathers absent. Moynihan, "The Negro Family," 6–11, Daniel P. Moynihan Papers, LOC, Box 66, Folder 7.

[90] This passage was inspired by the work of Kenneth B. Clark, but Moynihan refers to him only occasionally. On this topic, see below.

stantly getting worse. Due to broken families and the large number of single mothers, dependency on social welfare was steadily increasing.[91]

Moynihan's basic idea was that only stable families could form the basis of an orderly community, and consequently only an intact family structure could help reduce welfare payments. So far, he saw such coherent structures as limited exclusively to the white upper and middle classes and a steadily growing black middle class, which, he asserted, placed even greater value on stability and upward mobility than the white middle class.[92] In view of the severity of the problems faced by poor African American families, decisive and, above all, coordinated action was essential:

> In a word, a national effort towards the problems of Negro Americans must be directed towards the question of family structure. The object should be to strengthen the Negro family so as to enable it to raise and support its members as do other families.[93]

To this end, Moynihan wished to propose a new national policy vis-à-vis the black minority, which would be characterized by two features: consistency of measures and a focus on family structure:

> A national effort is required that will give a unity of purpose to the many activities of the Federal government in this area, directed to a new kind of national goal: the establishment of a stable Negro family structure.[94]

The sources

Looking at the content of the report, which was so controversial in 1965, the first feature that stands out is Moynihan's attempt to substantiate his arguments with reference to a large number of sources and statistics, though at times he merely condensed the memoranda produced by his assistants Ellen Broderick and Paul Barton into a text of his own. They had worked up the relevant social scientific literature for Moynihan and compiled statistics.[95] Thus, the report's argumentative structure borrows from the studies produced by black sociologists such as W. E. B. DuBois

---

91 Moynihan, "The Negro Family," 12–14, Daniel P. Moynihan Papers, LOC, Box 66, Folder 7.
92 This point had already been made very strongly by E. Franklin Frazier and, following Frazier, by Myrdal. On this, see below.
93 Moynihan, "Negro Family," 47, Daniel P. Moynihan Papers, LOC, Box 66, Folder 7.
94 Moynihan, "Negro Family," preface, Rainwater and Yankey, *Moynihan Report*, 43.
95 Ellen Broderick and Paul Barton were Moynihan's assistants at the Department of Labor; their excerpts and research are included in Moynihan's estate. Daniel P. Moynihan Papers, LOC, Box 66, Folder 8, Folder 9.

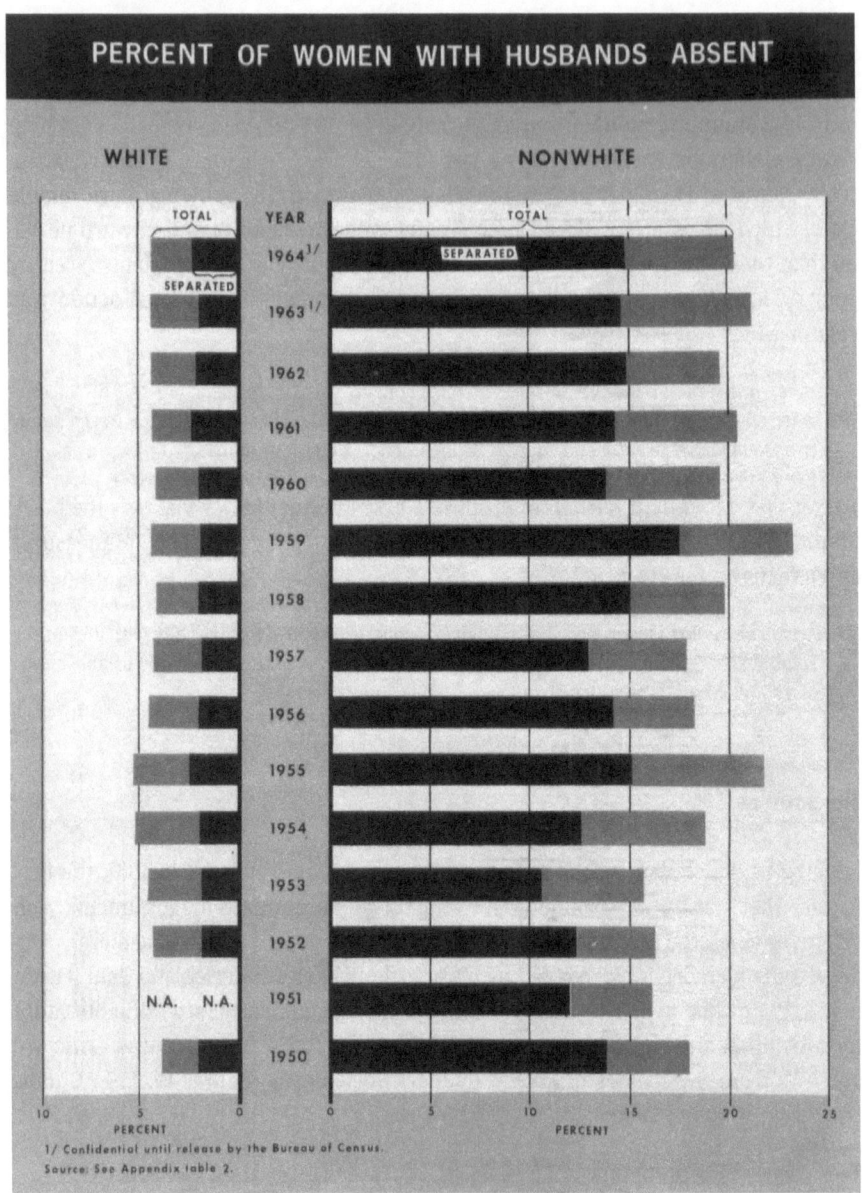

Fig. 4.4: Absentee fathers in white and African American families according to Moynihan.

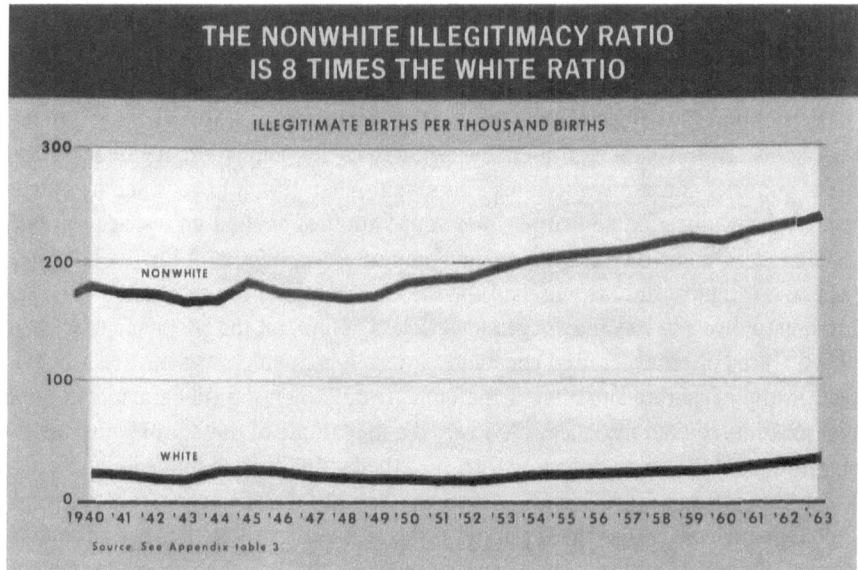

Fig. 4.5: Trends in the illegitimacy rate of the white majority and African American minority according to Moynihan.

and especially E. Franklin Frazier.[96] Moynihan linked their reflections with the work of Gunnar Myrdal and Arnold M. Rose; in *An American Dilemma,* they too had in fact mainly referred to Frazier's theses on the African American family.[97] Moynihan already quoted Myrdal in the preface as stating that America must decide for itself whether it would view the black minority in the future as a financial and moral burden or as an opportunity for national advancement.[98]

In addition, Moynihan reflected on the arguments made by civil rights activists such as Whitney M. Young and Bayard Rustin, but above all he drew on the studies penned by sociologist Nathan Glazer, with whom he had published an analysis of the population composition of the city of New York shortly before.[99] Glazer's passage in that text on New York's black population ("The Negroes") contained as-

---

[96] Frazier, *The Negro Family*. Frazier, "Problems and Needs," 269–277. Frazier, *Black Bourgeoisie*.
[97] Myrdal, *American Dilemma*, 931–935. Rose, *The Negro in America*, 294–296.
[98] Moynihan, "Negro Family," preface, Rainwater and Yankey, *Moynihan Report*, 43.
[99] Glazer, Nathan and Moynihan, Daniel P., *Beyond the Melting Pot. The Negroes, Puerto Ricans, Jews, Italians and Irish of New York City 1963* (Cambridge 1963). Young, Whitney, *To be Equal* (New York 1964). Rustin, Bayard, "From Protest to Politics. The Future of the Civil Rights Movement," *Commentary* 39 (1965), 1, 25–31. There is also an unmistakable echo of the work of Myrdal, who referred mainly to Frazier when it came to the "Negro family."

sumptions and propositions that were disseminated by the Moynihan Report a short time later: a quarter of all "Negro families" consisted of only one mother and her children, whereas this applied to less than 10 percent of white families; the proportion of out-of-wedlock births among African Americans was very high, at fourteen or fifteen times the figure for the white majority population; members of the black minority constantly faced discrimination when trying to get a job or obtain housing; the education and employment opportunities of children (especially male youths) were poor; the juvenile delinquency rate was high; and the overall prospects were significantly worse than for the U.S. population in general.[100] The real problem, however, was the "Negro lower class." Here, all the problems described above were concentrated and constantly intensifying, which was particularly evident in the desperate situation of the family: "But when the fundamental core of organization, the family, is already weak, the magnitude of these problems may be staggering."[101] Glazer explained this crisis of the family (though limited to the black lower class), citing Frazier, with reference to the history of slavery.[102] Also revealing is his insistence that the black minority, and especially its upper and middle classes, must make their own efforts to improve the life chances of the "Negro lower-class family" in particular.[103]

In terms of content, Moynihan's text is essentially based on the thinking of African American psychologist Kenneth B. Clark, who, together with his wife, had achieved national prominence through experiments intended to assess the self-esteem of black children in the 1940s.[104] In the early 1960s, Clark was commissioned

---

100 Glazer and Moynihan, *Melting Pot*, 24–85, esp. 50–51.
101 Glazer and Moynihan, *Melting Pot*, 52.
102 The same argument can be found in the text by civil rights activist Bayard Rustin, "From Protest to Politics," also cited by Moynihan, in which, at the beginning of 1965, Rustin puts forward a new perspective for the civil rights movement directed toward political-social change: "The Negro family structure was totally destroyed by slavery and with it the possibility of cultural transmission (the right of Negroes to marry and rear children is barely a century old)." Rustin, "From Protest to Politics."
103 Glazer and Moynihan, *Melting Pot*, 84–85. For a trenchant critique of the so-called "self-help" approach of white liberals, see the text by Bayard Rustin, who argues that real "self-help" can only seek to achieve social change, while everything else fails to go beyond (ineffective) calls for "self-improvement." Rustin, "From Protest to Politics," 27.
104 Kenneth Bancroft Clark (1914–2005) studied psychology at Howard University and was the first African American to teach as a full professor at the City College of New York. There he directed the Social Dynamics Research Institute. He was active in the civil rights movement, founded the organization HARYOU (Harlem Youth Opportunities Unlimited) with his wife, and became the first black president of the American Psychological Association. He and his wife Mamie Phipps Clark (1917–1983) became famous for their experiments with African American schoolchildren, in which they showed that black children preferred playing with white dolls—which they put down to the

by the government to analyze the social and economic disadvantages of African Americans in U.S. society and their effects on life in the big-city ghettos in particular.[105] Although Moynihan makes no explicit mention of Clark or his major work *Dark Ghetto*, which appeared around the same time the report was released to the public, Clark's research was definitely known to Moynihan. As it happens, Clark and not Moynihan was the originator of the term "tangle of pathology," through which the Moynihan Report later attained its contested renown.[106] In *Dark Ghetto*, Clark had described this as "institutionalized pathology, [. . .] chronic self-perpetuating poverty."[107] The psychologist was able to draw on his own experiences in this regard and he described his study as "a summation of my personal and lifelong experiences and observations as a prisoner within the ghetto long before I was aware that I really was a prisoner."[108] Clark attached particular significance to the connection between unemployment, racial discrimination, and the breakdown of family structures, a link he observed during his research in Harlem. This, he believed, had serious effects on children, who lacked the sense of a secure home, affection, and reliable role models. They were unable to establish stable families for themselves since they had never known an orderly life:

> Children and young people who grow up in a community in which a large proportion of families have no father in the home, a community in which 40 percent of the men and 47 percent of the women aged 14 and over are unmarried, find it difficult, if not almost impossible, to know what an "adequate" family is like. The cycle of family instability continues uninterrupted.[109]

---

persistence of racist stereotypes in U.S. society. Their work formed one of the bases of the desegregation of education through the Supreme Court *Brown v. Board of Education* ruling (1954). Clark, *Dark Ghetto*. Moynihan referred explicitly to a publication on the social ills of the Harlem ghetto, a study for which Clark was responsible but which did not appear under his name: HARYOU (Harlem Youth Opportunities Unlimited Inc.), *Youth in the Ghetto. A Study of Powerlessness and a Blueprint for Change* (Harlem Youth Opportunities Unlimited Inc, 1964).

105 Clark was commissioned by the President's Committee on Juvenile Delinquency and the Mayor of New York to study the living conditions of young people in Harlem from 1962 to 1964 in order to determine the financing requirements for reform programs. Clark and his colleagues subsequently managed to secure a total of $4 million in funding. Clark, *Dark Ghetto*, xiii–xiv.

106 Clark coined the term in his report *Youth in the Ghetto* for the HARYOU initiative. Moynihan, Daniel P., "Employment, Income, and the Ordeal of the Negro Family," in Clark, Kenneth B. and Parsons, Talcott (eds.), *The Negro American* (Boston 1966), 134–159, here 151. Estes, *I am a Man!*, 205.

107 Clark, *Dark Ghetto*, 81.

108 Clark, *Dark Ghetto*, xv.

109 Clark, *Dark Ghetto*, 48.

At the same time, the breakdown of many families and ubiquitous poverty led to a strong, ever-increasing dependence on welfare. New programs and better education were urgently needed to give people back their self-confidence and initiative and, in the longer term, to bring about true participation in the economy and society.[110] Clark's findings here made a seamless fit with Moynihan's demands, but they were received quite differently by the African American community because they were formulated more cautiously and presented as the result of many years of research by a respected black psychologist.

Moynihan's thinking, meanwhile, shifted from a focus on juvenile delinquency, poverty among single mothers, and the economic difficulties of large families, to the importance of family values in preventing violence and hopelessness in the urban ghettos.[111] His original idea was to address the financial problems facing the "Negro family" primarily through aid programs and birth control for "large families" within the framework of the War on Poverty.[112] For Moynihan, birth control in particular was "a major factor in the War on Poverty," and he took a keen interest in the relevant advances in research.[113] As he saw it, previous welfare and relief programs (especially Aid to Families with Dependent Children or AFDC) tended to be a hindrance to problem families because in a sense they privileged the absence of fathers: "For the past 25 years [. . .] the remedy proposed has been based on the 'insane' idea that to help the family, the father

---

110 Clark, *Dark Ghetto*, 50–62.
111 Rodney H. Clurman, Consultant, Juvenile Delinquency Planning Board of the United Planning Organization, to Moynihan, March 25, 1963. Daniel P. Moynihan Papers, LOC, Box 24, Folder 8. See also Moynihan's correspondence with Jack Melzer, Director of the Center for Urban Studies at Chicago University, January and March 1964, on poverty in the inner-city ghettos of major cities. Daniel P. Moynihan Papers, LOC, Box 26, Folder 2, Folder 3. See also a memorandum from Daniel P. Moynihan to Lyndon B. Johnson, February 14, 1972. Daniel P. Moynihan Papers, LOC, Box 176, Folder 3.
112 See Moynihan's 1964 plans for a "Family Size and Family Income Conference," which he then organized at the Harvard-MIT Joint Center for Urban Studies in 1965. Daniel P. Moynihan Papers, LOC, Box 50, Folder 10.
113 Waite, Elmont, "Poverty's Link with Fertility, Professor's View," *San Francisco Chronicle*, March 1, 1965. Papers of Daniel P. Moynihan. LOC, Box 16, Folder 3. Joyce Haney, Research Associate to DPM, to Dr. Leon Gerdis, Sinai Hospital, Baltimore, June 2, 1967, requesting information on a birth control project distributing "birth control pills to unmarried adolescent girls." Papers of Daniel P. Moynihan. LOC, Box 413, Folder 11. See also letter from Joint Center for Urban Studies, MIT/HU, June 19, 1968, attn. Katharine G. Bauer, Project Coordinator, Health Information System Project, to Henry Wechsler, Medical Foundation, regarding research on birth control underway at the Center. Papers of Daniel P. Moynihan. LOC, Box 414, Folder 2.

must be required to stay away from the family."[114] The AFDC—the most important welfare program in the U.S., whose origins lay in the New Deal era—was in fact based on the idea that women would receive support for themselves and their children only if the fathers did not live in the same household.[115]

The civil rights movement could easily build on these ideas, since it, too, was highly critical of welfare policies and, in particular, the AFDC program. Thus, at the end of 1964, the labor secretary of the NAACP, Herbert Hill, complained to Moynihan about the "savage welfare policies of the Federal Government" and requested information about "available data relating to the correlation between unemployment and Negro family dis-integration."[116] Yet this was where the core problem of Moynihan's entire argument lay. He claimed that there was a correlation between the breakdown of the African American family due to the absence of fathers, the disproportionate increase in the share of black children receiving support from the AFDC welfare program, and the dismal circumstances of many blacks in the major urban centers. But precise statistical evidence of this link was lacking, even after the report was published, no matter how hard he had his assistants search for it.[117] In a handwritten note composed in late summer 1965, he self-critically noted:

---

114 Waite, Elmont, "Poverty's Link with Fertility, Professor's View," *San Francisco Chronicle*, March 1, 1965. Papers of Daniel P. Moynihan. LOC, Box 16, Folder 3. On this, see also the letter from the dean of the School of Social Work, University of Connecticut, Harleigh B. Trecker, to Moynihan, December 17, 1965, in which Trecker expresses indignation at Moynihan's assertion in the NYT, December 12, 1965, that welfare programs "contribute to family breakdown by putting a premium on fatherless homes." Papers of Daniel P. Moynihan. LOC, Box 92, Folder 5.

115 Chappell, *War on Welfare*. Mittelstadt, Jennifer, *From Welfare to Workfare. The Unintended Consequences of Liberal Reform, 1945–1965* (Chapel Hill 2005). Nadasen, Premilla, Mittelstadt, Jennifer, and Marisa Chappell (eds.), *Welfare in the United States. A History with Documents* (New York 2009).

116 Herbert Hill, Labor Secretary, NAACP, to Moynihan, December 4, 1964. Daniel P. Moynihan Papers, LOC, Box 66, Folder 8.

117 On this point, see Barton's research reports for Moynihan of March 22, 1965, and November 4, 1965. Barton explained that while the increase in AFDC families between 1948 and 1961 was disproportionately caused by African American families, their share rising from 31 percent (1948) to 46 percent (1961) of the total number of families receiving such benefits, he had to concede that there were no statistics that listed children and youth receiving AFDC separately by ethnicity, so it could not be concluded that the living situation of black children was particularly grave. Daniel P. Moynihan Papers, LOC, Box 92, Folder 6. See also another memorandum by Barton dated February 1, 1965, in which he explains to Moynihan that there is no statistical correspondence between "separation rates" and "poverty rates, education, percentage of migrants, unemployment, family size, relative size of nonwhite population, and divorce rates"—but this did not prevent Moynihan from making this very argument in his report. Daniel P. Moynihan Papers, LOC, Box 66, Folder 9.

> No one knows what the ADC figures mean, because no one knows [what] that the real universe of ADC children is: i.e. how many truly dependent children are there, of these how many get ADC payments. Social class is a bat [sic] invention of sociology.[118]

Yet he was aided by the social sciences. Sociologist Harold L. Sheppard, for example, wrote to him in reference to a study by the Office of Economic Opportunity on Hough, "the Watts of Cleveland," Ohio, an overwhelmingly African American neighborhood.[119] According to Sheppard, the alleged link between social problems, poverty, and fatherless families was readily demonstrable there:

> The Cleveland Study, without saying so, seems to me to back up Moynihan: among Negro families in Hough with a male head, the percentage in poverty registered only a very slight increase from 1959 to 1964—from 20.5 to 21.8; but among those with a female head, the extent of poverty had increased at a much higher rate, from 65.9 to 75.3. In other words, nearly all of the increase in the percentage of Negro families living in poverty was associated with the rise in fatherless families.
>
> What may be just as important, between 1960 and 1965, the percentage of all Negro families with a female head increased in Hough, from 22.5 to 32.1. Similar shifts occurred in the other contiguous parts of the Cleveland "Poverty Area" (selected by the Census Bureau for its work for OEO [Office of Economic Opportunity])![120]

Psychologist Urie Bronfenbrenner also found Moynihan's argument convincing in principle, although with respect to the details he questioned whether the separation of men from their families was truly a consequence of their unemployment or vice versa—and whether any conclusions could be drawn about this at all.[121] Above all, however, he criticized the vehement reactions of white liberal social scientists to Moynihan as a person and to the report:

---

[118] Handwritten note by Moynihan during his semester at Wesleyan University, undated (late summer 1965). Daniel P. Moynihan Papers, LOC, Box 92, Folder 6.

[119] Harold L. Sheppard (1922–2000), whom President Carter appointed Counselor to the President on Aging in 1980, was a sociologist and specialist in gerontology. After teaching as a sociology professor at Wayne State University and holding various positions in government-related advisory institutions, he worked at the W. E. Upjohn Institute for Employment Research from 1963 to 1975, where he focused especially on the relationship between age and the world of work. Jimmy Carter: "Counselor to the President on Aging Appointment of Harold L. Sheppard," April 18, 1980. Online at Gerhard Peters and John T. Woolley, "The American Presidency Project," <www.presidency.ucsb.edu/ws/?pid=33293>.

[120] Memorandum from Harold L. Sheppard, The W. E. Upjohn Institute for Employment Research (Washington, D. C.), undated (1966). Daniel P. Moynihan Papers, LOC, Box 184, Folder 4.

[121] Urie Bronfenbrenner (1917–2005) was a psychologist who taught at Cornell University. His work on early childhood development was incorporated into the Head Start Program, which was intended to improve educational opportunities for disadvantaged children as part of the Johnson administration's War on Poverty. <www.bctr.cornell.edu/about-us/urie-bronfenbrenner/>.

I have often thought of the high price you had to pay for acting on your thoroughly unracist convictions. What struck me as the most unjust and the most instructive was that the attack came from some of our most so-called "liberal" white colleagues. Sometimes I have the feeling that many liberals are more concerned with convincing others and themselves of the intensity of their beliefs than with contributing to the solution of an objective situation.[122]

Hence, a key insight arising from analysis of the text and its sources that has as yet gone unacknowledged by researchers is that Moynihan not only developed his ideas on the structure and values of the African American family in the context of the War on Poverty and the growing focus on the causes of poverty, but also sought to improve public policy with the help of experts. Further, he was keen to use urban sociology and population policy to address the problems at issue through a large-scale interdisciplinary effort. This is exemplified by the conferences led by Moynihan in the mid-1960s at the Joint Center for Urban Studies at Harvard University and MIT and at Wesleyan University.[123] At the same time, the publication of the Moynihan Report occurred during a period when scholars in numerous disciplines were considering possible solutions to society's most pressing problems, discursively linking poverty, violence, racial discrimination, and overpopulation. The solution always seemed to lie in the relationship between individual and community, that is, in the family.[124]

But how did the black community respond to the sudden spotlighting of its family structures?

4.5 Perceptions of the Moynihan Report in the African American community

Unlike the formerly confidential Moynihan Report, which the White House deliberately leaked to the press in mid-August 1965, immediately triggering a heated debate, the presidential speech of June 4, 1965, was initially received very positively by the American public and, in particular, by the civil rights movement and repre-

---

[122] Letter from Uri Bronfenbrenner, Cornell University, New York State College of Home Economics, Department of Child Development, to Moynihan, November 29, 1966. Daniel P. Moynihan Papers, LOC, Box 414, Folder 2.
[123] Conference on Family Size and Family Income, Harvard-MIT Joint Center for Urban Studies, 1965. Daniel P. Moynihan Papers, LOC, Box 50, Folder 10. Conference on Problems of the Lower Class Negro Family, Wesleyan University, 1966. Daniel P. Moynihan Papers, LOC, Box 460, Folder 11, Box 461, Folders 4 and 5. Conference on Social Statistics and the City, Washington D. C., 1967. Daniel P. Moynihan Papers, LOC, Box 154, Folder 1.
[124] On this point, see the comments in chapter five of this book.

sentatives of the black minority.[125] The two major national daily newspapers, the *New York Times* and the *Washington Post*, printed the text of the speech and published exclusively laudatory comments.[126] However, the focus here was not on Johnson's remarks on the structure of the African American family, but on his promise to follow up efforts to achieve legal equality with programs to improve the social situation. The *Washington Post* was alone in pointing out that Johnson had described the "breakdown of the Negro family structure" as the "most important wound, radiating into every part of life."[127] White America, however, according to the president, bore responsibility for this in view of centuries of oppression and discrimination, especially with respect to the "Negro man," who had been deprived of his dignity and the ability to provide for his family. In the weeks that followed, the first explicit discussions of the "breakdown of the Negro family structures" (*Washington Star*, June 11, 1965), the "deterioration of the Negro family" (*New York Times*, July 19, 1965), and the "disintegration of Negro families" (*Newsweek*, August 9, 1965) appeared in the national press.[128] The debate was still relatively open and positive, the explosive material concealed within it only coming to light against the background of the race riots in August 1965.

When black youths and police fought fierce street battles in Watts, Los Angeles, from August 11 to 17, 1965, brought to an end only by the deployment of 14,000 National Guard soldiers, Johnson's reflections on the embattled African American family took on a different significance.[129] By the time the Watts race riots had ended, thirty-four people had died, while some 1,000 individuals had suffered injuries and 4,000 had been arrested (almost all of them black); the ma-

---

[125] The report itself was to be kept strictly confidential. Of the 100 copies initially printed, only White House Press Secretary Bill Moyers received one. He decided that President Johnson should receive an abridged memorandum. Rainwater and Yankey, *The Moynihan Report*, 3–4.

[126] Johnson's Address to Howard University Graduates, NYT, June 5, 1965, 14. President's Address at Howard U., WP, June 5, 1965, C41. Tom Wicker, "Johnson Pledges to Help Negroes to Full Equality. Says Legal Freedom is Not Enough—Plans A Special Conference in the Fall," NYT, 5.6.1965, 1, 14. "Mr. Johnson's Candle," WP, June 6, 1965, E6. "To Fulfill These Rights," NYT, June 6, 1965, E10. Tom Wicker, "Johnson's View of Negro. President Takes the Advanced Position Assumed by High Court in School Case," NYT, June 7, 1965, 27.

[127] Edward T. Folliard, "President Announces Fall Conference on Negro Rights. Tells Howard Class Isolation is Rising Despite Progress," WP, June 5, 1965, A1, A4.

[128] For a good overview of the debate, see Rainwater and Yankey, *Moynihan Report*, 133–154, 369–394. Mary McGrory, "President Talks Frankly to Negroes," *The Washington Star*, June 6, 1965, John D. Pomfret, "Drive for Negro Family Stability Spurred by White House," NYT, July 19, 1965. *Newsweek*, August 9, 1965.

[129] Rustin, "The Watts 'Manifesto.'" See also Estes, *I am a Man!*, 116. D'Emilio, John, *Lost Prophet. The Life and Times of Bayard Rustin* (New York 2003), 418–425.

terial damage was estimated at over $200 million. Bill Moyers, the White House press secretary, began distributing the first copies of the Moynihan Report to journalists on August 17, 1965, providing a kind of intellectual background to the dramatic events.[130] Observers noted that it was chiefly black youths—without jobs or prospects—who made up the majority of the protesters, in other words, precisely the group that the Moynihan Report had placed at the center of its account of the alleged decline of the African American family.[131]

The ensuing debate on the report and on conditions in the urban ghettos essentially divided according to political ideology. One argumentative pole was represented by conservative journalists, politicians and, in general, opponents of the Johnson administration's equal rights policies. They argued that while Moynihan had aptly described the "pathology" of blacks, the call for further government welfare programs derived from this was misguided. The African American minority, wrote Mary McGrory in the *Washington Star*, did not need new government programs, but had to develop solutions to their own problems: "President Johnson suggested that the time had come for them to come to grips with their own worst problem, the breakdown of Negro family life."[132] Her colleague Richard Wilson concluded in the same paper that the question was "how to cause Negroes to help themselves, how to cause them to create for themselves, in their own communities, an ordered society based upon a stable family structure."[133] This task, he averred, fell mainly to the black middle class. Private citizens also responded to Moynihan by writing to him and submitting readers' letters to various publications. Of particular interest is a letter from Jackie Boudreaux of White Springs, California, who doubted the existence of a "Negro family" *per se*, while also criticizing Moynihan's approach as a social scientist:

> Dear Sir, people like you make me sick. You go to school most of your life and have a lot of foolish learning, but you know about as much about the Negro as I know about Eskimos. There has never been a Negro family to deteriorate, that is, not as white people know a family and I've known Negroes all my life and they have never been any different.[134]

---

[130] As Moynihan himself recalls: Estes, *I am a Man!*, 117. Moynihan, Daniel P. *Family and Nation. The Godkin Lectures, Harvard University* (San Diego etc. 1986), 34.
[131] Rustin, "Watts 'Manifesto.'".
[132] Mary McGrory, "President Talks Frankly to Negroes," *Washington Star*, June 6, 1965. Reprinted in Rainwater and Yancey, *Moynihan Report*, 369–371.
[133] Richard Wilson, "Gloomy Study Faces Parley on Negroes," *Washington Star*, September 24, 1965. Rainwater and Yancey, *Moynihan Report*, 152.
[134] Jackie Boudreaux to Moynihan, White Springs, CA, September 5, 1965. Daniel P. Moynihan Papers, LOC, Box 184, Folder 1.

The other ideological pole was that espoused by civil rights activists, liberal journalists, and liberal politicians, who disapproved of Moynihan's cool, analytical tone in discussing the problems of the ghettos and criticized the tenor of his argument. For instance, civil rights activist Floyd McKissick, chairman of the Congress on Racial Equality (CORE), stated:

> My major criticism of the report is that it assumes that middle class American values are the correct ones for everyone in America. Just because Moynihan believes in the middle class values doesn't mean that they are the best for everyone in America.[135]

Bayard Rustin, another prominent civil rights activist and union official, took the problem of transferring white middle-class values to the African American underclass to another level:

> One important point that must be made is that what may seem to be a disease to the white middle class may be a healthy adaptation of the Negro lower class. [. . .] Finally, we must talk about the poor family, not simply the Negro family. Poverty is a problem. It is amazing to me that Negro families exist at all.[136]

For Rustin, a stable family structure was only conceivable with a male breadwinner at its head, and policies ought to focus on this: "the Negro family can be reconstructed only when the Negro male is permitted to be the economic head of the family."[137] This position was also backed by Alan Gartner, like Floyd McKissick a representative of CORE: "Provide satisfying, decent-paying, steady jobs for Negro men and the so-called 'pathology' of the Negro family will vanish [. . .]."[138] What is interesting about these statements is that here male representatives of the civil rights movement not only affirmed the ideal of the male breadwinner prevalent in white majority society at the time, but also explicitly took up the re-

---

[135] Floyd McKissick, quoted in Rainwater and Yancey, *Moynihan Report*, 200. Floyd Bixler McKissick (1922–1991) became chairman of CORE in 1966, which he reoriented from a civil rights organization committed to nonviolence toward the militant course pursued by the young Black Power movement. McKissick was the first African American student to gain admission to the University of North Carolina Law School in 1951 and began working as a civil rights attorney in 1955.
[136] Bayard Rustin, quoted in Rainwater and Yancey, *Moynihan Report*, 200. Bayard Rustin (1912–1987) was a well-known African American civil rights activist who advocated nonviolence and pacifism. He was a member of the SCLC and one of the chief strategists of the civil rights movement. Among other things, he organized the 1963 March on Washington for Jobs and Freedom, and from 1966 to 1968 he directed the A. Philip Randolph Institute of the AFL-CIO, which advocated the integration of blacks into the white union system. Arrested for homosexual conduct in 1953, he became a prominent advocate for gay rights in the 1970s.
[137] Bayard Rustin, "Why Don't Negroes . . ., " *America. The National Catholic Weekly Review*, June 4, 1966. Reprinted in Rainwater and Yancey, *Moynihan Report*, 417–426.
[138] Alan Gartner, reader's letter in the NYT, December 12, 1965.

port's criticism of the supposed "matriarchy of the Negro family."[139] Moynihan himself, influenced by the violent racial unrest of the summer of 1965, had also sharpened his critique of allegedly matrifocal family structures in the ghettos, as his article in *America* magazine makes clear:

> A community that allows a large number of young men to grow up in broken families, dominated by women, never acquiring any stable relationship to male authority, never acquiring any set of rational expectations about the future—that community asks for and gets chaos.[140]

Meanwhile, the reactions of the Southern Christian Leadership Conference (SCLC) to the Moynihan Report were surprisingly reserved. In some speeches, the president of the SCLC, Martin Luther King, indirectly criticized the report, but he adopted its statistics on divorce and illegitimacy rates, the supposed matriarchal family structure, and dependence on government welfare.[141]

Four core elements characterized his arguments on the state of the African American family in the years 1965 to 1968. First, King repeatedly emphasized the achievements and strengths of black families, which, against all odds, had ultimately fought collectively for civil rights: "The Negro family is scarred, it is submerged, but it struggles to survive. It is working against greater odds than perhaps

---

[139] This demand was not only in line with Moynihan's thinking, but with the concepts of white and black social scientists in general, on which see below in this chapter.

[140] Moynihan, Daniel P., "A Family Policy for the Nation," *America. The National Catholic Weekly Review*, September 18, 1966. Reprinted in Rainwater and Yancey, *Moynihan Report*, 385–394, here 393.

[141] Martin Luther King, Jr. (1929–1968) was the most prominent representative of the civil rights movement and the most important advocate of the tactic of non-violent protest. After leading the Montgomery bus boycott of 1955, which was ignited by the segregation of public transportation in Alabama—and that, in a sense, served as the initial spark for a national civil rights movement—he co-founded the SCLC, of which he became the first president in 1957. He led the civil rights movement until his assassination in 1968. Among other things, he organized the 1962 protests in Birmingham, Alabama, which brought the brutal actions of the police to the attention of a national public. During the 1963 March on Washington, he delivered his famous "I Have a Dream" speech. He was awarded the Nobel Peace Prize in 1964 for his advocacy of nonviolent protest against racial discrimination in the United States. King had studied sociology at Morehouse College in Atlanta and theology at Crozer Theological Seminary in Chester, Pennsylvania. In 1955, he received his doctorate in systematic theology from Boston University. In 1954, he took up a post as pastor in Montgomery, Alabama, then from 1960 at Ebenezer Baptist Church in Atlanta, where his father had also served in the same role. Some of his personal papers are in the collection of AUC Atlanta, Woodruff Library, and at the King Center in Atlanta. The SCLC's papers, meanwhile, can be found at Emory University, Atlanta, MARBL. From the multitude of literature on King, see Kirk, John A. (ed.), *Martin Luther King Jr. and the Civil Rights Movement. Controversies and Debates* (New York 2007). Hodgson, Godfrey, *Martin Luther King* (London 2009). Waldschmidt-Nelson, Britta, *Dreams and Nightmares. Martin Luther King, Jr, Malcolm X and the Struggle for Black Equality in America* (Gainesville, FL 2012).

any other family experienced in all civilized history."[142] Second, he repeatedly referred to the economic oppression of African Americans throughout the nation, which impacted on their family life, as in this quote directly influenced by the eruptions of violence in Watts:

> But let us not assume that this is a situation peculiar to Los Angeles alone. It is a national problem. At a time when the Negro's aspirations are at peak, his actual conditions of employment, education and housing are worsening. The paramount problem is one of economic stability for this sector of our society. All other progress in education, family life, and the moral climate of the community is dependent upon the ability of the masses of Negroes to earn a living in this wealthy society of ours.[143]

The disastrous housing conditions in the ghettos as well as the lack of access to affordable housing in the suburbs or better neighborhoods were—third—another heavy burden on families:

> The kind of house a man lives in, along with the quality of his employment, determines, to a large degree, the quality of his family life. I have known too many people in my own parish in Atlanta who, because they were living in overcrowded conditions apartments [sic], were constantly bickering with other members of their families—a situation that produced many severe dysfunctions in family relations. And yet I have seen these same families achieve harmony when they were able to afford a house allowing for a little personal privacy and freedom of movement.[144]

With this argument, King joined the overall societal discussion on masculinity, which considered home ownership a key criterion of the independence of the American man and father. Finally, the SCLC president criticized welfare legislation at state level, which, he asserted, often encouraged the breakup of poor families:

> The concern of white Americans for the problems of the Negro family would be somewhat more compelling if the welfare laws in many state did not promote separation and divorce by denying children aid so long as there is a male in the house.[145]

---

142 Martin Luther King, "Address at Abbott House, Westchester County, New York, October 29, 1965." Reprinted in Rainwater and Yancey, *Moynihan Report*, 402–409, here 408. See also a similar speech at the University of Chicago, January 27, 1966. LOC Daniel Patrick Moynihan Papers, Series I, Box 464, Folder 5.
143 "Statement to the Press by Dr. Martin Luther King Jr, August 20, 1965, Los Angeles, California." Emory University, Atlanta, MARBL, MS 1083, Box 11, Folder 26.
144 Martin Luther King, "A Testament of Hope" (undated, 1968). Emory University, Atlanta, MARBL, MSS 1083, Box 11, Folder 25. For a later edition, see King, Martin Luther, *A Testament of Hope. The Essential Writings and Speeches of Martin Luther King, Jr.*, edited by James Melvin Washington (New York 1986).
145 First draft of statement by SCLC President to U.S. President, Congress, and Supreme Court, February 6, 1968, Emory University, Atlanta, MARBL, MS 1083, Box 574, Folder 3.

Another key organization in the civil rights movement, the National Urban League under Whitney M. Young, also followed Moynihan's lead in making the stabilization of the black family the object of its activism. Shortly after the release of the report and the events at Watts, *Jet* magazine, which was aimed primarily at "working class" African American readers, reported under the headline "Urban League Places Premium on Stabilizing Negro Family," that:

> The League's dominant interest centered on devising practical techniques to strengthen the weakening Negro family unit, with special emphasis on ways to mend and save the "spiritually castrated" Negro male family head.[146]

The comments of leading representatives of the civil rights movement on the Moynihan Report reflect, on the one hand, an attempt to repel criticism of African American family values that they perceived as unwarranted. On the other hand, however, we can also clearly discern civil rights activists' emphasis on the importance of the breadwinner father to the well-being of the family (and their call for the strengthening of the position of the black father through apt social policies). King, Young, and others thus consciously placed themselves within the discourse at large within the wider society, which linked masculinity to economic performance.

The "To Fulfill These Rights" White House Conference of June 1966

When the "To Fulfill These Rights" White House Conference finally took place in Washington D. C. from June 1 to 2, 1966, it did not officially include the African American family as one of its topics.[147] The approximately 2,500 delegates discussed the four central themes of the conference in twelve different forums: "Economic Security and Welfare, Education, Housing, Administration of Justice." The planning session on November 17 and 18, 1965, at which some 200 scholars, social experts, and civil rights activists discussed possible topics for the White House Conference, had resulted in the family being removed from the agenda as an unsuitable theme.[148] In the run-up to this planning session and also during the dis-

---

[146] National Report, "LBJ Calls Negro Leaders to White House," *Jet*, August 19, 1965, 3–10, here 8.
[147] On the conference, see especially Yuill, Kevin L., "The 1966 White House Conference on Civil Rights," *The Historical Journal* 41 (1998), 1, 259–282. Estes, *I Am a Man!*, 120–123. Patterson, *Freedom is not Enough*, 65–89. The transcripts of the individual panels are held at the Johnson Presidential Library, Austin, Texas.
[148] Representing the SCLC at the Planning Session were Program Director Randolph T. Blackwell and the Director of the SCLC's Washington Office, Reverend Walter Fauntroy. Emory University, Atlanta, MARBL, MSS 1083, Box 541, Folder 15.

cussions it featured, there had been intense wrangling over the extent to which the "Negro Family" might represent a suitable subject for the conference. In particular, the text by New York church representative Daniel Payton and psychologist William Ryan's critique of the Moynihan Report inflamed passions in the "Family" section of the November 1965 preparatory meeting, which was chaired by Hylan G. Lewis, professor of sociology at Howard University.[149] Confronted by his critics, Moynihan explained that his report was absolutely about improving the socioeconomic conditions of the black minority, particularly when it came to "jobs" and "decent housing," because

> we can measure our success and failure as a society, not in terms of the gross national product, not in terms of income level, and not in the prettiness or attractiveness or peacefulness of our people, but in the health, and the living, loving reality of our families.[150]

Just as Moynihan was unable to placate his critics, the participants were unable to agree on a unified approach to fortifying the socioeconomic bedrock of the African American family, and not even the palliative final report could hide that fact:

> The President has accurately described the problems confronting Negro Americans as "a seamless web." The strands of this web reach into every arena of American life, and none of these interrelated aspects of the problems is without its urgent and anguishing features. Yet no single conference could productively trace the thread of Negro disadvantage through the whole fabric of society. In order to achieve a common focus on specific action efforts, it was necessary to select a manageable number of areas of concentration.[151]

---

[149] Ryan, William, "Savage Discovery. The Moynihan Report," *The Nation*, November 22, 1965. Cf. the long version of the text: Ryan, William, "The New Genteel Racism," *The Crisis*, 12 (1965), 622–644. Payton, Benjamin F., "The President, the Social Experts, and the Ghetto. An Analysis of an Emerging Strategy in Civil Rights," October 14, 1965 (unpublished). Payton, Benjamin F., "New Trends in Civil Rights," *The Crisis*, 12 (1965). Payton, then director of the Office of Religion and Race of the Protestant Council of New York, called vehemently for the issue of "Negro family stability" to be struck from the agenda of the White House Conference and managed to push this through at the November 1965 Planning Session. On this point, see the discussion in Rainwater and Yankey, *Moynihan Report*, 220–270.

[150] Moynihan at the Planning Session of the White House Conference on Civil Rights, Washington, D. C., November 18, 1966, quoted in Rainwater and Yankey, *Moynihan Report*, 253. On the Planning Session prior to the conference, see also Daniel P. Moynihan Papers, Library of Congress, Manuscript Division (LOC), Box 431, Folder 9.

[151] Statement by the Council to the Conference, Emory University, Atlanta, MARBL, MSS 1083, Box 172, Folder 16. See also the final report by Session Chairman Hylan G. Lewis, "The Family—Resources for Change." Daniel P. Moynihan Papers, Library of Congress, Manuscript Division (LOC), Box 431, Folder 5.

As one observer noted in the *Washington Post*, this was no longer a civil rights conference in the strict sense, but rather a discussion of social reforms that were intended to enable the black minority to participate fully in society: "This conference talked mainly about social reform. Legal discrimination no longer is the leading issue, the conference talked about economic and social discrimination."[152] In principle, this shift in topics dovetailed with the objectives of the moderate civil rights movement around the SCLC and the black trade union movement, whose hopes for binding resolutions were, however, disappointed. Even before the conference began, Bayard Rustin—head of the AFL-CIO's A. Philip Randolph Institute and one of the leading strategists of the civil rights movement—had warned that the conference would be a "total and abysmal failure" if it did not make recommendations for far-reaching economic reforms such as the introduction of a "guaranteed annual income" and free schooling. The *Washington Post* quoted him as advocating comprehensive social engineering: "The Nation must make a point of better social planning to avoid such mistakes as sending people into the Job Corps but providing no jobs."[153]

The press essentially considered the conference a success for the government, although, like representatives of the civil rights movement, many journalists criticized the event as a talking shop devoid of binding resolutions.[154] In any case, it was becoming clear that the Johnson administration's civil rights policy was in a state of serious crisis, with cracks already beginning to appear in the liberal "civil rights coalition."[155] At the conference itself, apart from the numerous invited social experts, the most audible participants were the moderate, pro-government faction of the civil rights movement. Its more radical representatives had stayed away from the conference anyway, like the SNCC, or failed to win over their co-participants to their critique of the government. For example, the anti-Vietnam resolution proposed by Floyd McKissick, chairman of CORE, failed to sway the panels. Martin Luther King was not among the invited closing speakers, which meant that he did not actively participate in the second day of the conference, instead retiring to his hotel room.[156] Observers explained this evident slight to King as due to his critical stance on the

---

152 "Civil Rights and Beyond," WP, June 3, 1966, A24.
153 Robert E. Baker: "White House Conference is Urged to Meet Basic Problems," WP, May 18, 1966, A8.
154 Robert E. Baker, "Sensitive Situation. Johnson Puts His Stamp on Meeting," WP, June 3, 1966, A1. John Herbers, "Rights Conference Averts Showdown on War Policy," NYT, June 3, 1966, 1, 21. Rowland Evans and Robert Novak, "Inside Report: 'Better Than Nothing,'" WP, June 7, 1966, A19.
155 Yuill, "White House Conference," provides a compelling account of this.
156 At least according to press reports. The SCLC files contain documents on the conference, but no personal comments or statements by King. Herbers, John, "Rights Conference Averts Showdown on War Policy," NYT, June 3, 1966, 1, 21. Evans, Rowland and Novak, Robert, "Inside Report:

Vietnam War and the organizers' eagerness not to discredit the conference results through a clear anti-war resolution.[157]

However, there were also a few voices in the press that enumerated the alleged shortcomings of the conference from a different perspective. Arthur Krock, writing in the *New York Times*, faulted the gathering for failing to confront the civil rights movement's tolerance of violence as well as its narrowing of the concept of "civil rights" to the interests of African Americans and dependence on government programs. Moreover, he was disturbed by the fact that "the breakdown of Negro family life, as Daniel P. Moynihan pointed out" was not addressed as a "basic source of juvenile delinquency"—as manifest at the time in Washington, D.C., in the form of increased capital crimes and vandalism.[158]

Overall, one gains the impression that the conference represented the lowest common denominator of the debate on the lot of the black minority. All the participants, however, consciously avoided setting concrete economic or political goals and put the family and its values on the back burner.

Effects of the report

The debate on the state and values of the African American family and their consequences for the American nation, which unfolded between the publication of the Moynihan Report in the summer of 1965 and the White House Conference a year later, not only illustrates what happens when social scientific ideas are taken out of context and instrumentalized in a politically one-sided way. Above all, this controversy shows that something changed in the mid-1960s in the prevailing ideal of the American family and in ideas about black families.

First of all, Moynihan's text, President Johnson's speech, and the responses to them vividly demonstrate that by the mid-1960s African Americans were seen as part of society. Only a few decades earlier, no social scientist or politician would have thought of suggesting that black families should have the same family structure, the same values, as the white middle class—quite apart from the fact that their

---

'Better Than Nothing,'" WP, June 7, 1966, A19. Emory University, Atlanta, MARBL, MSS 1083, Box 541, Folder 15.
157 Yuill, "White House Conference," 278. On King's mounting criticism of the Vietnam War in the course of his involvement with the Poor People's Campaign, see Robbins, Mary Susannah, *Against the Vietnam War: Writings by Activists* (New York 2007). King's programmatic speech of April 4, 1967 "Beyond Vietnam—A Time to Break Silence" is available online at <www.americanrhetoric.com/speeches/mlkatimetobreaksilence.htm>.
158 Arthur Krock, "In the Nation. Missing the Target," NYT, June 5, 1966.

very recognition as "families" would have been problematic in itself. Further, it was not until the 1960s that a sociology emerged that genuinely addressed the structures, values, and problems of black families rather than merely calling for assimilation.[159]

The debate ensured that after 1965 it was no longer such a straightforward matter to unreflectingly transfer the white middle-class family ideal to family life in the urban ghettos. Thanks to this public discourse, social scientists and politicians gained a broader view of coping strategies and ethnic diversity in both family patterns and family values. They began to think about extended kinship networks, community structures, and the importance of more flexible gender relations (a high degree of female self-reliance and fathers' informal support of their children). They also began to grasp that the problematic living conditions and fragile family structures experienced by black Americans had much to do with socioeconomic status, as indicated in the statements of Rustin and Gartner quoted above. Consequently, the notion of "the" African American family was replaced by more nuanced analyses.

However, calls to consider the black family in terms of its individual living conditions rather than dismissing it across the board had little impact on policy itself in the 1960s. On the contrary, after the Johnson Era, programs intended to promote equal economic and social opportunities were either slashed or abandoned. The long-term effects of the debate were an immense increase in the research literature on the topic of "black families" (in a sense, this was first discovered as a research subject as a result of this controversial discourse),[160] but also the integration of supposed "black family pathologies" into the discussion of social welfare legislation and the dismantling of the welfare state.[161]

During the racial unrest of 1965 to 1968, however, Daniel P. Moynihan rose to become the most in-demand expert supposedly capable of explaining the meaning of these conflicts to white America. The mayor of Detroit, for example, had him flown in as an advisor after severe riots there in the summer of 1967.[162] Moynihan himself commented: "People are now saying that I was right and that my report on the disintegration of the Negro family predicted the riots, [. . .]. For the moment, I'm a good guy." In an article for *Commentary* magazine in 1967, he made it clear that in his view—due to the hesitancy of white liberals and the militancy of the

---

[159] Billingsley, *Black Families*, 198–207.
[160] See Finzsch, Norbert, "Gouvernementalität, der Moynihan-Report und die Welfare Queen im Cadillac," in Martschukat, Jürgen (ed.), *Geschichte schreiben mit Foucault* (Frankfurt a. M. 2002), 257–282.
[161] On this point, see the comments below.
[162] Powledge, Fred, "A Troubled Nation Turns to Pat Moynihan. Idea Broker in the Race Crisis," *Life*, November 3, 1967, 72–82. Hoyt William Fuller collection, Box 44, Folder 23.

civil rights movement in 1965—a historic opportunity had been squandered to take the decisive steps toward economic equality for African Americans. The initiative embodied in the presidential speech, he went on, had failed to get off the ground because of Americans' refusal to accept a targeted federal family policy to the benefit of black families: "Family is not a subject Americans tend to consider appropriate as an area of public policy. Family affairs are private."[163] At the same time, he averred, the black community would also have to make its own contribution, either adapting or taking care of its problem families itself:

> The country is not fair to Negroes and will exploit any weaknesses they display. Hence they simply cannot afford the luxury of having a large lower class that is at once deviant and dependent. If they do not wish to bring it into line with the working class (not the middle class) world around them, they must devise ways to support it from within.[164]

This reflects the ambivalence typical of Moynihan's political thinking as a whole: he stood up for African Americans, even in the face of considerable opposition, but at the same time he was fiercely critical and tended toward deliberate public provocation, so that he always eluded simple attributions.

This ambivalence can also be discerned in his own perception of his role in bringing about the report and composing Johnson's Howard University speech. While he described the speech in his usual immodest manner as the president's "only decent civil rights speech" and highlighted his authorship, he concurrently emphasized the political damage caused by the leaking of the confidential report to the press and denied any responsibility for it:

> It is not only a great event in your life, but one in mine as well. I left for the United Nations conference in Yugoslavia just an hour before you were scheduled to speak, and only when I got to Rome (where the event was front-page news) did I learn that you had indeed used the text we had prepared the night before. I was away three weeks and returned to a rather different Washington. Somehow word had got to the press that I had helped draft the speech. As best I can reconstruct, the leak came from the White House and was meant to be a friendly act. But you were distressed, as you had every right to be.[165]

Moynihan's typical inconsistency was on display again a few years later, when another confidential expert report from his pen was leaked to the public in a calcu-

---

163 Daniel P. Moynihan, "The President & The Negro. The Moment Lost. A *Commentary* Report," February 1967. AUC, Woodruff Library, Hoyt William Fuller collection, Box 44, Folder 23. <https://www.commentarymagazine.com/article/the-president-the-negro-the-moment-lost/>.
164 Daniel P. Moynihan, "The President & The Negro: The Moment Lost. A *Commentary* Report," February 1967. AUC, Woodruff Library, Hoyt William Fuller collection, Box 44, Folder 23.
165 Moynihan to Lyndon B. Johnson, March 8, 1972. See also memorandum from Moynihan to Lyndon B. Johnson, February 14, 1972. Daniel P. Moynihan Papers, LOC, Box 176, Folder 3.

lated way. At the end of 1969, in a memo for President Richard Nixon, whom he was now serving as scientific advisor, Moynihan had argued—in view of the confrontations with an increasingly militant black civil rights movement and the race riots—that the "antisocial behavior among young black males" was harming the minority, as was the large number of "female-headed families" living in poverty. Conversely, he underscored, blacks suffered disproportionately from unemployment, poor education, and a broken welfare system. The memo culminated in a call for a new government study on the situation of African Americans, coupled with advice that again earned Moynihan the accusation of "covert racism": "The time may have come when the issue of race could benefit from a period of benign neglect."[166]

Moynihan's persistent ambivalence is also evident in the longer-term discussion of his text. Two decades later, for example, in a series of lectures at Harvard University, he again commented on the report's intentions and expressed regret over the missed opportunity to sustainably improve the economic lot of black families through bold policies. At the same time, he reiterated his call for a proactive national family policy to combat poverty, socio-structural problems, and dependence on welfare benefits, since for him the intact family was the only guarantor of an intact society.[167]

But the moderate civil rights movement also attached great importance to intact families and family values, as illustrated not least by the SCLC's Poor People's Campaign in the early summer of 1968.[168] In December 1967, King had announced a large-scale, nonviolent protest by residents of the country's ghettos in Washington, D. C., to draw attention to the lack of economic and social equality. Core demands included an adequate supply of jobs, guaranteed income for the poorest, social security, and affordable, modern housing. The protests began in the spring of 1968, with King leading the campaign until his assassination in April of that year; his successor as SCLC president, Ralph D. Abernathy, took over his role through June 1968.

The centerpiece of the campaign was a tent city on the National Mall in Washington, D.C., the so-called Resurrection City, in which over 2,000 people

---

166 "U.S. News & World Report," March 16, 1970. AUC, Woodruff Library, Johnson Publishing Company Clipping Files, Folder: Daniel P. Moynihan.
167 Moynihan, *Family and Nation*. Here chapter 1: "The Moment Lost," 1–60, esp. 25–35. See also Mark Starr, "Moynihan: I Told You So," *Newsweek*, April 22, 1985, 30. Starr quotes Moynihan as saying, "What would I prescribe? Nothing different now from then."
168 On the Poor People's Campaign, see McKnight, Gerald, *The Last Crusade: Martin Luther King, Jr., the FBI, and the Poor People's Campaign* (Boulder, CO 1998). Honey, Michael K., *Going Down Jericho Road: The Memphis Strike, Martin Luther King's Last Campaign* (New York 2007). Risen, Clay, *A Nation on Fire. America in the Wake of the King Assassination* (Hoboken 2009). Mantler, Gordon K., *Power to the Poor. Black-Brown Coalition and the Fight for Economic Justice, 1960–1974* (Chapel Hill 2013).

lived between May and June.¹⁶⁹ The organizing principle of this site, in which complete strangers lived together in large tents, as well as the frame of reference for the entire campaign, was the intact family under an ideally male family head.¹⁷⁰ This emerges from the rules for living in Resurrection City as well as from reports by contemporary witnesses. For example, those staying in each tent had to elect a "head of household" who was responsible for keeping the tent tidy and clean, for passing on information, and for reporting problems. The tent community was considered a "family," and the individual tent residents were considered "individuals in the family."¹⁷¹ One resident of Resurrection City described it as "an oasis in most of our lives"—in contrast to his previous life experiences: "Living in Resurrection City is like living in one big happy family who believes in

Fig. 4.6: Resurrection City, Poor People's Campaign, Washington D. C.

---

169 On the Poor People's Campaign, see Emory University, MARBL, MSS 1083, Boxes 571 to 575.
170 The plans made for the campaign already focused on strengthening the family and justified the demand for a "guaranteed income" with reference to the positive effects on the affected families and especially the children. "Proposal of a Declaration of the Poor People's Campaign," April 28, 1968. Emory University, MARBL, MSS 1083, Box 571, Folder 8.
171 "Community Representation of Resurrection City," draft, 1968. Emory University, MARBL, MSS 1083, Box 571, Folder 15.

taking care of each other. And we're not going to leave until our homes around America are this way."[172] The tent city thus represented a utopian vision of an invigorated poor (black) family in the United States. This family was conceived as moderately hierarchical (under an elected head), more extended than nuclear, more "elective kinship" than biological family, and was oriented toward solidarity and mutual support among family members. The way in which the functioning tent family was described as essential to the overall success of Resurrection City, however, recalls the equation of family and nation that characterized the debate on family in the United States throughout the twentieth century.

4.6 Plans to improve the African American family as a key example of the "scientification of the social" in the mid-1960s

The plans to reform the black family formulated by Kenneth B. Clark, Nathan Glazer, and especially Daniel P. Moynihan in the 1960s must be understood in the context of the "scientification of the social" described by Lutz Raphael and others for Western societies.[173] The notion that society can be rationally planned and improved peaked in the 1960s, precisely when the Moynihan Report appeared. Updating and internationalizing his ideas, first published in 1996, Lutz Raphael recently defined the "scientification of the social" as "a larger process that has transformed an esoteric, academic knowledge about man [sic] in society into public categories, professional routines, and behavioral patterns." Social experts, mostly "academically trained professionals," played a key role in this process, linking the arguments put forward in the social sciences (Raphael literally refers to the "human sciences" as the "sciences of the human being") to practice, as well as translating them into action.[174]

How this transfer worked can be demonstrated paradigmatically if we look at the arguments presented in the Moynihan Report—although it is interesting that this contextualization is absent from the existing, very extensive research literature on

---

[172] Gordon White, "The Cry of Resurrection City Residents" (1968). Emory University, MARBL, MSS 1083, Box 571, Folder 20.
[173] Raphael, "Verwissenschaftlichung." Raphael, "Embedding." See also Etzemüller (ed.), *Die Ordnungen der Moderne*. Etzemüller, Thomas, *Romantik der Rationalität*. On the United States, see Welskopp and Lesoff, *Fractured Modernity*.
[174] Raphael, "Embedding," 41, 45.

the report.[175] So far, only Norbert Finzsch, in an intriguing essay, has argued for a reading of the treatment of black families, and particularly the negative stereotyping of African American single mothers as "welfare queens" under the Reagan administration, as an example of governmentality as conceived by Foucault.[176] This is undoubtedly apposite and illuminating. Yet in the case of the Moynihan Report, what we can discern is not so much the attempt to trigger a specific behavior via governmentality—in this case, the adoption of white middle-class family values. Rather, the social experts, government advisors, and civil rights activists involved initially negotiated the potential and limits of expert-led government intervention in the family structures, values, and socioeconomic conditions of the black minority. Thus, the term "social engineering" or, more broadly, the "scientification of the social" seems more appropriate here, though U.S. historical research has not seen it that way.

The significance of "social engineering" to Moynihan, who understood it as science-guided intervention in the living conditions of the African American family, is exemplified by a text written by sociologist Nathan Glazer, who in turn referred to one of Moynihan's ideas. In a preface he wrote in 1966 for the new edition of E. Franklin Frazier's *The Negro Family in the United States*, Glazer contended that while the potential of "social engineering" was widely known, there should be limits on government intervention, especially in the case of the family. He then referenced a proposal by Moynihan, who had suggested introducing a second daily mail delivery to create 50,000 new jobs for black men, who would provide for their families and thus act as pillars of the community:

> I think E. Franklin Frazier would have liked this form of social engineering, which left the structure of the Negro family to each family, but which set conditions that we know produce the opportunity for stability, better education and higher income.[177]

While such a measure would not have directly intervened in the structure of the affected families, it would have cemented the existing normative order (of the white middle class) via the transported ideal of the "male breadwinner" as the foundation of the family *and* society. Hence, in the eyes of Moynihan and his predecessors, given the continued social and economic discrimination against and depravation of African Americans, an expansion of government programs aimed at strengthening the black nuclear family did not represent an unwarranted encroachment on a minority's rights and family structures, but appeared

---

[175] Patterson, *Freedom is not Enough*. Estes, *I am a Man!* Massey and Sampson, "Moynihan Report Revisited." Lawson, *Civil Rights Crossroads*, 31–55.
[176] Finzsch, "Gouvernementalität," 257–282.
[177] Nathan Glazer, "Foreword," in Frazier, *The Negro Family* (1966, first edition New York 1939), xvi–xvii, reprinted in Rainwater and Yancey, *Moynihan Report*, 312–313.

to be the only conceivable way to effectively improve their living conditions. The political and normative background was the Johnson administration's civil rights policy and the president's efforts in 1965 to follow up legal equality with greater economic participation (the War on Poverty program).[178] The problematic aspect of Moynihan's treatise and its reception, however, was the tendency to equate family structure and family values, as well as socioeconomic parameters (living conditions in the ghettos and ongoing discrimination in terms of education, housing, and social participation) and individual dispositions, which fostered numerous misunderstandings and misinterpretations.

Moynihan—very much in the manner of the social expert analyzed by Raphael, who saw themself as a scientist and practitioner in equal measure and worked toward the practical implementation of their analyses—did not leave it at a description of the difficulties of African American families but tried to go beyond the report to generate solutions and a new policy program. After his stint as assistant secretary of labor, he directed the Joint Center for Urban Studies at Harvard University and the Massachusetts Institute of Technology (MIT) from its founding in 1965 until he joined the Nixon administration in 1969. The center saw itself explicitly as a social scientific think tank, a link between scholarship and policy. Funded by the Ford Foundation, scholars and practitioners from a wide range of disciplines worked on interdisciplinary approaches to the problems of modern cities—a perfect example of the "scientification of the social." In 1967, for example, Moynihan organized an interdisciplinary conference on "Social Statistics and the City," which was intended to advance the "improvement of social statistics concerning the Negro and other deprived ethnic groups" in advance of the 1970 census. The background to this was the "underenumeration of young Negro males in the young adult group," that is, his observation that young black males in particular were underrepresented in the voter rolls because often they were unable to provide a permanent address.[179] The piquancy of this argument consisted in the fact that many young men chose not to live with their families to enable them to receive benefits from the Aid to Families with Dependent Children (AFDC) program, which required

---

[178] On the Johnson administration's "War on Poverty" and its assumptions about the importance of early childhood education, as well as about the link between social disadvantage and children's psychological deformation, see Raz, Mical, *What's Wrong with the Poor? Psychiatry, Race and the War on Poverty* (Chapel Hill 2013).

[179] See Daniel P. Moynihan's letters as Director of the Joint Center for Urban Studies of the Massachusetts Institute of Technology and Harvard University to SCLC President Martin Luther King, May 27, 1967, and July 6, 1967, AUC Atlanta, Morehouse College. Woodruff Library, Martin Luther King Jr. Collection, Subseries 1.1: Correspondence, 1.1.0.33710, fol. 001–017.

the absence of a (male) breadwinner.[180] It is interesting that this time Moynihan made great efforts to bring representatives of the civil rights movement on board, notably inviting Martin Luther King.[181] With the exception of Hylan G. Lewis, however, the movement's high-ranking figures stayed away from the conference, whose outcome was as ambivalent as Moynihan himself.[182] King himself considered the event "apologetic," as he wrote in the margin of his invitation, by which he presumably meant that it was a mere façade that failed to propose effective solutions to the problems facing black Americans. The goal of improving the representation of African Americans on the electoral rolls—and thus empowering them to exercise their civic rights—was to be achieved by expanding the "vital statistics" on minority groups, that is, by collecting sensitive data on illegitimacy, reproductive rates, divorce rates, and ethnicity. The conference resolution, which Moynihan forwarded to King, thus reads like a manual on "social engineering" (recording the characteristics of a specific population group using modern data processing methods and deriving policy proposals from this) in the language of the civil rights movement:

> In a modern society statistical information is not only a primary guide to public and private actions, in itself it profoundly influences patterns of thought and basic assumptions as to the way things are and the way they are likely to be. [. . .] As it happens, however, where American population statistics are inadequate, they will normally be found to be so in terms of the under-enumeration and under-estimation of minority groups, defined in terms of race, or national origin, and concentrated in specific neighborhoods, usually in densely populated central city areas. They are also, characteristically, defined by poverty. But a larger issue than that simply of efficiency and convenience must enter the consideration of this subject. A constitutional issue enters.[183]

Martin Luther King and the SCLC also referred to "social engineering" approaches (understood as a positive tool) when it came to the question of how to improve the lot of black families. Thus, in May 1966, at a conference on "Social Change and the Role of the Behavioral Scientist" in Atlanta, King elucidated his expectations of social scientists: "We ask you to make society's problems your laboratory. We ask you to translate your data into direction, direction for action." In view of the continuing

---

180 On the AFDC program and welfare policy toward the African American minority, see Chappell, *War on Welfare*.
181 For relevant correspondence featuring the invitation as well as the final report on the conference, see Martin Luther King's papers. AUC Atlanta, Morehouse College, Woodruff Library, Martin Luther King Jr. Collection, Subseries 1.1: Correspondence, 1.1.0.33710, fol. 001–017.
182 See the summary of the results of the conference, the resolutions it adopted, and the list of participants, in Daniel P. Moynihan Papers, LOC, Box 154, Folder 1.
183 AUC Atlanta, Morehouse College, Martin Luther King Jr. Collection, Subseries 1.1: Correspondence, 1.1.0.33710, fol. 005.

struggle of African Americans for equal rights and the still troubling conditions in the big-city ghettos, King contended, new perspectives had opened up in the sense that "the social scientist can render an invaluable contribution to our social order by being a catalyst, by becoming an activist, by stimulating, uplifting, reconciling, democratic change." Specifically, he underscored, the family offered a rich field with respect to both research and practical proposals for change:

> What about the Negro family, its too often matriarchal character, its strengths, its weaknesses, its extended family, and welfare dependency? What institutional changes can be effected to cope with discrimination in a society leading to the so-called "breakdown" of the Negro family? Have Negro families broken down in actual fact, or are they a major source of support? Where this family support is lacking, how can social scientists assist in overcoming this?[184]

As background to this highly positive view of social scientists, it is important to note that King attributed the Supreme Court's landmark decision in *Brown v. Board of Education*, which declared educational segregation unconstitutional, in significant part to the findings of psychological research conducted by Kenneth B. Clark and others.[185] It is also revealing, however, that the commentator on King's contribution, Philip Hauser, a sociology professor at the University of Chicago and director of its Population Research and Training Center, emphasized the economic and social emasculation of the African American male. This, he averred, had to be overcome by means of "social engineering," such that Hauser was to a certain extent moving on classic Moynihan terrain:

> The target is clear enough. We need to adopt a whole series of measures that add up to the program of restoring the social and economic masculinity of the Negro male. Nothing can do more in my judgment to restore the Negro family than to give every Negro male some kind of steady income flow that he earns by the labor force contribution he can make and not as an inadequate dole.[186]

In contrast, sociologist Lee Rainwater of Harvard University, one of the editors of the annotated edition of the Moynihan Report, urged caution. After interviewing many of the approximately 10,000 residents of the predominantly African Ameri-

---

[184] King, Martin Luther, "The Social Activist and Social Change," Invitational Conference on Social Change and the Role of Behavioral Scientist, Atlanta, May 4–6, 1966. Emory University, Atlanta, MARBL, MS 1083, Box 801, Folder 27, 45–56, esp. 54.

[185] On this, see the arguments put forward in King, Martin Luther, "The Social Activist and Social Change," Invitational Conference on Social Change and the Role of Behavioral Scientist, Atlanta, May 4–6. 1966, Emory University, Atlanta, MARBL, MS 1083, Box 801, Folder 27, 47–48.

[186] Philip Hauser, "Response to Dr. King's Remarks," Invitational Conference on Social Change and the Role of Behavioral Scientist, Atlanta, May 4–6, 1966, Emory University, Atlanta, MARBL, MS 1083, Box 801, Folder 27, 57–70, here 66.

can Pruitt-Igo Housing Project in St. Louis over a two-year period about their family values and forms, he concluded that they were predominantly oriented toward the white middle class:

> It is important to recognize that lower-class Negroes know that their particular family forms are different from those of the rest of the society and that [. . .] they also think of the more stable family forms of the working class as more desirable. That is, lower-class Negroes know what the "normal American family" is supposed to be like, and they consider a stable, family-centered way of life superior to the conjugal and familial situations in which they often find themselves. Their conceptions of the good American life include the notion of a father-husband who functions as an adequate provider and interested member of the family, a hard-working, home-bound mother who is concerned about her children's welfare and her husband's needs, and children who look up to their parents and perform well in school and other outside places to reflect credit on their families.[187]

Since for many families, he underlined, the awareness that their family life deviated widely from the dominant ideal meant great pressure, social experts had to proceed with much caution:

> Unless they are careful, social workers and other professionals exacerbate the tendency to use the norms of "American family life" as weapons by supporting these norms in situations where they are in reality unsupportable, thus aggravating the sense of failing and being failed by others which is chronic for lower-class people.

It is also telling that representatives of the civil rights movement considered a civic form of "social engineering" to be an appropriate method for tackling the social and structural problems of African American families in the urban ghettos: for example, as a guest speaker at the first nationwide meeting of the SCLC, the mayor of Atlanta, Andrew Young, emphasized that this civil rights organization saw itself as a "consultative firm of social engineers":

> SCLC has been gifted with this tremendous power to mobilize and inspire, but we will not use it to attempt to take over the country. Rather, we will be a consultative firm of social engineers which will make its services available to the forces of good will within a community in projects of moral and spiritual urban renewal, redeeming the soul of America and constructing the social foundations of our beloved community.[188]

---

[187] Rainwater, Lee, "Crucible of Identity: The Negro Lower Class Family," in Clark, Kenneth B. and Parsons, Talcott (eds.), *The Negro American* (Boston 1966), 160–204, here 170–171, available as a copy at Emory University, Atlanta, MARBL, MSS 1083, Box 177, Folder 22.

[188] Young, Andrew J., "An Experiment in Power," Keynote Address, National Convention SCLC, Birmingham, Alabama, August 11, 1965. Emory University, Atlanta, MARBL, MSS 1083, Box 177, Folder 1. Andrew Jackson Young (b. 1932) is an American politician, civil rights activist, and pastor from Georgia. He has served as mayor of Atlanta, congressman for Georgia, and president of

It is evident from this statement that the SCLC—literally in the face of Watts and the Moynihan Report—still harbored no overt doubts about the efficacy and legitimacy of interventionist social planning in August 1965. The importance of the "lost masculinity" of black men (which supposedly required restoration) in the debates of the 1960s is, however, demonstrated particularly impressively by the writings of activists in the Black Power movement and those of African American feminists.

4.7 "Race genocide?" Black men and white concepts of masculinity in the 1960s

The Moynihan Report had already argued that many African American families were characterized by a matriarchal structure. Single mothers, the report underlined, were taking care of their families without the support of husbands or the fathers of their children—with all the associated side effects, from increased dependence on welfare to juvenile delinquency and a lack of prospects for male youths due to the absence of male role models.[189] As Moynihan saw it, there was a simple explanation:

> In essence, the Negro community has been forced into a matriarchal structure which, because it is so out of line with the rest of the American society, seriously retards the progress of the group as a whole, and imposes a crushing burden on the Negro male and, in consequence, on a great many women as well.[190]

The civil rights movement also evoked the notion of the "absent black male" who could not provide for his family and simply abandoned it.[191] No less a figure than the president of the SCLC, Martin Luther King, referred to the dilemma of the

---

the National Council of Churches USA. Young was a member of the SCLC and served as U.S. ambassador to the United Nations under President Carter.

189 The captions of relevant diagrams read "Almost one fourth of nonwhite families are headed by a woman" and "One third of non-white children live in broken homes." Moynihan, "The Negro Family," 9, 11, 18. Daniel P. Moynihan Papers, LOC, Box 66, Folder 7. Rainwater and Yancey, *Moynihan Report*, 55, 57, 64.

190 Moynihan, "The Negro Family", 29. Daniel P. Moynihan Papers, LOC, Box 66, Folder 7. Rainwater and Yancey, *Moynihan Report*, 75.

191 Lamented by contemporaries as early as the Civil War, social scientists had begun to examine this stereotype since the early work of W. E. B. DuBois. One line of argument explained the matrifocal structure of many black families in terms of the emasculation of the African American male due to his economic oppression. DuBois, *Negro Family*. Frazier, *The Negro Family*, 1951. Frazier, *Black Bourgeoisie*. Frazier, *On Race Relations*. Gutman, *The Black Family*. Marable, Manning, *Race, Reform and Rebellion. The Second Reconstruction in America 1945–1999* (Jackson, MS 1991). Weisbrot, Robert, *Freedom Bound. A History of America's Civil Rights Movement* (New York 1990).

man robbed of his masculinity in numerous speeches in the mid-1960s. At the SCLC annual conference in Jackson, Mississippi, in August 1966, for example, he declared that there were two Americas—one living in prosperity (that of the white majority society) and another America of poverty and oppression:

> It is an America inhabited by millions of people who are poverty stricken aliens in an affluent society; too poor even to rise with the society; too impoverished by the ages to be able to ascend by using their own resources. It is an America where millions are forced to live in depressing, rat-infested, vermin filled slums. This America is the home of the dispossessed, the disinherited and the disenchanted. This is the America where fathers are stripped of their masculinity because they cannot support their families. This is the America where unborn hopes have died and where radiant dreams of freedom have been deferred.[192]

In addition to Michael Harrington's *The Other America*, the Moynihan Report, which had been the subject of intense discussion only a year earlier, was obviously in the background here, so we can assume that King is alluding in particular to the masculinity of African American men and their need to act as breadwinners for their families.[193]

As Steve Estes has convincingly argued, it was in the wake of the civil rights movement that black men were for the first time able to proactively make their will and ability to support a family the subject of political protest. The equation of the family breadwinner role and individual masculinity reached its apogee in the slogan "I am a Man!" as used by striking garbage men in Memphis, Tennessee in March of 1968.[194]

The activists of the Black Power movement, on the other hand, evoked a very specific type of black hypermasculinity as an alternative to the image of the oppressed African American male.[195] A striking example is the charismatic pioneer of this movement and high-ranking member of the Black Panther Party, Eldridge Cleaver. In his collection of autobiographical essays, *Soul on Ice* (1968), he de-

---

[192] President's Annual Report by Dr. Martin Luther King Jr., President, Southern Christian Leadership Conference, Delivered in Jackson, Mississippi, August 10, 1966. Emory University, Atlanta, MARBL, MSS 1083, Box 167, Folder 2.

[193] Harrington, *Other America*.

[194] Estes, Steve, *I am a Man!*, esp. 131–151. See also the important studies by Wendt: Wendt, "'They Finally Found Out.'" Wendt, Simon, "Gewalt und schwarze Männlichkeit in der Black Power Bewegung," in Martschukat, Jürgen and Stieglitz, Olaf (eds.), *Väter, Soldaten, Liebhaber. Männer und Männlichkeiten in der Geschichte Nordamerikas* (Bielefeld 2007), 355–369.

[195] On the concept of hegemonic masculinity, see Connell, *Masculinities*. Connell and Messerschmidt, "Hegemonic Masculinity." Dinges, "Hegemoniale Männlichkeit," 7–36. Nagel, Joanne, "Masculinity and Nationalism. Gender and Sexuality in the Making of Nations," *Ethnic and Racial Studies* 21 (1998), 2, 242–269.

scribed a vision sharply different from the idea of the "suppressed and castrated black male," one centered on a self-confident, aggressive black masculinity: "We shall have our manhood. We shall have it or the earth will be leveled by our attempt to gain it."[196] In Cleaver's specific case, this included approval of rape (of white women) as a means of political protest:

> Rape was an insurrectionary act. It delighted me that I was defying and trampling upon the white man's law, upon his system of values, and that I was defiling his women — and this point, I believe, was the most satisfying to me because I was very resentful over the historical fact of how the white man has used the black woman. I felt I was getting revenge.[197]

This frequently quoted passage illustrates well how Cleaver fused an existentialist notion of masculinity with his personal desire for revenge and the armed struggle of the Black Power movement. Cleaver's ideal of masculinity made do without any reference to fatherhood and was focused exclusively on the young activists' generation. In this regard, his concept differed significantly from that of the civil rights movement, which explicitly linked masculinity, breadwinner function, and father role. It is true that the notion of masculinity typical of Black Power activists—armed young men in black uniforms who alluded explicitly to their sexual potency by striking powerful poses—could be effortlessly combined with community work that involved supposedly typical "feminine" activities, as Steve Estes has argued.[198] Yet even when activists served food at a children's recreational camp in a staged setting designed to attract media attention, they simultaneously insisted on the strictly biological roots of gender roles, which was perceived as overt sexism by many women within the movement. Simon Wendt in particular has shown that the hegemonic masculinity of Black Power activists was underpinned by a heteronormative ideal and a biological understanding of gender, that is, it was premised on the oppression of black women and homosexual men, though he has not systematically addressed the critique put forward by black

---

196 Cleaver, Leroy Eldridge, *Soul on Ice* (New York 1968), 61. Leroy Eldridge Cleaver (1935–1998) was an influential member of the Black Panther Party, of which he was a member from 1966 until his expulsion in 1971, among other things as "Minister of Information" and "Head of the International Section." Cleaver was particularly fascinated by the Panthers' commitment to armed struggle. Among other things, he led an armed ambush by the Panthers of Oakland police that ended with the death of one Panther and the wounding of two police officers. To avoid attempted murder charges, Cleaver fled first to Cuba and then to Algeria. In the mid-1970s, he returned to the U.S., renounced his radical past and became an evangelical Christian and Republican. Cleaver wrote the collection of essays *Soul on Ice*, which was published in 1968 by left-wing publishing house Ramparts, during a prison sentence for rape, from which he was released in 1966.
197 Cleaver, *Soul on Ice*, 216.
198 Estes, *I Am a Man!*, 171–173.

feminists. Meanwhile, Benita Roth has shown that the latter had to defend themselves both against marginalization by white feminists and gender discrimination by the Black Power movement.[199] The significance of references to family concepts and the national family ideal in this context, however, remains to be clarified, as evident in the discussion of "black genocide."

Black feminists close to the Black Power movement in particular had already begun to highlight the double, if not triple, oppression of African American women by the end of the 1960s. As Frances Beale and Patricia Robinson described, they faced discrimination as women, as black women, and as activists within the Black Power movement.[200] They were especially bitter about the way male activists reduced them exclusively to their reproductive function. For instance, the Nation of Islam, as one of the centers of gravity of black nationalism, declared that the most important task of African American women was "to prevent black genocide" through the highest possible birth rate—a message that resonated with countless male activists.[201]

Patricia Robinson, who combined her plea for equal rights for African American women with a sharp critique of capitalism (centered on the United States as a "male-dominated class society"), opposed both the attempts of black men to compensate for their own oppression by oppressing black women and the tendency of many poor black women to blame their marginal position exclusively on black men. Instead, she called for a root-and-branch questioning of the socio-economic system and of class and gender hierarchies, which entailed a clear gradation: the "white male in power, followed by the white female, then the black male and lastly the black female."[202]

---

199 Wendt, "Gewalt." Roth, *Separate Roads*, 80–100. Roth also considers the position of Chicana *feministas*, which is not the focus here.

200 Beale, "Double Jeopardy." Robinson, Patricia, *Poor Black Women* (Boston 1968). Excerpted in Albert and Albert, *Sixties Papers*, 481–483. Online at <www.library.duke.edu/digitalcollections/wlmpc_wlmms01008/>. The most important study of African American and also Mexican-born feminists' attempts to position themselves in the face of their marginalization by white feminists and in the light of gender discrimination by the Black Power movement is Roth, *Separate Roads*. On white feminists' experiences of oppression in social protest movements, see Evans, Sara M., *Personal Politics. The Roots of Women's Liberation in the Civil Rights Movement and the New Left* (New York 1980). Hayden, Casey and King, Mary, "Sex and Caste. A Kind of Memo," in Albert and Albert, *Sixties Papers*, 133–136. Lawson, *Civil Rights Crossroads*, 265–283.

201 A good analysis, especially of the resistance of African American women to their appropriation as a means of combating supposed "race suicide" can be found in Nelson, *Women of Color*. Silliman, Gerber Fried, Ross, and Gutiérrez (eds.), *Undivided Rights*.

202 Robinson, *Poor Black Women*, 481–482.

> All domestic and international political and economic decisions are made by men and enforced by males and their symbolic extensions—guns. Women have become the largest oppressed group in a dominant, male, aggressive, capitalistic culture.[203]

Beyond the contemporary revolutionary jargon, Robinson's statement is interesting because, much like Beale's pamphlet, her socio-economic analysis sought to empower African American women while challenging the gender roles and family values of mainstream society. Beale also viewed the oppression of African American men as a core element of the capitalist system:

> However, it is a gross distortion of fact to state that Black women have oppressed black men. The capitalist system found it expedient to enslave and oppress them and proceeded to do so without consultation or the signing of any agreements with Black women.[204]

Yet her critique of the fencing in of black women's scope of action as a key means of advancing the supposed "restoration" of African American men's masculinity was much harsher:

> Those who are exerting their "manhood" by telling Black women to step back into a domestic, submissive role are assuming a counterrevolutionary position. Black women likewise have been abused by the system and we must begin talking about the elimination of all kinds of suppression.[205]

The potency of traditional family values and concepts of nationhood as well as biologistic gender role notions within the Black Power movement is, however, clearly apparent in a letter from six African American women activists to their male comrades-in-arms in September 1968:

> The brothers are calling on the sisters not to take the pill. [. . .] To take the pill means that we are contributing to our own GENOCIDE. However, in not taking the pill, we must have a new sense of value. When we produce children, we are aiding the REVOLUTION in the form of NATIONbuilding.[206]

Disgusted by the overt machismo and irresponsible ideal of masculinity espoused by many African American men ("poor black men won't support their families, won't stick by their women—all they think about is the street, dope and liquor, women, a piece of ass, and their cars"), the letter writers claimed the right to decide for themselves whether or not to use contraception: "For us, birth control is freedom

---

[203] Robinson, *Poor Black Women*, 483.
[204] Beale, "Double Jeopardy," 502–503.
[205] Beale, "Double Jeopardy," 503.
[206] "Birth Control Pills and Black Children, The Sisters Reply, September 11, 1968," in Albert and Albert, *Sixties Papers*, 478–480, here 478.

to fight genocide of black women and children."[207] This argument was also embraced by representatives of the "middle-class" black women's movement, as exemplified by the autobiography of long-serving congresswoman Shirley Chisholm:[208]

> Which is more like genocide, I have asked some of my black brothers—this, the way things are, or the conditions I am fighting for in which the full range of family planning services is freely available to women of all classes and colors, starting with effective contraception and extending to safe, legal termination of undesired pregnancies, at a price they can afford?[209]

In much simpler terms than Chisholm the politician, Margaret Wright, a black activist from Los Angeles, summed up the connection between the Moynihan Report, the masculinity ideals of the Black Power movement, and her own dilemmas as a feminist. In a 1970 text, she stated:

> Some white man wrote this book about the black matriarchy, saying that black woman ran the community. Which is bull[shit]. We don't run no community. We went out and worked because they wouldn't give our men jobs. This is where some of us are different from the white women's liberation movement. We don't think work liberates you. We've been doing it so damned long. [. . .]
>
> Now the black man is saying he wants a family structure like the white man's. He's got to be head of the family and women have to be submissive and all that nonsense. Hell the white woman is already suppressed in that setup. [. . .]
>
> In black women's liberation we don't want to be equal with men, just like in black liberation we're not fighting to be equal with the white man. We're fighting for the right to be different and not be punished for it.[210]

This is another striking piece of evidence that African American feminists identified neither with the demands of the white women's movement nor with the gender role conceptions at large within the Black Power movement. Instead, they insisted on the right to be "different" in a positive sense but at the same time

---

207 "Birth Control Pills and Black Children," 479.
208 Shirley Chisholm (1924–2005) was a U.S. politician and civil rights activist. She was the first African American to run (unsuccessfully) for the Democratic presidential nomination in 1972. A member of the New York State Assembly since 1965, she was elected the first female black member of Congress in 1968 and served there until 1982. She was one of the co-founders of NOW; a committed advocate for the rights of African Americans, the poor and women, she also campaigned against the Vietnam War. Her autobiography echoed the slogan of her campaign for the presidential nomination: Chisholm, Shirley, *Unbought and Unbossed* (Boston 1970).
209 Chisholm, Shirley, *Unbought and Unbossed* (Boston 1970), cited in Lerner, Gerda (ed.), *Black Women in White America. A Documentary History* (New York 1972), 606–607.
210 Wright, Margaret: "I Want the Right to Be Black and Me," originally published in Reinholz, Mary, "Storming the All Electric Dollhouse," *West Magazine, Los Angeles Times*, June 7, 1970, reprinted in Lerner, *Black Women*, 607–608. See also Roth, *Separate Roads*, 97.

accepted. In this struggle for the right "to be black and me" and to overcome "double jeopardy," however, neither white feminists, black activists, nor social experts were of any help.

4.8 Interim conclusion: toward an expansion of the national ideal of the family

In the late 1960s, the national family ideal remained a highly normative construct, though the U.S. conception of family did expand to include a greater range of ethnicities. Thus, the Moynihan Report, Johnson's speech, and, with some qualifications, the White House Conference on Civil Rights, together represented the first political attempt in U.S. history to include African American families in the national family ideal. The problem, however, was that instead of accepting diverse family structures, values, and gender norms, the concept of the "modern isolated nuclear family" as described by Talcott Parsons was declared the measure of all things and a prerequisite for socio-economic advancement. This not only ignored the poverty afflicting the majority of black families but entailed a failure to recognize and problematize the practical effects of "race" and "class" as categories of difference.

This perspective was anything but preordained when the debate began, as we have seen from the analysis of the sources of the Moynihan Report. Moynihan developed his ideas about the structure and values of the African American family specifically in light of research into the causes of poverty, initially identifying a large number of children per family as a key factor in making people poor. He wished to tackle this through a targeted combination of "population planning" and "urban planning." Social scientists from a wide range of disciplines discussed relevant proposals under his guidance, but repeatedly identified the family as the core of the problem.

Finally, a common paradigm among social experts in the 1960s was the critique of the matriarchy supposedly prevailing in black families, in a sense reversing the momism debate of the 1940s. Through their strength and dominance, so the argument went, African American women were themselves largely responsible for their deficient family structures and the failure of their sons in particular. The latter allegedly lacked adequate role models and socialization opportunities. This criticism of matriarchy was shared even by moderate civil rights activists, who were also quite willing to accept the expertise of social scientists when it came to ways of "improving" family structures. Unlike white experts, however, they always linked this with calls to improve the socioeconomic conditions of blacks, attaching a decidedly positive meaning to the term "social engineering." In contrast, the Black Power movement vehemently rejected the stereotype of the African American male, who was either absent and weak (in the case of fathers) or disoriented and delinquent (in the case of sons), as evoked by white experts and assimilationist black civil rights activists. The concept of black hypermasculinity hailed by Black Power activists privileged the powerful demonstration of African American men's agency, self-confidence, and sexuality. One shadow side of this conception, however, was to reduce African American women from the outset to a strictly biologistic role as the mothers of new fighters for the movement. Black women thus faced multiple forms of discrimination from predominantly white social experts and from black activists—not to mention their marginalization by the white women's movement. This starting point is crucial if we wish to understand the conflicts between white and African American feminists within the women's movement's shared struggle over access to abortion and contraception and for reproductive control more generally (including the right to motherhood) in the 1970s. This is the task of the following chapter.

5 "From reproductive choice to reproductive rights": abortion, reproduction, and the role of women in family and society in the 1970s and 1980s

In November 1972, a small revolution occurred on American evening television.[1] Maude Findley, the eponymous heroine of a CBS sitcom, found herself unintentionally pregnant at the age of forty-seven. After intense self-questioning and discussions with her adult daughter Carol, a staunch feminist, as well as her husband Walter, Maude decided to have an abortion.[2] This did not bring her into conflict with the law, since the fictional Maude lived in the small town of Tuckahoe in Westchester County, New York State, where abortion had been legal since 1970.[3] But the broadcast of the two "abortion episodes" triggered heated viewer discussions and a public debate. Producer Norman Lear, who often addressed socially relevant topics in his shows, had personally lobbied for the subject to be tackled in the sitcom and had managed to push through the broadcast at CBS—no doubt with one eye on the likely ratings.[4] Lear explained to the *New York Times*: "I realized the only way to engage the audience's interest was to let Maude get pregnant."[5]

The immediate result was a significant increase in viewing figures and a flood of readers' letters to national newspapers debating not only the pros and cons of abortion, but also the extent to which such a serious topic should be tackled in a television comedy.[6] The Catholic Church in particular was up in arms

---

[1] Excerpts of the following section in Heinemann, "American Family Values," 278–283.
[2] *Maude* was produced by Norman Lear and ran from September 1972 to April 1978 on CBS. The two episodes centered on Maude's abortion were first broadcast on November 16 and 23, 1972.
[3] Legalization at the federal level did not occur until the Supreme Court's landmark *Roe v. Wade* ruling on January 22, 1973. See below in this chapter.
[4] Spangler, Lynn, *Television Women from Lucy to Friends. Fifty Years of Sitcoms and Feminism* (Westport 2003), 109. Mitz, Rick, *The Great TV Sitcom Book* (New York 1980), 254. Alley, Robert and Brown, Irby, *Women Television Producers. Transformation of the Male Medium* (Rochester NY 2001), 86.
[5] Aljean Harmetz, "Maude Didn't Leave 'Em All Laughing," NYT, December 10, 1972, D3.
[6] CBS alone received 7,000 letters protesting the initial broadcast. Les Brown, "Wood, C.B.S.-TV Head, Defends 'Mature' Shows," NYT, October 16, 1973, 87. The "abortion episodes" were also subject to intense discussion in readers' letters printed in the national press. See, for example, the critical letters received in response to a favorable article on *Maude* in the NYT of December 1972. Aljean Harmetz, "Maude Didn't Leave 'Em All Laughing," NYT, December 10, 1972, D3. Readers' letters were sent in, for example, by Carol Gieger, The Bronx, N.Y., Sheila Marron, Florham Park, N. J., Maria J. Grieco, Co-Chairman, Voice for the Innocent Victims of Abortion; all in NYT, Decem-

about this "open propaganda for abortion and vasectomy," to quote the Archbishop of New York.[7] Bishop James S. Rausch, secretary general of the United States Conference of Catholic Bishops, declared that "advocacy of abortion is unacceptable in a situation-comedy format aired at prime viewing hours."[8] The Catholic press urged church members to protest.

In the summer of 1973, a good six months after the Supreme Court legalized abortion, CBS decided to rebroadcast the episodes. This time there was uproar: no fewer than thirty-nine local stations refused to go on air. All sponsors (including companies such as Pepsi Cola and American Home Products) withdrew their commercials, and CBS received 17,000 critical letters from outraged viewers.[9] Abortion opponents and supporters demonstrated not only in front of CBS headquarters, but also outside smaller TV stations to impede or demand the broadcast of the episodes.[10] The most powerful intervention came from the National Catholic Conference, which led a coalition of anti-abortion organizations.[11]

Ten years later, however, in 1982, the same theme could be addressed in the movie *Take Your Best Shot*, also on CBS, without triggering the slightest controversy:[12] the hero, an unsuccessful actor in the midst of a marital crisis, met a young colleague who candidly told him about the abortion she had just undergone, after which they embarked on a brief affair. In contrast to the *Maude* episodes, the film caused no public stir whatsoever, as a laconic article in the

---

ber 24, 1972, D8. Another critical text was the article by Tom Donnelly, "Mirth and Maude," WP, December 5, 1972, B1.

7 Letter from New York Bishop Monsignor Eugene V. Clark, November 21, 1972, to Richard W. Jencks, president of the CBS Broadcast Group. Cited in Montgomery, Kathryn, *Target: Prime Time: Advocacy Groups and the Struggle Over Entertainment Television* (New York 1989), 35.

8 Albin Krebs, "'Maude' Sponsorship Decline Laid to Abortion Foes," NYT, August 10, 1973, 61.

9 Albin Krebs, "25 C.B.S. Affiliates Won't Show 'Maude' Episodes on Abortion," NYT, August 14, 1973, 67. John Carmody, "Two-Part Problem," WP, August 14, 1973, B7. "Censoring 'Maude,'" NYT, August 15, 1973, 36. "'Maude' Sponsors Who Backed Out Now Face Boycott," NYT, August 18, 1973, 53. Albin Krebs, "5 Diverse Groups Urge Action to Counter Censorship of TV," NYT, August 30, 1973. 67. Les Brown, "Wood, C.B.S.-TV Head, Defends 'Mature' Shows," NYT, October 16, 1973.

10 Marjorie Hyer, "240 Picket WTOP Over Abortion," WP, August 22, 1973, A22. "300 Anti-Abortionists March on C.B.S. in 'Maude' Protest," NYT, August 22, 1973, 75. See also readers' letters from J. J. Reilly, Bellport, Long Island, reprinted in the NYT, August 27, 1973, 28, and from C.V.A. Avedikian and Robert Harmon in the WP of August 30, 1973, A19.

11 Montgomery, *Prime Time*, 28–50.

12 According to the research of Sisson and Kimport, a total of eight film and television productions in 1982 addressed the topic of "abortion," with negative consequences of the decision to have one (such as the death of the protagonist) being presented disproportionately often. Sisson, Gretchen and Kimport, Katrina, "Telling Stories about Abortion: Abortion Related Plots in American Film and Television, 1916–2013," *Contraception* 89 (2014), 413–418, here 417.

New York Times stated.¹³ So had the public debate on abortion changed profoundly in the space of ten years? If so, does this indicate a broad change in social values?

When it comes to what could be portrayed on television and in terms of viewing habits, the answer is yes in both cases. Media historian Kathryn Montgomery, for example, argues that entertainment television in the 1970s increasingly tackled politically controversial topics. She explains this, not least with reference to *Maude*, as due to socio-political interest groups' influence on the portrayal of key themes and to broadcasters' attempt to maximize their financial interests, as they could attain sky-high ratings by airing controversial shows.¹⁴ *Maude* can also be seen as an example of how social change altered the visualization of family life on TV: the head of the CBS television division, Robert Wood, explained in 1973 that his goal in rebroadcasting the abortion episodes was in part to respond to viewer criticism that entertainment programs were boring and neglected socially significant topics.¹⁵

But the public debate on abortion in the United States since the mid-1960s has been much more nuanced and heterogeneous than the reception of *Maude* suggests. A particularly important role in this regard was played by the women's movement, which made the right to abortion one of its core objectives—along with anchoring equality in the constitution and fighting all discrimination against women.¹⁶ In addition to the nationwide legalization of abortion by the Supreme Court in January 1973—after the first broadcast of the two *Maude* episodes—the introduction of the Pill in 1960–61 and the sexual revolution of the 1960s in general

---

13 John J. Connor, "Yesterday's Taboos are Taken for Granted Now: What Used to be Called the 'New Permissiveness' Has Entered the Television Mainstream with Remarkable Ease," NYT, November 7, 1982.
14 Montgomery, *Prime Time*, 49–50. While Montgomery cites the national debate on *Maude* essentially as evidence of pro-lifers' clout, Susan Staggenborg approaches it as part of the pro-choice movement's campaign. Staggenborg, Suzanne, *The Pro-Choice Movement. Organization and Activism in the Abortion Conflict* (Oxford 1991), 69–72.
15 NYT, October 16, 1973. Similar arguments are made by Marc, David and Thompson, Robert, *Prime Time, Prime Movers. From I Love Lucy to L.A. Law—America's Greatest TV Shows and the People Who Created Them* (Syracuse, NY 1992), 51.
16 Evans, Sarah, *Personal Politics. The Roots of Women's Liberation in the Civil Rights Movement and the New Left* (New York 1980). Echols, Alice, *Daring to be Bad. Radical Feminism in America 1967–1975* (Minneapolis, MN 1989). Cott, Nancy, *The Grounding of Modern Feminism* (New Haven, CT 1987). Chafe, *Paradox of Change*.

are widely regarded as landmarks in a seismic process of social liberalization.[17] At the same time, however, there was also an increase in protests—predominantly of a religiously conservative nature—against the legalization of abortion, a phenomenon that persists to this day.[18]

In any case, a perspective on the twentieth century as a whole reveals that abortion remained deeply controversial in the United States even after 1973, making it impossible to refer straightforwardly to a profound change in values with respect to this topic.[19] It is also apparent that access to comprehensive reproductive control (in the form of abortion, contraception, sterilization, artificial insemination, and adoption) has always been and remains strongly segmented by race and class.[20] For example, prior to the legalization of abortion, it was generally white women of the middle and upper classes who were able to have illegal abortions because they had the necessary financial means. If this step was out of the question, it was primarily white parents who forced their daughters to give up their babies through adoption in order to avoid the stigma of illegitimacy.[21] At the same time, white women who sought voluntary sterilization as a means of intentional birth control were often unable to sway skeptical doctors and the authorities, whereas non-white women became the target of forced sterilizations.[22] After *Roe v. Wade*, meanwhile, it was once again white, educated women who had bet-

---

17 May, Elaine Tyler, *America and the Pill. A History of Promise, Peril, and Liberation* (New York 2010). Watkins, Elizabeth, *On the Pill. A Social History of Oral Contraceptives, 1950–1970* (Baltimore 1998). Bailey, *Sex in the Heartland*. Tone, Andrea, *Devices and Desires. A History of Contraceptives in America* (New York 2002). Gordon, Linda, *The Moral Property of Women. A History of Birth Control Politics in America* (Urbana and Chicago 2002). Solinger, Rickie, *Pregnancy and Power. A Short History of Reproductive Politics in America* (New York 2005).
18 Riesebrodt, Martin, *Die Rückkehr der Religionen. Fundamentalismus und der "Kampf der Kulturen"* (Munich 2004). Ronald Inglehart's analysis, meanwhile, deviates from this: he postulates a continuing trend toward secularization within the framework of his model of changing values. Inglehart, *Kultureller Umbruch*, 259–260. Blanchard, Dallas A., *The Anti-Abortion Movement and the Rise of the Religious Right* (New York 1994). Wilcox, Clyde, *Onward Christian Soldiers. The Religious Right in American Politics* (Boulder 1996).
19 This is in contrast to the position taken so far by Ronald Inglehart. Inglehart, *Kultureller Umbruch*, 259–268. Inglehart, Ronald and Fischer, Ivonne, *Modernisierung und Postmodernisierung: Kultureller, wirtschaftlicher und politischer Wandel in 43 Gesellschaften* (New York and Frankfurt a. M. 1997), 384–389.
20 Solinger, *Beggars and Choosers*. Solinger, *Pregnancy and Power*. On sterilization policy, see Schoen, *Choice and Coercion*. Stern, *Eugenic Nation*; see also the book by historian Molly Ladd-Taylor, *Fixing the Poor*, on the connection between welfare policy and eugenics in the 1930s.
21 Solinger, Rickie, *Wake up, Little Suzie. Single Pregnancy before Roe vs. Wade* (New York 1992). Fessler, Anne, *The Girls Who Went Away: The Hidden History of Women Who Surrendered Children for Adoption in the Decades Before Roe v. Wade* (New York 2006).
22 Schoen, "Choice and Coercion." Schoen, *Choice and Coercion*.

ter access to this form of reproductive control, while welfare recipients received no financial aid for abortions.[23]

At the same time, from the beginning of the twentieth century until the 1970s, the reproduction of chiefly nonwhite women was often the focus of intervention by social experts as well as media portrayals.[24] Measures taken in individual states ranged from calculated discrimination against and pathologization of nonwhite mothers to the sterilization of welfare recipients.[25] Forced sterilizations of African American and Mexican American women into the 1970s were legitimized on the basis of the associated expert discourse.[26] In the 1970s, however, protest movements made up of those affected used demonstrations, press reports and overall public pressure to force the states to end this practice and to consider apologies and compensation payments—which can certainly be viewed as an expression of both social change and normative change.[27]

It is the task of this chapter to examine the national discussion on reproduction and abortion in the 1960s and 1970s and to determine to what extent this provides us with evidence of a lasting change in family values and gender roles. To this end, I not only trace the relevant expert discourses on the legal permissibility of abortion, on women's right to self-determination, and on population policy objectives. Crucially, I also analyze women's scope for action within the national struggle over reproduction. This ranged from the engagement of representatives of the women's movements in the form of the National Organization of Women (NOW) and the activism of organized abortion advocates—considered here by reference to the National Abortion Rights Action League (NARAL) and its suborganizations—to the demands of African American and Mexican-born women. Equally interesting are the positions of female opponents of abortion as expressed in churches, grassroots movements across the spectrum of the religious right, and nationally active conservative organizations. I contrast the demand for women's self-determination and

---

23 For more details, see below.
24 Roberts, *Killing the Black Body*. Solinger, *Beggars and Choosers*. Nelson, *Women of Color*. Gutiérrez, *Fertile Matters*. Chavez, Leo, *Covering Immigration. Popular Images and the Politics of the Nation* (Berkeley 2001). Heinemann, Isabel, "Social Experts and Modern Women's Reproduction: From Working Women's Neurosis to the Abortion Debate 1950–1980," in Heinemann, Isabel (ed.), *Inventing the Modern American Family. Family Values and Social Change in 20th Century United States* (Frankfurt a. M. 2012), 124–151.
25 Gutiérrez, *Fertile Matters*. Solinger, *Beggars and Choosers*. Chappell, *War on Welfare*. Roesch, *Macho Men*. Overbeck, *At the Heart of It All*.
26 Stern, *Eugenic Nation*. Roberts, *Killing the Black Body*. Gutiérrez, *Fertile Matters*. Kluchin, Rebecca M., *Fit to Be Tied. Sterilization and Reproductive Rights in America, 1950–1980* (New Brunswick and London 2011).
27 Stern, *Eugenic Nation*.

freedom of choice with respect to their own reproduction, as articulated by NOW and NARAL in particular, with the postulates of population scientists and relevant politicians, in order to bring out organizational synergies and programmatic overlaps and to clarify why the population control movement, which drew much of its inspiration from eugenics and an imperialist understanding of modernization theory, proved to be particularly compatible with the campaigns pursued by liberal women's rights and abortion activists.

The source material for this chapter thus consists of the files of NOW and NARAL as well as the various organizations making up the population control movement (the Population Research Bureau, the Population Council, Zero Population Growth, and the Planned Parenthood Federation of America), plus the papers of social experts (notably Margaret Mead and Robert C. Cook); all of these actors advocated population control from a variety of perspectives. The chapter commences with a brief overview of the profound changes in reproductive decision-making options in the United States since 1960 brought about by the "Pill" and the legalization of abortion.

5.1 "Sexual revolution" and "women's health": social change in the use of contraceptives and in access to legal abortion since the 1960s

A far-reaching change in the lives of U.S. families and women in particular occurred through the introduction of the hormonal contraceptive Enovid—"the Pill" for short—in the early 1960s.[28] The availability of the Pill and thus the decoupling of sexuality and reproduction represented the true "sexual revolution" of the 1960s, although the term was primarily coined to describe the generational conflict between an academically educated youth and their parents' generation in the 1960s.[29] Both the pioneers of liberalized sexuality and the developers of the new contraceptive, however, belonged to an earlier generation. This applied first and foremost to analysts of sexuality such as Alfred Kinsey,[30] William Masters,

---

[28] Watkins, *On the Pill*. Tone, *Devices and Desires*. May, *The Pill*. Eig, Jonathan, *The Birth of the Pill. How Four Crusaders Reinvented Sex and Launched a Revolution* (New York 2014).

[29] Bailey, Beth, "Sexual Revolution(s)," in Farber, David (ed.), *The Sixties. From Memory to History* (Chapel Hill and London 1994), 235–262. Bailey, *Sex in the Heartland*. McLaren, Angus, *Twentieth-Century Sexuality. A History* (Malden, MA 1999).

[30] Alfred Kinsey (1894–1956) was originally a biologist; he founded the Institute for Sex Research at Indiana University. He is considered the first U.S. sexuality researcher, his studies on the sexuality of women and men enabling both further research and a broad social discussion about sex.

and Virginia Johnson,[31] whose studies had attracted massive attention since the 1950s. The same went for those considered the Pill's "midwives," ranging from key figures in the birth control movement such as Margaret Sanger[32] and Katharine McCormick[33] to researchers such as John Rock and Gregory Pincus,[34] who ultimately developed the hormonal contraceptive.

Kinsey, *Sexual Behavior in the Human Female*. Kinsey, *Sexual Behavior in the Human Male*. Christenson, Cornelia, *Kinsey. A Biography* (Bloomington 1971). Robinson, *Modernization of Sex*. Hegarty, Peter, *Gentlemen's Disagreement. Alfred Kinsey, Lewis Terman, and the Sexual Politics of Smart Men* (Chicago 2013). Drucker, Donna, *The Classification of Sex. Alfred Kinsey and the Organization of Knowledge* (Pittsburg, PA 2014).

31 William H. Masters (1915–2001) and Virginia E. Johnson (1925–2013) explored human sexuality and sexual dysfunction through empirical experiments beginning in the 1950s. Masters taught as a gynecologist at Washington University, St. Louis, and Johnson became his assistant in 1957. In the years that followed, they worked extremely successfully as a team, and from 1971 to 1993 they were a married couple. They described the "human sexual response circle" and in 1964 founded their own research institute in St. Louis, the Reproductive Biology Research Foundation. Masters and Johnson, *Human Sexual Response*. Masters and Johnson, *Human Sexual Inadequacy*. Masters, William H. and Johnson, Virginia, *The Pleasure Bond* (New York 1970). Maier, Thomas, *Masters of Sex. The Life and Times of William Masters and Virginia Johnson, the Couple Who Taught America How to Love* (New York 2013).

32 Margaret Higgins Sanger (1879–1966) is considered *the* pioneer of the birth control movement in the United States. A trained nurse, social reformer, and feminist, she opened the first family counseling clinic in the U.S. in Brooklyn, New York, in 1916. Sanger's goal was to provide women with the option of legal birth control through education and contraceptives. In 1917, she began publishing the journal *Birth Control Review*. The American Birth Control League, which she founded in 1921, evolved into the Planned Parenthood Federation of America, which she headed until 1962. Sanger also directed the International Planned Parenthood Federation from 1952 to 1959. A member of the American Eugenic Society, she combined her fight for birth control with eugenic goals. Sanger, Margaret, *My Fight for Birth Control* (London 1932). McCann, Carole R., *Birth Control Politics in the United States 1916–1945* (Ithaca 1994). Frank, Angela, *Margaret Sanger's Eugenic Legacy. The Control of Female Fertility* (Jefferson 2005). Chesler, Ellen, *Woman of Valor. Margaret Sanger and the Birth Control Movement in America* (New York 2007, first edition 1992).

33 Katharine McCormick (1875–1967) was a biologist, women's rights activist, and birth control campaigner who worked closely with Sanger from the 1920s onward. Thanks to her inherited fortune, she became a patron of medical research that led to the development of hormonal contraceptives. Eig, *Birth of the Pill*.

34 Gregory Goodwin Pincus (1903–1967) conducted research as a biologist at Harvard University. Supported by a generous McCormick grant, he developed and tested the hormone preparation Enovid together with John Rock (1890–1984), a gynecologist in Brookline, Massachusetts. Clinical trials began in Brookline among Rock's patients, then expanded to Puerto Rico, and later to Haiti, Mexico, and Los Angeles. Because of the high hormone dose, many users suffered serious side effects, but it was to be some time before this was discussed publicly. Originally approved as a drug for menstrual cramps, from 1960 onward Enovid became known as a hormonal contracep-

Shortly after its release as a contraceptive by the Food and Drug Administration in May 1960, women of all ages began to use the Pill. This applied to the young, unmarried, well-educated, and self-confident woman who, in the style of Helen Gurley Brown's *Sex and the Single Girl* (1962), was cultivating a new, metropolitan lifestyle,[35] as well as to the wife and mother who, thanks to this innovation, now had no need to fear another pregnancy.[36] By 1969, the pill already had 8.5 million users in the U.S.[37] However, the practice of prescribing and using the oral contraceptive initially remained at the very least an ambivalent matter: it was mainly white, well-educated women who could afford it, while doctors prescribed it chiefly to married women. Moreover, until well into the 1970s, parents, doctors, social workers, and college administrators had serious concerns about the sexuality of unmarried women and girls, so that the latter gained access to the Pill only after a long struggle, as Beth Bailey, for example, has shown in the case of students at the University of Kansas, Lawrence. But it was not only Midwestern states that restricted access to contraceptives to married women; Catholic New England states such as Massachusetts, Rhode Island, and Connecticut initially did so as well. This led to heated public debates there as elsewhere from the mid-1960s onward, mostly ignited by the question of whether or not college health services could prescribe the pill to female students.[38] Many of the Southern states with a high proportion of rural black communities (North Carolina, South Carolina, Mississippi, and Alabama), on the other hand, had particularly liberal laws and generous public funding for birth control.[39]

At the legal level, the Supreme Court's 1965 decision in *Griswold v. Connecticut* was decisive. Citing the right to privacy, the court ruled that married couples could legally obtain contraceptives, thus eliminating the hitherto valid state-level provisions of the Comstock Laws, dating from the nineteenth century.[40] However, this was not associated with a liberalization of attitudes toward the sexuality of unmar-

---

tive and as "the Pill." Briggs, Laura, *Reproducing Empire: Race, Sex Science, and U.S. Imperialism in Puerto Rico* (Los Angeles 2002). Marsh, Margaret and Wanner, Ronda, *The Fertility Doctor: John Rock and the Reproductive Revolution* (Baltimore 2008).
35 Brown, Helen Gurley, *Sex and the Single Girl* (New York 1962).
36 May, *America and the Pill*, 70–80.
37 Bailey, *Sex in the Heartland*, 105.
38 Bailey, *Sex in the Heartland*, 105–132. Watkins, *On the Pill*, 64–67. Prescott, Heather Munro, *Student Bodies. The Impact of Student Health on American Society and Medicine* (Ann Arbor 2007).
39 Schoen, *Choice and Coercion*, 21–74. Solinger, *Pregnancy and Power*, 131–162.
40 On the Comstock Laws and the practice of censoring supposedly "obscene" practices and information, see Beisel, Nicola, *Imperiled Innocents. Anthony Comstock and Family Reproduction in Victorian America* (Princeton 1997). Friedman, Andrea, *Prurient Interests. Gender, Democracy, and Obscenity in New York City, 1909–1945* (New York 2000).

ried people, on the contrary. As Marc Stein has brought out, this move buttressed a heteronormative ideal of sexuality and linked it to marriage: the family continued to be regarded as the only legitimate site of reproduction—and its prevention.[41] It was not until the late 1960s onward, when female students at ever more colleges and universities won their fight for access to the oral contraceptive, and the women's movement as a whole demanded the right to sexual and reproductive self-determination, that the Pill truly became part of the sexual revolution.[42]

Yet the debate on hormonal contraception also had its dark side. Trials of the contraceptive in Puerto Rico that failed to provide the test subjects with proper information about its health implications are a good example of the export of Western medical technology to control population growth in developing countries.[43] At the same time, the Pill reinforced women's responsibility for reproduction and its prevention through contraception. Hence, a biologistic view of gender roles was propagated as the ovum was raised to the status of core problem. The longtime president of the Planned Parenthood Federation of America, physician Alan F. Guttmacher,[44] had argued as early as February 1960, in an article for the *Saturday Review* on the potential of oral contraceptives, that the obligation to limit international population growth was essentially a matter for women: "Key to the problem: the human female egg."[45]

---

[41] Stein, Marc, *Sexual Injustice. Supreme Court Decisions from Griswold to Roe* (Chapel Hill 2010), 29–34.
[42] May, *America and the Pill*, 89–90.
[43] Briggs, *Reproducing Empire*.
[44] Alan Frank Guttmacher (1898–1974) was one of the most prominent population-focused politicians and supporters of the birth control movement in the United States. After serving as chief gynecologist at Mount Sinai Hospital in New York, he succeeded Margaret Sanger as president of the Planned Parenthood Federation in 1962, a position he held until his death in 1974. He also headed the Medical Committee of the International Planned Parenthood Foundation from 1964 to 1968. The Center for Family Planning Program Development, founded under his presidency, exists today as the independent Guttmacher Institute with an annual budget of $17 million. It funds research and policy planning in the fields of "reproductive and sexual health worldwide." Guttmacher also founded the American Association of Planned Parenthood Physicians, which now operates under the name Association of Reproductive Health Professionals. Guttmacher, Alan F., *Babies by Choice or Chance* (Garden City 1959). Guttmacher, Alan F., *Complete Book of Birth Control* (New York 1961). Guttmacher, Alan F., *Planning Your Family* (New York 1964). Parry, Manon, *Broadcasting Birth Control. Mass Media and Family Planning* (New Brunswick, NJ 2013). Guttmacher Institute: <www.guttmacher.org/index.html>. The Guttmacher papers are housed at Harvard University, Francis A. Countway Library of Medicine, Center for the History of Medicine, H MS c155.
[45] Alan F. Guttmacher, "Pills for Population Control?" *Saturday Review*, February 6, 1960, 50–51. Robert C. Cook Papers, Library of Congress, Manuscript Division, Box 44, Folder 13.

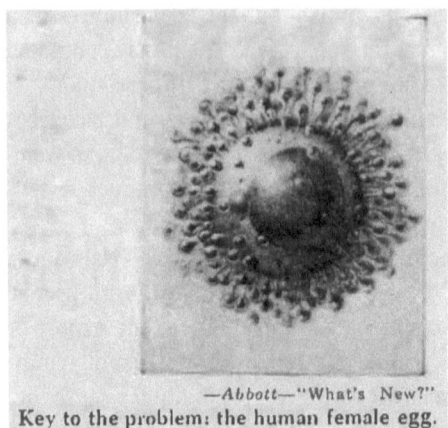

—*Abbott*—"What's New?"
Key to the problem: the human female egg.

Fig. 5.1: The female egg as the core of the population problem.

Like many representatives of the birth control movement, Guttmacher had been involved in the eugenics movement since the 1930s, including a stint as vice president of the American Eugenics Society (as late as 1958) and as a member of the Association for Voluntary Sterilization, itself the successor to the eugenics-focused Human Betterment Foundation.[46] In his writings, concern for the health of women and families (based on his experience as chief gynecologist of a large clinic) merged with growing concern about an anticipated global population explosion, which led him to view birth control as a key means of maintaining the gender and social order. This entailed, first, a clear commitment to reproductive control as a woman's right:

> No woman is completely free unless she is wholly capable of controlling her fertility and [. . .] no baby receives its full birthright unless it is born gleefully wanted by its parents.[47]

Second, it seemed essential to Guttmacher to use birth control methods to reduce global population growth, if necessary by force:

---

[46] Franks, Angela, *Margaret Sanger's Eugenic Legacy. The Control of Female Fertility* (Jefferson 2005), 76. Guttmacher, Alan F., *Babies by Choice or Chance* (New York 1961, first edition Garden City 1959), 11. On the Human Betterment Foundation, see section 2.4 of the present book.

[47] This quote, attributed to Guttmacher, is cited on the Guttmacher Institute website without citation or dating and has since been quoted everywhere in the secondary literature as the core of his commitment to birth control. <www.guttmacher.org/who-was-alan-guttmacher>. However, Guttmacher expressed a very similar view as early as 1961 in his guidebook, when he emphasized that "the practice of birth control for family planning is recognized by almost all Americans as a personal right" and encouraged American women "to make each of your children a truly wanted child." Guttmacher, Alan F., *The Complete Book of Birth Control* (New York 1961), 4.

I would like to give our voluntary means of population control full opportunity in the next 10 to 12 years. Then, if these don't succeed, we may have to go into some kind of coercion, not worldwide, but possibly in such places as India, Pakistan, and Indonesia, where pressures are the greatest. [. . .] There is no question that birth rates can be reduced all over the world if legal abortion is introduced.[48]

The first study of contraceptive use in the U.S.—which built on data from 1955, 1960, and 1965—was published in 1967.[49] It appeared in *"Studies in Family Planning"*, the journal of the Population Council.[50] For this study, researchers had asked women in the New York metropolitan area about their contraceptive practices. Nearly 2,000 white married women aged 18 to 39 were interviewed in 1955 and 1960, and almost 2,500 in 1965. In 1960, the authors expanded their sample and also interviewed 160 women whom they classified as "nonwhite" ("Negro women" in the text); by 1965, the figure had grown to 651. The first interesting aspect of this is that the fertility of African American women did not appear to be of interest at all in the context of this study until 1960, yet in 1965, a disproportionately high number of such women were interviewed (the sample was 27% African American, despite a population share in 1965 of only about 12%).[51]

Comparison of contraceptives "ever used" by ethnicity shows that in 1965 most white women declared that they had already made use of condoms, then in roughly equal proportions the Pill, the rhythm method (a calendar-based approach based on logging the menstrual cycle), vaginal douching, and the dia-

---

48 Guttmacher, Alan F., "Family Planning: The Needs and the Methods," *American Journal of Nursing*, vol. 69, 6. (June 1969), 1229–1234, quote on 1234. This article was also distributed as an offprint by Planned Parenthood.
49 I thank my colleague Claudia Roesch for the reference. Westhoff, Charles F. and Ryder, Norman B., "United States: Methods of Fertility Control, 1955, 1960, & 1965," *Studies in Family Planning. A Publication of the Population Council*, February 1967, 1–5. The two authors had directed the National Fertility Survey in 1965.
50 The Population Council (PC) was one of the key institutions of population planning and research in the United States. It was founded in 1952 with funds from the Rockefeller Foundation and counted many former eugenicists among its members. For more on the PC, see later in this chapter.
51 U.S. Census Bureau, *Statistical Abstracts of the United States, 2003, Mini Historical Statistics, HS-2. Population Characteristics: 1900 to 2002*, 5. Although the fertility of African Americans was the subject of research even before the 1960s, it was always viewed in the context of paternalistic measures aimed at reducing the fertility rate, such as the "Negro Project" launched by the American Birth Control League (ABCL) in 1939. On this, see the papers of Clarence Gamble, who directed some of the ABCL's projects in the Southern states, at the Harvard University Medical Library, and the Margaret Sanger Papers at New York University. Clarence Gamble papers, 1920–1970s. H MS c23. Harvard Medical Library, Francis A. Countway Library of Medicine, Boston, MA.

phragm. A comparison of the "most recently used contraceptives" among white women showed that by 1965 the Pill had clearly outstripped all other methods—particularly at the expense of the condom, diaphragm, and rhythm method.[52] Among non-white women, vaginal douching was used more than the condom and the Pill in 1965—while the rhythm method played virtually no role.[53]

However, it was not only ethnicity and thus socio-economic circumstances that were decisive to the choice of contraceptive method. Major differences were still evident in 1965 on the basis of women's religious affiliation as well. While Protestant women mainly resorted to the Pill in that year, 71% of Jewish couples used either condoms or diaphragms (among Protestant couples, the figure was only 31%). In contrast, the Catholic Church referred its faithful to the rhythm method as the only acceptable contraceptive practice. Yet in 1965, little more than a third of all Catholic women (36%) still relied on this technique, compared with 54% in 1955. This prompted the authors to conclude that "nearly two thirds of the Catholic women who report having used some method of fertility control have at some time employed practices inconsistent with traditional Church doctrine."[54] They also identified the biggest increase in the use of the oral contraceptive among Catholics: not only were more couples than ever before using contraception as a means of family planning, but the Pill also enjoyed the highest popularity among all contraceptive options.

A 2000 study by the Center for Disease Control and Prevention (CDC)—based on a variety of data drawn from the National Vital Statistics System—shows that in the 1990s, the popularity of the Pill as the primary contraceptive among unmarried women aged 15 to 44 years experienced a slight decline. In 1995, 36% of women still relied on this hormone preparation, down from 48% in 1988. In contrast, sterilization and the use of hormone implants and condoms experienced an upswing.[55]

In 2004, another investigation by the same institution found a significant disparity in the use of contraceptives by ethnicity: more than 7,600 women had been surveyed for this study in 2002.[56] It too confirmed that contraceptives were generally highly popular, with 98% of sexually active women using some form of them.

---

[52] Westhoff, Charles F. and Ryder, Norman B., "United States: Methods of Fertility Control, 1955, 1960, & 1965," *Studies in Family Planning. A Publication of the Population Council*, February 1967, 4.
[53] Westhoff and Ryder, "Methods," 3.
[54] Westhoff and Ryder, "Methods," 4.
[55] Ventura, Stephanie J. et al., *Nonmarital Childbearing in the United States, 1940–99*. National Vital Statistics Report from the Center for Disease Control and Prevention, National Center for Health Statistics, National Vital Statistics System, 48, no. 16, October 18, 2000.
[56] Mosher, William D. et al., "Use of Contraception and Use of Family Planning Services in the United States: 1982–2002," *Advanced Data from Vital and Health Statistics* 350, December 10, 2004.

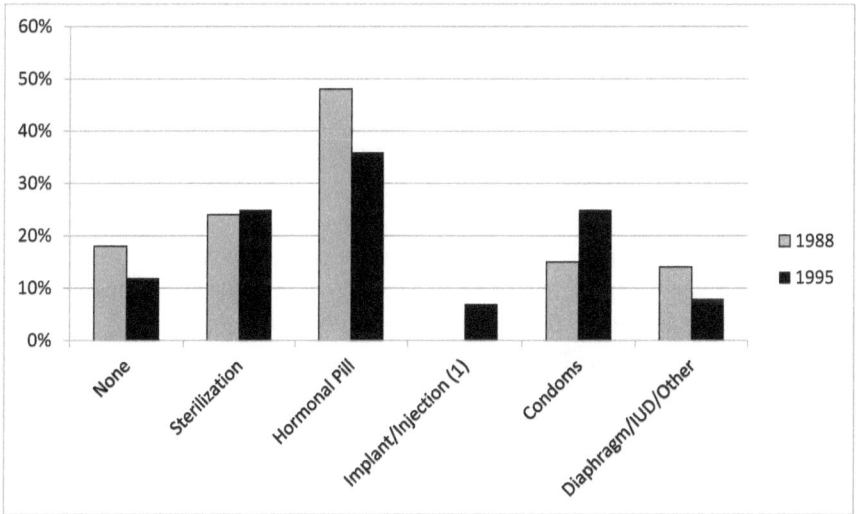

Fig. 5.2: Contraceptive use by unmarried women aged 15–44, 1988 and 1995.

In 2002, 11.6 million women in the U.S. were on the Pill, and 10.3 million women were sterilized. Yet while sterilization played virtually no role as a contraceptive method for white women, a disproportionate number of African American and Mexican American women used this method to prevent unintended pregnancy.[57] This raises the question of what the consequences of "non-consented sterilizations" may have been, particularly for members of ethnic minorities, a point I will be discussing later in the chapter. In contrast, more black and Mexican American women used the three-monthly hormone injection Depo-Provera (much less expensive than the Pill) than white women, who used the Pill in significantly larger numbers.[58] This finding too raises questions about the everyday effects of racial discrimination and social disadvantage in access to "reproductive rights" and "women's health care," issues I discuss below.

For the period from 2002 to 2012, the Guttmacher Institute (named after longtime Planned Parenthood chairman Alan F. Guttmacher) found an increase in this trend toward the use of long-term contraceptive methods (hormone implant or IUD). While the use of such devices was a low 2.4% in 2002, it had increased to

---

57 Mosher, "Use of Contraception," 8.
58 Mosher, "Use of Contraception," 6.

11.6% by 2012.⁵⁹ Meanwhile, long-term contraceptive methods have been discussed primarily in connection with the number of children borne by welfare recipients. As early as the 1990s and 2000s, both state and federal governments debated the feasibility and desirability of requiring women on welfare to use hormone implants (NORPLANT) to stem the birth of more needy individuals. Civil rights activists and scholars in particular have accurately described these musings as veiled "attempts to curb the black population."⁶⁰

Overall, contraceptive use prior to 1980 has only been sparsely researched and the majority of comparative statistics refer to the 1990s and 2000s. In contrast, legal abortions in the United States are much better documented. The Center for Disease Control and Prevention, a subdivision of the Department of Health and Human Services, has been recording legally performed abortions since 1969. A look at the data shows that after the legalization of abortion in 1973, the abortion rate (calculated per 1,000 live births) increased (from 180 in 1972 to 196 in 1973). However, a dramatic increase to about 350 abortions per 1,000 births did not occur until the late 1970s. Abortion figures then remained at this level until the early 1990s, before dropping significantly thereafter (2000: 246, 2012: 210). It is interesting to note that despite Ronald Reagan's anti-abortion rhetoric and the aggressive anti-abortion movement, which did not shy away from violence against individuals and abortion clinics, the 1980s did not see a collapse in the abortion rate.⁶¹ However, this did occur in the 1990s and 2000s as a result of intensified sex education and better access to contraceptives.

---

59 Kavanaugh, Megan L. et al., "Guttmacher Institute: Changes in Use of Long-Acting Reversible Contraceptive Methods among United States Women, 2008–2012." <www.guttmacher.org/article/2015/11/changes-use-long-acting-reversible-contraceptive-methods-among-united-states-women>.
60 On this subject, see later in this chapter. Roberts, *Killing the Black Body*. Overbeck, *At the Heart of It All*.
61 On the anti-abortion movement of the 1980s, see Schoen, *Abortion after Roe*. Hale, Grace E., *A Nation of Outsiders. How the White Middle Class Fell in Love with Rebellion in Postwar America* (Oxford and New York 2011). Critchlow, Donald T., *Intended Consequences. Birth Control, Abortion, and the Federal Government in Modern America* (Oxford and New York 1999).

Tab. 5.1: Number of abortions recorded by the Center for Disease Control and Prevention, 1970–2010.

Year	Number of abortions	Abortions per 1,000 live births
1970	193,491	52
1971	485,816	137
1972	586,760	180
1973	615,831	196
1974	763,476	242
1975	654,853	272
1976	988,267	312
1977	1,079,430	325
1978	1,157,776	347
1979	1,251,921	358
1980	1,297,606	359
1985	1,328,570	364
1990	1,429,247	345
1995	1,210,833	311
2000	857,475	246
2005	820,151	233
2010	765,651	228

5.2 "From reproductive choice to reproductive rights": the U.S. women's movement and the struggle over access to self-determined reproduction

The founding of the National Organization for Women (NOW) on June 30, 1966, occurred in the context of the Johnson administration's equal rights policy.[62] At the annual meeting of the Commission on the Status of Women, which had been appointed by President John F. Kennedy to investigate discrimination against women in the United States, twenty-eight female participants decided to form NOW as a "civil rights organization" for women.[63] In October 1966, just three months later, at the official founding conference in Washington, D.C., 300 members elected journal-

---

[62] On the establishment of NOW, see also section 3.6 of this book.
[63] NOW Origins: A Chronology of NOW, 1966–1985. Schlesinger Library, Radcliffe Institute, Harvard University (SLHU), MC 496, Box 1, Folder 1. NOW Statement of Purpose (written 1966), adopted at conference October 29–30, 1967 in Washington, D.C. NOW, The First Five Years, 1966–1971, prepared by Aileen C. Hernandez and Letitia P. Somers, NOW, Chicago (1971), SLHU, MC 496, Box 1, Folder 1. Online at <www.now.org/about/history/statement-of-purpose/>.

ist Betty Friedan as NOW's first president. NOW justified its self-imposed mission, to campaign as a "civil rights organization" for the normative and legal renegotiation of women's status in society, partly in light of the accelerated social and normative change that US society was undergoing at the time.[64]

> We, 300 men and women, [. . .] believe that the time has come for a new movement toward true equality for all women in America, and toward a fully equal partnership of the sexes, as part of the worldwide revolution of human rights now taking place within and beyond our national borders.

In the spirit of the presidential Commission on the Status of Women, the activists first wanted to highlight and overcome discrimination against women in the labor market due to unequal wages and hiring opportunities, as well as poorer education and wholly inadequate childcare.

> We organize [. . .] to break through the silken curtain of prejudice and discrimination against women in government, industry, the professions, the churches, the political parties, the judiciary, the labor unions, in education, science, medicine, law, religion and every other field of importance in American society.[65]

NOW's second conference in 1967, now with 1,200 members in attendance, identified two new goals in addition to the fight to end discrimination against women: a constitutional amendment that would formally enshrine equal rights for women (an equal rights amendment or ERA), and the legalization of abortion. Point viii of the NOW Bill of Rights adopted at the conference called for: "The right of women to control their own reproductive lives by removing from the penal code laws limiting access to contraceptive information and devices, and laws governing abortion."[66] The discussion at the conference itself went even further. It was affirmed that a fetus is not yet a legal person or a human being, so the mother's right to bodily self-determination was clearly superior to any supposed rights of the fetus. While abortion, the conference discussants contended, was not an appropriate birth control technique, banning it did not prevent it, but only harmed the health of women, who were forced to turn to illegal providers. NOW estimated the number of unreported abortions at between 200,000 and one million annually despite the practice's prohibition.[67]

---

[64] NOW, An Invitation to Join, November 1966, SLHU, MC 496, Box 1, Folder 2.
[65] NOW, An Invitation to Join, November 1966, SLHU, MC 496, Box 1, Folder 2.
[66] NOW Bill of Rights (1967), SLHU, MC 496, Box 1, Folder 2.
[67] NOW: The Right of a Woman to Determine Her Own Reproductive Process, undated (1967). SLHU, MC 496, Box 49, Folder 16.

However, criminal abortion laws clearly have proven to be ineffectual in eliminating the use of abortion as a means of birth control, and have driven women to unskilled practitioners, handicapped doctors in practicing their profession, and have made a mockery of the law.[68]

The fact that the right to reproductive self-determination through contraception and abortion was included in the NOW Bill of Rights in 1967 was due to an initiative by Alex Rossi,[69] chairwoman of the Task Force on Family Life, who won through with her proposal in a close vote—meaning that the members were by no means of one mind on this issue. After the related deliberations, NOW, passing a motion by Rossi, affirmed that

> it is a basic right of every woman to control her reproductive life, and therefore, NOW supports the furthering of the sexual revolution of our century by pressing for widespread sex education, provision of birth control information and contraceptives, and urges that all laws penalizing abortion be repealed.[70]

After this spectacular result, however, in 1968 and 1969 NOW took a more tentative approach to demanding the legalization of abortion. Certainly, the "repeal of abortion laws" was still one of the items discussed at the 1968 annual meeting in Atlanta and was still in the "Women's Bill of Rights," which was also supposed to apply to 1969. But that year—billed as "a militant 1969" by NOW's leadership—was to set other "priorities for action." These were, first, the demand for reform of divorce and alimony laws and, second, the fight to end discrimination against women in the labor market, which NOW assailed as a violation of the Civil Rights Act of 1964.[71]

---

68 NOW: The Right of a Woman to Determine Her Own Reproductive Process, undated (1967). SLHU, MC 496, Box 49, Folder 16.
69 Sociology professor Alice S. Rossi was a close friend and confidant of Friedan's; a co-founder of NOW, she became a member of NOW's Board of Directors in 1967. As early as 1964, she had made her mark with an essay on "Equality Between the Sexes: An Immodest Proposal," which, like Friedan's *The Feminine Mystique*, became one of the key texts of feminism. On Friedan and Rossi, see section 3.6 of this book. On Rossi's expertise on the question of reproductive control, see also Alice Rossi, Sociological Argument in Support of Effect of Denial of Right to a Woman to Control her Own Reproductive Life, SLHU, MC 496, Box 49, Folder 16.
70 Minutes of National Conference of NOW held at the Mayflower Hotel, Washington D.C., November 18 & 19, 1967. SLHU, MC 496, Box 23, Folder 2.
71 See the summary of the Third National Conference, Atlanta, Georgia, December 6–8, 1968, by Wilma Heide. See also E. Betty Berry's report to the 1968 National NOW Conference, Atlanta, Georgia, for NOW New York's Subcommittee on Divorce, Alimony, and Child Support, December 7, 1968. SLHU, MC 496, Box 23, Folder 7. Press release by Betty Friedan and Jean Faust on the results of the conference, December 10, 1968. SLHU, MC 496, Box 23, Folder 8.

In 1968, after only two years of existence, NOW saw itself as the leading national women's rights organization, fighting for equality for women at the political, legal, and social level. The organization already had forty-seven regional subdivisions and, according to its own figures, had attracted no less than 15,000 members by 1971.[72] But at its 1968 conference the new "civil rights organization," as it saw itself, had to deal with the accusation that it was a "'middle-class organization' and as such it [could not] give adequate leadership on basic problems."[73] This perception was not entirely unfounded, since only a few leading members of NOW were African American or of Mexican descent (Aileen C. Hernández, Pauli Murray, and Shirley Chisholm, among others), whereas the bulk of its functionaries belonged to the white middle class. That a sore point was being touched on here was underscored by Kathryn F. Clarenbach, chair of the board of directors, in her 1968 annual report:

> Our concerns for employed women, for low-income families, social security legislation, women in poverty, unemployed girls are not traditional middle-class concerns. From the very outset we have made conscious efforts to encourage active participation of a wide range of people and to guard against domination of white, well educated, professional, middle-class, middle-aged females. We need to increase these efforts for an even wider range of representation in our membership and our leadership.[74]

Although Clarenbach vigorously rejected the claim that the organization represented only the interests of the white middle class, she explicitly affirmed a set of values that she described—referring to an article in *New York Times Magazine*—as "middle class values": "education, competence, responsibility, improvement, optimism."

Yet NOW not only used the tactics of the civil rights movement, such as demonstrations and protest marches, but also consciously drew parallels between the concerns of the two movements. The statements made by NOW representatives sometimes have a troubling undertone from today's perspective, as they considered sexism in American society to be a significantly greater problem than racism. The newly elected "national membership chairman" [sic] Karen DeCrow, for instance, declared shortly after the 1968 annual conference: "Women are more oppressed than the black men." Since the top positions in society were held exclusively by white men, she averred, there was a dramatic parallel between "the

---

[72] NOW, The First Five Years, 1966–1971, prepared by Aileen C. Hernandez and Letitia P. Somers, NOW, Chicago (1971), SLHU, MC 496, Box 1, Folder 1.
[73] Annual Report of the Chairman of Board (Dr. Kathryn F. Clarenbach), 1968. SLHU, MC 496, Box 23, Folder 7.
[74] Annual Report of the Chairman of Board (Dr. Kathryn F. Clarenbach), 1968. SLHU, MC 496, Box 23, Folder 7.

black second class citizen and the female second class citizen."[75] This equation between the civil rights movement's struggle and the women's movement's advocacy for equal rights and free access to abortion was also made by Betty Friedan as NOW chair in her keynote speech at the First National Conference for the Repeal of Abortion Laws in Chicago in 1969, which she titled "Abortion: A Woman's Civil Right." She interpreted opposition to existing abortion laws as a radical step:

> This is a radical change in the terms of the debate. This is like what has happened when the blacks began to say it the way it is and not permit even the white liberals to tell them the way it should be.[76]

At the same time, Friedan insisted that legalizing abortion should be seen as part of the "unfinished revolution of sexual equality." A woman's right to decide about her reproduction had to be recognized as a fundamental human right. This, in turn, could only happen if it was above all the voices of women themselves that were heard:

> There is only one voice that needs to be heard on the question of the final decision as to whether a woman will or will not bear a child and that is the voice of the woman herself. Her own consciousness, her own conscious choice.

This focus on the woman as an independent decision-maker, she contended, changed the understanding of the family and gender relations, but did not make the family as such obsolete—as Friedan once again clearly delineated the position of the bourgeois women's movement of the 1960s:

> This is revolutionary. It cannot happen without radical changes in the family as we know it today; in our concepts of marriage, in our very concepts of love, in our architecture, our plans of cities, in our theology, in our politics, in our art. [. . .] But, it's bound to be a different politics, when women's voices are equally heard: 51% of the population. They are bound to be much more varied [. . .] the dimension of human relationship—when women and men are allowed to relate to each other beyond the strict confines of the *Ladies Home Journal*'s definition of the mamma and papa and Junior and Janie marriage [. . .].

> But, if we are both people and if we are allowed finally to become full people, I would imagine, not only will there be children born and continue to be born and brought up with more love and responsibility than today, but we will break out of the confines of that sterile little suburban family to relate to each other in terms of all of the possible dimensions of our

---

[75] Carolyn Jay, "Her Big Campaign—Winning Women's Rights," *Miami News Observer*, December 19, 1968. SLHU, MC 496, Box 23, Folder 8.
[76] Keynote Speech, Betty Friedan, First National Conference for Repeal of Abortion Laws Chicago, Ill., February 14, 1969, "Abortion: A Woman's Civil Right." SLHU, MC 496, Box 49, Folder 16.

personalities—male and female, as comrades, as colleagues, as friends, as lovers, in a life span that is now 75 years and that is going to be a 100 years.[77]

Contrary to the sense of a new era dawning invoked in the chairwoman's rhetoric, it was not until the fourth annual conference in March 1970 that the NOW leadership could bring itself to organize a workshop on "Abortion: Tactics & Strategy."[78] The resolution it drew up, "Human Reproduction," declared the self-determined, prosecution- and risk-free termination of an unwanted pregnancy to be a "basic human right."[79] It is interesting that there was no mention here of a right to make a self-determined decision *for* a pregnancy, an issue of particular relevance to African American and Mexican-born women, who found themselves doubly restricted in their reproductive freedom of choice.

In the summer of 1971, NOW's fight for reproductive control stepped up several gears. A "National Task Force on Reproduction and its Control" was established under Lucinda Cisler, one of the largest thematic task forces maintained by NOW.[80] Together with the Women's National Abortion Action Coalition (WONAAC),[81] the task force fought for the repeal of national and state laws making abortion and contraceptive use punishable offenses.[82] It is clear from NOW's files that in the first instance the members' overriding task was to establish a solid foundation of information on the legal situation and policies in the field of reproductive control and to build networks. When Cisler called for activists to get involved in a WONAAC conference scheduled for July 1971, she argued that the exchange of information alone was worth the effort—invoking a revealing parallel with the first wave of the women's movement:

---

[77] Keynote Speech, Betty Friedan, First National Conference for Repeal of Abortion Laws Chicago, Ill., February 14, 1969, "Abortion: A Woman's Civil Right." SLHU, MC 496, Box 49, Folder 16.

[78] Letter of Invitation from NOW President Betty Friedan to fourth annual NOW Conference 1970, January 28, 1970. SLHU, MC 496, Box 23, Folder 9.

[79] Action resolutions passed by the members of the National Organization for Women at the Fourth Annual Conference, March 20–11, 1970. SLHU, MC 496, Box 23, Folder 11.

[80] While NOW's National Task Force on Reproduction and its Control had been headed by Lucinda Cisler since 1971, in 1973 Jan Liebman, who was also Program Director for Planned Parenthood and thus had substantial expertise on the matter, took over. Letter from Ann Scott to Del Martin, August 10, 1973. SLHU, MC 496, Box 49, Folder 16.

[81] Founded in 1971 with mass participation by members of the Socialist Workers Party (SWP), as well as NOW and other women's groups, WONAAC existed until shortly after the Supreme Court's *Roe v. Wade* ruling of 1973. Letter from Nancy Rolf, Rose Weber, and Terry Bruce, National Office of WONAAC to NOW Executive Board, June 25, 1972. SLHU, MC 496, Box 49, Folder 16. Staggenborg, *The Pro-Choice Movement*, 26. Keetley and Pettigrew, *Public Women, Public Words*, vol. 2, 217–218.

[82] NOW, National Task Force on Reproduction and its Control, Coordinator Lucinda Cisler to Chapter Presidents, June 6, 1971. SLHU, MC 496, Box 49, Folder 16.

The situation is much like that of the early suffragists: we must go about it with horse and buggy, meeting face-to-face and exchanging tactical ideas.[83]

Task force co-coordinator Lana C. Phelan took a different approach by convening a regional conference of NOW chapters from the western part of the country in Seattle, Washington, in 1972, on the subject of "Reproduction," "in order to get some consensus of opinion on this apparently still controversial subject."[84] Those gathered in Seattle were first supposed to develop a common position on "new methods of contraception, general family planning, abortion, and the principles embodied in the new self-help clinics being undertaken in some areas by women themselves." Also crucial, she underscored, was a shared stock of information on legal regulations and changes in laws on contraception and abortion in the U.S. and internationally. Furthermore, the goals of other organizations such as Planned Parenthood and Zero Population Growth should be analyzed and discussed in order to sound out the potential for cooperation. Above all, however, it was vital to agree on the meaning of terms such as "birth control," which "last year served to inflame emotions in such manner as to make rational discussion almost impossible among members attending the conference."[85] Here, we can clearly discern feminists' difficulties agreeing on concrete measures and terms, even with regard to such a sensitive issue as reproductive control. At the same time, it is clear that NOW members were also divided by a generational conflict. At the previous year's meeting in San Francisco, according to Phelan, the debate had been hampered by "unfortunate disagreements stemming from misunderstandings from newer member of past NOW philosophies in the field of human reproduction, or perhaps those unaware of new developments in this fast-changing area of women's rights."[86]

These observations of major clashes over attitudes toward reproduction between different members of NOW, which Phelan described here using the example of NOW's western chapters, also applied to the organization as a whole. Generally speaking, the key confrontation was between activists of the so-called second wave of the 1960s women's movement (following the Progressive-Era suffragettes) and the more recent Women's Liberation movement. While the former pursued legal reform by demanding the legalization of abortion and the passage of the ERA, and foregrounded political mobilization, the latter formulated their

---

83 NOW, National Task Force on Reproduction and its Control, Coordinator Lucinda Cisler to Chapter Presidents, June 6, 1971. SLHU, MC 496, Box 49, Folder 16.
84 Lana C. Phelan, Co-Coordinator National Task Force on Reproduction, to Board of Directors, NOW, February 20, 1972. Western Regional Conference, Seattle, Washington, March 3–4, 1972, Proposed Workshop on Reproduction. SLHU, MC 496, Box 49, Folder 16.
85 Phelan to Board of Directors, NOW, February 20, 1972. SLHU, MC 496, Box 49, Folder 16.
86 Phelan to Board of Directors, NOW, February 20, 1972. SLHU, MC 496, Box 49, Folder 16.

political goals more uncompromisingly from the early 1970s onward and also backed them up with more radical forms of activism.

In the early 1970s, younger feminists such as Kate Millett, Anne Koedt, Shulamith Firestone, and Frances Beale thus called for a revolution in gender roles and society, making them icons of the Women's Liberation movement.[87] Under the rallying cry "the personal is the political," they opposed not only patriarchy and the oppression of women, but above all the biological rationale for gender inequality in society, which they discerned, among other things, in expert discourses and the national media. Although they shared the goals of the bourgeois women's movement around NOW—legalization of abortion, equal rights in the labor market, and the adoption of the ERA—these did not amount to the social revolution they had in mind.[88] On the other side of the political spectrum, NOW too came under pressure, as conservative women's and family organizations accused them of seeking precisely this sort of social revolution. For the latter groups, NOW's advocacy of the ERA and the legalization of abortion threatened to overturn gender roles and devalue the family as the basis of the nation.[89]

In fact, after both houses of Congress passed it in 1971 and 1972, the ERA subsequently failed because of the unwillingness of a number of states to ratify it—despite an extension of the ratification deadline from 1979 to 1982 and despite NOW's unwaveringly intensive lobbying.[90] The conservative opposition to the ERA, especially the "STOP ERA" movement led by lawyer Phyllis Schlafly, was eloquent and at least as well organized and financed as NOW.[91] The most effective

---

87 Millett, Kate, "Sexual Politics: A Manifesto for Revolution." Koedt, Anne, "The Myth of the Vaginal Orgasm," both in Firestone, Shulamith and Koedt, Anne (eds.), *Notes from the Second Year* (New York 1970), 37–41 and 111–112. Firestone, Shulamith, *The Dialectic of Sex* (New York 1970), 1–12. Beale, Frances M., "Double Jeopardy: To Be Black and Female," in Cade, Toni (ed.), *The Black Woman. An Anthology* (New York 1970), 90–100.

88 On women's liberation, see, among others, Valk, Anne, *Radical Sisters. Second-Wave Feminism and Black Liberation in Washington, D.C.* (Urbana 2008). Echols, Alice, *Daring to Be Bad. Radical Feminism in America 1967–1975* (Minneapolis 1989). Echols, Alice, "Nothing Distant About It: Woman's Liberation and Sixties Radicalism," in Farber, David (ed.), *The Sixties. From Memory to History* (Chapel Hill and London 1994), 149–174.

89 Critchlow, Donald T., "Conservatism Reconsidered. Phillis Schlafly and Grassroot Conservatism," in Farber, David and Roche, Jeff (eds.), *The Conservative Sixties* (New York 2003), 108–126.

90 Mathews and De Hart, *Sex, Gender, and the Politics of ERA*. Mansbridge, Jane J., *Why We lost the ERA* (Chicago 1986).

91 Phyllis Schlafly (1924–2016) was until her death president of the conservative Eagle Forum, which she founded in 1972 and whose slogan is "Leading the pro-family movement since 1972." <www.eagleforum.org>. In the 1970s, the law graduate was already one of America's best-known conservative voices; her monograph *A Choice, Not an Echo* had made her suddenly famous in 1964. In it, she had opposed the candidacy of East Coast Republican Nelson Rockefeller, whom she ac-

Fig. 5.3: Pro-choice protesters at Union Square, New York, May 1972.

argument made by the opponents of ERA around Schlafly was to point to the perceived threat to traditional gender roles: women would be drafted into the military and would face disagreeable "leveling down" forms of egalitarianism in the future, including unwelcome impositions such as unisex public restrooms. Furthermore, in the event of divorce, they would no longer be entitled to alimony

---

cused of corruption and globalism, during the 1964 presidential campaign, and had spoken out in favor of right-wing conservative Barry Goldwater. Beginning in 1967, she regularly addressed her fan base through a monthly newsletter (*The Phyllis Schlafly Report*) along with numerous newspaper columns and media appearances. Critchlow, *Phillis Schlafly*. Rymph, Catherine, *Republican Women. Feminism and Conservatism from Suffrage to the Rise of the New Right* (Chapel Hill, 2006).

and would thus lose their protected position in marriage and family.[92] Schlafly channeled and propagated the protest in an extremely effective way under the slogan "STOP ERA" (with the first element functioning as an acronym for "Stop Taking Our Privileges"), deploying her activists to demonstrate while displaying the traditional insignia of housewifery. In those states where ratification of the ERA was subject to heated debate, they showed up outside politicians' offices with their children in tow and home-cooked meals, holding signs reading "I am for Mom and Apple Pie."[93] In 1972, Schlafly transformed her "STOP ERA" movement into a conservative interest group called "Eagle Forum: People for the American Way," of which she served as president until her death in 2016.[94]

But while NOW was defeated on the ERA, in 1973 it scored an important victory in the struggle for self-determination and reproductive control when the Supreme Court legalized abortion. This act of law placed gender relations and the debate over women's reproductive function on a new footing. For the first time in U.S. history, women across the country could have an unwanted pregnancy terminated at abortion clinics in a legal and medically safe manner. In the case of poor women, the state initially covered the cost of the procedure. But the Supreme Court's ruling—more than any legal act before it—led to fierce cultural conflicts between supporters and opponents, and between a number of states and the federal government.[95]

---

[92] Eilperin, Juliet, "New Drive Afoot to Pass Equal Rights Amendment," WP, March 28, 2007. Levenstein, Lisa, "'Don't Agonize, Organize!' The Displaced Homemakers Campaign and the Contested Goals of Postwar Feminism," *Journal of American History* 100 (2014), 4, 1114–1138.

[93] Rosenberg, Rosalind, *Divided Lives. American Women in the Twentieth Century* (New York 1992), 225.

[94] Diamond, Sara, *Roads to Dominion. Right Wing Movements and Political Power in the United States* (New York 1994).

[95] Schoen, *Choice and Coercion*. Cline, David P., *Creating Choice. A Community Responds to the Need for Abortion and Birth Control, 1961–1973* (New York 2006). Critchlow, T. Donald, *Intended Consequences. Birth Control, Abortion, and the Federal Government in Modern America* (New York 1999). Marx Ferree, Myra et al., *Shaping Abortion Discourse. Democracy and the Public Sphere in Germany and the United States* (Cambridge 2001). Solinger, Rickie (ed.), *Abortion Wars. A Half Century of Struggle, 1950–2000* (Berkeley 1998). Reagan, *When Abortion was a Crime*. Shapiro, Ian, *Abortion. The Supreme Court Decisions* (Indianapolis 1995). Rubin, Eva R., *The Abortion Controversy. A Documentary History* (Westport 1994). Ginsburg, Faye D., *Contested Lives. The Abortion Debate in an American Community* (Berkeley CA 1989). Petchesky, Rosalind Pollack, *Abortion and Woman's Choice. The State, Sexuality, and Reproductive Freedom* (London 1986).

5.3 Legal framework: *Roe v. Wade* and the implications for the negotiation of gender roles

On January 22, 1973, in the case of *Roe v. Wade*, the Supreme Court ruled that an abortion could legally be performed at the request of the pregnant woman up to the end of the first trimester of pregnancy and, under certain conditions, thereafter.[96] Invoking the woman's personal freedom of choice (right to privacy), the court thus rescinded the federal abortion ban of the late nineteenth century and the strict abortion laws of the individual states. This had been preceded by a lengthy and highly contentious debate over the right to abortion, in which feminists, family planners, as well as liberal scholars, politicians, and publicists had clashed bitterly with conservative physicians, politicians, clergy, and civic groups. The debate over the pros and cons of abortion continues to this day.

The case was tried under the pseudonym Jane Roe. It was inspired by Texas resident Norma McCorvey's[97] third unintended pregnancy in 1969 at the age of 21, which she was unable to legally terminate due to the state's abortion ban. Young lawyers Sarah Weddington and Linda Coffee selected McCorvey's case to fight for an overhaul of Texas state abortion laws on her behalf.[98] They first filed suit in a Dallas federal district court in the name of "Jane Roe" against district attorney Henry Wade—hence the case's name. While the court declared Texas's abortion laws unconstitutional, it did not derive any specific consequences from this. When the Supreme Court finally took up the case in 1971, not only did the two lawyers and the plaintiff gain national prominence, but the court's decision became nationally binding, forcing a legal overhaul throughout the states.[99] NOW

---

[96] The court's ruling stated that until the end of the first trimester the decision on whether to carry out an abortion was up to the "medical judgment of the pregnant woman's attending physician." In subsequent stages of pregnancy, meanwhile, the state, given its interest in preserving the health of the mother, could regulate abortion "in ways that are reasonably related to maternal health." Finally, once the fetus reached viability, the state was permitted "(to) regulate, and even proscribe, abortion." However, the court underlined, late-term abortions that were necessary to preserve the life or health of the mother must be permitted. Full text of the ruling at <www.supreme.justia.com/cases/federal/us/410/113/>.

[97] Norma McCorvey (1947–2017) later distanced herself from the Supreme Court decision and became an outspoken opponent of abortion and activist for the pro-life movement. See her monograph: McCorvey, Norma, *I am Roe. My Life, Roe v. Wade, and Freedom of Choice* (New York 1994).

[98] The two lawyers were not members of NOW, but Coffee was a member of the Women's Equity Action League (WEAL), a spin-off of NOW. This had been founded by women's rights activists in Cleveland, Ohio in 1968 to advance women's equality through education, litigation, and law reform. WEAL members explicitly distanced themselves from the fight to legalize abortion as pursued by NOW. Women's Equity Action League Records, SLHU, MC 500.

[99] Stein, *Sexual Injustice*, 51–56.

supported the enterprise from the beginning, mobilizing members of its regional chapters through the "Task Force on Reproduction," writing petitions, staging demonstrations, and undertaking an array of behind-the-scenes lobbying.[100]

After the announcement of the verdict in *Roe v. Wade*, initially the national dailies had surprisingly little to say. The *Washington Post* devoted only a brief report to the event and an op-ed article a few days later.[101] The *New York Times*, meanwhile, at least informed its readers about the main points of the ruling and printed excerpts from the majority opinion authored by Justice Harry A. Blackmun.[102] It was not until a few weeks later that the paper published a letter of protest by a law professor and Jesuit, who complained bitterly that the Supreme Court had set itself up as the moral judge of the value of the unborn child's life and was thus reducing the citizens of the United States to the status of minor children.[103] The *Washington Post*, on the other hand, published a critical article that addressed the value conflicts within the Catholic Church, commenting on them from a feminist perspective.[104] It was in fact to be quite some time before feminists explicitly defended the law in the press, though the focus of their articles and op-eds was mainly on newly established abortion clinics.[105]

Recent scholarship, however, has not only characterized the Supreme Court's decision in *Roe v. Wade* as a liberal achievement, but has also pointed to its era-specific downsides. While Johanna Schoen describes Roe as a positive sign of the inclusion of legal abortion in women's health care, Mary Ziegler views the decision as the beginning of a long process of reorienting the women's movement toward "choice" as a form of "single-issue politics."[106] In contrast, Marc Stein criticizes the judges for pursuing a "classed, gendered, and racialized doctrine of

---

[100] On this point, see the diverse material on NOW's lobbying efforts in pursuit of the legalization of abortion in the organization's papers. NOW Papers, SLHU MC 496, Boxes 23, 49.

[101] Mackenzie, John P., "Supreme Court Allows Early-Stage Abortions," WP, January 23, 1973, A1. Kraft, Joseph, "'Conservative' on Abortion," WP, January 25, 1973, A15.

[102] "Excerpts from Abortion Case." Special to the New York Times, NYT, January 23, 1973, 20. "Summary of Actions Taken by the Supreme Court," NYT, January 23, 1973, 22.

[103] Degnan, Daniel A., "The Supreme Court as Moral Arbiter," NYT, March 10, 1973, 31.

[104] Hyer, Marjorie, "Abortion: A Conflict of Values," WP, February 18, 1973, B3.

[105] See, for example, Kiernan, Laura A., "1st Clinic for Abortion Set in Fairfax," WP, May 28, 1973. Day, Emily Ann, "Abortion," WP, September 1, 1973. On the *Roe v. Wade* debate in the U.S., see Condit, Celeste Michelle, *Decoding Abortion Rhetoric. Communicating Social Change* (Urbana and Chicago 1990). Gorney, Cynthia, *Articles of Faith. A Frontline History of the Abortion Wars* (New York 1998). Burns, Gene, *The Moral Veto. Stalemate and Change in American Debates over Contraception and Abortion* (New York 2002). Marx Ferree, *Shaping Abortion Discourse*. Ziegler, Mary, *After Roe. The Lost History of the Abortion Debate* (Cambridge and London 2015).

[106] Schoen, *Abortion after Roe*, 10–11. Ziegler, *After Roe*.

heteronormative supremacy."[107] Roe, he contends, was aimed less at women's reproductive autonomy than at their role in family, marriage, and society. Yet here Stein disregards the fact that in 1973 marriage and family still constituted the national normative lodestone of both politics and jurisprudence. Still, his observations highlight a fundamental problem in the women's movement's campaign for the right to abortion: for white activists, the practice had a quite different—exclusively positive—quality than for their African American or Mexican-born comrades-in-arms, who first had to struggle to achieve the right to reproduction itself.[108] Stein also points out that although the Supreme Court justices based their decision on the "right to privacy," they placed the final decision on abortion in the hands of the doctor.[109] Detailing future abortion procedures in the first trimester of a pregnancy, the court stated: "the abortion decision and its effectuation must be left to the pregnant woman's attending physician."[110]

Even before *Roe v. Wade*, an active women's health movement had developed in the early 1970s, driven on the one hand by the demand for legal, universally accessible abortion, and on the other by a general critique by women of contemporary paternalistic gynecology and obstetrics.[111] Starting with the Boston Women's Health Book Collective and their guidebook *Our Bodies, Ourselves* (first published in 1973 and followed by numerous new and revised editions), women had begun to acquire medical expertise themselves or, as doctors, to pass it on in consultations and abortion clinics.[112] This was intended to counteract the reduction of women to the status of mere patients, who typically had to submit to the decision of a male doctor. For the bourgeois women's movement around NOW in particular, however, the *Roe v. Wade* decision remained *the* milestone in the struggle for legal abortion, one that had to be preserved against all attacks from

---

107 Stein, *Sexual Injustice*, 55–56.
108 Solinger, *Beggars and Choosers*. Solinger, *Pregnancy and Power*. Stein, *Sexual Injustice*, 54.
109 Stein, *Sexual Injustice*, 55.
110 Supreme Court decision in *Roe v. Wade*, quoted in Stein, *Sexual Injustice*, 55.
111 For an early feminist critique of male expert advice to women, see Ehrenreich, Barbara and English, Deirdre, *For Her Own Good. Two Centuries of the Expert's Advice to Women* (New York 2005, first edition 1978). The genesis of the women's health movement is the focus of numerous recent publications. See Morgen, Sandra, *Into Our Own Hands: The Women's Health Movement in the United States, 1969–1990* (New Brunswick, N. J. and London 2002). Kline, Wendy, *Bodies of Knowledge. Sexuality, Reproduction, and Women's Health in the Second Wave* (Chicago 2010). Nelson, *More Than Medicine* (New York 2015).
112 Boston Women's Health Collective Collections, SLHU MC 503. See also Prescott, *Student Bodies*. Davis, Kathy, *The Making of Our Bodies, Ourselves. How Feminism Travels Across Borders* (Durham 2008). Kline, *Bodies of Knowledge*, 9–40.

anti-abortionists and conservative states.[113] To this day, NOW devotes a significant portion of its resources and engagement to the defense of Roe and to women's reproductive rights in general.[114]

The backlash from conservative social forces—especially the Catholic Church, but also Protestant fundamentalists—and the formation of a bitterly hostile anti-abortion movement ensued immediately,[115] with anti-abortion activists euphemistically referring to themselves as the "pro-life" movement (as opposed to pro-choice). The most visible expression of anti-abortion protest at the national level was the March for Life, which was first held in 1974 and has since taken the form of an annual rally in Washington, D.C., on January 22 to mark the anniversary of the Supreme Court ruling, now with up to 250,000 participants.[116]

The most radical outgrowths of anti-abortion protests are the attacks on abortion clinics, doctors, nurses, and patients, which have occurred repeatedly since the 1980s and have already claimed a number of lives, the perpetrators mostly identifying with Christian fundamentalism.[117] Recently, Johanna Schoen has shown how "abortion

---

[113] Mary Ziegler recently published an interesting study of the consequences of the Roe ruling for the women's movement. She argues that Roe had ambivalent effects, such as forcing the pro-abortion women's movement to reposition itself while at the same time impeding compromises between pro- and anti-abortion activists on other women's health and legal equality issues for years. Ziegler, *After Roe*, 157–218.

[114] See NOW's self-portrayal on its website <now.org>. For example, in 1979 NOW's Human Rights Committee dedicated 80 percent of its annual budget to the fight for reproductive rights. Report of the NOW Human Rights Board Committee Meeting of May 19, 1979, signed by the Chair of the Human Rights Committee, Sue Errington, May 31, 1979. SLHU MC 496, Box 42, Folder 30.

[115] The best-known body within the movement, the National Right to Life Committee, was founded as early as 1968 at the behest of the National Conference of Catholic Bishops but did not achieve recognition as a nonprofit organization until 1973. The magazine *National Right to Life News* has been published since 1973. <www.nrlc.org/abortion/history/>. See also the papers of its long term President Mildred Jefferson, SLHU MC 696. On the anti-abortion movement, see Blanchard, *Anti-Abortion Movement*.

[116] McGrory, Mary, "The Wind Chill Factor of the Abortion Issue," WP, January 23, 1976. McGrory, Mary, "Mr. Carter on Abortion," WP, September 10, 1976. McGrory, Mary, "There Is No Middle Ground in Volatile Politics of Abortion," *Washington Star*, February 2, 1979. LOC Mary McGrory Papers, Box 54, Folder 1.

[117] A clear-eyed observer of violence among anti-abortion activists was *Washington Post* journalist Mary McGrory, who repeatedly critiqued violence as a means of achieving political goals. See her writings on abortion in her papers: LOC Mary McGrory Papers, Box 54, Folders 1 and 2. See also McGrory, Mary, "Tolerance, Aborted," WP, January 23, 1984. Nice, David C., "Abortion Clinic Bombings as Political Violence," *American Journal of Political Science* 32 (1988), 1, 178–195. Jefferis, Jennifer L., *Armed for Life: The Army of God and Anti-Abortion Terror in the United States* (Santa Barbara 2011). Hale, Grace E., *A Nation of Outsiders: How the White Middle Class Fell in Love with Rebellion in Postwar America* (Oxford and New York 2011), 277–308.

Fig. 5.4: Anti-abortion demonstrator in front of St. Patrick's Church in New York, March 9, 1976.

providers" were and continue to be pressured by an increasingly virulent anti-abortion movement, taking countless regional forms, in the decades following Roe.[118] To be sure, there were anti-abortion activists who combined their belief that abortion was "murder" with a fundamental commitment to women's rights, as asserted by the demonstrator in New York pictured here. But NOW activists were skeptical. In the face of the anti-abortion protests organized so rapidly in 1973, they had already come to the conclusion that anti-abortionists and anti-ERA activists largely consisted of the same group of people:

---

118 Schoen, *Abortion after Roe*, 155–198.

> The Right-to-Lifers and the anti-Era forces are by and large the same people (and their money) and are anxious to tie the two issues together through their usual tactic—hysteria. That may work in the field, but by and large congress responds coolly to their tactics.[119]

The self-styled "right-to-life" faction and especially the National Catholic Conference of Bishops made a huge effort to persuade the 93rd Congress (1973–1975) to pass a constitutional amendment that would overturn the Supreme Court decision. NOW fought this tooth and nail and in 1973–1974 devised a wide range of activities to preserve legal access to abortion.[120] The organization's key objectives are conveyed in the following bullet points:

1. Contraception, sterilization and abortion be made available at public hospitals to anyone requesting them.
2. A network of local public clinics be established to offer these services.
3. Widespread publicizing of the availability of these services.
4. Public funds to promote research into safer methods of contraception, sterilization and abortion which would be made easily available.
5. Repeal of all laws prohibiting or restricting abortions.[121]

Of signal importance in this context was the strategy of informing the press about NOW's goals and actions at an early stage, for example through the NOW News Service, to which newspapers and television stations could subscribe.[122] The organization also developed a "Right to Choose" kit for journalists, which was presented to the press in 1974. The kit featured information about NOW's position on abortion and a woman's right to choose, but also provided medical and legal background information.[123]

Internally, NOW's primary goal was to encourage members to engage in targeted lobbying of their members of Congress in order to persuade them to support legal abortion. To furnish NOW activists with precise and relevant information, they received, among other things, an "Abortion Action Kit" (to help them prepare

---

[119] Letter from Ann Scott to Del Martin about abortion, August 10, 1973. SLHU MC 496, Box 49, Folder. 16.
[120] Inaugural statement by Jan Liebman, June 20, 1973, as new coordinator of Task Force on Reproduction and Population for NOW. SLHU MC 496, Box 49, Folder 16.
[121] Statement by Dian Terry and Jan Liebman, NOW Task Force on Reproduction and Population, November 1973. SLHU MC 496, Box 49, Folder 17.
[122] NOW Reproduction Task Force: Legal Arguments against the Constitutional Amendment on Abortion (undated, 1974). NOW Reproduction Task Force: The Abortion Issue and the 93rd Congress. SLHU MC 496, Box 49, Folder 16.
[123] Letter from Dian Terry to Press Representatives on Right-To-Choose Kit, April 5, 1974. SLHU MC 496, Box 49, Folder 16.

for possible meetings with their members of Congress),[124] a "Political Action Resource Kit" (a detailed handout explaining how to talk to politicians), and a "Chapter Action Kit" (with suggestions on local activities and lobbying techniques).[125] NOW members also launched a petition in Congress in 1974, which urged representatives of that body to defend the "right to choose."[126] The importance NOW attached to its members' personal engagement is illustrated by a letter from the leadership in March 1974:

> Constituent lobbying—meeting personally as NOW chapter delegation with your Representative at home is the most effective lobbying technique you can employ. NOW's effectiveness in Washington depends on these meetings, and our growing impact is clearly a result of your effort.[127]

In addition, NOW declared October 9, 1974, the "lobby day for the right to choose." Representatives of all 700 NOW chapters assembled on Capitol Hill on that date to put pressure on senators who were discussing the possible revision of the Roe decision in the Senate Subcommittee on Constitutional Amendments on Abortion.[128] In subsequent years, these activities were pursued annually on or around Margaret Sanger's birthday on September 14. On the other side of the spectrum, adversaries of legal abortion organized the "National March for Life," held annually in Washington on the anniversary of Roe, January 22, from 1974 onward.

With their constant lobbying, NOW activists built on the practices they had used in the struggle for the Equal Rights Amendment. Another characteristic feature was NOW's frequent collection—and circulation among its members—of information on abortion clinics in the different states, pro- and anti-abortion organizations,

---

[124] This was regularly updated and expanded in subsequent years. See the various versions in SLHU MC 496, Box 49, Folder 17.
[125] Ann Scott and Jan Liebman: Abortion: NOW National Lobbying Program, February 15, 1975, to all State Legislative Coordinators. Chapter Abortion Resource Kit, Installment Folder 1, Ann Scott and Jan Liebman to Chapter Presidents, February 15, 1974. SLHU MC 496, Box 49, Folder 17.
[126] Petition to the Members of the U.S. Congress, undated (1974). SLHU, MC 496, Box 49, Folder 16.
[127] Legislative Office to All Chapters, March 26, 1974, Attn. Ann Scott, Jan Liebman, Plan NOW to Meet with Your Congressional Representative. Washington Blue Sheet, Abortion: NOW Action Program [1974]. Ann Scott and Jan Liebman, Abortion: NOW National Lobbying Program, February 15, 1975, to all State Legislative Coordinators. SLHU MC 496, Box 49, Folder 17.
[128] NOW Legislative Office, Washington DC, Ann Scott, Vice President Legislation and Jan Liebman, National Task Force Coordinator, Reproduction, Loss of Control of our Bodies Threatened! October Lobby Day, October 9, 1974. SLHU MC 496, Box 49, Folder 16. On the number of chapters in 1974, see the fundraising letter from NOW President Wilma Scott Heide, March 2, 1974. SLHU MC 496, Box 49, Folder 17.

concrete legislative initiatives, and press reports.[129] As early as the summer of 1974, NOW had produced a comprehensive "Right to Choose" pamphlet that amalgamated all the information concerning abortion in a readily understandable form.[130] Its activists were especially eager to furnish women with information on abortion in this way to enable them to make a responsible decision.

While NOW, as a social movement, to some extent pursued a moderate reformist course, members of the National Abortion Rights Action League (NARAL) were less restrained in their choice of strategies as they fought for the right to abortion in the early 1970s.[131] Through the instrument of PACs (political action committees), moreover, NARAL was more focused than NOW on influencing policy directly through support for pro-choice politicians and maintained an office in Washington DC to that end. How NARAL stepped up its mobilization efforts in the face of pro-life activism is well illustrated by the 1973 protests against the broadcast of the "abortion episodes" of the *Maude* series, described earlier. After the first broadcast in November 1972, the first substantial response was that of Catholic pastors, who urged their parishioners to write letters of protest to the broadcaster and its advertising clients. Anti-abortion activists soon jumped on this bandwagon and launched a campaign targeting the CBS network, producer Norman Lear, and the show's actors. Unwilling to take this lying down, the NARAL leadership launched their own program of action in an attempt to put a brake on the "pro-lifers"—as they saw it, the progress achieved through *Maude* in terms of the media thematization of abortion seemed too important to give up without a fight. Executive Director Lee Gidding wrote to the organization's board and circle of supporters in January 1973:

---

[129] SLHU MC 496, Box 49, Folders 20, 22, 23, 25, 26, 27. Box 95, 96 For details, see Organizations supporting abortion rights [1980], SLHU MC 496, Box 49, Folder 19. NOW Rates First Trimester Abortion Facilities—Spring 1973. SLHU MC 496, Box 49, Folder 17. Federal Abortion Legislation [1971] and Organizations Supporting Right to Choose Abortion/Organizations Opposing Abortion (undated). SLHU MC 496, Box 49, Folder 16.

[130] Letter from Dian Terry to Chairpersons of the NOC, July 29, 1974: First Right to Choose Brochure. SLHU MC 496, Box 49, Folder 18. Brochure in SLHU MC 496, Box 49, Folder 23.

[131] NARAL was founded in 1969 as the National Association for the Repeal of Abortion Laws at the First National Conference on Abortion Laws in Chicago, mentioned above. Under its first executive director, Lee Gidding, the organization established its office in New York. NARAL's sole purpose was to advocate for legal abortion and for the abolition of restrictive state legislation. In 1973, after the Supreme Court decision in favor of legal abortions, NARAL renamed itself the National Abortion Rights Action League. By the end of 1973, it had about 4,000 members and numerous subdivisions, such as the Massachusetts state-level group MORAL, which became MORAL Mass Choice in 1984. The NARAL papers are housed at Harvard University's Schlesinger Library, particularly in holdings MC 313 and MC 714, while those of MORAL Mass Choice are in MC 659.

The case of Maude is important. It is the first TV entertainment to deal with abortion in a way that reflects changing attitudes of society, and the decision of the sympathetic dramatic character affirms our position. If the opposition wins its campaign against Maude, networks and sponsors will back off from all but conventional treatment of abortion.[132]

Amid the conflict over the rebroadcast of the episodes in the summer of 1973, NARAL launched its own letter-writing campaign featuring missives of solidarity to CBS and Lear, as well as letters of protest to the companies that had withdrawn their advertising from the series.[133] In addition, a boycott of the products of these same companies, including giants such as American Home Products and General Mills, was coupled with an attempt to put additional pressure on them through targeted reportage (for example, in the feminist *Ms.* magazine).[134] As the third pillar of its protest strategy, NARAL invited the directors of the country's ten largest abortion clinics to solicit letters of support from clients, which were then forwarded to a given state's political representatives.[135] NARAL chairman Lawrence Lader articulated the goal of the campaign as follows: "Let's prove that the legalized abortion movement can equal the power of the Catholic Church."[136] This was in fact done, with letters of support and criticism roughly balancing each other out in the summer of 1973, as the new NARAL executive director, Roxanne Olivo noted with satisfaction.[137]

But it was not only the anti-abortionists' letter-writing campaign that galvanized NARAL. Its activists felt particularly challenged by the often extreme actions of the "pro-life" faction, which inflamed public debates on abortion by deploying dramatic images and films. Particularly popular among anti-abortionists—in addition to recordings of fetal heartbeats and reports on premature babies born alive—

---

[132] Memo from Lee Gidding, Executive Director NARAL, to NARAL Directors and Organization Supporters, re: CBS-TV program Maude, January 1973. SLHU MC 313, Carton 7, folder "Maude." Emphasis in original.
[133] Memo by Lawrence Lader, Chairman of the Board, NARAL, August 17, 1973, The "Maude" CBS-TV Boycott. Letter from NARAL, Executive Director Roxanne Olivo, to NARAL Directors, Organization Members and Supporters, August 28, 1973. Re Maude Show. SLHU MC 313, Carton 7, Folder "Maude."
[134] Memo by NARAL, August 17, 1973, A Boycott of CBS TV's Maude Show on Abortion Arouses Counter Boycott by ten National Organizations. Letter from Executive Director NARAL, Roxanne Olivo, to *Ms.* Magazine, September 5, 1973. SLHU MC 313, Carton 7, Folder "Maude."
[135] Memo by Lawrence Lader, Chairman of the Board, NARAL, August 17, 1973, The "Maude" CBS-TV Boycott. SLHU MC 313, Carton 7, Folder "Maude."
[136] Memo by Lawrence Lader, Chairman of the Board, NARAL, August 17, 1973, The "Maude" CBS-TV Boycott. SLHU MC 313, Carton 7, Folder "Maude."
[137] Memo by Roxanne Olivo, Executive Director NARAL, A Follow Up on Maude (undated, 1973). SLHU MC 313, Carton 7, Folder "Maude."

was the distribution of a four-page pamphlet with a high shock value, featuring photographs of aborted fetuses (long before the release of the tendentious anti-abortion film *The Silent Scream* in 1984).[138] Thus, in November 1972, NARAL chairman Lawrence Lader suggested that the drastic strategies adopted by anti-abortionists should be countered by corresponding actions, such as emptying out units of human blood on camera to demonstrate the life-threatening blood loss suffered by a patient who had undergone an illegal abortion.[139] Already in the context of the first anti-*Maude* protests in January 1973 (and thus even before the Supreme Court decision), the then NARAL executive director Lee Gidding had announced a new strategy:

> To counter the impact of "Right to Life's" four page pamphlet of fetus horror pictures [. . .] NARAL will soon have the "dummy" of a four-page pamphlet with our own shock approach. The NARAL Executive Committee, as well as many state affiliates, are convinced we must now adopt the hard line.[140]

To this end, she requested that members provide NARAL with "slides and photos [. . .], which illustrate the tragedy of illegal abortion, or are useful in challenging the opponent's arguments." The pamphlet was promptly printed, but its use was not entirely unproblematic, as Karen Mulhauser, co-director of NARAL, noted only a year later:

> Enclosed is our "shock brochure" which we have found to be effective in some situations and ineffective in others. It should be used selectively and only if the opposition has previously shown their fetus pictures. In a debate, it is preferable that no visuals be used but if the fetus pictures are used, the Pro Choice debater can be equally effective by illustrating the tragedy of a mother's death by botched abortion or of infanticide.[141]

---

138 On this topic, see the comments in chapter 6.
139 In his letter, Lader bitterly lamented the damage done to the abortion movement by the clumsy presentation of the findings of the Presidential Commission Report on *Population and the American Future* on PBS, November 29, 1972. Larry Lader, NARAL, Chairman of the Board, to NARAL Board Members et al., undated (1972), Subject: The Damage to the Abortion Movement from the Second Hour of the TV Report of the Commission on Population Growth and the American Future (aired PBS November 29, 1972). SLHU MC 131, Carton 8, Folder "President's Commission on Population and the American Future." Of similar concern were the activities of pro-lifers in the state of Michigan, where a referendum to repeal abortion bans held in late 1972 failed due to pro-lifers' public relations campaigns.
140 Memo from Lee Gidding, Executive Director NARAL, to NARAL Directors and Organization Supporters, re: CBS-TV-program Maude, January 1973. SLHU MC 313, Carton 7, folder "Maude."
141 Memo by Karen Mulhauser, NARAL Co-Director to participants in St. Louis and Washington ZPG/Planned Parenthood media workshops, n.d. (1974). SLHU MC 313, Box 9, Folder "Zero Population Growth."

It is evident here that in the first instance the anti-abortion movement used strategies typical of the civil rights movement (protests, mass letters) and later the pro-choice movement in turn drew on their opponents' radical public relations ("shock brochure"). Hence, when it came to devising the most effective mobilization techniques, the learning processes were reciprocal rather than unilinear.

Significantly, a coalition of feminists and representatives of the population control movement emerged amid the struggle for abortion rights. One indication of this was a 1974 letter from NOW President Wilma Scott Heide to the Zero Population Growth (ZPG) movement, the most influential grassroots movement in the field. Here she laid out a vision of the year 2000 in which biologistic gender roles were no longer of any import and all American children were the product of conscious choices by their parents. The final sentence was crucial: "Meanwhile, for NOW I'm glad that ZPG and NOW are working together in our many areas where we have common cause."[142] NARAL Chairman Lawrence Lader had already enthusiastically welcomed cooperation "with our old allies, ZPG, NOW, and other feminist, religious, and population groups" during the anti-*Maude* protests.[143]

The overlaps in content and personnel between the women's movement, "pro-choice" activism, and advocacy for limiting national and global population growth form the focus of the following section.

5.4 The campaign to reduce global population growth, the role of population experts, and the reproduction of the white American woman

> Any and every drop in the birth rate is desirable. We've got enough people in the world and in this country so that there is no danger that we'll ever run out. We have lots of people, what we need is high-caliber individuals contributing as individuals. We need quality; quantity takes care of itself.[144]

In May 1966, with her call for the lowering of the national and global birth rate and the concurrent strengthening of the "quality" of offspring in *Time* magazine, anthropologist Margaret Mead built on a number of discourses at once. First, the

---

[142] Letter Wilma Scott Heide to Meg Letterman, Editor, *The National Reporter*, ZPG, Palo Alto, CA, October 10, 1974. SLHU MC 496, Box 49, Folder 17.
[143] Memo by Lawrence Lader, Chairman of the Board, NARAL, August 17, 1973, The "Maude" CBS-TV Boycott. SLHU MC 313, Carton 7, Folder "Maude."
[144] Margaret Mead, quoted in the article "Welcome Decline," *Time*, May 6, 1966. See also Blake, *Family Size*, 66.

convinced feminist Mead reflected the discourse of the women's movement concerning the right to reproductive control and self-determined reproduction as a milestone on the way to equal rights for women. Second, she was referring to a contemporary population discourse centered on the reduction of global population growth, a discourse that was unfolding in various private and semi-public organizations that together formed the population control movement.[145] Population policy concepts, often advocated and developed by the same experts who supported the right to abortion, were aimed above all at reducing the reproduction of socially disadvantaged groups in the United States and the inhabitants of developing countries. Finally, hints of a conservative family discourse can be discerned in Mead's statement, one that offered points of connection both with debates on "race suicide" and "fitter families" among eugenicists and discussions of the benefits of the traditional nuclear family.

In what follows, I elaborate how exactly the discursive link between reproductive control, women's equality, and population policy operated, to what extent the emphasis was once again on the values and experiences of white middle-class America, and why even liberal intellectuals such as Margaret Mead saw this discourse as relevant to them.

In the United States, the desire for scientific "population control" grew out of concerns about uncontrolled population growth both domestically (due to high birth rates among ethnic minorities and welfare recipients) and internationally (as a result of high birth rates in developing countries). In 1966, for example, Hugh Moore, president of the Association for Voluntary Sterilization (successor to the Human Betterment Foundation), warned that the U.S. population would double within the next three decades:

> Over-crowded cities, polluted air and water, countless unwanted and suffering children, skyrocketing taxes for welfare! Half of the babies now born in some cities are from indigent families on relief.[146]

On this view, it was vital to step up efforts to promote voluntary sterilization among Americans—though it was clear that Moore primarily had "poor indigent families" in mind, in other words predominantly African American ones. In 1968, at the invitation of the Planned Parenthood Federation, Margaret Mead was much more cautious, but she too called for effective "family size limitation"—chiefly through contraception and the increased integration of women into the labor market:

---

145 For organizations in the population control movement, see later in this chapter.
146 Letter from AVS President Hugh Moore to donors, November 1966. Margaret Mead Papers, Library of Congress, E 104, Folder 3.

The social climate will change in response to pressures on the land, in space, on food, on personnel. Today [. . .] it has become self-evident that the present rate of population growth endangers the quality of life in the most affluent countries, and the very existence of millions in poorer countries.[147]

To conduct scientific research and document the problem, as well as to provide concrete advice—which meant propagating birth control through sterilization and contraception—numerous privately and publicly funded organizations were formed, such as the Population Reference Bureau (or PRB, founded in 1929),[148] the Population Council (PC, founded in 1952),[149] Zero Population Growth (ZPG, founded in 1969),[150] which had strong public appeal, and the Population Institute (founded in 1969).[151] The Planned Parenthood Federation, due to its focus on birth control and women's reproductive rights and the fact that it helped fund most of the other institutions, played a significant role in this development.[152] Supporters of the ZPG were especially vigorous in their support for the *Roe v. Wade* ruling, emphasizing that freely available abortions and contraceptives were not only "absolutely desirable and necessary" as "mechanisms to achieve ZPG," but also served "to increase personal freedom and improve the quality of life."[153] The ZPG, which by 1973 claimed to have no fewer than 300 branches and 21,000 members throughout the country, con-

---

[147] Speech by Margaret Mead at a Planned Parenthood Federation luncheon, November 15, 1968, typescript. Margaret Mead Papers, Library of Congress, E 104, Folder 3.
[148] The organization's documents in the Robert C. Cook Papers, Library of Congress, Manuscript Division.
[149] The organization still exists today and is primarily involved in development aid, women's health, and control of global population growth; its annual budget is US $74 million. <www.popcouncil.org> Founded in 1952 by John D. Rockefeller, the body counted among its presidents several former eugenicists of distinction, such as Frederick Osborn (1957–1959), founding member of the American Eugenics Society and editor of the *Eugenics Quarterly* journal (since 1954), and Frank Notestein (1959–1968), demographer and former director of the American Eugenics Society. The PC's research was instrumental in the development of the intrauterine device (IUD), which was then prescribed to millions of women in the United States and the developing world as a form of contraception. The PC also contributed to the development of hormone implants such as Norplant.
[150] Folder "Zero Population Growth, 1969–1974" in NARAL files: SLHU MC 313, Box 9. Also included here are rules of procedure (1974) and initial reports by the executive director of the ZPG (1969).
[151] Margaret Mead Papers, Library of Congress, Manuscript Division, E 106.
[152] Margaret Mead Papers, Library of Congress, Manuscript Division, E 105. Robert C. Cook Papers, Library of Congress, Manuscript Division, Box 12, Folder 3.
[153] According to ZPG vice president, Judith Senderowitz, quoted by Jack Rosenthal, "Each Change Has Vast Impact," NYT, March 4, 1973, 201.

sciously saw itself as a grassroots movement. Although founded only in 1969, it had an office in New York and maintained close contacts with NARAL from the outset.[154]

In the mid-1970s, numerous mergers occurred among the "population organizations," which were also closely networked in terms of personnel and at the local level. In an attempt to influence government agenda-setting on population issues, the Population Oriented Organization People (POOP) was founded in 1975, which was made up of representatives of the PRB, PC, ZPG, NARAL, the Population Institute, the Religious Coalition for Abortion Rights, and the Population Crisis Committee. Between 1975 and 1977, its members met regularly for so-called "population lunches" in Washington, D.C.[155] This "population coalition" (which also referred to itself as such) attempted to promote issues such as abortion, contraception, and population control through targeted lobbying and public relations, while at the same time carefully avoiding the appearance that it was working toward the expert-supported planning of national population growth—although that was precisely its aim.[156]

In addition, in the course of the 1970s population policy concepts were incorporated into U.S. development policy. Many population experts who had initially advocated abortion and birth control in the United States, such as pro-choice veteran and physician Christopher Tietze,[157] whose research on abortion was one of the sources of inspiration for the Supreme Court decision, became involved in international population policy. Tietze was made deputy director of the New York-based

---

[154] Folder "Zero Population Growth, 1969–1974" in NARAL files. SLHU MC 313, Box 9. See also SLHU MC 714, Box 53, Folder 14 and Box 48, Folder 8 for information on the work of the ZPG from 1975 to 1980.

[155] Minutes, for example, in the NARAL papers, SLHU 714, Box 48, Folder 8: Population Coalition 1975–1978.

[156] Staggenborg, *The Pro-Choice Movement*, 162–165.

[157] Christopher Tietze (1908–1984) was a U.S. physician. Together with his wife, Sarah Lewit Tietze, he was a dedicated advocate of efforts to control population growth and disseminate knowledge about birth control and abortion. The two jointly received the Planned Parenthood Federation's Margaret Sanger Award in 1973 for their work. <www.plannedparenthood.org/about-us/newsroom/politics-policy-issues/ppfa-margaret-sanger-award-winners-4840.htm>. In the 1960s, Tietze acted as research director of the National Committee on Maternal Health and associate director of the PRB. He also served on the Legal and Social Scientific Committee of the Association for Voluntary Sterilization (AVS). Letter from Tietze to Robert C. Cook, December 16, 1960. Library of Congress, Manuscript Division, Robert C. Cook Papers, Box 11, Folder 9, ibid. Box 12, Folder 5. AVS annual conference program, December 17, 1966. Library of Congress, Manuscript Division, Margaret Mead Papers, Box E 105, Folder 3. SLHU MC 714 Box 59, Folder 9. Tietze, Christopher, "Contraceptive Practice in the Context of a Nonrestrictive Abortion Law: Age Specific Pregnancy Rates in New York City, 1971–1973," *Family Planning Perspectives*, vol. 7, 5 (1975), 197–202. Tietze, Christopher and Lewit, Sarah, "Legal Abortion," *Scientific American*, vol. 236, 1 (1977), 21–27.

Population Council, an international non-governmental organization founded by John D. Rockefeller and funded by the Rockefeller Foundation, which still exports birth control projects to developing countries in the name of women's health.[158]

For other population experts and physicians such as Robert C. Cook, the population control movement provided a welcome opportunity to shape society. Cook had succeeded Paul B. Popenoe[159] as editor of the *Journal of Heredity* in 1922 and later rose to become the long-serving director and president of the Population Reference Bureau (or PRB, which he headed from 1951 to 1968).[160] As a young man, he had willingly exchanged the medical profession for the role of eugenicist and population expert, as he acknowledged in retrospect to Wilson Popenoe, Paul B. Popenoe's brother:

> It has been a long time since you had a powerful influence in turning me away from the yearning for the practice of medicine—in about 1922. I can report that your advice was sound. This has been a hell of a lot more fun than listening to old ladies' sundry complaints, painting with iodine and reporting for duty.[161]

As early as 1961, Cook and a group of scientists (including Tietze for the Population Council and Alan Guttmacher of the Planned Parenthood Federation of America, as well as John Rock and Gregory Pincus, the developers of the Pill)[162] were commissioned by the National Institute of Health (NIH) to compile a report on the potential for effective contraception. The background was governmental approval of the pill in 1960 and the question of how hormonal contraception

---

158 Tietze, Christopher, "The Effects of Legalization of Abortion on Population Growth and Public Health," *Family Planning Perspectives* 7 (1975), no. 3, 123–127. On Tietze's role at the PC, see Robert C. Cook Papers, Library of Congress, Manuscript Division, Box 12, Folder 5. Recently, Mario Faust-Scalisi has explored the cooperation between the Ford Foundation and the PC, but he does not consider the experts involved and their programmatic goals, instead focusing solely on funding practices. Faust-Scalisi, Mario, "Die Ford Foundationund der Population Council. Zwei Institutionen, die gemeinsam globale Bevölkerungsdiskurseprägten," in Etzemüller, Thomas, *Vom "Volk" zur "Population". Interventionistische Bevölkerungspolitik der Nachkriegszeit* (Münster 2015), 135–157.
159 On Paul B. Popenoe, see section 2.5.
160 Robert C. Cook (1898–1991) was an American demographer and geneticist who served first as director (1951–1958), then as president (1958–1968) of the Population Reference Bureau (PRB). Cook was also an extremely active publicist and a politician with a strong focus on population who wrote several books and a large number of periodical articles. From 1922 to 1962 he edited the eugenic *Journal of Heredity*, and from 1951 to 1968 the PRB's journal, the *Population Bulletin*. On Cook, see the very good biographical sketch in the finding aid for his papers in the Library of Congress, Manuscript Division, Robert C. Cook Papers. Cook, Robert C., *Human Fertility: The Modern Dilemma* (New York 1951).
161 Robert C. Cook to Wilson Popenoe, Escuela Agricola Panamericana, Honduras, October 20, 1965. Robert C. Cook Papers, Library of Congress, Manuscript Division, Box 12, Folder 4.
162 Tietze, Rock, and Pincus also served as advisors to Planned Parenthood in the 1960s. I thank Claudia Roesch for pointing this out.

could best be used in the context of international population policy.¹⁶³ The scientists met in New York in August 1961 at the invitation of the Ford Foundation, harboring hopes of establishing a national Human Reproduction Institute, though these were to go unfulfilled. In the study itself, they mulled the most favorable family structure (which they identified as the nuclear family) and the potential to export birth control techniques to developing countries.¹⁶⁴ To the scientists' great frustration, the NIH declined to publish the report—a political decision intended to avoid triggering a debate on contraceptive methods, the progress of medicine, and government funding of birth control practices, especially in the field of population policy.¹⁶⁵

Cook also became involved with the PRB in relation to other issues of human genetics and population policy, such as the classic notion of preventing disability as a result of genetic defects. In 1959, for example, the national director of the Planned Parenthood Federation, William A. Vogt, asked Cook for information on the number of children born each year with disabilities caused by parental genetic defects or diseases—in his eyes "one of the worst forms of irresponsible parenthood."¹⁶⁶ Cook responded by underlining that "effective fertility control would prevent the perpetuation of defective genes and the births of many tragically afflicted children." This, he averred, was currently "one of the greatest challenges for the development of a better human race." Potential responses included "abstaining from reproduction or [. . .] the use of artificial insemination to assure that no defective children would be born." Cook linked this plea for "positive eugenics" with the help of modern science to a harsh critique of the supposedly meager general knowledge about the potential of modern human genetics:

> Ignorance regarding these simple genetic propositions is almost complete at the moment, and that includes most of the medical profession. In summary it can be said that the enlightened application of what now is known regarding human genetics could prevent the births of several billion [sic] defective children per generation in the United States.¹⁶⁷

---

163 Memorandum, September 17, 1961: "The need for new funds in research and training in population and fertility control." Robert C. Cook Papers, Library of Congress, Manuscript Division, Box 44, Folder. 13.
164 National Institute of Health, Report on Contraception, undated. Robert C. Cook Papers, Library of Congress, Manuscript Division, Box 44, Folder 13.
165 Letter from Robert C. Cook to Christopher Tietze, August 9, 1961. Cook Papers, Library of Congress, Manuscript Division. Cook Papers, Library of Congress, Manuscript Division, Box 44, Folder 12. WP, September 7, 1962: "Lengthy Birth Control Report is Shelved by Health Service."
166 Letter from national director PPF, William Vogt, to Cook, president, PRB, September 8, 1959. Robert C. Cook Papers, Library of Congress, Manuscript Division, Box 12, Folder 3.
167 Draft reply from Cook to William Vogt, September 15, 1959. Robert C. Cook Papers, Library of Congress, Manuscript Division, Box 12, Folder 3.

This exchange of letters shows how self-evidently eugenic ideas could still be mobilized in 1959 under the guise of modern human genetics—with reference to the healthy family and responsible parenthood. Very similar debates can be traced in Germany around the same time.[168]

Another revealing example of the fusion of family values and population policy is the discussion conducted by the PRB and PC in 1963 on a Women Strike for Peace activist's project to impart contraceptive knowledge to illiterate women. Betty Kindleberger-Stone had approached both organizations requesting their support.[169] Her self-developed concept of "baby planning beads," originally intended to popularize knowledge about birth control among illiterate U.S. families, she asserted, was also suitable for export to developing countries. By means of a home-made bead bracelet—to be hung above the marital bed—women were to get to know their menstrual cycle and determine their fertile days: green beads for the latter, a blue bead for the day of ovulation, white beads for infertile days, and red for menstruation. They were then supposed to pass this knowledge on to their husbands to help them understand the necessity for abstinence on fertile days.[170] Kindleberger-Stone did not leave it at theory, but promoted her invention in the *Washington Post*—as a means of curbing national population growth:

> Our most tragic agricultural surplus is our surplus crop of country-slum-bred farm children, white, Negro and Indian, children unplanned, ill-housed, ill-fed, undereducated and destined [. . .] to swell the numbers of unemployed multi-problem families on relief in our bursting city slums.
>
> Surplus children cannot be "ploughed under" or "dumped"; they must be stopped at the source. [. . .]
>
> Color-coded beads are now available for teaching rhythm to "functional illiterates"; information on them is obtainable from the Population Council, 230 Park Ave, New York.[171]

On the one hand, Cook reacted with reserve to this "interesting 'do it yourself' in fertility control" and expressed surprise that Kindleberger-Stone cited the PC as an

---

168 See the minutes of the meetings of the Eugenics Working Group of the Diakonisches Werk der Evanglischen Kirche in the papers of Otmar Freiherr von Verschuer, Archive of the Max Planck Society, Berlin, AMPG III-86 A-39,1 and 39,2.
169 Anne Fookson, "Women Strike for Peace," to PRB, November 20, 1963. Cook to the President of the PC, Bernard Berelson, November 26, 1963. Robert C. Cook Papers, Library of Congress, Manuscript Division, Box 42, Folder 3.
170 "Directions for Making and Teaching Baby Planning Beads" by Betty Kindleberger-Stone [undated, 1963]. Robert C. Cook Papers, Library of Congress, Manuscript Division, Box 42, Folder 3.
171 Stone, Betty K., "Surplus Children," letter to the editor, *Washington Post*, January 13, 1964.

official reference. At the same time, he marveled at this evidence that the organization had indeed reached the "grass roots level."[172]

Both organizations, the PRB and PC, subsequently intensified their efforts to raise public awareness of population issues—in the United States and worldwide. They cooperated, for instance, on the production of a series of six educational films, each thirty minutes long, on *The Population Problem*, which were shown from 1965 onwards and provided a didactic take on every field of the PC's activities. In addition to India, Brazil, and Japan, they also featured Europe and the United States. The final installment constituted, so to speak, the apotheosis of population policy under the title *The Gift of Choice*. This gift, it was claimed, was possible thanks to the engagement of experts and the export of modern contraceptives to developing countries (especially the IUD, since it was semi-permanent and could also be used by illiterate women).[173]

It is also important to note that in the summer of 1965, at exactly the same time as the heated debates surrounding the Moynihan Report,[174] a Population Crisis Committee under former Senator Kenneth B. Keating—later headed by General William H. Draper—published a proposal to establish a national "Family Development and Planning Service" within the Department of Health. Once again, this initiative was justified with the argument that the poor in the United States were having too many children.[175] The years 1965 and 1966 were in fact crucial to discussions on the control of population growth at the national and international levels.[176] These discussions, in turn, provided an important reference point for the debates—sparked by the Moynihan Report—on "deviant" African American families and the outbreaks of violence in the ghettos of major cities and vice versa. This is an insight hitherto absent from the research.

This link was also evident in the enthusiastic reception of a speech by anthropologist Margaret Mead as keynote speaker at the annual conference of the Planned

---

172 Cook to Bernard Berelson, Population Council, November 23, 1963. Cook to David Yaukey, Population Council, December 12, 1963. Cook to Dudley Kirk, Population Council, January 14, 1964. Robert C. Cook Papers, Library of Congress, Manuscript Division, Box 42, Folder 3.
173 Robert C. Cook Papers, Library of Congress, Manuscript Division, Box 47, Folder 8. The individual films covered: 1) The European Experience, 2) Answer in the Orient, 3) Brazil: The Gathering Millions, 4) India: Writings on the Sand, 5) USA: Seeds of Change, 6) The Gift of Choice.
174 For more on this, see chapter 4 of the present book.
175 Robert C. Cook Papers, Library of Congress, Manuscript Division, Box 47, Folder 10.
176 On this point, see also Heinrich Hartmann's study of contacts between the Population Crisis Committee, IPPF, and the West German government in the 1960s. Hartmann, Heinrich A. "In einem gewissen Sinne politisch belastet: Bevölkerungswissenschaft und Bevölkerungspolitik zwischen Entwicklungshilfe und bundesrepublikanischer Sozialpolitik (1960er und 1970er Jahre)," HZ, vol. 303 (2016), 98–125, 106–107.

Parenthood Federation in October 1966. At the time, the organization traded under the programmatic name of Planned Parenthood World Population (PPWP)—the result of a 1963 naming contest that underscored the organization's goal of limiting international population growth.[177] The 1966 conference was dedicated to PPWP's supposed 50th anniversary—as calculated from the establishment of the first birth control clinic by Margaret Sanger in 1916—and its overarching theme was "The Population Crisis: 20th Century Challenge." At Guttmacher's invitation, Mead spoke on the topic of "Women as Individuals in the Population Crisis."[178] Her reflections on childlessness as an opportunity for women in modern society delighted her audience, as documented by the enthusiastic reactions and reports.[179] Specifically, Mead argued that for the first time in history having few or no children was desirable for the well-being of the nation:

> Meanwhile this is, with a very few exceptions, the first time in history when the well-being of a society demands fewer children rather than more children. Where society in the past could not afford very many women to withdraw from reproductivity, there can now be active support for fewer children per household, or even no children at all.[180]

However, she averred, it was crucial that intelligent and well-educated individuals foster the further development of modern society—and this high "quality" of the requisite individuals necessitated restrictions on the number of children through birth control as a "social necessity for the well-being of the entire society":

---

177 After merging with the World Population Emergency Campaign in 1961. On the renaming, see communication from Planned Parenthood-World Population to PPFA Affiliates and Board, June 28, 1963. Planned Parenthood Federation of America Records, 1918–1974 (PPFA I), MS 371. I thank Claudia Roesch for the document.

178 Letter of invitation from President Guttmacher, PPWP, May 24, 1966, Letter of invitation from Executive Vice President, PPWP, Winfield Best, September 28, 1966. Cf. PPWP fiftieth Anniversary brochure, *Building Stronger Families, Happier Children*. Margaret Mead Papers, Library of Congress, Manuscript Division, Box E 105, Folder 3.

179 Letter of thanks from executive vice president, PPWP, Winfield Best to Mead, October 26, 1966. Press release October 19, 1966, on Mead's Luncheon Speech at the Roosevelt Hotel. The theme of the conference was "The Population Crisis: 20th Century Challenge." Two years later, the speech was still considered legendary among population policy experts. See, for example, executive vice president, PPWP, Winfield Best's letter to Mead dated October 4, 1968, through which he persuaded her to speak at the 1968 annual conference. Margaret Mead Papers, Library of Congress, Manuscript Division, Box E 105, Folder 3.

180 Excerpts of Margaret Mead's speech "Women as Individuals in the Population Crisis," sent by her assistant Patrice Woeppel on October 6, 1966, to executive vice president, PPWP, Best. Margaret Mead Papers, Library of Congress, Manuscript Division, Box E 105, Folder 3.

> Furthermore, our society is in great need of adults who will themselves contribute—as individuals, intelligent and trained and dedicated—to the rapid development of new institutional forms. Under these circumstances conception control becomes not a concession to the individual wishes of particular women, to whom we concede autonomy, nor a means of protection to the health of mothers and children in too large families, but a social necessity for the well-being of the entire society and the entire world.[181]

Here, we can clearly discern the connection with Mead's reflections in *Time* magazine in May of the same year, quoted at the beginning of this section, on the reduction of population growth in the United States to help ensure a higher "quality" of individuals. What is new, however, is that she now ascribed to American women in particular a pioneering role in birth control:

> Women all over the world look to the American women as style setters; it is essential that the first steps toward a new ethic of individual responsibility be taken in the United States.[182]

While this speech still focused on women's individual responsibility, in another speech just two years later at the PPWP's annual conference in New York on November 15, 1968, Mead addressed the question of how to get people to limit their family size without coercion. The organizers had tasked her with reflecting on "whether or not the two-child family will become culturally fashionable, throughout the population, once contraception becomes available and thoroughly acceptable to everyone."[183] The background to this was the PPWP's ideas on how the principle of voluntariness—understood as guided voluntarism—could be better anchored in population policy. This was the organization's response to accusations from the civil rights movement (articulated above all by the militant Black Panthers and the Nation of Islam, but also by representatives of the Student Non-Violent Coordinating Committee [SNCC] and the National Association for the Advancement of Colored People [NAACP]) that PPWP was committing "race genocide" among the African American minority by aggressively disseminating contraceptives and contraceptive methods.[184]

---

181 Mead, "Women as Individuals in the Population Crisis," October 19, 1966. Margaret Mead Papers, Library of Congress, Manuscript Division, Box E 105, Folder 3.
182 Mead, "Women as Individuals in the Population Crisis," October 19, 1966. Margaret Mead Papers, Library of Congress, Manuscript Division, Box E 105, Folder 3.
183 Invitation to Mead by executive vice president, PPWP, Best, October 4, 1968, to give Luncheon Speech, November 14, 1968. Margaret Mead Papers, Library of Congress, Manuscript Division, Box E 105, Folder 3.
184 Caron, Simone M., "Birth Control and the Black Community in the 1960s: Genocide or Power Politics?" *Journal of Social History* 31 (1998), no. 3, 545–569. Critchlow, Donald T., *Intended Consequences: Birth Control, Abortion, and the Federal Government in Modern America* (Oxford and New York 1999). Silliman, Gerber Fried, Ross, and Gutiérrez (eds.), *Undivided Rights*.

To help her prepare for her speech, Mead received an outline from the PPWP that asked, among other things, "How to make voluntarism work?" In retrospect, the ideas discussed here can be described, with reference to Michel Foucault, as a population *dispositive*—an attempt to induce people, through the provision of a governmental framework, to get themselves to embrace binding norms:

> Though current birth rates are showing a marked decline, concern is being expressed by some fertility control experts that the extension of voluntary conception to all adults will not automatically decelerate population growth enough to avoid serious overpopulation in America. [. . .] What other voluntary inducements could bring individual, personal micro-politics on family size in line with an optimum social macro-policy on population?[185]

Margaret Mead responded to the organizers' request and chose the title "Personal Decisions About Family Size" for her luncheon speech. First, she referred to the couple's personal right to decide, which was worth protecting:

> Decisions about parenthood are personal decisions, made by two persons about their own lives and the lives of their children. The injection of governmental coercion into such a choice is feared and condemned both in the name of individual religious freedom and in the name of civil rights.[186]

Immediately afterwards, however, Mead stressed that it was the task of social experts, abortion activists, and the government to create a "climate of opinion" that would enable couples and families to align themselves with the ideal of the wanted child. Ultimately, she stated, this would make a crucial contribution to reducing global population growth:

> If we can establish sufficiently [sic], so that no married pair ever have a child that they do not want [. . .], we would go a long way towards setting up a climate of opinion in which the idea of choice of whether or not to be a parent, ever, once, several times, was moved into the center of public consciousness. Once every couple with children could make such decisions, almost every couple would accept them as decisions to be made. Just as the shift in governmental pressures was the first step, the development of reliable contraception the second, the widespread acceptance of the right to choose will be the third step towards a balanced world population.[187]

---

185 Attachment, "Voluntary Parenthood and Population Policy," September 1968, to Mead's invitation from executive vice president, PPWP, Best, October 4, 1968, to hold Luncheon Speech, November 14, 1968. Margaret Mead Papers, Library of Congress, Manuscript Division, Box E 105, Folder 3.
186 Margaret Mead, "Personal Decisions About Family Size," November 15, 1968. Margaret Mead Papers, Library of Congress, Manuscript Division, Box E 105, Folder 3.
187 Margaret Mead, "Personal Decisions About Family Size," November 15, 1968. Margaret Mead Papers, Library of Congress, Manuscript Division, Box E 105, Folder 3.

But Mead did not limit her involvement with Planned Parenthood to occasional speeches; in the 1960s and 1970s she repeatedly authored fundraising letters for the organization.[188] What is less well known is that she maintained contacts with the broader population policy milieu in the United States: she was on the mailing list of the Association for Voluntary Sterilization (AVS) in the 1960s and also corresponded with the PRB.[189] In addition, from 1971 to 1978 she sat on the board of directors of another population policy organization, the Population Institute, which attempted to disseminate knowledge about population growth through the entertainment industry—with the help of TV producer Norman Lear, among others.[190]

Margaret Mead's reflections are testimony to the urgency with which the problem of international population growth was perceived in the 1960s, even among liberal human scientists. For Mead, birth control, contraception and, if necessary, abortion seemed to constitute an apt response; her fight for women's rights and advocacy of the ideal of the nuclear family (and individuals' autonomous alignment with it) entered into a revealing fusion. Careers such as that of Robert C. Cook, meanwhile, are striking evidence of how well eugenic goals could be combined with the curbing of population growth and thus, in a sense, modernized: through the advocacy of a healthy and thus harmonious family that would fulfill its obligations to society. Other eugenic institutions, such as the Association for Voluntary Sterilization,[191] whose members included Paul B. Popenoe and Christopher Tietze and that, after the Second World War, continued to collect the sterilization statistics begun by the now defunct Human Betterment Foundation,[192] emphasized the economic significance of modern population planning through birth control (sterilization), especially among the poor, socially disadvantaged population of America. Thus, eugenics in its modern guise helped the government to cut costs.[193] Biologistic family concepts continued to make an impact on modern notions of reproduction, as particularly evident in debates on the reproductive rights of non-white women.

---

[188] Collection of such letters from PPWP and PPFA, all signed and edited by Mead, in Margaret Mead Papers, Library of Congress, Manuscript Division, Box E 105, Folder 3, Folder 4.
[189] Margaret Mead Papers, Library of Congress, Manuscript Division, Box E 105, Folders 3 and 4.
[190] Margaret Mead Papers, Library of Congress, Manuscript Division, Box E 106, Folder 4.
[191] The former Sterilization League of New Jersey from 1937, then the Human Betterment Association of America from 1950, the Human Betterment Association for Voluntary Sterilization from 1950 to 1962, and finally the Association for Voluntary Sterilization (AVS) from 1965. See section 2.4.
[192] Records of the AVS in the Elmer L. Andersen Library, University of Minnesota.
[193] Kluchin, *Fit to be Tied*, 26–31.

5.5 "Race," "class," and "reproductive rights." African American women and their struggle for access to self-determined reproduction

On August 29, 1977, when *Time* magazine led with the headline "The Underclass: Destitute and Desperate in the Land of Plenty," the journalists involved were concerned first and foremost with the question of why the urban centers of the United States were home to a steadily growing number of poor people.[194] The article described the existence of an "underclass," estimated at seven to eight million people, as a pressing social problem in the United States. These people, it was argued, had simply not been reached by the War on Poverty welfare measures since the 1960s, and they lacked the self-confidence, discipline, and education to take advantage of opportunities for upward mobility in the first place.

The article did not regard factors of structural inequality—such as persistent racism, discrimination in the labor and housing markets, poor schooling and vocational training, neglect of urban centers in terms of urban planning and social policy—as an explanation for the dire economic situation of many members of the "underclass." Instead, the problem appeared to the journalists to lie in supposedly deficient family values. They lamented the inability of most members of the "underclass" to form a stable family structure based on a male breadwinner, to maintain this structure and pass it on to their children.[195] In addition, there was a supposed "culture of poverty," which merely reproduced penury and prevented social advancement—as sociologist Oscar Lewis had already described in the 1950s using the example of Mexican families.[196] According to the article, since its values were out of sync with those of the majority society and its family structure was fundamentally deficient, the "underclass," produced "a highly disproportionate number of the Nation's juvenile delinquents, school dropouts, drug addicts and welfare mothers and much of the adult crime, family disruption, urban decay and demand for social expenditures."[197]

Hence, underlying this discovery, which caught the public imagination, of a new social stratum lay something quite different, namely concern about the sup-

---

[194] "The American Underclass, Destitute and Desperate in the Land of Plenty," *Time*, vol. 110, issue 9, August 29, 1977, 34–41. See also Chappell, *War on Welfare*, 139–143.
[195] Auletta, Ken, *The Underclass* (New York 1982).
[196] Lewis himself had warned against applying his model without modification to the African American minority, but this did not prevent the "culture of poverty" from taking on a discursive life of its own. Lewis, "Five Families." Lewis, "The Culture of Poverty," 187–220. See section 4.3 of the present book.
[197] "The American Underclass," *Time*, August 28, 1977, 18. See also Chappell, *War on Welfare*, 140.

posed disintegration of the family and its values, especially among the African American minority. The journalists argued that the majority society was facing a double social and economic cost, first in the form of a further rise in juvenile delinquency (assaults, drug abuse), and second in the shape of an increase in the welfare budget to remedy the consequences, which worsened the burden on taxpayers.

Fig. 5.5: "Three Generations on Welfare—Discrimination's Sad Testament." Illustration for the article "The American Underclass" in *Time* magazine, August 29, 1977.

As *Time* saw things, the so-called "underclass" consisted essentially of non-white, single mothers. The journalists drew a direct link between the familial and economic situation of the poor in America's cities: poverty was majority black, female, and had many children. This interpretation was illustrated by a photograph of a three-generation black family—grandmother, mother, child—with the caption: "Three generations on welfare: discrimination's sad testament."[198] Such family set-ups, it was averred, were detrimental to society in the long term, because "welfare moms" were incapable of instilling in their children a work ethic or hope for advancement; due to the absence of the father, they were also unable to impart adequate family values.

> For many women of the underclass, welfare has turned illegitimate pregnancy into a virtual career. Says Barbara Wright, a welfare mother of four in Brooklyn: "A lot of young girls in the ghetto believe that the only way for them to get something in this society is by becoming pregnant and getting on welfare."[199]

Thus, "welfare moms" also appeared as an economic burden on the community: *Time* argued that a total of 1.5 million African American women in this category constituted the largest group (44.3 percent) of clients of the federal Aid to Families with Dependent Children (AFDC) program, which was claimed to cost the country $10.3 billion annually.[200]

This example of the (re)discovery of the "underclass" in the 1970s is a good illustration of how effectively discrimination on the basis of "race, class, and gender" still functioned in the second half of the twentieth century. The existence of an ever-growing underclass appeared not simply as a socioeconomic problem that could be addressed through educational, housing, and labor market programs, but as a moral dilemma with a clear ethnic encoding: the failure of black mothers in the big-city ghettos was said to be one of the main reasons for the social powder keg that was exploding into race riots, juvenile delinquency, and drug use.

This discourse was by no means new.[201] In the Americanization debates of the early twentieth century, social experts had repeatedly referred to the importance of immigrant women to the successful integration of the entire family into U.S. society and had developed corresponding educational and retraining programs.[202] In the 1960s, Assistant Secretary of Labor Daniel Patrick Moynihan's reflections on the supposedly deficient structure of the black family in the urban ghettos had sparked an intense debate on the structure and values of these families.[203] Finally, in the

---

198 Reprinted in Chappell, *War on Welfare*, 142.
199 "The American Underclass," *Time*, August 28, 1977.
200 On the conflicts surrounding the AFDC, see also section 6.1.
201 For more detail, see Overbeck, *At the Heart of It All*.
202 Roesch, "Americanization through Homemaking," 59–81. Sanchéz, "'Go after the Women'".
203 On this, see chapter 4 of the present book. Rainwater and Yancey (eds.), *The Moynihan Report*. Estes, Steve, *I am a Man! Race, Manhood, and the Civil Rights Movement* (Chapel Hill 2005). Patterson, *Freedom is not Enough*.

1980s, Ronald Reagan successfully mobilized votes with his polemical attacks on the alleged "welfare queen" who abused the welfare system.[204]

African American and also Mexican-born women faced multiple forms of discrimination with regard to their reproduction. First, there were the statements of white experts who sought to deny them access to self-determined reproduction as "hyperfertile breeders," "welfare recipients," or "incompetent mothers." This is starkly illustrated by the sterilization practices widespread in many states until the early 1970s.[205] Black, Native American, Mexican American, and Puerto Rican women were victims of so-called "non-consented" sterilizations either without their prior consent (for example, during a cesarean section or gynecological surgery) or in cases where their consent was obtained under pretext (for example, during labor, in the absence of sufficient information from the attending physicians, without receiving information in Spanish, or with reference to welfare benefits that would otherwise be denied them).[206] This practice affected hundreds of thousands of mothers throughout the U.S. in the 1960s and 1970s alone, and led to a number of important court cases in which victims sued for compensation and recognition of the violation of their personal rights.[207] The practice of sterilization combined eugenic, racist, and economic-utilitarian arguments. As a result, "women of color" across the country faced serious attacks on their reproductive autonomy. At the same time, they had to fight for their right to have children as they saw fit, as well as their right to access contraception and legal abortion. This made them quite different from their white counterparts.[208] For while the legalization of access to contraception and abortion essentially addressed the needs of white middle-class women, the needs of non-white women, such as protection against forced sterilization and the right to decide how many children they had, were long neglected. By 1963, a total of 64,000 people had fallen victim to forced sterilization in the United States; since 1930, these had been predominantly women, and since 1940 mostly African Americans, but also Mexican Americans and Puerto Ricans.[209]

---

[204] Finzsch, Norbert, "Gouvernementalität, der Moynihan-Report und die Welfare Queen im Cadillac," in Martschukat, Jürgen (ed.), *Geschichte schreiben mit Foucault* (Frankfurt a. M. 2002), 257–282. Chappell, *War on Welfare*. On this, see chapter 6.
[205] Schoen, *Choice and Coercion*. Stern, *Eugenic Nation*, 198–210, Velez-Ibañez, "Se Me Acabó." Carey, "Gender." Kluchin, *Fit to Be Tied*.
[206] Kluchin, Rebecca M., "Locating the Voices of the Sterilized," *The Public Historian* 29 (2007), no. 3, 131–144.
[207] Shapiro, *Population Control Politics*. Kluchin, *Fit to be Tied*, 151–183.
[208] Solinger, *Beggars and Choosers*.
[209] Kluchin, *Fit to be tied*.

The double-edged nature of the sterilization debate in the United States became apparent in 1977, when Secretary of Health, Education, and Welfare Joseph A. Califano called for an overhaul of sterilization practices in order to prevent "publicly funded coerced sterilizations" in the future.[210] The secretary also wanted to make so-called "voluntary sterilizations" more difficult through longer waiting periods and additional declarations of consent (for mothers under twenty-one years of age and mentally disabled women). Both NARAL and the Population Council firmly opposed this, valuing the option of conscious reproductive planning and the woman's freedom of choice more highly than the protection against coercion sought by Califano.[211] While Christopher Tietze of the Population Council insisted that it must be possible to sterilize mentally disabled mothers, Karen Mulhauser of NARAL underscored the individual's freedom to choose sterilization, which she claimed was once again being restricted according to racial and social criteria: "the same women, who are discriminated against with the Hyde amendment, are affected by these regs [regulations]."[212]

The effects of the debate on how to control the fertility of nonwhite women were still evident in the 1990s, when numerous states attempted to enact legislation to encourage (predominantly nonwhite) women on welfare to implant the hormonal contraceptive Norplant if they wished to continue receiving benefits. Lawyer Dorothy Roberts has argued that such legislative initiatives and the accompanying public debate violated the reproductive autonomy of African American women and girls in particular: "Black women's reproduction is a proper arena for social regulation: Perhaps this is the greatest danger of Norplant incentives: they reinforce the belief that the solution to Black poverty is to curb Black reproduction."[213]

While African American women on welfare began to organize and fight for their reproductive rights in the 1970s and 1980s, by the late 1960s African American feminists had already begun to point out the double, if not triple, oppression of African American women. As Frances Beale and Patricia Robinson described, they faced discrimination as women in U.S. society, as black women in white

---

210 Press Release of the Department of Health, Education and Welfare (HEW), Attn. Joseph A. Califano, December 1, 1977. Press release HEW, January 3, 1978, on proposed change in approach to sterilization. SLHU MC 714, Box 52, Folder 11.
211 Notes of protest from Karen Mulhauser, Chair of NARAL, January 6, 1978, to Marylin Martin of Public Health Service and from Christopher Tietze, deputy director of PC, January 3, 1978, also to Martin. SLHU MC 714, Box 52, Folder 11.
212 "Testimony before the Dept. of HEW for Public Hearings on Proposed Sterilization Regulations by Karen Mulhauser, executive director NARAL," January 17, 1978 (Draft). SLHU MC 714, Box 52, Folder 11.
213 Roberts, *Killing the Black Body*, 138.

America, and as activists within the Black Power movement.[214] While the white majority society's population experts tended to focus on reducing the minority's birth rate, African American women faced accusations of "black genocide" from black activists if they chose to use contraception.[215]

Welfare policy also demonstrates the extent to which the reproductive rights of non-white, poor women have been and continue to be restricted. First, the 1976 Hyde Amendment stipulated that Medicaid could not cover abortion costs for the poor, thus depriving women welfare recipients of a potential means of access to reproductive control. At the same time, there was a general lack of affordable, quality childcare for low-income mothers, while racist welfare policies criminalized single mothers in particular.[216] Even the liberal "welfare coalition" of the 1960s and 1970s, through its adherence to the ideal of the "family wage," that is, the principle of the father as breadwinner, helped stymie any effective reworking of welfare policy to better help families and single parents; the "welfare reform" of 1996 then repudiated the idea of a welfare state and introduced an obligation to work for recipients of support.[217] Marisa Chappell has convincingly brought out this "cultural conservatism" of 1960s liberals on issues of family structure and gender roles, identifying it as another cause of the undermining of the United States' most important welfare program, Aid to Families with Dependent Children (AFDC).[218] The finding that the entire twentieth-century debate on U.S. welfare policy remained centered on the breadwinner principle underscores with striking clarity the long-term social significance of the family values examined in this book.

The great influence still exerted by the ideal of the nuclear family featuring a male breadwinner in the early 1980s is vividly illustrated in the following state-

---

214 Beale, "Double Jeopardy." Robinson, "Poor Black Women," 481–483. Roth, *Separate Roads*. For more detail, see section 4.7.
215 On this topic, see chapter 4 of the present book.
216 Chappell, *War on Welfare*.
217 The Personal Responsibility and Work Opportunity Reconciliation Act (PRWORA) of 1996 ended the understanding of welfare as an "entitlement," replacing it with a Temporary Assistance for Needy Families (TANF) provision. This included a duty to provide for oneself through labor, including work requirements for welfare recipients. In addition, the federal government delegated to the states the form to be taken by payments, so that since then benefits have varied widely across the country. PRWORA [H.R. 3734], August 22, 1996, reprinted in Nadasen, Premilla, Mittelstadt, Jennifer, and Chappell, Marisa (eds.), *Welfare in the United States. A History with Documents* (New York 2009), 214–216.
218 Chappell's work is the best analysis of the undermining of the Aid to Families with Dependent Children (AFDC) welfare program, precisely because she demonstrates the proximity between liberal and conservative values with respect to family and welfare. Chappell, *War on Welfare*. See also Mittelstadt, *From Welfare to Workfare*.

ment by an African American woman. In her response to an ad from the Boston Women's Health Book Collective (BWHBC), which was seeking comments from "minority women" for a revised edition of its guidebook *Our Bodies, Ourselves*, Candace Lance, a Chicago-based public accountant, described the many difficulties faced by black women. Her statement is particularly significant because while Lance was an educated and articulate "professional woman," she was not a political activist but an "ordinary" contemporary who approached the BWHBC on her own initiative. Lance identified the biggest problem as "the extreme difficulty black women face in attempting to establish a solid relationship with a suitable mate, and hence to set up a stable family unit." Men, she stated, were often so ruined by the experience of ongoing discrimination that they failed as fathers and breadwinners:

> It really appears that minority—especially black—women just cannot expect to experience any of the benefits of being women in this country. We are always cheapened sadly, [sic] both by black and other races of men too. We're always seen as just an easy lay, a nothing, a "black bitch."[219]

However, apart from the fact that policies neglected the needs of African American women; many men ruthlessly exploited them; and an unattainable family ideal put them under additional pressure, Lance also lamented that the women's movement was not interested in the concerns of "minority women."

> I also feel that the Women's Movement has not seriously addressed the real and special problems of black women and other minority women. This is why many black women have not been quick to join the Women's Movement.[220]

Separate women's and women's health movements made up chiefly of African American women and mainly of Mexican American women had in fact already emerged since the 1970s. Here, activists protested against serious discrimination in access to reproductive control, healthcare, and welfare, as well as the neglect of their interests in the white abortion and women's health movements.[221] By contrast, in the 1980s, collaborations began between white "health feminists" and women of color in multiethnic forums. These were short-lived, however, as black

---

219 Letter from Candace Lance to BWHBC, November 19, 1981. SLHU MC 503, Box 109, Folder 27.
220 Letter from Candace Lance to BWHBC, November 19, 1981. SLHU MC 503, Box 109, Folder 27.
221 On the black women's health movement, see Nelson, *More than Medicine*, esp. 167–192, Springer, Kimberly, *Living for the Revolution. Black Feminist Organizations, 1968–1980* (Durham 2005). Roth, *Separate Roads*. On the Mexican American women's health Movement, see Gutiérrez, *Fertile Matters*. Espinoza, Dionne, "'Revolutionary Sisters': Women's Solidarity and Collective Identification among Chicana Brown Berets in East Los Angeles, 1967–1970," *Aztlan* 26 (2001), no. 1, 17–57.

feminists such as Loretta Ross, frustrated by the unwillingness of NOW's "mainstream feminists" to cooperate, withdrew from these ventures in the late 1980s.[222] Ross and many others became involved in the emerging "movement for reproductive justice," which focused more on the concerns of women of color.[223]

Candace Lance, meanwhile, was still optimistic in 1981, foreseeing that white women would soon face problems similar to those confronting their African American counterparts, "since now many white women are beginning to face some of the problems black women have always faced—divorce, working outside the home etc."[224]

Lance was quite right. Divorce and the risks associated with it had been developing into a core problem for many women since the early 1970s, even if they were not members of a minority group and did not live in socially precarious circumstances.

5.6 "Dramatic shift in the American temperament": the debates on divorce and the introduction of no-fault divorce

In late 1969, no less a figure than Ronald Reagan, as governor of the state of California, signed a law that was to revolutionize divorce throughout the U.S. and is generally regarded as an expression of a fundamental change in family values. The California Family Law Act initially stipulated for the state of California that, starting in 1970, a divorce no longer, as previously common, had to be obtained in court on the basis of a small number of recognized grounds for divorce, conclud-

---

[222] Loretta Ross (b. 1953) is an African American feminist and human rights activist. Herself a victim of rape, incest, and Dalkon Shield IUD-induced sterility, she has translated her personal experiences into political activism since the 1970s, including as director of the Rape Crisis Center in Washington, D.C. From 1985 to 1989, she directed NOW's Women of Color Program, in which capacity she organized the first national conference on "Women of Color and Reproductive Rights" in 1987. From 1989 to 1990, she worked for the National Black Women's Health Project. Since the 1990s, she has been involved in the "reproductive justice" movement, among other things as director of the Sister Song Women of Color Reproductive Health Collective (since 2004). Her papers are in the Sophia B. Smith Collection in Northampton, MA, where an extensive oral history interview with Ross is also archived. See biographical sketch <www.smith.edu/library/libs/ssc/pwv/pwv-ross.html>. On Ross, see also Nelson, *More than Medicine*, 167–192. For a recent work co-authored by Ross herself, see Ross and Solinger, *Reproductive Justice*.
[223] Nelson, *More than Medicine*, 193–220. Silliman, Gerber Fried, Ross, and Gutiérrez (eds.), *Undivided Rights*.
[224] Letter from Candace Lance to BWHBC, November 19, 1981. SLHU MC 503, Box 109, Folder 27.

ing with a verdict and the identification of a guilty party.[225] The so-called "no-fault divorce" replaced grounds for divorce and court proceedings with an expedited procedure in which spouses could apply for divorce quickly and unbureaucratically by referring to "irreconcilable differences." Family assets were divided equally, as there was no "guilty party" *per se* who could be forced to pay alimony.[226] Starting in California, most states liberalized their divorce laws in the 1970s, and by 1975, forty-five of the fifty states had established a form of no-fault arrangement.[227] At the same time, they replaced the term "divorce," with its negative connotations, with the more neutral "dissolution." By 1974, the *New York Times* was diagnosing a massive social change:

> One of the more dramatic shifts in the American temperament in the last five years is the increasing tendency of couples to seek divorce and the tendency of courts and state legislatures to make it easier for them to do so.[228]

On the very day that divorce reform went into effect in California, the same paper already identified a shift in values specifically among Californians, contending that:

> To many lawyers and sociologists, the law reflects the increasing instability of American family life, particularly in the booming and burgeoning states of the restless West. [. . .] Many experts here believe that the new divorce law mirrors a change in mores and morals of Californians.[229]

At first glance, the rapid nationwide introduction of no-fault divorce in the first half of the 1970s can indeed be read as an expression of a fundamental change in values, as recognition of the equal rights of both spouses, as criticism of the previously highly patriarchal family, and as a reaction to the individualization and pluralization of modern society. However, if we adopt a long-term historical perspective, this development loses much of its singularity and dramatic quality. Although national divorce rates did rise in the 1970s, they did so within a secular trend that had been

---

225 On the impact of the California Family Law Act from the perspective of contemporaries, see Hogoboom, William P., "The California Family Law Act of 1970: 21 Months of Experience," *Family Court Review* 9 (1971), No. 1 <www.onlinelibrary.wiley.com/doi/10.1111/j.174-1617.1971.tb00720.x/pdf>.
226 Phillips, *Untying the Knot*. Celello, Kristin, *Making Marriage Work. A History of Marriage and Divorce in the Twentieth-Century United States* (Chapel Hill, NC 2009). Riley, *Divorce*.
227 Warren, Virginia Lee, "Taking Some of the Pain out of Divorce. 'No-Fault' is a Growing Reality," *New York Times* (NYT), March 19, 1975.
228 King, Wayne, "Demand for Divorce Brings Laws to Make it Easier and Cheaper," NYT, January 5, 1974. 16.
229 Roberts, Steven V., "Divorce, California Style, Called A Reflection of the Restless West," NYT, January 1, 1970.

observed since data collection began in 1867. It was the 1980s that represented the real turnaround, as it was then that the divorce rate began its long-term decline; previously, only the 1950s and early 1960s had seen a temporary fall in the number of divorces. The debate over the pros and cons of liberalizing the divorce process and its impact on the family as the nucleus of the nation was by no means new either. The first publication of national divorce statistics in 1889 had triggered an initial public debate, in the course of which social experts in particular discovered the family as an object of analysis and advocated divorce as a remedy for ending intolerable relationships.[230] Liberal sociologists such as George E. Howard and Charlotte Perkins Gilman already linked their plea for the right to divorce to demands for women's rights and greater gender equality overall at the beginning of the century.[231] This first divorce debate of the twentieth century ended in victory for divorce advocates and the marginalization of their opponents as religiously and culturally conservative. Divorce law itself initially remained highly fragmented regionally, as it was regulated by the states, though most of them permitted fault-based divorce in principle on the basis of varyingly broad grounds for divorce.[232]

The widespread introduction of no-fault divorce in the 1970s was not without controversy. Particularly severe was the criticism from certain representatives of the women's movement, who argued that women would be massively disadvantaged economically by the abolition of the man's basic obligation to pay maintenance—which the principle of fault had guaranteed them in most cases.[233] As early as 1973, the *Los Angeles Times* pointed out that while California divorce judges divided the family assets equally between the partners, in doing so they disregarded factual inequalities such as poorer opportunities on the labor market and women's lower level of education. The paper quoted a Santa Monica-based (female) divorce lawyer as saying:

> Ten years ago, judges were breaking their necks to see that a woman could stay home and take care of preschool children. [. . .] Now, if I'm lucky, I can get enough money to cover the child care and the woman is left to cover the rest of support.[234]

---

[230] Lichtenberger, *Divorce*. On the divorce debates of the Progressive Era, see chapter 1 of the present book.
[231] Howard, George Elliott, "Is the Freer Granting of Divorce an Evil?" *American Journal of Sociology* 14 (1908–9), 766–796. Gilman, "Home Conditions."
[232] A still essential work is O'Neill, *Divorce in the Progressive Era*. Riley, *Divorce*.
[233] Weitzman, Lenore J., *The Divorce Revolution. The Unexpected Social and Economic Consequences for Women and Children in America* (New York 1985).
[234] Durant, Celeste, "New Feminism Benefits Men in Divorce Actions," *Los Angeles Times*, December 30, 1973.

NOW, too, had recognized that the sustenance of divorced women posed a serious problem and gravely jeopardized the desired equality of the sexes. Therefore, from 1970 to the mid-1970s, the NOW Task Force on Marriage, Divorce, and Family Relations gave a great deal of thought to how to remedy the glaring inequality of treatment of women in the new divorce regime.[235] In addition to questions of economic security for women, the activists were always concerned with how to strengthen their position vis-à-vis their spouses' unilateral desire for divorce, or how to prevent women from being divorced against their will after many years of marriage and then facing social and economic ruin.[236] Also important here was the highlighting of ongoing discrimination against women in the labor market and the lack of policies to help them re-enter the working world after divorce, which drastically worsened the economic starting point of divorced women obliged to work compared to that of their ex-husbands.[237] But female lifeways as a whole also appeared to be in danger. In 1975, the coordinator of the NOW Task Force on Marriage and Divorce, Elizabeth Coxe Spalding, even argued that divorce reform threatened the way of life of the housewife and mother—an astonishing statement coming from a feminist:

> The current wave of divorce "reform" bills has put "instant" gratification into divorce law; "throw-away" marriage into our culture and added "endangered species": the homemaker wife/mother. The divorce legislation completes the phasing out of family life that began with the decline of the extended family, followed by the isolation of the nuclear family and then the single parent. By increasing the ex-wife's obligation to provide support without giving her property rights during the marriage or recompense in the divorce settlement, married women must go to work. They cannot stay at home and take care of their husbands and children, they must keep their working skills sharp at all times. The role of the homemaker for women has been phased out by these "reform" divorce laws.[238]

From a historical perspective, it is clear that the marriage law reform of the early 1970s did indeed facilitate the divorce procedure and made legal divorce generally more accessible, so that it was less dependent than before on economic resources and place of residence. But at the same time, it reinforced economic

---

[235] See correspondence and drafts in SLHU MC 496, Box 47, Folders 42, 43, and 45.
[236] Letter from Ellen Sim Dewey, Nebraska chair person, NOW Task Force on Marriage, Divorce and Family Relations, June 20, 1975, to Task Force coordinator. Letter from Ellen Sim Dewey, Nebraska, to Barbara Cox, NOW executive director Legislative Development Task Force, December 16, 1974. SLHU MC 496, Box 47, Folder 43.
[237] "An Explanation of No-Fault Divorce," prepared by Betty Berry, national coordinator of the Marriage, Divorce and Family Relations Task Force of the NOW, undated [1973]. SLHU MC 496, Box 47, Folder 45.
[238] NOW Task Force on Marriage and Divorce, Elisabeth Coxe Spalding, national coordinator, January 15, 1975. SLHU MC 496, Box 47, Folder 45.

inequalities by massively reducing the support payments that men were required to pay their ex-wives and for the upkeep of their children and by presupposing equal opportunities for male and female divorcees to earn income, which did not correspond to reality (child rearing, poorer education, lower wages).

Hence, we can discern in the 1970s an important aspect of normative pluralization in the sense of a changed social understanding of roles. Unlike in the first third of the twentieth century, men and women were now regarded by divorce judges as formally equal partners—an extraordinary step in the renegotiation of gender norms. In practice, however, this equality was interpreted primarily in economic terms, as expressed in the distribution of marital property. On the other hand, the refusal of most judges to recognize persistent inequalities, such as the fact that child-rearing mostly remained the task of the woman, was a major blow to many women.

5.7 Interim conclusion: abortion as a constitutional right

Overall, the discourse on abortion and reproduction shows that throughout the twentieth century, the main emphasis was on the reproduction of white women and their contribution to securing the American family as the foundation of the nation. Non-white families, in contrast, were devalued or restricted in their choices. Looking at the debate in terms of its racial inequalities, the change in values in the field of sexuality and reproduction that culminated in the legalization of abortion appears less dramatic, since initially only white, middle-class women gained greater reproductive choice. Meanwhile, repressive measures were used against ethnically, racially, and socially defined minorities, with the spectrum ranging from coercive sterilization to mandatory contraception (through parole conditions or the mass administration of IUDs and hormone implants to African American teenagers, "welfare mothers," prisoners, and immigrant women). Coercive measures and lack of access to reproductive control thus reinforced each other. In this context, the organized women's movement around NOW initially played an ambivalent role, primarily representing the requirements and interests of white middle-class women, and only being motivated to broaden its focus to include the needs and desires of non-white women by the protests of African American feminists. At the same time, experts on population policy in particular—many of them with roots in the eugenics movement—played a major role in shaping the debate over "birth control" and "reproduction," bringing a biologistic understanding of "quality" into play. The idea that the quality of the population had to be increased, but not its quantity, was also far from alien to liberal social scientists, as the example of anthropologist Margaret Mead underlines.

Contrary to the demands of the women's and student movements, the gender norms contained in the family ideal had hardly changed by the end of the 1960s. This is shown, among other things, by the statements of white social scientists as well as the demands of male African American civil rights and Black Power activists, all of whom cleaved to an unequal gender relationship—whether by highlighting the importance of the man's role as breadwinner ("family wage") or envisaging and promoting a specific African American "hypermasculinity" as a counter-image to the idea of the weak black man. In both concepts, women appeared at best as biologistically tied to reproduction and childrearing, but not as equal partners. This is where the women's movement of the late 1960s and early 1970s had to begin in order to pursue crucial renegotiations of gender relations under the watchwords of "equality" and "reproductive control." Key gender-related changes materialized first in antidiscrimination policies in the workplace, which were based on Johnson's Executive Order 11375 of 1967, then in the introduction of no-fault divorce in 1970, and finally in the Supreme Court's legalization of first-trimester abortion in the 1973 *Roe v. Wade* ruling.

In the course of the 1970s, liberal conceptions of women's employment and abortion found their way into the national understanding of family. In the debate over the August 1973 rebroadcast of the "abortion episodes" of the popular *Maude* television series, for example, one reader wrote in arguing that for her abortion no longer constituted a scandal, but simply a constitutional right:

> For most of us, abortion is no longer an issue. It is a right, pure and simple. Not only because it is a woman's right to control her own body, but because it is the right of every child to be wanted and loved from the start.[239]

But the most profound indication of a change in social values that we can discern in the public debates about divorce and abortion in the 1970s lies in a gradual, and by no means conflict-free, privileging of the right to individual self-determination over the importance of the common good—albeit within narrow discursive limits. The representatives of the women's movement played a key role in this, since they not only discursively occupied the topic of reproduction, but concurrently disseminated information about contraceptive practices, medical fundamentals, and legal frameworks among activists. In doing so, little by little they undermined the authority of population experts in this field. In general, from the late 1960s onward, expert discourses and decisions in the field of reproductive policy (relating to the prescription of contraceptives, access to abortion, and sterilization practices) were

---

239 Reader's letter from C.V.A. Avedikian, Kensington, on the occasion of the rebroadcast of the "abortion episode" on August 21, 1973, to WP, August 30, 1973, A19.

increasingly challenged by grassroots movements, which seized most of this discursive terrain, prompting many experts to focus on exporting birth control techniques to the Third World.

The initial question of the extent to which debates and actors increasingly made recourse to individual values must therefore be answered with some ambivalence for the 1970s. While liberal experts in principle granted white women greater individual decision-making rights in the managing of their reproduction (and many women also energetically demanded these rights), the situation was quite different for non-white women. To be sure, non-white activists actively demanded enhanced rights and the cessation of coercive measures, from sterilization to welfare cuts. But many experts and relevant sections of U.S. society simply refused to recognize such aspirations. Individual rights in the field of reproduction thus remained segmented along "race" and "class" lines even in the 1970s. In this regard, then, one can refer only to a "partial change in values."

The politically and culturally explosive nature of individual reproductive decisions for U.S. society as a whole is demonstrated by the fierce abortion debates that continue to this day. Starting with the failure of the Carter administration's first "National Conference on Families" in 1980 and its liberal family values, the following chapter analyzes the conflict over family values in the culture wars of the 1980s. The contrast made by Ronald Reagan between abortion (as selfish individualism) and giving one's child up for adoption (as altruistic service to the community), and the commentary on this view by the various social movements constitutes a particularly potent basis for investigating the conflicting ideas about individual rights and collective values.

6 "Culture wars?" Debates on the American family in the 1980s

On March 4, 1977, anthropologist Margaret Mead received an invitation from Secretary of Health, Education, and Welfare Joseph A. Califano to participate in a planned "White House Conference on Families."

> The intent of this conference will be to focus attention on the ways in which policies and institutions affect American families. It will seek to help us understand better the trends and forces which influence families and the problems and opportunities that result. Most importantly, it will be designed to help translate the knowledge into policies which strengthen families rather than weaken them.

To this end, the government was now seeking the cooperation of proven specialists and experts working in the field of the family:

> This is, as you know, a very important but exceedingly complex task. We need to understand the pluralistic nature of American families, as well as diverse, pluralistic, and sometimes conflicting opinions about them.[1]

The realization that U.S. families were diverse and that there were many divergent opinions about their structure and values represented an important insight into the reality of people's lives and, at the same time, a key lesson learned from the social protest movements and debates of the 1960s and 1970s. Anyone wishing to publicly mull families in modern society could only do so in a pluralistic and, to a certain extent, "grassroots" manner. This was precisely what Califano and Carter sought to do—but they failed spectacularly. The conference triggered a storm of protest, and Carter was ultimately defeated in the 1980 presidential election by his Republican challenger Ronald Reagan, who scored points with his conservative family rhetoric.[2] As I will argue here, this can be explained by the finding that while the right to individual freedom of choice in matters of reproduction, divorce, and family life represented a crucial achievement of the 1970s (with the qualifications set out in chapter 5), it made a nationally binding family

---
[1] Secretary of Health, Education, and Welfare Joseph A. Califano Jr. to Margaret Mead, March 4, 1977. Letter of reply from Mead, March 14, 1977. Margaret Mead Papers, Library of Congress (LOC), Manuscript Division, Box E 92, Folder 5.
[2] On the significance of the religious right to the failure of Carter's family policy and the rise of Ronald Reagan, see Flippen, J. Brooks, *Jimmy Carter, the Politics of Family, and the Rise of the Religious Right* (Athens and London 2011). Ribuffo, Leo P., "Family Policy Past as Prologue. Jimmy Carter, the White House Conference on Families, and the Mobilization of the New Christian Right," *Review of Policy Research* 23 (2006), no. 2, 311–338.

policy impossible in the 1980s—by then, the gulf between prevailing ideologies and political platforms had grown too wide.

Today, the debates on cultural, religious, and especially family values in the 1980s and 1990s are most often referred to as the "culture wars."[3] Put simply, the idea here is that two social camps faced off that represented sharply divergent attitudes toward gender norms, affirmative action, abortion, homosexuality, public support for culture and the arts, and the importance of religious education. On this view, while an alliance of conservative Republicans, religious fundamentalists, and the New Christian Right advocated moral and religious values, liberal Democrats continued to champion pluralistic values at the level of both government policy and the family. Despite the undeniable acrimony of the interpretive conflicts fought out in the public sphere and the tendency toward violent protests, outside abortion clinics and courts for example, in recent years a growing number of social scientific analyses have questioned whether we should be thinking in terms of two clearly demarcated fronts and have thus cast doubt on the aptness of the term "culture wars." Recent studies in public opinion research, meanwhile, indicate that the attitudes of most Americans on issues such as abortion, homosexuality, and so on were too internally inconsistent to be clearly assigned to a specific camp.[4]

For historical analysis, the term's primary advantage is that it focuses our attention on changes in the public debate on individual rights and collective values, individual and government, and family and nation in the 1980s. At the same time, it includes a historical perspective on the socio-cultural changes of the 1960s and 1970s: the "culture wars" explicitly grappled with the changes in norms and values spawned during that period.[5] Finally, the term can help us assess the extent to which social conflicts in the United States in the 1980s differed significantly from protests against changing family values and gender norms in other Western

---

[3] The term "culture wars" was coined by sociologist of religion James Davison Hunter in 1991 and apostrophized as the "War for the Soul of America" by Patrick Buchanan, then seeking the Republican presidential nomination, at the 1992 Republican convention. Hunter, *Culture Wars*. Another text from a sociology-of-religion perspective is Browning, et al., *From Culture Wars to Common Ground*. For a contemporary history angle, meanwhile, see Hartman, *War*.

[4] For a comprehensive critique of the "culture wars" paradigm, see Thomson, *Culture Wars*. Mouw and Sobel had already argued that even the abortion debate polarized people less than previously assumed. Mouw, Ted and Sobel, Michael E., "Culture Wars and Opinion Polarization," *American Journal of Sociology* 106, 4 (2001), 913–943, esp. 938.

[5] Hartman, *War*. For an insightful analysis of the controversy over public funding for the humanities and arts by the National Endowment for the Humanities and the National Endowment for the Arts, both Johnson administration agencies, see Jensen, Richard, "The Culture Wars, 1965–1995: A Historian's Map," *Journal of Social History* 29 (1995), 17–37.

societies, in other words, it can help us determine whether the "culture wars" were primarily an American phenomenon. This chapter, then, probes the family as an object of the "culture wars," seeking to gauge the fault lines of value change and its limits—and examining historically the alternative concepts offered by conservative critics in the form of "traditional family values."

The first question is thus what difficulties the Carter Conference faced at the beginning of the 1980s as it attempted to develop key parameters for a nationally uniform, liberal-pluralist family policy. Second, it is imperative to scrutinize the content and consequences of Reagan's symbolic family policy and to explore how the women's and pro-choice movements, in particular, responded to it. The third essential step is to clarify to what extent the president's privileging of adoption over abortion actually changed the framework for reproductive decision-making in the United States and perhaps the national ideal of the family as well.

To this end I will be evaluating the following source materials: the files of the Carter administration departments in charge of the Family Conference, Margaret Mead's literary estate, Ronald Reagan's speeches and proclamations, and the files of the organizations Concerned United Birthparents (CUB), National Abortion Rights Action League (NARAL), and the local abortion rights movement in Boston known as NARAL Mass Choice. First, however, a brief overview of the socioeconomic situation of American families in the 1980s provides key background to this analysis.

6.1 "Dual earners and welfare moms": the social history of the family in the 1980s

The social history of the family in the 1980s was determined to a large extent by two developments that can be summarized under the catchwords "welfare and work." First, the number of families with two incomes increased significantly in the 1980s, and the "dual earner family" prevailed as the majority model over the "male breadwinner." Whereas in 1969 just under 70 percent of married couples with children under 18 still depended on the husband's sole earnings and the mother was employed in just under 25 percent of these families, the share of co-earning mothers was to rise steadily over the next twenty years. In 1980, things evened out, with about 45 percent of families with a male breadwinner, compared to the same number with dual incomes. The share of married couples with children who depended solely on the mother's income had also risen, from just under 2 percent to about 4 percent. From 1980 onward, the trend toward two household incomes (and thus toward women's employment) continued. In 2011, just under 60 percent of all married couples with children had two incomes, with just over 30 percent living on the father's salary alone and just under 7 percent on the mother's earnings alone.[6] Social history data further shows that better-educated women began to earn higher wages over the long term: while in 1980, 3.8 percent of mothers of minor children earned more than their husbands, by 1990 this figure had risen to 16 percent—with an upward trend.[7]

At the other end of the spectrum, the 1980s also saw a consistently high demand for government assistance through the Aid to Families with Dependent Children (AFDC) program. This, along with widespread fears of "welfare fraud," in turn inspired the political diagnosis of a "welfare crisis," in other words a ruinous expansion of government welfare spending. This envisaged crisis, in turn, led to calls for major changes to the welfare system.[8] When the 1996 welfare reform under President Bill Clinton heralded the "end of welfare as we know it," it included a conscious departure from the principle of "entitlement." The Personal Responsibility and Work Opportunity Reconciliation Act (PRWORA) limited the duration of welfare payments to a maximum of five years, including no more than two consecutive years. The new Temporary Assistance for Needy Families (TANF) program included only short-term assistance for the needy and work requirements ("welfare to work").[9]

Statistics show, however, that welfare payments had been far from inflationary. The number of families dependent on government assistance (mostly mothers plus their minor children) initially fell briefly at the start of the 1980s, before rising again moderately only toward the end of the decade.[10] As a look at the number of children relying on AFDC shows, a significant increase did not occur until the years 1990–1994: in 1980, some 7 million children received aid from the AFDC program, and by 1989 the figure was still only 7.2 million; in 1993 and 1994, by contrast, it had risen to 9.4 million.[11]

---

[6] Wang, Wendy, Parker, Kim, and Taylor, Paul, *Breadwinner Moms. Mothers Are the Sole or Primary Provider in Four-in-Ten Households with Children; Public Conflicted about the Growing Trend*, PEW Research Center, March 29, 2013, 20. www.pewsocialtrends.org.

[7] Wang, Parker, and Taylor, *Breadwinner Moms*, 12.

[8] The best work on the undermining of AFDC by the reform debate is Chappell, *War on Welfare*. See also the sourcebook Nadasen, Mittelstadt, and Chappell, *Welfare in the United States*. Nadasen, Premilla, *Welfare Warriors. The Welfare Rights Movement in the United States* (New York 2005).

[9] PRWORA (H.R. 3734), August 22, 1996, reprinted in Nadasen, Premilla, Mittelstadt, Jennifer, and Marisa Chappell (eds.), *Welfare in the United States. A History with Documents* (New York 2009), 214–216.

[10] Page, Stephen B. and Larner, Mary B., "Introduction to the AFDC Program," *The Future of Children. Welfare to Work*, vol. 7, 1 (1997), 20–27, 24.

[11] Child Trends Data Bank, *Child Recipients of Welfare (AFDC/TANF): Indicators on Children and Youth*, updated December 2015, 4 <www.childtrends.org>.

The trend toward both parents in employment and the increasing dependence of single mothers in particular on AFDC welfare benefits did not go unchallenged. The associated discourses on "dual earner families" and "welfare mothers" were highly infused with racial stereotypes and carried a profound moral charge. While the inexorable rise of the dual-earner household was consistent with the primacy of economic policy under Ronald Reagan, it stood in latent contradiction to the "traditional family values" he proclaimed.[12] The unmistakable end of the "male breadwinner" once again fueled fears of disintegrating families and unsupervised children. In particular, the question of childcare for the offspring of working parents stoked passions, since here the traditional role of mother was at issue.[13] Consequently, members of the Reagan administration and representatives of the Christian right emphasized the importance of marriage and family as the foundation of the nation. This was flanked by an affirmation of heteronormative notions of partnership and a critique of single parenthood.[14]

Racial and social prejudices were even more prominent in the debate on welfare than in the discussion of working mothers. This is illustrated by the stereotype of the so-called "welfare queen," who, supposedly by making astute use of government resources, led an amoral life at the expense of ordinary, hardworking people.[15] In the cliché embraced by large numbers of Americans, these were virtually always non-white women, a belief that shone through subcutaneously in the debates.[16] This conception was prominently hatched by none other

---

[12] For more on this, see later in this chapter. On Reagan's presidency, see Brownlee, Elliott, *The Reagan Presidency. Pragmatic Conservatism and Its Legacies* (Lawrence 2003). Collins, Robert M., *Transforming America. Politics and Culture in the Reagan Years* (New York 2007). Ehrman, John, *The Eighties. America in the Age of Reagan* (New Haven etc. 2005).

[13] See also Dobson, James and Bauer, Gary, *Children at Risk. The Battle for the Hearts and Minds of Our Kids* (Dallas etc. 1990), 129–147. Schlafly, Phyllis (ed.), *Who Will Rock the Cradle? The Battle for Control of Childcare in America* (Nashville 1990). Popenoe, David, "American Family Decline, 1960–1990. A Review and Appraisal," *Journal of Marriage and the Family* 55 (1993), no. 3, 527–542. For an early critique, see Lasch, Christopher, *Haven in a Heartless World. The Family Besieged* (New York 1977), 137–139.

[14] See the expert report compiled under the direction of Gary Bauer: US Executive Office of the President, *The Family. Preserving America's Future. A Report to the President from the White House Working Group on the Family* (Washington DC, Domestic Policy Council, December 1986).

[15] On the wealth of literature, see Finzsch, Norbert, "Gouvernementalität, der Moynihan-Report und die Welfare Queen im Cadillac," in Martschukat, Jürgen (ed.), *Geschichte schreiben mit Foucault* (Frankfurt a. M. 2002), 257–282. Hancock, Ange-Marie, *The Politics of Disgust. The Public Identity of the Welfare Queen* (New York and London 2004). Kohler-Hausmann, Julilly, "Welfare Crises, Penal Solutions and the Origins of the 'Welfare Queen,'" *Journal of Urban History*, vol. 4, 5 (2015), 756–771.

[16] Quadagno, *Color of Welfare*.

than Ronald Reagan, first during his campaign for governor of California and then in 1976 during his first bid for nomination as Republican presidential candidate. In a radio address on October 18, 1976, Reagan told the story of a "welfare queen from Chicago," who "used 127 names, posed as a mother of 14 children at one time, 7 at another [. . .]. She has 3 new cars, a full length mink coat, and her take is estimated at a million dollars."[17] Although the identity of this woman (assuming she existed) was never established, the notion of the criminal "welfare queen" took on a life of its own in the contemporary debate on the supposed "welfare crisis" and paved the way for the reform of the 1990s.[18]

But how can we best characterize women welfare recipients in terms of ethnic and social structure? First, poverty was (and is) measurably linked to ethnic discrimination. While 18 percent of all American children lived in poverty in 1980, this was true of 42 percent of all African American children and only 13 percent of all white children. By 1982, the number of socially disadvantaged children had risen to 21 percent: 47 percent of African American children but only 17 percent of white children were considered poor. While 46 percent of all black mothers raised their children on their own that year, only 5 percent of white mothers did so. Nationally, single mothers accounted for no less than 19 percent of all mothers.[19]

Many nonwhite women and their children did in fact receive AFDC in the 1980s, but by no means exclusively. In fact, the percentage of African Americans among AFDC recipients had been significantly higher from 1965 to 1975. During this period, it had exceeded the 45 percent mark before subsequently falling.[20] By the end of the 1980s, it was below 40 percent, and by 1992, only 37 percent of AFDC recipients were African American, while 37 percent were white and 18 percent were Mexican American.[21] Most families on AFDC tended to be small, with 43 percent of them containing only one child. In addition, many women used AFDC only temporarily, either to bridge financial crises after a separation (45 percent) or the birth of a child (30 percent), as a 1983 survey indicated. Even before

---

17 Quoted in Crafton, William, "The Incremental Revolution. Ronald Reagan and Welfare Reform in the 1970s," *Journal of Policy History*, vol. 26, 1 (2014), 27–47, 27. See also the *Washington Star* report on a comparable statement by Reagan during the election campaign on February 14, 1976, cited in Nadasen, Mittelstadt, and Chappell, *Welfare*, 189–191.
18 Kohler-Hausmann, "Welfare Crises." Crafton, "Incremental Revolution." Gilens, Martin, *Why Americans Hate Welfare. Race, Media, and the Politics of Antipoverty Policy* (Chicago and London 1999).
19 Kimmich, Madeleine H., *America's Children. Who Cares? Growing Needs and Declining Assistance in the Reagan Era* (Washington D.C. 1985), 10.
20 Quadagno, *Color of Welfare*, 119–125, 175–176. For a survey of the proportion of African Americans among AFDC recipients between 1936 and 1995, see Gilens, *Why Americans Hate Welfare*, 106.
21 Page and Larner, "Introduction to the AFDC Program," 22–23.

6.1 "Dual earners and welfare moms": the social history of the family in the 1980s — 337

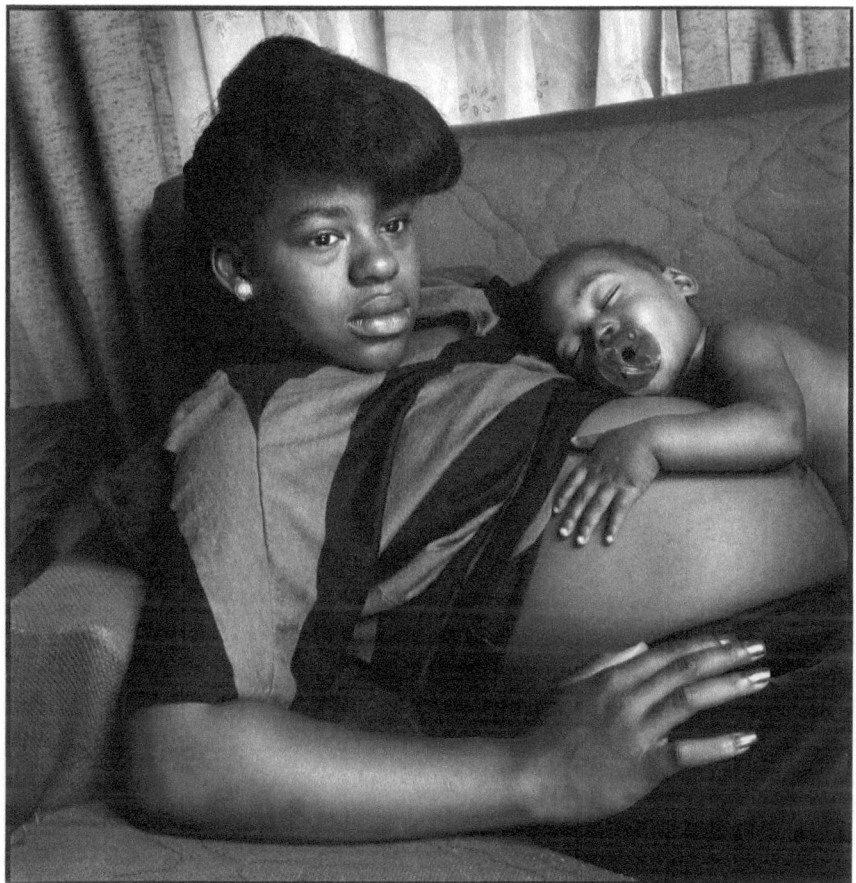

Fig. 6.1: Photograph of pregnant teenage mother accompanying *Fortune* magazine article "America's Underclass," May 11, 1987.

1996, many welfare recipients stopped using this program when they formed new relationships or when their youngest child turned eighteen.²²

Despite this, the image of the female welfare recipient in media reports and published opinion was mostly that of an African American woman, typically underage and already the mother of several children. This impression is conveyed ideal-typically by a photograph accompanying a 1987 *Fortune* magazine article that once again spotlighted "America's Underclass."²³

---

22 Quoted in Page and Larner, "Introduction to the AFDC Program," 23.
23 Magnet Myron, "America's Underclass: What to do?" *Fortune*, May 11, 1987.

Further, the notion of AFDC as a "program for blacks" contributed to a continuous decline in the acceptance of welfare measures among the general population, as recent studies have demonstrated.[24] At the same time, however, the benefits provided by the program declined steadily from 1970, while demand increased significantly until 1975 and then again from 1989 onward.[25] Whereas an eligible household could expect to receive an average of $800 per month in 1970, by 1995 this had halved to $400 per month.[26]

It is important to note that, contrary to the heated public debates on the supposed "decline of the family" and the alleged threat to the nation posed by the incidence of legal abortions, neither the abortion figures nor the divorce rate increased significantly in the 1980s; in fact, the latter declined substantially. While national abortion numbers rose moderately from about 1.3 million in 1980 to just over 1.4 million in 1990, the divorce figures fell from 1.18 million in 1980 to 1.17 million in 1990 in absolute terms.[27] Due to the increase in population, the reduction in the national divorce rate was significant, from 5.2 divorces (1980) to 4.7 divorces (1990) per 1,000 people annually.

In contrast, the number of births out of wedlock increased substantially: while only 5 percent of all children were born to unmarried women in 1960, this figure was no less than 41 percent in 2010.[28] Although the share of mothers who were divorced, separated or widowed and lived alone with their children remained constant at around 12 percent between 1980 and 1990,[29] the proportion of single mothers who had never been married among all households with minor children in the U.S. rose from 4 percent to around 7 percent. This group of people was particularly affected by poverty and therefore constituted a significant proportion of women recipients of AFDC.[30]

---

[24] Gilens, *Why Americans Hate Welfare*. Hancock, *Politics of Disgust*. Quadagno, *Color of Welfare*, 171–173, 194–196.

[25] Page and Larner, "Introduction to the AFDC Program," 23.

[26] Gilens, *Why Americans Hate Welfare*, 19. Gilens' calculation, based on the *Statistical Abstracts of the United States*, was in "constant 1997 dollars."

[27] On the development of abortion data, see the detailed discussion in chapter 5 of the present book. Statistics at Center for Disease Control and Prevention, *Abortion Surveillance—United States, 2005* <www.cdc.gov/mmwr/preview/mmwrhtml/ss5713a1.htm>. Center for Disease Control and Prevention, *Abortion Surveillance—United States, 2012* <www.cdc. gov/mmwr/preview/mmwrhtml/ss6410a1.htm?s_cid=ss6410a1_w>. On the divorce rate, see U.S. Department of Health and Human Services, National Center for Health Statistics, according to Information Please Database, 2007, Pearson Education Inc. <www.infoplease.com/ipa/A0005044. html>.

[28] Wang, Parker, and Taylor, *Breadwinner Moms*, 17.

[29] Wang, Parker, and Taylor, *Breadwinner Moms*, 17.

[30] Wang, Parker, and Taylor, *Breadwinner Moms*, 17.

Once again, the 1996 welfare reform promised to remedy the situation: the PRWORA was aimed quite explicitly at protecting marriage and combating "teen pregnancies," declaring:

1) Marriage is the foundation of a successful society.
2) Marriage is an essential institution of a successful society which promotes the interests of children.

The focus was on mothers of illegitimate children in particular: "The negative consequences of an out-of-wedlock birth on the mother, the family, and society are well documented." The avowed aim of the reorganization of welfare benefits away from longer-term support payments toward short-term bridging assistance was therefore "[to] prevent and reduce the incidence of out-of-wedlock pregnancies [. . .] and encourage the formation and maintenance of two-parent families."[31]

At the end of its existence, the AFDC program's "founding flaw" finally caught up with it—the linking of benefits to the existence of a family without a male breadwinner (a system originally designed to provide for white widows and orphans). Families on welfare, too, were now supposed to conform to the ideal of the nuclear family.

The responses of those affected: the welfare rights movement and Family Adoption Program

As early as the 1960s, a dedicated welfare rights movement had sprung up that strove to enhance benefits, but also to improve the public image of welfare recipients.[32] An important argument made by this movement in the early years was that African Americans were underrepresented in the programs rolled out as part of Lyndon B. Johnson's War on Poverty and were inadequately informed about their rights, leaving them with insufficient support.[33] In 1969, the largest organization in this field, the National Welfare Rights Organization (NWRO),

---

[31] PRWORA (H.R. 3734), August 22, 1996, reprinted in Nadasen, Mittelstadt, and Chappell, *Welfare*, 214–216.
[32] Nadasen, Premilla, "Expanding the Boundaries of the Women's Movement. Black Feminism and the Struggle for Welfare Rights," *Feminist Studies* 28 (2002), 271–301. Nadasen, *Welfare Warriors*. Nadasen, Mittelstadt, and Chappell, *Welfare*, 63–84.
[33] Quadagno, *Color of Welfare*, 14. Cloward, Richard A. and Piven, Frances Fox, "A Strategy to End Poverty," *The Nation*, May 2, 1966, quoted in Nadasen, Mittelstadt, and Chappell, *Welfare*, 143–146. Raz, Mical, *What's Wrong with the Poor? Psychiatry, Race, and the War on Poverty* (Chapel Hill 2013).

came up with a proposal to improve the situation of welfare recipients: AFDC should be replaced by a Guaranteed Adequate Income of $5,500 per year for a family of four.[34] Shortly after, President Richard Nixon put forward a Family Assistance Plan (FAP) as part of his envisaged welfare reform,[35] which was also based on a guaranteed minimum income for families, though the amount involved would have left them well below the poverty line. Neither plan was implemented. In the 1980s, meanwhile, welfare rights activists focused chiefly on demanding good jobs as a route out of poverty.[36]

In 1986, television journalist Bill Moyers[37]—White House press secretary in the mid-1960s and thus at the time of the Moynihan Report—scrutinized the African American family in a CBS TV documentary. In it, he raised the question of the connection between economic disadvantage, lack of educational opportunity, dismal housing conditions and poorly targeted welfare spending. The one-hour-thirty-minute documentary, *The Vanishing Family: Crisis in Black America*, was shown on U.S. evening television that same year, garnering a generally favorable response.[38]

In his report, Moyers focused on single mothers, particularly "teenage mothers," and absent fathers. In detailed interviews, the protagonists described their behavior as the result of conscious decisions, but the subtext of the documentary was that a massive change in mentality, namely a decline in family values, was taking place at the heart of the African American minority: men did not want to be fathers, and teenage mothers chose motherhood without marriage because, after all, they could fall back on welfare.[39]

---

34 NWRO's Guaranteed Adequate Income Plan, 1969, cited in Nadasen, Mittelstadt, Chappell, *Welfare*, 158–162.
35 Zaretsky, *No Direction Home*, 94–95, Chappell, *War on Welfare*, 65–79.
36 Chappell, *War on Welfare*, 214–228.
37 Bill Moyers (b. 1934) is a journalist, television commentator, and former press secretary to President Johnson. He was White House press secretary when the Moynihan Report was released. After a rift with Johnson over the continuation of the Vietnam War, which Moyers opposed, he began working as a journalist for television network PBS from 1971 and then for CBS from 1976.
38 Very positive response from Corry, John, "TV: 'CB Reports' Examines Black Families," January 25, 1986. For a critical take, see gender historian Patricia Hill Collins, who compared the Moynihan Report and the CBS report and argued that both texts "provide fairly straightforward examples of how defenders of white male privilege can use race, gender and class interactively to explain Black economic disadvantage." Hill Collins, Patricia, "A Comparison of Two Works on Black Family Life," *Signs*, vol. 14, 4, *Common Grounds and Crossroads: Race, Ethnicity, and Class in Women's Lives* (Summer 1989), 875–884.
39 The documentary itself can be viewed in its entirety on YouTube, for example, at <www.youtube.com/watch?v=k9BKXQ8ROlw>. Journalist Bill Moyers, who wrote, filmed, and commented on the documentary, provides a clip and the transcript on his homepage: <billmoyers.com/content/the-vanishing-family-crisis-in-black-america>.

> It's been a startling change in values. Twenty-five years ago you would not have heard such things said so freely, because they were not embraced so widely [the interviewed single mothers' statements that they did not need fathers for their children, and the men's statements that they spurned contraception and that women were responsible for whether they had children or not]. The strong family was still the backbone of black America, and three out of four children had both parents at home. That is true no longer, and most black children are now growing up without their fathers.[40]

But Moyers did not stop at lamenting the changing family values of the African American community. At the very end of the documentary, Ed Pitt, who was responsible in 1986 among other things for the National Urban League's "adolescent male responsibilities program", and Byllye Avery, director of the National Black Women's Health Program in Atlanta and single mother of two children, discussed the change in values in society as a whole with respect to the family.[41] Both agreed that "poor people" in particular were viewed as unacceptable in this context, because society demanded higher moral standards from them, while, as Ed Pitt explained, "the rest of society is experimenting with all kinds of family forms." Pitt put it in a nutshell:

> The fact of the matter is, the family—the concept of family, the definition of family is in a state of change in this society. And the only people who are being held to a rigid formula for what a family is are poor people who are receiving welfare.[42]

This statement is significant, as it clearly reveals the social and ethnic "double standard" of U.S. society, which assumed that only those who embodied society's (ideal) values were deserving of support. Those who were poor and neither fulfilled nor aspired to the ideal of the nuclear family—that is, supposedly, African American teenage mothers—provoked moral condemnation (and, over the long term, drastic cuts in welfare benefits). White and middle-class families, by contrast, were not viewed with the same moral rigor. To have clearly brought out this core contradiction in the U.S. debate over welfare is one of the documentary's signal achievements.

---

40 <billmoyers.com/content/the-vanishing-family-crisis-in-black-america>.
41 Byllye Y. Avery (b. 1937) is a noted African American civil rights activist and co-founder of the women's health movement. Among other things, she advocated for abortion rights before *Roe v. Wade*, served on the board of the National Women's Health Network, and founded the Gainesville Women's Health Center abortion clinic in 1974 as well as the Birthplace birth center in 1978. In 1983, she chaired the first nationwide conference on black women's health issues and co-founded the Black Women's Health Project in Atlanta, Georgia. See Loretta Ross's 2005 interview with Byllye Avery as part of the Voices of Feminism Oral History Project in the Sophia B. Smith Collection, Smith College, Northampton, MA. <www.smith.edu/library/libs/ssc/vof/transcripts/Avery.pdf>.
42 <www.billmoyers.com/content/the-vanishing-family-crisis-in-black-america>.

In addition, some of the "welfare mothers" at issue and scholars such as gender historian Patricia Hill Collins put forward searing critiques of the broadcast. Welfare rights activist Barbara Omolade objected to Moyers' problematization of families headed by single mothers. She described functioning networks of women with reference to the Sisterhood of Black Single Mothers self-help organization in Brooklyn, as well as the functionality of "extended family networks" and neighborhood support. Above all, however, she warned against a new patriarchal understanding of the family as the basis for social policy measures: promoting the male breadwinner, for example through job programs, should not be at the expense of women. Moreover, no new patriarchal structures of oppression should be established. "Appeals to black men to find their manhood in employment so as to reassert their dominance over black women can only increase the number of Black single mothers." Her vision, in contrast, was for the coexistence of the sexes on the basis of equality:

> In a society where men are taught to dominate and women to follow, we all have a lot to overcome in learning to build relationships, with each other and with our children, based on love and justice. For many Black single mothers, this is what the struggle is about.[43]

Another initiative intended to empower poor African American families emerged in the greater Atlanta area, the "Family Adoption Project": in 1985, an initially private association made up of a "group of concerned Atlantans" was founded, one "united in response to a crisis in the black community [. . .] the disintegration of the Black family." The members' primary concern was to strengthen problem families in the Atlanta area through activities at the community level: "They felt the community, as a whole, was at risk, and if this were true . . . what did it mean for the future quality of life in our community?"[44] This gave rise to the "Black Family Project, Inc.", based at Atlanta University's School of Social Work. The latter project was in turn a source of inspiration for the Atlanta-based Southern Christian Leadership Conference (SCLC), which, as part of its "Wings of Hope" anti-drug scheme (1989–1995), launched the "Family Adoption Program" in 1990 to promote solidarity between families.[45]

---

[43] Omolade, Barbara, "It's a Family Affair: The Real Lives of Black Single Mothers" (1986), in Nadasen, Mittelstadt, and Chappell, *Welfare*, 201–207.
[44] *Black Family Project* pamphlet, undated. MARBL, Woodruff Library, Emory University, MS 1083 Box 586, Folder 7.
[45] Letter from Executive Director of the Black Family Project, Amelia Tucker-Shaw, M.A. and Rev. Richard C. Dalton, SCLC Drug Prevention Program Coordinator, Atlanta, Georgia, May 9, 1989, MARBL, Woodruff Library, Emory University, MS 1083 Box 586, Folder 7.

To the main initiator of this project within the SCLC and leader of the "Wings of Hope" campaign, Reverend Richard C. Dalton, it was obvious that solutions to the problems of the African American family would in part have to come from the African American community itself. Among other things, he wished to see a black "think tank to craft solutions to [the] Black family and [the] Black community." He identified the failed attempts at "social engineering" and economic governance by the white majority society as one of the key causes of the difficulties facing black people: "Social/economic engineering has placed black family, black community in self destruct mode."[46]

What is interesting about the SCLC's Family Adoption Program is that it consciously acknowledged the diverse structures of African American families, all of which were regarded as valuable, livable and deserving of support. Families or groups within church congregations were to "adopt" individual "high risk families" in Atlanta's deprived areas and support them in their development:

> Many families, we believe, need an extra boost to make it in our complex and socially ill society. Many urban families have the same dreams and aspirations as suburban families. Hover, urban high risk families lack the economic wherewithal to obtain those dreams. In a number of cases, many have fallen into the poverty trap and the welfare syndrome and seem "stuck" unable to rise to a level of independence and self-sufficiency.[47]

The program explicitly refrained from privileging a specific family structure among the participants, instead embracing diversity. The only prerequisite for acceptance into the program was the desire for advancement: this meant eschewing drugs, a commitment to education for children, gainful employment and "maintaining a functional family life":

> The shape, make-up and composition of the participating high risk families will be diverse: some of the families will be single parent families, some two parent households, while others may be families with a recovering member (parent or child). In all cases, these families are struggling to provide the necessary sustenance to "make it." Making it suggests overcoming the impact of drugs, helping their children obtain a quality education and go on to college, securing meaningful employment, and maintaining a functional family life.

The program included close supervision by the SCLC of the individuals and families who "adopted" problem families. Among other things, "adopters" were meant

---

[46] MARBL, Woodruff Library, Emory University, MS 1083 Box 586, Folder 8: "The Black Family and the Drug Culture Outline," undated. The report was forwarded with a request to give a talk on November 8, 1993, by Richard C. Dalton to Lee P. Brown of the Office of National Drug Control Policy.
[47] MARBL, Woodruff Library, Emory University, MS 1083 Box 587, Folder 13: "Family Adoption Program," undated (1990).

to support the families through conversation, hands-on involvement, outings, as well as through prayer and by providing living role models. At the same time, highly practical "action plans" were developed to help support single mothers and young people.⁴⁸ Congregations and congregation members willing to adopt received carefully crafted "Family Adoption Training," which even concluded with exams.⁴⁹ Lists of "adoptive families" and the assigned congregations are contained in the files of the SCLC, in addition to a number of testimonials by "mentors," which were circulated along with the training materials. The engagement of the "mentors" extended, among other things, to help with job and housing searches, visits to authorities, healthcare, and so on.⁵⁰ Yet new "paternalistic" relationships between "adopted" family and "mentors" are also evident. For example, Richard C. Dalton, the program manager for the SCLC, told of how he resolutely made the "right" decisions for "his" family. The head of "his" family, a single mother of three children, had been raped by a relative:

> About two weeks later I received a call from Ms. Lawson [the tenants' representative at the Herndon Homes public housing complex, Atlanta, where the "adoptive family" lived]. She said the mother of our family had been raped by her first cousin. I made an immediate investigation. I talked to Mrs. Pintrup, the manager of Herndon Homes, to get more details. I also contacted the Grady Rape Crisis Center to get her an appointment. Then I called the mother and asked her what has happened, she told me she would be open to getting counseling from the Rape Crisis Center at Grady Hospital.⁵¹

Regardless of all the positive commitment to problem families, the familiar asymmetry shines through in this quotation. Dalton (or the member of the SCLC who wrote the report, which is not signed) first talks to the tenant representative of the housing complex, then to the manager, then to the Rape Crisis Center—before even speaking to the mother of the "adoptive family." He then takes her to counseling. Brushing aside her less than positive experiences with it, "I told her it takes time to develop trust with people, but if she gave herself and the counselor

---

48 "Family Adoption Discussion Outline, Instructors Guide." MARBL, Woodruff Library, Emory University, MS 1083 Box 587, Folder 13: "Family Adoption Program," undated (1990).
49 See the "Family Adoption Training Schedule April–July" (1990), MARBL, Woodruff Library, Emory University, MS 1083 Box 587, Folder 13: "Family Adoption Program," undated (1990).
50 Letter of thanks from Laura Lawson, President of Herndon Homes, Atlanta, one of the social housing complexes referred to in SCLC's "Family Adoption Program," September 20, 1990. MARBL, Woodruff Library, Emory University, MS 1083 Box 587, Folder 13: "Family Adoption Program," undated (1990).
51 "Wings of Hope Adopted Family," "SCLC Adopted Family," Rev. Richard C. Dalton, MARBL, Woodruff Library, Emory University, MS 1083 Box 587, Folder 13: "Family Adoption Program," undated (1990).

more time things would get better."⁵² We have come full circle with respect to the "social engineering" of the white majority society, which Dalton had previously criticized so vehemently—here, too, we can discern paternalistic intervention in the affairs of a "welfare mother," albeit with the best of intentions.

Given the discrepancy between the social-historical data and the public debate on the state of the family in the 1980s, a number of questions arise. First, if neither abortion numbers nor divorce rates increased significantly, where did the notion of the end of the family and a general decline in values, which Reagan sought to oppose with his rhetoric of "traditional family values," come from? Second, if the AFDC figures did not increase as dramatically as claimed, and the numbers of African American women on welfare actually decreased in the 1980s, what was the source of the concerns about black welfare queens? Third, many of those affected by no means passively insisted on their right to welfare benefits, with the welfare rights movement and individual civil rights organizations such as the SCLC discussing a wide variety of proposals for tailored support and assistance for African American families and single mothers. What, then, was the reason for the outrage over "welfare fraud" as a supposedly national blight? To answer these questions, we first have to examine the negotiation of family values and gender norms, as coupled with concepts of "race" and "class," in the 1980s. The failure of the liberal Carter Conference, which is the main subject of this chapter, helps provide an explanation, as do Reagan's family rhetoric and the fierce conflicts over abortion and adoption.

6.2 Jimmy Carter's White House Conference on families and the U.S. family in the early 1980s

Anthropologist Margaret Mead, long considered a national authority on the family because of her research and public presence, had been invited to a presidential family conference once before. At the 1948 National Conference on Family Life held under President Harry S. Truman, she had moderated the closing panel.⁵³ It is inter-

---

52 "Wings of Hope Adopted Family," "SCLC Adopted Family," Rev. Richard C. Dalton, MARBL, Woodruff Library, Emory University, MS 1083 Box 587, Folder 13: "Family Adoption Program," undated (1990).
53 Mead moderated the panel "Our Role in Strengthening Family Life," apparently with great success. "Highlights of the National Conference on Family Life" pamphlet, May 1948, 4. Letter from the Program Coordinator of the National Conference on Family Life, Ernest G. Osborne, to Mead, April 5, 1948, asking her to moderate the final panel. Letter of thanks from Osborne to Mead, June 9, 1948. Margaret Mead Papers, LOC, Box E 92, Folder 3.

esting to note that this first family conference, which was not explicitly billed as a White House Conference but was held with presidential support, ran its course without any public controversy.[54] Similar to the Carter Conference, its objective was "to discover specific means by which the American family may be strengthened for the benefit of its individual members and society," though in the context of "modern postwar society."[55] The Woman's Foundation[56] and the National Planning Association[57] had been laying the ground for the conference at the behest of the American Home Economics Association since 1946. It was held in Washington, D.C., from May 6 to 8, 1948, with about 1,000 people attending. While the role of the American housewife, wife, and mother was a major focus—among other things, the conference advocated better opportunities for part-time work—and the role of fathers in their families was also to be strengthened ("to rehabilitate the father as an actively functioning family member") the problems of non-white families received at best only marginal attention.[58] Reproductive control, contraception and abortion, on the other hand, were not yet considered explicitly; instead, there was a far more general discussion of "family counseling" and "education for marriage." Only in the debate on "the use of contraceptive advice in marriage counseling" did the first signs of conflict emerge.[59] The Statement of Purpose makes it clear that the main goal was to define clear objectives for the development of postwar families, to gain and disseminate expert knowledge, and to consider how best to use resources. Specifically, the conference addressed the following issues:

1. The importance of successful family living in the practice of democracy.
2. The environment and daily activities (American housing, nutrition, child-care etc.) and stability of the families.
3. Defining desirable objectives towards which the family may move [. . .].
4. Surveying and planning kinds of community resources that strengthen families [. . .].

---

54 See the notes on the conference in the Margaret Mead Papers, LOC, Box E 92, Folders 2 to 4.
55 "Highlights of the National Conference on Family Life" pamphlet, May 1948, Margaret Mead Papers, LOC, Box E 92, Folder 3.
56 A philanthropic organization still active today that promotes women's rights worldwide <www.womensfoundation.org>.
57 Founded in 1934 as an independent planning organization in the fields of agriculture, business, and labor in Washington D.C.
58 "Highlights of the National Conference on Family Life" pamphlet, May 1948, Margaret Mead Papers, LOC, Box E 92, Folder 3.
59 "Highlights of the National Conference on Family Life" pamphlet, May 1948, Margaret Mead Papers, LOC, Box E 92, Folder 3, 6–7, 11–13. See also *The American Family. A Factual Background. Report of Inter-Agency Committee on Background Materials. National Conference on Family Life, May 1948* (Westport 1949).

5. The use of the resources of education for the development of satisfactory family life for persons of all ages.
6. The training of professional workers in the fields of marriage and family life education, research, counseling, and related services.[60]

This clear emphasis on mobilizing and disseminating expert knowledge to improve the family clearly distinguished the 1948 conference from that of 1980. The summary of the 1948 conference results stated:

> But even more universal was the feeling that individuals, organizations, and communities should encourage in every field the basic research which is necessary to increase our knowledge, equipment, and skills for dealing with problems of family living in modern complex society.[61]

Almost thirty years later, during the 1976 presidential election, Democratic candidate Jimmy Carter announced that he would hold a new conference on ways to strengthen the U.S. family if he were elected.[62] The background this time was not the difficulties of the family during the Cold War, but the notion of a "family crisis" spread by conservative academics and publicists, as well as the effects of the recession on families in general.[63] Carter was also keen to occupy the family issue from a liberal perspective and challenge the emerging discursive hegemony of the religious right, anti-abortion activists, and conservative grassroots organizations.

Particularly on the issue of abortion, Carter tried to demonstrate his liberal credentials, while at the same time taking the values of abortion opponents seriously. During the election campaign, he thus declared that he believed abortion was fundamentally wrong, but he insisted that it must be an option:

> I believe that abortion is the doctor's treatment for failed birth control, and that in the long run the need for abortion services can be minimized by providing better family planning services. This means stronger family planning programs, more accessible services, and improved contraceptive technology.[64]

---

60 "Statement of Purpose," National Conference on Family Life, May 5–8, 1948. "Program National Conference on Family Life," May 5–8, 1948. Margaret Mead Papers, LOC, Box E 92, Folder 3.
61 "Highlights of the National Conference on Family Life" pamphlet, May 1948, Margaret Mead Papers, LOC, Box E 92, Folder 3, 15.
62 "Remarks by Jimmy Carter on the American Family, Manchester, New Hampshire," August 3, 1976. Carter Presidential Library. Records of the White House Press Office, Annette Samuels' Subject Files. Box 3.
63 Lasch, *Haven in a Heartless World*. For an analysis, see Zaretsky, *No Direction Home*, 183–221.
64 "The Presidential Campaign 1976," Volume One, Part One, Carter Presidential Library, Records of the Speechwriter's Office, Achsah Nesmith Files, Box 7, 97, 107.

Carter's official announcement on January 30, 1978, that he would hold a White House Conference on Families not only drew criticism in the media but also sparked internal opposition. A presidential staffer, Steve Hersh, approached the First Lady's aide, urging her to persuade the latter to talk Carter out of the venture:

> With the President's decision to run for a second term [. . .] the last thing he needs is to publicly float another banner issue that has the characteristics of a Family Conference. It will provide a very convenient "sink" into which all political opposition [. . .] can pour all the kinds of distortions, stimulating fears, misinterpretations, exaggerated misinterpretations about his intentions, his plans for interfering with committees on that "sacred-of-sacreds" the mythical American family.[65]

Carter had his way, however, and after some delays a team led by Catholic politician John Carr as executive director and Congressman James (Jim) Guy Tucker as conference chairman was appointed in 1979.[66] Carter signaled both internally and externally that his entire government apparatus was behind the project:

> A major goal of the White House Conference on Families, which I called for in my campaign for the Presidency, is to identify public policies which strengthen and support families as well as those which harm or neglect family life, and to recommend appropriate changes. To achieve this goal, the Conference must have the support and assistance of every Department and Agency within the government.[67]

The preparation for the conference can fairly be described as a "national effort." Carter's advisors decided to hold a total of three decentralized conferences in different parts of the U.S.—instead of one major event in Washington DC. The conference in Baltimore in June 1980 was followed by one in Minneapolis and another in Los Angeles. Over 200 meetings were scheduled at state level in preparation, and the National Advisory Committee under Tucker alone included no less than 40 people.[68] The total of 1179 delegates featured a disproportionate number

---

65 Memo from Steve P. Hersh to Kathy Cade, December 21, 1978. Carter Presidential Library, Records of the First Lady's Office, Kathy Cade's Project Office Subject Files, Box 18, 26.
66 Memo for Kathy Cade from Ellen Goldstein, subject: White House Conference on Families, October 25, 1979: "John and Jim Tucker, the Conference National Chairperson, have virtually saved this Conference for us and it now looks like it will be a very valuable, successful venture. [. . .] The Conference needs, and deserves, our support and interest." Carter Presidential Library, Records of the Domestic Policy Staff, Ellen Goldstein's Subject Files, Box 13.
67 The White House, October 15, 1979, signed Carter, Memorandum for the Heads of Executive Departments and Agencies. Carter Presidential Library, Records of the Council of Economic Advisors, Charles L. Schultze's Meeting Files, Box 143.
68 White House Conference on Families, National Advisory Committee [undated, 1979], Carter Presidential Library, Office of the Special Assistant for Ethnic Affairs, Stephen Aiello's Subject Files, Box 4.

of women (64 percent), members of ethnic minorities were also strongly represented (24.8 percent), while other categories included "Single Parent" and "Low Income."[69] Seven hearings were held to identify topics for the three regional conferences, and a preliminary agenda was established: out in front were "Sensitivity of the Government" and "Economic Pressures," followed by "Support for Specific Family Structures" and "Child Care." The item "Abortion," on the other hand, was in the middle of the range of topics selected at the hearings.[70]

The fact that the issues of work, unemployment, and welfare, in particular, were perceived as burdens on the family reflected the general economic situation. Ellen Goldstein, a member of Carter's Domestic Policy Staff involved in preparing for the conference, thus noted in March 1980, "Biggest Issues: The workplace becoming the most popular issue, not abortion, tax, child care, foster care, domestic violence, elderly care."[71] Anne Wexler, special assistant to the president, in her speech opening the second regional conference in Minneapolis, Minnesota in mid-June 1980, referred to the government's accomplishments in fortifying the economic foundations of American families:

> We have tried to cushion the sharp blows of unemployment, inflation and poverty, which tear at the fabric of family life. The efforts of this administration have produced 8 Million new jobs—We have sought to reform our nation's ineffective, inefficient welfare programs—Programs that for too long have been anti-work, anti-family.[72]

Meanwhile, Patricia Robert Harris, secretary of health and human services, went a step further in her speech inaugurating the third conference in Los Angeles, CA, on July 10, 1980. She came out strongly in favor of welfare programs to strengthen poor families, defending in particular the widely criticized Aid to Families with Dependent Children (AFDC) program:

> If we are sincere about wanting to strengthen family life, the time has come to demonstrate that sincerity by restoring respect to the programs designed to help families. The example

---

[69] Infosheet John Carr, undated: Briefing on White House Conference on Families. Carter Presidential Library, Records of the White House Press Office, Bradley Woodward's Subject Files, Box 6.
[70] White House Conference on Families, Jim Guy Tucker, Chairperson/John L. Carr, Executive Director, to the National Advisory Committee, Conference Format, April 3, 1980. Carter Presidential Library, Records of the Office of the Assistant to the President for Women's Affairs (Sarah Weddington), Bill Albers Files, Box 58.
[71] Ellen Goldstein's notes on a Meeting with John Carr, March 10, 1980. Carter Presidential Library, Records of the Domestic Policy Staff, Ellen Goldstein's Subject Files, Box 13.
[72] Opening Speech of Anne Wexler, Minneapolis MN, White House Conference on Families, June 19, 1980, Carter Presidential Library, Records of Anne Wexler as Special Assistant to the President, Michael Channin's Subject Files, Box 182.

of the Aid to Families with Dependent Children program makes the point as clearly as any I know. It is the major welfare program in the United States, designed to support children whose families lack the resources to support those children by their own efforts.

I can think of no more maligned program in the United States. We have developed a myth in this country which pictures so-called welfare mothers—welfare queens—driving around in Cadillacs, choosing to increase the size of their families in order to increase the size of their benefit checks. The myth is vicious, often racist, and blatantly false.[73]

After the programmatic opening speeches and days of intense debate, numerous resolutions were adopted at the conferences. Here it emerged, first, that delegates were concerned not only about economic security (jobs, social security) but also about education and childcare for working mothers. As Goldstein had surmised, balancing the demands of family and work was a core topic of discussion at all three conferences. Second, meanwhile, in the deliberations on the status of the housewife and on counterbalancing the consequences of liberalized divorce laws (that is, economic disadvantages mostly for the woman), it emerged that conservative groups in particular had major reservations about the gradual liberalization of the prevailing concept of the family. Third, the discussion on reproduction and abortion, which was dealt with in the context of healthcare, had a similarly polarizing effect. In Baltimore, for example, the delegates passed no less than three resolutions in favor of abortion as an expression of individual freedom of choice over one's own reproduction, while in Los Angeles a resolution was at least passed in favor of legal abortion.[74] In Minneapolis, the topic was never on the agenda. Most interesting of all, however, are the minority reports, which distanced themselves from the positive resolutions.

Here, in the case of abortion, it was mainly conservative women's associations that articulated their views, referring to the fetus's right to life while stylizing themselves as grassroots organizations, but civil rights organizations made up of African Americans and Mexican Americans also made their voices heard through calls for the safeguarding of their reproductive rights.[75] In general, however, the level of approval for the abortion resolutions was fairly high and out of

---

73 Carter Presidential Library, Records of the Domestic Policy Staff, Ellen Goldstein's Subject Files, Box 14.
74 White House Conference on Families, Los Angeles, CA, Recommendations, Abortion and Family Planning in Recommendation No. 38, which was adopted by a vote of 308 in favor to 192 against. Carter Presidential Library, Records of the Domestic Policy Staff, Ellen Goldstein's Subject Files, Box 14, Folder 5.
75 See the minority reports on the three conferences in Ellen Goldstein's files, especially the "Pro Family Position Paper: Grass Roots Report" and the "Hispanic Caucus Report" as Minority Reports 31 and 33 on the Los Angeles conference. Carter Presidential Library, Records of the Domestic Policy Staff, Ellen Goldstein's Subject Files, Box 14, Folder 4.

all proportion to the confrontations they triggered. Carter himself largely refrained from commenting on the results of the conferences and the votes held there. He had personally opened the first conference in Baltimore on June 5, 1980, after some initial hesitation[76] and he spoke again when the final reports of all three conferences were published on October 22, 1980.[77] The organizers of the event, Carr and Tucker, however, worried about the conferences' political impact, especially the evident lack of political benefit to Carter's presidential campaign:

> This concern for families is a new emphasis, a contribution of this Administration, and an area where the President's commitment and courage are obvious. His vision in calling the Conference and his full support during its implementation, has made a real beginning which will outlast his term of office, as will the broad consensus which developed on a number of Conference issues. No other President, despite all the rhetoric, has done more for families or gone directly to families to determine their needs.[78]

It is only at second glance that it becomes clear why Carter's commitment to the American family did not translate into political capital. The White House Conference on Families failed not despite but precisely because of its grassroots approach. Carter consciously eschewed the idea of prescribing a uniform definition of the family or of desirable political interventions. Instead, he let the delegates decide for themselves—with the result that the debates furnished the religious right and conservative organizations such as Phyllis Schlafly's Eagle Forum with a forum to communicate their views to a national public.[79]

Finally, if we compare the two national family conferences of 1948 and 1980, it is clear that the architects of the Carter Conference, like their predecessors,

---

[76] Memo from Stuart Eizenstat to Mrs. Carter, May 31, 1980, and to the President, May 31, 1980, urging him to attend the first of the three regional conferences and give the opening address. Carter's speech in Baltimore, June 5, 1980. Carter Presidential Library, Records of the Domestic Policy Staff, Ellen Goldstein's Subject Files, Box 14. Office of the White House Press Secretary, Baltimore, MD, June 5, 1980. Remarks of the President to the White House Conference on Families, Baltimore Convention Center, June 5, 1980. Carter Presidential Library, Records of the Speechwriter's Office, Achsah Nesmith Files, Box 70.

[77] Office of the White House Press Secretary, October 22, 1980, Statement of the President upon Reception of the Conference Report, Carter Presidential Library, Office of the Special Assistant for Ethnic Affairs, Stephen Aiello's Subject Files, Box 4. See also list of delegates May 22, 1978, Carter Presidential Library, Records of Anne Wexler as Special Assistant to the President, 1977–81, Jane D. Wales' Subject Files, Box 209.

[78] Jim Guy Tucker and John L. Carr, Memo to Stuart Eizenstat, November 19, 1980. Carter Presidential Library, Records of the Domestic Policy Staff, Ellen Goldstein's Subject Files, Box 14.

[79] Carter Presidential Library, Records of the First Lady's Office, Kathy Cade's Project Office Subject Files, Box 18.

were trying to come up with appropriate responses to the complexity of life in a modern society. But now the emphasis was more on the changes in family and gender roles—so that research and expert advice, while not superfluous, had to be reconciled with the needs and expectations of those concerned through a permanent process of negotiation: "American society is dynamic, constantly changing. The roles and structure of families and individual family members are growing, adapting and evolving in new and different ways."[80] This principle was honorable, but it was not the best way to win elections.

6.3 Ronald Reagan's "traditional family values" campaign and its place in the "culture wars"

The election of Ronald Reagan as the fortieth president of the United States in November 1980 is generally regarded as a major turning point in the country's social history and as the beginning of a reorientation of conservatism, one that found expression chiefly in the field of the family and its norms and values.[81] Political science and historiography in particular have long characterized Reagan's presidency as a "conservative revolution," in the course of which the president scaled back state intervention and emphasized citizens' individual freedoms, with disastrous consequences for the welfare state, which was poorly developed in the first place. The core of the "Reagan Revolution" was typically seen as economic consolidation and the reestablishment of the U.S. self-image as a leading nation in the world—in large part through Reagan's morally charged rhetoric.[82] However, in recent years historians have increasing argued that, rather than simply accepting that the 1980s were a conservative decade, we need to delve deeper into social debates and processes of negotiation.[83] Here, they point to the long-

---

80 Pamphlet titled "White House Conference on Families, Families: Foundation of Society," undated, Carter Presidential Library, Records of the Domestic Policy Staff, Ellen Goldstein's Subject Files, Box 13.
81 On the wide range of literature, see Faludi, Susan, *Backlash. The Undeclared War Against American Women* (New York 1991). Stacey, *In the Name of the Family*. Hale, Grace E., *A Nation of Outsiders. How the White Middle Class Fell in Love with Rebellion in Postwar America* (Oxford and New York 2011).
82 Tygiel, Jules, *Ronald Reagan and the Triumph of American Conservatism* (New York 2006). Hayward, Steven F., *The Age of Reagan. The Conservative Counterrevolution 1980–1988* (New York 2009). Troy, Gil, *The Reagan Revolution. A Very Short Introduction* (Oxford and New York 2009).
83 Andre Dechert, for example, makes this the starting point for his analysis of the debates surrounding portrayals of fatherhood in family-centered series of the 1980s and early 1990s. Dechert, *Dad on TV*, 6. Similar arguments were already made by Troy, Gil, *Morning in America. How*

term processes of social liberalization and pluralization that ran in parallel to Reagan's conservative policies. Four fields illustrate this ambivalence very well. First, despite his anti-abortion rhetoric, Reagan left the controversial *Roe v. Wade* ruling untouched, so that first-trimester abortions remained legal.[84] Second, while the president defended the heterosexual nuclear family as the foundation of the nation, he could not prevent the trend toward divorce, out-of-wedlock births, and alternative family forms, nor the growth in the number of families headed by gay couples or individuals. Third, while he geared his social and economic policies toward the "male breadwinner," this did not curb women's employment or the rise of the "dual earner family."[85] Fourth, attempts at cultural restoration through the extolling of an idealized past failed due to the diversification and pluralization of media topics, discourses, and forms of presentation. Andre Dechert's dissertation has shown impressively that in the 1980s and early 1990s, representations of family and fatherhood in popular family sitcoms underwent a process of pluralization by integrating minorities and including both single mothers and gays. Within this media context, these groups were in turn required to conform as much as possible to the ideal of the nuclear family.[86]

The task of the following section is thus to compare Ronald Reagan's family *rhetoric* with his administration's family *policy* and to probe to what extent changes occurred in the underlying family ideal or the family ideal exalted by conservative actors.

What exactly did the president mean by the "traditional family values" he so often invoked? In sum, Reagan was keen to strengthen the "traditional" family with its clearly structured gender roles, to promote adoption rather than abortion, and to revive "Christian" values in childrearing and schooling.[87] At the same time, however, he carefully avoided presenting himself as a religious fundamen-

---

Reagan Invented the 1980s (New York 2005). Collins, Robert M., *Transforming America. Politics and Culture in the Reagan Years* (New York 2007). Martin, Bradford, *The Other Eighties. A Secret History of America in the Age of Reagan* (New York 2011).
84 Even today, the issue of abortion is of central importance in public discourse, especially after the crucial *Dobbs v. Jackson Women's Health Center* decision by the Supreme Court (2022), which ended legal abortion on a national level and thus brought five decades of conservative lobbying against *Roe* to a close.
85 Chappell, Marisa, *War on Welfare*, 200–201.
86 Dechert, *Dad on TV*, 205–206.
87 See Reagan's statements in his radio addresses: Reagan, Ronald, "Radio Address to the Nation on the American Family," June 16, 1984. Reagan, Ronald, "Radio Address to the Nation on Family Values," December 20, 1986. In *Ronald Reagan. Public Papers of the Presidents of the United States. 1984*, vol. 1 (Washington D.C. 1986), 860–861. 1986, vol. 2 (Washington D.C. 1989), 1637–1638.

Fig. 6.2: The Reagan family, Christmas 1983.

talist, though he repeatedly sought proximity with evangelical Christians and religiously conservative organizations.[88]

As early as the 1980 presidential campaign, Reagan had identified the strengthening of "values and the virtues handed down to us by our families" as the way out of the economic and social crisis.[89] The Republican election manifesto reinforced this rhetoric, while branding the Democrats' social programs inadmissible state intervention in the family, indeed a threat to the family:

---

[88] Ehrman, John, *The Eighties. America in the Age of Reagan* (New Haven et al. 2005). 178. See especially his careful positioning on the topic at the Annual Convention of the National Association of Evangelicals in Orlando in 1983. Ronald Reagan, "Remarks at the Annual Convention of the National Association of Evangelicals in Orlando, Florida," March 8, 1983. Online at Gerhard Peters and John T. Woolley, The American Presidency Project <www.presidency.ucsb.edu/ws/?pid=41023>. Manfred Brocker, however, sees this as a purely strategic electoral calculation. Brocker, Manfred, *Protest—Anpassung—Etablierung. Die Christliche Rechte im politischen System der USA* (Frankfurt a. M. etc. 2004), 106–110.

[89] He also described "work and family" as the "center of our lives" and the "foundation of our dignity as a free people." Ronald Reagan, "Address Accepting the Presidential Nomination at the Republican National Convention in Detroit," July 17, 1980. Online at Gerhard Peters and John T. Woolley, The American Presidency Project <www.presidency.ucsb.edu/ws/?pid=25970>.

> The family is the foundation of our social order. It is the school of democracy. [. . .] But the Democrats have shunted the family aside. They have given its power to the bureaucracy, its jurisdiction to the courts, and its resources to government grantors. For the first time in our history, there is real concern that the family may not survive.[90]

In contrast, the Republicans and their candidate emphasized their commitment to the family and the individual as an alternative to state welfare policy:

> We will reemphasize those vital communities like the family, the neighborhood, the workplace, and others which are found at the center of society, between government and the individual. We will restore and strengthen their ability to solve problems in the places where people spend their daily lives and can turn to each other for support and help.

After taking office, Reagan stepped up his family values rhetoric. In a radio address on January 22, 1983, the tenth anniversary of the *Roe v. Wade* ruling, for example, he called the family "still the basic unit of religious and moral values that hold our society together."[91] In late 1983, in another radio address, he declared during Advent:

> Families stand at the center of society, so building our future must begin by preserving family values. [. . .] If we strengthen families, we'll help reduce poverty and the whole range of other social problems.[92]

For him, these "other social problems" were self-evidently aggravated, if not caused, by Democratic welfare policies. In addition, he blamed the steadily increasing number of single mothers for the deterioration of their families and the delinquency of their children. Neither the commitment to the family as the central unit of society nor criticism of the supposed excesses of government welfare (nor references to the re-

---

90 "Republican Party Platforms: Republican Party Platform of 1980," July 15, 1980. Online at Gerhard Peters and John T. Woolley, The American Presidency Project <www.presidency.ucsb.edu/ws/?pid=25844>.
91 Ronald Reagan, "Address to the Nation on Domestic Social Issues," January 22, 1983. Online at Gerhard Peters and John T. Woolley, The American Presidency Project <www.presidency.ucsb.edu/ws/index.php?pid=41643>.
92 Ronald Reagan, "Address to the Nation on the American Family," December 3, 1983. Online at Gerhard Peters and John T. Woolley, The American Presidency Project <www.presidency.ucsb.edu/ws/index.php?pid=4082>. The avowal in his address a year later uses very similar words: "Families have always stood at the center of our society, preserving good and worthy traditions from our past, entrusting those traditions to our children, our greatest hope for the future." Ronald Reagan, "Radio Address to the Nation on the American Family," June 16, 1984. <www.presidency.ucsb.edu/ws/index.php?pid=40053>. Again, very similar is the beginning of Reagan's 1984 National Adoption Week speech. Ronald Reagan, "Proclamation 5280—National Adoption Week 1984," November 13, 1984. <www.presidency.ucsb.edu/ws/index.php?pid=39423>. On this, see later in the present chapter.

sponsibility of many women and mothers for this) distinguished him from his Republican predecessors: Nixon had made the same claims.[93] What set the president apart from his forerunners was the fact that he viewed the intergenerational transmission of family values as a potent countermovement to social change. This was new:

> Family life has changed much down through the years. The days when we could expect to live in only one home and hold only one job are probably gone forever. Perhaps we will not go back to the old family ways, but I think we can and should preserve family values—values of faith, honesty, responsibility, tolerance, kindness, and love. And we'll keep on trying to do better, trying to create a better life for those who follow.[94]

In 1986, to establish how the government could support families even more effectively and to provide argumentative backing for his classical image of the family, Reagan set up a commission of experts led by his under secretary of education and adviser Gary L. Bauer,[95] which included some representatives of the religious right.[96] The commission submitted its final report, *The Family: Preserving America's Future*, to the president in December 1986. This text, often referred to as the "Bauer Report," is considered by researchers, along with Ronald Reagan's "Execu-

---

[93] See the lucid analysis of the undermining of the AFDC program by both liberal and conservative critics in the name of the family by Chappell, *War on Welfare*, on Nixon esp. 103–105. See also Zaretsky, *No Direction Home*, 239–241.

[94] Ronald Reagan, "Radio Address to the Nation on the American Family," June 16, 1984. <www.presidency.ucsb.edu/ws/index.php?pid=40053>.

[95] Gary Lee Bauer (b. 1946) became a member of Ronald Reagan's staff of advisors in 1980. He served the Reagan administration in various capacities, including Deputy Undersecretary for Planning and Budget and Undersecretary in the Department of Education, as well as domestic policy advisor. During his time at the Department of Education, Reagan appointed him to head his Special Working Group on the Family. Bauer is believed to have been the principal author of its report, *The Family: Preserving America's Future*. Subsequently, Bauer directed the ultraconservative and Christian Family Research Council (founded in 1981 by James Dobson, recognized as a nonprofit in 1983, and incorporated into Dobson's Focus on the Family in 1988) from 1988 to 1999 and he ran unsuccessfully in the 1999 primaries as a candidate for the Republican presidential nomination. Bauer is a conservative Christian, an avowed opponent of abortion and gay marriage, and a self-proclaimed champion of conservative family values and "traditional marriage." He has published widely, including the Focus on the Family publication *Our Hopes, Our Dreams: A Vision for America* (Washington D.C. 1996). See also Dobson and Bauer, *Children at Risk*. On Bauer, Dobson, Focus on the Family, and the Family Research Council, see Weber, Paul J. and Landis Jones, W. (eds.), *U.S. Religious Interest Groups. Institutional Profiles* (Westport and London 1994), 77–80. Utter, Glenn H. and Storey, John (eds.), *The Religious Right. A Reference Handbook* (Millerton 2007), 78–80, 86–87.

[96] "Members of the Working Group," in US Executive Office of the President, *The Family. Preserving America's Future. A Report to the President from the White House Working Group on the Family* (Washington DC, Domestic Policy Council, December 1986), 51–52. Cf. Self, *All in the Family*, 238–383.

tive Order 12606"⁹⁷ and the "Family Support Act," to be the expression and foundation of the Reagan administration's family policy.⁹⁸ This policy differed greatly from that of his Democratic predecessor. In keeping with Reagan's conviction that too much government intervention was to be avoided at all costs, the three measures advocated strengthening the family by withdrawing the state. The Bauer Report argued chiefly for further tax cuts and defended the reduction of welfare spending on families—while insisting on the "male breadwinner" model and the basic idea of the "family wage."

Allegedly aiming "to preserve and protect the American family," Bauer and the other commission members lamented the family's loss of autonomy in the face of the many forms of government intervention and the decline of the family institution itself, portraying them as a result of the "abrasive experiments of two liberal decades."⁹⁹ The American family, they contended, was endangered by the women's movement, female employment, rising numbers of illegitimate births and abortions, higher numbers of single parents, and by a lax sexual morality. Very much like the Moynihan Report of 1965, the authors first postulated a "pathology affecting many American families" and drew a gloomy picture of 3.6 million children starting school in 1986:

> 14 percent were children of unmarried parents.
>
> 40 percent will live in a broken home before they reach 18.
>
> Between one-quarter and one-third are latchkey children with no one to greet them when they come home from school.¹⁰⁰

In contrast to the Moynihan Report, however, Bauer and the commission were not interested in drafting a policy to assist African American, minority, or problem families. Their goal was to promote the idealized white middle-class nuclear family as the foundation and prerequisite of a neo-liberal market economy: "Strong families make economic progress possible by passing on the values central to a free economy."¹⁰¹ While on this view welfare measures generally ruined the family, tax

---

97 On Executive Order 12606 and the Family Support Act of 1987, see later in this chapter.
98 Wisensale, Steven K., *Family Leave Policy: The Political Economy of Work and Family in America* (New York 2015), 40–44.
99 US Executive Office of the President, *The Family. Preserving America's Future. A Report to the President from the White House Working Group on the Family* (Washington DC, Domestic Policy Council, December 1986), 6. See also Gary L. Bauer to President Ronald Reagan, December 2, 1986, cover letter accompanying report upon its submission. Ibid, no pagination.
100 *The Family*, 2.
101 *The Family*, 9.

breaks (for intact middle-class families) were the prerequisite for the formation and maintenance of strong families. A further core element here was the idea that the individual should serve the community: "It is as simple as this: private choices have public effects. The way our fellow citizens choose to live affects many other lives."[102] This allowed for the drastic curtailment of individual choices (abortion, out-of-wedlock pregnancy, childrearing) for those who needed state assistance, in other words poor families, minority families and single mothers. For the intact nuclear family, however, the report emphasized the primacy of individual rights over government intervention—without explicitly addressing this contradiction: "First and most important, a pro-family policy must recognize that the rights of the family are anterior, and superior, to those of the state."[103]

Although the report identified social programs since Lyndon B. Johnson's "Great Society," coupled with individualism and the sexual revolution, as the root of the crisis of the American family, it also heaped criticism on the Carter administration's "White House Conference on Families" for its "radical redefinition of 'family'": "It reached the peak of confusion when the White House Conference on Families foundered on the fundamental question of what constitutes a family and what makes for good family life."[104]

Reagan responded to the crisis of the family diagnosed by his experts not only by intensifying his family-centered rhetoric but also by issuing an executive order to protect the family.[105] In Executive Order 12606, "The Family," of September 2, 1987, Reagan decreed that any government action that might have an impact on the living conditions of families in the United States should be assessed with reference to a range of criteria. Are families and marriages being strengthened? Is parental authority and autonomy vis-à-vis the government being restricted or enhanced? What image of the family is being conveyed?[106] Local authorities and states were thus to be encouraged to factor the family into all political actions. Here, the presi-

---

102 *The Family*, 2.
103 *The Family*, 4.
104 *The Family*, 1.
105 A telling example (among many) of Reagan's family rhetoric is his year-end 1986 radio address, in which he referred directly to the Bauer Report and the supposed crisis of the family: Ronald Reagan, "Radio Address to the Nation on Family Values," December 20, 1986. <www.presidency.ucsb.edu/ws/index.php?pid=36826>.
106 Executive Order 12606 "The Family". <www.archives.gov/federal-register/codification/executive-order/12606.html>.

dent not only took up a key demand made in the Bauer Report[107] but also took his cue from the Family Protection Act of 1981, which Congress had discussed but not passed.[108] This act had assailed the threat to the American family posed by government intervention and identified as its goal "the strengthening of the American family and the elimination of governmental policies which diminish its strength and prosperity." To this end, access to contraception, abortion, and welfare benefits was to be drastically reduced, while parental rights were to be strengthened. Contemporary critics, especially from the ranks of the women's movement, clearly recognized at the time that the goal was to restore classic gender roles and curtail women's rights under the cloak of the "family values" program and under the banner of a supposed "family protection movement."[109] With his 1987 executive order in the wake of the Bauer Report, Reagan achieved a conservative turnaround in family policy, which in 1981 had been rejected by a majority in both houses of Congress.[110] It is also striking that the 1987 executive order revived a core demand of the Carter Conference for a "family impact statement," albeit within quite different aims in mind. Thus, according to the new regulations, it was not the federal government that had to take care of families, but—if at all—states and municipalities. Furthermore, parental authority was not to be restricted by the government, whose actions were considered potentially harmful to the family.[111]

Finally, the Family Support Act of October 13, 1988, stipulated that two-parent households could also receive AFDC in order to prevent the "disintegration" of poor families. At the same time, this law affirmed that poor mothers and fathers had to assume financial responsibility for their families, mothers through wage labor, fathers through alimony.[112] Although comprehensive regulation of manda-

---

107 "The Family," 4–5, 545–46.
108 The Family Protection Act was introduced in both the Senate and House of Representatives on June 17, 1981, but did not pass. In the House, Republican Albert Smith Jr. filed the bill as H.R. 3955; in the Senate, it was sponsored by Senators Roger Jepsen (Iowa) and Paul Laxalt (Nevada) <www.govtrack.us/congress/bills/97/hr3955>. On this topic, see also Flax, Karen, "Women's Rights and the Proposed Family Protection Act," *University of Miami Law Review* 36, 1 (1981), 141–163 <www.repository.law.miami.ecu/umlr/vol36/iss1/7>.
109 Flax, "Women's Rights," 141–143, 163.
110 Fox, Dennis R., "The Reagan Administration's Policy on Using the Family to Advance Capitalism." Paper Presented at the annual convention of the Law and Society Association (Vail, Colorado 1988) <www.dennisfox.net/papers/reagan-family.html>. For a sophisticated critique of the Bauer Report, see Johnson, Arthur T., "The Family. The Need for Sound Policy, Not Rhetoric and Ideology," *Public Administration Review* 47 (1987) 240–244.
111 Wisensale, *Family Leave Policy*, 41–42.
112 Wisensale, *Family Leave Policy*, 43. Wisensale quotes John Scanzoni as stating that the Family Support Act demonstrated the "use of the family as vehicle for social change," though from a conservative angle. Scanzoni, John, "Balancing the Policy Interests of Children and Adults," in

tory work for welfare recipients was not introduced until 1996, the Family Support Act responded to key reevaluations within the discourse on welfare in the Reagan Era, a "new consensus on welfare" that, however, completely and deliberately disregarded socioeconomic structural conditions. Here, welfare recipients appeared primarily as African American women and the "undeserving poor," the racist and gender stereotypes unmistakable.[113] As early as his campaign for the Republican presidential nomination in 1976, Reagan repeatedly referred to "welfare queens"[114] and invoked the alleged abuse of the AFDC welfare program as evidence of its shortcomings. Moreover, the wage labor of women welfare recipients could be legitimized (in a reversal of the arguments put forward by the women's movement, which advocated equal rights for women in the workforce) by the overall rise in women's employment.[115]

However, the practical effects of this reorientation of family policy under Reagan were less severe for white middle-class families than critics initially feared. Although the Reagan administration did not legislate on childcare or for the right to parental leave, the major reforms of the 1960s and 1970s remained officially in force. Abortion legislation, affirmative action, and no-fault divorce were untouched, while comprehensive welfare reform was not implemented until the Clinton administration.[116] What changed was the tone of the debate, which became increasingly emotional, and the extent to which religious values and beliefs were brought into play when determining the relationship between government and individual, and between personal liberties and the good of the community.[117] Here, the representatives of the new Christian right, especially evangelical Christians, came to the fore.[118] But radical anti-abortion activists from

---

Anderson, Elaine and Hula, Richard (eds.), *The Reconstruction of Family Policy* (Westport CT 1991), 11–22.
113 Nadasen, Mittelstadt, and Chappell, *Welfare*, 68–74.
114 "'Welfare Queen' Becomes Issue in Reagan Campaign," NYT, February 15, 1976, 51, reprinted in Nadasen et al, *Welfare*, 189–191. For a broader analysis of this trope, see Finzsch, Norbert, "Gouvernementalität, der Moynihan-Report und die Welfare Queen im Cadillac," in Martschukat, Jürgen (ed.), *Geschichte schreiben mit Foucault* (Frankfurt a. M. 2002), 257–282.
115 Wisensale, *Family Leave Policy*, 42–44.
116 In the shape of the Personal Responsibility and Work Opportunity Reconciliation Act (PRWORA) of 1996, which made it mandatory for welfare recipients to work even if they were mothers of young children. PRWORA (H.R. 3734), August 22, 1996, reprinted in Nadasen, Mittelstadt, and Chappell, *Welfare*, 214–216.
117 Brocker, *Protest*, 106–110.
118 On the rise of the religious right in the United States from the end of the 1960s, see Riesebrodt, Martin, *Protestantischer Fundamentalismus in den USA. Die religiöse Rechte im Zeitalter derelektronischen Medien* (Evangelische Zentralstelle für Weltanschauungsfragen, Stuttgart 1987). Riesebrodt, *Rückkehr der Religionen*. Wilcox, Clyde, *Onward Christian Soldiers. The Religious*

the ranks of Operation Rescue and other organizations also invoked religious values when defending the right to life of the fetus. In extreme cases, this did not prevent them from violently attacking doctors, nurses, and the clients of abortion clinics.[119]

Throughout Reagan's time in office, there was an intense debate about a return to supposed "traditional family values," especially between the two political camps, but also with massive participation by social movements and various religious groups. Both the liberal and conservative women's movements and the various factions of the religious right played a particularly prominent role here. This conflict demonstrates that while some elements of the conservative family concept were viewed as persuasive by broad swathes of society, even the conservative movements had differing ideas about just what a family ought to be. Although Reagan always focused on the ideal family of the white middle class, it became clear that sections of the working class and African American and Hispanic minorities identified with the Republican "moral values" agenda.[120] One aspect that held wide appeal in this regard was undoubtedly the constant emphasis on the importance of the mother as the "heart of the American family"[121] and the significance of raising children as a national duty, ideas unmissable if we examine the president's Mother's Day speeches. In his 1983 statement marking that occasion, for example, Reagan declared:

Right in American Politics (Boulder 1996). Hornung, Esther, *Bibelpolitik. Das Verhältnis des protestantischen Fundamentalismus zur nationalen Innenpolitik in den USA von 1980 bis 1996. Ein Fallbeispiel* (Frankfurt a.M. 2002). Brocker, *Protest*.

119 On the relationship between religious fundamentalists and the anti-abortion movement, see Blanchard, *Anti-Abortion Movement*. Jefferis, Jennifer L., *Armed for Life. The Army of God and Anti-Abortion Terror in the United States* (Santa Barbara 2011). Hale, Grace E., *A Nation of Outsiders. How the White Middle Class Fell in Love with Rebellion in Postwar America* (Oxford and New York 2011), esp. 227–302. Schoen, *Abortion after Roe*.

120 See, for example, the program of the Raza Unida Party, which in 1979 saw the family not only as the basis of society and the key institution for the transmission of values, but also as fundamentally endangered by the supposed decline of moral values. The Raza Unida Party itself was founded in 1970 by Mexican Americans as an alternative to the two traditional parties and achieved success primarily at the regional and local level in the states of Texas and California. On the family values propagated by the Raza Unida Party, see esp. Roesch, *Macho Men*, 463–444. Gonzales, Richard J., *Raza Rising: Chicanos in North Texas* (Denton 2016). With respect to African Americans, the TV sitcom *The Bill Cosby Show*, about an African American family, which enjoyed tremendous popularity in the 1980s, was interpreted as an expression of conservative family values. See Dechert, *Dad on TV*, 168–201. Inniss, Leslie B. and Feagin, Joe R., "The Cosby Show. The View from the Black Middle Class," *Journal of Black Studies* 25 (1995), 692–711.

121 Ronald Reagan, "Proclamation 4834, Mother's Day," April 13, 1981. John T. Wooley and Gerhard Peters, The American Presidency Project <www.presidency.ucsb.edu/ws/index.php?pid=43687>.

> Motherhood is both a great responsibility and one of the most rewarding and pleasurable experiences life has to offer. [. . .] The quality and scope of their activities, as well as their overriding concern for the well-being of their families and our country, inspires and strengthens us as individuals and as a Nation.[122]

On Mother's Day 1986, meanwhile, the President emphasized the changing role of the mother in modern society, but not without reaffirming her unchanging biological role as "heart of the family."

> The role of mother has changed constantly in our society, but its fundamental meaning abides: love and caring. The modern mother is conquering new worlds. She continues to be the heart of the family and hearth of the home.[123]

In the president's 1987 Mother's Day address, a year after the publication of the Bauer Report, stability, dedication, and morality took center stage as the core virtues of the U.S. mother and her national mission:

> As mothers help give their families a stability rooted in love, steadfastness, devotion, and morality, they strengthen communities and our Nation at the same time.[124]

Yet this tremendous emphasis on the importance of the mother and her parenting and caring role both to her children and to the welfare of the nation also had a serious downside: any decision to have an abortion posed a danger to the nation. As the following section brings out, for the president a woman's "right to decide" about her body was limited by her duty to carry even an unwanted pregnancy to term and then give the child up for adoption. With his emphasis on the "right to life of the fetus" over the "mother's right to decide," Reagan consciously opposed the women's movement and the Supreme Court decision of 1973.

6.4 Abortion and adoption as two poles of reproductive decision-making in the 1980s

> I, too, have always believed that God's greatest gift is human life and that we have a duty to protect the life of an unborn child. Until someone can prove the unborn child is not a life, shouldn't we give it the benefit of the doubt and assume it is? That's why I favored legisla-

---

[122] Ronald Reagan, "Proclamation 5042, Mother's Day," April 6, 1983. John T. Wooley and Gerhard Peters, The American Presidency Project <www.presidency.ucsb.edu/ws/?pid=41149>.
[123] Ronald Reagan, "Proclamation 5466, Mother's Day," April 22, 1983. John T. Wooley and Gerhard Peters, The American Presidency Project <www.presidency.ucsb.edu/ws/?pid=37164>.
[124] Ronald Reagan, "Proclamation 5641, Mother's Day," April 28, 1987. John T. Wooley and Gerhard Peters, The American Presidency Project <www.presidency.ucsb.edu/ws/?pid=34188>.

tion to end the practice of abortion on demand and why I will continue to support it in the new Congress.[125]

As this excerpt from his 1983 "Address to the Nation on Domestic Issues," delivered on the tenth anniversary of the Supreme Court's legalization of abortion, attests, Reagan staged himself during his two terms as U.S. president as a staunch anti-abortionist who championed the unborn's right to life.

Reagan had already developed his anti-abortion position during his time as governor of California. Although he signed the Therapeutic Abortion Act at the beginning of his term in 1967, which allowed legal abortions to protect the health of the mother, he later qualified this decision, for example in a radio address of April 1975, in which he explained to listeners how he had formed his opinion at the time:[126]

> My answer to what kind of abortion bill I could sign was one that recognized an abortion is the taking of a human life. [. . .] Therefore an abortion is justified when it is done in self-defense. My belief is that a woman has the right to protect her own life and health even against her own unborn child. [. . .] I can find no evidence whatsoever that a fetus is not a living human being with human rights.[127]

This section analyzes how Reagan, as president, tried to pursue his anti-abortion agenda and how the women's movement and anti-abortion activists reacted to it. Here, the files of "pro-choice" organizations such as NARAL, Mass Choice, and NOW come into play, as they not only provide information about the political campaigns and initiatives of organized women, but also contain numerous voices of women who defended and justified their decision to have an abortion. Also significant here are the Concerned United Birthparents (CUB), an organization of "birthmothers and -fathers" founded in 1976 in the context of the women's and self-help movements: drawing on their own experience, they assailed the notion of "adoption" as a straightforward alternative to "abortion."[128]

---

125 Ronald Reagan, "Address to the Nation on Domestic Social Issues," January 22, 1983. Online at Gerhard Peters and John T. Woolley, The American Presidency Project <www.presidency.ucsb.edu/ws/index.php?pid=41643>.
126 Between 1975 and 1979, Reagan delivered a total of more than 1,000 radio addresses, which he wrote himself and had distributed to radio stations via the media company O'Connor Creative Services. Originally intended to promote his nomination as Republican candidate for the 1976 presidential election, he subsequently continued to use this tool. The texts can be found in the Reagan Presidential Library, published in Skinner, Kiron K. et al. (eds.), *Reagan, In His Own Hand. The Writings of Ronald Reagan that Reveal His Revolutionary Vision for America* (New York et al. 2001).
127 Ronald Reagan, "Abortion Laws," April 1975, in Skinner, *Reagan, In His Own Hand*, 380–385.
128 For reasons of data protection, the names of letter writers who did not hold official positions in CUB or NARAL are abbreviated in what follows.

When Ronald Reagan was nominated as the Republican presidential candidate in 1980, the party platform already clearly bore his signature, as a passage on the question of the legality of abortion makes clear: it included a call for a "constitutional amendment to restore the protection of the right to life for unborn children." State funding of abortions for welfare recipients, on the other hand, came in for criticism. In addition, the only judges who should be nominated were those "who respect traditional family values and the sanctity of innocent human life"—an important topic, because over the next few years several new Supreme Court judges would likely have to be appointed.[129]

During his first term, Reagan already advocated major restrictions on the practice of abortion; among other things, he filled many key posts in the health system with declared opponents of abortion, appointed conservative jurist Sandra O'Day Connor to the Supreme Court, met repeatedly with members of the anti-abortion movements, and supported legislative initiatives that opposed abortion and its public funding.[130] Finally, on the tenth anniversary of the *Roe v. Wade* ruling, the president wrote an article on "Abortion and the Conscience of the Nation," which was published in 1984 in the anti-abortion journal *Human Life Review*.[131] Here, Reagan equated aborted fetuses with fallen soldiers, elevating them to the status of persons who had died for the nation:

> Since 1973, more than 15 million unborn children have had their lives snuffed out by legalized abortions. That is over ten times the number of American lost in all our nation's wars.

It is important to note that the president paid no attention here to the rights of women and mothers to physical integrity or free choice. All that counted for him was the fetus's right to life. On several occasions, the president used the term "holocaust" to describe abortion.[132] He always described this as entailing the late-term abortion of an already viable fetus, which he also called "infanticide." By contrast, the president ignored the fact that the overwhelming majority of abortions under *Roe* were first-trimester procedures. Reagan concluded his plea for

---

[129] Republican Party Platforms: "Republican Party Platform of 1980," July 15, 1980. Online at Gerhard Peters and John T. Woolley, The American Presidency Project <www.presidency.ucsb.edu/ws/?pid=25844>. See also NARAL National Leadership Caucus 1984, "Presidential Election Campaign: The Reagan Record on Abortion." SLHU MC 714, Box 83, Folder 3.

[130] Such as the Human Life Bill 1981 and the Respect Human Life Act 1983.

[131] Reagan, Ronald, "Abortion and the Conscience of the Nation," *The Human Life Review*, February 3, 1984, online at <www.humanlifereview.com/abortion-and-the-conscience-of-the-nation-ronald-reagan-the-10th-anniversary-of-the-supreme-court-decision-in-roe-v-wade-is-a-good-time-for-us-to-pause-and-reflect-our-nationwide-policy-of-abortion-o>.

[132] Though he always used the words of other authors, such as John Powell ("silent holocaust") and William Brennan ("human holocaust"). Reagan, "Abortion and the Conscience of the Nation," 4–5.

the reversal of *Roe v. Wade* with a commitment to freedom, which was in turn based on the "right to life of all human beings."

> My Administration is dedicated to the preservation of America as a free land, and there is no cause more important for preserving that freedom than affirming the transcendent right to life of all human beings, the right without which no other rights have any meaning.[133]

The article in turn formed the basis for a short book by the president of the same title, supplemented with contributions by Surgeon General C. Everett Koop (who was in charge of the public health system) and British writer Malcolm Muggeridge, which was published in 1984 by religiously conservative publisher Thomas Nelson.[134] Hence, in a way perceptible to the entire country, the President had consciously and unambiguously opposed the idea of abortion as something that flows from female freedom of choice and instead advocated a revision of the Supreme Court's *Roe v. Wade* ruling. Reagan declared the eleventh anniversary of that decision National Sanctity of Human Life Day, which was subsequently marked annually during his presidency and under his successor, George H. W. Bush. In the associated proclamation, he lamented the fate of aborted fetuses, whom he referred to as "children:" "These children [...] will never laugh, never sing, never experience the joy of human love; nor will they strive to heal the sick, or feed the poor, or make peace among nations."[135] Shortly after, in his State of the Union address before Congress of January 25, 1984, he called for "positive solutions to the tragedy of abortion."[136]

In view of the course he had set, the issue of "reproductive rights" took on a key significance for representatives of the women's movement and various pro-choice organizations in the presidential election campaign of 1983–84; Reagan's possible re-election appeared to them as a major threat to women's reproductive freedom.

"Ronald Reagan is a disaster for women."[137] This statement made in 1983 by Judy Goldsmith, president of the National Organization of Women (NOW), suc-

---

133 Reagan, Ronald, "Abortion and the Conscience of the Nation," 6.
134 Reagan, Ronald, *Abortion and the Conscience of the Nation* (Nashville 1984, new and revised edition Sacramento, CA 2001).
135 Ronald Reagan, "Proclamation 5147—National Sanctity of Human Life Day, 1984," January 13, 1984. Online at <reaganlibrary.archives.gov/archives/speeches/1984/11384c.htm>. On this, see also the "Reagan Record on Abortion" of the NARAL National Leadership Caucus, 1984, Presidential Election Campaign. SLHU MC 714, Box 83, Folder 3.
136 Ronald Reagan: "Address Before a Joint Session of the Congress on the State of the Union," January 25, 1984. Online at Gerhard Peters and John T. Woolley, The American Presidency Project <www.presidency.ucsb.edu/ws/?pid=40205>.
137 NOW News Release, June 30, 1983, Statement of Judy Goldsmith, President, National Organization for Women, Announcing the Women's Truth Squad on Reagan. SLHU MC 714, Box 78, Folder 16.

cinctly describes the perception of many members of the women's movement, especially advocates of abortion rights and female equality in general. To impede Reagan's reelection, NOW drew on its considerable experience in lobbying and political mobilization, but it also grounded its efforts in theory. In 1983, for example, the organization published a twenty-page pamphlet entitled *Women's Truth Squad on Reagan*. It meticulously listed and documented all of the government's measures that restricted women's social and economic equality as well as their reproductive freedom.[138] The women argued that the president was responsible, among other things, for women's rising poverty, their poorer educational and career opportunities, the reduction in affordable childcare and declining welfare spending, the thwarting of the Equal Rights Amendment, and, finally, the "gender gap." But above all they argued that he stood for increased government intervention in the private lives of many American women:

> The Reagan Administration actively promotes policies to deprive women and girls of access to adequate family planning services and safe, legal abortions. While rhetorically promoting "getting government off our backs," President Reagan advocates increasing government interference in our bedrooms.[139]

The National Abortion Rights Action League (NARAL), the largest and oldest national abortion rights advocacy group, launched a similar campaign to prevent Reagan's re-election. The activists justified this by citing his "anti-choice strategy," contending that "Ronald Reagan is the most anti-choice President in this country's history."[140]

> For anyone even peripherally involved with the right to choose, the threats posed by Ronald Reagan's re-election are clear. His strong support of the anti-choice opposition and his recent fueling of the emotional fires around the issue are of serious enough import.[141]

Moreover, they perceived the fact that he might appoint conservative Supreme Court justices if re-elected as particularly threatening.[142] "If an anti-choice President appoints several new anti-choice Justices, the stage would be set for a rever-

---

138 NOW pamphlet: "Women's Truth Squad on Reagan" (1983). SLHU MC 714, Box 78, Folder 16.
139 NOW pamphlet: "Women's Truth Squad on Reagan" (1983). SLHU MC 714, Box 78, Folder 16.
140 NARAL National Leadership Caucus, 1984, Presidential Election Campaign. SLHU MC 714, Box 83, Folder 3.
141 NARAL National Leadership Caucus 1984, Presidential Election Campaign. SLHU MC 714, Box 83, Folder 3.
142 NARAL National Leadership Caucus 1984, Presidential Election Campaign. SLHU MC 714, Box 83, Folder 3.

sal of Roe v. Wade."[143] But the activists saw themselves as well equipped to actively intervene in the election campaign:

> It is critical that the NARAL "network"—our political machinery that we have worked so hard to develop—be used to educate voters this fall about the real impact this election has on the right to choose. The next President's ability to shape the Supreme Court will determine the future of the right to choose.[144]

This concern was shared by religious pro-choice organizations such as the Religious Coalition for Abortion Rights (RCAR), which included members of all Christian churches as well as representatives of Jewish religious communities. In a 1984 leaflet, RCAR informed its members about *The Supreme Court and Reproductive Freedom* and warned that, in light of the impending appointment of new conservative justices, "the future for religious and reproductive rights may be at stake." This is an interesting argument when we consider that most abortion critics invoked religious values to *oppose* the right to reproductive self-determination.[145]

In preparation for the campaign to prevent Reagan's re-election, NARAL in particular attached great importance to learning how its activities and the issue of reproductive choice were viewed by the American public—as a means of better organizing their political work and especially their fundraising. Together with the Planned Parenthood Federation of America (PPFA), NARAL commissioned a survey on birth control in 1983.[146] From March 19 to 25, Boston-based polling institute Harrison and Goldberg asked a total of 1,199 people over the age of 18 by telephone about their attitudes to abortion and contraception. The survey found that respondents were overwhelmingly in favor of legal abortion and against a government ban. 71 percent opposed such a ban and 86 percent stated that abortion was "a private, personal choice that the government should stay out of." Yet Ronald Reagan enjoyed consistently high approval ratings, with 64 percent of respondents having a positive opinion of him. The survey also found that religion

---

[143] Memo to Nanette Falkenberg from Gail Harmon and William S. Jordan, III, June 7, 1984: "The Most Serious Threat to the Freedom of Choice." SLHU MC 714, Box 83, Folder 10.

[144] Memo from Nanette Falkenberg to NARAL Affiliates, NARAL Board, undated (1984), "Presidential Election Campaign." SLHU MC 714, Box 83, Folder 3.

[145] Religious Coalition for Abortion Rights pamphlet: "The Supreme Court and Reproductive Freedom," 1984. SLHU MC 714, Box 83, Folder 10.

[146] While NARAL and PPFA each contributed $10,000 in funding, another $20,000 came from the North Shore Unitarian Society. SLHU MC 714, Box 78, Folder 7. The organizations Catholics for a Free Choice, Religious Coalition for Abortion Rights, National Abortion Federation, and the Alan Guttmacher Institute also participated. NARAL, "Key Findings of a Poll on Issues related to Family Planning and Abortion, taken March 19–25, 1984," Confidential. SLHU MC 714, Box 78, Folder 9.

was a minor determinant of attitudes toward abortion—as many as 65 percent of Catholics were against a ban on the practice. However, the majority of respondents opposed public funding of abortions for the needy: 55 percent were against this idea, while 62 percent opposed public funding of abortion costs for welfare recipients.[147] The latter finding prompted PPFA and NARAL to refrain from publishing what they saw as otherwise positive findings:[148] they were unwilling to publicize the fact that a majority of respondents did not want public money spent on abortions—after all, maintaining the government funding ban for abortions (through the Hyde Amendment of 1976) was a core concern of the Reagan administration, which had now received backing from the survey data.[149] NARAL, PPFA, and RCAR, meanwhile, supported the Reproductive Health Equity Act (put before Congress in 1985 as H.R. 5745 but not passed), which aimed to reintroduce "public funding of abortions for poor women."[150]

The year before the large-scale telephone poll, NARAL and PPFA had jointly commissioned a much smaller survey. In 1983, they had an independent institution interview a total of 31 people in Chicago and Philadelphia in two rounds of talks on the topics of abortion rights and the pro-choice movement. These were people who had donated to one of the two organizations in 1981 and 1982, in other words who were in principle positively disposed toward their cause. The sample was highly homogeneous, consisting exclusively of whites, 23 women and 8 men. No fewer than 30 had college degrees and belonged to above-average income groups. An analysis of the transcripts of the originally tape-recorded discussion rounds is nevertheless revealing: the educated, high-income supporters of NARAL and PPFA emphasized three aspects in particular.

---

147 SLHU MC 714, Box 78, Folder 8: "National Poll re: Abortion/Birthcontrol, 1983–1984," vi-vii, 8–10, 32–34, 35–37.
148 In addition, 73 percent of respondents said they had a positive opinion of PPFA.
149 Planned Parenthood Memorandum, July 17, 1984, to the Pro-Choice Coalition: "Poll on Abortion Issues." PPFA, Faye Wattleton, President, to PPFA Board of Directors, July 13, 1984. Linda Davidoff, PPFA, Memorandum to Poll Coalition Members, June 6, 1984, Confidential. SLHU MC 714, Box 78, Folder 7. Nanette Falkenberg, NARAL, to NARAL Board, NARAL Affiliates, August 24, 1984: "Medicaid Funding Poll." NARAL, "Key Findings of a Poll on Issues related to Family Planning and Abortion, taken March 19–25, 1984," Confidential. SLHU MC 714, Box 78, Folder 9.
150 Memo Ron Fitzsimmons, NARAL Director of Government Relations, January 4, 1985, to NARAL Affiliates and Board Members. Memo, NARAL: "H.R 5745, The Reproductive Health Equity Act." Memo Ron Fitzsimmons, NARAL, "Legislative Update," January 11, 1985, "Reproductive Health Equity Act to be Reintroduced in House of Representatives." Statement NARAL, Nanette Falkenberg, May 30, 1984, on Introduction of RHEA. PPFA, Press Release, Statement Faye Wattleton, May 30, 1984. RCAR, Press Release, May 30, 1984: "Decade of Choice," in favor of RHEA. ACLU, May 30, 1984: Press Statement in Favor of RHEA as "historic act." SLHU MC 714 Box 84, Folder 2.

1) Abortion was a "matter of choice" that the government must not be allowed to regulate.
2) Abortion rights were more than a "feminist issue."
3) The "pro-life movement" was very well organized and thus more present and efficient than the "pro-choice" movement.[151]

In line with these views, one of the most successful NARAL campaigns of the 1980s came about through confrontation with an extremely effective anti-abortion movement, namely the "Silent No More" campaign of 1985. The background was the abortion-critical film *The Silent Scream* by former NARAL co-founder, "pro-choice" activist, and director of a New York abortion clinic, Bernhard Nathanson. He had gone from being an abortion practitioner to becoming one of the harshest critics of abortion in the United States.[152] According to Nathanson, it was Ronald Reagan's comments about the fetus feeling pain during an abortion, made in a speech to the National Religious Broadcasters in 1984,[153] that had motivated him to make this film.[154] *The Silent Scream* was first shown on television in 1984, with several networks broadcasting it as part of their early evening offerings.[155] The president himself then had it shown at the White House. The film was about an abortion, which viewers were able to experience "directly" by means of ultrasound images—accompanied by a commentary from Nathanson. In reality, virtually nothing could be seen on the pixelated black-and-white footage; it was effectively Nathanson's explanations that turned the event into a record of the abortion of a living fetus.[156]

---

151 NARAL, "Report of focus group on abortion rights and the pro-choice movement," 1983. SLHU MC 714, Box 84, Folder 1, 1–65.
152 Bernhard Nathanson (1926–2011) studied medicine before establishing himself as a gynecologist in New York, where he directed the Center for Reproductive and Sexual Health. In 1969, he was one of the founders of the National Association for the Repeal of Abortion Laws, later NARAL. According to his own statements, the change of heart that turned him into a "pro-life" activist was triggered by the development of ultrasound technology, which allowed him to experience the death of the fetus directly. Nathanson, Bernard, *Aborting America* (Garden City, 1979). On Nathanson, see Schoen, *Abortion after Roe*, 131–133.
153 "Medical science doctors confirm that when the lives of the unborn are snuffed out, they often feel pain, pain that is long and agonizing." Ronald Reagan: "Remarks at the Annual Convention of the National Religious Broadcasters," January 30, 1984. Online at Gerhard Peters and John T. Woolley, The American Presidency Project <www.presidency.ucsb.edu/ws/?pid=40394>.
154 Elizabeth Mehren and Betty Cuniberti, "He's the Force Behind 'The Silent Scream' Film: Doctor Who Performed Thousands of Abortions Narrates, Promotes Right-to-Life Sonogram Movie," *Time*, May 8, 1985. <www.articles.latimes.com/1985-08-08/news/vw-3552_1_silent-scream>.
155 Petchesky, Rosalind Pollack, "Fetal Images: The Power of Visual Culture in the Politics of Reproduction," *Feminist Studies* 13 (1987), no. 2, 263–292, 264.
156 Petchesky, "Fetal Images," 264.

For members of the women's movement and the pro-choice movement, *The Silent Scream* was a major irritant and at the same time an immensely successful propagandistic attack on women's freedom of choice. The activists of NARAL, NOW and PPFA criticized the fact that abortion was not shown correctly from a medical point of view.[157] In addition, they condemned the film's argument "that it is not necessary to include women's experiences in a discussion of abortion." The complete absence of women as individuals was unacceptable: "No woman's voice is heard at any time during the film. The movie simultaneously elevates fetuses to people and lowers women to speechless and senseless objects."[158]

This observation, reinforced by the film's huge popularity and the fact that it played directly into the hands of the "pro-life" movement, induced NARAL to launch a counter-campaign in 1984. Nanette Falkenberg, the body's executive director, reached out to sub-organizations and supporters:

> In recent months, NARAL has been flooded with phone calls and letters from concerned supporters, both women and men, who have expressed a concern about the current abortion debate which ignores women and misrepresents the reality of women's lives and family life in our society.[159]

Falkenberg's idea was to get 100,000 women who had chosen to have abortions to set out their personal reasons for doing so in a letter to the president. In the spring of 1985, she launched NARAL's national campaign:

> We must educate people that they are all real life cases, of real and good women who are making difficult but moral choices.
>
> [. . .]
>
> Remember, WE ARE THE MAJORITY.[160]

The notion that women who had abortions made their decisions as individuals but with and to the benefit of their family members was to be central to the campaign.

---

157 Memorandum PPFA, February 1985, to Affiliate Executive Directors, from Louise Tyrer, Vice President for Medical Affairs: "Expert Panel Critique of film 'The Silent Scream.'" Memorandum NOW, "The Silent Scream" (undated). SLHU MC 659, Box 16, Folder 13. See also criticism by medical student George P., who complained to President Reagan in 1985 as part of the Silent No More campaign that the film was based on medically false claims. George P. to President Reagan, [undated] 1985. SLHU MC 659, Box 17, Folder 17.
158 Memorandum NOW, "The Silent Scream" [undated]. SLHU MC 659, Box 16, Folder 13.
159 Memorandum Nanette Falkenberg, NARAL, to Members of the Media, March 20, 1985, "Re: Abortion Rights: Silent No More." SLHU MC 659, Box 16, Folder 13.
160 Letter from NARAL Leadership, signed Falkenberg, "Action," n.d. (1985). Falkenberg provided the specific figures in a letter to NARAL Leadership, May 3, 1985, Silent No More Mailing Folder 10. SLHU MC 659, Box 16, Folder 14.

> The action theme is a reminder that the 1.5 million women who have abortions each year are much more than faceless, nameless human beings. They are individuals who are important in our lives.[161]

At the time, on its own figures, NARAL had 150,000 members and 33 sub-organizations (such as Mass Choice), which had a further 100,000 members. Thus, the plan to send a total of 100,000 letters from women to the president in just a few months was ambitious, but not entirely far-fetched.[162] On May 21, 1985, some of the letters were to be read out in Washington, preceded by hearings and campaigns in the individual states. Some of the themes that NARAL provided the local activists with (in addition to a precise timetable and suggestions for organizing public relations and speak-outs), in the form of a kind of mantra, revolved around the normality of the women who opted to have an abortion and the seriousness and rationality of their decision:

> We are your mothers, your sisters, your daughter, your friends and we have chosen abortion. [. . .]
>
> We are decent, caring, intelligent women making responsible choices. [. . .]
>
> We will end the silence about abortion. Our stories must be heard.[163]

This project had a special significance in the state of Massachusetts, where a referendum on the implementation of the *Roe v. Wade* ruling was imminent in 1986. The Mass Choice movement there had about 5,000 members and was highly organized.[164] In accordance with its mission statement "to develop and sustain a grassroots constituency in Massachusetts that uses the political process to keep abortion

---

161 Memorandum from Nanette Falkenberg, NARAL, to Members of the Media, March 20, 1985, "Re: Abortion Rights: Silent No More." SLHU MC 659, Box 16, Folder 13.

162 Memorandum from Nanette Falkenberg, NARAL, to Members of the Media, March 20, 1985, "Re: Abortion Rights: Silent No More." SLHU MC 659, Box 16, Folder 13.

163 Material sent by NARAL to its state-level sub-organizations in preparation for the campaign: Binder, Abortion Rights: Silent No More, NARAL 2/1985. SLHU MC 659, Box 16, Folder 14. See also the material in SLHU MC 659, Box 16, Folder 15.

164 The local NARAL sub-organization in the state of Massachusetts, headquartered in Boston, was founded in 1972 as MORAL. From the beginning, it saw itself as a civil rights organization that tried out and refined "grass roots" techniques of mobilization at the local level. A so-called Political Action Committee (PAC) operated as its political arm, explicitly seeking to influence the election of pro-choice politicians. In 1984, MORAL renamed itself NARAL Mass Choice, then Mass NARAL in 1996, and NARAL Pro Choice Massachusetts in 2003. In 1985, the organization had about 5,000 members and was funded purely by donations, but still had an annual income of about $127,000 in 1985 and $134,400 in 1986. Pam Nourse was executive director of Mass Choice in 1985, Laura Jennings its president. "Mass Choice Annual Plan," April 1, 1985–March 31, 1986. SLHU MC 659, Box 3, Folder 1. Memorandum Laura Jennings to Pro Choice Individuals, April 5, 1985. SLHU MC 659, Box 3, Folder 3.

safe and legal," the activists of Mass Choice readily joined the campaign,[165] setting out to collect a total of 2,000 letters in just one month and send them to state senators. The aim was to make the politicians aware of "exactly what we are risking in Massachussetts if we take away the right to choose abortion."[166] On May 16, 1985, less than a week before the national hearing in Washington, the letters from Massachusetts were to be read out in front of the State House in Boston.[167] For Mass Choice too, the "Silent No More" campaign was intended to put women and their families back at the center of the abortion debate: "We want to shift the emphasis away from the picketers and hecklers, and back to the women and families who face a decision about abortion."[168] At the same time, the activists linked this to the goal of averting the Massachusetts amendment scheduled for November 1986 (which would have banned the use of Medicaid funding for abortions sought by poor women) and expanding Mass Choice's reach to the entire state.[169] Mass Choice formulated its critique of the Massachusetts referendum quite explicitly as a question of who would be allowed to decide about reproduction—the government or the woman: "Who will Control Reproductive Decision Making in Massachusetts? Individuals or State Government?"

> This Bill constitutes one more way in which the state legislature will expand its power and intrude into the private lives of the people of Massachusetts. Independent polls reveal that the overwhelming majority of Massachusetts residents—whether or not they would choose abortion themselves—believe that it is "a personal, private decision which state government should stay out of." But despite this mandate from its constituency, our state legislature is attempting to take control of individual childbearing and reproductive freedoms, usurping decisions which belong—morally as well as legally—to individuals and their families.[170]

The files of Mass Choice contain numerous copies of letters from the Silent No More campaign, written by women (and couples) through May 1985 and then sent to members of the state Senate and House of Representatives. Many people sent copies of their letters to political representatives to Mass Choice, which stored

---

165 "Mass Choice Mission Statement" (undated), SLHU MC 659, Box 3, Folder 5.
166 Mass Choice memorandum, Deborah Beard, April 17, 1985, Mass Choice News Release. When the planning began in March 1985, Mass Choice was still envisaging 3,000 letters. "Organizing Plan for the Call to Action," March 20, 1985. SLHU MC 659, Box 16, Folder 15.
167 Mass Choice memorandum, Deborah Beard, April 17, 1985, Mass Choice News Release. SLHU MC 659, Box 16, Folder 15.
168 Fundraising Letter from Pam Nourse to David Scondras, April 18, 1985. SLHU MC 659, Box 16, Folder 17.
169 "Mass Choice Annual Plan," April 1, 1985–March 31, 1986. SLHU MC 659, Box 3, Folder 1.
170 Mass Choice: "Who Will Control Reproductive Decision Making in Massachusetts? Individuals or State Government?" (1986). SLHU MC 659, Box 3, Folder 4.

them in its files.[171] The major themes were abortion as an individual right and as an element of individual family and career planning for women, as well as a desire for government to stay out of citizens' private life choices. For example, Hanna and Gustav P. of Lexington, MA, wrote to Representative Stephen Doran on May 14, 1985:

> We feel strongly that the government should not be the "third person" in bed with the couple. [. . .] Reproductive freedom is a vital part of personal freedom. Attempts to restrict reproductive freedom, by falsely claiming a role for government as an advocate of the unborn, represent attempts to limit individual freedom. The current struggle is really about the nature of state authority—not morality—and the role of the state in the most intimate personal decision.[172]

Charles F. D. of Springfield, MA, also wrote that the "right to choose" was an expression of the "right of the individual to live his own life free of government interference." At the same time, he expressed concern about "the violence which the militance of the hard-line Moral Majority and the 'New Right' has brought to the dispute over women's rights" and the fact that the Reagan administration was doing nothing to counter these excesses.[173] As early as April 17, 1985, Julie Z. of Somerville, MA, meanwhile, stated to her Senator Sal Albano—she had in fact worked for his election campaign—that abortion was simply a woman's right:

> The issue is the woman's right to choose abortion. [. . .] I see it as no different than the thousands of other personal rights we enjoy. NO one can tell us when to have children, how many to have, what sex they should be, or in what religion they should be raised. These are rights cherished by Americans of all persuasions. Abortion is an equally personal right.[174]

Liz S. of Pittsfield, MA, wrote to Pam Nourse of Mass Choice in May 1985:

> Personal goals include choosing a career and pursuing the necessary education to achieve that career. Personal goals also include planning a family, deciding how many children one wants or can afford and deciding when during one's career it is possible to stop and have that family.[175]

---

171 The entire bundle can be found in SLHU MC 659, Box 17, Folders 3 through 21.
172 Hanna P. and Gustav F. P., Lexington, MA, May 14, 1985, to Rep. Stephen Doran, c/o Mass Choice. Emphasis in original. Very similar letter from Joan C. E., Marblehead, MA, April 16, 1985, to Representative Lawrence Alexander. SLHU MC 659, Box 17, Folder 5.
173 Charles F. D., Springfield, MA to Mass Choice, June 4, 1985. SLHU MC 659, Box 17, Folder 5.
174 Julie Z., Somerville, MA, to Senator Sal Albano, Boston MA, April 17, 1985. SLHU MC 659, Box 17, Folder 4.
175 Liz S., Pittsfield, MA, to Pam Nourse, Executive Director, Mass Choice, May 28, 1985. SLHU MC 659, Box 17, Folder 5.

Claire B. of the Boston neighborhood of Brighton took a similarly pragmatic view, informing Democratic senator George Bachrach:

> Abortion is not a wonderful choice, but it is one of the few choices that this world currently affords us, and, often, it is the best choice, given the situation. [. . .] It is imperative that this choice remain available to all.[176]

Finally, in her letter, Mary M. expressed what many women in the abortion rights and women's movement thought: "Too many people these days seem to regard women as merely disposable containers for fetuses instead of as persons in their own right."[177]

However, when the approximately 1,000 letters were delivered to the Massachusetts state government on May 16, 1985, it was rather different statements that were read out. The total of eight letters, which were anonymized and recited in excerpts, referred to the misery of illegal abortions before *Roe* (a total of 5), abortion to end a pregnancy after rape (1), termination after taking medicines harmful to the embryo (1) and abortion due to the advanced age of the mother (1). Two of the selected testimonials acknowledged profound psychological doubts and feelings of guilt after a decision to have an abortion—but none of the excerpts forthrightly declared abortion a "personal right."[178] Apparently, Mass Choice was shying away from putting a woman's individual right to choose at the forefront of its campaign. NARAL was in fact to take a very similar tack for the speak-out at the federal level a few days later. But why? It may be that the activists did not want to furnish the anti-abortion movement with any new potential lines of attack and therefore retreated to morally "irreproachable" reasons for abortion (rape, effects of medication, advanced age) or wished to present illegal abortions as the real scandal.

The local Silent No More campaign, featuring the speak-out in Boston on May 16, 1985, was in fact a resounding success for Mass Choice. Chair Pam Nourse detailed this in her annual report:

> Both the local and national level received good press and 1,000 letters from prochoice men and women of Massachusetts were delivered to state legislators. The event also identified new prochoice activists, particularly on the North Shore and Western Massachusetts.[179]

---

176 Claire B., Brighton, MA, to State Senator Bachrach, April 8, 1985. SLHU MC 659, Box 17, Folder 4.
177 Mary M. to Pam Nourse, April 16, 1985. SLHU MC 659, Box 17, Folder 6.
178 Pam Nourse, Executive Director, Mass Choice: "Women speak out on Abortion," May 16, 1985, Press Release. SLHU MC 659, Box 17, Folder 21.
179 Minutes of Mass Choice Board Meeting, May 23, 1985. SLHU, MC 659, Box 2, Folder 18. Pam Nourse, Executive Director, Mass Choice: "Women speak out on Abortion," May 16, 1985, Press Release. SLHU MC 659, Box 17, Folder 21. See also press report by Frank Philipps, *Boston Herald*,

Mass Choice enjoyed even greater success when the 1986 amendment was defeated, for which it received recognition from NARAL for "Outstanding Grassroots Electoral Achievement" in 1987.[180] This helped spur plans by Mass Choice activists to take on larger issues, such as "reproductive rights" in general.[181]

The Silent No More letter campaign was also a success at the national level. Although the target of 100,000 letters was not reached, the roughly 45,000 total was substantial.[182] After a public speak-out was held in Washington DC on May 21, 1985, at which several women told of their decision to have an abortion and related their personal story, some of the letters were handed over to the president the following day. The response of the *Washington Post* and *New York Times* was basically positive, but also gave wide coverage to the press conference organized at the same time by the "pro-life" movement.[183] This event was organized by the Women Exploited By Abortions (WEBA) organization. Its members gave their own personal accounts of abortions they had regretted and their feelings of guilt.[184] The tensions between pro- and anti-abortionists remained acute in 1985 as they battled for interpretive dominance within the public sphere.

In this situation, Ronald Reagan increasingly tried to present adoption as *the* alternative to abortion and endeavored to create a positive social climate for the practice.[185] Thus, he declared the third week of November 1984 (around Thanksgiving on November 24, which traditionally serves to bring families together) the first National Adoption Week. His goal of "rebuilding families by promoting adoption," however, was not only meant to meet the needs of parentless children, especially those "with special needs," but above all to reduce the number of abortions:

May 17, 1985: "Pro Choice in a New Blitz. Testimony Dramatizes Lobby Effort," SLHU MC 659, Box 16, Folder 13.
180 However, of the $418,000 campaign costs, Mass Choice had raised only $88,000 itself. The rest came from Planned Parenthood ($200,000) and NARAL. Minutes of the Mass Choice Board Meeting, October 23, 1986. SLHU MC 659, Box 3, Folder 3.
181 NARAL Conference 1987, Mass Choice Minutes, July 29, 1987. SLHU MC 659, Box 3, Folder 5.
182 On this, see the NARAL papers in SLHU MC 714, Box 71, Folder 3, Box 219. Box 229, Folder 9 through Box 230, Folder 4.
183 Ruth Marcus, "Abortion Rights Rally Set: Campaign Comes to Washington Today," WP, May 21, 1985, C 1. Dudley Clendinen, "The Veterans of Abortion Fight Back by Speaking Up," NYT, May 26, 1985, E 5.
184 On WEBA, see Schoen, *Abortion after Roe*, 146–150.
185 He had already stated in his anti-abortion essay and subsequent book in 1983 and 1984 respectively that many families would gladly adopt a child, such that the "unwanted children" rationale for abortions was obsolete. Reagan, "Abortion and the Conscience of the Nation," 6.

> One aspect of the tragedy of the 1.5 million abortions performed each year is that so many women who undergo abortions are unaware of the many couples who desperately want to share their loving homes with a baby. No woman need fear that the child she carries is unwanted.[186]

In his proclamations of the National Adoption Week in 1985 and 1986, Reagan again emphasized the goal of preventing abortions through adoption and promised to provide more support for "single women facing crisis pregnancies."[187] In 1987, these then figured as "brave women who heroically choose life" and who deserved the full support of their fellow human beings and the entire nation.[188] The president thus consciously reversed the argument of NOW and NARAL, according to which a woman's right to decide about her body was the basic prerequisite for a responsible, carefully considered, and conscious reproductive decision: women finding themselves with an unintended pregnancy appeared in his rhetoric not as autonomous decision makers but as single women in a crisis situation. They could be relieved of the need to make a decision and granted the status of "heroic givers of life" through various forms of help and a functioning adoption program.

But here the president had not reckoned with those affected, the so-called birthmothers, in other words women who had given up their children for adoption after birth. In the 1980s, they increasingly spoke out, declaring that, rather than a "heroic" alternative to abortion, for mothers adoption was often a painful experience of loss. Their organization, Concerned United Birthparents (CUB), became an audible voice in the political discourse of the 1980s. Its members, for their part, resisted all too transparent attempts to instrumentalize them by demanding respect and discussing their experience of loss and the constraints imposed on them. One CUB staff member, Karen Kottmeier from Denver, summed this up in retrospect in 1992:

> But, I could not help but notice, that nobody cared about unwed mothers' relationship to their children until abortion was legalized in 1973. Suddenly, we were carrying a valuable

---

[186] Ronald Reagan: "Proclamation 5280—National Adoption Week, 1984," November 13, 1984. Online at Gerhard Peters and John T. Woolley, The American Presidency Project <www.presidency.ucsb.edu/ws/?pid=39423>.

[187] Ronald Reagan: "Proclamation 5411—National Adoption Week, 1985," November 15, 1985. Online at Gerhard Peters and John T. Woolley, The American Presidency Project <www.presidency.ucsb.edu/ws/?pid=38079>. Ronald Reagan, "Proclamation 5570—National Adoption Week, 1986," November 13, 1986. Online at Gerhard Peters and John T. Woolley, The American Presidency Project <www.presidency.ucsb.edu/ws/?pid=36726>. The quote is from Proclamation 5570 of 1986.

[188] Ronald Reagan, "Proclamation 5746—National Adoption Week, 1987," November 19, 1987. Online at Gerhard Peters and John T. Woolley, The American Presidency Project <www.presidency.ucsb.edu/ws/?pid=33714>.

person. Everyone in the pro-life movement jumped on the bandwagon to convince unwed, pregnant women to carry their children to term and then relinquish them to adoption—the "non-violent" alternative. At this time it was still assumed that the birthmother had no value to her child, once it was born, and that she should just "go on and forget" knowing that she "had done the right thing."

The last part of this chapter thus examines the reactions of "birthmothers" to Ronald Reagan's adoption promotion policy. How did these individuals feel about the legality of abortion, given that they had not opted to have one? The birthmothers' accounts of their experiences do in fact provide an important correlate to NARAL's statements, as they reflect the long-term impact of reproductive decisions and the tremendous effects of gender norms and family values from a complementary perspective.

In the United States—as in many Western countries—it was common until into the 1970s for young middle-class girls who became pregnant out of wedlock to conceal their pregnancy in order to preserve their honor and that of their family. In most cases, they then gave birth in a different location, in a home for unmarried girls or church institution.[189] To conceal the origin of the child, which was then given up for adoption, "sealed records" were created. Upon adoption, the child received a new birth certificate that identified the adoptive parents as the birth parents, while a document identifying the latter remained "sealed" at the registering authority of a given state—making the search for children and birth parents much more difficult.[190]

The fact that those affected organized themselves in the late 1970s and spoke out publicly, especially in the 1980s, can be explained by two factors. First, the social movements of the 1960s and 1970s, especially the women's movement, raised awareness of gender discrimination and family power relations and subjected them to a fundamental critique. Second, Reagan's emotive rhetoric about adoption, which condescendingly ascribed to women who had had to give up their children for adoption the status of "heroic single mothers," was hard to bear, especially for those women who had made their decision under difficult cir-

---

189 The following monograph brings together numerous moving testimonies of women's experiences: Fessler, Anne, *The Girls Who Went Away. The Hidden History of Women Who Surrendered Children for Adoption in the Decades Before Roe v. Wade* (New York 2006). On the practice of adoption imposed on girls, see Solinger, *Wake up, little Suzie*.
190 Carp, E. Wayne, *Family Matters: Secrecy and Disclosure in the History of Adoption* (Cambridge and London 2000), 102–137, esp. 109–110. On the history of adoption in the United States in general, see Carp, E. Wayne (ed.), *Adoption in America: Historical Perspectives* (Ann Arbor 2002). Carp, E. Wayne, *Jean Paton and the Struggle to Reform American Adoption* (Ann Arbor 2014). Herman, Ellen, *Kinship by Design: A History of Adoption in the Modern United States* (Chicago 2008) (up to 1970).

cumstances. The fact that the records were still closed and there was no uniform adoption law made things even more difficult for them.[191]

In 1976, a national association of former birth parents who had given their children up for adoption, Concerned United Birthparents Inc. (CUB), was founded in the United States.[192] Originally established as a local support group by Cape Cod elementary school teacher Lee Campbell, CUB soon developed into a visible national movement with branches (chapters and regions) in almost every state and several thousand members. The participants' goal was to exchange ideas and support each other, especially in the search for their relinquished children. At the same time, a political objective crystallized: recognition for the "forgotten people" in the adoption process, the birthmothers, along with the opening of the files to enable family reunions.

The organization, which was largely run by volunteers—one paid executive director was hired in 1984—published two magazines for its members. The *Communicator* appeared in 1977, primarily featuring members' personal experiences and appeals for assistance in finding children given up for adoption. The *Family Advocate* (1983–1989), meanwhile, was more geared toward the work of the individual chapters and regional associations and its reports were generally more factual in character.[193]

In the late 1970s, CUB lobbied hard for nationally binding regulation of the adoption process, while emphasizing the imperative of opening the records. In the 1980s, it also advocated for a National Birthparents Week as a means of giving members of this category greater visibility and recognition.[194] In a 1987 custody case involving a child carried by a surrogate mother, the so-called "Baby M. Case," CUB also played a significant role, arguing in favor of the biological mother's rights.

---

[191] On the history of adoption and foster families in the 1980s, see Briggs, *Somebody's Children*, 94–125. Dubinsky, Karen, *Babies without Borders. Adoption and Migration across the Americas* (New York 2010). Rymph, Catherine E., *Raising Government Children. A History of Foster Care and the American Welfare State* (Chapel Hill 2017).

[192] The institution's papers can be found at Harvard University's Schlesinger Library, where they have been accessible since 2015. SLHU MC 630. The organization also maintains a website, <www.cubirthparents.org>.

[193] Both periodicals are available at the Schlesinger Library, Harvard University, and were consulted there.

[194] After only a few governors responded to CUB's request to proclaim a Birthparents Week in 1984 and 1985, fifteen states decided to make the week of April 6–12, 1986, National Birthparents Week. Letter from CUB Vice President Janet Fenton to CUB President Carole Anderson, April 30, 1986. See also the instructions for requesting a National Birthparents Week for 1986: "List of outreach ideas, Press Release regarding Birthparents Week," April 7–13, 1985. SLHU MC630, Box 19, Folder 3.

In March 1979, the Model Adoption Legislation and Procedures Advisory Panel, of which CUB President Lee Campbell was a member, proposed replacing the term "birthparent" ("birthmother," "birthfather") with the term "biological parent."[195] In response, CUB received several hundred letters of protest from individuals who insisted on their status as "birthparents." The personal experiences of the "birthmothers" described in the letters not only tell of the consequences of societal double standards, but also reflect the tension between adoption and abortion. Bonnie Kay P. of Ogema, Wisconsin, for example, recounted how her father forced her to give up her child when she was sixteen years old:

> For almost 20 years now I have searched for my daughter, taken away from me at birth because I was "too young and immature" to care for her. I had nothing to say and knew none of the rights I had as her natural mother. I was told that if I didn't sign the relinquishment papers, she would be taken away from me anyway and I would be put in a home for girls and her father would be sent to prison. At 16 years of age I was so dumb as to believe everything my father told me in his fit of anger.[196]

Sarah M. from Merchantville, New Jersey, told a similar story and summarized: "We have never forgotten the child we had to relinquish. Many of us were actually forced by our parents, the social worker, the doctor, the lawyer, and others in authority. We were too young or too poor to fight back."[197]

In contrast, Carole J. Anderson, who became president of CUB in 1986, was able to convert her frustration at her "exploitation" by the adoption agency into feminist activism:

> I first became involved in women's issues because of the way I was exploited by the adoption agency, which felt that only women who are married ("owned" by men) are worthy of raising their much-loved children. I am now an active feminist and have taught Feminism and Women's History in a junior college and in a state university.

Most importantly, she presented the fact that she gave her son up for adoption as a conscious decision, which she saw as justifying the term "birthmother."

> Had I chosen to terminate my pregnancy, neither I nor my son's birthfather would now be birthparents, for there would be no child. It is because I chose to give birth to our son that his birthfather and I are now birthparents. This certainly is not sexist, it is simply factual.

---

195 See correspondence of the Model Adoption Legislation and Procedures Advisory Panel. SLHU, MC 630, Box 19, Folder 10, Box 20, Folder 2.
196 Letter from Bonnie Kay P., Ogema, WI to Lee Campbell, August 13, 1979. SLHU MC 630, Box 20, Folder 2.
197 Letter from Sarah M., Merchantville, NJ, June 18, 1979, to Lee Campbell. SLHU MC 630, Box 20, Folder 2.

> The term "birthparent," like the term "adoptive parent," is truthful yet humane; it recognizes loving, living people rather than cold machines. [. . .] Please, call me what I am—a birthparent.[198]

It is important that Anderson refers here to adoption as a conscious decision "to become a birthparent"—although abortion would have been a possibility. Similarly, Nancy L. N. insisted that she was the "birthmother" of a child and not only the "biological parent." However, she warned that the legal situation for "birthparents" was highly uncertain. There was a risk of an increase in the number of abortions:

> What kind of a warped societal system would make a prospective "life-giver" choose to end a baby's life (and all, or parts of her own, most likely) because the prospect of said system is so inhumane as to make death preferable?[199]

The abortion discourse thus allowed the "birthmothers" speaking here to present their decision to carry the child to term as a humane alternative to abortion. In this way, the women could also distance themselves from their experiences of powerlessness (vis-à-vis parents and adoption agencies) and from the stigma associated with a birth out of wedlock, while laying claim to respect and morality.

This was particularly evident in the controversy over the custody of "Baby M," Sara Elizabeth Whitehead/Melissa Elizabeth Stern, who was born in 1986 as a result of a surrogacy agreement. A married couple, Elizabeth and William Stern, had contracted Mary Beth Whitehead in 1985 to carry a child for them for a fee of $10,000 and to give them custody after the birth. It was a "traditional surrogacy contract," since Whitehead was inseminated with Stern's sperm (as opposed to "gestational surrogacy," when a fertilized egg is transferred). Elizabeth Stern, herself a pediatrician, suffered from multiple sclerosis and feared that a pregnancy would worsen her condition. After the birth of Sara/Melissa, Whitehead demanded that the baby previously handed over to the Sterns be returned to her and insisted on regaining custody. The Sterns brought an action against this, and the case was initially heard in New Jersey Superior Court, which granted custody to the Sterns in March 1987 "in the best interest of the child." In February 1988, the Supreme Court of New Jersey then declared the surrogacy contract incompatible with state law, upholding the biological mother's "parental rights." Yet the judges ruled that custody should remain with the Sterns, again in the best interest of the child. Mary Beth Whitehead was, however, granted visitation rights.[200]

---

[198] Letter from Carole J. Anderson to Lee Campbell, July 21, 1979. SLHU MC 630, Box 20, Folder 2.
[199] Nancy L.N. to CUB, August 30, 1979. SLHU MC 630, Box 19, Folder 3.
[200] For the details and on the legal wrangling, see Sanger, Carol, "Developing Markets in Baby-Making: In the Matter of Baby M," *Harvard Journal of Law and Gender* (30) 2007, 767–797.

6.4 Abortion and adoption as two poles of reproductive decision-making

CUB followed the case with great interest; to them, Mary Beth Whitehead was "a birthmother who has been denied her child."[201] Individual CUB chapters raised money and collected letters of support for Whitehead, and the organization's president, lawyer Allison Ward, became involved in Whitehead's defense.[202] For the hearing of the case before the Supreme Court of New Jersey in 1987, CUB wrote an *amicus curiae* brief, that is, a submission intended to influence the ruling. In it, the CUB activists first emphasized their expertise, since—they asserted—they knew from their own studies as well as from CUB members' experiences "that the separation and loss associated with severance of biological family ties have serious and adverse effects on all concerned."[203] They thus demanded that their voice be heard and suggested that "surrogacy agreements" be subject to strict legal rules, just like adoptions. After all, the parent-child relationship must be preserved at all costs. Whitehead's "parental rights" must therefore remain with Whitehead, though the child's place of residence could be determined in the light of the "best interests of the child."

CUB was particularly vehement about the "gender and wealth discrimination" that it saw as inherent in this case, since the surrogate mother was poor while the "clients" were necessarily wealthy. It should not, CUB averred, be assumed that it is always best for the child to remain with the wealthier parent.

> Based on the experiences of its members, CUB believes that wealth should never enter into a determination of the best interests of the child, particularly in a surrogacy arrangement. Given the economic reality of a surrogacy arrangement, the contracting father would necessarily be relatively affluent compared to the mother whose primary incentive to enter such an arrangement would be her need for compensation.[204]

Traditional gender stereotypes should not be used as an argument either, as otherwise the biological mother would lose custody and visitation rights "because of bias against her and [because of] the superior wealth or the stereotypical role of the father."

> Given the unusual maternal role of the mother in a surrogacy arrangement (who initially agreed to give away her child to a virtual stranger) compared to the traditional parental role

---

[201] CUB, Orange County, Empire Branch, Newsletter, May/June 1987. SLHU MC 630, Box 29, Folder 6.
[202] Allison Ward was president of CUB from 1986 to 1988. After her involvement with the Whitehead case, the dedicated opponent of surrogacy joined a law firm. Letter from Alison Ward to Janet Fenton, President CUB, April 18, 1991. SLHU MC 630, Box 18, Folder 5.
[203] Brief of Concerned United Birthparents, Inc. as Amicus Curiae, Supreme Court of New Jersey, Docket No. 27.050. SLHU, MC 630, Box 18, Folder 3, 1–2.
[204] Brief of Concerned United Birthparents, Inc. as Amicus Curiae, Supreme Court of New Jersey, Docket No. 27.050. SLHU, MC 630, Box 18, Folder 3, 42–43.

of the father in that situation, the use of gender stereotypes would only disfavor the woman on factors that are not probative of her ability to love, care for and nurture her child.

> Gender bias is reflected by the way our society treats scornfully a woman who surrenders her child, but does not criticize as harshly a man who agrees to the adoption of his child.[205]

While other *amicus curiae* briefs were filed, including a joint submission from conservative "pro-life organizations," including Phyllis Schlafly's Eagle Forum, the Family Research Council, and Concerned Women for America, all of which concurred in rejecting the surrogacy contract and emphasizing the "parental rights" of the biological mother, CUB was the only organization to address the connection between patriarchal gender norms and wealth, recognizing that differing family values were also at issue here.[206]

The result of the ruling, namely the affirmation of Whitehead's parental rights, the assigning of custody to the Sterns and the establishment of visitation rights for Whitehead, was considered a success by CUB, since the rights of the "birthmother" had been recognized.[207] The same did not necessarily apply to the policy of promoting adoption supported so vehemently by President Reagan. Here the "birthmothers" often felt instrumentalized, as Karen Kottmeier resignedly noted:

> This belief [that adoptive parents and adopted children are destined for each other as "family"] reduces the birthmother to an instrument, a mere vessel—an idea which, in combination with sealed records, denies the birthpartents' humanity entirely—we become, in people's minds, a means to an end, nothing more.[208]

To advance his project of promoting adoption[209] at the national level, in 1987 Reagan appointed a Federal Adoption Task Force.[210] In his statement establishing this body, the president once again juxtaposed the willingness of U.S. families to adopt with children's need for a stable family life:

---

[205] Brief of Concerned United Birthparents, Inc. as Amicus Curiae, Supreme Court of New Jersey, Docket No. 27.050. SLHU, MC 630, Box 18, Folder 3, 44–44.

[206] Brief Amici Curiae, Brief of Concerned Women for America, Eagle Forum, National Legal Foundation, Family Research Council of America, United Families Foundation, Juridical Reform Project, Supreme Court of New Jersey, Docket No. 27.050. SLHU MC 639, Box 18, Folder 4.

[207] On this topic, see the coverage in the CUB periodicals *Family Advocate* and *Communicator* in 1987 and 1988. SLHU, MC 630, Box 29, Folders 6 and 7. *Communicator* 1987 and 1988.

[208] Letter from Karen Kottmeier, Denver, CO, CUB Secretary, to Mrs. Pratt, November 25, 1992. SLHU MC 630, Box 17, Folder 1.

[209] This includes dedicated efforts to place older children and those with "special needs," who were viewed as requiring extra care and support.

[210] The Task Force, which included Gary Bauer, submitted its report to the President in November 1987: "America's Waiting Children—A Report to the President from the Interagency Task Force on Adoption," November 1987. SLHU MC 630, Box 19. folder 1.

> Americans are a warm hearted, caring people and for years, American couples have reached out to embrace children who otherwise would grow up without a stable family life. We must expand and broaden our efforts to make sure that America's family-less children are adopted.[211]

In the *Fact Sheet on Adoption* launched at the same time, however, the notion of "infant adoption as an alternative to pregnant women" reappeared. Here, though, the focus was on "birthmothers":

> Also, many birth mothers who would prefer to place a child for adoption are unaware of how to exercise that option and therefore do not so.[212]

This renewed portrayal of potential birthmothers as insecure and ignorant caused the CUB executive committee to fear opposition from the membership, as evident in the September 1987 issue of the *Communicator*. Here, CUB reprinted the Task Force's press release and its *Fact Sheet on Adoption*, both of which a CUB member had sent in for publication. But CUB president Carole Anderson felt compelled to ask members to exercise restraint. If they wanted to communicate their views on the task force to their political representatives, they should do so in a factual and polite manner. Otherwise, their common interest would be jeopardized: "If you can't make a friend, don't make an enemy."[213]

Initially, meanwhile, the CUB leadership had officially welcomed the initiative and sent materials to the head of the Task Force on Adoption, social policy expert Mary Gall.[214] Their key objective was to highlight the perspective of the "birthparents," because this was all too often ignored:

> We are easy to overlook because birthparents come from all social and economic classes. We are housewives, lawyers, social workers, teachers, plumbers, doctors, electricians, administrators and probably your neighbors. The vast majority of birthparents continue to love and care for their children, and none of us have forgotten either our children or the experience of being young, vulnerable and temporarily without the resources we needed to keep our families together.[215]

---

211 Statement by the Assistant to the President for Press Relations, The White House, Office of the Press Secretary, Santa Barbara, CA, August 24, 1987. SLHU MC 630, Box 19, Folder 1.
212 "Task Force on Adoption Fact Sheet," The White House, Office of the Press Secretary, Santa Barbara, CA, August 24, 1987. SLHU MC 630, Box 19, Folder 1.
213 Carole Anderson, "President's Task Force to Promote Adoptions," *Communicator*, September 1987, 12–13.
214 Janet Fenton, Vice President CUB, to Mary Gall, Chairperson of the "President's Task Force on Adoption," September 15, 1987. Letter of thanks from Gary Bauer for the Task Force to Janet Fenton of CUB, September 22, 1987. SLHU MC 630, Box 19, Folder 1.
215 Janet Fenton, Vice President CUB, to Mary Gall, Chairperson of the "President's Task Force on Adoption," September 15, 1987. SLHU MC 630, Box 19, Folder 1.

The task force was impressed, as evident in Mary Gall's response.[216] In fact, its final report, the glossy brochure *America's Waiting Children*, included a statement on page one by a "birthmother" who explained that she had made a decision to have her child adopted consciously and thanks to "good counseling"—rather than merely thinking short-term and ending the pregnancy through abortion.[217] As becomes clear as one reads through the report, however, the focus was not on the mother's freedom of decision. Instead, teenagers in particular were to be encouraged to carry their pregnancy to term and then give up their children.

"The promotion of adoption as an alternative for a crisis pregnancy" was also the first of three core goals that the task force described as the quintessence of its work—in addition to expanding the circle of potential adoptive parents to include older people, single people, the disabled, and members of ethnic minorities, and assessing foster children in particular for their adoptability. Its specific recommendations on how to reduce abortion and bolster adoption thus included greater availability of counseling for pregnant teenagers—the key target group to be persuaded to give up their children. In addition, there was a call to expand counseling at Crisis Pregnancy Centers. These institutions were run by the anti-abortion movement and advertised free pregnancy tests, but once a pregnancy had been established they primarily sought to persuade their clients to carry the child to term (and later give it up for adoption). According to the Task Force, the cost of the care and medical treatment of pregnant women who were willing to have their child adopted up to the time of birth was to be covered by the adoption fees.[218]

The report thus articulated the need to contain two developments perceived as undesirable: first, the increase in the number of abortions and, second, the spread of single motherhood, especially among teenagers. The idea of curbing the latter phe-

---

216 Personal letter of thanks from Mary Gall to Janet Fenton sent together with the report and featuring handwritten note: "Just wanted to let you know that the Task Force read with interest the materials provided by CUB—very moving and well done", December 8, 1987. SLHU MC 630, Box 19, Folder 1. Mary Sheila Gall had served both the Reagan administrations and the George H. W. Bush administration as a social policy official, ultimately as Assistant Secretary of Health and Human Services. She had previously been head of the Task Force on Adoption, Counselor to the Director of the United States Office of Personnel Management (1986–1989) and Deputy Domestic Policy Adviser in the Office of the Vice President (1981–1986). George H. W. Bush: "Nomination of Mary Sheila Gall to Be an Assistant Secretary of Health and Human Services," February 28, 1989. Online at Gerhard Peters and John T. Woolley, The American Presidency Project <www.presidency.ucsb.edu/ws/?pid=16706>.
217 "America's Waiting Children—A Report to the President from the Interagency Task Force on Adoption," November 1987. SLHU MC 630, Box 19. Folder 1, 1.
218 "America's Waiting Children—A Report to the President from the Interagency Task Force on Adoption," November 1987. SLHU MC 630, Box 19. Folder 1, 17–21.

nomenon must have reminded CUB members of their own experience of powerlessness and infantilization when, as young women, they themselves had been denied the capacity for motherhood. This was brought home clearly by CUB's district director, Laura Lewis, in a letter to CUB Vice President Janet Fenton in February 1988. Lewis was to report on her experiences as a "birthmother" at a conference organized by the official National Committee for Adoption (NCFA),[219] and she asked Fenton for advice on how to compose her contribution, which she was obviously struggling with:

> I'm giving a lot of thought to it, and trying to work myself into a frame of mind where I'll be able to express my feelings without sounding too angry, which I am. As much as I hate the NCFA, there'll be social workers there who deal day-to-day with pregnant teenagers.[220]

Lewis had had harrowing experiences of her own—voluntarily giving up her son to save him from a bleak family situation involving an abusive husband, dropping out of college and drug abuse, then a period of personal consolidation, the birth of another three children, and engagement as an activist for CUB. Lewis feared that her complicated life story might be exploited by the conference organizers to confirm negative stereotypes about teenage "birthmothers."

> I married an abusive man, dropped out of college, abused drugs, you name it. My life was a self-fulfilling prophecy of everything they imply about "unwed mothers." The only reason I'm glad my son was adopted is that my husband would have abused him. But if I hadn't let my kid be adopted, I doubt I would have married an abusive man! But these people could turn this against me and say, "See, it goes to show your kid was better off adopted!"

> At the same time, I want to show the terrible damage this does to women, I know they'll pounce on anything they see as personal weakness. I don't care what they think about me, but I do feel I'm representing other birthmothers and want to do right by them. I will, as [CUB president] Carole suggested, stress that families should never be separated in the first place, but, let's face it, these people are adoptive parents and agency workers. This is their first goal.

Instead of rushing pregnant teenagers into adoptions, Lewis believed, one should first try to preserve the mother-child relationship. Hence, she contended, the claim, mostly made by men, "that abortion was worse on women" was not entirely accurate.[221]

---

219 Lewis had been invited by the National Committee for Adoption (NCFA) as CUB representative to address a conference of social workers, adoption facilitators, and adoptive parents about her experiences as a "birthmother." The conference was a high-profile event, with Mary Gall, president of the National Task Force on Adoption, giving the keynote address. Invitation to Laura Lewis to speak at the Conference of the National Committee for Adoption, April 26, 1988, Washington D.C. Conference program: SLHU MC 630, Box 2, Folder 2.
220 Letter from Laura Lewis to Jan(et) Frenton, February 26, 1988. SLHU MC 630, Box 2, Folder 2.
221 Letter from Laura Lewis to Jan(et) Frenton, February 26, 1988. SLHU MC 630, Box 2, Folder 2.

Thus, CUB members too criticized the simplistic contrast made by the Reagan Administration, the Task Force, and adoption agencies between "adoption" as a positive reproductive decision and "abortion" as a negative one. The CUB activists' discomfort was fueled by their own experience of powerlessness vis-à-vis parents, social workers, and experts, and the pain of giving up their child. This prompted them to argue for strengthening women's right to decide rather than curtailing it. On this point, they were on the same page as representatives of the women's movement and supporters of abortion—but for different reasons.

6.5 Interim conclusion: the family as arena of the "culture wars"

The family policy and welfare policies of the Reagan administration in the 1980s exalted the traditionally structured nuclear family featuring a male breadwinner and thus adhered to an ethnically and socially exclusive model of the family. "Single mothers" in particular were portrayed as a grave threat to the nation (unwanted children, overburdened mothers, delinquent youth) and to the welfare state ("welfare queens"). At the same time, the U.S. economy could not do without the "dual earner family," and families, for their part, generally needed two incomes to maintain or achieve middle-class lifestyles. We can thus discern an immanent contradiction between social change (the spread of the "dual earner family") and the imperative of strengthening the classically structured nuclear family with its male breadwinner and traditional gender roles.

This demonstrates the foresight of the Carter Conference, which, as early as 1980, had sought concrete solutions to ease the living situation of families with two working parents and of single mothers, and had understood women's employment as an element of social liberalization and pluralization. This objective was not pursued further by the Reagan administration; on the contrary, the president's family policy agenda centered on a promise to roll back the "abrasive experiments of two liberal decades" with regard to family values. By cutting welfare spending and publicly discrediting abortion, the administration put many women under both economic and moral pressure. Yet Reagan's criticism of the supposed decline in values and its negative impact on the nation rested largely on baseless assertions. There is no sound social statistical data indicating that the community was threatened from within. The abortion rate remained stable, and the divorce rate fell slightly (albeit with significantly fewer marriages overall). By contrast, the number of births out of wedlock demonstrably increased. But whether this was read as the "end of the family" or as the result of a change in sexual morality and the younger generation's less rigid ways of living depended on the observer. Nor do social statistics back up the claim that a ubiquitous practice of "welfare fraud"—condensed into the racist and misogynistic trope of the supposed African American "welfare queen"—threatened the nation from within. Although the number of welfare recipients remained constant through the 1980s, the share of African Americans declined significantly. At the same time, black women were in fact more likely to be single parents than their white counterparts, and they and their children were more likely to be on welfare—even if only temporarily. But crucially, white and African American families were not judged by the same standards, either by social experts or in public discourse. The social and ethnic "double standard" of U.S. society when it came to welfare policy is well illustrated by the treatment of African American teenage mothers. Because they did not or could not conform to the ideal of the nuclear family, they were particularly hard hit by both moral condemnation and ultimately by cuts in welfare benefits. Their reproductive decisions were considered inherently uninformed, irrational, and flawed, and thus as harmful to the community as a whole.

In contrast, members of pro-abortion organizations from the milieu of the new women's movement highlighted a woman's right to decide in matters of reproduction. At a personal level, they asserted their capacity to make informed and rational decisions, but also to act in the interests of their families. The state should not intervene in this context and become the "third person in bed with the couple." Meanwhile, women who had been forced to give up their babies as young mothers and had joined other "birthparents" in the 1980s to advocate for "adoption rights" viewed the Reagan administration's crude contrast between abortion ("danger to the nation") and adoption ("blessing to the nation") with skepticism. Above all, they criticized the deliberate denigration of mothers of illegitimate children by government and president as backward-looking. Thus, we can discern an intense conflict over responsible reproductive choices that was, at its core, a clash over individual rights and their curtailment for the supposed benefit of the nation.

In the 1980s, the struggle over the right to "reproductive choice" made the family a key theater of the culture wars. This demonstrated once again the potency of ethnic and social stereotypes, but also the achievements of social movements in asserting the individual right of decision.

Conclusion: Value of the family—continuity and change in the family ideal in the twentieth-century United States

How did the notion of what norms and values should ideally characterize the American family change over the course of the twentieth century? Was there even a "change in values" with respect to the family and the gender norms linked to it?

Analysis of public debates and expert discourses on divorce, women's employment, and reproduction, to cite the first key finding of the present book, shows that the ideal of the white middle-class nuclear family—described by sociologist Talcott Parsons in the 1940s as the "modern isolated nuclear family"—remained the national norm and the discursive frame of reference in the United States throughout the twentieth century. This ideal acted upon members of society as a *dispositif* in the sense set out by Michel Foucault, a constellation of values and power to which they had to relate and toward which they had to gear their conduct. Even attempts to live consciously beyond the classical family entailed an implicit affirmation and actualization of this ideal, if only through actors' efforts to set themselves apart from it. The national family ideal was highly exclusive in ethnic and social terms, and in reality, only attainable and livable for a minority of Americans, but this did not diminish its potency. Social experts in particular, and the body of knowledge they generated, helped flesh out and disseminate this national ideal; their practical advice and guidelines mostly sought to perpetuate it.

In what follows, I condense the findings of the present study into nine propositions. First, an overview of the three empirical fields of the study—debates and expert discourses on divorce, women's employment, and reproduction—summarizes the main diachronic developments. The second section takes stock—with reference to the family—of the negotiation of norms, values, and social change. I then discuss the significance of the factors of "race, class, and gender" within the concept of the (nuclear) family before finally seeking to answer the book's fundamental question: can we discern a "change in family values"?

1 Debates and expert discourses on divorce, women's employment, and reproduction in the twentieth century—a diachronic overview

Divorce

As early as the beginning of the twentieth century, divorce mutated from a moral into a social problem and became central to efforts to grapple with the pluralization of sexual and gender norms. The rising number of divorces appeared to contemporaries as an expression of the individualism associated with modernity, but also as evidence that many individuals (especially women) were no longer willing to simply put up with intolerable private lives and were determined to dissolve their marriages. Evaluations of this topic depended on one's political and moral standpoint: while some perceived divorce as an attack on the family and thus on the nation ("race suicide") or regarded it as an expression of moral decay, others saw it as a timely "remedy for social ills." The issue that united all debates and expert statements was women's position in society—regardless of whether the actors involved were striving to enshrine biologistic legal provisions and gender roles or were pursuing equal rights and social equality for women. In the early debates of the Progressive Era, the center of discursive gravity clearly shifted away from churchmen, who gradually lost their moral supremacy, to social experts, especially representatives of the still young field of sociology. The latter made their mark as scientists and experts in the interpretation of social phenomena by collecting and analyzing empirical data for the first time. But the discussion of divorce rates in the twentieth century also had an ethnic component. In the 1960s, the incidence of divorce among African Americans (and other minorities) gradually began to match trends in the majority society. Yet from this point on, divorce received special attention in expert discourses on the state of the black family. The divorce rate of this minority now served experts as evidence of the supposedly deficient family structure and unsatisfactory family values of African Americans, which were in turn linked to the high number of black single mothers. There was a complete failure to acknowledge the connection between socioeconomic discrimination, restrictive welfare regulations, and family breakdown.

Overall, the increase in divorce rates represented a secular trend, but it was not as unique and ineluctable as contemporaries imagined. In fact, by the end of the 1980s, divorce rates were beginning to decline, and remarriage rates remained consistently high. Conversely, the introduction of no-fault divorce in most states in the early 1970s had a significant liberalizing effect, as couples could now dispense with torturous "courtroom battles," denigrating attributions of blame, and admissions of guilt that could have serious consequences. Yet the simplification of the divorce process also led to the relocation of social inequality, as the women's movement in particular rightly criticized. Divorced women were (and still are) often faced with serious economic problems, since they usually received no alimony and there was no attempt to factor in any child-rearing periods, though these were typically detrimental to their careers.

A change in values with respect to divorce—and this is my first proposition—cannot be demonstrated solely with reference to the no-fault divorce of the 1970s: the first two decades of the twentieth century identified divorce as a social (and no longer a moral) problem, while the 1980s saw the intensification of polemical attacks on "single mothers" and fragmented families.

Women's employment

The increase in women's gainful employment in the twentieth century was another secular trend. In 1980, for the first time, there were more families with children in which both parents worked than those that depended exclusively on a male breadwinner. Subsequently, there was an increase in both the number of high-earning women and those households in which women were the sole earners. At the same time, the fundamental difference in career opportunities and income between men and women, which the women's movement of the 1970s had so emphatically criticized, persisted.

The debates on women's employment reveal a profound shift in perception along the axes of "race" and "class." While the traditionally high labor market participation of working-class women and African Americans did not lead to a public debate in the U.S. at any time during the twentieth century but was taken as read or accepted unquestioningly by experts and the public alike, the growing employment of white women prompted interventions by demographers, physicians, and psychologists. Around the middle of the century, they linked their concerns over the increasing wage labor of mothers with the debate on the supposedly insufficient reproduction of white American women and on the future of the nation. The legitimacy or desirability of maternal employment played a major role as individuals and movements tussled over notions of desirable and undesirable motherhood. From the 1950s to the 1970s, (white, male) social experts demanded that white, middle-class women return to their reproductive role—and at most regarded part-time work as compatible with family life. Non-white women, meanwhile, had to provide for themselves, otherwise they risked being slandered as "welfare queens." If they raised their children alone and formed networks with other women, they were labeled "black matriarchs." Maternal dominance, in turn, provided an explanation for the deviance of children, especially sons. In the 1980s, the Reagan administration ramped up the "welfare queen" polemics and cut welfare spending. Widespread criticism of alleged "welfare fraud" later facilitated the reform of the 1990s, which made mothers' paid work a precondition for receiving benefits.

My second key proposition is that the debates on women's employment do not furnish us with clear evidence of value change since on close inspection it turns out that biologistic gender norms and both racist and social prejudices were often central to the associated discourse.

Reproduction

The debates and expert discourses on reproduction also permeated the entire twentieth century and were again strongly segmented according to "race" and "class." While the initial focus was on "reproductive morality" and eugenics, around the middle of the century the discussion was dominated by the goal of restricting the reproduction of non-white families, which was then superseded by the question of access to contraception and reproductive self-determination. In the field of reproduction in particular, there is abundant evidence that the women's movement contributed to many women patients turning away from male experts and toward the emerging women's health movements. At the same time, experts, politicians, grassroots movements, and ordinary Americans began to argue with particular ferocity over abortion, a woman's right to choose, and the embryo's right to life—a debate that remains just as hotly contested today. In the issue of the individual's right to decide about reproduction, notions of the family as the basis of the nation (primacy of the state) converged with concepts of self-determined decision-making (primacy of the individual).

If, on the other hand, we ask at what point reproduction constitutes a conscious decision, the conclusion must be that there is no one-dimensional answer. Throughout the twentieth century, race, class, and gender were key categories of difference when it came to reproductive decision-making. These categories made their impact in the form of different approaches to knowledge about reproduction and contraception, but also in clearly defined ideas about the "nuclear family" as the "basis of the nation," ideas that were overlain and shaped by the "scientification of the social."

These factors took varying forms at different times. Until the 1930s, a paternalistic expert discourse prevailed that affirmed traditional, biologistic gender role attributions. From World War I onward, the worldwide boom in eugenics brought an additional category of inequality into play, namely the distinction between healthy and sick, desirable and undesirable. After World War II, the experts' reasoning changed: instead of selection, conscious family planning was now supposed to contribute to the wellbeing of the American nation and the world. In the 1960s and 1970s, medical techniques and preparations increased the potential for individual reproductive decisions; at the same time, the continued practice of forced sterilization demonstrated the ongoing economization of the social in conjunction with racist exclusionary practices. The 1980s saw fierce clashes between abortion opponents and supporters. In addition, there was widespread criticism of the supposedly flawed reproductive choices of women welfare recipients and single mothers. This critique was opposed by representatives of various social movements such as the women's movement, the pro-choice movement, the women's health movement and, finally, the "birthparent movement."

Hence, my third proposition is that despite the expansion of reproductive choices in the 1960s and 1970s there can be no question of a straightforward change in values. The classical categories of inequality, namely "race, class, and gender," along with traditional family values and hegemonic expert knowledge, however, proved significant and long-lasting.

2 Family values and social change in the modern age

Liberal values and traditional forms

The family was *the* field in which the challenges of modernity—the pluralization of norms, dynamization of social structures, and individualization of lifestyles—were negotiated with particular intensity and with significant participation by social scientists. This is illustrated first of all by the divorce debate at the beginning of the twentieth century, when sociologists made their mark as new experts on social change. Ending the traditional moral monopoly of church representatives and jurists, they analyzed divorce as a social phenomenon and identified the family as a site of ambivalent responses to modernity. In the debates over reproduction and motherhood of the 1920s and 1930s, meanwhile, social experts ensured—against the backdrop of world war and economic crisis—that the government discovered the family as an object of policy. These experts provided contingency management through advice expressed in pragmatic form. We can draw a clear line between the call for "scientific motherhood" to improve pregnancy, childbirth, and child-rearing and the popularization of eugenics as a cutting-edge means of producing "high-quality" offspring for the nation, including coercive measures such as sterilization and marriage bans. Under the impact of Nazi racial policies and the privileging of family and privacy as a locus of national self-affirmation during the Cold War, eugenics in the United States then began to transform into genetically based marriage and family counseling.

The debate on the social pros and cons of women's employment made the effects of modernity particularly palpable. Part-time work by women and mothers, for example, gradually became socially acceptable in the 1950s and 1960s, albeit with reference to its economic necessity. In contrast, a powerful conservative coalition of physicians, psychologists, and demographers perceived so-called "modern women" who were striving for self-fulfillment and careers as a threat to the nation's survival because they posed a fundamental challenge to existing gender relations. In 1980, the Carter administration's White House Conference on Families marked a clear break with this conservative lament about the "crisis of the family" in the face of changing gender roles, bringing citizens together with experts in an attempt to meet the changing needs of the family. The resulting recommendations included expanding childcare to allow both parents to work, but crucially the conference also simply acknowledged that in 1980 the family could be far more diverse than Parson's nuclear model. Apparently, though, this acceptance of pluralistic family values and forms was not embraced by most Americans at the beginning of the 1980s. Ronald Reagan thus attracted widespread support with his call for a "restoration of the nuclear family," which seemed to many voters an apt response to the "unreasonable demands of modernity," which now manifested themselves in women's employment, divorce reform, and the legalization of abortion.

From the 1960s onward, experts cited the desperate situation of many African American families as another example of the dark side of modern society. Their predicament, they contended, was a result of economic disadvantages, inadequate housing in the urban ghettos, poor education, and inadequate social participation, but was due above all to deficient family values. A correlation was established that—in an analytically fuzzy and deliberately simplistic way—causally linked moral values and economic situation, without, however, considering the consequences of centuries of racial discrimination. In the context of the Johnson administration's War on Poverty, experts planned to document and combat these "social ills" on the basis of modern social scientific findings (on birth control, urban planning, and education). Their accomplishments were meager, however, because the government gradually withdrew funding for federal welfare and equality programs as a result of the Vietnam War and the change in policy under Nixon. Representatives of the civil rights and Black Power movements, meanwhile, underscored the negative effects of industrial modernity on the black minority, which led them to demand more and better social programs. At the same time, the civil rights movement in particular emphasized the importance of the nuclear family to achieving economic and social stability and—like the Black Power movement—propagated a strictly biologistic understanding of gender roles. In the 1980s, by contrast, conservative experts purposely detached their analyses of the lot of African American "single mothers" and women welfare recipients from structures of socioeconomic inequality. Instead, they put forward a moral critique of irresponsible "welfare queens" and "teenage mothers."

Hence, the debates analyzed in this book bring out the highly emotive and tension-filled nature of attempts to grapple with the impositions of modernity with reference to the family. Liberal values gained ground from the middle of the twentieth century onward (the official abolition of racial discrimination, the beginnings of gender equality, the strengthening of individuality and self-determination). But these values were always confronted by conservative ideas (expert criticism of female employment and self-realization, the anti-abortion movement, and neoconservative and religiously motivated concepts of the nuclear family—with its supposedly deep historical roots—as the basis of the nation). This ambivalent picture of liberal change and persistent conservatism, and this is my fourth proposition, explains the observation at the beginning of the book that at the end of the twentieth century the understanding of "family" in the United States could include liberal values but was always oriented toward a traditional structure.

Social practice and normative change

When it comes to the American family, what we find is a highly ambivalent relationship between processes of social change and normative evolution. Social transformation generated specific demands for normative change—the women's movement's call for the legalization of abortion against the background of the widespread practice of illegal abortions is a prime example of this. Conversely, normative changes could also bring social change in their wake, as when restrictive welfare legislation in the 1990s induced welfare recipients to increase their use of permanent or long-term contraceptive methods.

The various fields investigated here reveal how conflictive the relationship between social and normative change was. Expert discourses and debates on divorce show how it began to become established as a social practice in the Progressive era and, due to the development of demography and population statistics, also became empirically describable. This not only triggered the conservative evocation of crisis but prompted the new discipline of sociology to put forward scientific interpretations and inspired demands for normative adaptation. The latter, however, did not occur until the early 1970s, when the states gradually introduced no-fault divorce. New fears of social change arose as a result of this normative shift. The women's movement, for example, rightly assailed the economic disadvantage suffered by many divorced women because the new divorce laws eliminated the obligation to pay alimony.

In the debates on reproduction, meanwhile, it was the activities of the eugenics movement that first demonstrated how society could be segmented according to biologistic criteria. Eugenic knowledge penetrated into the heart of society through the Fitter Family contests, but above all due to the spread of marriage and family counseling informed by hereditary biology. The associated attempt to re-biologize gender norms suggests that the revival of traditional values (the refocusing of the white American family on its "duty" to reproduce) could be impelled by social change (declining birth rates among white American women in modern society). It also became abundantly clear that individual rights—to reproduction, physical integrity, and ultimately to life—were tied to these supposedly rational criteria (the good of the nation, the birth rate, hereditary desirability), which could in turn interface with traditions of racism. Thus, until the early 1970s, there was no social resistance to the forced sterilization of African American and Mexican American women, despite many social experts' profound concerns about the "low" reproductive rates of white American women.

In the same vein, the National Organization of Women (NOW) put forward its demands for legal equality for women essentially with a view to *white* women. NOW advocated job-related equality, reproductive choice (contraception and abortion), and an Equal Rights Amendment (ERA). While the ERA failed due to opposition from the conservative family-centered women's movement around publicist Phyllis Schlafly and the vetoes of numerous states, the progressive women's movement achieved a major victory when the Supreme Court legalized abortion. At the same time, women's groups began to acquire health-related knowledge, thus challenging the authority of predominantly male experts. Meanwhile, beginning in the 1970s, those affected by forced sterilization, mostly African American and Mexican-born women, began to protest against the interventions of social experts and physicians, and in some cases even won compensation in court and apologies from states for their racist population policies. It is important to note, however, that it was initially the *victims* of sterilization policies who spoke out. It was to be a long time before these victims and their concerns were heard within the majority society, with apologies and compensation payments by states having to wait until the twenty-first century.

Finally, the changing social valuation of women's employment and, in particular, of the gainful employment of the mothers of young children illustrates how, since the 1950s, changing social practices in the form of the increasing employment of women and mothers have necessitated gradual normative adjustments. These normative shifts were backed by the empirical studies produced by liberal social scientists and the second wave of the women's movement, beginning in the 1960s. Yet it was economic factors rather than those intended to liberalize the family ideal that set the pace: women's employment evolved from part-time to full-time ("dual earner couples") chiefly out of economic necessity.

Thus, my fifth proposition is that the twentieth-century family reveals a tense and by no means linear relationship between social practice and normative change. One clear trend we can identify, however, is the increasing importance of social movements, which from the 1960s onward began to challenge the position of (white, male) social experts as analysts of social change and pioneers of normative adaptation and called for their interests to be taken into account.

Social experts and clients

In the expert discourses and debates on the American family, social scientists did not limit themselves to diagnosing processes of change and social problems. They also recommended and implemented concrete measures to improve families and their values. In the early discussions of divorce, the unanimous demand for "social control," which was endowed with scientific and rational legitimacy, is striking. Even liberal experts were keen to restrict too much individuality and to tie individuals to their duty to society. Eugenics, meanwhile, planned to strengthen the U.S. family as the basis of the nation through the targeted promotion of "high-quality" families and their offspring and by preventing the reproduction of sick individuals or those considered "inferior." Here, the connection to the international racial discourse of the 1920s and 1930s is important, as is the fact that this ideology, in the form of hereditary biological marriage counseling and forced sterilization, endured into the 1970s.

Physicians, demographers, and psychologists asserted themselves in the debate on women's employment because they had new methods of diagnosis and therapy to offer the modern woman, who was, supposedly, psychologically disturbed and reproductively dysfunctional. Their efforts to renegotiate gender roles using the tools of modern science did not increase the rate of reproduction, but it did serve as a foundation for the conservative turn of the 1980s. Meanwhile, the Moynihan controversy over the supposed "pathology" of the African American family demonstrates the ambivalence of the relationship between social scientific analysis and normative reorientation. On the one hand, Moynihan triggered a bitter public tussle over the validity of the white nuclear family ideal. On the other hand, in the longer term the associated debate helped integrate African American families into this ideal—without, however, modifying it significantly as a result.

Although the Supreme Court ruled that in principle women could decide whether to continue or terminate their pregnancies, it did so with explicit reference to the overriding importance of medical advice. In line with this, clinicians made unilateral decisions about the forced sterilization of female welfare recipients and immigrant women on a scale that has only been rudimentarily studied. Further, social experts—more than a few of them with roots in the eugenics movement—played a key role in exporting contraceptive techniques to developing countries within the framework of international population policy. In this context, too, they disseminated their idea of the "modern isolated nuclear family" as the underpinning of society and made this the basis of their interventions.

Sociological careers like Edward E. Ross's, lives such as Paul B. Popenoe's, and the role of scholar/politician of the kind played by Daniel P. Moynihan impressively demonstrate the key function of social experts in dealing with and talking about the family. All were united by the desire to improve and nurture the family as the basis of society and the nucleus of the nation. To this end, all proposed a combination of modern scientific analysis and diagnostics plus apt reform measures. Ross argued around 1900 for the acceptance of divorce in conjunction with a simultaneous expansion of "social control"; Popenoe favored eugenics in the 1930s and, from 1940, hereditary-biological marriage counseling; Moynihan devised a social science-inspired reformist policy in the 1960s to stabilize African American nuclear families; and in the 1980s, Gary Bauer sought to hem in the family in moral terms while concurrently curbing welfare spending. All drew on the techniques of modern "social engineering." Ross's example shows the need to date the start of the "scientification of the social," which saw expert intervention on a large scale and is typically located between 1930 and 1960, earlier, namely by including the preceding period from the turn of the century, and to end it somewhat later.

Social experts' diagnoses and proposals were intensively received, commented on, and criticized by journalists and letter writers in the media as well as by social movements. The women's movement in particular intervened in the interpretive struggles over female gender roles, while the civil rights movement shone a critical light on proposals for "improving" African American families. What is interesting here, first, is that the early women's movement helped disseminate and popularize expert advice within the debate on divorce, demonstrating that social movements made an impact on the family ideal well before the 1960s. Second, there were clear limits to the normative changes envisaged by members of the women's and civil rights movements. For example, the representatives of the white women's movement of the 1960s completely disregarded black women's experience of discrimination. Through their struggle for female equality and self-determined reproduction, NOW activists actually reinforced the mechanisms of oppression to which African American women were subject in U.S. society. Unlike their white counterparts, the latter initially sought equality on the basis of "race" and pursued reproductive rights in the broadest sense, for which they were willing to make very different compromises than white feminists. Meanwhile, men within the civil rights and

Black Power movements were prepared to accept traditional, narrow definitions of gender in the name of strengthening the African American family—and in accordance with their own ideal of masculinity.

Expert advice on all aspects of the family was not only administered but was also appropriated by clients. Women, men, and families consciously accessed social technologies and used them to pursue their own ends. This is evident in efforts to reorganize child-rearing according to scientific principles in an attempt to achieve "scientific motherhood," as well as in the way couples and families used Fitter Family contests and hereditary-biological marriage and family counseling to obtain information about their ancestry and "hereditary health." Members of the civil rights movement, meanwhile, called on social scientists to intervene to improve the lives of the black minority. To this end, they developed their own understanding of desirable—"liberal"—social engineering, which was intended both to strengthen the African American family and fortify traditional gender roles ("male breadwinner"). Likewise, women and couples requested contraceptive knowledge and access to legal abortion or fertilization methods. All of this shows that individuals purposefully and consciously drew on expert knowledge to enhance their agency. Finally, the women's and women's health movements illustrate how, from the 1960s/1970s onward, individuals acquired expert knowledge and passed it on—beyond the traditionally patriarchal and hierarchical relationship between doctor and patient or expert and client.

The continuity of eugenic thinking and the associated expert advice far beyond the caesura of World War II, and this is my sixth proposition, is one of the most significant findings of the present study. Into the 1980s, experts used the family as a starting point for their ideas about eugenic, welfare, and health policy, which they presented as a population policy in keeping with the times. Individual reproductive desires were to be subordinated to the goal of containing supposedly perilous population growth and fostering the "healthy" family as the basis of the nation. It was the appropriation of expert knowledge by those affected that led to a rethinking here over the longer term.

3 The family as the basis of the nation and the significance of "race, class, and gender" as categories of inequality

Three fields illustrate the relevance of gender-related, social, and ethnic categories to the negotiation of the U.S. family ideal in the twentieth century: the relationship between state and individual, a fixation on the white middle-class family, and the still biologistic gender norm of the wife and mother within the family.

State and individual

The family was already being portrayed as the basis of the nation in the early twentieth-century debate on alleged "race suicide." At the end of the twentieth century, meanwhile, Ronald Reagan based his criticism of legal abortion on the family's crucial role as the foundation of state and society, with the woman's right to decide clearly of secondary import in this context. The question is whether there has been any change at all in the centrality of the family over the course of the twentieth century.

While the family remained the discursive frame for reflection on the nation's well-being throughout the period under study (which is the source of its implicit centrality to government policy and public debates), we can identify characteristic differences in both policies and discourses. For example, while in 1965 President Lyndon B. Johnson sought to use concerns about the African American family as a starting point for social policy interventions, two decades later Ronald Reagan argued that only by slashing welfare could the family be strengthened as the basis of the nation. Johnson and Reagan embodied two ideal-typical and opposing sociopolitical models, namely expert-backed social policy and welfare retrenchment, models that can be found in different gradations throughout the twentieth century in the United States. It is interesting to note that the normative sphere always received emphasis when the government reduced socioeconomic investments that benefited families. Thus, in the 1950s, against the backdrop of the Cold War, the "modern isolated nuclear family" was exalted as the family form best suited to the capitalist economy. The associated privileging of the "male breadwinner" confronted wife and children with traditional gender norms and dependency structures—condensed in ideal-typical form in the myth of the "golden age of the family" and embodied in contemporary sitcoms. In the 1980s, meanwhile, women welfare recipients were held to conservative moral criteria within the framework of an ethnic and social "double standard," with these criteria indirectly determining the granting of welfare benefits. While the government reduced welfare spending, an ultraconservative morality caused it to act as the "third person in bed with the couple" when it came to reproductive decisions. Individual decision-making rights tended to be enhanced when the government was more active in social policy terms, as in the New Deal era (key examples being the Social Security Act and the notion of welfare as an "entitlement") or during the Great Society era under Johnson (as embodied in civil rights laws, welfare legislation, and moves to achieve equal rights). Crucially in this context, the Supreme Court, with its direct lawmaking authority, was the key actor alongside president and Congress.

My seventh proposition, then, is that family norms and values have always served as a litmus test for the state of the nation. Yet the interplay of social policy and the propagation of certain familial norms does not exhibit a linear development, but rather a striking interweaving. At times of growing welfarist intervention, individual opportunities for participation increased, while the curbing of government spending on the family went hand in hand with a reduction in individual decision-making rights. Hence, at the end of the period considered in this book, the focus shifted from an emphasis on individual rights (to divorce, employment, and reproduction) back to privileging the interests of the "community" (the embryo's right to life, slashing the welfare budget). Again, this does not indicate a long-term change in values.

The hegemony of the white middle-class family

Ethnic and social inequality run like a thread through debates and expert discourses on family values. Early discussions of divorce already centered exclusively on the white middle class. Only a few years later, the eugenics movement viewed the upper- and middle-class white family as an "ancestral community" and affirmed the reproductive and economic role of marriage as crucial to the wellbeing of the nation. Ethnic minorities and lower-class families had no place in this "positive eugenics," appearing in debates exclusively as addressees of "negative eugenics," such as forced sterilization, or as the object of social policy interventions. This consciously selective perception of the factors of "race, class, and gender" in terms of their importance to the family and their linkage with the findings of modern reproductive medicine help explain what made careers like Paul B. Popenoe's (from eugenicist to nationally prominent marriage and family counselor) possible in the first place. His traditional interpretation of these three key categories fit well with the views of a majority of Americans in the middle decades of the twentieth century, and it was not until the 1970s that it was challenged on a broad social basis.

The women's movement of the 1960s, meanwhile, demanded social acceptance of mothers' employment. While this was in principle pertinent to working-class women and members of ethnic minorities, it failed to reflect their lack of access to affordable childcare. Hence, this demand implicitly fortified a racial and class-specific curtailing of the family ideal. In addition, from the mid-1950s through the 1970s, a discourse at large among medical professionals and demographers foregrounded the mental health and declining reproductive rates of white women and aired possible countermeasures. This discourse was consciously discriminatory in ethnic and social terms and, to a certain extent, saw itself as a perpetuation of "positive eugenics" using the tools of modern population science. It was an approach that dovetailed neatly with demands for forced sterilization—based on the supposed benefits to society, notably from a eugenic perspective—as well as for permanent contraceptives for female welfare recipients, since these measures were intended to prevent the reproduction of women who were neither white nor middle-class.

In the debate over the supposed decline of African American families, the effects of social and ethnic inequality were themselves the issue. While civil rights activists assailed social scientists' uncritical transfer of white middle-class values and norms to the black minority, they themselves insisted on the ideal of the "male breadwinner" as the objective for the black family and used this perspective to demand better jobs and earning opportunities for black men. Black women in the 1960s, on the other hand, often reacted with incomprehension to white housewives' complaints about their unfulfilling existence (Betty Friedan's "comfortable concentration camp"). After all, it was precisely the opportunity to run a household and raise children (rather than engaging in wage labor) that they viewed as desirable and unattainable. The welfare rights movement of the 1970s and 1980s also argued in favor of classical family structures when it called for the guaranteeing of a family income rather than inadequate welfare benefits. Similarly, the abortion advocates and "birthmothers" of the 1980s justified their decisions as "in the interests of their families" while gay couples, as Jürgen Martschukat has argued, embraced classical family arrangements as they sought to gain acceptance within society. For much of the twentieth century, Mexican American families too attempted to achieve upward mobility and respectability through the conscious adoption and demonstration of "American family values."

Although individual projects of social change such as the Black Power movement and the radical wing of the women's movement foregrounded alternative family values to differentiate themselves from a majority society they perceived as repressive, overall it was ethnic, social, and other minorities efforts' to gradually appropriate or at least constructively transform the majority ideal that predominated.

The constancy of the nuclear family ideal across all phases of socioeconomic transformation illustrates that even a markedly heterogeneous reality (the diversity of family life among Americans in the twentieth century) could be corralled by a highly homogeneous and homogenizing norm (the ideal of the white nuclear family) and interpreted on this basis. In this process, social experts provided concrete advice on how to maintain, expand, or transform norms. Another key player was the media as an arena of public debate and occasional site of expert discourse, along with advertising, which always had the interests of consumers in mind and addressed normative renegotiations with considerable sensitivity.

My eighth proposition is that all in all the ideal of the white middle-class family was so significant that it overarched and determined every debate on the family in the twentieth century. This was true even of the discourses of social movements and ethnic minorities.

The family as the "woman's domain"

Throughout the period investigated in this book, debates on family values were to a considerable extent struggles over the position of women in the family, their rights and tasks—regardless of whether they were centered on change or persistence. While the Progressive-era divorce debate echoed the early women's movement's goal of understanding women as individuals with rights and agency, the reproduction debate of the 1920s and 1930s reemphasized women's primary responsibility for the family, reproduction, and the stability of their marriages. Women became the priority target of expert advice and later marriage counseling, with experts such as Paul B. Popenoe specifically attempting to persuade advice-seekers to maintain traditional, supposedly "natural" gender norms, at most augmented by moderate concessions such as a partnership-based conception of marriage. When it came to female employment, women gained some self-determination and a wider range of options in the postwar period. Yet the discourse on the employed woman's reproduction from the 1950s to the 1970s rolled back some of the leeway that had just been attained as women's role was re-biologized. Finally, the most visible actors in the civil rights movement were men, most of whom advocated traditional gender roles to strengthen the African American family. The Black Power movement, on the other hand, championed black hypermasculinity as a means of social self-assertion and reduced women to their reproductive function. Together with the white women's movement's neglect and lack of understanding, this increased the pressure on African American women, as clearly articulated by the black women's movement. White social experts blamed the supposed matriarchy of African American women for the decline they identified in the black family. Finally, the women's movement of the 1960s and 1970s demanded comprehensive social equality for women but was itself ambivalent in its attitude toward the position of women in marriage and the family. Here a generational conflict arose between established activists and the more radical exponents of the women's liberation movement, as evinced by criticism of no-fault divorce (as a threat to the housewife and mother) and also by discussions of sexuality and responsibility for contraception.

Hence, we can discern a fundamental trend toward the liberalization of gender norms—starting with women's suffrage and followed by the rise of elementary principles of equality, changes in education and employment, and finally the struggle over reproductive choice. Yet countervailing developments and opposition are just as conspicuous. Of particular importance are attempts to constrain women's reproductive decision-making. These efforts were associated with an emphasis on women's primary responsibility for reproduction and contraception; restrictive practices of sterilization justified on eugenic grounds or with reference to the needs of society; and the privileging of the embryo's right to life over the mother's right to decide. But male gender norms also exhibit ruptures and renegotiations, as clearly visible in the de facto demise of the male breadwinner model—which is obsolete in real terms but still very much alive at the normative level ("gender pay gap," discussions of maternal labor). Men who were members of ethnic or social minorities were relentlessly confronted with white, heterosexual "hegemonic masculinity." This is apparent in the example of African American men: already struggling with their often precarious socio-economic status, they also had to negotiate their masculinity, as evinced by the civil rights movement's "I am a Man" campaign of 1968. At the same time, the aggressive masculinity extolled by the Black Power movement heaped further pressure on African American women. The latter already faced the "double jeopardy" (Frances Beale) of being women and black. African American (and Mexican American) women had to defend any enhanced freedoms in the sphere of gender relations against discriminatory tendencies, the latter palpable, for example, in references to the "black matriarch" (with her excessive decision-making power) and "hyperfertile breeders" (who thoughtlessly produced too many children).

My ninth proposition is that expert discourses and debates on the family revolved mainly around the position and role of women and mothers, their rights and duties. Yet the equation of women with the family and the idea that they had a fundamental duty to preserve the family was by no means solely a conservative trope. It can be found among both conservative social experts and feminists, Black Panthers and members of the anti-abortion movement. This finding is important because it demonstrates the persuasiveness and continuity of biologistic gender norms to the present day (the idea of women as solely responsible for reproduction), which coexists with a tendency toward the pluralization and liberalization of gender norms (with respect to both women and men) since the 1960s.

4 The value of the family rather than value change

The present study has shown that there was no single, definitive value change with respect to the family in the twentieth-century United States. Instead, multiple small waves or processes of normative and attitudinal change can be traced with regard to gender norms and family concepts. These were heterogeneous and conflict-ridden and by no means unaffected by political-economic, religious, and racist counter-movements—always against the background of the concept of the nuclear family.

The divorce debate demonstrates that at the beginning of the twentieth century divorce had already ceased to be regarded as a moral catastrophe and was instead viewed as a concomitant of modernity and thus as rationally manageable. It was in fact interpreted as a social policy "remedy" for intolerable relationships that ultimately harmed society, or as a means of dissolving marriages that were "undesirable" from a eugenic point of view. We can identify an important change in values in the fact that by the end of the Progressive Era divorce was no longer understood as a complete breakdown of the family and the social order but as a social policy device. The reproductive discourse of the 1920s and 1930s, on the other hand, exemplifies a restorative countermovement: eugenicists used the tools of modern science to evoke the re-establishment of a biologistic conception of gender that was intended to return women to a purely reproductive role and enshrine the idea of men as sole family breadwinners.

In the 1950s, advertising and magazines in particular lay bare an initial trend toward hedonistic values—long before the upheavals of the mid-1960s. Consumption, beauty, and the personal grooming and care of the modern woman and wife were already to the fore during this period, though this in no way challenged the ideal of the nuclear family. Meanwhile, social experts began to view African American families as "families" in the mid-1960s in one of the most significant expansions of the national family ideal. In this process, however, the ideal of the white nuclear family as described by Parsons was not superseded but was instead gradually adopted by the black minority.

By the same token, a look at the negotiation of reproduction and reproductive choice shows how long-lived biologistic gender roles and patterns of interpretation were, again subverting any simple notion of linear "value change." The continuation of eugenics with the means of modern population policy was based on a concept of the "healthy family" that consciously distinguished between value and lack of value. This was evident in the long-standing practice of forced sterilization as well as the measures taken by both the national and international movements to control population growth. The redefinition of the relationship between government and individual through two crucial legal decisions, the legalization of abortion and the introduction of no-fault divorce, points to a long-term change in values. Yet even these examples of fundamentally liberal norm-making have been and continue to be heavily criticized—by the pro-life movement, still vigorous today, and by the women's rights movement itself, which saw divorce practices as a threat to the socioeconomic survival of many women.

What matters from a historical perspective is not so much whether a liberal or conservative conception of the family will prevail over the long term, but to what extent the conflict-ridden negotiation processes centered on the family and gender roles permit—or perhaps even necessitate—new, alternative periodizations of American history. It is true that the 1960s and early 1970s constitute a significant period of transformation, and this includes the family and its values (moves toward equal rights, recognition of African American families as "families," a growing belief in women's reproductive decision-making rights, and the adoption of no-fault divorce). At the same time, liberalization processes that have so far received less attention can also be discerned in the period before World War I (the divorce debate), the 1950s (women as consumers), and even during the Reagan Era (birth mothers and "adoption rights"). Moreover, the classic "liberal decades" of the 1920s/1930s and the 1960s/1970s also feature attempts to (re)biologize gender roles and intervene radically in supposedly deficient families with the help of eugenics and "socially beneficial" sterilization.

Rather than working on the assumption of sweeping "value change" with respect to the family, then, we need to probe the "value of the family" in debates and discourses in an open-ended way. This enables us to reevaluate the caesuras of twentieth-century American history as well as individuals' room for maneuver within both family and society.

Acknowledgments

Producing *Family Values* has been an adventure at both the intellectual and human levels, one shaped in multiple ways by my families—my own family and my academic one. Reason enough to take this opportunity to thank all those who have given me advice and support over the years, discussed my ideas with me, and broadened my perspective. I began my first family-focused explorations of social change in the United States as a postdoc at the University of Freiburg. After writing my first book on Nazi race policies and the history of the holocaust, I thoroughly enjoyed the opportunity to switch perspectives and turn to family norms and the gender order as objects of scholarly analysis. Special thanks go to Ulrich Herbert and my colleagues in the working group on contemporary history at Freiburg for their critical feedback and constructive encouragement. Thanks also to the staff of the German Historical Institute in Washington D.C, who first opened my mind to U.S. social history as early as 2003 during a short stay as a postdoctoral fellow.

For my research on "Family Values and Social Change: the U.S. Family in the Twentieth Century," I received substantial funding from the German Research Foundation that enabled me to establish an Emmy Noether Research Group for early career scholars in 2009—for which I am immensely grateful. Special thanks go to those of my colleagues who wrote their dissertations within the framework of my Noether Group at the University of Münster and whose books are now available in German or English. Claudia Roesch worked on Mexican American Families, Andre Dechert on fatherhood in TV sitcoms, and Anne Overbeck on concepts of African American motherhood. Another study by Jana Hoffmann on changing family values and notions of gender in U.S. mainline Protestantism emerged in the context of the Noether Group and saw its completion at the University of Bielefeld. Working with my colleagues in the Noether Group—all of whom are now pursuing successful academic careers—not only taught me a great deal but was a genuine pleasure and great fun! My heartfelt thanks go to Anne, Claudia, Andre and Jana for the creative, collegial, and always pleasant working atmosphere at Rosenstraße 9. The same expressly goes for our student assistants, especially Anika Mester as the first and Lisa Peters as the last assistant to the Noether Group. The present book and the entire group owe a great deal to their attentiveness and enthusiasm. I am also grateful to Jana Hoffmann for her matchless organizational and scholarly support as research assistant when I had to attend to the needs of my newborn son.

Within the framework of the Noether Group, my team and I were able to organize a total of four international conferences on "Family in the 1960s and 1970s" (2009), "Concepts of Motherhood" (2010), "Masculinities" (2010), and "Processes of Social Change in the United States" (2013) at the University of Münster. The associated discussions significantly shaped our understanding of twentieth-century U.S. social history, while also enriching our overall perspective. For your comments and advice, I thank all my colleagues, especially Marisa Chappell, Ruth Feldstein, Grace Hale, Christina von Hodenberg, Michael Kimmel, Felix Krämer, Tracy Penny Light, Laura Lovett, Nina Mackert, Jürgen Martschukat, Joanne Meyerowitz, Jennifer Nelson, Christopher Neumaier, Rebecca Jo Plant, Till van Rahden, Catherine Rymph, Rickie Solinger, Olaf Stieglitz, Simon Wendt, and Natasha Zaretsky.

I was able to present my work at numerous university seminars and I would like to thank Patrick Wagner (Halle), Jürgen Martschukat (Erfurt), Andreas Rödder (Mainz), Andreas Wirsching (then Augsburg), Bernd Weisbrod and Dirk Schumann (Göttingen), Till Kössler (Bochum), Lutz Raphael, Ursula Lehmkuhl, and Christian Jansen (Trier) for key impulses and constructive feedback. In 2011, Elisabeth Timm initiated the establishment of the interdisciplinary colloquium "Family and Kinship: Historical and Contemporary Approaches" at the University of Münster. I owe many important insights and stimuli from the perspective of cultural anthropology to this forum and to our long-standing cooperation, for which I am truly grateful.

I had the pleasure of working in the following U.S. libraries and archives: Library of Congress, Washington D.C.; Schlesinger Library, Harvard University, Cambridge, MA; Countway Library, Harvard University, Boston, MA; Manuscript and Rare Books Collection, Stuart A. Rose Library, Emory University, Atlanta, GA; Woodruff Library, Atlanta University Colleges, Atlanta, GA; and the Jimmy Carter Presidential Library, Atlanta GA. My sincere thanks to the archivists for their helpfulness and expert assistance in obtaining both primary sources and relevant literature.

In composing the original manuscript and revising it for publication, I benefited from the suggestions and comments of numerous colleagues. First and foremost, I owe a special debt of gratitude to Lutz Raphael, who supervised my habilitation at the University of Trier as primary reviewer and chair of the post-doctoral panel. I would also like to thank Ursula Lehmkuhl and Norbert Finzsch for their expert assessments and positive support. Habilitating at the University of Trier was a thoroughly enjoyable experience. My thanks also to Jürgen Martschukat and Patrick Wagner, who read the entire manuscript in advance and gave helpful advice on its revision. A special thank you goes to Johanna Schoen, who not only read the manuscript in its entirety during a research stay at Münster in winter 2016, but also encouraged and supported the Noether group in a variety of ways from the outset.

The members of my working group in Münster also provided valuable suggestions for the final version of the original German-language book. My heartfelt thanks to Verena Limper and Marcel Brüntrup, who read and commented on individual sections of the manuscript. Lukas Alex's eagle eyes discovered many an error during the proofreading process, and he also created the comprehensive index. Marcel Brüntrup arranged the graphics. I owe both of them a debt of gratitude. My sincere thanks also to Rabea Rittgerodt and Anne Stroka at De Gruyter Verlag for their careful stewardship of the manuscript. I am deeply grateful to Alex Skinner, who not only produced a masterful translation into English, but also made invaluable editorial comments and suggestions that further benefited the manuscript. Special thanks go to Lea Mahn and Anja Gründl of my Bayreuth working group who created the English index and did the proofreading of the English manuscript.

I dedicate the book to my own family, who contributed to its realization in a variety of ways. First, I thank my children Flora, Magdalena, Hanno and Tristan, who were born while I was working on the original German version of the book and who (mostly) deal with the reality of a "working mom" with tremendous aplomb. I would especially like to thank my husband, Mario Ohlberger, who shares with me the joy both of raising our children and academic work. This is a mathematician who knows how to balance the equation of family life and scholarly engagement. Thank you, Mario.

Bayreuth, May 2023

Abbreviations

ACLU	American Civil Liberties Union
AES	American Eugenics Society
AFDC	Aid to Families with Dependent Children
AFL-CIO	A. Philip Randolph Institute
AIFR	American Institute for Family Relations
AMA	American Medical Association
ASA	American Sociological Association
AVS	Association for Voluntary Sterilization
BWHBC	Boston Women's Health Book Collective
CCA	Christian Coalition of America
CDC	Center for Disease Control and Prevention
CORE	Congress on Racial Equality
CUB	Concerned United Birthparents
ERA	Equal Rights Amendment
ERO	Eugenic Record Office
FAP	Family Assistance Plan
FOTF	Focus on the Family
HBCUs	Historically Black Colleges and Universities
HBF	Human Betterment Foundation
IFEO	International Federation of Eugenics Organizations
IPPF	International Planned Parenthood Federation
IUD	Intra Uterine Device
LOC	Library of Congress, Washington DC
MARBL	Manuscript and Rare Books Library, Emory University, Atlanta
MC	Manuscript Collection
MORAL/ Mass Choice	Massachusetts Organization for the Repeal of Abortion Laws
NAACP	National Association for the Advancement of Colored People
NARAL	National Abortion Rights Action League
NBFO	National Black Feminist Organization
NCFA	National Committee for Adoption
NOW	National Organization of Women
NWRO	National Welfare Rights Organization
NYT	*New York Times*
OEO	Office of Economic Opportunity
PAC	Political Action Committee
PFA	People for the American Way
PC	Population Council
POOP	Population Oriented Organization People
PPFA	Planned Parenthood Federation of America
PPWP	Planned Parenthood World Population
PRB	Population Research Bureau
PRWORA	Personal Responsibility and Work Opportunity Reconciliation Act
RCAR	Religious Coalition for Abortion Rights

RHEA	Reproductive Health Equity Act
SCLC	Southern Christian Leadership Conference
SLHU	Schlesinger Library, Harvard University
SNCC	Student Non-Violent Coordinating Committee
WAC	Women's Army Corps
WEBA	Women Exploited By Abortion
WONAAC	Women's National Abortion Action Coalition
WP	*Washington Post*
ZPG	Zero Population Growth

List of figures

Fig. 1.1 Number of divorces per 1,000 U.S. citizens, 1900–1960
Data in Alexander A. Plateris, *100 Years of Marriage and Divorce Statistics. United States 1867–1967*, U.S. Department of Health, Education and Welfare, National Center for Health Statistics (Rockville 1973), 22 —— **48**

Fig. 1.2 Number of divorces per 1,000 U.S. citizens, 1960–2008
Data in U.S. Census Bureau, *Statistical Abstract of the United States, 2012* (August 2011) —— **49**

Fig. 2.1 Population distribution 1900–2000 by ethnic group
Data in Frank Hobbs and Nicole Stoops, *U.S. Census Bureau, Census 2000 Special Reports, Series CENSR-4, Demographic Trends in the 20th Century* (Washington, D.C. 2002), 75, 141, 143 —— **103**

Fig. 2.2 Population trends and average household sizes, 1900–2000
Data in U.S. Census Bureau, *Statistical Abstracts of the United States 2003. U.S. Households by Size, 1790–2006* <www.infoplease.com/ipa/A0884238.html> —— **104**

Fig. 2.3 Fitter Family Medal, "Yea, I Have a Goodly Heritage." This medal was awarded to outstanding families by the American Eugenics Society
American Philosophical Society, Digital Collections, Graphics:1673, APSimg1539, Negative Number: 870.092. American Eugenics Society Records —— **120**

Fig. 2.4 Winners of the "small," "medium," and "large" family categories, Fitter Families Contest, Kansas Free Fair, 1923. Members of the winning families are holding their trophies
American Philosophical Society, Digital Collections, Graphics:1685, APSimg1542, Negative Number: 870.095. American Eugenics Society Records —— **121**

Fig. 2.5 Winner in the "large family" category, Texas State Fair, 1925. This is a good example of the connection evoked between nature, healthy bodies, and family. The message of the image is: this is what a hereditarily healthy family featuring lots of children looks like
American Philosophical Society, Digital Collections, Graphics:1681, APSimg1532, Negative Number: 870.085, American Eugenics Society Records —— **122**

Fig. 2.6 Installation with flashing lights, opening exhibit of the eugenics exhibition at the Fitter Families Contests
American Philosophical Society, Digital Collections, Graphics:1644, APSimg1491, Negative Number: 870.044. American Eugenics Society Records —— **123**

Fig. 2.7 Eugenics Building, Fitter Family Contests, Kansas Free Fair. A winning family (center) is shown with various dignitaries, representatives of the eugenics movement, and nurses involved in the contest
American Philosophical Society, Digital Collections, Graphics:1660, APSimg1502, Negative Number: 870.055. American Eugenics Society Records —— **124**

Fig. 2.8 Eugenic and Health Exhibit, Fitter Family Contests, Kansas Free Fair, 1929
American Philosophical Society, Digital Collections, Graphics:1661, APSimg1479, Negative Number: 870.023. American Eugenics Society Records —— **126**

List of figures

Fig. 2.9 Paul B. Popenoe explaining the basic principles of heredity to a couple planning to get married. This picture was published in 1930 to mark the foundation of the AIFR, and appeared, for example, in the German journal *Eugenik*.
Eugenik, Erblehre, Erbpflege 1 (1931), no. 8, 184 —— **145**

Fig. 3.1 Labor market participation of American women by race, 1972–2012
United States Department of Labor, Women's Bureau, *Facts over Time, Women in the Labor Force* <www.dol.gov/wb/stats/facts_over_time.htm> —— **164**

Fig. 4.1 Births per 1,000 women aged 15 to 44, 1960–1969
Center for Disease Control and Prevention, *Vital Statistics of the United States, Live Birth, Birth Rates, and Fertility Rates, by Race, United States, 1909–1994* <www.cdc.gov/nchs/data/statab/t941x01.pdf> —— **213**

Fig. 4.2 Proportion of out-of-wedlock births by ethnicity, 1960–2014
Child Trends Databank, *Births to Unmarried Women, 2015* <www.childtrends.org/?indicators=births-to-unmarried-women> —— **213**

Fig. 4.3 The affluent American family is white. Victims of the Ohio River flood of 1937 in Louisville, Kentucky, wait for food donations
Margaret Bourke White, At the Time of the Louisville Flood, 1937, Getty Images TMC: 92926162 —— **215**

Fig. 4.4 Absentee fathers in white and African American families according to Moynihan
Daniel Patrick Moynihan, "The Negro Family: The Case for National Action," 7. Daniel P. Moynihan Papers, Library of Congress, Washington D.C., Box 66, Folder 8 —— **236**

Fig. 4.5 Trends in the illegitimacy rate of the white majority and African American minority according to Moynihan
Daniel Patrick Moynihan, "The Negro Family: The Case for National Action by Daniel Patrick Moynihan," 9. Daniel P. Moynihan Papers, Library of Congress, Washington D.C., Box 66, Folder 8 —— **237**

Fig. 4.6 Resurrection City, Poor People's Campaign, Washington D. C
Bob Adelman Estate, Poor People's March, ppm014 —— **256**

Fig. 5.1 The female egg as the core of the population problem
Saturday Review, February 6, 1960, 50–51. Robert C. Cook Papers, Library of Congress, Manuscript Division, Box 44, Folder 13 —— **280**

Fig. 5.2 Contraceptive use by unmarried women aged 15–44, 1988 and 1995
Data in Stephanie J. Ventura et al., *Nonmarital Childbearing in the United States, 1940–99, National Vital Statistics Report from the Center for Disease Control and Prevention, National Center for Health Statistics, National Vital Statistics System*, 48, no. 16, October 18, 2000, 14 —— **283**

Fig. 5.3 Pro-choice protesters at Union Square, New York, May 1972
Bettye Lane, One of the first Abortion Demonstrations at Union Square, New York, May 6, 1972, Schlesinger Library, Harvard University, PC 320022 —— **293**

Fig. 5.4 Anti-abortion demonstrator in front of St. Patrick's Church in New York, March 9, 1976
Bettye Lane, Anti-Choice "Right to Life" at St. Patrick's Cathedral, March 9, 1976, Schlesinger Library, Harvard University, PC32-46-R3/f7 —— **299**

Fig. 5.5 "Three Generations on Welfare—Discrimination's Sad Testament." Illustration for the article "The American Underclass" in *Time* magazine, August 29, 1977
Bob Adelman Estate, UC_45-29a —— **318**

Fig. 6.1 Photograph of pregnant teenage mother accompanying *Fortune* magazine article "America's Underclass," May 11, 1987
Mary Ellen Mark, Urban Poverty —— **337**

Fig. 6.2 The Reagan family, Christmas 1983
The Reagan Family Christmas Portrait by the White House Residence Christmas Tree, December 25, 1983. Ronald Reagan Presidential Library, Simi Valley, CA: C19215-9 A —— **354**

List of tables

Tab. 1.1 Trends in marriage and divorce according to the two national statistical surveys of 1887 and 1909
Data in Alexander A. Plateris, *100 Years of Marriage and Divorce Statistics,United States 1867–1967*, U.S. Department of Health, Education and Welfare, NationalCenter for Health Statistics (Rockville 1973), 22. U.S. Department of Commerce andLabor, *Marriage and Divorce, 1867–1906* (Westport, Conn. 1909), reprinted 1978, vol. 1,7–8, 11–12 —— **47**

Tab. 1.2 Marriages and divorces, 1900–2009
Data in U.S. Department of Health and Human Services, National Center forHealth Statistics, Information Please Database, 2007 Pearson Education Inc. <www.infoplease.com/ipa/A0005044.html> —— **50**

Tab. 3.1 Women's share of the labor force, 1900–1970
Data in US Census Bureau, *Statistical Abstracts of the United States, MiniHistorical Statistics* (2003), 52 —— **160**

Tab. 5.1 Number of abortions recorded by the Center for Disease Control and Prevention, 1970–2010
Data in Center for Disease Control and Prevention, *Abortion Surveillance – United States, 2005* <www.cdc.gov/mmwr/preview/mmwrhtml/ss5713a1.htm.>. Center forDisease Control and Prevention, *Abortion Surveillance – United States, 2012* <www.cdc.gov/mmwr/preview/mmwrhtml/ss6410a1.htm?s_cid=ss6410a1_w> —— **285**

Bibliography

Unpublished sources

American Philosophical Society, Philadelphia, Digital Collections

American Eugenics Society Records
Eugenics Record Office Records

Library of Congress, Washington D. C.

Samuel W. Dike Papers
Daniel P. Moynihan Papers
Margaret Mead Papers
Robert C. Cook Papers
Mary McGrory Papers

Arthur and Elizabeth Schlesinger Library on the History of Women in America, Radcliff College, Cambridge, MA

Betty Friedan Papers MC 575
National Organization of Women (NOW) MC 496
National Abortion Rights Action League (NARAL) MC 313
National Abortion Rights Action League (NARAL), Additional Records MC 714
Concerned United Birthparents (CUB) MC 630
Boston Women's Health Book Collective Collections MC 503
NARAL Mass. Choice MC 659

Manuscript and Rare Books Library (MARBL), Emory University, Atlanta, GA

Southern Christian Leadership Conference MSS 1083

Carter Presidential Library, Atlanta, GA

Records of Anne Wexler as Special Assistant to the President
Records of the Assistant for Public Liaison
Records of the Council of Economic Advisors
Records of the Domestic Policy Staff: Ellen Goldstein's Subject Files
Records of the First Lady's Office
Records of the Office of Congressional Liaison

Records of the Office of the Assistant to the President for Women's Affairs
Records of the Special Assistant for Ethnic Affairs
Records of the Speechwriter's Office

Woodruff Library, Atlanta University Colleges, Atlanta, GA

Hoyt William Fuller Collection
Johnson Publishing Company Clipping Files Collection
Morehouse College Martin Luther King, Jr. Collection

Newspapers, magazines, and journals

Atlantic Monthly
Century
Chicago Tribune
Communicator
Ebony
Eugenical News
Eugenics
Family Advocate
Family Life
Good Housekeeping
Herald Tribune
Heredity
Jet
Journal of Heredity
Ladies' Home Journal
Los Angeles Times
Ms. Magazine
New York Times
New-York Tribune
North American Monthly
Time
US News and World Report
Washington Post

Published and primary sources

For the sake of clarity, all contemporary writings analyzed as sources are listed here. Hence, this listing includes those works by social scientists that served as sources for my analysis of expert discourses on family, divorce, women's work and reproduction, as well as key social scientific texts on changing values.

N.n., *Love, Marriage, and Divorce and the Sovereignty of the Individual. A Discussion Between Henry James, Horace Greeley, and Stephen Pearl Andrews* (Boston 1889).
N.n., *The American Family. A Factual Background. Report of the Inter-Agency Committee on Background Materials. National Conference on Family Life, May 1948* (Westport 1949).
Adler, Felix, "Marriage," in Johnson, Julia E. (ed.), *Selected Articles on Marriage and Divorce* (New York, 1925), quoted in *Hibbert Journal* 22 (1923), 20–43.
Adler, Felix, *Marriage and Divorce* (New York 1915).
Adler, Felix, "The Ethics of Divorce," *Ethical Record* 29 (1890), 200–209.
Ahlemeyer, Heinrich (ed.), *We Shall Overcome. Die amerikanische Friedensbewegung in Selbstzeugnissen* (Cologne 1983).
Albert, Judith and Stewart Albert (eds.), *The Sixties Papers. Documents of a Rebellious Decade* (Westport, CT and London 1984).
Alexander, Franz, *Psychosomatische Medizin. Grundlagen und Anwendungsgebiete. Mit einem Kapitel über die Funktionen des Sexualapparates und ihre Störungen von Therese Benedek* (Berlin 1951).
Ali, Tariq, *Street Fighting Years. Autobiographie eines 68ers* (Cologne 1998).
Ali, Tariq and Watkins, Susan, *1968. Marching in the Streets* (New York 1998).
Almond, Gabriel A. and Verba, Sidney (eds.), *The Civic Culture Revisited. An Analytic Study* (Boston and Toronto 1980).
Almond, Gabriel A. and Verba, Sidney, *The Civic Culture. Political Attitudes and Democracy in Five Nations* (Princeton 1963).
Amendt, Gerhard, *Black Power. Dokumente und Analysen* (Frankfurt a. M. 1970).
Ammon, Otto, *Die natürliche Auslese beim Menschen auf Grund der Ergebnisse der anthropologischen Untersuchungen der Wehrpflichtigen in Baden und anderer Materialien* (Jena 1893).
Anderson, Benedict, *Imagined Communities. Reflections on the Origin and Spread of Nationalism* (London 1983).
Anshen, Ruth Nanda, *The Family. Its Function and Destiny* (New York, 1949).
Baber, Ray Erwin, *Marriage and the Family* (New York 1939).
Bajema, Carl Jay, "Relation of Fertility to Educational Attainment," *Eugenics Quarterly* 13 (1966), no. 4, 306–315.
Ballantine, William, "The Hyperbolic Teaching of Jesus," *The North American Review* 179 (1904), 403.
Barrett, David M., *Lyndon B. Johnson's Vietnam Papers. A Documentary Collection* (College Station, TX 1997).
Beale, Frances M., "Double Jeopardy. To Be Black and Female," in Cade, Toni (ed.), *The Black Woman. An Anthology* (New York 1970), 90–100.
Bell, Daniel, *The Coming of Post-Industrial Society. A Venture in Social Forecasting* (New York 1971).
Bell, Daniel, *The End of Ideology. On the Exhaustion of Political Ideas in the Fifties* (Glencoe 1960).
Benedek, Therese, "Die Funktionen des Sexualapparates und ihre Störungen," in Alexander, Franz (ed.), *Psychosomatische Medizin. Grundlagen und Anwendungsgebiete* (Berlin 1951), 170–210 (first published as *Psychosomatic Medicine*, New York 1950).
Benedek, Therese, "Infertility as Psychosomatic Disease," *Fertility and Sterility* 3 (1952), 527–541.
Benedek, Therese, *Psychosexual Functions in Women* (New York 1952).

Benedek, Therese, "The Emotional Structure of the Family," in Anshen, Ruth Nanda (ed.), *The Family. Its Function and Destiny* (New York 1959, first edition 1949), 353–380.
Benedek, Therese, "The Psychobiology of Pregnancy, and Motherhood and Nurturing," in Anthony, Elwyn James (ed.), *Parenthood. Its Psychology and Psychopathology* (Boston 1970), 137–165.
Benedek, Therese and B. B. Rubenstein, *The Sexual Cycle in Women* (Washington 1942).
Bishop, Joel Prentis, *Commentaries on the Law of Marriage and Divorce*, vol. 1 (Boston 1881).
Blake, Judith, *Family Size and Achievement* (Studies in Demography 3, Berkeley 1989).
Blake, Judith, "Family Size in the 1960s. A Baffling Fad?" *Eugenics Quarterly* 14 (1967), no. 1, 60–73.
Blake, Judith, "Ideal Family Size among White Americans. A Quarter of a Century's Evidence," *Demography* 3 (1966), no. 1, 154–173.
Bloom, Alexander and Breines, Wini (eds.) *"Takin' it to the Streets." A Sixties Reader* (New York 1995).
Brown, Helen Gurley, *Sex and the Single Girl* (New York 1962).
Bureau of Labor Statistics, U.S. Department of Labor, "The Economics Daily. Unemployment Rates by Race and Ethnicity," Washington D. C. 2010 <www.bls.gov/opub/ted/2011/ted_20111005.htm>.
Burgess, Ernest W., "The Family as a Unity of Interacting Personalities," *The Family. Journal of Social Case Work* (1926), no. 7, 3–9.
Burr, Jane, *Letters of a Dakota Divorce* (Boston 1909).
Burton, Ernest D., "The Biblical Teachings Concerning Divorce. I. Old Testament Teaching and Jewish Usage," *Biblical World* 29 (1907), no. 2, 121–127.
Capper, Arthur, "Proposed Amendment to the Constitution," in Johnson, Julia E. (ed.), *Selected Articles on Marriage and Divorce* (New York 1925), 244–250.
Carmichael, Stokely, Hamilton, Charles V., and Ture, Kwame, *Black Power. The Politics of Liberation in America* (New York 1967).
Carpenter, Edward, *Love's Coming of Age* (New York 1911).
Carpenter, Elizabeth, "Marriage and Divorce from a Lay Point of View," *North American Review* 181 (1905), 123–124.
Carson, Rachel, *Silent Spring* (London 1962).
Caverno, Charles, "Uniform Divorce Law," *Bibliotheca Sacra* 69 (1912), 242–245.
Cayton, Horace R. and St. Clair Drake, *Black Metropolis. A Study of Negro Life in a Northern City* (New York 1945).
Ceplair, Larry (ed.), *Charlotte Perkins Gilman. A Nonfiction Reader* (New York 1992).
Chandler, Alfred D. and Galambos, Louis, *The Papers of Dwight David Eisenhower*, 21 vols. (Baltimore 1970–2001).
Chapin, Gerald H., "United States of Matrimony," in Johnson, Julia E., *Selected Articles on Marriage and Divorce* (New York 1915), 179–189.
Chapin, Lou V., "Uniform Marriage and Divorce Laws," *Good Form* 3 (1892), June, 50.
Child Trends Databank (2015), "Births to Unmarried Women" <www.childtrends.org/?indicators=births-to-unmarried-women>.
Child Trends Data Bank, "Child Recipients of Welfare (AFDC/TANF): Indicators on Children and Youth, Updated December 2015" <www.childtreds.org>.
Children's Bureau, U.S. Department of Labor, *Save the Youngest. Seven charts on Maternal and Infant Mortality, with explanatory comment* (Washington 1919).
Children's Bureau, U.S. Department of Labor and Lundberg, Emma Octavia, *Unemployment and Child Welfare. A Study made in a Middle-Western and an Eastern City during the Industrial Depression of 1921 and 1922* (Washington 1923).
Clark, Kenneth B., *Dark Ghetto. Dilemmas of Social Power* (New York and Evanston 1967, first edition 1965).

Clark, Kenneth B., "Introduction. The Dilemma of Power," in Clark, Kenneth B. and Parsons, Talcott (eds.), *The Negro American* (Boston 1966), xi–xviii.
Clark, Kenneth B., "The Civil Rights Movement. Momentum and Organization," in Clark, Kenneth B. and Parsons, Talcott (eds.), *The Negro American* (Boston 1966), 595–625.
Clark, Kenneth B. and Parsons, Talcott (eds.), *The Negro American* (Boston 1966).
Cohen, Robert (ed.), *Dear Mrs. Roosevelt. Letters from Children of the Great Depression* (Chapel Hill 2002).
Cohn, David L., *Love in America. An Informal Study of Manners and Morals in American Marriage* (New York 1943).
Cook, Joseph, *Christ and Modern Thought. The Boston Monday Lectures, 1880–1881* (Boston 1882).
Cook, Robert C., *Human Fertility. The Modern Dilemma* (New York 1951).
Cooper, Courtney Riley, "Man Who Is Casting Out Divorce," in Johnson, Julia E., *Selected Articles on Marriage and Divorce* (New York 1914), 227–239.
Cooper, John M., "Human Welfare and the Monogamous Ideal," *Social Hygiene* 6 (1920), no. 4, 457–468.
Cott, Nancy F., *Roots of Bitterness. Documents of the Social History of American Women* (Boston 1996).
Croly, Jane Cunningham, *The History of the Woman's Club Movement in America*, vol. 1 (New York 1898).
Davenport, Charles B., *Eugenics, Genetics and the Family. Second International Congress of Eugenics, Held at New York, Sept. 22–28 1921* (New York etc. 1921).
Davenport, Charles B., *Eugenics. The Science of Human Improvement by Better Breeding* (New York 1910).
Davenport, Charles B., *Guide to Physical Anthropometry and Anthroposcopy* (Cold Spring Harbor 1927).
Davenport, Charles B., *Heredity in Relation to Eugenics* (London 1912).
Davenport, Charles B., *Heredity of Constitutional Mental Disorders*, Eugenics Record Office (Cold Spring Harbor 1920).
Davenport, Charles B., *Naval Officers. Their Heredity and Development*, Carnegie Institution of Washington (Washington 1919).
Davenport, Charles B., *State Laws Limiting Marriage Selection. Examined in the Light of Eugenics* (Cold Spring Harbor 1913).
Davenport, Charles B., *The Family-History Book*, Eugenics Record Office (Cold Spring Harbor 1912).
Davenport, Charles B., *The Feebly Inhibited. Nomadism, or the Wandering Impulse, with Special Reference to Heredity, Inheritance of Temperament, with Special Reference to Twins and Suicides* (Washington 1915).
Davenport, Charles B. and Love, Albert G., *Defects Found in Drafted Men* (Washington 1920).
Davis, Katharine Bement, "A Study of the Sex Life of the Normal Married Woman. I. The Use of Contraceptives," *Journal of Social Hygiene* 8 (1922), no. 2, 173–189.
Davis, Katharine Bement, "A Study of the Sex Life of the Normal Married Woman. II. The Happiness of Married Life," *Journal of Social Hygiene* 9 (1923), no. 1, 1–26.
Davis, Katharine Bement, "A Study of the Sex Life of the Normal Married Woman. III. The Happiness of Married Life—continued," *Journal of Social Hygiene* 9 (1923), no. 3, 129–146.
Davis, Katharine Bement, *Factors in the Sex Life of Twenty-two Hundred Women* (New York 1929).
Deland, Margaret, "The Change in the Feminine Ideal," *The Atlantic Monthly* 105 (1910), 296.
Dike, Samuel W., *Important Features of the Divorce Question* (Royalton, 1885).
Dike, Samuel W., "Is the Freer Granting of Divorce an Evil?" *American Journal of Sociology* 14 (1909), no. 6, 766–796.
Dike, Samuel W., "Statistics of Divorce in the United States and Europe," *Journal of the American Statistical Association* 1 (1888/89), 206–214.
Doane, William C., *Kindred and Affinity. God's Law of Marriage* (New York 1891).
Doane, William C., "Remarriage after Divorce. Catholic Theory and Practice," *North American Review* 180 (1905), no. 4, 513–522.

Doane, William C., "The Question of Divorce and Remarriage," *New York Times*, November 26, 1899.
Dobson, James and Bauer, Gary, *Children at Risk. The Battle for the Hearts and Minds of Our Kids* (Dallas 1990).
Drummond, Isabel, *Getting a Divorce* (New York 1931).
DuBois, William Edward Burghardt, *The Negro Family in the United States* (London and New York 2005, first edition Atlanta 1908).
Dwight, Timothy, *Theology. Explained and Defended in a Series of Sermons*, vol. 3 (New York 1928).
Eisenhower, Dwight D., *Die Jahre im Weißen Haus, 1953-1956* (Düsseldorf 1964).
Eisenhower, Dwight D., *Public Papers of the Presidents of the United States. Dwight D. Eisenhower, 1960-61. Containing the Speeches, Public Messages, and Statements of the President*, 9 vols., 1953-1961 (Washington 1960-1978).
Ellis, Edith, *New Horizon in Love and Life* (New York 1921).
Ellis, Havelock, *Little Essays of Love and Virtue* (New York 1921).
Ellwood, Charles E., *Sociology and Modern Social Problems* (New York 1913).
Evans, W. S., *Organized Eugenics* (New Haven 1931).
Farnham, Marynia F. and Lundberg, Ferdinand, *Modern Woman. The Lost Sex* (New York 1947).
Firestone, Shulamith, *The Dialectic of Sex* (New York 1970).
Flanders Dunbar, Helen, "Comment on the Paper of Benedek," *Fertility and Sterility* 3 (1952), 538-541.
Frazier, Edward Franklin, *Black Bourgeoisie. The Rise of a New Middle Class in the United States* (Glencoe, IL 1957, first French edition 1955).
Frazier, Edward Franklin, *On Race Relations. Selected Writings* (Chicago 1968).
Frazier, Edward Franklin, "Problems and Needs of Negro Children and Youth Resulting from Family Disintegration," *Journal of Negro Education* 19 (1950), 269-277.
Frazier, Edward Franklin (ed.), *The Integration of the Negro into American Society* (Washington D. C. 1951).
Frazier, Edward Franklin, *The Negro Family in the United States* (New York 1966, first edition 1939).
Frazier, Edward Franklin, *The Negro in the United States* (New York 1949).
Friedan, Betty, *The Feminine Mystique* (New York 1963).
Galbraith, John Kenneth, *The Affluent Society* (Boston 1958).
Galton, Francis, *Essays in Eugenics* (London 1909).
Galton, Francis, *Hereditary Genius. An Inquiry into its Laws and Consequences* (London 1869).
Galton, Francis, *Inquiries into Human Faculty and Development* (London 1883).
Galton, Francis, *The Possible Improvement of the Human Breed under the Existing Conditions of Law and Sentiment*, Huxley Lecture at the Royal Anthropological Institute 1901, Annual Report of the Board of Regents of the Smithsonian Institution (Washington 1902), 523-538.
Gibbons, Cardinal James, "Divorce," *Century* 78 (1909), 145-149.
Gibbons, Cardinal James, Potter, Bishop Henry C., and Ingersoll, Colonel Robert G., "Is Divorce Wrong?" *North American Review* 149 (1889), 513-538.
Gillies, Mary Davis, *How to Keep House* (New York 1949).
Gilman, Charlotte Perkins, "How Home Conditions React Upon the Family," *American Journal of Sociology* 14 (1909), no. 5, 592-605.
Gilman, Charlotte Perkins, *The Diaries of Charlotte Perkins Gilman*. Edited by Denise D. Knight, vol. 2, *1890-1935* (Charlottesville and London 1994).
Gilman, Charlotte Perkins, *The Home. Its Work and Influence* (Chicago 1972, reprint of the 1903 edition, introduction by William L. O'Neill).

Gilman, Charlotte Perkins, *Women and Economics. A Study of the Economic Relation between Men and Women as a Factor in Social Evolution*. Edited by Carl N. Degler (New York etc. 1966, first edition Boston 1898).

Glazer, Nathan and Moynihan, Daniel P., *Beyond the Melting Pot: The Negroes, Puerto Ricans, Jews, Italians and Irish of New York City* (Cambridge 1963).

Goddard, Henry Herbert, "The Elimination of Feeble-Mindedness," *Annals of the American Academy of Political and Social Science* 37 (1911), no. 2, 261-272.

Goddard, Henry Herbert, *The Kallikak Family. A Study in the Heredity of Feeblemindedness* (New York 1912).

Goldberg, David, "Some Observations on Recent Changes in American Fertility Based on Sample Survey Data," *Eugenics Quarterly* 14 (1967), no. 4, 255-264.

Goodman, David, *A Parent's Guide to the Emotional Needs of Children. With an Introduction by Marynia Farnham, M. D.* (London 1959).

Goodsell, Willystine, *A History of the Family as a Social and Educational Institution* (New York 1915).

Goodwin, Doris Kearns, *The Johnson Presidential Press Conferences*, 2 vols. (London 1978).

Goodwin, Richard N., *Remembering America. A Voice from the Sixties* (Boston 1988).

Gosney, Ezra Seymour and Popenoe, Paul B., *Collected Papers on Eugenic Sterilization in California*, The Human Betterment Foundation (Pasadena 1930).

Gosney, Ezra Seymour and Popenoe, Paul B., *Sterilization for Human Betterment. A Summary of Results of 6,000 Operations in California, 1909-1929* (New York 1929), German translation Berlin 1930.

Gosney, Ezra Seymour and Popenoe, Paul B., *Twenty-Eight Years of Sterilization in California*, The Human Betterment Foundation (Pasadena 1938).

Grabill, Wilson H., Kiser, Clyde V., and Whelpton, Pascal K., *The Fertility of American Women* (New York and London 1958).

Grant, Madison, *The Passing of the Great Race or the Racial Basis of European History. Fourth Revised Edition with A Documentary Supplement, with Prefaces by Henry Fairfield Osborn* (New York 1924, first edition 1916).

Grant, Robert, "Marriage and Divorce," *Scribner's Magazine* 66 (1919), 193-198.

Greeley, Horace, *Recollections of a Busy Life* (New York 1869).

Groves, Ernest R. and Ogburn, William F., *American Marriage and Family Relationships* (New York 1928).

Guttmacher, Alan F., *Babies by Choice or Chance* (New York 1961, first edition: Garden City 1959).

Guttmacher, Alan F., "Family Planning: The Needs and the Methods," *The American Journal of Nursing*, vol. 69, no. 6, (June 1969), 1229-1234.

Guttmacher, Alan F., *Planning Your Family* (New York 1964).

Guttmacher, Alan F., *The Complete Book of Birth Control* (New York 1961).

Hall, Kermit L. (ed.), *American Legal History. Cases and Materials* (New York and Oxford 1996).

Halsey, Margaret, *Color Blind. A White Woman Looks at the Negro* (New York 1946).

Halverson, H. Jeanette, "The Prolificacy of Dependent Families," *The American Journal of Sociology* 29 (1923), no. 3, 338-344.

Harding Davis, Rebecca et al., "Are Women to Blame?" *North American Review* 148 (1889), 622-642.

Harper Cooley, Winnifred, "The Younger Suffragists (1913)," in Keetley, Dawn and Pettegrew, John (eds.), *Public Women, Public Words. A Documentary History of American Feminism*, vol. 2, 1900 to 1960 (Lanham etc. 2002), 16-19.

Harrington, Michael, *The Other America. Poverty in the United States* (New York 1962).

HARYOU (Harlem Youth Opportunities Unlimited Inc.), *Youth in the Ghetto. A Study of Powerlessness and a Blueprint for Change, Harlem Youth Opportunities Unlimited Incorporation* (New York 1964).

Havelock, Ellis, *Little Essays of Love and Virtue* (New York 1921).

Hawley, James H., "Uniformity of Marriage and Divorce Laws," in Johnson, Julia E. (ed.), *Selected Articles on Marriage and Divorce* (New York, 1925), 160–164 (first published in *Proceedings of the Governor's Conference 1912*, 162–173).

Hayden, Tom, *Reunion. A Memoir* (New York 1988).

Henderson, Charles Richmond, "Are Modern Industry and City Life Unfavorable to the Family?" *The American Journal of Sociology* 14 (1909), no. 5, 668–680.

Henderson, Charles Richmond, *Social Duties* (Chicago 1909).

Henderson, Charles Richmond, *Social Elements, Institution, Characters, Progress* (Cambridge 1898).

Hollinger, David A. (ed.), *The American Intellectual Tradition. A Source Book*, 2 vols. (New York 1997).

Horney, Karen, *The Neurotic Personality of Our Time* (New York 1937).

Houck, Davis W., *Actor, Ideologue, Politician. The Public Speeches of Ronald Reagan* (Westport 1993).

Howard, George, *A History of Matrimonial Institutions*, 3 vols. (Chicago 1904).

Howard, George Elliott, "Bad Marriage and Quick Divorce," *Journal of Applied Sociology* 6 (1921), 1–10.

Howard, George Elliott, "Is the Freer Granting of Divorce an Evil?" *The American Journal of Sociology* 14 (1908/09), no. 6, 766–796.

Howard, George Elliott, "Is the Freer Granting of Divorce and Evil?" *Papers and Proceedings, Third Annual Meeting, American Sociological Society, held at Atlantic City, N. J. December 28 –30, 1908* (Chicago and New York 1909, reprinted 1971, *Publications of the American Sociological Society* 3), 150–180.

Hutchinson, Woods, "Evidences of Race Degeneration in the United States," *Annals of the Academy of Political and Social Science* 34 (1909), no. 1, 43–47.

Hutchinson, Woods, "Evolutionary Ethics of Marriage and Divorce," *Contemporary Review* 88 (1905), 398.

Ingersoll, Robert G. et al., "Is Divorce Wrong?" *North American Review* 149 (1889), 513–538.

Inglehart, Ronald, *Culture Shift in Advanced Industrial Society* (Princeton 1990).

Inglehart, Ronald (ed.), *Human Values and Social Change. Findings from the Values Surveys* (Leiden 2003).

Inglehart, Ronald, *Kultureller Umbruch. Wertewandel in der westlichen Welt* (Frankfurt a. M. and New York 1989).

Inglehart, Ronald, *The Silent Revolution. Changing Values and Political Styles among Western Publics* (Princeton 1977).

Inglehart, Ronald, "The Silent Revolution in Europe. Intergenerational Change in Post-Industrial Societies," *American Political Science Review* 65 (1971), 991–1017.

Inglehart, Ronald and Norris, Pippa, *Rising Tide. Gender Equality and Cultural Change Around the World* (Cambridge 2003).

Jacobs, Paul and Landau, Saul, *Die neue Linke in den USA. Analyse und Dokumentation* (Munich 1969).

Johnson, H. W., "Fitter Family for Future Firesides. The Kansas Eugenics Contest," *Journal of Heredity* 16 (1925), no. 1, 457–60.

Johnson, Julia E. (ed.), *Selected Articles on Marriage and Divorce* (New York 1925).

Johnson, Lyndon B., *Public Papers of the Presidents of the United States. Lyndon B. Johnson. Containing the Public Messages, Speeches, and Statements of the President*, 11 vols., 1963–1969 (Washington D. C. 1965–1978).

Johnson, Lyndon B., "Remarks of the President at Howard University, June 4, 1965. To Fulfill These Rights," in Rainwater, Lee and Yancey, William (ed.), *The Moynihan Report and the Politics of Controversy. A Trans-Action Social Science and Public Policy Report. Including the Full Text of The Negro Family. The Case for National Action by Daniel P. Moynihan* (Cambridge and London 1967), 125–132.

Johnson, Roswell Hill, "Eugenic Aspect of Sexual Immorality," *Journal of Heredity* 8 (1917), no. 3, 121–122.

Johnson, Roswell Hill, "The Determination of Disputed Parentage as a Factor in Reducing Infant Mortality," *Journal of Heredity* 10 (1919), no. 3, 121–124.
Keely, Dawn and Pettegrew, John (ed.), *Public Women, Public Words. A Documentary History of American Feminism*, 3 vols., 1997–2002.
Kennan, George F., *Rebellen ohne Programm. Demokratie und studentische Linke* (Stuttgart 1968).
Kennedy, John F., *Legacy of a President. The Memorable Words of John Fitzgerald Kennedy* (United States Information Agency, n. p., n. d.).
Kennedy, John F., *Profiles in Courage* (London 1955).
Kennedy, John F., *Public Papers of the Presidents of the United States. John F. Kennedy. Containing the Public Messages, Speeches and Statements of the President*. 4 vols. 1961–1963 (Washington D. C. 1962–1977).
Kennedy, John F., *The Burden and the Glory* (New York 1964).
Kennedy, John F., *The Strategy of Peace* (New York 1960).
Kennedy, John F., *To Turn the Tide* (New York 1962).
Kesaris, Paul and Gibson, Joan, *A Guide to the Minutes and Documents of the Cabinet Meetings of President Eisenhower, 1953–1961* (Washington 1980).
Key, Ellen, *Das Jahrhundert des Kindes* (Berlin, 1902, English edition: *The Century of the Child*, New York and London 1909, first appeared as *Barnets århundrade*, 1900).
King, Martin Luther, *A Testament of Hope: The Essential Writings and Speeches of Martin Luther King, Jr.*, edited by James Melvin Washington (New York 1986).
Kinsey, Alfred, *Sexual Behavior in the Human Female* (Philadelphia and Bloomington 1953).
Kinsey, Alfred, *Sexual Behavior in the Human Male* (Philadelphia and Bloomington 1948).
Kirkpatrick, Clifford, *The Family as Process and Institution* (New York 1955).
Kiser, Clyde V., "Trends in Fertility Differentials by Color and Socioeconomic Status in the United States," *Eugenics Quarterly* 15 (1968), no. 4, 221–226.
Knight, Denise D., "Declaration of Sentiments," in Gabler-Hover, Janet and Sattelmeyer, Robert (eds.), *American History through Literature 1820–1870*, vol. 1 (New York 2006), 316–320.
Koedt, Anne, "The Myth of the Vaginal Orgasm," in Firestone, Shulamith and Koedt, Anne (eds.), *Notes from the Second Year* (New York 1970), 111–112.
Koehn, George L., "Is Divorce a Social Menace?" in Johnson, Julia E., *Selected Articles on Marriage and Divorce* (New York 1925), 189–200 (first appeared in *Current History Magazine, New York Times* 16 [1922], 294–299).
Komarovsky, Mirra, *Blue Collar Marriage* (New York 1964).
Komarovsky, Mirra, *Dilemmas of Masculinity. A Study of College Youth* (New York 1976).
Komarovsky, Mirra, *The Unemployed Man and His Family: The Effect of Unemployment Upon the Status of the Man in Fifty-nine Families* (New York 1940, reprinted 1973).
Komarovsky, Mirra, *Women in College. Shaping New Feminine Identities* (New York 1985).
Komarovsky, Mirra, *Women in the Modern World. Their Education and Dilemmas* (Ann Arbor 1953).
Kupinski, Stanley (ed.), *The Fertility of Working Women. A Synthesis of International Research* (New York 1977).
Kupinski, Stanley, "The Fertility of Working Women in the United States. Historical Trends and Theoretical Perspectives," in Kupinski, Stanley (ed.), *The Fertility of Working Women. A Synthesis of International Research* (New York 1977), 188–249.
Lasch, Christopher, *Haven in a Heartless World. The Family Besieged* (New York 1977).
Lasch, Christopher, *The Culture of Narcissism. American Life in an Age of Diminishing Expectations* (New York 1978).
Lasch, Christopher, *The New Radicalism in America, 1889–1963. The Intellectual as a Social Type* (London 1966).

Laughlin, Harry H., *Eugenical Sterilization in the United States* (Psychopathic Laboratory of the Municipal Court of Chicago, Chicago 1922).
Laughlin, Harry H., *Eugenics and Infant Mortality* (Eugenics Record Office, Cold Spring Harbor 1912).
Laughlin, Harry H., *Immigration and Conquest. A Study of the United States as the Receiver of Old World Emigrants Who Became the Parents of Future-born Americans* (Chamber of Commerce of the State of New York, New York 1939).
Laughlin, Harry H., *Official Records in the History of the Eugenics Record Office* (Cold Spring Harbor 1939).
Laughlin, Harry H., *The Legal, Legislative and Administrative Aspects of Sterilization* (Eugenics Record Office, Cold Spring Harbor 1914).
Laughlin, Harry H., *The Legal Status of Eugenical Sterilization. History and Analysis of Litigation under the Virginia Sterilization Statute, Which Led to a Decision of the Supreme Court of the United States Upholding the Statute* (Chicago 1930).
Laughlin, Harry H., *The Present Status of Eugenical Sterilization in the United States* (Cold Spring Harbor 1923, first appeared as *Eugenics in Race and State*, vol. 2, 1923).
Laughlin, Harry H., "The Socially Inadequate. How Shall We Designate and Sort Them?" *American Journal of Sociology* 27 (1921), no. 1, 54–70.
Lee, Margaret, *Divorce; or, Faithful and Unfaithful* (New York, 1889).
Lee, Margaret, "Final Words on Divorce," *North American Review* 150 (1890), no. 2, 263–268.
Lenroot, Katherine F., "Social Responsibility for the Protection of Children Handicapped by Illegitimate Birth," *Annals of the American Academy of Political and Social Science* 98 (1921), 120–128.
Lewis, Oscar, *Five Families. Mexican Case Studies in the Culture of Poverty* (New York 1959).
Lewis, Oscar, "The Culture of Poverty," in Moynihan, Daniel P., *On Understanding Poverty: Perspectives from the Social Sciences* (New York 1969), 187–220.
Lewotin, Richard, Kirk, Dudley, and Crow, James, "Selective Mating, Assortative Mating, and Inbreeding. Definitions and Implications," *Eugenics Quarterly* 15 (1968), no. 2, 141–143.
Lichtenberger, James P., "Divorce. A Study in Social Causation," *Columbia University Studies in History, Economics and Public Law* 25, no. 3 (New York 1909).
Lichtenberger, James P., "Is the Freer Granting of Divorce an Evil?" *The American Journal of Sociology* 14 (1909), no. 6, 785–789.
Lipset, Seymour Martin, *Rebellion in the University. A History of Student Activism in America* (London 1972).
Lipset, Seymour Martin and Wolin, Sheldon S. (eds.), *The Berkeley Student Revolt* (Garden City 1965).
Livermore, Mary A. et al., "Women's View of Divorce," *North American Review* 150 (1890), no. 1, 110–135.
Lowitt, Richard and Beasly, Maurine (eds.), *One Third of a Nation: Lorina Hickok Reports on the Great Depression* (Urbana 1981).
Luce, Henry, "The American Century," *Life Magazine*, 10 (1941), no. 7, February 17, 1941, 61–65.
Lynd, Robert S. and Lynd, Helen Merrell, *Middletown. A Study in Contemporary American Culture* (New York 1929).
Lynd, Robert S. and Lynd, Helen Merell, *Middletown in Transition. A Study in Cultural Conflicts* (New York 1937).
Malcolm X and Haley, Alex, *The Autobiography of Malcolm X* (New York 1965).
Malinowski, Bronislaw, *The Family Among the Australian Aborigines. A Sociological Study* (London 1913).
Mansbridge, Jane J., *Why We Lost the ERA* (Chicago 1986).

Martschukat, Jürgen, *Väter, Soldaten, Liebhaber. Männer und Männlichkeiten in der Geschichte Nordamerikas. Ein Reader* (Bielefeld 2007).
Massey, Douglas S. (ed.), *The Moynihan Report Revisited. Lessons and Reflections after Four Decades* (Thousand Oaks 2009).
Masters, William H. and Johnson, Virginia, *Homosexuality in Perspective* (Boston 1979).
Masters, William H. and Johnson, Virginia, *Human Sexual Inadequacy* (Boston 1970).
Masters, William H. and Johnson, Virginia, *Human Sexuality* (Toronto 1982).
Masters, William H. and Johnson, Virginia, *Human Sexual Response* (Boston 1966).
Masters, William H. and Johnson, Virginia, "Settling Sexual Conflicts," *The Reader's Digest* (1975), no. 4, 84–87.
Masters, William H. and Johnson, Virginia, *The Pleasure Bond* (New York 1970).
McCorvey, Norma, *I am Roe. My Life, Roe vs. Wade, and Freedom of Choice* (New York 1994).
Mead, Margaret, *And Keep Your Powder Dry: An Anthropologist Looks at America* (New York 1942).
Mead, Margaret, *Male and Female. A Study of the Sexes in a Changing World* (London 1949).
Mead, Margaret, "What is Happening to the American Family? Religion Is the Support of the Family, but the Family is also the Support of Religion," *Pastoral Psychology* 1 (1950), no. 5, 40–50 (first published in 1947 in the *Journal of Social Casework*).
Mead, Margaret, "What's the Matter with the Family?" *Harper's Magazine* 190 (1945), April, 393–399.
Mead, Margaret and Heyman, Ken, *Family* (New York 1965).
Mead, Margaret and Wolfenstein, Martha (eds.), *Childhood in Contemporary Cultures* (Chicago and London 1955).
Mehren, Elizabeth and Cuniberti, Betty, "He's the Force Behind 'The Silent Scream' Film: Doctor Who Performed Thousands of Abortions Narrates, Promotes Right-to-Life Sonogram Movie," *TIME*, May 8, 1985 https://articles.latimes.com/1985-08-08/news/vw-3552_1_silentscream.
Merriam, Eve, "'The Matriarchal Myth' or the Case of the Vanishing Male," *The Nation*, November 8, 1958, 332.
Meyer, Agnes E., *Education for a New Morality* (New York, 1957).
Meyer, Agnes E., *Out of These Roots. The Autobiography of an American Woman* (Boston, MA 1953).
Meyer, Agnes E., "Women Aren't Men," *Atlantic Monthly* 194 (1950), August, 32–36.
Millett, Kate, "Sexual Politics. A Manifesto for Revolution," in Firestone, Shulamith and Koedt, Anne (eds.), *Notes from the Second Year* (New York 1970), 37–41.
Mills, Charles W., *Power, Politics and People. The Collected Essays of C. Wright Mills* (New York 1963).
Mills, Charles W., *The Power Elite* (New York 1957).
Mills, Charles W., *The Racial Contract* (Ithaca 1997).
Mills, Charles W., *White Collar. The American Middle Classes* (New York 1952).
Mink, Gwendolyn and Solinger, Rickie (eds.), *Welfare. A Documentary History of U.S. Policy and Politics* (New York 2003).
Mitra, S., "Child-Bearing Pattern of American Woman," *Eugenics Quarterly* 13 (1966), no. 2, 133–140.
Mitra, S., "Education and Fertility in the United States," *Eugenics Quarterly* 13 (1966), no. 4, 214–222.
Mitra, S., "Income, Socioeconomic Status, and Fertility in the United States," *Eugenics Quarterly* 13 (1966), no. 4, 223–230.
Mitra, S., "Occupation and Fertility in the United States," *Eugenics Quarterly* 13 (1966), no. 2, 141–146.
Morgan, J. W., "Ministers and Divorce," *Homiletic Review* 63 (1912), 76–77.
Morgan, Robin et al. (eds.), *Sisterhood is Powerful: An Anthology of Writings from the Women's Liberation Movement* (New York 1970).
Morgan, Winona, *The Family Meets the Depression. A Study of a Group of Highly Selected Families* (Westport 1939).

Morrow, Prince A., "The Relations of Social Diseases to the Family," *The American Journal of Sociology* 14 (1909), no. 5, 622–637.
Moynihan, Daniel P., "Employment, Income, and the Ordeal of the Negro Family," in Clark, Kenneth B. and Parsons, Talcott (eds.), *The Negro American* (Boston 1966), 134–159.
Moynihan, Daniel P., *Family and Nation. The Goodkin Lectures, Harvard University* (San Diego etc. 1986).
Moynihan, Daniel P., *Maximum Feasible Misunderstanding. Community Action in the War on Poverty* (New York 1969).
Moynihan, Daniel P., *On Understanding Poverty. Perspectives from the Social Sciences* (New York 1969).
Moynihan, Daniel P., *Toward a National Urban Policy* (New York 1970).
Murdock, George P., *Social Structure* (New York 1949).
Murray, Bill, *Up Front* (New York 1945).
Myrdal, Gunnar, *An American Dilemma. The Negro Problem and Modern Democracy* (New York 1944).
Myrdal, Gunnar, *Social Trends in America and Strategic Approaches to the Negro* Problem. *Phylon*, vol. 9, no. 3 (1948), 196–214.
Nadasen, Premilla, Mittelstadt, Jennifer, and Marisa Chappell (eds.), *Welfare in the United* States. *A History with Documents* (New York 2009).
Nathanson, Bernard, *Aborting America* (Garden City 1979).
National Commission on the Causes and Prevention of Violence, *To Establish Justice, To Insure Domestic Tranquility. The Final Report* (New York 1970).
Neptune, Donna Wicks and Popenoe, Paul B., "Acquaintance and Betrothal," *Social Forces* 16 (1938), no. 4, 552–555.
Norris, George W., "Divorce and the Means of Diminishing It," *Editorial Review* 5 (1911), 1081–1084.
Northcote, Hugh, *Christianity and Sex Problems* (Philadelphia, 1907).
Noyes, Hilda H, "The Development of Useful Citizenship," *Journal of Heredity* 11 (1920), no. 2, 88–91.
Nye, F. Ivan and Hoffman, Lois Wladis (eds.), *The Employed Mother in America* (Chicago 1963).
Park, Robert, *Race Relations and the Race Problem. A Definition and an Analysis, with Edgar Tristram Thompson* (Durham, NC 1939).
Parsons, Elsie Clews, "Higher Education of Women and the Family," *The American Journal of Sociology* 14 (1909), no. 6, 758–763.
Parsons, Elsie Clews, *The Family. An Ethnographical and Historical Outline with Descriptive Notes. Planned as a Text-book for the Use of College Lecturers and of Directors of Home-reading Clubs* (New York and London 1906).
Parsons, Talcott, "Age and Sex in the Social Structure of the United States," *American Sociological Review* 7, no. 5 (October 1942), 604–616.
Parsons, Talcott, "Full Citizenship for the Negro American? A Sociological Problem," in Clark, Kenneth B. and Parsons, Talcott (eds.), *The Negro American* (Boston 1967), 709–754.
Parsons, Talcott, "Introduction. Why 'Freedom Now,' Not Yesterday?" in Clark, Kenneth B. and Parsons, Talcott (eds.), *The Negro American* (Boston 1967), xix–xxviii.
Parsons, Talcott, "The American Family. Its Relations to Personality and the Social Structure," in Parsons, Talcott and R. F. Bales (eds.), *Family, Socialization and Interaction Process* (New York and London 1955), 3–33.
Parsons, Talcott, "The Kinship System of the Contemporary United States," *American Anthropologist* 45 (1943), no. 1, 22–38.
Parsons, Talcott (ed.), *The Negro American* (Boston, 1966), 160–204.
Parsons, Talcott, "The Normal American Family," in Skolnick, Arlene S. and Skolnick, Jerome H. (eds.), *Family in Transition. Rethinking Marriage, Sexuality, Child Rearing and Family Organization* (Boston 1971), 397–403.

Parsons, Talcott, "The Social Structure of the Family," in Anshen, Ruth Nanda (ed.), *The Family. Its Function and Destiny* (New York 1949), 173–201.
Parsons, Talcott and Bales R. F. (eds.), *Family, Socialization and Interaction Process* (New York and London 1955).
Peabody, Francis, *Jesus Christ and the Social Question* (New York 1903).
Pohlmann, Edward, "Mobilizing Social Pressures toward Small Families," *Eugenics Quarterly* 13 (1966), no. 2, 122–127.
Pohlmann, Edward, "The Timing of First Birth. A Review of Effects," *Eugenics Quarterly* 15 (1968), no. 4, 252–263.
Ponsett, Alex, "A Despised Minority. Unwed Mothers are Targets of Abuse from a Harsh Society," *Ebony*, August 1966, 48–54.
Popenoe, Paul B., "Assortative Mating for Occupational Level," *Journal of Social Psychology. Political, Racial and Differential Psychology* 8 (1937), no. 2, 270–274.
Popenoe, Paul B., "A Study of 738 Elopements," *American Sociological Review* 3 (1938), no. 1, 47–53.
Popenoe, Paul B., "Divorce and Remarriage from a Eugenic Point of View," *Social Forces* 12 (1933), no. 1, 48–50.
Popenoe, Paul B., *Divorce. 17 Ways to Avoid It* (Los Angeles 1959).
Popenoe, Paul B., "Education and Eugenics," *Journal of Educational Sociology* 8 (1935), no. 8, 451–458.
Popenoe, Paul B., "Eugenics and Family Relations," *Journal of Heredity* 31 (1940), no. 12, 532–536.
Popenoe, Paul B., "Eugenics and Human Morality," *Journal of Heredity* 13 (1922), no. 2, 77–81.
Popenoe, Paul B., "Family or Companionate?" *Journal of Social Hygiene* 11 (1925), no. 3, 129–138.
Popenoe, Paul B., "Heredity in Relation to the Family," *Living* 1 (1939), no. 2/3, 46.
Popenoe, Paul B., *Marriage. Before and After* (New York 1943).
Popenoe, Paul B., *Marriage Is What You Make It* (New York 1950).
Popenoe, Paul B., "Mate Selection," *American Sociological Review* 2 (1937), no. 5, 735–743.
Popenoe, Paul B., *Modern Marriage. A Handbook* (New York 1925).
Popenoe, Paul B., *Modern Marriage. A Handbook for Men, Revised and Entirely Rewritten* (New York 1940).
Popenoe, Paul B., *Practical Applications of Heredity* (Baltimore 1930).
Popenoe, Paul B., *Preparing for Marriage* (Los Angeles 1938).
Popenoe, Paul B., *Problems of Human Reproduction* (Baltimore 1926).
Popenoe, Paul B., "Remarriage of Divorcees to Each Other," *American Sociological Review* 3 (1938), no. 5, 695–699.
Popenoe, Paul B., *Sex, Love and Marriage* (New York 1963).
Popenoe, Paul B., *Sexual Inadequacy of the Male. A Manual for Counselors* (Los Angeles 1946).
Popenoe, Paul B., "Should Boys Grow up to Be Men?" *The Phi Delta Kappan* 27 (1945), no. 4, 120.
Popenoe, Paul B., *Social Life for High School Girls and Boys* (The American Social Hygiene Association, New York 1941).
Popenoe, Paul B., *The Child's Heredity* (Baltimore 1929).
Popenoe, Paul B., *The Conservation of the Family* (Baltimore 1926).
Popenoe, Paul B., "The Foster Child," *Scientific Monthly* 29 (1929), no. 3, 243–248.
Popenoe, Paul B., "The German Sterilization Law," *Journal of Heredity* 25 (1934), no. 7, 257–260.
Popenoe, Paul B., "The Institute of Family Relations," *Journal of Home Economics* 22 (1930), no. 11, 906–907.
Popenoe, Paul B., "Trends in Teaching Family Relations," *Marriage and Family Living* 8 (1946), no. 2, 35–36.
Popenoe, Paul B., "Where are the Marriageable Men?" *Social Forces* 14 (1935), no. 2, 257–262.

Popenoe, Paul P. and Disney, Dorothy Cameron, *Can this Marriage Be Saved?* (New York 1960).
Popenoe, Paul B. and Johnson, Roswell H., *Applied Eugenics* (New York 1918, new, revised edition New York 1933).
Popenoe, Paul B. and Williams, Ellen Morton, "Fecundity of Families Dependent on Public Charity," *The American Journal of Sociology* 40 (1934), no. 2, 214–220.
Potter, Henry, "'Is Divorce Wrong?'" *North American Review* 149 (1889), 513–538.
Rainwater, Lee, "Crucible of Identity. The Negro Lower Class Family," in Clark, Kenneth B. and Ralph, James R., *Northern Protest. Martin Luther King Jr., Chicago and the Civil Rights Movement* (Cambridge 1993).
Rainwater, Lee and Yancey, William L. (eds.), *The Moynihan Report and the Politics of Controversy. Including the Full Text of The Negro Family. The Case for National Action by Daniel Patrick Moynihan* (Cambridge and London 1967).
Reagan, Ronald, "Abortion and the Conscience of the Nation," *The Human Life Review*, February 3, 1984.
Reagan, Ronald, *Abortion and the Conscience of the Nation* (Nashville, 1984, new, revised edition Sacramento, CA 2001).
Reagan, Ronald, *Public Papers of the Presidents of the United States. Ronald Reagan, 1981–1989*, 11 vols. (Washington 1982–1991).
Richardson, A. S., *Better Babies and Their Care* (New York 1914).
Riesman, David, *The Lonely Crowd. A Study of the Changing American Character* (Garden City 1954 [1950]).
Rogers, Anna B., *Why American Marriages Fail* (Boston 1909).
Roosevelt, Theodore, "Race Decadence. Review of 'Racial Decay' by Octavius Charles Beale in the *Outlook*, April 8, 1911, in Roosevelt, Theodore, *Literary Essays* (*The National Edition of Roosevelt's Works*, vol. 12, New York 1926), 184–196.
Roosevelt, Theodore, "Sixth Annual Message," December 3, 1906, *State Papers as Governor and President, 1899–1909* (*The National Edition of Roosevelt's Works*, vol. 15, New York 1926), 377–378.
Rose, Arnold, *The Negro in America. A Condensation of An American Dilemma, by Gunnar Myrdal with the assistance of Richard Sterner and Arnold Rose* (London 1948).
Ross, Arthur M., "The Changing Pattern of Negro Employment," *Ebony*, July 1967, 38–39.
Ross, Edward Alsworth, *Das Buch der Gesellschaft. Grundlagen der Soziologie und Sozialreform* (Karlsruhe 1926, first English edition: *Principles of Sociology*, 1924).
Ross, Edward Alsworth, "Is the Freer Granting of Divorce an Evil?" *American Journal of Sociology* 14 (1909), no. 6, 793–794.
Ross, Edward Alsworth, *Social Control. A Survey of the Foundations of Order* (Cleveland and London 1969, [1901]).
Ross, Edward Alsworth, "The Causes of Race Superiority," *Annals of the American Academy of Political and Social Science* 18 (1901), 67–89.
Ross, Edward Alsworth, "The Significance of Increasing Divorce," *Century* 78 (1909), 149–152.
Rossi, Alice, "Equality Between the Sexes. An Immodest Proposal," *Daedalus* 93 (1964), no. 2, 607–652.
Rossi, Alice S., "Gender and Parenthood," *American Sociological Review* 49 (1984), February, 1–19.
Russell, Bertrand, "Marriage and the Population Question," *International Journal of Ethics* 26 (1916), 443–461.
Rustin, Bayard, "From Protest to Politics. The Future of the Civil Rights Movement," *Commentary* 39 (1965), no. 1, 25–31.
Rustin, Bayard, "The Watts 'Manifesto' & the McCone Report," *Commentary* 41 (1966), no. 3, 29–35.

Sanford, Elias B., *Origin and History of the Federal Council of Churches of Christ in America* (Hartford 1916).
Sanger, Margaret, *Birth Control Comes of Age, 1928-1939* (Urbana etc. 2006 [1966]).
Sanger, Margaret, *Family Limitation* (New York 1914).
Sanger, Margaret, *Motherhood in Bondage* (New York 1928).
Sanger, Margaret, *My Fight for Birth Control* (London 1932).
Sanger, Margaret, *The Pivot of Civilization* (New York 1922).
Sanger, Margaret, *What Every Girl Should Know* (New York 1920).
Sanger, Margaret, "Why Not Birth Control Clinics in America?" *Birth Control Review* 3 (1919), no. 5, 10-11.
Sanger, Margaret, *Woman and the New Race* (New York 1920).
Sanger, Margaret and Russell, Winter, *Debate on Birth Control* (New York 1921).
Scanlon, Jennifer (ed.), *The Gender and Consumer Culture Reader* (New York and London 2000).
Schlafly, Phyllis, *A Choice, Not an Echo* (Alton, IL 1964).
Schlafly, Phyllis (ed.), *Who Will Rock the Cradle? The Battle for Control of Childcare in America* (Nashville 1990).
Schlapp, Max G., "Causes of Defective Children. Prenatal Development Affected by Glandular Disturbances in the Mother—Induced by Unfavorable Environment," *The Journal of Heredity* 14 (1923), no. 9, 387-398.
Schlesinger, Arthur M. Jr., *Robert Kennedy and His Times* (Boston 1978).
Schlesinger, Arthur M.Jr., "The American Male. Why do Women Dominate Him?" *Look*, March 1959.
Schlesinger, Arthur M. Jr., "The Crisis of American Masculinity," in Schlesinger, Arthur M. Jr. (ed.), *The Politics of Hope* (Boston 1963), 237-246.
Schlesinger, Arthur M. Jr., "The Crisis of American Masculinity," *Esquire* 51, January 1959.
Schreiner, Olive, *Woman and Labour* (Leipzig 1911).
Seward, Georgine, "Sex Roles in Postwar Planning," *Journal of Social Psychology* 19 (1944), 163-185.
Sherbon, Florence B., "Popular Education," *Eugenics* 1.1 (1928), 33-35.
Siegel, Alberta E. and Meek Stolz, Lois, *Research Issues Related to the Effects of Maternal Employment on Children. A Symposium Presented at the Biennial Meeting of the Society for Research in Child Development, March 16, 1961* (Pennsylvania State University, University Park, PA 1961).
Siegel, Alberta Engvall, Meek Stolz, Lois, and Hitchcock, Ethel Alice et al., "Dependence and Independence in Children" in Nye, F. Ivan and Hoffman, Lois Waldis (eds.), *The Employed Mother in America* (Chicago 1963), 67-81.
Skinner, Kiron (ed.), *Reagan. A Life in Letters* (New York 2004).
Skinner, Kiron, *Reagan, in His Own* Hand. *The Writings of Ronald Reagan that Reveal His Revolutionary Vision for America* (New York 2001).
Small, Albion W., *Adam Smith and Modern Sociology* (Chicago 1907).
Small, Albion W., *General Sociology* (Chicago 1905).
Small, Albion W., *The Cameralists* (Chicago 1909).
Small, Albion W., *The Meaning of the Social Sciences* (Chicago 1910).
Smith, Walter George, "Ethics of Divorce," *Case and Comment* 21 (1914), 3-6.
Smith, Walter George, "Is the Freer Granting of Divorce an Evil?" *The American Journal of Sociology* 14 (1909), no. 6, 789-793.
Smith, Walter George, *Uniform Marriage and Divorce Laws: Address* (Columbus, 1909) <www.galenet.galegroup.com/servlet/MOML?af=RN&aeF3752545864&srchtp=a&ste=14>.
Spencer, Anna Garlin, "Problems of Marriage and Divorce," *Forum* 48 (1912), 188-204.

Spencer, Anna Garlin, "The Social Education of Women," *Publications of the American Sociological Society* 13 (1918), 11–27.
Spock, Benjamin, *Säuglings- und Kinderpflege*, vol. 1 (*Pflege und Behandlung des Säuglings*, Frankfurt a. M. 1957).
Spock, Benjamin, *Säuglings- und Kinderpflege*, vol. 2 (*Probleme der Kindheit und Jugend*, Frankfurt a. M. 1957).
Spock, Benjamin, *The Commonsense Book of Baby and Child Care* (New York 1946).
Stanton, Elizabeth Cady, "Are Homogenous Divorce Laws in All the States Desirable?" *North American Review* 170 (1900), 405–409.
Stanton, Elizabeth Cady, "Divorce vs. Domestic Warfare," *Arena* 1 (1890), 560–569.
Stanton, Elizabeth Cady, Anthony, Susan Brownell, and Gordon, Ann Dexter, *The Selected Papers of Elizabeth Cady Stanton and Susan B. Anthony*, vol. 1–3 *(1840–1873)* (New Brunswick 1997–2000).
Stoddard, Lothrop, *Into the Darkness. Nazi Germany Today* (New York 1940).
Stoddard, Lothrop, *The Rising Tide of Color against White Supremacy* (Brighton 1981 [reprint], first edition New York 1920).
Stolz, Lois Meek, "Effects of Maternal Employment on Children: Evidence from Research," *Child Development* 31 (1960), no. 4, 749–782.
Stone Blackwell, Alice, "The Threefold Menace (1913)," in Keetley, Dawn and Pettegrew, John (eds.), *Public Women, Public Words. A Documentary History of American Feminism*, vol. 2, 1900 to 1960 (Lanham etc. 2002), 186–189.
Strecker, Edward, *Their Mother's Sons: The Psychiatrist Examines an American Problem* (New York 1946).
Sturgis, Somers H. and Menzer-Benaron, Doris, *The Gynecological Patient. A Psycho-Endocrine Study* (New York and London 1962).
Sumner, William G., "The Family and Social Change," *Publications of the American Sociological Society. Papers and Proceedings, Volume III: Third Annual Meeting of the American Sociological Society, held at Atlantic City, N. J., December 28–30, 1908* (New York and London 1971, first edition Chicago and New York 1909), 1–15.
Sumner, William, "The Family and Social Change," *The American Journal of Sociology* 14 (1909), no. 5, 577–591.
Terkel, Studs, *Hard Times. An Oral History of the Great Depression* (New York 1970).
Terkel, Studs, *Race. How Blacks and Whites Think and Feel about the American Obsession* (New York 1992).
Terkel, Studs, *The Good War. An Oral History of World War II* (New York 1984).
The Race Betterment Foundation, *Proceedings of the First National Conference on Race Betterment* (Battle Creek 1914).
Tietze, Christopher, "Contraceptive Practice in the Context of a Nonrestrictive Abortion Law: Age Specific Pregnancy Rates in New York City, 1971–1973," *Family Planning Perspectives*, vol. 7, no. 5 (1975), 197–202.
Tietze, Christopher, "The Effects of Legalization of Abortion on Population Growth and Public Health," *Family Planning Perspectives* 7 (1975), no. 3, 123–127.
Tietze, Christopher and Lewit, Sarah, "Legal Abortion," *Scientific American*, vol. 236, no. 1 (1977), 21–27.
Trumbull, Benjamin, *An Appeal to the Public. Especially the Learned on the Unlawfulness of Divorce* (New Haven 1788).
U.S. Department of Commerce and Labor, *Marriage and Divorce, 1867–1906*, 2 vols. (Westport 1909, reprinted 1978).
U.S. Department of Labor, "Women's Bureau: Facts over Time," *Women in the Labor Force* (2012).
Unger, Irwin and Unger, Debi (eds.), *The Times Are a Changin'. The Sixties Reader* (New York 1998).

Vaget, Hans R. (ed.), *Thomas Mann, Agnes E. Meyer. Briefwechsel 1937–1955* (Frankfurt a. M. 1992).
Ventura, Stephanie J. et al., *Nonmarital Childbearing in the United States, 1940–99. National Vital Statistics Report from the Center for Disease Control and Prevention, National Center for Health Statistics, National Vital Statistics System*, 48 (2000), no. 16.
Vespa, Jonathan et al., *America's Family and Living Arrangements: 2012. Current Population Reports*, P20–570. (U.S. Census Bureau, Washington D. C).
Weisman, Steven R. (ed.), *Daniel Patrick Moynihan. A Portrait in Letters of an American Visionary* (New York 2010).
Wells, Kate Gannett, "Some Comments on Divorce," *North American Review* 173 (1901), no. 4, 508–517.
West, Mary Mills (Mrs. Max West) and U.S. Department of Labor, *Children's Bureau: Infant Care* (Washington 1914).
White House Working Group on the Family, *The Family. Preserving America's Future. A Report to the President from the White House Working Group on the Family* (Washington 1986).
White, Mrs. Edward Franklin, "Marriage and Divorce" (Amendment to the Constitution. Hearing before a Subcommittee on S. J. Res. 5, 68th Congress, 1st Session. January 11, 1924, 11–14), in Johnson, Julia E. (ed.), *Selected Articles on Marriage and Divorce* (New York 1925), 250–253.
Wiggam, A. E., *The New Decalogue of Science* (New York 1922).
Wilkinson, Marguerite O.B., "Education as a Preventive of Divorce," *The Craftsman* 21 (1912), no. 5, 473–481.
Wise, Jennings C., "Shall Congress Be Given Power To Establish Uniform State Laws?" *Central Law Journal* 70 (1910), 93–99.
Wright, Caroll D., *Outline of Practical Sociology* (New York 1900).
Wylie, Philip, *Generation of Vipers* (Champaign and London, 2007 first edition 1942).
Young, Whitney, *To be Equal* (New York and Toronto, London 1964).

Research literature

Ahlburg, Dennis A. and DeVita, Carol J., "'New Realities of the American Family,'" *Population Bulletin* 47, no. 2 (August 1992), 15.
Allen, Ann Taylor, *Feminism and Motherhood in Western Europe 1890–1970. The Maternal Dilemma* (New York 2005).
Allen, Ann Taylor, "Feminism, Social Science, and the Meanings of Modernity. The Debate on the Origin of the Family in Europe and the United States, 1860–1914," *American Historical Review* 104 (1999), no. 4, 1085–1113.
Allen, Ann Taylor and Baader, Meike Sophie (eds.), *Ellen Keys reformpädagogische Vision. Das "Jahrhundert des Kindes" und seine Wirkung* (Weinheim 2000).
Allen, Garland, "Eugenics Comes to America," in Jacoby, Russell and Glauberman, Naomi (eds.), *The Bell Curve Debate. History, Documents, Opinions* (New York 1995), 441–475.
Allen, Garland, "The Biological Basis of Crime. An Historical and Methodological Study," *History of Social and Physical Science* 31 (2001), no. 2, 183–222.
Allen, Garland, "The Eugenics Record Office at Cold Spring Harbor, 1910–1940. An Essay on Institutional History," *Osiris* 2 (1986), no. 2, 225–264.
Allen, Garland, "The Ideology of Elimination: American and German Eugenics, 1900–1945," in Nicosia, Frances and Heuner, Jonathan (eds.), *Medicine and Medical Ethics in Nazi Germany.Origins, Practices, Legacies* (New York 2002) 13–39.

Allen, Garland, "The Reception of Mendelism in the United States, 1900–1930," *Life Science* 323 (2000), no. 12, 1081–1088.

Allen, Katherine and Demo, David, "The Families of Lesbians and Gay Men. A New Frontier in Family Research," *Journal of Marriage and the Family* 57 (1995), no. 1, 111–127.

Allerbeck, Klaus, *Soziologie radikaler Studentenbewegungen. Eine vergleichende Untersuchung in der Bundesrepublik Deutschland und den Vereinigten Staaten* (Munich 1973).

Alley, Robert and Brown, Irby, *Women Television Producers. Transformation of the Male Medium* (Rochester 2001).

Allit, Patrick, *Catholic Intellectuals and Conservative Politics in America 1950–1985* (Ithaca 1993).

Amato, Paul, *Alone Together. How Marriage in America is Changing* (Boston 2009).

Amireh, Amal, *The Factory Girl and the Seamstress. Imagining Gender and Class in Nineteenth Century American Fiction* (New York 2000).

Ammerman, Nancy, "North American Protestant Fundamentalism," in Marty, Martin E. and Appelby, R. Scott (eds.), *Fundamentalisms Observed. Fundamentalism Project*, vol. 1, (Chicago 1991), 1–65.

Anderson, Karen, *Changing Woman. A History of Racial Ethnic Women in Modern America* (New York 1996).

Anderson, Karen, *Wartime Women. Sex Roles, Family Relations, and the Status of Women During World War II* (Westport 1981).

Anderson, Karen T., "Last Hired, First Fired. Black Women Workers during World War II," *Journal of American History* 69 (1982), no. 1, 83–97.

Anderson, Terry H., *The Movement and the Sixties* (New York 1995).

Andrew, John A., "Resurgent Conservatism," in Kupiec Cayton, Mary and Williams, Peter (eds.), *Encyclopedia of American Cultural and Intellectual History*, vol. 2 (New York etc. 2001), 205–213.

Andrew, John A., *The Other Side of the Sixties. Young Americans for Freedom and the Rise of Conservative Politics* (New York 1997).

Apple, Rima, "Constructing Mothers. Scientific Motherhood in the Nineteenth and Twentieth Centuries," *Social History of Medicine* 8 (1995), no. 2, 161–178.

Apple, Rima, "Constructing Mothers. Scientific Motherhood in the Nineteenth and Twentieth Centuries," in Apple, Rima and Golden, Janet (eds.), *Mothers and Motherhood. Readings in American History* (Columbus 1997), 90–110.

Apple, Rima, *Perfect Motherhood: Science and Childrearing in America* (Piscataway 2006).

Apple, Rima, "Physicians and Mothers Construct 'Scientific Motherhood,'" in Warner, John and Tighe, Janet, *Major Problems in the History of American Medicine and Public Health* (Boston and New York 2001), 332–339.

Apple, Rima and Golden, Janet (eds.), *Mothers and Motherhood. Readings in American History* (Columbus 1997).

Appy, Christian G., *Cold War Constructions. The Political Culture of United States Imperialism 1945–1966* (Amherst, MA 2000).

Ariès, Philippe, *Centuries of Childhood. A Social History of Family Life* (New York 1962).

Arnold, Laura and Weisberg, Herbert, "Parenthood, Family Values and the 1992 Presidential Election," *American Politics Quarterly* 24 (1996), no. 2, 194–220.

Aronson, Amy Beth, *Taking Liberties. Early American Women's Magazines and their Readers* (Westport 2002).

Aschenbrenner, Joyce, "Extended Families among Black Americans," *Journal of Comparative Family Studies* 4 (1973), no. 2, 257–268.

Aschenbrenner, Joyce, *Lifelines. Black Families in Chicago* (New York 1975).

Auga, Ulrike (ed.), *Das Geschlecht der Wissenschaften. Zur Geschichte von Akademikerinnen im 19. und 20. Jahrhundert* (Frankfurt a. M. 2010).
Auletta, Ken, *The Underclass* (New York 1982).
Badger, Anthony J., *The New Deal. The Depression Years, 1933–1940* (Basingstoke 1989).
Bailey, Beth, *From Front Porch to Back Seat. Courtship in Twentieth Century America* (Baltimore 1988).
Bailey, Beth, *Sex in the Heartland* (Cambridge etc. 2004).
Bailey, Beth, "Sexual Revolution(s)," in Farber, David (ed.), *The Sixties. From Memory to History* (Chapel Hill and London 1994), 235–262.
Bailey, Beth and Farber, David, *America in the Seventies* (Lawrence 2004).
Bailey, Martha J. and Danziger, Sheldon (eds.), *Legacies of the War on Poverty* (New York 2013).
Baker, Ellen, *On Strike and on Film. Mexican American Families and Blacklisted Filmmakers in Cold War America* (North Carolina 2007).
Balbier, Uta, "Billy Graham's Crusades in the 1950s: Neo-Evangelicalism between Civil Religion, Media, and Consumerism," *Bulletin of the German Historical Institute Washington D. C.* 44 (2009), 71–80.
Balitzer, Alfred and Bonnetto, Gerald, *A Time for Choosing. The Speeches of Ronald Reagan* (Chicago 1983).
Ballaster, Ros et al., *Women's Worlds. Ideology, Femininity and the Woman's Magazine* (Basingstoke etc. 1991).
Banks, J. A., *Victorian Values. Secularism and the Size of Families* (London 1981).
Bashford, Alison and Levine, Philippa (eds.), *The Oxford Handbook of the History of Eugenics* (Oxford 2010).
Bassimir, Anja-Maria, *Evangelical News: Politics, Gender, and Bioethics in Conservative Christian Magazines of the 1970s and 1980s* (Tuscaloosa 2022).
Bateman, Fred and Taylor, Jason E., "The New Deal at War. Alphabet Agencies' Expenditure Patterns 1940–1945," *Explorations in Economic History* 40 (2003), no. 3, 251–278.
Bauman, John F. and Coode, Thomas H., *In the Eye of the Great Depression. New Deal Reporters and the Agony of the American People* (DeKalb 1988).
Baumann, Zygmunt, *Moderne und Ambivalenz: Das Ende der Eindeutigkeit* (Hamburg 2005, first edition *Modernity and Ambivalence*, 1991).
Baumol, William J., *Welfare Economics and the Theory of the State with a New Introduction. Welfare and the State Revisited* (London 1965).
Baxandall, Rosalyn and Ewen, Elizabeth, *Picture Windows. How the Suburbs Happened* (New York 2000).
Baxandall, Rosalyn Fraad, *America's Working Women. A Documentary History, 1600 to the Present* (New York 1995).
Bean, Frank D. and Frisbie, W. Parker (eds.), *The Demography of Racial and Ethnic Groups* (New York etc. 1978).
Beard, Mary, *Women as Force in History* (New York 1946).
Beattie, Keith, *The Scar that Binds. American Culture and the Vietnam War* (New York 1998).
Beck, Ulrich, "Das Zeitalter des 'eigenen Lebens.' Individualisierung als 'paradoxe Sozialstruktur' und andere offene Fragen," *Aus Politik und Zeitgeschichte* B 29 (2001), 3–6.
Beck, Ulrich, "Jenseits von Frauen- und Männerrollen. Die Zukunft der Familie," *Universitas* 1 (1991), 1–9.
Beck, Ulrich, *Risikogesellschaft. Auf dem Weg in eine andere Moderne* (Frankfurt a. M. 1986).
Beck, Ulrich and Beck-Gernsheim, Elisabeth, "Individualisierung in modernen Gesellschaften. Perspektiven und Kontroversen einer subjektorientierten Soziologie," in Beck, Ulrich and Beck-Gernsheim, Elisabeth (eds.), *Riskante Freiheiten* (Frankfurt a. M. 1994, 10–39).

Beck-Gernsheim, Elisabeth, "Auf dem Weg in die postfamiliale Familie. Von der Notgemeinschaft zur Wahlverwandtschaft," in Beck-Gernsheim, Elisabeth and Beck, Ulrich (eds.), *Riskante Freiheiten* (Frankfurt a. M. 1994), 115–138.
Beck-Gernsheim, Elisabeth and Beck, Ulrich (eds.), *Riskante Freiheiten. Individualisierung in modernen Gesellschaften* (Frankfurt a. M. 1994), esp. 10–39.
Bederman, Gail, *Manliness and Civilization. A Cultural History of Gender and Race in the United States 1880–1917* (Chicago 1995).
Beisel, Nicola, *Imperiled Innocents: Anthony Comstock and Family Reproduction in Victorian America* (Princeton 1997).
Bell, Daniel, "Zur Auflösung der Widersprüche von Modernität und Modernismus: Das Beispiel Amerikas," in Bell, Daniel and Meier, Heinrich (eds.), *Zur Diagnose der Moderne* (Munich 1990), 21–68.
Bell, Rudolph and Yans, Virginia (eds.), *Women on Their Own. Interdisciplinary Perspectives on Being Single* (New York 2008).
Bendroth, Margaret Lamberts, *Growing Up Protestant. Parents, Children, and Mainline Churches* (New Brunswick 2002).
Benedict, Hans-Jürgen, "Vom Protest zum Widerstand. Die Vietnamkriegs-Opposition in den USA und in der BRD," *Friedensanalysen* 4 (1977), 79–106.
Bengtson, Vern L., Biblarz, Timothy J., and Roberts, Robert E. L., *How Families Still Matter. A Longitudinal Study of Youth in Two Generations* (Cambridge 2002).
Benkov, Laura, *Reinventing the Family. Lesbian and Gay Parents* (New York 1994).
Bennett, David H., *The Party of Fear. From Nativist Movements to the New Rights in American History* (Chapel Hill 1988).
Bennett, William, *Our Children and Our Country. Improving America's Schools and Affirming the Common Culture* (New York 1988).
Bensel, Richard Franklin, *The Political Economy of American Industrialization 1877–1900* (Cambridge 2000).
Berg, Allison, *Mothering the Race. Women's Narratives of Reproduction 1890–1930* (Illinois 2002).
Berg, Manfred, "1968. A Turning Point in American Race Relations?" in Fink, Carole, Gassert, Philipp, and Junker, Detlef (eds.), *1968. The World Transformed* (Publications of the German Historical Institute, Cambridge 1998), 397–420.
Berg, Manfred, *The Ticket to Freedom. Die NAACP und das Wahlrecht der Afro-Amerikaner* (Frankfurt a. M. 2000).
Berg, Manfred, *Two Cultures of Rights. The Quest for Inclusion and Participation in Modern America and Germany* (Cambridge, MA 2002).
Berger, Maurice, *How Art Becomes History. Essays on Art, Society, and Culture in Post-New Deal America* (New York 1992).
Berghahn, Volker R., *America and the Cold Wars in Europe. Shepard Stone between Philanthropy, Academy and Diplomacy* (Princeton 2001).
Berman, William, *America's Right Turn. From Nixon to Bush* (Baltimore 1994).
Bernanke, Ben S., *Essays on the Great Depression* (Princeton 2000).
Bernstein, Irving, *Guns or Butter. The Presidency of Lyndon Johnson* (Oxford and New York 1996).
Berzon, Betty, "Sharing Your Lesbian Identity with your Children," in Vida, Ginny (ed.), *Our Right to Love. A Lesbian Resource Book* (Englewood Cliffs 1978) 69–74.
Besharov, Douglas A. and West, Andrew, *African American Marriage Patterns* <www.hoover.org/sites/default/files/uploads/documents/0817998721_95.pdf>.
Betts, Paul Robert (ed.), *Domestic Dreamworlds. Notions of Home in Post-1945 Europe* (London 2005).

Biblarz, Timothy J. and Stacey, Judith (eds.), "How Does the Gender of Parents Matter?" *Journal of Marriage and Family*, vol. 72, 1 (2010), 3–22.
Biles, Roger, *A New Deal for the American People* (DeKalb 1991).
Biles, Roger, *The South and the New Deal* (Lexington 1994).
Billingsley, Andrew, *Black Families in White America* (Englewood Cliffs 1968).
Birnbaum, Norman, *After Progress. American Social Reform and European Socialism in the Twentieth Century* (Oxford 2001).
Birnbaum, Norman, "Der protestantische Fundamentalismus in den USA," in Meyer, Thomas (ed.), *Fundamentalismus in der modernen Welt* (Frankfurt a. M. 1989), 121–154.
Birnbaum, Norman, "Verlust mit Folgen. Das Vermächtnis des New Deal in der amerikanischen Politik," *Gewerkschaftliche Monatshefte* 55 (2004), 344–370.
Bix, Amy Sue, "Experiences and Voices of Eugenic Field-Workers. 'Women's Work' in Biology," *Social Studies of Science* 27 (1997), 625–668.
Black, Edwin, *War Against the Weak. Eugenics and America's Campaign to Create a Master Race* (New York and London 2003).
Black, Jason Edward, "Authoritarian Fatherhood. Andrew Jackson's Early Familial Lectures to America's 'Red Children,'" *Journal of Family History* 30 (2005), no. 3, 247–264.
Blackwelder, Julia Kirk, *Now Hiring: The Feminization of Work in the United States, 1990–1995* (College Station 1997).
Blair, Karen, *The Clubwoman as Feminist. True Womanhood Redefined 1868–1914* (New York 1980).
Blake, Nelson M., *The Road to Reno. A History of Divorce in the United States* (New York 1962).
Blanchard, Dallas A., *The Anti-Abortion Movement and the Rise of the Religious Right* (New York 1994).
Blankenhorn, David, *Fatherless America. Confronting Our Most Urgent Social Problem* (New York 1995).
Block, James E., *The Crucible of Consent. American Child Rearing and the Forging of Liberal Society* (Cambridge, MA 2012).
Blossfeld, Hans-Peter (ed.), *Between Equalization and Marginalization. Women Working Part-time in Europe and the United States of America* (Oxford 1997).
Blum, John Morton, *Years of Discord. American Politics and Society 1961–1974* (New York 1991).
Booker, Keith M., *The Post-Utopian Imagination. American Culture in the Long 1950s* (Westport 2002).
Boris, Eileen and Klein, Jennifer, *Caring for America. Home Health Workers in the Shadow of the Welfare State* (New York 2012).
Boswell, Angela, "Married Women's Property Rights and the Challenge to the Patriarchal Order: Colorado County, Texas," in Coryell, Janet L. (ed.), *Negotiating Boundaries of Southern Womanhood: Dealing with the Powers That Be* (Columbia, MO 2000), 89–109.
Boudreau, Erica Bicchieri, "'Yea, I have a Goodly Heritage.' Health Versus Heredity in the Fitter Family Contests 1920–1928," *Journal of Family History* 30 (2005), no. 4, 366–387.
Bourdieu, Pierre, *La Domination Masculine* (Paris 1998).
Bowman-Kruhm, Mary, *Margaret Mead. A Biography* (Westport and London 2003).
Boydston, Jeanne, "Gender as a Question of Historical Analysis," in Shepard, Alexandra and Garthine, Walker (eds.), *Gender and Change. Agency, Chronology, and Periodization* (Malden 2009), 133–165.
Boydston, Jeanne, *Home and Work. Housework, Wages, and the Ideology of Labor in the Early Republic* (New York 1994).
Boyer, Paul, *By the Bomb's Early Light. American Thought and Culture at the Dawn of the Atomic Age* (New York 1985).
Bozett, Frederick W., *Gay and Lesbian Parents* (New York 1987).

Bracke, Maud Ann, "Women's Rights, Family Planning, and Population Control: The Emergence of Reproductive Rights in the United Nations (1960s–70s)," *The International History Review*, 2021, DOI: 10.1080/07075332.2021.1985585.
Braeman, John, "The New Deal Revisited," *Continuity* 23 (1999), 1–63.
Brandt, Allen M., *No Magic Bullet. A Social History of Venereal Disease in the United States since 1880* (New York 1987).
Braunstein, Peter and Doyle, Michael William (eds.), *Imagine Nation. The American Counterculture of the 1960s and '70s* (New York 2002).
Breines, Winifred, *The Trouble between Us. An Uneasy History of White and Black Women in the Feminist Movement* (Oxford 2007).
Brennan, Mary, *Wives, Mothers, and the Red Menace. Conservative Women and the Crusade against Communism* (Colorado 2008).
Bridenthal, Renate and Claudia Koontz (eds.), *Becoming Visible. Women in European History* (Boston 1987).
Briggs, Laura, "Mother, Child, Race, Nation. The Visual Iconography of Rescue and the Politics of Transnational and Transracial Adoption," *Gender & History* 15 (2003), no. 2, 179–200.
Briggs, Laura, *Reproducing Empire. Race, Sex Science, and U.S. Imperialism in Puerto Rico* (Los Angeles 2002).
Briggs, Laura, *Somebody's Children. The Politics of Transracial and Transnational Adoption*, Durham (London 2012).
Brinkley, Alan, *The End of Reform. New Deal Liberalism in Recession and War* (New York 1995).
Brinkley, Alan, "The Problem of American Conservatism," *American Historical Review* 99 (1994), no. 2, 409–429.
Bristow, Nancy K., *Making Men Moral. Social Engineering During the Great War* (New York and London 1996).
Brock, William R., *Welfare, Democracy, and the New Deal* (Cambridge and New York 1988).
Brocker, Manfred, *Protest—Anpassung—Etablierung. Die Christliche Rechte im politischen System der USA* (Frankfurt a. M. etc. 2004).
Bronfen, Elisabet, *Das verknotete Subjekt. Hysterie in der Moderne* (Berlin 1998).
Bronner, Stephen Eric, "US-amerikanischer Blick zurück. 1968 dreißig Jahre danach," in Faber, Richard and Stölting, Erhard (eds.), *Die Phantasie an die Macht? 1968. Versuch einer Bilanz* (Berlin and Vienna 2002).
Bronski, Michael, *A Queer History of the United States* (Boston 2011).
Brooks, Marla, *The American Family on Television. A Chronology of 121 Shows 1948–2004* (Jefferson and London 2004).
Brooks, Tim and Marsh, Earl, *The Complete Directory to Prime Time Network and Cable TV Shows. 1946-Present* (New York 2003).
Brosco, Jeff, "Weight Charts and Well Child Care. When the Pediatrician Became the Expert in Child Health," in Stern, Alexandra Minna and Markel, Howard (eds.), *Formative Years. The History of Children's Health in the United States 1880–2000* (Ann Arbor, 2002), 91–121.
Brown, Bruce W., *Images of Family Life in Magazine Advertising 1920–1978* (New York 1981).
Brown, Laura, "Lesbians and Family," *NWSA Journal* 1 (1988), no. 1, 103–108.
Brown, Nikki, *Private Politics and Public Voices. Black Women's Activism from World War I to the New Deal* (Bloomington, IN 2006).
Browning, Don and Clairmont, David A., *American Religions and the Family. How Faith Traditions Cope with Modernization and Democracy* (Columbia 2006).

Browning, Don S. et al, *From Culture Wars to Common Ground: Religion and the American Family Debate* (Louisville, KY 1997).
Brownlee, Elliott, *The Reagan Presidency. Pragmatic Conservatism and Its Legacies* (Lawrence 2003).
Brückmann, Rebecca, *Massive Resistance and Southern Womanhood. White Women, Class, and Segregation* (Athens 2021).
Brueckweh, Kerstin et al. (eds.), *Engineering Society. The Role of the Human and Social Sciences in Modern Societies 1880–1980* (New York 2012).
Brumberg, Johanna, *Die Vermessung einer Generation. Die Babyboomer und die Ordnung der Gesellschaft im US-Zensus zwischen 1940 und 1980* (Göttingen 2015).
Bryson, Thomas A., *Walter George Smith* (Washington 1977).
Buch, Friedrich W. and Nave-Herz, Rosemarie (eds.), *Familie und Gesellschaft. Beiträge zur Familienforschung* (Oldenburg 2005).
Buhle, Mari Jo, *Feminism and Its Discontents: A Century of Struggle with Psychoanalysis* (Cambridge 1999).
Bullard, Catherine S., "Children's Future, Nation's Future. Race, Citizenship and the United States Children's Bureau," in Schumann, Dirk (ed.), *Raising Citizens in the "Century of the Child." The United States and German Central Europe in Comparative Perspective* (New York 2010), 53–67.
Bullard, Robert D. (ed.), *The Black Metropolis in the Twenty-First Century. Race, Power, and Politics of Place* (Lanham, MD and Plymouth, UK 2007).
Burke, Phyllis, *Family Values. A Lesbian Mother's Fight for Her Son* (New York 1993).
Burkes, George R. Jr., "Family Values," in Kutler, Stanley I. (ed.), *Dictionary of American History*, vol. 3 (New York 2003), 316–317.
Burkholder, Zoe, *Color in the Classroom. How American Schools Taught Race 1900–1954* (Oxford 2011).
Burner, David, *Making Peace with the '60s* (Princeton 1996).
Burns, Gene, *The Moral Veto. Stalemate and Change in American Debates over Contraception and Abortion* (New York 2002).
Büschges, Christian et al. (eds.), *Die Ethnisierung des Politischen. Identitätspolitiken in Lateinamerika, Asien und den USA* (Frankfurt a. M. 2007).
Bush, William S., *Who Gets a Childhood? Race and Juvenile Justice in Twentieth-Century Texas* (Athens, GA 2010).
Butler, Judith, *Bodies that Matter. On the Discursive Limits of "Sex"* (New York 1993).
Butler, Judith, *Undoing Gender* (New York, London 2004).
Butler, Judith, *Gender Trouble. Feminism and the Subversion of Identity* (New York 1990).
Calhoun, Craig (ed.), *Sociology in America. A History* (Chicago 2007).
Cameron, Ardis (ed.), *Looking for America. The Visual Production of Nation and People* (Malden 2005).
Canaday, Margot, *The Straight State. Sexuality and Citizenship in Twentieth-Century America* (Princeton 2009).
Canning, Kathleen, "Feminist History after the Linguistic Turn. Historicizing Discourse and Experience," *Signs* 19 (1994), no. 2, 368–404.
Canning, Kathleen, *Gender History in Practice. Historical Perspectives on Bodies, Class, and Citizenship* (Ithaca and London 2005).
Caplow, Theodore, *Recent Social Trends in the United States 1960–1990* (Montréal 1994).
Caplow, Theodore, Bahr, Howard, and Chadwick, Bruce (eds.), *Middletown Families. Fifty Years of Change and Continuity* (Minneapolis 1982).
Carbone, June, *From Partners to Parents. The Second Revolution in Family Law* (New York 2000).
Carey, Allison C., "Gender and Compulsory Sterilization Programs in America 1907–1950," *Journal of Historical Sociology* 11 (1998), no. 3, 74–105.

Carey, Allison C., *On the Margins of Citizenship. Intellectual Disability and Civil Rights in Twentieth Century America* (Philadelphia 2010).

Carlson, Elof Axel, *The Unfit. A History of a Bad Idea* (Cold Spring Harbor) 2001.

Carlson, Elof Axel, *Times of Triumph. Times of Doubt. Science and the Battle for the Public Trust* (Cold Spring Harbor 2006).

Carlson, Elof Axel and Micklos, David, "Engineering American Society. The Lesson of Eugenics," *Nature Review and Genetics* 1 (2000), 153–158.

Caron, Simone M., "Birth Control and the Black Community in the 1960s. Genocide or Power Politics?" *Journal of Social History* 31 (1998), no. 3, 545–569.

Caron, Simone M., *Who Chooses? American Reproductive History since 1830* (Gainesville 2008).

Carp, E. Wayne (ed.), *Adoption in America. Historical Perspectives* (Ann Arbor 2002).

Carp, E. Wayne, *Family Matters. Secrecy and Disclosure in the History of Adoption* (second edition Cambridge and London 2000).

Carp, E. Wayne, *Jean Paton and the Struggle to Reform American Adoption* (Ann Arbor 2014).

Carter, Dale, *War and Cold War in American Foreign Policy 1942-62* (Basingstoke 2002).

Carter, Julian, *The Heart of Whiteness. Normal Sexuality and Race in America 1890-1940* (Durham 2007).

Casey, Steven, *Franklin D. Roosevelt. American Public Opinion, and the War Against Nazi Germany* (Oxford 2001).

Cashin, Joan E. (ed.), *The Family in the American South* (Thousand Oaks 2003).

Cashman, Sean Dennis, *America in the Age of the Titans. The Progressive Era and World War I* (New York 1988).

Cavan, Ruth Shonle, *The American Family* (New York 1969).

Cayton, Mary Kupiec and Williams, Peter W. (eds.), *Encyclopedia of American Cultural and Intellectual History* (New York et al. 2001).

Cecora, J. (ed.), *Changing Values and Attitudes in Family Households with Rural Peer Groups, Social Networks, and Action Spaces. Implications of Institutional Transition in East and West for Value Formation and Transmission* (Bonn 1994).

Celello, Kristin, *Making Marriage Work. A History of Marriage and Divorce in the Twentieth-Century United States* (Chapel Hill 2009).

Chadwick, Bruce A. and Heaton, Tim B. (eds.), *Statistical Handbook on the American Family* (Phoenix 1992, second edition 1999).

Chafe, William H., "Eleanor Roosevelt," in Kerber, Linda K. and De Hart, Mathews (eds.), *Women's America. Refocusing the Past* (New York 1987), 364–374.

Chafe, William H., *The American Woman. Her Changing Social, Economic, and Political Roles 1920-1970* (London 1974).

Chafe, William H., *The Paradox of Change. American Women in the 20th Century* (New York 1991).

Chafe, William H., *The Unfinished Journey. America since World War II* (New York and Oxford 2003).

Chafe, William H., *Women and Equality. Changing Patterns in American Culture* (New York 1977).

Chafe, William H. and Sitkoff, Harvard, *A History of Our Time. Readings on Postwar America* (New York 1999).

Chandler, Ralph Clark, "The Wicked Shall Not Bear Rule. The Fundamentalist Heritage of the New Christian Right," in Bromley, David G. and Shupe, Anson (eds.), *New Christian Politics* (Macon 1984).

Chappell, Marisa, *The War on Welfare. Family, Poverty, and Politics in Modern America* (Philadelphia 2010).

Cherlin, Andrew J., "American Marriage in the Early Twenty-First Century," in *The Future of Children—Marriage and Child Wellbeing* 15 (2005), no. 2, 33–55.

Cherlin, Andrew J., *Public and Private Families. An Introduction* (sixth edition, New York, 2010).
Cherlin, Andrew J., "Public Display. The Picture-Perfect American Family? These Days, It Doesn't Exist," WP, September 7, 2008 <www.washingtonpost.com/wp-dyn/content/article/2008/09/05/AR2008090502652.html>.
Cherlin, Andrew J., "The Deinstitutionalization of American Marriage," *Journal of Marriage and the Family* 66 (2004), 848–861.
Cherlin, Andrew J., *The Marriage-Go-Round. The State of Marriage and the Family in America Today* (New York 2009).
Chesler, Ellen, *Woman of Valor. Margaret Sanger and the Birth Control Movement in American* (New York 2007, first edition 1992).
Cho, Sumi, Crenshaw, Kimberlé, and McCall, Leslie, "Towards a Field of Intersectionality Studies: Theory, Applications, and Praxis," *Signs* 38 (2013), no. 4, 785–810.
Christenson, Cornelia, *Kinsey: A Biography* (Bloomington 1971).
Clark, Clifford Edward, *The American Family Home 1800–1960* (Chapel Hill and London 1986).
Clarke, Adele, *Disciplining Reproduction. Modernity, American Life Sciences, and the Problem of Sex* (Berkeley 1998).
Cline, David P., *Creating Choice. A Community Responds to the Need for Abortion and Birth Control, 1961–1973* (New York 2006).
Clunis, Merilee and Green Dorsey, D., *Lesbian Couples* (Seattle 1988).
Cobble, Dorothy Sue, *The Other Women's Movement. Workplace Justice and Social Rights in Modern America* (Princeton 2004).
Coffman, Elesha J., *The Christian Century and the Rise of the Protestant Mainline* (New York et al. 2013).
Cogdell, Christine, *Eugenic Design. Streamlining America in the 1930s* (Philadelphia 2004).
Cohan, Steve, *Masked Men. Masculinity and the Movies in the Fifties* (Bloomington 1997).
Cohen, Jerry and Murphy, William S., *Burn, Baby, Burn! The Los Angeles Race Riot, August 1965* (New York 1966).
Cohen, Lizabeth, *A Consumers' Republic. The Politics of Mass Consumption in Postwar America* (New York 2003).
Colburn, David R. and Pozzetta, George D. *Reform and Reformers in the Progressive Era* (Westport 1983).
Collier, Jane, Rosaldo, Michelle Z., and Yanagisako, Sylvia, "Is There a Family? New Anthropological Views," in Thorne, Barry and Yalom, Marilyn (eds.), *Rethinking the Family. Some Feminist Questions* (Boston 1992), 31–48.
Collins, Robert M., *Transforming America. Politics and Culture in the Reagan Years* (New York 2007).
Coltrane, Scott and Adams, Michele, "Men's Family Work. Child-Centered Fathering and the Sharing of Domestic Labor," in Hertz, Rosanna and Marshall, Namy L. (eds.), *Working Families. The Transformation of the American Home* (Berkeley 2001), 72–99.
Condit, Celeste Michelle, *Decoding Abortion Rhetoric. Communicating Social Change* (Urbana and Chicago 1990).
Connell, R. W. and Messerschmidt, James W., "Hegemonic Masculinity. Rethinking the Concept," *Gender & Society* 19 (2005), 829–859.
Connell, Robert, *Masculinities* (Cambridge 1995).
Connelly, Mark Thomas, *The Response to Prostitution in the Progressive Era* (Chapel Hill 1980).
Connelly, Matthew, *Fatal Misconception. The Struggle to Control World Population* (Cambridge and London 2008).
Conrad, Sebastian and Randeria, Shalini (eds.), *Jenseits des Eurozentrismus. Postkoloniale Perspektiven in den Geschichts- und Kulturwissenschaften* (Frankfurt a. M. 2002).

Cook, Blanche Wiesen, *Eleanor Roosevelt 1884-1933* (London 1992).
Cook, Blanche Wiesen, *The Defining Years 1933-1938* (London 2000).
Coontz, Stephanie, *A Strange Stirring. The Feminine Mystique and American Women at the Dawn of the 1960s* (New York 2011).
Coontz, Stephanie, *Die Entstehung des Privaten. Amerikanisches Familienleben vom 17. bis zum ausgehenden 19. Jahrhundert* (Münster 1994).
Coontz, Stephanie, *Marriage, A History. From Obedience to Intimacy or How Love Conquered Marriage* (New York 2005).
Coontz, Stephanie, *The Social Origins of Private Life. A History of American Families 1600-1900* (London 1988).
Coontz, Stephanie, *The Way We Never Were. American Families and the Nostalgia Trap* (New York 1992).
Coontz, Stephanie, *The Way We Really Are. Coming to Terms with America's Changing Families* (New York 1997).
Coontz, Stephanie, Parson, Maya, and Raley, Gabrielle (eds.), *American Families. A Multicultural Reader* (New York 1998, new, revised edition New York 2008).
Corber, Robert J., *Homosexuality in Cold War America. Resistance and the Crisis of Masculinity* (Durham 1997).
Corcoran, May, "The Economic Progress of African American Women," in Browne, Irene (ed.), *Latinas and African American Woman at Work. Race, Gender, and Economic Inequality* (New York 2000), 35-60.
Costin, Lela, *Two Sisters for Social Justice. A Biography of Grace and Edith Abbott* (Chicago 1983).
Cott, Nancy F. et al., "Considering the State of U.S. Women's History," *Journal of Women's History* 15 (2003), 145-163.
Cott, Nancy F. (ed.), *No Small Courage. A History of Women in the United States* (Oxford 2000).
Cott, Nancy F., *Public Vows. A History of Marriage and the Nation* (Cambridge and London, 2000).
Cott, Nancy F., *The Grounding of Modern Feminism* (New Haven 1987).
Crafton, William, "The Incremental Revolution. Ronald Reagan and Welfare Reform in the 1970s," *Journal of Policy History*, vol. 26, no. 1 (2014), 27-47.
Crenshaw, Kimberlé, "Demarginalizing the Intersection of Race and Sex: A Black Feminist Critique of Antidiscrimination Doctrine, Feminist Theory and Antiracist Politics," *University of Chicago Legal Forum 1989*, no. 1, 139-167.
Critchlow, Donald T., "Conservatism Reconsidered. Phillis Schlafly and Grassroot Conservatism," in Farber, David and Roche, Jeff (eds.), *The Conservative Sixties* (New York 2003), 108-126.
Critchlow, Donald T., *Intended Consequences. Birth Control, Abortion, and the Federal Government in Modern America* (Oxford and New York 1999).
Critchlow, Donald T., *Phillis Schlafly and Grassroots Conservatism. A Woman's Crusade* (Princeton and Oxford 2005).
Cross, Gary S., *Time and Money. The Making of Consumer Culture* (London 1993).
Cuordileone, Kyle, "Politics in an Age of Anxiety. Cold War Political Culture and the Crisis in American Masculinity 1949-1960," *Journal of American History* 87 (2000), no. 2, 515-545.
Curran, Laura, "Feminine Women, Hard Workers. Foster Motherhood in Midcentury America 1946-1963," *Journal of Family History*, 31 (2006), no. 4, 386-412.
Currell Susan and Cogdell, Christina (eds.), *Popular Eugenics. National Efficiency and American Mass Culture in the 1930s* (Athens 2006).
Curtis, Bruce, "Victorians Abed. William Graham Sumner on the Family, Women and Sex," *American Studies* 18 (1977), no. 1, 101-122.
D'Emilio, John, *Lost Prophet. The Life and Times of Bayard Rustin* (New York 2003).

D'Emilio, John and Freedman, Estelle, *Intimate Matters. A History of Sexuality in America* (Chicago 1997).
Dabel, Jane, *A Respectable Woman. The Public Roles of African American Women in 19th Century New York* (New York 2008).
Dale, Clare A. (ed.), *The Military and the Family* (Thousand Oaks 2002).
Dallek, Robert, *Flawed Giant. Lyndon Johnson and His Times 1961-1973* (New York and Oxford 1998).
Dallek, Robert, *John F. Kennedy. Ein unvollendetes Leben* (Munich 2003).
Dallek, Robert, *Lone Star Rising. Lyndon Johnson and His Times 1908-1960* (New York and Oxford 1991).
Dallek, Robert, *Lyndon B. Johnson. Portrait of a President* (Oxford and New York 2004).
Damon-Moore, Helen, *Magazines for the Millions. Gender and Commerce in the Ladies' Home Journal and the Saturday Evening Post 1880-1910* (New York 1994).
Daniel, Ute, *Kompendium Kulturgeschichte. Theorien, Praxis, Schlüsselwörter* (Frankfurt a. M. 2001).
Daniels, Roger, *Prisoners Without Trial. Japanese Americans in World War II* (New York 1994).
Daniels, Roger and Yang Murray, Alice, *What Did the Internment of Japanese Americans Mean?* (Boston 2000).
Dau-Schmidt, Kenneth G. and Sherman, Ryland, "The Employment and Economic Advancement of African-Americans in the 20th Century," *Articles by Maurer Faculty, Paper 1292*, 2013 <www.repository.law.indiana.edu/facpub/1292>.
Davidson, Chandler and Grofman, Bernard (ed.), *Quiet Revolution in the South. The Impact of the Voting Rights Act 1965-1990* (Princeton, NJ 1994).
Davis, Allen F., *Spearheads for Reform. The Social Settlements and the Progressive Movement 1890-1914* (New York 1967).
Davis, Angela Y., *Women, Race, and Class* (New York 1983).
Davis, Kathy, *The Making of Our Bodies, Ourselves. How Feminism Travels Across Borders* (Durham 2008).
Davis, Natalie Zemon, "'Women's History' in Transition. The European Case," *Feminist Studies* 3 (1976), no. 3-4, 83-103.
Davis, Rebecca L., *More Perfect Unions. The American Search for Marital Bliss* (Cambridge and London 2010).
Davis, Sue, *The Political Thought of Elizabeth Cady Stanton. Women's Rights and the American Political Traditions* (New York 2010).
Dawson, Doyne, "Evolutionary Theory and Group Selection. The Question of Warfare," *History and Theory* 38 (1999), no. 4, 79-100.
Dayton, Cornelia H. and Levenstein, Lisa, "The Big Tent of U.S. Women's and Gender History. A State of the Field," *Journal of American History* (2012), 793-817.
Dechert, Andre, "Family Man: The Popular Reception of 'Home Improvement,' 1991-1992, and the Debate about Fatherhood," in Heinemann, Isabel (ed.), *Inventing the Modern American Family. Family Values and Social Change in 20th Century United States* (Frankfurt a. M., 2012), 265-288.
Dechert, Andre, "'The good father in every way except . . .': Sitcoms, Vaterschaft und das Ideal der Kernfamilie in den USA, 1981-1992" (Dissertation University of Münster, completed August 2016, published in 2018 under the title *Dad on TV: Sitcoms, Vaterschaft und das Ideal der Kernfamilie in den USA, 1981-1992*, Berlin and Boston 2018).
Dechert, Andre, "Von der zeitgenössischen Fiktion zur Dokumentation historischer Realität? Gender in US-amerikanischen Family Sitcoms der 1950er und frühen 1960er Jahre," in Cheauré, Elisabeth, Paletschek, Sylvia, and Reusch, Nina (eds.), *Geschlecht und Geschichte in populären Medien* (Bielefeld 2013), 209-232.
Degele, Nina and Dries, Christian, *Modernisierungstheorie. Eine Einführung* (Munich 2005).
Degler, Carl N., *At Odds. Women and the Family in America from the Revolution to the Present* (New York 1980).

Degler, Carl N., "Charlotte Perkins Gilman on the Theory and Practice of Feminism," *American Quarterly* 8 (1956), 21–39.
Del Castillo, Adelaida R., "Sterilization. An Overview," in Del Castillo, Adelaida R. and Mora, Magdalena (eds.), *Mexican Women in the United States. Struggles Past and Present* (Los Angeles 1980), 65–70.
Demos, John, *Past, Present and Personal. The Family and the Life Course in American History* (New York 1986).
Demtriou, Demetrakis Z., "Connell's Concept of Hegemonic Masculinity. A Critique," *Theory and Society* 30 (2001), no. 3, 337–361.
Dermott, Esther, *Intimate Fatherhood. A Sociological Analysis* (New York 2008).
Deth, Jan van, "Wertewandel im internationalen Vergleich. Ein deutscher Sonderweg?" *Aus Politik und Zeitgeschichte* B 29 (2001), 23–30.
Deth, Jan van and Scarbrough, Elinor (eds.), *The Impact of Values* (Oxford and New York 1995).
Deutsch, Sarah Jane, "From Ballots to Breadlines 1920–1940," in Cott, Nancy F. (ed.), *No Small Courage. A History of Women in the United States* (Oxford 2000), 413–473.
Diamond, Sara, *Roads to Dominion. Right Wing Movements and Political Power in the United States* (New York 1994).
Dietz, Bernhard and Neumaier, Christopher, "Vom Nutzen der Sozialwissenschaften für die Zeitgeschichte. Werte und Wertewandel als Gegenstand historischer Forschung," *Vierteljahrshefte für Zeitgeschichte* 60 (2012), 293–304.
Dietz, Bernhard, Neumaier, Christopher, and Rödder, Andreas (eds.), *Gab es den Wertewandel? Neue Forschungen zum gesellschaftlich-kulturellen Wandel seit den 1960er Jahren* (Munich 2013).
Dietze, Gabriele, *Weiße Frauen in Bewegung. Genealogien und Konkurrenzen von Race- und Genderpolitiken* (Bielefeld 2013).
Dikain, Edward L., *The Myth of Family Decline. Understanding Families in a World of Rapid Social Change* (Lexington 1990).
Dikötter, Frank, "Race Culture. Recent Perspectives on the History of Eugenics," *The American Historical Review* 103 (1998), no. 2, 467–478.
Dill, Bonnie Thornton, "Race, Class, and Gender. Prospects for an All-Inclusive Sisterhood," *Feminist Studies* 9 (1983), 131–150.
Dinges, Martin, "'Hegemoniale Männlichkeit'—ein Konzept auf dem Prüfstand," in Dinges, Martin (ed.), *Männer—Macht—Körper. Hegemoniale Männlichkeiten vom Mittelalter bis Heute* (Frankfurt a. M. 2005), 7–36.
Dinges, Martin (ed.), *Männer—Macht—Körper. Hegemoniale Männlichkeiten vom Mittelalter bis Heute* (Frankfurt a. M. 2005).
Dipper, Christof, "Die deutsche Geschichtswissenschaft und die Moderne," *Internationales Archiv für die Sozialgeschichte der Literatur*, vol. 37 (2012), 37–62.
Dipper, Christof, "Moderne, Version: 1.0," *Docupedia-Zeitgeschichte*, August 25, 2010 http://docupedia.de/zg/Moderne?oldid=97426.
Dobriner, William, *The Suburban Community* (New York 1958).
Doering-Manteuffel, Anselm, "Konturen von 'Ordnung' in den Zeitschichten des 20. Jahrhunderts," in Etzemüller, Thomas (ed.), *Die Ordnungen der Moderne. Social Engineering im 20. Jahrhundert* (Bielefeld 2009), 41–64.
Doering-Manteuffel, Anselm, "Nach dem Boom. Brüche und Kontinuitäten der Industriemoderne seit 1970," *Vierteljahrshefte für Zeitgeschichte* 55 (2007), no. 4, 559–581.
Doering-Manteuffel, Anselm, *Wie westlich sind die Deutschen? Amerikanisierung und Westernisierung im 20. Jahrhundert* (Göttingen 1999).

Doering-Manteuffel, Anselm and Raphael, Lutz, *Nach dem Boom. Perspektiven auf die Zeitgeschichte seit 1970* (Göttingen 2010).
Doering-Manteuffel, Anselm, Raphael, Lutz, and Schlemmer, Thomas (eds.), *Vorgeschichte der Gegenwart. Dimensionen des Strukturbruchs nach dem Boom* (Göttingen 2016).
Donaldson, Scott, *The Suburban Myth* (New York and London 1969).
Dorr, Gregory Michael and Logan, Angela, "'Quality, not mere quantity, counts.' Black Eugenics and the NAACP Baby Contests," in Lombardo, Paul (ed.), *A Century of Eugenics in America. From the Indiana Experiment to the Human Genome Era* (Bloomington 2011), 68–92.
Dossett, Kate, *Bridging Race Divides. Black Nationalism, Feminism, and Integration in the United States, 1896–1935* (Florida 2008).
Dowbiggin, Ian Robert, *A Merciful End. The Euthanasia Movement in Modern America* (New York 2003).
Dowbiggin, Ian Robert, "'A Rational Coalition'. Euthanasia, Eugenics, and Birth Control in America, 1940–1970," *Journal of Policy History* 14 (2002), no. 3, 223–260.
Dowbiggin, Ian Robert, *The Quest for Mental Health. A Tale of Science, Medicine, Scandal, Sorrow, and Mass Society* (Cambridge 2011).
Dowland, Seth, *Family Values and the Rise of the Christian Right* (Philadelphia 2015).
Downey, Douglas B. and Powell, Brian, "Do Children in Single-Parent Households Fare Better Living with Same-Sex Parents?" *Journal of Marriage and the Family* 55 (1999), no. 1, 55–71.
Downs, Donald Alexander, *Cornell '69. Liberalism and the Crisis of the American University* (Ithaca 1999).
Doyle, Laura, "The Long Arm of Eugenics," *American Literary History* 16 (2004), no. 3, 520–535.
Drake, W. Magruder (ed.), "A Discourse on Divorce: Orleans Territorial Legislature, 1806," *The Journal of the Louisiana Historical Association* 22 (1981), no. 4, 434–437.
Drucker, Donna, *The Classification of Sex. Alfred Kinsey and the Organization of Knowledge* (Pittsburg, PA 2014).
Dubinsky, Karen, *Babies without Borders. Adoption and Migration across the Americas* (New York 2010).
Dudink, Stefan, Hagemann, Karen, and Tosh, John (eds.), *Masculinities and Politics in War. Gendering Modern History* (New York 2004).
Durkheim, Emile, *Die Regeln der soziologischen Methode* (Frankfurt 1984).
Dwyer, Jeffrey W. (ed.), *Gender, Families and Elder Care* (Newbury Park 1992).
Eagles, Charles W. (ed.), *The Civil Rights Movement in America* (Jackson 1986).
Echols, Alice, *Daring to Be Bad. Radical Feminism in America 1967–1975* (Minneapolis 1989).
Echols, Alice, "Nothing Distant about it: Woman's Liberation and Sixties Radicalism," in Farber, David (ed.), *The Sixties. From Memory to History* (Chapel Hill and London 1994), 149–174.
Edsforth, Ronald, *The New Deal. America's Response to the Great Depression* (Malden 2000).
Ehmer, Josef, *Bevölkerungsgeschichte und Historische Demographie 1800–2000* (Munich 2004).
Ehrenreich, Barbara, "Legacies of the Sixties. New Rights and New Lefts," in Tischler, Barbara L. (ed.), *Sights on the Sixties* (New Brunswick 1992), 227–234.
Ehrenreich, Barbara, *Nickled and Dimed. On Not Getting by in America* (New York 2001).
Ehrenreich, Barbara, *The Hearts of Men. American Dreams and the Flight from Commitment* (New York 1983).
Ehrenreich, Barbara and Ehrenreich, John, *Long March, Short Spring. The Student Uprising at Home and Abroad* (New York 1969).
Ehrenreich, Barbara and English, Deirdre, *For Her Own Good. Two Centuries of the Expert's Advice to Women* (New York 2005, first edition 1978).
Ehrman, John, *The Eighties. America in the Age of Reagan* (New Haven etc. 2005).
Eig, Jonathan, *The Birth of the Pill: How Four Crusaders Reinvented Sex and Launched a Revolution* (New York 2014).

Eisenstadt, Shmuel N., "Multiple Modernities," *Daedalus* 129 (2000), no. 1, 1–30.
Eliott, Diana B. et al., "Historical Marriage Trends from 1890–2010. A Focus on Race Differences." SEHSD Working Paper 2012-12 <www.census.gov/hhes/socdemo/marriage/data/acs/Elliottetal PAA2012paper.pdf>.
Ender, Hanna, "'The American Woman? Not for this GI!'—GIs, Fräuleins und der Geschlechterdiskurs in den USA," *Fastforeword* (2010), no. 1, 18–28.
Engelhardt, Tom, *The End of Victory Culture. Cold War America and the Disillusioning of a Generation* (New York 1995).
Engerman, David C., *Know Your Enemy. The Rise and Fall of America's Soviet Experts* (New York 2009).
Engerman, David C., Gilman, Nils, Haefele, Mark H., and Latham, Michael (eds.), *Staging Growth. Modernization, Development, and the Global Cold War* (Amherst 2003).
England, Paula and Farkas, George, *Households, Employment, and Gender. A Social, Economic, and Demographic View* (New York 1986).
Enke, Anne, *Finding the Movement. Sexuality, Contested Space, and Feminist Activism* (Durham 2007).
Erlich, John and Erlich, Susan (eds.), *Student Power, Participation and Revolution* (New York 1971).
Espinoza, Dionne, "'Revolutionary Sisters'. Women's Solidarity and Collective Identification among Chicana Brown Berets in East Los Angeles, 1967–1970," *Aztlan* 26 (2001), no. 1, 17–57.
Estes, Steve, "A Question of Honor. Masculinity and Massive Resistance to Integration," in Watts, Trent, *White Masculinity in the Recent South* (Kansas 2008), 99–120.
Estes, Steve, *I Am a Man! Race, Manhood, and the Civil Rights Movement* (Chapel Hill 2005).
Etges, Andreas, "The Wound that Won't Heal. Neue Forschungen zum Vietnamkrieg und seinen Folgen," *Neue Politische Literatur* 47 (2002), 93–105.
Etzemüller, Thomas, "Auf den Spuren einer gesellschaftspolitisch problematischen Formation: social engineering 1920–1960," *Potsdamer Almanach des Zentrums für Zeithistorische Forschungen* (Göttingen 2008), 39–47.
Etzemüller, Thomas (ed.), *Die Ordnungen der Moderne. Social Engineering im 20. Jahrhundert* (Bielefeld 2009).
Etzemüller, Thomas, *Die Romantik der Rationalität. Alva & Gunnar Myrdal—Social Engineering in Schweden* (Bielefeld 2010).
Etzemüller, Thomas, "Die Romantik des Reißbretts. Social engineering und demokratische Volksgemeinschaft in Schweden: Das Beispiel Alva und Gunnar Myrdal (1930–1960)," *Geschichte und Gesellschaft* 32 (2006), 445–466.
Etzemüller, Thomas, "Social Engineering als Verhaltenslehre des kühlen Kopfes. Eine einleitende Skizze," in Etzemüller, Thomas (ed.), *Die Ordnungen der Moderne. Social Engineering im 20. Jahrhundert* (Bielefeld 2009).
Etzemüller, Thomas, "Social Engineering, Version: 1.0," *Docupedia-Zeitgeschichte. Begriffe, Methoden und Debatten der zeithistorischen Forschung* <www.docupedia.de/zg/Social_engineering>.
Etzemüller, Thomas, *Vom "Volk" zur "Population." Interventionistische Bevölkerungspolitik der Nachkriegszeit* (Münster 2015).
Evans, Sara M., *Born for Liberty. A History of Women in America* (New York 1991).
Evans, Sara M., *Personal Politics. The Roots of Women's Liberation in the Civil Rights Movement and the New Left* (New York 1980).
Fairclough, Adam, "Historians and the Civil Rights Movement," *Journal of American Studies* 24 (1990), 387–398.
Faludi, Susan, *Backlash. The Undeclared War Against American Women* (New York 1991).
Farber, David, *Chicago '68* (Chicago 1988).
Farber, David, *The Age of Great Dreams. America in the 1960s* (New York 1994).

Farber, David, *The Rise and Fall of Modern American Conservatism. A Short History* (Princeton 2010).
Farber, David (ed.), *The Sixties. From Memory to History* (Chapel Hill 1994).
Farber, David and Bailey Beth, *Columbia Guide to America in the Sixties* (New York 2001).
Farber, David and Roche, Jeff, *The Conservative Sixties* (New York 2003).
Fass, Paula S. and Mason, Mary Ann (eds.), *Childhood in America* (New York 2000).
Faust-Scalisi, Mario, "Die Ford Foundation und der Population Council. Zwei Institutionen, die gemeinsam globale Bevölkerungsdiskurse prägten," in Etzemüller, Thomas, *Vom "Volk" zur "Population." Interventionistische Bevölkerungspolitik der Nachkriegszeit* (Münster 2015), 135–157.
Faver, Catherine A., *Women in Transition. Career, Family, and Life Satisfaction in Three Cohorts* (New York 1984).
Feidel, Frank, *Franklin D. Roosevelt. A Rendezvous with Destiny* (Boston 1990).
Feldhaus, Michael and Nave-Herz, Rosemarie, *Blickrichtung Familie. Vielfalt eines Forschungsgegenstandes, Festschrift für Rosemarie Nave-Herz anlässlich ihrer Emeritierung* (Würzburg 2003).
Feldstein, Ruth, *Motherhood in Black and White. Race and Sex in American Liberalism, 1930–1965* (Ithaca 2000).
Felsenthal, Carol, *The Sweetheart of the Silent Majority. The Biography of Phyllis Schlafly* (New York 1981).
Fenske, Uta, *Mannsbilder. Eine geschlechterhistorische Betrachtung von Hollywoodfilmen 1946–1960* (Bielefeld 2008).
Ferguson, Marjorie, *Forever Feminine. Women's Magazines and the Cult of Femininity* (London 1983).
Ferreira da Silva, Denise, *Unpayable Debt* (London 2022).
Ferriss, Abbott L., *Indicators of Change in the American Family* (New York 1970).
Fessler, Anne, *The Girls Who Went Away: The Hidden History of Women Who Surrendered Children for Adoption in the Decades Before Roe v. Wade* (New York 2006).
Fiebig-von-Hase, Ragnild and Heideking, Jürgen (eds.), *Zwei Wege in die Moderne. Aspekte der deutsch-amerikanischen Beziehungen 1900–1918* (Trier 1998).
Fields, Barbara J., "Ideology and Race in American History," in Kousser, J. Morgan and McPherson, James (eds.), *Region, Race, and Reconstruction. Essays in Honor of C. Vann Woodward* (New York 1982), 143–147.
Fiese, Barbara, *Family Routines and Rituals* (New Haven 2006).
Fink, Carole, Gassert, Philipp, and Junker, Detlef (eds.), *1968. The World Transformed* (Cambridge 1998).
Finlay, Barbara, *Before the Second Wave. Gender in the Sociological Tradition* (Upper Saddle River, NJ 2007).
Finzsch, Norbert, "Gouvernementalität, der Moynihan-Report und die Welfare Queen im Cadillac," in Martschukat, Jürgen (ed.), *Geschichte schreiben mit Foucault* (Frankfurt a. M. 2002), 257–282.
Fishback, Price V., Horrace, William C., and Kantor, Shawn, "Did New Deal Grant Programs Stimulate Local Economies? A Study of Federal Grants and Retail Sales During the Great Depression," *The Journal of Economic History* 65 (2005), 36–72.
Flax, Karen, "Women's Rights and the Proposed Family Protection Act," *University of Miami Law Review* 36, 1 (1981), 141–163 http://repository.law.miami.ecu/umlr/vol36/iss1/7.
Flippen, J. Brooks, *Jimmy Carter, the Politics of Family, and the Rise of the Religious Right* (Athens and London 2011).
Fogel, Robert William, *Stability and Change in the Family. Proceedings of a Symposium Held in Annapolis, MD, March 22–24, 1979* (New York 1981).
Foleno, Louis A., *A Critical Review of Selected Literature on College Student Unrest in the United States 1968–1970* (San Francisco 1992).

Folly, Martin, *The United States and World War II. The Awakening Giant* (Edinburgh 2002).
Forbes, Jack D., *Black Africans and Native Americans. Color, Race and Caste in the Evolution of Red-Black Peoples* (Oxford 1988).
Forman, James, *The Making of Black Revolutionaries* (Seattle 1990).
Foucault, Michel, *Archäologie des Wissens* (Frankfurt a. M. 1981, *Archéologie du savoir*, 1969).
Foucault, Michel, *Der Wille zum Wissen (Sexualität und Wahrheit*, vol. I), (Frankfurt 1977, *La Volonté du savoir* 1976).
Foucault, Michel, *Die Ordnung der Dinge* (Frankfurt a. M. 1971, *Les mots et les choses*, 1966).
Foucault, Michel, *Die Ordnung des Diskurses* (Frankfurt a. M. 1992, *L'ordre du discours*, 1972).
Foucault, Michel, *Dits et Écrits: Schriften*, vol. 3, (Frankfurt a. M. 2003).
Foucault, Michel, *Il faut defender la société. Cours au Collège de France 1976* (Paris 1976).
Fout, John C. and Tantillo, Maura Shaw, *American Sexual Politics. Sex, Gender and Race since the Civil War* (Chicago 1993).
Francois, Etienne et al. (eds.), *1968—ein europäisches Jahr?* (Leipzig 1997).
Francome, Colin, *Abortion in the USA and the UK* (Burlington 2004).
Frank, Nathaniel, *Awakening: How Gays and Lesbians Brought Marriage Equality to America* (Cambridge, MA 2017).
Frank, Thomas, *What's the Matter with Kansas. How Conservatives Won the Heart of America* (New York 2004).
Frankel, Noralee and Dye, Nancy S. (eds.), *Gender, Class, Race and Reform in the Progressive Era* (Lexington 1991).
Franklin, Donna L., *Ensuring Inequality. The Structural Transformation of the African-American Family* (New York 1997).
Franks, Angela, *Margaret Sanger's Eugenic Legacy. The Control of Female Fertility* (Jefferson 2005).
Fraser, Ronald, *1968—A Student Generation in Revolt. An International Oral History* (London 1988).
Freedman, Laurence, *Kennedy's Wars. Berlin, Cuba, Laos, and Vietnam* (New York 2000).
Freeman, Richard B., "Changes in the Labor Market for Black Americans, 1948–72," *Brooking Papers on Economic Activity* 1 (1973), 67–132.
Freeman, Susan, *Sex Goes to School: Girls and Sex Education Before the 1960s* (Illinois 2008).
Frey, Marc, "Der Vietnamkrieg im Spiegel der amerikanischen Forschung," *Neue Politische Literatur* 42 (1997), no. 1, 29–47.
Frey, Marc, *Die Geschichte des Vietnamkrieges* (Munich 2000).
Friedman, Andrea, *Prurient Interests. Gender, Democracy, and Obscenity in New York City, 1909–1945* (New York, 2000).
Friedman, Andrea, "Sadists and Sissies. Anti-Pornography Campaigns in Cold War America," *Gender & History* 15 (2003), no. 2, 210–227.
Frölich, Margrit, Middel, Reinhard, and Visarius, Karsten (eds.), *Family Affairs. Ansichten der Familie im Film* (Marburg 2004).
Fuller, Linda K., *The Cosby Show. Audiences, Impact, and Implications* (Westport, CN 1992).
Furstenberg, Frank F. and Chelin, Andrew J., *Geteilte Familien* (Stuttgart 1993).
Gaines, Kevin K., *Uplifting the Race. Black Leadership, Politics, and Culture in the Twentieth Century* (Chapel Hill 1996).
García, Alma M. (ed.), *Chicana Feminist Thought: The Basic Historical Writings* (New York 1997).
Garrison, Dee, "Our Skirts Gave Them Courage. The Civil Defense Protest Movement in New York City, 1955–1961," in Meyerowitz, Joanne (ed.), *Not June Cleaver. Women and Gender in Postwar America. 1945–1960* (Philadelphia 1994), 201–227.

Garrow, David J., *Protest at Selma. Martin Luther King, Jr., and the Voting Rights Act of 1965* (New Haven, CT and London 1978).
Gates, Henry Louis (ed.), *"Race." Writing, and Difference* (Chicago 1986).
Gauthier, Anne Helene, "Towards Renewed Fears of Population and Family Decline," *European Journal of Population* 9 (1993), no. 2, 143–167.
Geasy, David: "'Becoming International Again'. C. Wright Mills and the Emergence of a Global New Left, 1956–62," *Journal of American History* 95 (2008), no. 3, 710–736.
Gebhardt, Miriam, *Die Angst vor dem kindlichen Tyrannen. Eine Geschichte der Erziehung im 20. Jahrhundert* (Munich 2009).
Gembries, Ann-Katrin, Theuke, Theresie, and Heinemann, Isabel (eds.), *Children by Choice? Changing Values, Reproduction, and Family Planning in the 20th Century* (Berlin and Boston 2018).
Gerhardt, Uta, "Die deutsche Familie und die Gewalt. Konkurrenz der Erklärungsmodelle?" in Gerhardt, Uta (ed.), *Wirklichkeit(en)—Soziologie und Geschichte* (Baden-Baden 2014), 23–40.
Gerhardt, Uta, *Talcott Parsons—An Intellectual Biography* (New York 2002).
Gerhardt, Uta, *The Social Thought of Talcott Parsons. Methodology and American Ethos* (Farnham, Surrey 2011).
Gerson, Deborah A., "Is Family Devotion Now Subversive? Familialism against McCarthyism," in Meyerowitz, Joanne (ed.), *Not June Cleaver. Women and Gender in Postwar America, 1945–1960* (Philadelphia 1994), 151–176.
Gerson, Kathleen, *No Man's Land. Men's Changing Commitments to Family and Work* (New York 1993).
Gerstle, Gary, *American Crucible. Race and Nation in the Twentieth Century* (Princeton 2001).
Gestrich, Andreas, "Geschichte der Familie im 19. und 20. Jahrhundert," in Gall, Lothar (ed.), *Enzyklopädie deutscher Geschichte*, vol. 50 (Munich 1999).
Gestrich, Andreas, Krause, Jens-Uwe, and Mitterauer, Michael, *Geschichte der Familie* (Stuttgart 2003).
Gettleman, Marvin E. and Mermelstein, David (eds.), *The Great Society Reader. The Failure of American Liberalism* (New York 1967).
Gilbert, Dennis and Kahl, Joseph A., *The American Class Structure. A New Synthesis* (Homewood 1982).
Gilbert, James, *A Cycle of Outrage: America's Reaction to the Juvenile Delinquent in the 1950s* (New York and Oxford 1986).
Gilbert, James Burkhart, *Men in the Middle. Searching for Masculinity in the 1950s* (Chicago and London 2005).
Gilbert, Marc Jason and Head, William, *The Tet Offensive* (Westport 1996).
Gilcher-Holtey, Ingrid (ed.), "1968. Vom Ereignis zum Gegenstand der Geschichtswissenschaft," *Geschichte und Gesellschaft: Sonderheft* 17 (Göttingen 1998).
Gilcher-Holtey, Ingrid, *Die 68er Bewegung. Deutschland, Westeuropa, USA* (Munich 2001).
Gilcher-Holtey, Ingrid, "Plädoyer für eine dynamische Mentalitätsgeschichte," *Geschichte und Gesellschaft* 24 (1998), no. 3, 476–497.
Gilens, Martin, *Why Americans Hate Welfare. Race, Media, and the Politics of Antipoverty Policy* (Chicago and London 1999).
Gillis, John R., *A World of Their Own Making. A History of Myth and Ritual in Family Life* (Oxford and New York 1997).
Gilman, Sander L., "Black Bodies—White Bodies. Toward an Iconography of Female Sexuality in Late Nineteen Century Art, Medicine and Literature," in Henry Louis Gates (ed.), *"Race," Writing, and Difference* (Chicago 1986), 223–240.
Gilmore, Stephanie (ed.), *Feminist Coalitions. Historical Perspectives on Second-Wave Feminism in the United States* (Urbana 2008).
Gitlin, Todd, *Sixties. Years of Hope, Days of Rage* (New York 1993).

Gitlin, Todd, *The Whole World is Watching. Mass Media in the Making and Unmaking of the New Left* (Berkeley 1980).
Glasrud, Bruce and Pitre, Merline (eds.), *Black Women in Texas History* (Texas 2008).
Glazer, Deborah and Drescher, Jack, *Gay and Lesbian Parenting* (New York 2001).
Glenn, Evelyn Nakano, *Forced to Care. Coercion and Caregiving in America* (Cambridge 2010).
Glick, Paul C., "Fifty Years of Family Demography. A Record of Social Change," *Journal of Marriage and the Family* 50 (1988), no. 4, 861–873.
Gluck, Sherna, *Rosie the Riveter Revisited. Women, the War, and Social Change* (Boston 1987).
Goff, Philip, *The Blackwell Companion to Religion in America* (Malden 2010).
Goldin, Claudia, *Understanding the Gender Gap. An Economic History of American Women* (New York 1990).
Goldman, Eric, *The Crucial Decade. America 1945–1955* (New York 1965).
Goldscheider, Frances K. and Waite, Linda J., *New Families, No Families? The Transformation of the American Home* (Berkeley 1991).
Goldstein, Carolyn M, *Creating Consumers. Home Economists in Twentieth-Century America* (Chapel Hill 2012).
Goldthorpe, John E., *Family Life in Western Societies. A Historical Sociology of Family Relationships in Britain and North America* (Cambridge 1987).
Goodwin, Doris K., *No Ordinary Time—Franklin and Eleanor Roosevelt. The Home Front in World War II* (New York 1994).
Goodwin, Doris Kearns, *Lyndon Johnson and the American Dream* (London 1979).
Goody, Jack, *Geschichte der Familie* (Munich 2002).
Gordon, Linda, *Heroes of Their Own Lives. The Politics and History of Family Violence* (Boston 1880–1960, Urbana 2002).
Gordon, Linda, *Pitied but Not Entitled. Single Mothers and the History of Welfare, 1890–1935* (New York 1994).
Gordon, Linda, *The Great Arizona Orphan Abduction* (Princeton 2001).
Gordon, Linda, *The Moral Property of Women. A History of Birth Control Politics in America* (Urbana and Chicago 2002).
Gordon, Linda, "Why 19th Century Feminists Did Not Support 'Birth Control' and 20th Century Feminists Do. Feminism, Reproduction and the Family," in Thorne, Barrie and Yaloom, Marilyn (eds.), *Rethinking the Family* (New York 1982), 140–154.
Gordon, Linda, *Women's Body, Women's Right. A Social History of Birth Control in America* (New York 1976).
Gordon, Linda and Amott, Teresa L. (eds.), *Women, the State, and Welfare* (Madison 1990).
Gordon, Lynn D., *Gender and Higher Education in the Progressive Era* (New Haven 1990).
Gordon, Michael, *Das Wesen der Ehe. Die wechselnde Auffassung vom Wesen der Ehe im Wandel der Verfassungsepochen des 20. Jahrhunderts* (Berlin 1978).
Gordon, Michael (ed.), *The American Family in Social-Historical Perspective* (New York 1978).
Gordon, William A., *Four Dead in Ohio. Was There a Conspiracy at Kent State?* (Laguna Hills 1995).
Gorney, Cynthia, *Articles of Faith. A Frontline History of the Abortion Wars* (New York 1998).
Görtemarker, Manfred, *Geschichte der Bundesrepublik Deutschland. Von der Gründung bis zu Gegenwart* (Munich 1999).
Gosse, Van and Moser, Richard, *The World the Sixties Made. Culture and Politics in Recent America* (Philadelphia 2003).
Gould, Lewis L., *America in the Progressive Era, 1890–1914* (New York 2001).

Graf, Rüdiger and Priemel, Kim, "Zeitgeschichte in der Welt der Sozialwissenschaften. Legitimität und Originalität einer Disziplin," *Vierteljahrshefte für Zeitgeschichte* 59 (2011), no. 4, 479–495, esp. 486–488.

Graff, Agnieska and Korolczuk, Elżbieta, *Anti-Gender Politics in the Populist Moment* (London 2021). DOI: 10.4324/9781003133520.

Graham, Hugh Davis, *The Civil Rights Era. Origins and Development of National Policy 1960–1972* (New York 1990).

Graham, Margaret Baker, *Victorian America. A Family Record from the Heartland* (Kirksville 2003).

Grant, Julia, *Raising Baby by the Book. The Education of American Mothers* (New Haven and London 1998).

Gratton, Brian, Gutmann, Myron P., and Skop, Emily, "Immigrants, Their Children, and Theories of Assimilation. Family Structure in the United States 1880–1970," *The History of the Family* 12 (2007), no. 3, 203–222.

Gray, Herman, "Television and the New Black Man. Black Male Images in Prime-Time Situation Comedy," *Media, Culture & Society* 8 (1986), no. 2, 223–242.

Gray, Herman, *Watching Race. Television and the Struggle for "Blackness"* (Minneapolis 1995).

Green, Adam, *Selling the Race. Culture, Community, and Black Chicago, 1940–1955* (Chicago 2007).

Greiner, Bernd, "'You'll Never Walk Alone'. Amerikanische Reaktionen auf Kriegsverbrechen in Vietnam," *Mittelweg 36* (2000), no. 5, 49–71.

Griffith, Elisabeth, "Elizabeth Cady Stanton on Marriage and Divorce. Feminist Theory and Domestic Experience," in Kelley, Mary (ed.), *Woman's Being, Woman's Place* (Boston 1979), 233–251.

Griffith, Robert and Baker, Paula (eds.), *Major Problems in American History since 1945* (Boston and New York 2007).

Griswold del Castillo, Richard, *La Familia. Chicano Families in the Urban South West* (Notre Dame 1984).

Griswold, Robert L., *Family and Divorce in California 1850–1890. Victorian Illusions and Everyday Realities* (Albany 1982).

Griswold, Robert L., *Fatherhood in America. A History* (New York 1993).

Griswold, Robert L., "Law, Sex, Cruelty, and Divorce in Victorian America 1840–1900," *American Quarterly* 38 (1986), no. 5, 771–745.

Griswold, Robert L., *The History of Fatherhood* (Thousand Oaks 1999).

Grossberg, David, *Governing the Hearth. Law and Family in Nineteenth-Century America* (Chapel Hill 1988).

Grossman, Joanna L. and Friedman, Lawrence M., *Inside the Castle. Law and Family in 20th Century America* (Princeton, NJ 2011).

Grove, Robert D. and Hetzel, Alice, *Vital Statistics Rates in the United States 1940–1960. National Center for Health Statistics* (Washington D. C. 1968).

Grube, Norbert, "Das Institut für Demoskopie Allensbach und die 'Deutschen Lehrerbriefe' als Instrumente staatsbürgerlicher Erziehung? Ansprüche und Umsetzungen 1947 bis 1969," *Jahrbuch für historische Bildungsforschung* 13 (2007), 267–288.

Gruhzit-Hoyt, Olga, *A Time Remembered. American Women and the Vietnam War* (Novato 1999).

Gullett, Gayle, "Women Progressives and the Politics of Americanization in California 1915–1920," *The Pacific Historical Review* 64 (1995), no. 1, 71–94.

Gumbrecht, Hans Ulrich, "Modern, Modernität, Moderne," *Geschichtliche Grundbegriffe*, vol. IV, Stuttgart 1978, 93–131, esp. 126–127.

Gurr, Barbara, *Reproductive Justice. The Politics of Health Care for Native American Women* (New Brunswick 2014).

Gutiérrez, Elena R., *Fertile Matters. The Politics of Mexican-Origin Women's Reproduction* (Austin 2008).

Gutman, Herbert G., *The Black Family in Slavery and Freedom 1750–1925* (New York 1976).
Hagemann, Karen and Michel, Sonya, *Gender and the Long Postwar: The United States and the Two Germanys, 1945–1989* (Baltimore 2014).
Hajo, Cathy Moran, *Birth Control on Main Street. Organizing Clinics in the United States 1916–1939* (Urbana 2010).
Hale, Grace E., *A Nation of Outsiders. How the White Middle Class Fell in Love with Rebellion in Postwar America* (Oxford and New York 2011).
Hall, Catherine, *White, Male and Middle-Class. Explorations in Feminism and History* (Cambridge 1992, first edition 1988).
Hall, Marny, "Lesbian Families. Cultural and Clinical Issues," *Social Work* 23 (1978), no. 4, 380–385.
Halloway, John and Keppel, Ben (eds.), *Black Scholars on the Line. Race, Social Science, and American Thought in the Twentieth Century* (Notre Dame 2007).
Hancock, Ange-Marie, *The Politics of Disgust: The Public Identity of the Welfare Queen* (New York and London 2004).
Haney, David Paul, *The Americanization of Social Science. Intellectuals and Public Responsibility in the Postwar United States* (Philadelphia 2008).
Hanhardt, Christina B., "Queer History," https://www.oah.org/tah/issues/2019/may/queer-history/.
Hanhardt, Christina B., *Safe Space: Gay Neighborhood History and the Politics of Violence* (Durham 2013).
Hanscombe, Gillian E. and Forster, Jackie, *Rocking the Cradle. Lesbian Mothers—A Challenge in Family Living* (Boston 1982).
Haralovich, Mary Beth, "Sit-coms and Suburbs. Positioning the 1950s Homemaker," in Cameron, Ardis (ed.), *Looking for America. The Visual Production of Nation and People* (London and Boston 2004), 238–263.
Haralovich, Mary Beth and Rabinovitz, Lauren, *Television, History, and American Culture. Feminist Critical Essays* (Durham 1999).
Hardacre, Helen, "The Impact of Fundamentalisms on Women, the Family and Interpersonal Relations," in Marty, Martin E. and Appleby, R. Scott (eds.), *Fundamentalisms and Society. Reclaiming the Sciences, the Family, and Education, The Fundamentalism Project*, vol. 2, The American Academy of Arts and Sciences (Chicago and London 1993), 129–150.
Hardy-Fanta, Carol, "Intersectionality and Politics. Recent Research on Gender, Race, and Political Representation in the United States," *Journal of Women, Politics & Policy* 28 (2006), no. 3–4, 7–41.
Hareven, Tamara K., "The History of the Family and the Complexity of Social Change," *American Historical Review* 96 (1991), no. 1, 95–124.
Harris, John (ed.), *The Family. A Social History of the Twentieth Century* (New York and Oxford 1991).
Harris, M. J., Mitchell, Franklin D., and Schechter, Steven J. (eds.), *The Home Front. America during World War II* (New York 1984).
Hartman, Andrew, *A War for the Soul of America: A History of the Culture Wars* (Chicago and London 2015).
Hartman, Susan M., "Women's Employment and the Domestic Ideal in the Early Cold War Years," in Meyerowitz, Joanne (ed.), *Not June Cleaver. Women and Gender in Postwar America, 1945–1960* (Philadelphia 1994), 84–100.
Hartmann, Betsy, *Reproductive Rights and Wrongs: The Global Politics of Population Control*, third edition (Chicago 2016, first edition 1987).
Hartmann, Heinrich A., "In einem gewissen Sinne politisch belastet. Bevölkerungswissenschaft und Bevölkerungspolitik zwischen Entwicklungshilfe und bundesrepublikanischer Sozialpolitik (1960er und 1970er Jahre)," HZ, vol. 303 (2016), 98–125.

Hartog, Hendrik, *Man and Wife in America. A History* (Boston 2000).
Harwood, Sarah, *Family Fictions. Representations of the Family in 1980s Hollywood Cinema* (Basingstoke 1997).
Hasian, Marouf Arif Jr., *The Rhetoric of Eugenics in Anglo-American Thought* (Athens 1996).
Haskell, Thomas (ed.), *The Authority of Experts. Studies in History and Theory* (Bloomington 1984).
Hausen, Karin, "Family and Role-Division. The Polarization of Sexual Stereotypes in the Nineteenth Century. An Aspect of Dissociation of Work and Family Life," in Richard J. Evans and W. R. Lee (eds.), *Social History of the Family in Nineteenth and Twentieth Centuries Germany* (London 1981, first German edition 1976), 51–83.
Hausen, Karin, "Öffentlichkeit und Privatheit. Gesellschaftspolitische Konstruktionen und die Geschichte der Geschlechterbeziehungen," in Hausen, Karin and Wunder, Heide (eds.), *Frauengeschichte—Geschlechtergeschichte* (Frankfurt a. M., 1992), 81–88.
Hausen, Karin and Wunder, Heide (eds.), *Frauengeschichte—Geschlechtergeschichte* (Frankfurt a. M. 1992), 81–88.
Hausen, Karin and Wunder, Heide (eds.), *Frauengeschichte—Geschlechtergeschichte* (Frankfurt a. M. 1992).
Havens, Timothy, "'The Biggest Show in the World'. Race and the Global Popularity of The Cosby Show," *Media, Culture & Society* 22 (2000), no. 4, 371–391.
Hawes, Joseph M. (ed.), *The Family in America. An Encyclopedia*, 2 vols. (Santa Barbara 2002).
Hawes, Joseph M. and Nybakken, Elizabeth I. (eds.), *American Families. A Research Guide and Historical Handbook* (New York 1991).
Hawes, Joseph M. and Nybakken, Elizabeth I. (eds.), *Family and Society in American History* (Chicago 2001).
Hayward, Steven F., *The Age of Reagan: The Conservative Counterrevolution 1980-1988* (New York 2009).
Heale, Michael J., *American Anticommunism. Combating the Enemy within 1830–1970* (Baltimore 1990).
Heale, Michael J., *McCarthy's Americans. Red Scare Politics in State and Nation 1935–1965* (Basingstoke 1998).
Heale, Michael J., *The Sixties in America. History, Politics and Protest* (Edinburgh 2001).
Hegarty, Marilyn E., *Victory Girls, Khaki-Wackies, and Patriotutes. The Regulation of Female Sexuality During World War II* (New York 2008).
Hegarty, Peter, *Gentlemen's Disagreement: Alfred Kinsey, Lewis Terman, and the Sexual Politics of Smart Men* (Chicago 2013).
Heideking, Jürgen (ed.), *The Sixties Revisited. Culture—Society—Politics* (Heidelberg 2001).
Heinemann, Isabel, "American Family Values and Social Change. Gab es den Wertewandel in den USA?" in Dietz, Bernhard, Neumaier, Christopher, and Rödder, Andreas (eds.), *Gab es den Wertewandel? Neue Forschungen zum gesellschaftlich-kulturellen Wandel seit den 1960er Jahren* Munich 2013, 269–284.
Heinemann, Isabel, "'Concepts of Motherhood'. Öffentliche Debatten, Expertendiskurse und die Veränderung von Familienwerten in den USA 1890-1970," *Zeithistorische Forschungen/Studies in Contemporary History* 8 (2011), no. 1, 60–87.
Heinemann, Isabel, "Familie in den USA. Zwischen Hegemonie der Kernfamilie und Wandel der Familienwerte," in Hill, Paul B. and Kopp, Johannes (eds.), *Handbuch der Familiensoziologie* (Wiesbaden 2014), 91–123.
Heinemann, Isabel, "From 'Children by Choice' to 'Families by Choice'? 20th Century Reproductive Decision-Making between Social Change and Normative Transitions in Comparative Perspective," in Gembries, Ann-Katrin, Heinemann, Isabel, and Theuke, Theresia (eds.), *Children*

by Choice? Changing Values, Reproduction, and Family Planning in the 20th Century* (Berlin and Boston 2018), 215–236.

Heinemann, Isabel, "Introduction. Inventing the Modern American Family—Family Values and Social Change in 20th Century United States," in Heinemann, Isabel (ed.), *Inventing the Modern American Family. Family Values and Social Change in 20th Century USA* (Frankfurt a. M. 2012), 7–29.

Heinemann, Isabel (ed.), *Inventing the Modern American Family. Family Values and Social Change in 20th Century USA* (Frankfurt a. M. 2012).

Heinemann, Isabel, "'Modernizing Mom'? Der Einfluss von Expertendiskursen und Werbung auf die Familienwerte in den USA des 20. Jahrhunderts," in Baader, Meike Sophie, Götte, Petra, and Groppe, Carola (eds.), *Familientraditionen und Familienkulturen. Theoretische Konzeptionen, historische und aktuelle Analysen* (Wiesbaden 2013), 235–255.

Heinemann, Isabel, "Preserving Family and Nation. Eugenic Masculinity Concepts, Expert Intervention, and the Hegemonic American Family in the United States, 1900–1960," in Dominquez, Pablo and Wendt, Simon (eds.), *Masculinities and the Nation in the Modern World, 1800–1945* (New York 2015), 71–92.

Heinemann, Isabel, "Social Experts and Modern Women's Reproduction. From 'Working Women's Neurosis' to the Abortion Debate 1950–1980," in Heinemann, Isabel (ed.), *Inventing the Modern American Family. Family Values and Social Change in 20th Century USA* (Frankfurt a. M. 2012), 124–151.

Heinemann, Isabel, "Vom 'Good War' zum 'American Century.' Die US-Gesellschaft und der Zweite Weltkrieg," in Martin, Bernd (ed.), *Der Zweite Weltkrieg und seine Folgen. Ereignisse—Auswirkungen —Reflexionen* (Freiburg 2006), 173–194.

Heinemann, Isabel, "Wertewandel, Version: 1.0," *Docupedia-Zeitgeschichte*, October 22, 2012 <www.docupedia.de/zg/Wertewandel?oldid=84709>.

Heinemann, Isabel and Stern, Alexandra Minna, "Gender and Far Right Nationalism: Historical and International Dimensions, in *Special Issue: Gender and Far Right Nationalism, Journal of Modern European History* (JMEH), Issue 3, 20 (2022), 311–321. DOI: 10.1177and16118944221110721.

Heinrich-Böll-Stiftung (ed.), *Prag—Berlin—Paris—1968. Internationale Konferenz am 21. And 22. Mai 1993 in Prag* (Prague 1993).

Helsing, Jeffrey W., *Johnson's War/Johnson's Great Society. The Guns and Butter Trap* (Westport and London 2000).

Hequembourg, Amy and Farrell, Michael P, "Lesbian Motherhood. Negotiating Marginal-Mainstream Identities," *Gender and Society* 13 (1999), no. 4, 540–557.

Herbert, Ulrich, "Europe in High Modernity. Reflections on a Theory of the 20th Century," *Journal of Modern European History* (2007), no. 5, 5–21.

Herbert, Ulrich, "Liberalisierung als Lernprozeß. Die Bundesrepublik in der deutschen Geschichte— eine Skizze," in Herbert, Ulrich (ed.), *Wandlungsprozesse in Westdeutschland. Belastung, Integration, Liberalisierung 1945–1980* (Göttingen 2002), 7–49.

Herbert, Ulrich (ed.), *Wandlungsprozesse in Westdeutschland. Belastung, Integration, Liberalisierung 1945–1980* (Göttingen 2002), 7–49.

Herbst, Jürgen, "Francis Greenwood Peabody. Harvard's Theologian of the Social Gospel," *The Harvard Theological Review* 54 (1961), no. 1, 45–69.

Herman, Ellen, *Kinship by Design. A History of Adoption in the Modern United States* (Chicago 2008).

Herman, Ellen, *The Romance of American Psychology. Political Culture in the Age of Experts* (Berkeley 1995).

Hernandez, Donald J., *America's Children—Resources from Family, Government and the Economy. For the National Committee for Research on the 1980 Census* (New York 1993).

Herring, George C., "Tet and the Crisis of Hegemony," in Fink, Carole, Gassert, Philipp, and Junker, Detlef (eds.), *1968. The World Transformed* (Cambridge 1998), 31–53.
Herskovits, Melville J., *The Myth of the Negro Past* (Boston 1972).
Hertz, Rosanna and Marshall, Namy L. (eds.), *Working Families. The Transformation of the American Home* (Berkeley 2001).
Hesse-Biber, Sharlene and Carter, Gregg Lee, *Working Women in America. Split Dreams* (New York 2000).
Hettlage, Robert and Lenz, Karl, *Erving Goffman. Ein soziologischer Klassiker in der zweiten Generation* (Stuttgart and Bern 1991).
Hewitt, Nancy A. (ed.), *A Companion to American Women's History* (Malden 2005).
Hewitt, Nancy A., *No Permanent Waves. Recasting the Histories of U.S. Feminism* (New Brunswick 2010).
Higginbotham, Evelyn Brooks, "African-American Women's History and the Metalanguage of Race," *Signs* 17 (1992), no. 2, 251–274.
Hill Collins, Patricia, "A Comparison of Two Works on Black Family Life," *Signs*, vol. 14, no. 4, *Common Grounds and Crossroads. Race, Ethnicity, and Class in Women's Lives* (Summer 1989), 875–884.
Hill Collins, Patricia, *Black Feminist Thought. Knowledge, Consciousness, and the Politics of Empowering* (New York 2000).
Hill Collins, Patricia, *From Black Power to Hip Hop. Racism, Nationalism, and Feminism* (Philadelphia 2006).
Hill Collins, Patricia, "Shifting the Center. Race, Class, and Feminist Theorizing about Motherhood," in Coontz, Stephanie, Parson, Maya, and Raley, Gabrielle (eds.), *American Families. A Multicultural Reader* (New York 2008), 173–187.
Hill Collins, Patricia, "The Difference That Power Makes: Intersectionality and Participatory Democracy," in Olena Hankivsky and Julia S. Jordan-Zachery (eds.), *The Palgrave Handbook of Intersectionality in Public Policy* (London 2019, first edition 2017), 167–192.
Hill, Daniel Delis, *Advertising to the American Woman 1900–1999* (Columbus 2002).
Hill, Mary A., *Charlotte Perkins Gilman. The Making of a Radical Feminist 1860–1896* (Philadelphia 1980).
Hill, Shirley, *Black Intimacies. A Gender Perspective on Families and Relationships* (Lanham 2005).
Himmelstein, Jerome L., *To the Right. The Transformation of American Conservatism* (Berkeley 1990).
Hinton, Elizabeth, *America on Fire. The Untold History of Police Violence and Black Rebellion since the 1960s* (New York, NY 2021).
Hixon, William B., *The Search for the American Right Wing. An Analysis of the Social Science Record 1955–1987* (Princeton 1992).
Hixson, Walter L., *Parting the Curtain. Propaganda, Culture, and the Cold War, 1945–1961* (Basingstoke 1997).
Hochgeschwender, Michael, "The Noblest Philosophy and Its Efficient Use. Zur Geschichte des Social Engineering in den USA, 1910–1965," in Etzemüller, Thomas (ed.), *Die Ordnung der Moderne. Social Engineering im 20. Jahrhundert* (Bielefeld 2009), 171–197.
Hochschild, Arlie Russell, *The Time Bind. When Work Becomes Home and Home Becomes Work* (New York 1997).
Hodenberg, Christina von, "'Ekel Alfred und die Kulturrevolution: Unterhaltungsfernsehen als Sprachrohr der 68er-Bewegung?'" GWU 62 (2011), 557–572.
Hodenberg, Christina von, "Fernsehrezeption, Frauenrolle und Wertewandel in den 1970er Jahren: Das Beispiel 'All in the Family,'" in Dietz, Bernhard, Neumaier, Christopher, and Rödder, Andreas (eds.), *Gab es den Wertewandel? Neue Forschungen zum gesellschaftlich-kulturellen Wandel seit den 1960er Jahren* Munich 2013, 285–306.

Hodenberg, Christina von, *Television's Moment. Sitcom Audiences and the Sixties Cultural Revolution* (Oxford and New York 2015).
Hodenberg, Christina von, "Television Viewers and Feminism in 1970s North America: How All in the Family Drove Value Change,'" in Vasudevan, Ravi (ed.), *Media and the Constitution of the Political. South Asia and Beyond* (New Delhi 2022), 195–217.
Hodgson, Godfrey, *America in Our Time* (New York 1978).
Hodgson, Godfrey, *Martin Luther King* (London 2009).
Hodgson, Godfrey, *The Gentleman From New York. Daniel Patrick Moynihan. A Biography* (Boston 2000).
Hodgson, Godfrey, *The World Turned Right Side Up. A History of the Conservative Ascendancy in America* (Boston 1996).
Hoerder, Dirk, "'A Genuine Respect for the People': The Columbia University Scholars' Transcultural Approach to Migrants," *Journal of Migration History* 1 (2015), no. 2, 136–170.
Hoerder, Dirk, "Migration History as a Transcultural History of Societies: New Perspectives on the Field's United States Origin." *Journal of Migration History* 1 (2015), no. 2. 121–135.
Hoeveler, J. David Jr., *Watch on the Right. Conservative Intellectuals in the Reagan Era* (Madson 1991).
Hoffman, Jana, *Sexing Religion: Sexualität, Familie und Geschlecht im amerikanischen Mainline-Protestantismus* (Berlin and Boston 2021).
Hoffman, Katherine, *Concepts of Identity. Historical and Contemporary Images and Portraits of Self and Family* (New York 1996).
Hofstadter, Richard, *The American Political Tradition and the Men Who Made It* (London 1962).
Hoganson, Kristin L., *Consumers' Imperium. The Global Production of American Domesticity, 1865–1920* (Chapel Hill 2007).
Hoganson, Kristin L., *Fighting for American Manhood. How Gender Politics Provoked the Spanish-American and Philippine-American Wars* (New Haven 1998).
Holtfrerich, Carl-Ludwig (ed.), *Wirtschaft USA. Strukturen, Institutionen und Prozesse* (Munich 1991).
Honegger, Claudia and Arni, Caroline (eds.), *Gender. Die Tücken einer Kategorie* (Zürich 2001).
Honey, Maureen, *Creating Rosie the Riveter. Class, Gender, and Propaganda During World War II* (Amherst 1984).
Honey, Michael K., *Going Down Jericho Road. The Memphis Strike. Martin Luther King's Last Campaign* (New York 2007).
Hoover, Stewart M., Schofield Clark, Lynn, and Alters, Diane et al. (eds.), *Media, Home, and Family* (New York 2004).
Horne, Gerald, *Fire This Time. The Watts Uprising and the 1960s* (Charlottesville 1995).
Hornung, Esther, *Bibelpolitik. Das Verhältnis des protestantischen Fundamentalismus zur nationalen Innenpolitik in den USA von 1980 bis 1996. Ein Fallbeispiel* (Frankfurt a. M. 2002).
Horowitz, Daniel, *Betty Friedan and the Making of the Feminine Mystique. The American Left, the Cold War, and Modern Feminism* (Amherst 1998).
Horowitz, Daniel, "Rethinking Betty Friedan and the Feminine Mystique. Labor Union Radicalism and Feminism in Cold War America," *American Quarterly* 48 (1996), no. 1, 1–42.
Howard, Angela, Tarrant, Adams, and Ranae, Sasha, *Redefining the New Woman, 1920–1963* (New York 1997).
Howard, Vicki, *Brides, Inc. American Weddings and the Business of Tradition* (Philadelphia 2006).
Hradil, Stefan, "Vom Wandel des Wertewandels. Die Individualisierung und eine ihrer Gegenbewegungen," in Glatzer, Wolfgang et al. (eds.), *Sozialer Wandel und gesellschaftliche Dauerbeobachtung* (Opladen 2002), 31–47.
Hull, N. E. H. and Hoffer, Peter Charles, *Roe v. Wade. The Abortion Rights Controversy in American History* (Lawrence 2001).

Hüning, Louisa, *Die Diskussion um Mutterschaft in den 1950er Jahren in den USA am Beispiel von "Chicago Tribune" und "Washington Post"* (bachelor thesis, Münster 2010).
Hunt, Alan, *Governing Morals. A Social History of Moral Regulation* (Cambridge 1999).
Hunter, James Davison, *Culture Wars. The Struggle to Define America. Making Sense of the Battles over the Family, Art, Education, Law and Politics* (New York 1991).
Hunter, James Davison, *Evangelicalism. The Coming Generation* (Chicago and London 1987).
Hurm, Gerd and Fallon, Ann Marie (eds.), *Rebels without a Cause? Renegotiating the American 1950s* (Bern 2007).
Hylton, Kevin, *"Race" and Sport. Critical Race Theory* (London 2009).
Igo, Sarah, *The Averaged American. Surveys, Citizens, and the Making of a Mass Public* (Cambridge 2007).
Igra, Anna, *Wives without Husbands. Marriage, Desertion, and Welfare in New York, 1900–1935* (Chapel Hill 2007).
Inniss, Leslie B. and Feagin, Joe R., "The Cosby Show. The View from the Black Middle Class," *Journal of Black Studies* 25 (1995), 692–711.
Irving, Katrina, *Immigrant Mothers. Narratives of Race and Maternity, 1890–1925* (Champaign 2000).
Isenstadt, Sandy, *The Modern American House. Spaciousness and Middle-Class Identity* (*Modern American Architecture and Cultural Identity*) (New York 2006).
Jackson, Kenneth, *Crabgrass Frontier. The Suburbanization of the United States* (New York and Oxford 1985).
Jackson, Walter A., *Gunnar Myrdal and America's Conscience. Social Engineering and Racial Liberalism, 1938–1987* (Chapel Hill 1990).
Jacob, Herbert, *Silent Revolution. The Transformation of Divorce Law in the United States* (Chicago 1988).
Jaeger, Friedrich, *Amerikanischer Liberalismus und zivile Gesellschaft. Perspektiven sozialer Reform zu Beginn des 20. Jahrhunderts* (Göttingen 2001).
Jäger, Jens, "Bilder als historische Quellen? Ein Problemaufriss," in Jäger, Jens and Knauer, Martin (eds.), *Bilder als Historische Quellen? Dimension der Debatten um historische Bildforschung* (Munich 2009), 7–23.
Jahning, Anica, "Antifeminismus in der Southern Baptist Convention," *Fastforeword* 3 (2010), no. 1, 29–36.
Jamison, Andrew and Eyermann, Ron, *Seeds of the Sixties* (Berkeley, Los Angeles, and London 1994).
Jefferis, Jennifer L., *Armed for Life. The Army of God and Anti-Abortion Terror in the United States* (Santa Barbara 2011).
Jenkins, Philip, *Decade of Nightmares. The End of the Sixties and the Making of Eighties Americas* (New York 2006).
Jensen, Richard, "The Culture Wars, 1965–1995. A Historian's Map," *Journal of Social History* 29 (1995), 17–37.
Jhally, Sut and Lewis, Justin, *Enlightened Racism. The Cosby Show, Audiences, and the Myth of the American Dream* (Boulder 1992).
Joas, Hans, *Die Entstehung der Werte* (Frankfurt a.M. 1999).
Jobs, Sebastian and Lüdtke, Alf, *Unsettling History. Archiving and Narrating in Historiography* (Frankfurt a. M. 2010).
Joel, Charles, *Fertility Disturbances in Men and Women. A Textbook with Special Reference to Etiology, Diagnosis and Treatment* (New York and Basel 1971).
Johnson, Arthur T., "The Family. The Need for Sound Policy, Not Rhetoric and Ideology," *Public Administration Review* 47 (1987), no. 3, 240–244.
Johnson, Doyle Paul, *Contemporary Sociological Theory. An Integrated Multi-Level Approach* (New York 2008).

Johnson, Robert D., *Washington 20. Januar 1961. Der amerikanische Traum* (Munich 1999).
Jones, Charles O., *The Reagan Legacy. Promise and Performance* (Chatham 1988).
Jones, Jacqueline, *Labor of Love, Labor of Sorrow. Black Women, Work, and the Family from Slavery to the Present* (New York 1995).
Jones, Jacqueline, "Race and Gender in Modern America," *Reviews in American History* 26 (1998), no. 1, 220–238.
Jones, James H., *Bad Blood. The Tuskegee Syphilis Experiment* (New York 1981).
Jones, James M., *Prejudice and Racism* (Reading, MA 1972).
Jones, Martha, *All Bound Up Together. The Woman Question in African American Public Culture, 1830–1900* (Chapel Hill 2007).
Jordan, John, *Machine-Age Ideology. Social Engineering and American Liberalism, 1911–1939* (Chapel Hill and London 1994).
Jorstad, Erling, *Holding Fast, Pressing On. Religion in America in the 1980s* (New York, Westport, and London 1990).
Juchler, Ingo, *Die Studentenbewegung in den Vereinigten Staaten und der Bundesrepublik Deutschland der sechziger Jahre. Eine Untersuchung hinsichtlich ihrer Beeinflussung durch Befreiungsbewegungen und -theorien aus der Dritten Welt* (Berlin 1996).
Junker, Detlef (ed.), *Die USA und Deutschland im Zeitalter des Kalten Krieges. Ein Handbuch*, 2 vols. (Stuttgart and Munich 2001).
Kaelble, Hartmut, *Sozialgeschichte Europas 1945 bis zur Gegenwart* (Munich 2007).
Kaiser, David, *American Tragedy. Kennedy, Johnson, and the Origins of the Vietnam War* (Cambridge 2000).
Kaledin, Eugenia, *Mothers and More. American Women in the 1950s* (Boston 1984).
Kammler, Clemens, Parr, Rolf, and Schneider, Ulrich Johannes (eds.), *Foucault Handbuch. Leben—Werk—Wirkung* (Stuttgart 2008).
Kaplan, Laura, *The Story of Jane. The Legendary Underground Feminist Abortion Service* (Chicago 1995).
Kaschuba, Wolfgang, "Konsum—Lebensstil—Bedürfnis. Zum Problem materieller Indikatoren in der Kultur- und Mentalitätsgeschichte," *Sozialwissenschaftliche Informationen* 17 (1988), no. 3, 133–138.
Katsiaficas, George, *The Imagination of the New Left. A Global Analysis of 1968* (Boston 1987).
Katz, Michael B., Stern, Mark J., and Fader, Jamie J., "The New African American Inequality," *The Journal of American History* 92,1 (2005), 75–108.
Katzmann, Robert A. (ed.), *Daniel Patrick Moynihan. The Intellectual in Public Life* (Baltimore 2004).
Katznelson, Ira, *When Affirmative Action was White. The Untold History of Racial Inequality in Twentieth Century America* (New York 2005).
Kavanaugh, Megan L. et al., *Guttmacher Institute: Changes in Use of Long-acting Reversible Contraceptive Methods among United States Women, 2000–2012* <www.guttmacher.org/article/2015/11/changes-use-long-acting-reversible-contraceptive-methods-among-unitedstates-women>.
Kazin, Michael, "The Grass-Roots Right. New Histories of U.S. Conservatism in the Twentieth Century," *American Historical Review* 97 (1992), no. 1, 136–155.
Keddie, Nikki R., "The New Religious Politics. Where, When, Why Do 'Fundamentalisms' Appear?" *Comparative Studies in Society and History* 40 (1998), no. 4, 696–723.
Kelly, Joan, "Did Women Have a Renaissance?" in Bridenthal, Renate and Koontz, Claudia (eds.), *Becoming Visible. Women in European History* (Boston 1987), 137–164.
Kennedy, David M., *Freedom from Fear. The American People in Depression and War, 1929–1945* (Oxford 2001).
Kennedy, David M., *Progressivism. The Critical Issues* (Boston 1971).

Kennedy, David M. and Bailey, Thomas A. (eds.), *The American Spirit. Volume II. Since 1865* (Boston and New York 2002).
Kerber, Linda K., *Women of the Republic. Intellect and Ideology in Revolutionary America* (Chapel Hill 1980).
Kerber, Linda K. and De Hart, Jane Sherron (eds.), *Women's America. Refocusing on the Past* (New York 1987).
Kerner, Ina, "Alles intersektional? Zum Verhältnis von Rassismus und Sexismus," *Feministische Studien* 27 (2009), no. 1, 36–50.
Kesselman, Mark, "The Silent Revolution. Changing Values and Political Styles Among Western Publics by Ronald Inglehart," *Political Science Review* 72 (1979), no. 1, 284–286.
Kessler-Harris, Alice, *In Pursuit of Equity. Women, Men, and the Quest for Economic Citizenship in 20th Century America* (New York 2001).
Kessler-Harris, Alice, *Out to Work. A History of Wage-Earning Women in the United States* (Oxford 1982).
Kevles, Daniel, *In the Name of Eugenics. Genetics and the Use of Human Heredity* (New York 1985).
Kielmannsegg, Peter Graf, *Nach der Katastrophe. Eine Geschichte des geteilten Deutschlands* (Berlin 2000).
Kimball, Jeffrey P., *Nixon's Vietnam War* (Lawrence 1998).
Kimball, Roger, *The Long March. How the Cultural Revolution of the 1960s Changed America* (San Francisco 2000).
Kimmel, Michael, *Guyland. The Perilous World Where Boys Become Men* (New York 2008).
Kimmel, Michael, *Manhood in America. A Cultural History* (New York 1996).
Kimmel, Michael, *Studentenbewegungen der 60er Jahre. Frankreich, BRD und USA im Vergleich* (Vienna 1998).
Kimmel, Michael and Aronson, Amy, *The Gendered Society Reader* (New York 2000).
Kimmel, Michael, Hearn, Jeff, and Connell, Robert William (eds.), *Handbook of Studies on Men & Masculinities* (Thousand Oaks 2005).
King, Desmond, *Making Americans. Immigration, Race, and the Origins of Diverse Democracy* (Cambridge and London 2000).
King, Wilma, *The Essence of Liberty. Free Black Women during the Slave Era* (Missouri 2006).
Kirk, John A. (ed.), *Martin Luther King Jr. and the Civil Rights Movement. Controversies and Debates* (New York 2007).
Klages, Helmut, "Brauchen wir eine Rückkehr zu traditionellen Werten?" *Aus Politik und Zeitgeschichte* B 29 (2001), 7–14.
Klages, Helmuth, *Wertedynamik. Über die Wandelbarkeit des Selbstverständlichen* (Zurich 1988).
Klages, Helmut, "Werte und Wertewandel," in Schäfers, Bernhard and Zapf, Wolfgang (eds.), *Handwörterbuch zu Gesellschaft Deutschlands* (Opladen 2001), 726–738.
Klages, Helmut, *Wertorientierungen im Wandel. Rückblick, Gegenwartsanalyse, Prognosen* (Frankfurt a. M. 1984).
Klages, Helmut and Kmieciak, Peter (eds.), *Wertewandel und gesellschaftlicher Wandel* (Frankfurt a. M. and New York 1981).
Klages, Helmut, Hippler, Hans-Jürgen, and Herbert, Willi (eds.), *Werte und Wandel. Ergebnisse und Methoden einer Forschungstradition* (Frankfurt 1992).
Klatch, Rebecca E., *A Generation Divided. The New Left, the New Right, and the 1960s* (Berkeley 1999).
Kleemann, Susanne, *Ursachen und Formen der amerikanischen Studentenopposition* (Frankfurt a. M. 1971).
Klein, Thomas, "Auswirkungen des Wertewandels auf die Familienbildung," in Klages, Helmut, Hippler, Hans-Jürgen, and Herbert, Willi (eds.), *Werte und Wandel. Ergebnisse und Methoden einer Forschungstradition* (Frankfurt 1992), 579–594.

Kleinberg, Jay S., Boris, Eileen, and Ruiz, Vicki L. (eds.), *The Practice of U.S. Women's History. Narratives, Intersections, and Dialogues* (New Brunswick 2007).
Kline, Wendy, *Bodies of Knowledge. Sexuality, Reproduction, and Women's Health in the Second Wave* (Chicago 2010).
Kline, Wendy, *Building a Better Race. Gender, Sexuality, and Eugenics from the Turn of the Century to the Baby Boom* (Berkeley 2001).
Kluchin, Rebecca M., *Fit to Be Tied. Sterilization and Reproductive Rights in America, 1950–1980* (New Brunswick and London 2011).
Kluchin, Rebecca M., "Locating the Voices of the Sterilized," *The Public Historian* 29 (2007), no. 3, 131–144.
Kluckhohn, Clyde, "Values and Value Orientations in the Theory of Action. An Exploration in Definition and Classification," in Parsons, Talcott and Shils, Edward A. (eds.), *Toward A General Theory of Action* (Cambridge, MA 1962), 388–433.
Knapp, Gudrun-Axeli, "'Intersectionality'—Ein neues Paradigma feministischer Theorie? Zur transatlantischen Reise von 'Race, Class, Gender,'" *Feministische Studien* 2005, no. 1, 68–81.
Knapp, Gudrun-Axeli, "Travelling Theories. Anmerkungen zur neueren Diskussion über 'Race, Class and Gender,'" *Österreichische Zeitschrift für Geschichtswissenschaft* 16 (2005), no. 1, 88–110.
Knupfer, Anne and Woyshner, Christine, *The Educational Work of Women's Organizations, 1890–1960* (New York 2007).
Koenen, Gerd, *Das Rote Jahrzehnt. Unsere kleine deutsche Kulturrevolution, 1967–1977* (Cologne 2001).
Kohler-Hausmann, Julily, "Welfare Crises, Penal Solutions and the Origins of the 'Welfare Queen,'" *Journal of Urban History*, vol. 4, no. 5 (2915), 756–771.
Koops, Willem and Zuckerman, Michael (eds.), *Beyond the Century of the Child. Cultural History and Developmental Psychology* (Philadelphia 2003).
Koschorke, Albrecht, *Vor der Familie. Grenzbedingungen einer modernen Institution* (Konstanz 2010).
Kotz, Nick, *Judgement Days. Lyndon Baines Johnson, Martin Luther King Jr., and the Laws that Changed America* (New York 2005).
Kousser, J. Morgan and McPherson, James (eds.), *Region, Race, and Reconstruction. Essays in Honor of C. Vann Woodward* (New York 1982).
Kozol, Wendy, *Life's America. Family and Nation in Postwar Photojournalism* (Philadelphia 1994).
Kraft, Claudia, Lüdtke, Alf, and Martschukat, Jürgen (eds), *Kolonialgeschichte. Regionale Perspektiven auf ein globales Phänomen* (Frankfurt a. M. 2010).
Krämer, Felix, "Playboy Tells His Story. Geschichte eines Krisenszenarios um die hegemoniale US-Männlichkeit der 1970er Jahre," *Feministische Studien* 27 (2009), no. 1, 83–96.
Krugman, Paul, *The Age of Diminished Expectations. US Economic Policy in the 1990s* (Cambridge 1998).
Kuchenbuch, David, "Eine Moderne nach 'menschlichem Maß.' Ordnungsdenken und social engineering in Architektur und Stadtplanung Deutschland und Schweden, 1920er bis 1950er Jahre," in Etzemüller, Thomas (ed.), *Die Ordnung der Moderne. Social Engineering im 20. Jahrhundert* (Bielefeld 2009), 109–128.
Kuchenbuch, David, *Geordnete Gemeinschaft. Architekten als Sozialingenieure, Deutschland und Schweden im 20. Jahrhundert* (Bielefeld 2010).
Kühl, Stefan, *Die Internationale der Rassisten. Aufstieg und Niedergang der internationalen Bewegung für Eugenik und Rassenhygiene im 20. Jahrhundert* (Frankfurt a. M. 1997).
Kühl, Stefan, *The Nazi Connection. Eugenics, American Racism, and National Socialism* (New York 1994).
Kuhn, Barbara, *The "Liberated" Woman of 1914. Prominent Women in the Progressive Era* (London 1979).
Kuller, Christiane, *Familienpolitik im föderativen Sozialstaat. Die Formierung eines Politikfeldes in der Bundesrepublik 1949–1975* (Studien zur Zeitgeschichte 67, Munich 2004).

Kunzel, Regina G., *Fallen Women, Problem Girls. Unmarried Mothers and the Professionalization of Social Work, 1890–1945* (New Haven 1993).
Ladd-Taylor, Molly, "Fitter Family Contests" (April 29, 2014) <www.eugenicsarchive.ca/discover/connections/535eebfb7095aa0000000228>.
Ladd-Taylor, Molly, "Eugenics, Sterilization and the Modern Marriage in the USA. The Strange Career of Paul Popenoe," *Gender and History* 13 (2001), no. 2, 298–327.
Ladd-Taylor, Molly, *Mother-Work. Women, Child Welfare and the State, 1890–1930* (Champaign 1994).
Ladd-Taylor, Molly, "Saving Babies and Sterilizing Mothers. Eugenics and Welfare Politics in the Interwar United States," *Social Politics* 4 (1997), no. 1, 136–153.
Ladd-Taylor, Molly and Umansky, Lauri (eds.), *Bad Mothers. The Politics of Blame in Twentieth-Century America* (New York 1998).
Laird, Joan, *Lesbians and Lesbian Families. Reflections on Theory and Practice* (New York 1999).
Landry, Bart, *Black Working Wives. Pioneers of the American Family Revolution* (Berkeley and Los Angeles 2000).
Lane, Ann J., *To Herland and Beyond. The Life and Work of Charlotte Perkins Gilman* (New York 1990).
Lareau, Annette, *Unequal Childhoods. Class, Race, and Family Life* (Berkeley 2003).
LaRossa, Ralph, *Of War and Men. World War II in the Lives of Fathers and Their Families* (Chicago 2011).
LaRossa, Ralph, "The Changing Culture of Fatherhood in Comic-Strip Families. A Six-Decade Analysis," *Japanese Journal of Family Sociology* 62 (2000), no. 2, 375–387.
LaRossa, Ralph, "The Culture and Conduct of Fatherhood in America, 1800 to 1960," *Japanese Journal of Family Sociology* 19 (2007), no. 2, 87–98.
LaRossa, Ralph, "The Culture of Fatherhood in the Fifties. A Closer Look," *Journal of Family History* 29 (2004), no. 1, 47–70.
LaRossa, Ralph, *The Modernization of Fatherhood. A Social and Political History* (London 1997).
Larson, Edward J., "'In the Finest, Most Womanly Way'. Women in the Southern Eugenics Movement," *The American Journal of Legal History* 39 (1995), no. 2, 19–147.
Larson, Edward J., *Sex, Race, and Science. Eugenics in the Deep South* (Baltimore 1995).
Lasch-Quinn, Elisabeth, "Family," in Kupiec Cayton, Mary and William, Peter W. (eds.), *Encyclopedia of American Cultural and Intellectual History*, vol. 3, (New York etc. 2001), 73–82.
Laslett, Peter, "Social Structural Time. An Attempt at Classifying Types of Social Change by their Characteristic Paces," in Young, Michael and Schuller, Tom (eds.), *The Rhythms of Society* (London 1988), 17–36.
Latham, Michael E., *Modernization as Ideology. American Social Science and "Nation Building" in the Kennedy Era* (Chapel Hill 2000).
Laughlin, Kathleen A. et al., "Is It Time to Jump Ship? Historians Rethink the Waves Metaphor," *Feminist Formations* 22 (2010), 76–135.
Lawson, Steven F., *Civil Rights Crossroads. Nation, Community, and the Black Freedom Struggle* (Lexington, KY 2003).
Lawson, Steven F., "Freedom Then, Freedom Now. The Historiography of the Civil Rights Movement," *American Historical Review* 96 (1991), no. 2, 456–471.
Lawson, Steven F., *Running for Freedom. Civil Rights and Black Politics in America Since 1941* (New York 1997).
Leff, Mark H., "The Politics of Sacrifice on the American Home Front in World War II," *Journal of American History* 77 (1991), no. 4, 1296–1318.
Leibfried, Stephan, *Die angepaßte Universität. Zur Situation der Hochschulen in der Bundesrepublik und den USA* (Frankfurt a. M. 1969).
Leibman, Nina C., *Living Room Lectures. The Fifties Family in Film and Television* (Austin 1995).

Lemons, J. Stanley, "The Sheppard-Towner Act. Progressivism in the 1920s," *The Journal of American History* 55 (1969), no. 4, 776–786.
Lerner, Gerda (ed.), *Black Women in White America. A Documentary History* (New York 1972).
Lerner, Gerda, "Placing Women in History," *Feminist Studies* 3 (1975), no. 1–2, 5–14.
Lerner, Gerda, *The Majority Finds its Past* (New York 1979).
Leslie, Gerald R., *The Family in Social Context* (New York 1979).
Lessoff, Alan, "American Progressivism. Transnational, Modernization, and Americanist Perspectives," in Welskopp, Thomas and Lessoff, Alan, *Fractured Modernity. America Confronts Modern Times, 1890s to 1940s* (Munich 2013), 61–80.
Leuchtenberg, William E., *Franklin D. Roosevelt and the New Deal, 1932–1940* (Basingstoke 1989).
Leuchtenburg, William E., *The FDR Years. On Roosevelt and his Legacy* (New York 1995).
Levenstein, Lisa, "'Don't Agonize, Organize!' The Displaced Homemakers Campaign and the Contested Goals of Postwar Feminism," *Journal of American History* 100 (2014), no. 4, 1114–1138.
Levine, Peter, *The New Progressive Era. Toward a Fair and Deliberative Democracy* (Lanham 2000).
Lewin, Ellen, *Lesbian Mothers. Accounts of Gender in American Culture* (Ithaca 1993).
Lewin, Ellen and Lyons, Terri, "Everything in Its Place. The Coexistence of Lesbianism and Motherhood," in Paul, William and Weinreich, James (eds.), *Homosexuality. Social, Psychological, and Biological Issues* (Beverly Hills 1982), 249–273.
Lewis, David Levering, *W. E. B. Du Bois. The Fight for Equality and the American Century 1919–1963* (New York 2001).
Lewis, Jan, *The Pursuit of Happiness. Family and Values in Jefferson's Virginia* (Cambridge 1983).
Liard, Joan, "Lesbian and Gay Families," in Walsh, Froma (ed.), *Normal Family Processes* (New York 1993), 157–188.
Lichtenstein, Nelson et al. (eds.), *Industrial Democracy in America. The Ambiguous Promise* (Washington D. C. 1993).
Liebman, Robert and Wuthnow, Robert (eds.), *The New Christian Right. Mobilization and Legitimation* (New York 1983).
Lienesch, Michael, "Right-Wing Religion. Christian Conservatism as a Political Movement," *Political Science Quarterly* 97 (1982), no. 3, 403–426.
Limper, Verena, *Verantwortung für Körper, Kind, Nation. Mutter-Werden in der Kommunikation zwischen dem United States Children's Bureau und amerikanischen Frauen zu Beginn des 20. Jahrhunderts* (Master's thesis, Bielefeld University 2012).
Linde, Hans, "Familie und Haushalt als Gegenstand bevölkerungsgeschichtlicher Forschung," in Conze, Werner (ed.), *Sozialgeschichte der Familie in der Neuzeit Europas* (Stuttgart 1976), 32–52.
Lindenmeyer, Kriste, *A Right to Childhood. The U.S. Children's Bureau and Child Welfare, 1912–1930* (Urbana and Chicago 1997).
Lipset, Seymour Martin, *American Exceptionalism. A Double-Edged Sword* (New York 1996).
Livingston, Gretchen and Cohn, D'Vera, *The New Demography of American Motherhood* (Pew Research Center, 2010) <www.pewsocialtrends.org/2010/05/06/the-new-demography-of-american-motherhood/>.
Loch, Paul Rogat, *Generation at the Crossroads. Apathy and Action on the American Campus* (New Brunswick 1994).
Loevy, Robert D. (ed.), *The Civil Rights Act of 1964. The Passage of the Law That Ended Racial Segregation* (Albany and New York 1997).
Loevy, Robert D., *To End All Segregation. The Politics of the Passage of The Civil Rights Act of 1964* (Lanham, MD 1990).

Kunzel, Regina G., *Fallen Women, Problem Girls. Unmarried Mothers and the Professionalization of Social Work, 1890–1945* (New Haven 1993).
Ladd-Taylor, Molly, "Fitter Family Contests" (April 29, 2014) <www.eugenicsarchive.ca/discover/connections/535eebfb7095aa0000000228>.
Ladd-Taylor, Molly, "Eugenics, Sterilization and the Modern Marriage in the USA. The Strange Career of Paul Popenoe," *Gender and History* 13 (2001), no. 2, 298–327.
Ladd-Taylor, Molly, *Mother-Work. Women, Child Welfare and the State, 1890–1930* (Champaign 1994).
Ladd-Taylor, Molly, "Saving Babies and Sterilizing Mothers. Eugenics and Welfare Politics in the Interwar United States," *Social Politics* 4 (1997), no. 1, 136–153.
Ladd-Taylor, Molly and Umansky, Lauri (eds.), *Bad Mothers. The Politics of Blame in Twentieth-Century America* (New York 1998).
Laird, Joan, *Lesbians and Lesbian Families. Reflections on Theory and Practice* (New York 1999).
Landry, Bart, *Black Working Wives. Pioneers of the American Family Revolution* (Berkeley and Los Angeles 2000).
Lane, Ann J., *To Herland and Beyond. The Life and Work of Charlotte Perkins Gilman* (New York 1990).
Lareau, Annette, *Unequal Childhoods. Class, Race, and Family Life* (Berkeley 2003).
LaRossa, Ralph, *Of War and Men. World War II in the Lives of Fathers and Their Families* (Chicago 2011).
LaRossa, Ralph, "The Changing Culture of Fatherhood in Comic-Strip Families. A Six-Decade Analysis," *Japanese Journal of Family Sociology* 62 (2000), no. 2, 375–387.
LaRossa, Ralph, "The Culture and Conduct of Fatherhood in America, 1800 to 1960," *Japanese Journal of Family Sociology* 19 (2007), no. 2, 87–98.
LaRossa, Ralph, "The Culture of Fatherhood in the Fifties. A Closer Look," *Journal of Family History* 29 (2004), no. 1, 47–70.
LaRossa, Ralph, *The Modernization of Fatherhood. A Social and Political History* (London 1997).
Larson, Edward J., "'In the Finest, Most Womanly Way'. Women in the Southern Eugenics Movement," *The American Journal of Legal History* 39 (1995), no. 2, 19–147.
Larson, Edward J., *Sex, Race, and Science. Eugenics in the Deep South* (Baltimore 1995).
Lasch-Quinn, Elisabeth, "Family," in Kupiec Cayton, Mary and William, Peter W. (eds.), *Encyclopedia of American Cultural and Intellectual History*, vol. 3, (New York etc. 2001), 73–82.
Laslett, Peter, "Social Structural Time. An Attempt at Classifying Types of Social Change by their Characteristic Paces," in Young, Michael and Schuller, Tom (eds.), *The Rhythms of Society* (London 1988), 17–36.
Latham, Michael E., *Modernization as Ideology. American Social Science and "Nation Building" in the Kennedy Era* (Chapel Hill 2000).
Laughlin, Kathleen A. et al., "Is It Time to Jump Ship? Historians Rethink the Waves Metaphor," *Feminist Formations* 22 (2010), 76–135.
Lawson, Steven F., *Civil Rights Crossroads. Nation, Community, and the Black Freedom Struggle* (Lexington, KY 2003).
Lawson, Steven F., "Freedom Then, Freedom Now. The Historiography of the Civil Rights Movement," *American Historical Review* 96 (1991), no. 2, 456–471.
Lawson, Steven F., *Running for Freedom. Civil Rights and Black Politics in America Since 1941* (New York 1997).
Leff, Mark H., "The Politics of Sacrifice on the American Home Front in World War II," *Journal of American History* 77 (1991), no. 4, 1296–1318.
Leibfried, Stephan, *Die angepaßte Universität. Zur Situation der Hochschulen in der Bundesrepublik und den USA* (Frankfurt a. M. 1969).
Leibman, Nina C., *Living Room Lectures. The Fifties Family in Film and Television* (Austin 1995).

Lemons, J. Stanley, "The Sheppard-Towner Act. Progressivism in the 1920s," *The Journal of American History* 55 (1969), no. 4, 776–786.
Lerner, Gerda (ed.), *Black Women in White America. A Documentary History* (New York 1972).
Lerner, Gerda, "Placing Women in History," *Feminist Studies* 3 (1975), no. 1–2, 5–14.
Lerner, Gerda, *The Majority Finds its Past* (New York 1979).
Leslie, Gerald R., *The Family in Social Context* (New York 1979).
Lessoff, Alan, "American Progressivism. Transnational, Modernization, and Americanist Perspectives," in Welskopp, Thomas and Lessoff, Alan, *Fractured Modernity. America Confronts Modern Times, 1890s to 1940s* (Munich 2013), 61–80.
Leuchtenberg, William E., *Franklin D. Roosevelt and the New Deal, 1932–1940* (Basingstoke 1989).
Leuchtenburg, William E., *The FDR Years. On Roosevelt and his Legacy* (New York 1995).
Levenstein, Lisa, "'Don't Agonize, Organize!' The Displaced Homemakers Campaign and the Contested Goals of Postwar Feminism," *Journal of American History* 100 (2014), no. 4, 1114–1138.
Levine, Peter, *The New Progressive Era. Toward a Fair and Deliberative Democracy* (Lanham 2000).
Lewin, Ellen, *Lesbian Mothers. Accounts of Gender in American Culture* (Ithaca 1993).
Lewin, Ellen and Lyons, Terri, "Everything in Its Place. The Coexistence of Lesbianism and Motherhood," in Paul, William and Weinreich, James (eds.), *Homosexuality. Social, Psychological, and Biological Issues* (Beverly Hills 1982), 249–273.
Lewis, David Levering, *W. E. B. Du Bois. The Fight for Equality and the American Century 1919–1963* (New York 2001).
Lewis, Jan, *The Pursuit of Happiness. Family and Values in Jefferson's Virginia* (Cambridge 1983).
Liard, Joan, "Lesbian and Gay Families," in Walsh, Froma (ed.), *Normal Family Processes* (New York 1993), 157–188.
Lichtenstein, Nelson et al. (eds.), *Industrial Democracy in America. The Ambiguous Promise* (Washington D. C. 1993).
Liebman, Robert and Wuthnow, Robert (eds.), *The New Christian Right. Mobilization and Legitimation* (New York 1983).
Lienesch, Michael, "Right-Wing Religion. Christian Conservatism as a Political Movement," *Political Science Quarterly* 97 (1982), no. 3, 403–426.
Limper, Verena, *Verantwortung für Körper, Kind, Nation. Mutter-Werden in der Kommunikation zwischen dem United States Children's Bureau und amerikanischen Frauen zu Beginn des 20. Jahrhunderts* (Master's thesis, Bielefeld University 2012).
Linde, Hans, "Familie und Haushalt als Gegenstand bevölkerungsgeschichtlicher Forschung," in Conze, Werner (ed.), *Sozialgeschichte der Familie in der Neuzeit Europas* (Stuttgart 1976), 32–52.
Lindenmeyer, Kriste, *A Right to Childhood. The U.S. Children's Bureau and Child Welfare, 1912–1930* (Urbana and Chicago 1997).
Lipset, Seymour Martin, *American Exceptionalism. A Double-Edged Sword* (New York 1996).
Livingston, Gretchen and Cohn, D'Vera, *The New Demography of American Motherhood* (Pew Research Center, 2010) <www.pewsocialtrends.org/2010/05/06/the-new-demography-of-american-motherhood/>.
Loch, Paul Rogat, *Generation at the Crossroads. Apathy and Action on the American Campus* (New Brunswick 1994).
Loevy, Robert D. (ed.), *The Civil Rights Act of 1964. The Passage of the Law That Ended Racial Segregation* (Albany and New York 1997).
Loevy, Robert D., *To End All Segregation. The Politics of the Passage of The Civil Rights Act of 1964* (Lanham, MD 1990).

Logevall, Fredrik, *Choosing War. The Lost Chance for Peace and the Escalation of War in Vietnam* (Berkeley 1999).
Lombardo, Paul A. (ed.), *A Century of Eugenics in America. From the Indiana Experiment to the Human Genome Era* (Bloomington 2011).
Lombardo, Paul A., "Medicine, Eugenics, and the Supreme Court. From Coercive Sterilization to Reproductive Freedom," *Journal of Contemporary Health Law and Policy* 13 (1996), no. 1, 1–25.
Lombardo, Paul A., "Taking Eugenics Seriously. 'Three Generations of Imbeciles Are Enough,'" *Florida State University Law Review* 30 (2003), no. 2, 191–218.
Lombardo, Paul A., "'The American Breed'. Nazi Eugenics and the Origins of the Pioneer Fund," *Albany Law Review* 65 (2002), no. 3, 743–830.
Lombardo, Paul A., "Three Generations, No Imbeciles. New Light on Buck vs. Bell," *New York University Law Review* 60 (1985), no. 1, 31–62.
Lovett, Laura L., *Conceiving the Future. Pronatalism, Reproduction and the Family in the United States 1890–1938* (Chapel Hill 2007).
Lovett, Laura L., "'Fitter Families for Future Firesides?' Florence Sherbon and Popular Eugenics," *The Public Historian* 29 (2007), no. 3, 69–85.
Luks, Timo, *Der Betrieb als Ort der Moderne. Zur Geschichte von Industriearbeit, Ordnungsdenken und Social Engineering im 20. Jahrhundert* (Bielefeld 2010).
Lüscher, Kurt, Schultheis, Franz, and Wehrspaun, Michael (eds.), *Die "postmoderne" Familie. Familiale Strategien und Familienpolitik in einer Übergangszeit* (Konstanz 1988).
Lüthi, Barbara, *Invading Bodies. Medizin und Immigration in den USA, 1880–1920* (Frankfurt a. M. and New York 2009).
Lutz, Hartmut, *"Indianer" und "Native Americans." Zur sozial- und literarhistorischen Vermittlung eines Stereotyps* (Hildesheim 1985).
Lutz, Helma, *Framing Intersectionality. Debates on a Multi-Faceted Concept in Gender Studies* (Farnham 2011).
Lyden, Fremont J. and Legters, Lyman H., *Native Americans and Public Policy* (Pittsburgh 1992).
Lytle Hernández, Kelly Anne, *Entangling Bodies and Borders. Racial Profiling and the US Border Patrol 1924–1955* (Dissertation, University of California, Los Angeles 2002).
Macedo, Stephen (ed.), *Child, Family, and State* (New York 2003).
Macedo, Stephen, *Reassessing the Sixties. Debating the Political and Cultural Legacy* (New York and London 1997).
Mackert, Nina, "'But recall the kinds of parents we have to deal with . . .'—Juvenile Delinquency, Interdependent Masculinity and the Government of Families in the Postwar U.S.," in Heinemann, Isabel (ed.), *Inventing the Modern American Family. Family Values and Social Change in 20th Century United States* (Frankfurt a. M. and New York 2012), 196–219.
Mackert, Nina, "Danger and Hope. White Middle-Class Juvenile Delinquency and Parental Anxiety in the Postwar U.S.," in Ellis, Heather and Chang, Lily (eds.), *Juvenile Delinquency and Western Modernity, 1800–2000* (New York 2013).
Mackert, Nina, *Jugenddelinquenz. Die Produktivität eines Problems in den USA der späten 1940er bis 1960er Jahre* (Konstanz 2014).
Macklin, Ruth and Gaylin, Willard (eds.), *Mental Retardation and Sterilization. A Problem of Competency and Paternalism* (New York 1981).
MacLean, Mavis (ed.), *Family Law and Family Values* (Oxford 2005).
Maier, Charles, "Consigning the Twentieth Century to History. Alternative Narratives for the Modern Era," *The American Historical Review* 105 (2000), no. 3, 807–831.

Maier, Thomas, *Masters of Sex. The Life and Times of William Masters and Virginia Johnson, the Couple that Taught America How to Love* (New York 2013).
Manley, John F., "Marx in America. The New Deal," *Science & Society* 67 (2003), no. 1, 9–39.
Mantler, Gordon K., *Power to the Poor: Black-Brown Coalition and the Fight for Economic Justice, 1960–1974* (Chapel Hill 2013).
Marable, Manning, *Race, Reform and Rebellion. The Second Reconstruction in America, 1945–1990* (Jackson 1991).
Marable, Manning, *W. E. B. Du Bois—Black Radical Democrat* (New York 2005).
Marc, David and Thompson, Robert, *Prime Time, Prime Movers. From I Love Lucy to L. A. Law America's Greatest TV Shows and People Who Created Them* (Boston 1992).
Marling, Karal Ann, *As Seen on TV. Visual Culture of Everyday Life in the 1950s* (Cambridge and London 1994).
Marsden, George M., *Fundamentalism and American Culture* (Oxford 2006, second edition).
Marsden, George M., *The Twilight of the American Enlightenment. The 1950s and the Crisis of Liberal Belief* (New York 2014).
Marsh, Margaret and Wanner, Ronda, *The Fertility Doctor. John Rock and the Reproductive Revolution* (Baltimore 2008).
Martin, April, *The Lesbian and Gay Parenting Handbook. Creating and Raising our Children* (New York 1993).
Martin, Bradford, *The Other Eighties. A Secret History of America in the Age of Reagan* (New York 2011).
Martschukat, Jürgen, *Die Ordnung des Sozialen. Väter und Familien in der amerikanischen Geschichte seit 1770* (Frankfurt a. M. 2013, English: *American Fatherhood. A History*, New York 2019).
Martschukat, Jürgen and Stieglitz, Olaf, *"Es ist ein Junge!" Einführung in die Geschichte der Männlichkeiten in der Neuzeit* (Tübingen 2005).
Martschukat, Jürgen and Stieglitz, Olaf, *Geschichte der Männlichkeiten* (Frankfurt a. M. 2008).
Marty, Martin E. and Appleby, R. Scott (eds.), *Fundamentalisms and Society. Reclaiming the Sciences, the Family, and Education. The Fundamentalism Project*, 3 vols. (Chicago and London 1993).
Marwick, Arthur, *The Sixties. Cultural Revolution in Britain, France, Italy, and the United States, 1958–1974* (Oxford 1998).
Marx Ferree, Myra et al., *Shaping Abortion Discourse. Democracy and the Public Sphere in Germany and the United States* (Cambridge 2001).
Marx, Christoph, "Fundamentalismus und Nationalstaat," *Geschichte und Gesellschaft* 27 (2001), no. 1, 87–117.
Massey, Douglas S. and Denton, Nancy A., *American Apartheid. Segregation and the Making of the Underclass* (Cambridge, MA 1993).
Masur, Louis P, *The Challenge of American History* (Baltimore and London 1999).
Mathews, Donald G. and De Hart, Jane Sherron, *Sex, Gender, and the Politics of ERA. A State and the Nation* (Oxford 1993).
Matthews, Jean, *The Rise of the New Woman. The Women's Movement in America, 1875–1930* (Chicago 2003).
Matusow, Allen J., *The Unraveling of America. A History of Liberalism in the 1960s* (New York 1984).
Mauch, Christof and Patel, Kiran Klaus (eds.), *Competing Modernities. The United States of America and Germany, 1890–2000* (New York 2010).
Mauch, Christof and Patel, Kiran Klaus (eds.), *Wettlauf um die Moderne. Die USA und Deutschland 1890 bis heute* (Munich 2008).
Mausbach, Wilfried, "Historicising '1968,'" *Contemporary European History* 11 (2002), no. 1, 177–187.
May, Elaine Tyler, *America and the Pill. A History of the Promise, Peril, and Liberation* (New York 2010).
May, Elaine Tyler, *Barren in the Promised Land* (New York 1995).

May, Elaine Tyler, "Explosive Issues. Sex, Women and the Bomb," in May, Larry (ed.), *Recasting America. Culture and Politics in the Age of the Cold War* (Chicago and London 1998), 154–169.
May, Elaine Tyler, *Great Expectations. Marriage and Divorce in Post-Victorian America* (Chicago 1980).
May, Elaine Tyler, *Homeward Bound. American Families in the Cold War Era* (Boston 1988).
May, Elaine Tyler, "In-Laws and Out-Laws. Divorce in New Jersey, 1890–1925," in Murrin, Mary R. (ed.), *Women in New Jersey History* (Trenton 1985), 31–41.
May, Elaine Tyler, *Pushing the Limits. American Women 1940–1961* (New York 1994).
May, Elaine Tyler, "The Pressure to Provide. Class, Consumerism, and Divorce in Urban America," *Journal of Social History* 12 (1978), no. 2, 180–193.
May, Lary, *Recasting America. Culture and Politics in the Age of Cold War* (Chicago 1989).
Mayeri, Serena, *Reasoning from Race. Feminism, Law and the Civil Rights Revolution* (Harvard 2011).
McAdoo, Harriette P., *Black Families* (Thousand Oaks 1997 [1981]).
McAdoo, Harriette P. (ed.), *Family Ethnicity. Strength in Diversity* (Thousand Oaks, London, and New Delhi 1999).
McCann, Carole R., *Birth Control Politics in the United States 1916–1945* (Ithaca 1994).
McCarthy, Desmond F., *Reconstructing the Family in Contemporary American Fiction* (New York et al. 1997).
McCarthy, Thomas A., "Introduction," in Habermas, Jürgen, *The Theory of Communicative Action* (Boston 1984), vol. 1, v–xxxvii.
McCarthy, Thomas A., "Reflections on Rationalization in the Theory of Communicative Action," *Praxis International*, 4 (1984), no. 2, 177–191.
McClymer, John, *War and Welfare. Social Engineering in America, 1890–1925* (Greenwood Press, Westport 1980).
McCormick, Thomas J., *America's Half Century. United States Foreign Policy of the Cold War* (Baltimore and London 1995).
McCracken, Ellen, *Decoding Women's Magazines. From Mademoiselle to Ms.* (Houndmills 1995).
McEaney, Laura, *"Civil Defense Begins at Home." Militarization Meets Everyday Life in the Fifties* (Princeton 2000).
McGirr, Lisa, *Suburban Warriors. The Origins of the New American Right* (Princeton 2001).
McGreevy, John T., "Faith and Morals in the United States, 1865–Present," *Reviews in American History* 26 (1998), no. 1, 239–254.
McGuire, Danielle L., *At the Dark End of the Street: Black Women, Rape and Resistance. A New History of the Civil Rights Movement from Rosa Parks to the Rise of Black Power* (New York 2010).
McKnight, Gerald, *The Last Crusade. Martin Luther King, Jr., the FBI, and the Poor People's Campaign* (Boulder, CO 1998).
McLaren, Angus, *Twentieth-Century Sexuality. A History* (Malden, MA 1999).
McMahon, Sean H., *Social Control & Public Intellect. The Legacy of Edward A. Ross* (New Brunswick and London 1999).
McNamara, Robert S. (ed.), *Argument Without End. In Search of Answers to the Vietnam Tragedy* (New York 1999).
Meckel, Richard A., *Save the Babies. American Public Health Reform and the Prevention of Infant Mortality, 1850–1929* (Baltimore 1990).
Medick, Hans (ed.), *Emotionen und materielle Interessen. Sozialanthropologische und historische Beiträge zur Familienforschung* (Göttingen 1984).
Meriwether, James H., "'Worth a Lot of Negro Votes'. Black Voters, Africa, and the 1960 Presidential Campaign," *Journal of American History* (2008), no. 3, 737–763.

Merritt, Bishetta and Stroman, Carolyn A., "Black Family Imagery and Interactions on the Television," *Journal of Black Studies* 23/4 (1993), 492–499.
Mertin, Katja, *Zwischen Anpassung und Konfrontation. Die religiöse Rechte in der amerikanischen Politik* (Wiesbaden 2004).
Mester, Anika, *Die Veränderung von Mutterkonzepten in den 1950er und 1960er Jahren in den amerikanischen Women's Magazines: Die Bedeutung der Werbung. Abschlussarbeit zur Erlangung eines Grades als Master Artium* (University of Münster 2013).
Metzl, Jonathan M., "'Mother's Little Helper'. The Crisis of Psychoanalysis and the Miltown Resolution," *Gender & History* 15 (2003), no. 2, 228–255.
Metzl, Jonathan M., *Prozac on the Couch. Prescribing Gender in the Era of Wonder Drugs* (Durham 2003).
Metzl, Jonathan M., *The Protest Psychosis. How Schizophrenia became a Black Disease* (Boston 2009).
Meyering, Sheryl L. (ed.), *Charlotte Perkins Gilman. The Woman and Her Work* (Ann Arbor 1989).
Meyerowitz, Joanne, "Beyond the Feminine Mystique. A Reassessment of Postwar Mass Culture 1946–1958," *Journal of American History* 79 (1993), no. 4, 1455–1482.
Meyerowitz, Joanne, "Beyond the Feminine Mystique. A Reassessment of Postwar Mass Culture, 1946–1958," in Meyerowitz, Joanne (ed.), *Not June Cleaver. Women and Gender in Postwar America, 1945–1960* (Philadelphia 1994), 229–262.
Meyerowitz, Joanne, "'How Common Culture Shapes the Separate Lives'. Sexuality, Race, and Mid-Twentieth-Century Social Constructionist Thought," *The Journal of American History* 96 (2010), no. 4, 1057–1084.
Meyerowitz, Joanne (ed.), *Not June Cleaver. Women and Gender in Postwar America, 1945–1960* (Philadelphia 1994).
Meyerowitz, Joanne, "The Liberal 1950s? Reinterpreting Postwar U.S. Sexual Culture,'" in Hagemann, Karen and Michel, Sonya (eds.), *Gender and the Long Postwar: Reconsiderations of the United States and the Two Germanys, 1945–1989* (Baltimore 2014), 297–319.
Meyerowitz, Joanne, "Sex, Gender and Cold War Language of Reform," in Gilbert, James and Kuznick, Peter (eds.), *Rethinking Cold War Culture* (Washington 2001), 106–123.
Meyerowitz, Joanne, "Transnational Sex and US History," *American Historical Review* (2009), 1273–1286.
Meyerowitz, Joanne, *Women Adrift. Independent Wage Earners in Chicago, 1880–1930* (Chicago 1988).
Meyerowitz, Joanne, "Women, Cheesecake and Borderline Material. Responses to Girlie Pictures in the Mid-Twentieth-Century US," *Journal of Women's History* 8 (1996), no. 3, 9–35.
Mezey, Nancy, *New Choices, New Families. How Lesbians Decide about Motherhood* (Baltimore 2008).
Mikos, Lothar, *Es wird dein Leben! Familienserien im Fernsehen und im Alltag der Zuschauer* (Münster 1994).
Mikos, Lothar, "Familienbilder im Fernsehen," in Frölich, Magrit, Middel, Reinhard, and Visarius, Karsten (eds.), *Family Affairs. Ansichten der Familie im Film* (Marburg 2004), 37–52.
Mikos, Lothar, "Familienserien—Familienbilder," in Baacke, Dieter and Lauffer, Jürgen (eds.), *Familien im Mediennetz?* (Opladen 1988), 109–124.
Miles, Michael W., *The Radical Probe. The Logic of Student Rebellion* (New York 1973).
Millar, Jane, *Keeping Track of Welfare Reform. The New Deal Programmes* (York 2000).
Miller, James, *Democracy Is in the Streets. From Port Huron to the Siege of Chicago* (New York 1987).
Miller, Kenneth E., "The Silent Revolution. Changing Values and Political Styles Among Western Publics by Ronald Inglehart," *The Journal of Politics* 40, no. 3 (1978), 801–803.
Miller, Melody, Moon, Phyllis, and Dempster McLain, Donna, "Motherhood, Multiple Roles, and Maternal Well-Being. Women of the 1950s," *Gender and Society* 5 (1991), no. 4, 565–582.
Mindick, Burton, *Social Engineering in Family Matters* (New York et al. 1986).

Mink, Gwendolyn, "The Lady and the Tramp. Gender, Race, and the Origins of the American Welfare State," in Gordon, Linda (ed.), *Women, the State, and Welfare* (Madison 1990), 92–122.

Minkenberg, Michael, *Die neue radikale Rechte im Vergleich. USA, Frankreich, Deutschland* (Opladen and Wiesbaden 1998).

Mintz, Steven, *A Prison of Expectations. The Family in Victorian Culture* (New York 1983).

Mintz, Steven, *Huck's Raft. A History of American Childhood* (Cambridge 2004).

Mintz, Steven, "Regulating the American Family," in Hawes, Joseph M. and Nybakken, Elizabeth I. (eds.), *Family and Society in American History* (Chicago 2001), 9–36.

Mintz, Steven and Kellog, Susan, *Domestic Revolutions. A Social History of American Family Life* (New York 1988).

Miser, Keith M., *Student Affairs and Campus Dissent. Reflection of the Past and Challenge for the Future* (Washington D. C. 1988).

Mitchell Mary, *Raising Freedom's Child. Black Children and Visions of the Future after Slavery* (New York 2010).

Mittelstadt, Jennifer, *From Welfare to Workfare. The Unintended Consequences of Liberal Reform, 1945–1965* (Chapel Hill 2005).

Mitz, Rick, *The Great TV Sitcom Book* (New York 1980).

Modell, John, *Into One's Own. From Youth to Adulthood in the United States, 1920–1975* (Berkeley 1989).

Moeller, Robert G., *Geschützte Mütter. Frauen und Familien in der westdeutschen Nachkriegspolitik* (Munich 1993).

Moise, Edwin, *Tonkin Gulf and the Escalation of the Vietnam War* (Chapel Hill 1997).

Momeni, Jamshid A., *Demography of the Black Population in the United States. An Annotated Bibliography with a Review Essay* (Westport and London 1983).

Montejano, David, *Quixote's Soldiers. A Local History of the Chicano Movement, 1966–1981* (Austin 2010).

Montgomery, Kathryn, *Target. Prime Time. Advocacy Groups in the Struggle Over Entertainment Television* (New York 1989).

Moran, Gerald F. and Vinovskis, Maris A., *Religion, Family, and the Life Course. Explorations in the Social History of Early America* (Ann Arbor 1992).

More, Elizabeth Singer, *Best Interests. Feminism, Social Science, and the Revaluing of Working Mothers in Modern America* (Dissertation Harvard University 2012).

More, Elizabeth Singer, "'The Necessary Factfinding Has Only Just Begun'. Women, Social Science, and the Reinvention of the 'Working Mother' in the 1950s," *Women's Studies* 40 (2011), no. 8, 974–1005.

Morgen, Sandra, *Into Our Own Hands. The Women's Health Movement in the United States, 1969–1990* (New Brunswick, N. J. and London 2002).

Morris, Aldon D., "Sociology of Race and W. E. B. DuBois. The Path Not Taken," in Calhoun, Craig (ed.), *Sociology in America. A History* (Chicago, 2007), 503–534.

Moskowitz, Eva, *In Therapy We Trust. America's Obsession with Self-Fulfillment* (Baltimore 2001).

Mouw, Ted and Sobel, Michael E., "Culture Wars and Opinion Polarization," *American Journal of Sociology* 106, no. 4 (2001), 913–943.

Müller, Jürgen, *Die Geschichte des Student Non-Violent Coordinating Committee. Ein Kapitel der Bürgerrechtsbewegung in den Vereinigten Staaten* (Stuttgart 1978).

Murch, Donna Jean, *Living for the City. Migration, Education, and the Rise of the Black Panther Party in Oakland, California* (Chapel Hill 2010).

Murray, Heather, *Not in this Family. Gays and the Meaning of Kinship in Postwar North America* (Philadelphia and Oxford 2010).

Myers-Shirk, Susan E., "Sexuality," in Kupiec Cayton, Mary and Williams, Peter (eds.), *Encyclopedia of American Cultural and Intellectual History*, vol. 3 (New York 2001), 83–92.

Nadasen, Premilla, "Expanding the Boundaries of the Women's Movement. Black Feminism and the Struggle for Welfare Rights," *Feminist Studies* 28 (2002), 271–301.

Nadasen, Premilla, *Welfare Warriors. The Welfare Rights Movement in the United States* (New York 2005).

Nash, George H., *The Conservative Intellectual Movement in America since 1945* (New York 1976).

Nate, Richard, *Amerikanische Träume. Die Kultur der Vereinigten Staaten in der Zeit des New Deal* (Würzburg 2003).

Nave-Herz, Rosemarie, *Familie zwischen Tradition und Moderne* (Oldenburg 2003).

Neale, Steve, *Genre and Hollywood* (London and New York 2000).

Neidhardt, Friedrich and Rucht, Dieter, "The Analysis of Social Movements. The State of the Art and Some Perspectives of Further Research," in Rucht, Dieter (ed.), *Research on Social Movements. The State of the Art in Western Europe and the USA* (Boulder 1991), 421–464.

Nelson, Deborah, *Pursuing Privacy in Cold War America* (New York 2002).

Nelson, Jennifer, "'All this that has happened to me shouldn't happen to nobody else': Loretta Ross and the Women of Color Reproductive Freedom Movement of the 1980s," *Journal of Women's History*, vol. 22 (3), Fall 2010, 136–160.

Nelson, Jennifer, *More Than Medicine. A History of the Feminist Women's Health Movement* (New York 2015).

Nelson, Jennifer, *Women of Color and the Reproductive Rights Movement* (New York 2003).

Neu, Charles E. (ed.), *After Vietnam. Legacies of a Lost War* (Baltimore 2000).

Neuhaus, Jessamyn, "The Way to a Man's Heart. Gender Roles, Domestic Ideology, and Cookbooks in the 1950s," *Journal of Social History* 32 (1998), no. 3, 529–555.

Newkirk, M. Glenn, "The Silent Revolution. Changing Values and Political Styles Among Western Publics by Ronald Inglehart," *The Public Opinion Quarterly* 42, no. 4 (1978), 568–569.

Nice, David C., "Abortion Clinic Bombings as Political Violence," *American Journal of Political Science* 32 (1988), no. 1, 178–195.

Nicholas, Phil Jr., "The Agency That Kept on Going. The Late New Deal SEC and Shareholder Democracy," *Journal of Policy History* 16 (2004), no. 3, 212–239.

Nicholas, Susan C., Price, Allice M., and Rubin, Rachel, *Rights and Wrongs. Women's Struggle for Legal Equality* (Old Westbury etc. 1979).

Niehuss, Merith, *Familie, Frau und Gesellschaft. Studien zur Strukturgeschichte der Familie in Westdeutschland, 1945–1960* (Göttingen 2001).

Nock, Steven, Sanchez, Laura, and James D. Wright, *Covenant Marriage. The Movement to Reclaim Tradition in America* (New York 2008).

Noelle-Neumann, Elisabeth, *Werden wir alle Proletarier? Wertewandel in unserer Gesellschaft* (Zurich 1978).

Noelle-Neumann, Elisabeth, "Zeitenwende. Der Wertewandel 30 Jahre später," *Aus Politik und Zeitgeschichte* B 29 (2001), 15–22, esp. 16–18.

Nolte, Paul, *Die Ordnung der deutschen Gesellschaft. Selbstentwurf und Selbstbeschreibung im 20. Jahrhundert* (Munich 2000).

Nolte, Paul, "Öffentlichkeit und Privatheit. Deutschland im 20. Jahrhundert," *ZeitRäume. Potsdamer Almanach des Zentrums für Zeithistorische Forschungen* 2 (2006), 127–136.

Norton, Mary B., *A People and a Nation. A History of the United States* (Boston 1994).

Norton, Mary B., *Major Problems in American Women's History. Documents and Essays* (Lexington 1996).

Nye, Joseph S., *Bound to Lead. The Changing Nature of American Power* (New York 1990).

O'Brien, Kenneth Paul (ed.), *The Home-Front War. World War II and American Society* (Westport 1995).

O'Neill, William L., "Divorce and the Professionalization of the Social Scientist," *Journal of the Behavioral Sciences* 2 (1966), no. 4, 291–302.

O'Neill, William L., *Divorce in the Progressive Era* (New Haven and London 1967).

O'Neill, William L., *The Progressive Years. America Comes of Age* (New York 1975).

O'Connor, Alice, *Poverty Knowledge. Social Science, Social Policy, and the Poor in Twentieth-Century US History* (Princeton 2001).

O'Day, Rosemary, *The Family and Family Relationships, 1500–1900. England, France and the United States of America* (Houndmills 1994).

Odem, Mary E., *Delinquent Daughters: Protecting and Policing Adolescent Female Sexuality in the United States, 1885–1920* (Chapel Hill and London 1995).

Odland, Sarah Burke, "Unassailable Motherhood, Ambivalent Domesticity. The Construction of Maternal Identity in Ladies' Home Journal in 1946," *Journal of Communication Inquiry* 34 (2010), no. 1, 61–84.

Oertzen, Christine von, *Teilzeitarbeit und die Lust am Zuverdienen. Geschlechterpolitik und gesellschaftlicher Wandel in Westdeutschland 1948–1969* (Göttingen 1999).

Oertzen, Christine von, *The Pleasures of a Surplus Income. Part-time Work, Gender Politics, and Social Change in West Germany, 1955–1969* (New York 2007).

Ogbar, Jeffrey O. G., *Black Power: Radical Politics and African American Identity* (Baltimore 2004).

Olasky, Marvin N., *The Press and Abortion 1838–1988* (Hillsdale 1988).

Olson, James Stuart (ed.), *Historical Dictionary of the 1920s. From World War I to the New Deal, 1919–1933* (New York 1988).

Olson, James Stuart (ed.), *Historical Dictionary of the Great Depression 1929–1940* (Westport 2001).

Olson, James Stuart (ed.), *Historical Dictionary of the New Deal. From Inauguration to Preparation of War* (Westport 1985).

Opitz, Claudia, *Geschlechtergeschichte* (Frankfurt and New York 2010).

Opitz, Claudia, *Um-Ordnungen der Geschlechter. Einführung in die Geschlechtergeschichte* (Tübingen 2005).

Oppenheimer, Valerie, *Work and the Family. A Study in Social Demography* (New York 1982).

Ordover, Nancy, *American Eugenics. Race, Queer Anatomy, and the Science of Nationalism* (Minneapolis 2003).

Orleck, Annelise and Hazirjian, Lisa Gayle (eds.), *The War on Poverty: A New Grassroots History, 1964–1980* (Athens, GA 2011).

Ormrod, Susan, "'Let's Nuke the Dinner'. Discursive Practices of Gender in the Creation of a New Cooking Process," in Cockburn, Cynthia and Dillic, Ruza Fürst (eds.), *Bringing Technology Home. Gender and Technology in a Changing Europe* (Buckingham 1994), 42–59.

Ortiz, Ana Teresa and Briggs, Laura, "The Culture of Poverty, Crack Babies, and Welfare Cheats. The Making of the 'Healthy White Baby Crisis,'" *Social Text* 75 (2003), no. 3, 39–57.

Ortiz, Paul, *An African American and Latinx History of the United States* (Boston 2018).

Overbeck, Anne, *At the Heart of It All: Discourses on the Reproductive Rights of African American Women* (Berlin and Boston 2019).

Overbeck, Anne, "'The Enemy Within'. African American Motherhood and the Crack Baby Crisis," in Heinemann, Isabel (ed.), *Inventing the Modern American Family. Family Values and Social Change in 20th Century United States* (Frankfurt a. M. and New York 2012), 155–176.

Overbeck, Anne, *Mothering the Race. Eugenics and the Discourse on the Reproductive Rights of African American Women in the 20th Century* (Dissertation, Münster 2017).

Pach, Chester J. Jr., "Tet on TV. U.S. Nightly News Reporting and Presidential Policy Making," in Fink, Carole, Gassert, Philipp, and Junker, Detlef (eds.), *1968. The World Transformed* (Cambridge 1998), 55–81.

Packard, Vance, *Verlust der Geborgenheit. Unsere kinderkranke Gesellschaft. Was die Vernachlässigung der Familie für unsere Kinder und die Zukunft der Gesellschaft bedeutet* (Bern 1984).
Page, Stephen B. and Larner, Mary B., "Introduction to the AFDC Program," *The Future of Children. Welfare to Work*, vol. 7, no. 1 (1997), 20–27.
Parker, Randall E., *Reflections on the Great Depression* (Cheltenham 2002).
Parker, Richard, *The Myth of the Middle Class. Notes on Affluence and Equality* (New York 1972).
Parkin, Katherine J., *Food is Love. Advertising and Gender Roles in Modern America* (Philadelphia 2007).
Parry, Manon, *Broadcasting Birth Control. Mass Media and Family Planning* (New Brunswick, NJ 2013).
Pascoe, Peggy, *What Comes Naturally. Miscegenation Law and the Making of Race in America* (New York 2008).
Patterson, Charlotte J., "Children of Lesbian and Gay Parents," *Current Directions in Psychological Science* 15 (2006), no. 5, 241–244.
Patterson, Charlotte J., "Family Relationships of Lesbians and Gay Men," *Journal of Marriage and the Family* 62 (2000), no. 4, 1052–1069.
Patterson, James T., *Brown v. Board of Education. A Civil Rights Milestone and Its Troubled Legacy* (New York 2001).
Patterson, James T., *Freedom is not Enough. The Moynihan Report and America's Struggle over Black Family Life from LBJ to Obama* (New York 2010).
Patterson, James T., *Grand Expectations. The United States 1945–1974* (Oxford 1996).
Patterson, James T., *Restless Giant. The United States from Watergate to Bush vs. Gore* (Oxford 2005).
Paul, Gerhard, *Das visuelle Zeitalter. Punkt und Pixel* (Göttingen 2016).
Paul, Gerhard (ed.), *Visual History. Ein Studienbuch* (Göttingen 2006).
Paul, Gerhard, "Visual History, Version: 3.0," *Docupedia-Zeitgeschichte*, March 13, 2014 <www.docupedia.de/zg/paul_visual_history_v3_de_2014>.
Pegg, Robert, *Comical Co-Stars of Television. From Norton to Kramer* (Jefferson 2002).
Peiss, Kathy, Simmons, Christina, and Padgug, Robert A., *Passion and Power. Sexuality in History* (Philadelphia 1989).
Pelka, Suzanne, "Sharing Motherhood. Maternal Jealousy among Lesbian Co-Mothers," *Journal of Homosexuality* 56 (2009), no. 2, 195–217.
Pells, Richard H., *The Liberal Mind in a Conservative Age. American Intellectuals in the 1940s and 1950s* (Middletown 1989).
Penley, Constance, *The Future of an Illusion. Film, Feminism, and Psychoanalysis* (Minneapolis 1990).
Pernick, Martin S., *The Black Stork. Eugenics and the Death of Defective Babies in American Medicine and Motion Pictures since 1915* (New York 1996).
Petchesky, Rosalind Pollack, "Fetal Images. The Power of Visual Culture in the Politics of Reproduction," *Feminist Studies* 13 (1987), no. 2, 263–292.
Peters, Uwe Henrik, *Psychiatrie im Exil. Die Emigration der dynamischen Psychiatrie aus Deutschland 1933–1939* (Düsseldorf 1992).
Peterson, Theodore, *Magazines in the Twentieth Century* (Urbana 1956).
Philipps, Roderick, *Putting Asunder. A History of Divorce in Western Society* (Cambridge 1988).
Phoenix, Ann, "Intersectionality," *European Journal of Women's Studies* 13 (2006), no. 3, 187–192.
Pierce, Jenifer Burek, "Science, Advocacy, and 'The Sacred Things of Life': Representing Motherhood as a Progressive Era Cause in Women's Magazines," *American Periodicals* 18 (2008), no. 1, 69–94.
Pivar, David J., *Purity and Hygiene. Women, Prostitution, and the "American Plan" 1900–1930* (Westport 2002).
Plant, Rebecca Jo, *Mom. The Transformation of Motherhood in Modern America* (Chicago 2010).

Plateris, Alexander A., *100 Years of Marriage and Divorce Statistics. United States 1867-1967*, U.S. Department of Health, Education and Welfare, National Center for Health Statistics (Rockville 1973).
Platt, Jennifer, *A History of Sociological Research Methods in America, 1920-1960* (Cambridge et al. 1996).
Pleck, Elizabeth H., *Celebrating the Family. Ethnicity, Consumer Culture, and Family Rituals* (Cambridge and London 2000).
Pleck, Elizabeth, *Domestic Tyranny. The Making of American Social Policy against Family Violence from Colonial Times to the Present* (New York 1987).
Poiger, Uta G., *Jazz, Rock and Rebels. Cold war Politics and American Culture in a Divided Germany* (Berkeley 2000).
Polatnick, Pivka M., "Diversity in Women's Liberation Ideology. How a Black and a White Group of the 1960s Viewed Motherhood," *Signs* 21 (1996), no. 3, 679-706.
Pollack, Sandra (ed.), *Politics of the Heart. A Lesbian Parenting Anthology* (Ithaca 1987).
Popenoe, David, "American Family Decline, 1960-1990. A Review and Appraisal," *Journal of Marriage and the Family* 55 (1993), no. 3, 527-542.
Popenoe, David, *Disturbing the Nest. Family Change and Decline in Modern Societies* (New York 1988).
Popenoe, David, *Life Without Father. Compelling New Evidence that Fatherhood and Marriage are Indispensable for the Good of Children and Society* (New York 1996).
Popenoe, David, "Modern Marriage. Revising the Cultural Script," in Popenoe, David, Elshtain, Jean Bethke, and Blankenhorn, David (eds.), *Promises to Keep. Decline and Renewal of Marriage in America* (Lanham 1996), 247-270.
Popenoe, David, "Remembering My Father. An Intellectual Portrait of 'The Man Who Saved Marriages,'" in Popenoe, David, *War Over the Family* (New Brunswick 2005), 227-244.
Popenoe, David, *War Over the Family* (New Brunswick 2005).
Powell, Brian et al., *Counted Out. Same Sex Relations and American Definitions of Family* (New York 2010).
Prescott, Heather Munro, *Student Bodies. The Impact of Student Health on American Society and Medicine* (Ann Arbor 2007).
Press, Andrea and Cole, Elizabeth, *Speaking of Abortion. Television and Authority in the Lives of Women* (Chicago 1999).
Priemel, Isabel and Schuster, Annette, *Frauen zwischen Erwerbstätigkeit und Familie. Historische und aktuelle Entwicklungen* (Pfaffenweiler 1990).
Quadagno, Jill, *The Color of Welfare. How Racism Undermined the War on Poverty* (New York 1994).
Raab, Jürgen, *Erving Goffman* (Konstanz 2007).
Raeithel, Gerd, *Geschichte der nordamerikanischen Kultur*, vol. 3, *Vom New Deal bis zur Gegenwart, 1930-1988* (Weinheim and Berlin 1989).
Rafkin, Louise, *Different Mothers. Sons and Daughters of Lesbians Talk about their Lives* (Pittsburgh 1990).
Raley, R. Kelly and Bumpass, Larry, "The Topography of the Divorce Plateau. Levels and Trends in Union Stability in the United States after 1980," *Demographic Research* 8 (2003), 245-260 <www.demographic-research.org/Volumes/Vol8/8/>.
Randeria, Shalini, "Geteilte Geschichte und verwobene Moderne," in Rüsen, Jörn et al. (eds.), *Zukunftsentwürfe. Ideen für eine Kultur der Veränderung* (Frankfurt a. M. 2000), 87-96.
Raphael, Lutz, "Das Ende des Deutschen Reiches als Zäsur nationaler Expertenkulturen? Überlegungen zu den Folgen des politischen Umbruchs 1945 für Technik und Wissenschaft in Deutschland," in Doering-Manteuffel, Anselm (ed.), *Strukturmerkmale der deutschen Geschichte des 20. Jahrhunderts* (Munich 2006), 181-195.

Raphael, Lutz, "Die Verwissenschaftlichung des Sozialen als methodische und konzeptionelle Herausforderung für eine Sozialgeschichte des 20. Jahrhunderts," *Geschichte und Gesellschaft* 22 (1996), 165–193.

Raphael, Lutz, "Embedding the Human and Social Sciences in Western Societies, 1880–1980. Reflections on Trends and Methods of Current Research," in Brueckweh, Kerstin (ed.), *Engineering Society. The Role of the Human and Social Sciences in Modern Societies, 1880–1980* (New York 2012), 41–56.

Raphael, Lutz, "Experten im Sozialstaat," in Hockerts, Hans-Günther (ed.), *Drei Wege deutscher Sozialstaatlichkeit. NS-Diktatur, Bundesrepublik und DDR im Vergleich* (Munich 1998), 231–258.

Raphael, Lutz, *Geschichtswissenschaft im Zeitalter der Extreme* (Munich 2003).

Raphael, Lutz, "Ordnungsmuster der 'Hochmoderne'? Die Theorie der Moderne und die Geschichte der europäischen Gesellschaften im 20. Jahrhundert," in Schneider, Ute and Raphael, Lutz (eds.), *Dimensionen der Moderne. Festschrift für Christof Dipper* (Frankfurt a. M. 2008), 73–91.

Raphael, Lutz, "'Ordnung' zwischen Geist und Rasse. Kulturwissenschaftliche Ordnungssemantik im Nationalsozialismus," in Lehmann, Hartmut and Oexle, Otto Gerhard (eds.), *Nationalsozialismus in den Kulturwissenschaften*, vol. 2, (Göttingen 2004), 115–137.

Raphael, Lutz, "Radikales Ordnungsdenken und die Organisation totalitärer Herrschaft. Weltanschauungseliten und Humanwissenschaftler im NS-Regime," *Geschichte und Gesellschaft* 27 (2001), 5–40.

Raphael, Lutz, "Sozialexperten in Deutschland zwischen konservativem Ordnungsdenken und rassistischer Utopie (1918–1945)," in Hardtwig, Wolfgang (ed.), *Utopie und politische Herrschaft im Europa der Zwischenkriegszeit* (Schriften des Historischen Kollegs, Kolloquien 56, Munich 2003), 327–346.

Raphael, Lutz, "Zwischen Sozialaufklärung und radikalem Ordnungsdenken. Die Verwissenschaftlichung des Sozialen im Europa der ideologischen Extreme," in Hübinger, Gangolf (ed.), *Europäische Wissenschaftskulturen und politische Ordnungen der Moderne (1890–1970)* (Munich 2013), 29–50.

Raphael, Lutz and Pleinen, Jenny, "Zeithistoriker in den Archiven der Sozialwissenschaften. Erkenntnispotentiale und Relevanzgewinne für die Disziplin," *VfZ* 62 (2014), 173–196.

Rapp, Rayna, "Family and Class in Contemporary America," in Coontz, Stephanie, Parson, Maya, and Raley, Gabrielle (eds.), *American Families. A Multicultural Reader* (New York 2008), 188–200.

Raschke, Joachim, *Soziale Bewegungen. Ein historisch-systematischer Grundriß* (Frankfurt a. M. 1985).

Raulff, Ulrich and Burguière, André (eds.), *Mentalitäten-Geschichte. Zur historischen Rekonstruktion geistiger Prozesse* (Berlin 1989).

Reagan, Leslie J., *Dangerous Pregnancies. Mothers, Disabilities, and Abortion in Modern America* (Berkeley 2010).

Reagan, Leslie J., *When Abortion Was a Crime. Women, Medicine and the Law in the United States, 1867–1973* (Berkeley and Los Angeles 1997).

Reagan, Patrick D., *Designing a New America. The Origins of New Deal Planning, 1890–1943* (Amherst 1999).

Reese, William J. (ed.), *American Education in the Twentieth Century. Progressive Legacies* (Abingdon 2003).

Register, Cheri, "Motherhood at Center. Ellen Key's Social Vision," *Women's Studies Int. Forum* 5 (1982), no. 6, 599–610.

Reilly, Philip R., *The Surgical Solution. A History of Involuntary Sterilization in the United States* (Baltimore and London 1991).

Reiman, Richard A., *The New Deal and American Youth. Ideas and Ideals in a Depression Decade* (Athens 1992).

Reinarman, Craig and Levine, Harry, *Crack in America. Demon Drugs and Social Justice* (London 1997).

Reinecke, Christiane and Mergel, Thomas, "Das Soziale vorstellen, darstellen, herstellen: Sozialwissenschaften und gesellschaftliche Ungleichheit im 20. Jahrhundert," in Reinecke, Christiane and MergelThomas, *Das Soziale Ordnen. Sozialwissenschaften und gesellschaftliche Ungleichheit im 20. Jahrhundert* (Frankfurt a. M. 2012), 7–31.

Reiss, David (ed.), *The American Family. Dying or Developing? Proceedings of the Conference Held in Washington, D. C. on June 10–11, 1978* (New York 1979).

Rhoades, Lawrence J., *A History of the American Sociological Association, 1905–1980* <www.asanet.org/about/Rhoades_History.cfm>.

Richelson, Jeffrey T. (ed.), *Presidential Directives on National Security from Truman to Clinton* (Washington D. C. 1994).

Riesebrodt, Martin, *Die Rückkehr der Religionen. Fundamentalismus und der "Kampf der Kulturen"* (Munich 2000).

Riesebrodt, Martin, *Fundamentalismus als patriarchalische Protestbewegung. Amerikanische Protestanten (1910–28) und iranische Schiiten (1961–79) im Vergleich* (Tübingen 1990).

Riesebrodt, Martin, *Protestantischer Fundamentalismus in den USA. Die religiöse Rechte im Zeitalter der elektronischen Medien*, Evangelische Zentralstelle für Weltanschauungsfragen, Information no. 102 (Stuttgart 1987).

Riley, Glenda, *Divorce. An American Tradition* (New York and Oxford 1991).

Risen, Clay, *A Nation on Fire. America in the Wake of the King Assassination* (Hoboken 2009).

Risen, James and Thomas, Judy L., *Wrath of Angels. The American Abortion War* (New York 1998).

Robbins, Mary Susannah, *Against the Vietnam War. Writings by Activists* (New York 2007).

Roberts, Dorothy, *Fatal Invention. How Science, Politics, and Big Business Re-create Race in the Twenty-first Century* (New York, London 2011).

Roberts, Dorothy, *Killing the Black Body. Race, Reproduction, and the Meaning of Liberty* (New York 1999).

Roberts, Dorothy, *Shattered Bonds. The Color of Child Welfare* (New York 2002).

Robin, Ron Theodore, *The Making of the Cold War Enemy. Culture and Politics in the Military-Intellectual Complex* (Princeton 2001).

Robinson, Armstead L. and Sullivan, Patricia (eds.), *New Directions in Civil Rights Studies* (Charlottesville 1991).

Robinson, Paul, *The Modernization of Sex. Havelock Ellis, Alfred Kinsey, William Masters, and Virginia Johnson* (New York 1976).

Rödder, Andreas, "Vom Materialismus zum Postmaterialismus? Ronald Ingleharts Diagnosen des Wertewandels, ihre Grenzen und ihre Perspektiven," *Zeithistorische Forschungen* 3 (2006), no. 3, 280–285.

Rödder, Andreas, "Werte und Wertewandel. Historisch-Politische Perspektiven," in Rödder, Andreas and Elz, Wolfgang (eds.), *Alte Werte—Neue Werte. Schlaglichter des Wertewandels* (Göttingen 2008), 9–25.

Rödder, Andreas, *Wertewandel in der Postmoderne. Gesellschaft und Kultur der Bundesrepublik Deutschland 1965–1990* (Stuttgart 2004).

Rödder, Andreas, "Wertewandel in historischer Perspektive. Ein Forschungskonzept," in Dietz, Bernhard, Neumaier, Christopher, and Rödder, Andreas (eds.), *Gab es den Wertewandel? Neue Forschungen zum gesellschaftlich-kulturellen Wandel seit den 1960er Jahren* (Munich 2013), 17–39.

Rödder, Andreas and Elz, Wolfgang (eds.), *Alte Werte—Neue Werte. Schlaglichter des Wertewandels* (Göttingen 2008).

Roderick, Phillips, *Untying the Knot. A Short History of Divorce* (New York 1991).

Rodríguez, Richard T., *Next of Kin: The Family in Chicano/a Cultural Politics* (Durham, NC 2009).

Roesch, Claudia, "'Americanization through Homemaking'. Mexican American Mothers as Major Factors in Americanization Programs," in Isabel Heinemann (ed.), *Inventing the Modern American Family. Family Values and Social Change in 20th Century United States* (Campus Verlag, Frankfurt a. M. and New York 2012), 59–81.

Roesch, Claudia, "'Failure to Provide.' Mexican Immigration, Americanization and Marginalized Masculinities in the Interwar United States," in Dominguez Andersen, Pablo and Wendt, Simon (ed.), *Masculinities and the Nation in the Modern World. Between Hegemony and Marginalization* (New York 2015), 149–170.

Roesch, Claudia, "Macho Man? Repräsentationen mexikanischer Familienstrukturen durch Sozialexperten, Sozialarbeiter und Bürgerrechtsaktivisten in den USA, 1940–1980," in Gabriele Metzler (ed.), *Das Andere denken. Repräsentationen von Migration in Westeuropa und den USA im 20. Jahrhundert* (Frankfurt a. M. and New York 2013), 87–118.

Roesch, Claudia, *Macho Men and Modern Women. Mexican Immigration, Social Experts and Changing Family Values in the 20th Century United States* (Berlin and Boston 2015).

Roesch, Claudia, *Mexican Immigrant Families, Social Experts, Social Work, and Changing Family Values in the 20th Century USA* (Dissertation, Münster 2014).

Romesberg, Don (ed.), *The Routledge History of Queer America (New York 2019)*.

Romo, Harriett D., *Transformations of la Familia on the U.S.-Mexico Border* (Notre Dame 2008).

Rorabaugh, William J., *Berkeley at War* (New York and Oxford 1989).

Rorabaugh, William J., *Kennedy and the Promise of the Sixties* (Cambridge 2002).

Rosaldo, Michelle, "The Use and Abuse of Anthropology. Reflections on Feminism and Cross Cultural Understanding," *Signs* 5 (1980), no. 3, 392–416.

Rosas, Ana Elizabeth, *Abrazando El Espiritu. Bracero Families Confront the US-Mexico Border* (California 2014).

Rosas, Ana Elizabeth, "Breaking the Silence: Mexican Children and Women's Confrontation of Bracero Family Separation, 1942–1964," *Gender & History*, August 2011, Vol. 23, Issue 2, 382–400.

Rosenberg, C., *No Other Gods. On Science and American Social Thought* (Baltimore 1961).

Rosenberg, Rainer, Münz-Koenen, Inge, and Boden, Petra (eds.), *Der Geist der Unruhe. 1968 im Vergleich. Wissenschaft, Literatur, Medien* (Berlin 2000).

Rosenberg, Rosalind, *Beyond Separate Spheres. Intellectual Roots of Modern Feminism* (New Haven and London 1982).

Rosenberg, Rosalind, *Divided Lives. American Women in the Twentieth Century* (New York 1992).

Rosenfeld, Michael, *The Age of Independence. Interracial Unions, Same-Sex Unions, and the Changing American Family* (Cambridge 2009).

Ross, Dorothy, *The Origins of American Social Science* Cambridge (University Press, New York 1991).

Ross, Loretta and Solinger, Rickie, *Reproductive Justice. An Introduction* (Oakland, CA 2017).

Rossinow, Douglas, *The Politics of Authenticity. Liberalism, Christianity and the New Left in America* (New York 1998).

Rossiter, Margaret, *Women Scientists in America. Struggles and Strategies to 1940* (Baltimore 1982).

Roth, Benita, *Separate Roads to Feminism. Black, Chicana, and White Feminist Movements in America's Second Wave* (Cambridge 2004).

Rothman, Sheila M., *Women's Proper Place. A History of Changing Ideals and Practices, 1870 to Present* (New York 1978).

Rotundo, Anthony, *American Manhood. Transformations in Masculinity from the Revolution to the Modern Era* (New York 1994).

Rubin, Eva R., *The Supreme Court and the American Family. Ideology and Issues* (New York 1986).

Rubin, Lillian B., "Getting Younger while Getting Older. Family-Building at Midlife," in Hertz, Rosanna and Marshall, Namy L. (eds.), *Working Families. The Transformation of the American Home* (Berkeley 2001), 58–71.

Rucht, Dieter (ed.), *Research on Social Movements. The State of the Art in Western Europe and the USA* (Boulder 1991).

Ruggles, Steven, "The Transformation of American Family Structure," *American Historical Review* 99 (1994), no. 1, 103–128.

Rugh, Susan, *Are We There Yet? The Golden Age of American Family Vacations* (Lawrence 2008).

Ruiz, Vicki L., *Cannery Women, Cannery Lives. Mexican Women, Unionization, and California Food Processing Industry, 1930–1950* (Albuquerque, NM 1987).

Ruiz, Vicki L. and DuBois, Carol (eds.), *Unequal Sisters. A Multicultural Reader in U.S. Women's History* (New York 2008).

Rupp, Leila, *Mobilizing Women for War. German and American Propaganda, 1939–1945* (Princeton 1978).

Ryan, Patrick J., "How New Is the 'New' Social Study of Childhood? The Myth of a Paradigm Shift," *Journal of Interdisciplinary History* 38 (2008), no. 4, 553–576.

Ryan, Patrick J., "'Six Blacks from Home.' Childhood, Motherhood, and Eugenics in America," *The Journal of Policy History* 19 (2007), no. 3, 253–275.

Ryan, William, *Blaming the Victim* (New York 1971).

Ryan-Flood, Roisin, *Lesbian Motherhood. Gender, Families and Sexual Relationship* (Basingstoke 2009).

Ryback, Timothy W., *Hitlers Bücher. Seine Bibliothek—sein Denken* (Cologne 2010).

Rymph, Catherine E., "From 'Economic Want' to 'Family Pathology.' Foster Family Care, the New Deal and the Emergence of a Public Child Welfare System," *Journal of Policy History* 24 (2012), no. 1, 7–25.

Rymph, Catherine E., *Raising Government Children. A History of Foster Care and the American Welfare State* (Chapel Hill, NC 2017).

Rymph, Catherine E., *Republican Women, Feminism and Conservatism from Suffrage through the Rise of the New Right* (Chapel Hill 2006).

Saldern, Aldelheid von, Lüdke, Alf, and Marsolek, Inge (eds.), *Amerikanisierung. Traum und Alptraum im Deutschland des 20. Jahrhunderts* (Stuttgart 1996).

Samuel, Lawrence A., *The American Middle Class. A Cultural History* (New York 2014).

Sanchéz, George J., *Becoming Mexican American: Ethnicity, Culture, and Identity in Chicano Los Angeles* (New York and Oxford 1993).

Sanchéz, George J., "'Go after the Women'. Americanization and the Mexican Immigrant Woman, 1915–1929," in Apple, Rima and Golden, Janet (eds.), *Mothers and Motherhood. Readings in American History* (Columbus 1997), 475–494.

Sanders, Randy, "'The Sad Duty of Politics.' Jimmy Carter and the Issue of Race in his 1970 Gubernatorial Campaign," *The Georgia Historical Quarterly* 76 (1992), no. 3, 612–638.

Sanger, Carol, "Developing Markets in Baby-Making. In the Matter of Baby M," *Harvard Journal of Law and Gender* (30) 2007, 767–797.

Sarasin, Philipp, *Michel Foucault zur Einführung. 5. vollständig überarbeitete Neuausgabe* (Hamburg 2013).

Sarasin, Philipp, *Wie weiter mit Michel Foucault?* (Hamburg 2008).

Sarasin, Philipp, "Zweierlei Rassismus? Die Selektion des Fremden als Problem in Michel Foucaults Verbindung von Biopolitik und Rassismus," in Stingelin, Martin (ed.), *Biopolitik und Rassismus* (Frankfurt a. M. 2003).

Sarasohn, David, *The Party of Reform. The Democrats in the Progressive Era* (Jackson 1989).

Sartain, Lee, *Invisible Activists. Women of the Louisiana NAACP and the Struggle for Civil Rights, 1915–1945* (Baton Rouge 2007).

Saunt, Claudio, *Black, White, and Indian. Race and the Unmaking of an American Family* (Oxford 2006).
Scanlon, Jennifer, *Inarticulate Longings. The Ladies' Home Journal, Gender, and the Promises of Consumer Culture* (New York 1995).
Scanzoni, John, "Balancing the Policy Interests of Children and Adults," in Anderson, Elaine and Hula, Richard (eds.), *The Reconstruction of Family Policy* (Westport, CT 1991), 11–22.
Scanzoni, John H., *The Black Family in Modern Society. Patterns of Stability and Security* (Chicago 1977).
Schäfer, Axel R., *American Progressives and German Social Reform, 1875-1920. Social Ethics, Moral Control, and the Regulatory State in a Transatlantic Context* (Stuttgart 2000).
Schäfer, Peter, *Alltag in den Vereinigten Staaten. Von der Kolonialzeit bis zur Gegenwart* (Graz 1998).
Schermer, Elisabeth Tandy, "Origins of the Conservative Ascendancy. Barry Goldwater's Early Senate Career and the De-legitimization of Organized Labor," *The Journal of American History* 95 (2008), no. 3, 678–709.
Schildt, Georg, *Zwischen Freiheit des Einzelnen und Wohlfahrtsstaat. Amerikanische Sozialpolitik im 20. Jahrhundert* (Paderborn 2003).
Schivelbusch, Wolfgang, *Entfernte Verwandtschaft. Faschismus, Nationalsozialismus, New Deal, 1933-1939* (Munich 2005).
Schlimm, Annette, *Verkehrsraum—Sozialer Raum. Social Engineering und die Ordnung der Gesellschaft im 20. Jahrhundert* (Bielefeld 2011).
Schmuhl, Hans-Walter, *Rassenkunde, Nationalsozialismus, Euthanasie. Von der Verhütung zur Vernichtung "lebensunwerten Lebens," 1890-1945* (Göttingen 1987).
Schneider, Gregory L., *American Conservatism since the 1930s. A Reader* (New York 2003).
Schneider, Gregory L., *Cadres for Conservatism. Young Americans for Freedom and the Rise of the Contemporary Right* (New York 1999).
Schoen, Johanna, *Abortion after Roe* (Chapel Hill 2015).
Schoen, Johanna, *Choice and Coercion. Birth Control, Sterilization and Abortion in Public Health and Welfare*, University of North Carolina Press (Chapel Hill 2005).
Schoen, Johanna, "Choice and Coercion. Women and the Politics of Sterilization in North Carolina, 1929-1975," *Journal of Women's History* 13 (2001), no. 1, 132–156.
Schoen, Johanna, "From the Footnotes to the Headlines: Sterilization Apologies and Their Lessons," *Sexuality Research and Social Policy* 3 (2006), no. 3 <doi:10.1525/srsp.2006.3.3.7.>
Schrecker, Ellen, *Many are the Crimes. McCarthyism in America* (Boston 1998).
Schrecker, Ellen, *The Age of McCarthyism. A Brief History with Documents* (Boston 1994).
Schulman, Bruce, *The Seventies. The Great Shift in American Culture, Society, and Politics* (New York 2001).
Schulman, Bruce and Zelizer, Julian (eds.), *Rightward Bound. Making America Conservative in the 1970s* (Harvard 2008).
Schumann, Dirk (ed.), *Raising Citizens in the "Century of the Child." The United States and German Central Europe in Comparative Perspective* (New York 2010).
Schwartz, Barry (ed.), *The Changing Face of the Suburbs* (Chicago and London 1976).
Schwartz, Richard Alan, *Cold War Culture. Media and the Arts, 1945-1990* (New York 1998).
Scott, Anne Firor, *Natural Allies. Women's Associations in American History* (Urbana 1991).
Scott, James C., *Seeing Like a State. How Certain Schemes to Improve the Human Condition Have Failed* (New Haven 1998).
Scott, Joan W., "Gender. A Useful Category of Historical Analysis," *American Historical Review* 91 (1986), no. 5, 1053–1075.
Scott, Joan W., "Gender. Eine nützliche Kategorie der historischen Analyse," in Kaiser, Nancy (ed.), *Selbst Bewusst. Frauen in den USA* (Leipzig 1994), 27–75.

Scott, Joan W., "Millenial Fantasies. The Future of 'Gender' in the 21st Century," in Honegger, Claudia and Arni, Caroline (eds.), *Gender. Die Tücken einer Kategorie* (Zürich 2001), 19–38.
Scott, Joan W., "Unanswered Questions, Contribution to AHR Forum, Revisiting 'Gender: A Useful Category of Historical Analysis,'" *American Historical Review* 113 (2008), no. 5, 1422–1430.
Sealander, Judith, *The Failed Century of the Child. Governing America's Young in the Twentieth Century* (Cambridge 2003).
Segalen, Martine, *Die Familie. Geschichte, Soziologie, Anthropologie* (Frankfurt a. M. 1990).
Selden, Steven, "Transforming Better Babies into Fitter Families. Archival Resources and the History of American Eugenics Movement, 1908–1930," *Proceedings of the American Philosophical Society* 149 (2005), no. 2, 199–225.
Self, Robert O., *All in the Family. The Realignment of American Democracy since the 1960s* (New York 2012).
Seward, Rudy R., *The American Family. A Demographic History* (Beverly Hills 1978).
Sharp, Lawrence J. and Nye, F. Ivan, "Maternal Mental Health," in Nye, F. Ivan and Hoffman, Lois Wladis, *The Employed Mother in America* 309–319.
Shaw, David Gary, "The Return of Science," *History and Theory* 38 (1999), no. 4, 1–10.
Shepard, Alexandra and Walker, Garthine (eds.), *Gender and Change. Agency Chronology and Periodization* (Malden 2009).
Shore, Bradd, *Culture in Mind. Cognition, Culture, and the Problem of Meaning* (New York 1996).
Sidbury, James, *Becoming African in America. Race and Nation in the Early Black Atlantic* (Oxford 2009).
Sidel, Ruth, *Unsung Heroines. Single Mothers and the American Dream* (Berkeley and Los Angeles 2006).
Siff, Ezra Y., *Why the Senate Slept. The Gulf of Tonkin Resolution and the Beginning of America's Vietnam War* (Westport 1999).
Silliman, Jael, Gerber Fried, Marlene, Ross, Loretta and Gutiérrez, Elena R. (eds.), *Undivided Rights. Women of Color Organizing for Reproductive Justice* (New York 2004).
Silva, Elizabeth B., "The Cook, the Cooker and the Gendering of the Kitchen," *Sociological Review* 48 (2001), no. 4, 612–628.
Singh, Gopal K. and van Dyck, Peter C., *Infant Mortality in the United States, 1935–2007. Our Seven Decades of Progress and Disparities*. U.S. Department of Health and Human Services, Health Resources and Service Administration, Maternal and Child Health Bureau (Rockville, Maryland 2010) <www.mchb.hrsa.gov>.
Sisson, Gretchen and Kimport, Katrina, "Telling Stories About Abortion. Abortion Related Plots in American Film and Television, 1916–2013," *Contraception* 89 (2014), 413–418.
Sitkoff, Harvard, *A New Deal for Blacks. The Emergence of Civil Rights as a National Issue*, vol. 1, *The Depression Decade* (New York 1978).
Sitkoff, Harvard (ed.), *Fifty Years Later. The New Deal Evaluated* (Philadelphia 1985).
Sitkoff, Harvard (ed.), *Perspectives on Modern America. Making Sense of the Twentieth Century* (New York and Oxford 2001).
Sitkoff, Harvard, *The Struggle for Black Equality 1954–1992* (New York 1993).
Sklar, Martin J., *United States as a Developing Country. Studies in U.S. History in the Progressive Era and the 1920s* (Cambridge 1992).
Skolnick, Arlene, *Embattled Paradise. The American Family in an Age of Uncertainty* (New York 1991).
Skolnick, Arlene, *The Intimate Environment. Exploring Marriage and the Family* (Boston 1987).
Skolnick, Arlene S. and Skolnick, Jerome H. (eds.), *Family in Transition. Rethinking Marriage, Sexuality, Child Rearing and Family Organization* (Boston 1971).
Skolnick, Arlene S. and Skolnick, Jerome H. (eds.), *Intimacy, Family, and Society* (Boston 1974).
Smith, Beretta Eileen, *Shaded Lives. Objectification and Agency in the Television Representation of African-American Women, 1980–1994* (Los Angeles 1997).

Smith, Daniel Scott, "Recent Change and the Periodization of American Family History," *Journal of Family History* 20 (1995), no. 4, 329–346.
Smith, Daniel Scott, "The Meanings of Family and Household. Change and Continuity in the Mirror of the American Census," *Population and Development Review* 18 (1992), no. 3, 421–456.
Smith, Geoffrey S., "National Security and Personal Isolation. Sex, Gender and Disease in the Cold War United States," *International History Review* 14 (1992), no. 2, 1–15.
Smith, Shawn Michelle, *American Archives. Gender, Race, and Class in Visual Culture* (Princeton 1999).
Smith, Tony, *America's Mission. The United States and the Worldwide Struggle for Democracy in the Twentieth Century* (Princeton 1994).
Smulyan, Susan, *Popular Ideologies. Mass Culture at Mid-Century* (Pennsylvania 2007).
Snay, Mitchell, *Horace Greeley and the Politics of Reform in Nineteenth Century America* (Lanham etc. 2011).
Sokoll, Thomas, "Historische Demographie und historische Sozialwissenschaft," *Archiv für Sozialgeschichte* 32 (1992), 405–425.
Sokoll, Thomas and Gehrmann, Rolf, "Historische Demographie und quantitative Methoden," in Maurer, Michael (ed.), *Aufriß der Historischen Wissenschaften*, vol. 7 (Stuttgart 2003), 152–229.
Solinger, Rickie (ed.), *Abortion Wars. A Half Century of Struggle, 1950–2000* (Berkeley 1998).
Solinger, Rickie, *Beggars and Choosers. How the Politics of Choice Shapes Adoption, Abortion, and Welfare in the United States* (New York 2001).
Solinger, Rickie, *Pregnancy and Power. A Short History of Reproductive Politics in America* (New York 2007).
Solinger, Rickie, *Wake up, little Suzie. Single Pregnancy before Roe vs. Wade* (New York 1992).
Solinger, Rickie and Nakachi, Mie, *Reproductive States. Global Perspectives on the Invention and Implementation of Population Policy* (New York 2016).
Sorensen, John and Sealander, Judith (eds.), *The Grace Abbott Reader* (Lincoln 2008).
Southern, David W., *Gunnar Myrdal and Black-White Relations. The Use and Abuse of An American Dilemma, 1944–1969* (Baton Rouge and London 1987).
Spain, Daphne and Bianchi, Suzanne, *Balancing Act. Motherhood, Marriage, and Employment among American Women* (New York 1996).
Spangler, Lynn, *Television Women from Lucy to Friends. Fifty Years of Sitcoms and Feminism* (Westport 2003).
Spelman, Elizabeth, *Inessential Woman. Problems of Exclusion in Feminist Thought* (Boston 1988).
Spender, Stephen, *The Year of the Young Rebels* (Berkeley 1984).
Speth, Linda E, "The Married Women's Property Acts, 1839–1865: Reform, Reaction, or Revolution?," in Lindgren, J. Ralph et al. (eds.), *The Law of Sex Discrimination* (Wadsworth 2011), 12–15.
Spigel, Lynn, *Make Room for TV. Television and the Family Ideal in Postwar America* (Chicago and London 1992).
Spiro, Jonathan P., *Defending the Master Race. Conservation, Eugenics, and the Legacy of Madison Grant* (Hannover 2008).
Springer, Kimberly, *Living for the Revolution. Black Feminists Organizations, 1968–1980* (Durham 2005).
Stacey, Judith, *Brave New Families. Stories of Domestic Upheaval in Late Twentieth Century America* (New York 1990).
Stacey, Judith, "Good Riddance to 'the Family'. A Response to David Popenoe," *Journal of Marriage and the Family* 55 (1993), no. 3, 545–547.
Stacey, Judith, *In the Name of the Family. Rethinking Family Values in the Postmodern Age* (Boston 1996).
Stacey, Judith, *Unhitched—Love, Marriage, and Family Values from West Hollywood to Western China* (New York 2011).
Staggenborg, Suzanne, *The Pro-Choice Movement. Organization and Activism in the Abortion Conflict* (New York 1991).

Stansell, Christine, *The Feminist Promise. 1792 to the Present* (New York 2010).
Starr, Kevin, *Inventing the Dream. California through the Progressive Era* (Oxford 1985).
Starrels, Marjorie E., Bould, Sally, and Nicholas, Leon J., "The Feminization of Poverty in the United States. Gender, Race, Ethnicity, and Family Factors," *Journal of Family Issues* 15 (1994), no. 4, 590–607.
Stebner, Eleanor J., *The Women of Hull House. A Study in Spirituality, Vocation, and Friendship* (Albany 1997).
Stein, Marc, *Sexual Injustice. Supreme Court Decisions from Griswold to Roe* (Chapel Hill 2010).
Stemmer, Peter, "Die Rechtfertigung moralischer Normen," *Zeitschrift für Philosophische Forschung* 58, no. 4 (2004), 483–504.
Stern, Alexandra Minna, "Beauty is not Always Better. Perfect Babies and the Tyranny of Pediatric Norms," *Patterns of Prejudice* 36 (2002), no. 1, 68–78.
Stern, Alexandra Minna, *Eugenic Nation. Faults and Frontiers of Better Breeding in Modern America* (Berkeley 2005).
Stern, Alexandra Minna, "Gender and the Far-Right in the United States: Female Extremists and the Mainstreaming of Contemporary White Nationalism," *Journal of Modern European History*, 20(3), 322–334. DOI: 10.1177/16118944221110101.
Stern, Alexandra Minna, "Making Better Babies. Public Health and Race Betterment in Indiana, 1920–1935," *American Journal of Public Health* 92 (2002), no. 5, 742–752.
Stern, Alexandra Minna, *Telling Genes. The Story of Genetic Counseling in America* (Baltimore 2012).
Stern, Alexandra Minna and Markel, Howard (eds.), *Formative Years. The History of Children's Health in the United States, 1880–2000* (Ann Arbor 2002).
Stevenson, Brenda E., *Life in Black and White. Family and Community in the Slave South* (New York 1996).
Stieglitz, Olaf, "Is Mom to Blame? Anti-Communist Law-Enforcement and the Representation of Motherhood in Early Cold War U.S. Film," in Heinemann, Isabel (ed.), *Inventing the Modern American Family. Family Values and Social Change in 20th Century USA* (Frankfurt a. M. and New York 2012), 244–264.
Stone, Pamela, *Opting Out. Why Women Really Quit Careers and Head Home* (Berkeley 2008).
Strasser, Susan, *Never Done. A History of American Housework* (New York 1982).
Strasser, Susan, *Satisfaction Guaranteed. The Making of the American Mass Market* (New York 1989).
Stremlau, Rose, "'To Domesticate and Civilize Wild Indians'. Allotment and the Campaign to Reform Indian Families, 1875–1887," *Journal of Family History* 30 (2005), no. 3, 265–286.
Stryker, Susan, *Transgender History. The Roots of Today's Revolution* (revised edition, Boston 2017, first edition 2008).
Sudarkasa, Niara, "Family. African Roots," in Salzman, Jack, Smith, David Lionel, and West, Cornel (eds.), *Encyclopedia of Afro-American Culture and History*, vol. 2 (New York et al. 1996), 928–932.
Sudarkasa, Niara, "Interpreting the African Heritage in Afro-American Family Organziation," in McAdoo, Harriette P. (ed.), *Black Families* (Thousand Oaks 1997), 9–40.
Sufian, Sandra M., *Familial Fitness: Disability, Adoption, and Family in Modern America* (Chicago 2022).
Sugrue, Thomas J., "Crabgrass-Roots Politics. Race, Rights and the Reaction against Liberalism in the Urban North, 1940–1964," *Journal of American History* 82 (1995), no. 2, 551–578.
Sullivan, Patricia, *Days of Hope. Race and Democracy in the New Deal Era* (Chapel Hill 1996).
Sweet, James A., "Indicators of Family and Household Structure of Racial and Ethnic Minorities in the United States," in Bean, Frank D. and Frisbie, W. Parker (eds.), *The Demography of Racial and Ethnic Groups* (New York 1978), 221–259.
Taylor, Ella, *Prime Time Families. Television Culture in Postwar America* (Berkeley and Los Angeles and London 1989).

Taylor, Henry Louis, *Historical Roots of the Urban Crisis. African Americans in the Industrial City, 1900–1950* (New York and London 2000).
Taylor, Paul, *The Decline of Marriage and the Rise of New Families* (PEW Research Center 2010) <www.pewsocialtrends.org/files/2010/11/pew-social-trends-2010-families.pdf>.
Terry, Jennifer, "'Momism' and the Making of Treasonous Homosexuals," in Ladd-Taylor, Molly and Umansky, Lauri (eds.), *Bad Mothers. The Politics of Blame in Twentieth-Century America* (New York 1998), 169–190.
Testi, Arnaldo, "The Gender of Reform Politics. Theodore Roosevelt and the Culture of Masculinity," *Journal of American History* 81, no. 4 (1995), 1509–1533.
Tetrault, Lisa, *The Myth of Seneca Falls: Memory and the Women's Suffrage Movement* (Chapel Hill 2014).
Thistle, Susan, *From Marriage to the Market. The Transformation of Women's Lives and Work* (California 2006).
Thomas, Susan L., "Race, Gender, and Welfare Reform. The Antinatalist Response," *Journal of Black Studies* 28 (1998), no. 4, 419–446.
Thomas-Maddox, Candice and Blau, Nicole, "We're not like the Cleavers Anymore. Diversity and Parenting Communication in ABC's Modern Family," in González, Alberto and Harris, Tina M. (eds.), *Mediating Cultures. Parenting in Intercultural Contexts* (Lanham, MD 2013), 109–121.
Thome, Helmut, "Ein von Niklas Luhmann inspirierter Vorschlag für die engere Verknüpfung von Theorie und Empirie," *Zeitschrift für Soziologie* 32,1 (2003), 4–28.
Thome, Helmut, "Wandel zu postmaterialistischen Werten? Theoretische und empirische Einwände gegen Ingleharts Theorie-Versuch," *Soziale Welt* 1 (1985), 27–59.
Thompson, Linda, "Conceptualizing Gender in Marriage. The Case of Maternal Care," *Journal of Marriage and the Family* 55 (1993), no. 3, 557–569.
Thomson, Irene Taviss, *Culture Wars and Enduring American Dilemmas* (Ann Arbor 2010).
Thornton, Arland, "Changing Attitudes Toward Family Issues in the United States," *Journal of Marriage and the Family* 51 (1989), no. 4, 873–893.
Thornton, Arland and Young-DeMarco, Linda, "Four Decades of Trends in Attitudes toward Family Issues in the United States. The 1960s through the 1990s," *Journal of Marriage and the Family* 63 (2001), no. 4, 1009–1037.
Tipton, Steven M. and Witte Jr., John (eds.), *Family Transformed. Religion, Values, and Society in American Life* (Washington 2007).
Tischler, Barbara L., *Sights on the Sixties* (New Brunswick 1992).
Tobey, Ronald C., *Technology as Freedom. The New Deal and the Electrical Modernization of the American Home* (Berkeley 1996).
Tomaschke, Dirk, *In der Gesellschaft der Gene. Räume und Subjekte der Humangenetik in Deutschland und Dänemark, 1950–1990* (Bielefeld 2014).
Tone, Andrea (ed.), *Controlling Reproduction. An American History* (Wilmington 1997).
Tone, Andrea, *Devices and Desires. A History of Contraceptives in America* (New York 2002).
Tone, Andrea, *The Age of Anxiety. A History of America's Turbulent Affair with Tranquilizers* (New York 2009).
Tosh, John, "Hegemonic Masculinity and the History of Gender," in Dudink, Stefan, Hagemann, Karen, and Tosh, John (eds.), *Masculinities and Politics in War. Gendering Modern History* (New York 2004), 41–58.
Traister, Bryce, "Academic Viagra. The Rise of American Masculinity Studies," *American Quarterly* 52 (2000), no. 2, 274–304.
Trotha, Trutz von, "Zum Wandel der Familie," *Kölner Zeitschrift für Soziologie und Sozialpsychologie* 42 (1990), no. 3, 452–473.
Troy, Gil, *Morning in America. How Reagan Invented the 1980s* (New York 2005).

Troy, Gil, *The Reagan Revolution. A Very Short Introduction* (Oxford and New York 2009).
Tucker, Lauren R., "Was the Revolution Televised? Professional Criticism about 'The Cosby Show' and the Essentialization of Black Cultural Expression," *Journal of Broadcasting & Electronic Media* 41 (1997), no. 1, 90–109.
Tufte, Virginia, *Changing Images of the Family* (New Haven 1979).
Tygiel, Jules, *Ronald Reagan and the Triumph of American Conservatism* (New York 2006).
Umansky, Lauri, *Motherhood Reconceived. Feminism and the Legacies of the Sixties* (New York 1996).
Unger, Corinna, "Family Planning. A Rational Choice? The Influence of Systems Approaches, Behavioralism, and Rational Choice Thinking on Mid-twentieth Century Family Planning Programs," in: Hartmann, Heinrich and Unger, Corinna (eds.), *A World of Populations. Transnational Perspectives on Demography in the Twentieth Century* (New York 2014), 58–82.
Utter, Glenn H. and Storey, John (ed.), *The Religious Right. A Reference Handbook* (Millerton 2007).
Valk, Anne, *Radical Sisters. Second-Wave Feminism and Black Liberation in Washington D. C.* (Urbana 2008).
Van Horn, Susan Householder, *Women, Work and Fertility 1900–1986* (New York 1988).
Vance Dorey, Annette K., *Better Babies Contests. The Scientific Quest for Perfect Childhood Health in the Early Twentieth Century* (Jefferson 1999).
Vandenberg-Davis, Jodi, *Modern Motherhood. An American History* (New Brunswick, NJ 2014).
Varenne, Hervé, "Love and Liberty. Die moderne amerikanische Familie," in Burguiere, André (ed.), *Geschichte der Familie*, vol. 4, *20. Jahrhundert* (Frankfurt a. M., New York and Paris 1998), 59–90.
Vatter, Harold G. (ed.), *History of the U.S. Economy since World War II* (Armonk 1996).
Vatter, Harold G., *The US Economy in the 1950s. An Economic History* (Chicago 1985).
Velez-Ibañez, Carlos G., "Se me acabó la canción. An Ethnography of Non-consenting Sterilizations among Mexican Women in Los Angeles," in Del Castillo, Adelaida R. and Mora, Magdalena (eds.), *Mexican Women in the United States. Struggles Past and Present* (Los Angeles 1980), 71–91.
Verburgge, Martha H., *Active Bodies. A History of Women's Physical Education in Twentieth-Century America* (New York 2012).
Victor, Barbara, *Beten im Oval Office. Christlicher Fundamentalismus in den USA und die internationale Politik* (Munich and Zürich 2005).
Villie, Charles V., *Black and White Families. A Study in Complementarity* (New York 1985).
Von Eschen, Penny M., *Race Against Empire. Black Americans and Anticolonialism, 1937–1957* (Ithaca 1997).
Waddell, Brian, *The War against the New Deal. World War II and American Democracy* (DeKalb 2001).
Waite, Linda J. and Nielsen, Mark, "The Rise of the Dual-Earner Family, 1963–1997," in Hertz, Rosanna and Marshall, Namy L. (eds.), *Working Families. The Transformation of the American Home* (Berkeley 2001), 23–41.
Walgenbach, Katharina, "Gender als interdependente Kategorie," in Walgenbach, Katharina (ed.), *Gender als interdependente Kategorie. Neue Perspektiven auf Intersektionalität, Diversität und Heterogenität* (Opladen 2007), 23–64.
Walker, Nancy, *Shaping our Mothers' World. American Women's Magazines* (Jackson 2000).
Walker, Susannah, *Style and Status. Selling Beauty to African American Women, 1920–1975* (Lexington 2007).
Wallerstein, Judith S. and Blakeslee, Sandra, *Second Chances. Men, Women, and Children a Decade after Divorce* (New York 1989).
Wandersee, Winifred D., *Women's Work and Family Values, 1920–1940* (Cambridge 1981).
Warren, Holly George, *The Rolling Stone Book of the Beats. The Beat Generation and the Counterculture* (London 1999).
Watkins, Elizabeth Siegel, *On the Pill. A Social History of Oral Contraceptives, 1950–1970* (Baltimore 1998).
Watson, Jamie and Arp, Robert, *What's Good on TV? Understanding Ethics through Television* (Malden 2011).

Watts, Trent, *White Masculinity in the Recent South* (Kansas 2008).
Weber, Paul J. and Landis Jones, W. (eds.), *U.S. Religious Interest Groups. Institutional Profiles* (Westport and London 1994).
Weber-Kellermann, Ingeborg, *Die Familie. Geschichte, Geschichten und Bilder* (Frankfurt a. M. 1990).
Weidemann, Doris, *Leben und Werk von Therese Benedek 1892–1977. Weibliche Sexualität und Psychologie des Weiblichen* (Frankfurt a. M. 1988).
Weigel-Klinck, Nicole, "'Sir, do we get to win this time?' Die Aufarbeitung des Vietnamkrieges im US-amerikanischen Spielfilm," *1999* 17 (2002), no. 2, 44–72.
Weiler, Michael (ed.), *Reagan and Public Discourse in America* (Tuscaloosa 1992).
Weiner, Lynn, *From Working Girl to Working Mother. The Female Labor Force in the United States, 1820–1980* (Chapel Hill 1985).
Weisbrot, Robert, *Freedom Bound. A History of America's Civil Rights Movement* (New York 1990).
Weiss, Heather B. (ed.), *Evaluating Family Programs* (New York 1988).
Weiss, Jessica, "'A Drop-In Catering Job'. Middle-Class Women and Fatherhood, 1950–1980," *Journal of Family History* 24 (1999), no. 3, 374–390.
Weiss, Jessica, *To Have and to Hold. Marriage, the Baby Boom and Social Change* (Chicago and London 2000).
Weiss, Nancy Pottishman, "Mother, the Invention of Necessity. Doctor Benjamin Spock's Baby and Child Care," *American Quarterly* 29 (1977), no. 5, 519–546.
Weitzman, Lenore J., *The Divorce Revolution. The Unexpected Social and Economic Consequences for Women and Children in America* (New York 1985).
Weitzman, Lenore J. and Maclean, Mavis (eds.), *Economic Consequences of Divorce. The International Perspective* (Oxford 1992).
Wellman, Judith, *The Road to Seneca Falls: Elizabeth Cady Stanton and the First Woman's Rights Convention* (Urbana 2004).
Welskopp, Thomas and Lessoff, Alan, *Fractured Modernity. America Confronts Modern Times, 1890s to 1940s* (Munich 2013).
Welter, Barbara, "The Cult of True Womanhood 1820–1860," *American Quarterly* 18 (1966), no. 2, part 1, 151–174.
Wendt, Simon, "Gewalt und Männlichkeit in der Black Power Bewegung," in Martschukat, Jürgen and Stieglitz, Olaf (eds.), *Väter, Soldaten, Liebhaber. Männer und Männlichkeiten in der Geschichte Nordamerikas* (Bielefeld 2007), 355–369.
Wendt, Simon, "'They Finally Found Out that We Really Are Men'. Violence, Non-Violence and Black Manhood in the Civil Rights Era," *Gender & History* 19 (2007), 543–564.
Wesley C. Hogan, *Many Minds, One Heart. SNCCs Dream for a New America* (Chapel Hill 2007).
Westby, David L., *The Clouded Vision. The Student Movement in the United States in the 1960s* (Lewisburg 1976).
Weston, Kathleen, *Families We Choose. Lesbians, Gays, Kinship* (New York 1991).
Wetzel, James R., "American Families. 75 Years of Change," *Monthly Labor Review* 113 (1990), no. 3, 4–13.
Whitfield, Stephen J., *The Culture of the Cold War* (Baltimore 1991).
Wickberg, Daniel, "Heterosexual White Male. Some Recent Inversions in American Cultural History," *The Journal of American History* 92 (2005), no. 1, 136–159.
Wilcox, Clyde, *God's Warriors* (Baltimore 1992).
Wilcox, Clyde, *Onward Christian Soldiers. The Religious Right in American Politics* (Boulder 1996).
Willekens, Harry (ed.), *Family Law. The Present's Past and the Past's Present* (Thousand Oaks 2003), 4–13.

Willems, Herbert, *Rahmen und Habitus. Zum theoretischen und methodischen Ansatz Erving Goffmans, Vergleiche, Anschlüsse und Anwendungen* (Berlin 1997).
Willems, Ulrich et al. (ed.), *Moderne und Religion. Kontroversen um Modernität und Säkularisierung* (Bielefeld 2013).
Wilmoth, John R. and Ball, Patrick, "The Population Debate in American Popular Magazines, 1946–1990," *Population and Development Review* 18 (1992), no. 4, 631–668.
Wilson, William J., *The Truly Disadvantaged. The Inner City, the Underclass, and Public Policy* (Chicago 1987).
Winters, Donald E., *The Soul of the Wobblies. The I. W., W., Religion, and American Culture in the Progressive Era, 1905–1917* (Westport 1985).
Wirsching, Andreas, *Agrarischer Protest und Krise der Familie. Zwei Versuche zur Geschichte der Moderne* (Wiesbaden 2004).
Wisensale, Steven K., *Family Leave Policy: The Political Economy of Work and Family in America* (New York 2015).
Witkowski, Jan A., *Davenport's Dream. 21st Century Reflections on Heredity and Eugenics* (New York 2008).
Witte, James C, *Labor Force Integration and Marital Choices in the United States and Germany* (Frankfurt a. M. and Boulder 1992).
Wittner, Lawrence S., *Resisting the Bomb. A History of the World Nuclear Disarmament Movement, 1954–1970* (Stanford 1997).
Wofford, Harris, *Of Kennedys and Kings. Making Sense of the Sixties* (New York 1980).
Wolf, Thomas P., Pederson, William D., and Daynes, Byron W. (eds.), *Franklin D. Roosevelt and Congress. The New Deal and Its Aftermath* (Armonk 2000).
Wolfrum, Edgar, *Die geglückte Demokratie. Geschichte der Bundesrepublik Deutschland von ihren Anfängen bis zur Gegenwart* (Stuttgart 2006).
Wollons, Roberta (ed.), *Kindergartens and Cultures. The Global Diffusion of an Idea* (New Haven 2000).
Wright, James D., "The Political Consciousness of Post-Industrialism. The Silent Revolution. Changing Values and Political Styles Among Western Publics by Ronald Inglehart," *Contemporary Sociology* 7 (1978), no. 3, 270–273.
Wuthnow, Robert and Evans, John H. (eds.), *The Quiet Hand of God. Faith-Based Activism and the Public Role of Mainline Protestantism* (Berkeley et al. 2002).
Wynn, Neil A., *From Progressivism to Prosperity. World War I and American Society* (New York 1986).
Yamin, Priscilla, *American Marriage. A Political Institution* (Philadelphia 2012).
Yuill, Kevin L., "The 1966 White House Conference on Civil Rights," *The Historical Journal* 41 (1998), no. 1, 259–282.
Zamir, Shamoon (ed.), *The Cambridge Companion to W. E. B. Du Bois* (Cambridge et al. 2008).
Zapf, Wolfgang (ed.), *Die Modernisierung moderner Gesellschaften. Verhandlungen des 25. Deutschen Soziologentages in Frankfurt a. M. 1990* (Frankfurt a. M. and New York 1991).
Zaretsky, Eli, *Secrets of the Soul. A Social and Cultural History of Psychoanalysis* (New York 2004).
Zaretsky, Natasha, *No Direction Home. The American Family and the Fear of National Decline, 1968–1980* (Philadelphia 2007).
Zavella, Patricia, *Women's Work and Chicano Families. Cannery Workers of the Santa Clara Valley* (Ithaca 1987).
Zeul, Mechthild, "Der unmögliche Dialog. Versuch einer psychoanalytischen Deutung von Kramer gegen Kramer," *Arnoldshainer Filmgespräche* vol. 5 (Frankfurt a. M. 1988), 66–75.
Ziegler, Mary Joe, *Abortion and the Law in America: Roe v. Wade to the Present* (Cambridge 2022).
Ziegler, Mary Joe, *After Roe. The Lost History of the Abortion Debate* (Cambridge and London 2015).
Ziegler, Mary Joe, "Roe v. Wade and the Rise of Arguments," in Ziegler, Mary Joe, *Abortion and the Law in America: Roe v. Wade to the Present* (Cambridge 2022), 11–26.

Zimmerman, Jonathan, *Too Hot to Handle. A Global History of Sex Education* (Princeton 2015).
Zimmermann, Christine, *Familie als Konfliktfeld im amerikanischen Kulturkampf. Eine Diskursanalyse* (Wiesbaden 2010).
Zolberg, Aristide, *A Nation by Design: Immigration Policy in the Fashioning of America* (Cambridge, MA 2006).
Zunz, Olivier (ed.), *Social Contracts under Stress. The Middle Classes of America, Europe and Japan at the Turn of the Century* (New York 2002).

Person Index

Abbott, Grace 112
Abernathy, Ralph D. 255
Almond, Gabriel 17
Ammon, Otto 115
Anderson, Carole J. 379
Anderson, Karen 160
Andrews, Stephen Pearl 53
Avery, Byllye 341

Bailey, Beth 278
Ballantine, William Gay 83
Barr, Amelia Edith 57–60
Barton, Paul 235
Bauer, Gary L. 356, 397
Baumann, Zygmunt 35
Beale, Frances 208–210, 266f., 292, 321, 403
Beck, Ulrich 19
Benedek, Therese 186–188
Benedict, Ruth 158
Birney, Alice McLellan 110
Bix, Amy 127
Blackmun, Harry A. 296
Bolzendahl, Catherine 10
Boudreaux, Jackie 245
Bourdieu, Pierre 23
Broderick, Ellen 235
Bronfenbrenner, Urie 242
Brown, Helen Gurley 278
Buck, Carrie 133–137
Burton, Ernest DeWitt 83f.
Bush, George 365
Butler, Judith 23

Califano, Joseph A. 321, 331
Campbell, Lee 378f.
Capper, Arthur 79
Carr, John 348
Carter, Jimmy 345, 347, 408
Cayton, Horace R. 225
Chappel, Marisa 322, 408
Cherlin, Andrew J. 10
Chisholm, Shirley 268, 288
Cisler, Lucinda 290
Clarenbach, Kathryn F. 288

Clark, Kenneth B. 232, 238–240, 257, 261
Cleaver, Eldridge 264f.
Coffee, Linda 295
Cohen, Robert 99
Cohn, David L. 176
Collier, Virginia McMakin 117
Collins, Patricia Hill 24, 342
Connell, Raewyn 25
Connor, Sandra O'Day 364
Cook, Robert C. 37, 276, 309–311, 316
Cooke, Rose Terry 57, 59
Coontz, Stephanie 29, 31, 200
Cooper, Frankie 162

Dalton, Richard C. 343–345
Davenport, Charles Benedikt 79, 97, 101, 118, 127
DeCrow, Karen 288
Degler, Carl 229
Dejarnette, Dr. J. S. 135
Deth, Jan van 16
Dike, Samuel A. 37
Dike, Samuel W. 44, 54–56, 60f., 83, 85–87, 93
Dill, Bonnie Thornton 24
Doane, William Croswell 61, 82f.
Douthat, Ross 1
Draper, William H. 312
DuBois, William Edward Burghardt 217–220, 226, 235
Durkheim, Emile 16
Dye, Sarah 4

Efron, Edith 166f.
Eisenstadt, Shmuel N. 35
Estes, Steve 264f.
Etzemüller, Thomas 27, 42

Farnham, Marynia 185, 187
Fenton, Janet 385
Findley, Maude 271
Finzsch, Norbert 258, 408
Firestone, Shulamit 292
Foucault, Michel 27, 30, 33, 158, 258, 315, 388
Franklin, John Hope 228

Frazier, Edward Franklin 219–221, 224, 226, 230, 232, 237, 238, 258
Freud, Sigmund 167
Friedan, Betty 37, 191, 196–200, 286, 289, 401
Fromm, Erich 158

Gaither, Frances 225
Gall, Mary 383f.
Galton, Francis 69, 115, 118, 131
Garmo, Mary De 125
Gartner, Alan 246, 253
Geist, Claudia 10
Gibbons, James Cardinal 56f., 59, 82, 91
Gidding, Lee 302, 304
Gillies, Mary Davis 169
Gilman, Charlotte Perkins 44, 71, 74, 326
Glazer, Nathan 237f., 257f.
Golding, Illiam H. 177
Goldstein, Ellen 349f.
Goodman, David 37, 187f.
Goodwin, Richard M. 231
Gosney, Ezra Seymour 131f., 143
Grant, Madison 118
Greeley, Horace 53
Griswold, Robert L. 93
Grube, Norbert 19
Guttmacher, Alan F. 279f., 283, 309, 313

Haiselden, Dr. Harry J. 137
Harrington, Michael 232, 264
Harris, Patricia Robert 349
Hartman, Susan M. 162
Hausen, Karin 23
Hauser, Philip 261
Hawley, James H. 78
Haworth, Mary 169, 180
Heide, Wilma Scott 305
Herbert, Ulrich 34
Higginbotham, Evelyn Brooks 24
Hill, Herbert 241
Hitler, Adolf 119
Hodenberg, Christina von 21, 408
Hoffman, Lois Wladis 191f., 196
Holmes Jr., Oliver Wendell 134
Horney, Karen 158, 166f.

Howard, George Elliott 44, 64–66, 69, 77, 84, 88, 91, 93, 326
Hutchinson, Woods 76f.

Ingersoll, Robert G. 59, 91
Inglehart, Ronald 17–19, 21

Jackson, Walter A. 223
James Jr., Henry 53
Joas, Hans 19
Johnson, John H. 204
Johnson, Lyndon B. 230, 339, 358, 399
Johnson, Roswell H. 101, 129, 140, 148
Johnson, Virginia 184, 277
June, Jennie (Cunningham Croly, Jane) 57

Kardiner, Abraham 158
Keating, Kenneth B. 312
Kennedy, John F. 285
Key, Ellen 114
Keyserling, Mary 205
Khrushchev, Nikita 173
Kimmel, Michael 25, 209, 408
Kindleberger-Stone, Betty 311
King, Martin Luther 37, 247, 251, 260, 263
Kinsey, Alfred 184, 276
Kluckhohn, Clyde 16
Knapp, Gudrun-Axeli 24
Koedt, Anne 292
Komarovsky, Mirra 37, 99, 189–191, 196, 198, 201
Koop, C. Everett 365
Kottmeier, Karen 376, 382
Krock, Arthur 252
Kupinski, Stanley 194

Ladd-Taylor, Molly 114
Lader, Lawrence 303–305
Lance, Candace 323f.
LaRossa, Ralph 99
Lathrop, Julia 111–113
Laughlin, Harry H. 97, 118, 132–134
Lear, Norman 6, 271, 302, 316
Lee, Margaret 57
Lerner, Gerda 200
Lessoff, Alan 35f.
Lewis, Hylan G. 250, 260

Lewis, Laura 385
Lewis, Oscar 227f., 232, 317
Lichtenberger, James Pendelton 44, 66f., 69, 88, 91, 93
Lindsay, Malvina 168f., 177, 181
Livermore, Mary A. 57–59
Lombardo, Paul A. 134
Lokteff, Lana 4
Luhmann, Niklas 19
Lundberg, Ferdinand 37, 177, 185
Lynd, Helen Merrell 107
Lynd, Robert S. 107
Lynn, Lacey 4

Martschukat, Jürgen 25, 29–31, 99, 401, 408
Maslow, Adam 18
Masters, William 184, 276
Mauch, Christoph 35
Maudsley, Henry 115
Maulsby, Ann 166
McCormick, Katharine 277
McCorvey, Norma 295
McGrory, Mary 245
McKissick, Floyd Bixler 246, 251
Mead, Margaret 37, 154, 158, 276, 305f., 312, 315f., 328, 331, 333, 345
Meyer, Agnes E. 178f.
Meyerowitz, Joanne 31, 158, 170, 173, 183, 408
Millett, Kate 292
Mills, C. Wright 155
Montague, Ashley 158
Moore, Hugh 306
Moxom, Philip Stafford 57f.
Moyers, Bill 245, 340
Moynihan, Daniel Patrick 37, 228, 231, 233, 319
Muggeridge, Malcolm 365
Murray, Pauli 288
Myrdal, Gunnar 210, 221, 226, 237

Nathanson, Bernhard 369
Nixon, Richard 34, 173, 255, 340
Norris, George W. 81
Nye, Francis Ivan 191f., 196

O'Neill, William 83, 93
Olivo, Roxanne 303

Omolade, Barbara 342
Owen, Robert Dale 53

Park, Robert Ezra 218, 221
Parry, Carl E. 70f.
Parsons, Elise Clews 72, 74
Parsons, Talcott 8f., 155, 269, 388, 404
Patel, Kiran Klaus 35
Payton, Daniel 250
Peabody, Francis G. 84f.
Perlman Shafton, Marjorie 1
Pernick, Martin S. 137
Pettibone, Brittany 4
Phelan, Lana C. 291
Phelps, Elizabeth Stuart 57
Pitt, Ed 341
Plant, Rebecca 176, 408
Popenoe, Paul B. 37, 96, 101, 129, 131f., 138–152, 172, 309, 316, 397, 400, 402
Potter, Henry Codman 57f.
Powell, Brian 10

Raderia, Shalinia 35
Rainwater, Lee 261
Raphael, Lutz 26f., 42, 158, 257, 259, 408
Rausch, James S. 272
Reagan, Ronald 34, 37, 156, 284, 320, 324, 330f., 333, 335f., 352f., 356, 364–367, 369, 375, 377, 393, 399
Riesman, David 155
Riley, Glenda 63, 93
Rinehart, Mary Ella Roberts 177
Roberts, Dorothy 321
Robertson, Pat 6
Robinson, Patricia 266f., 321
Rockefeller, John D. 309
Rödder, Andreas 16, 21, 408
Roosevelt, Eleanore 99
Roosevelt, Theodore 46, 61, 78–80
Rosaldo, Michelle 23
Rose, Arnold Marshall 227, 237
Ross, Edward Alsworth 44, 66f., 78, 91, 93, 130, 141
Ross, Edward E. 37, 397
Ross, Loretta 324
Rossi, Alice S. 197f.
Rossiter, Margaret 127

Roth, Benita 266
Rustin, Bayard 237, 246, 251, 253
Ryan, William 250
Ryback, Timothy 119

Sanger, Margaret 277, 301, 313
Scarbrough, Elinor 16
Schlafly, Phyllis 292–294, 351, 382, 395
Schlapp, Max G. 116
Schoen, Johanna 296, 298, 408
Schreiner, Olive 76
Scott, James C. 34
Scott, Joan W. 22, 150
Self, Robert O. 30
Sheppard, Harold L. 242
Sherbon, Dr. Florence Brown 125–127
Siegel, Alberta Engvall 189
Small, Albion Woodbury 70, 93
Smith, Walter George 62, 80
Sontag, Lester Warren 177
Spalding, Elizabeth Coxe 327
Spencer, Anna Garlin 71, 74, 77
Spencer, Herbert 67
Spock, Benjamin 106
Stanton, Elisabeth Cady 53, 75
Strecker, Edward 174f.
Steelmann, Lala Carr 10
Stein, Marc 279, 296
Stein, Robert 194
Steinbeck, John 172f.
Stern, Alexandra Minna 4, 98, 125
Stern, Elizabeth 380
Stern, William 380
Stoddard, Lothrop Theodore 118f.
Stolz, Lois Meek 189, 196
Sullivan, Harry Stack 158
Sumner, William Graham 40–42, 70

Thome, Helmut 19
Tietze, Christopher 308f., 316, 321
Tosh, John 25
Tucker, James 348, 351

Verba, Sidney 17
Vogt, William A. 310

Wade, Henry 295
Wallace, Alfred Russel 115
Ward, Allison 381
Watts, Mary Tirell 125–127
Weddington, Sarah 295
Wells, Kate Gannett 75
Welskopp, Thomas 35f.
Wendt, Simon 265, 408
West, Mary Mills 112
Wexler, Anne 349
White, Edward Franklin 79
Whitehead, Mary Beth 380f.
Wilkinson, Maguerite 76f., 80
Wilson, Richard 245
Wood, Robert 273
Woods, Howard B. 204
Wright, Carroll D. 46
Wright, Margaret 268
Wylie, Philip 174–176
Wyzanski Jr., Charles Edward 227

Young, Andrew 262
Young, Whitney M. 237, 249

Zaretsky, Natasha 30, 408
Ziegler, Mary 296

Subject Index

A. Philip Randolph Institute (AFL-CIO) 251
Abortion
- Abortion 1–3, 5, 12f., 15, 34, 37–39, 52, 150, 196, 270–276, 284–287, 289–292, 294–308, 315f. 320, 322f., 328–330, 332f., 338, 345–347, 349f., 353, 357–377, 379f., 384–387, 391–395, 398f., 401, 403f.
- Abortion clinics 284, 294, 296–298, 301, 303, 332, 361
- Abortion providers 298f.
- Abortion rights 37, 275, 302, 305, 308, 333, 366–369, 374
- Therapeutic Abortion Act 363
- First trimester abortion 3, 12, 329, 353
Affirmative action 332, 360
African American
- African American colleges 216
- African American family 28, 37, 203, 205, 207–210, 217, 237, 241, 243–245, 247, 249f., 252f., 257f., 269, 340, 343, 396, 398f., 402
- African American women 38, 50, 105, 160–162, 165, 184, 199, 201, 203f., 206, 208, 211f., 214, 266f., 269f., 281, 317, 319, 321–323, 345, 360, 397, 402f.
- African Americans 50, 102, 108, 136, 150, 202f., 211f., 218–220, 222f., 225f., 228f., 231f., 238f., 248, 252, 254f., 258, 260f., 320, 336, 339, 350, 387, 389, 390
Aid to Families with Dependent Children (AFDC) 100f., 240f., 259, 319, 322, 334–336, 338–340, 345, 349, 359f.
American
- American Century 36
- American Creed 223, 225
- American Dilemma 210, 221–226, 229, 237
- American Eugenics Society 37, 101, 117, 120, 126, 148, 159, 280
- American exceptionalism 36
- American Home Economics Association 346
- American Journal of Sociology 226
- American Sociological Association (ASA) 40, 44, 64, 73
- Americanism 36
- Americanization 14, 95, 319

America's Waiting Children (report) 384
Amicus curiae brief 381f.
Anthropologist 16, 23, 34, 37, 72, 115, 118, 154f., 228, 305, 312, 328, 331, 345
Anti-abortion movement 284, 298f., 305, 364
Archbishop 272
Artificial insemination 274, 310
Association for Voluntary Sterilization (AVS) 280, 306, 316
Atlanta University Negro Conference 218

Baby boom 14, 31, 46, 104f., 156, 183, 193, 197, 206, 212
Baby M. Case 378
Baby planning beads 311
Bauer-Report 356f., 359, 362
Biopolitics 158
Birth/s
- Birth control 134, 240, 267, 274, 277f., 280, 286f., 291, 307–311, 313f., 316, 328, 330, 347, 367, 393
- Birth control movement 277, 280
- Birth rate/s 61, 78, 80, 99, 105, 110, 131, 152, 193, 194, 206, 211, 212, 214, 266, 281, 305f., 315, 322, 395
Black
- Black family pathologies 208f., 211, 253
- Black Family Project 342
- Black Feminism 3
- Black genocide 266, 322
- Black hyperfertility 211
- Black hypermasculinity 264, 270, 402
- Black nationalism 266
- Black Panther Party 264
- Black Power movement 38, 209, 263–269, 322, 393, 401–403
Boston Women's Health Book Collective (BWHBC) 37, 297, 323
Brown vs. Board of Education 106, 214, 229, 261
Bureau of the Census 46, 161, 164

Can this Marriage be Saved? (newspaper column) 139, 172

Subject Index

California 49, 51, 98f., 131f., 135f., 139f., 142, 144, 146, 152, 204, 245, 324–326, 336, 363
California Family Law Act 324
Catholic Church 56, 61, 82, 135, 271, 282, 296, 298, 303
Catholic press 272
CBS 271–273, 302f., 340
Census
– Census data 194
– Census Report 193
Center for Disease Control and Prevention (CDC) 282, 284
Chicago School of Sociology 218, 221
Chicago Tribune 137, 159, 168
Children
– Childlessness 152, 187, 218, 313
– Upbringing / parenting 106, 109, 158, 190, 362
Christian Coalition of America (CCA) 6
Civil Rights Act 195f., 214, 231, 287
Civil rights movement 38, 204, 209f., 225, 227, 229, 241, 243, 246, 249, 251, 254f., 260, 262–265, 288, 305, 314, 393, 397f., 402
Cold War 31, 152, 156, 161, 163, 173, 184, 347, 392, 399
Commercial 272
Commission on the Status of Women 285f.
Comstock Laws 278
Conceptions of social order 27
Concerned United Birthparents (CUB) 37, 333, 363, 376, 378
Concerned Women for America 382
Congress on Racial Equality (CORE) 246, 251
Constitutional Amendment 55, 81, 90, 286, 300, 364
Consumer culture 159, 163, 178
Contraception 15, 38, 267f., 270, 274, 279, 282, 287, 291, 300, 306–309, 314–316, 320, 322, 328, 341, 346, 359, 367, 391, 395, 402f.
Contraceptive/s 276–279, 281–284, 286f., 290, 307, 310–312, 314, 321, 329, 346f., 394, 397f., 401
Counselor 37, 96, 138f., 142, 146, 151f. 344, 400
Crisis Pregnancy Center 384
Culture of poverty 228, 232, 317
Culture wars 5, 22, 34, 39, 330–332, 333, 352, 386f.

Demographers 183, 193f., 201, 206, 390, 393, 396, 400
Demography 27, 184, 394
Department of Health and Human Services 284
Department of Labor 46, 95, 111, 117, 162, 169, 205, 233
Depo-Provera 283
Dispositif / dispositive 27, 29, 33, 315, 388
Divorce
– Divorce 5f., 12–15, 32–34, 37–41, 43–71, 73–93, 108–110, 144, 147f., 152, 157, 161, 166, 179, 185, 206f., 211, 338, 345, 350, 353, 360, 386, 388–390, 392–394, 396f., 400, 402, 404f.
– Divorce debate 44, 52, 59f., 73f., 90, 207, 326, 392, 402, 404f.
– Divorce laws 47, 54, 62–64, 74f., 80–83, 90, 325, 327, 350, 394
Dobbs v. Jackson Women's Health Center 2
Double jeopardy 208, 210, 269, 403
Dual earner family 163, 165, 333, 353, 386

Eagle Forum 294, 351, 382
Ebony 159, 202f., 205
Economic crisis 30, 33, 96, 98f., 392
Economic Opportunity Act 230
Employment 38
Enovid 276
Equal Rights Amendment (ERA) 34, 196, 286, 301, 366, 395
Eugenics
– Eugenics 37, 73f., 96, 101, 110, 119, 121f., 127, 130f., 132, 138, 140, 142, 148, 151f., 306, 309, 400, 404
– Eugenics Movement 76f., 79, 94–96, 101, 110, 115, 117–119, 126f., 131, 148f., 151f., 158, 201, 280, 328, 395, 397, 400
– Eugenics Quarterly 159, 201
Executive Order 329, 358f.
Expert
– Expert advice 12, 27, 79, 109f., 169, 352, 397f., 402
– Expert cultures 22, 26
– Expert discourses 6, 11–13, 32, 37, 117, 154f., 159, 205, 275, 292, 329, 388f., 391, 394, 396, 400, 403

Subject Index — **493**

Family
- Family adoption program 339, 342f.
- Family adoption training 344
- Family as the basis of the nation 6, 13, 150, 292, 391, 396, 398
- Family assistance plan (FAP) 340
- Family, golden age of the 5, 31, 156, 178, 399
- Family, healthy 117, 147, 311, 398, 404
- Family, heteronormative nuclear 5
- Family home 163, 217
- Family ideal 7, 11f., 30–33, 36–38, 43, 74 88, 92, 104, 127, 158, 168, 206, 208–210, 253, 266, 269, 323, 329, 353, 388, 396–398, 400f., 404
- Family ideology 192
- Family, modern isolated nuclear 8f., 157, 269, 388, 397, 399
- Family, nuclear 5, 7–10, 12, 14, 26, 30, 33, 101, 104, 128, 157, 171, 178, 183, 200, 206f., 258, 269, 306, 310, 316, 322, 327, 339, 341, 353, 357f., 386f., 388, 391, 393f., 396f., 399, 401, 404
- Family policy 39, 114, 141, 143, 254f., 333, 353, 357–360, 386
- Family Protection Act 359
- Family Research Council 382
- Family sociologists 10, 66
- Family support act 357, 359f.
- Family values 1f., 5–7, 10–15, 28–32, 34, 38–41, 63, 92, 101, 108, 128, 152f., 155, 159, 180f., 207, 240, 249, 253, 255, 258f., 262, 267, 275, 311, 317, 319, 322, 324, 330, 332f., 335, 340f., 345, 352f., 355f., 359, 361, 364, 377, 382, 386, 388f., 392f., 400–402, 407
- Family: Preserving America's Future, The (report) 356
Father knows best (sitcom) 156
Fatherhood 14, 30, 107, 156, 265, 353, 407
Fathers 29f., 40, 99f., 107, 155, 169, 171, 182, 220, 222, 234, 240f., 253, 263f., 270, 323, 340f., 346, 359, 363
Female employment/employment of women/ maternal employment 38, 73, 76, 78, 93
Feminine Mystique, The (monograph) 191, 196–198, 200f., 203
Femininity 12, 173, 203, 208

Feminists 12, 24, 71, 73–75, 157, 191, 196, 199f., 206, 210, 263, 266, 268, 271, 296, 303, 305f., 327, 369, 379
Fertility 1, 102, 105, 151, 159, 184, 187, 193f., 201, 205, 211, 280–282, 310f., 315, 321
Fetus 286, 304, 361–364, 369
First-trimester procedures 364
Fitter family contest/s 120, 122, 124f., 127, 129, 136, 152, 395, 398
Focus on the Family (FOTF) 5
Food and Drug Administration 278
Forced sterilization 114, 135–137, 139, 320, 392, 395–397, 400, 404
Ford Foundation 259, 310

Gender
- Gender concept/s / conceptions 31, 190, 209
- Gender hierarchy 7, 192
- Gender relation/s 13, 31, 88, 253, 289, 294, 329, 393, 403
- Gender relationship 329
- Gender roles 4, 42, 59f., 90, 94, 99, 109, 113, 127, 136, 140f., 146f., 150, 156f., 159, 169, 178f., 188, 191, 200, 206f., 265, 267, 275, 279, 292f., 295, 305, 322, 352f., 359, 386, 389, 393, 396–398, 402, 404f.
- Gender studies 22–25
Generation of Vipers 174, 176
Gestational Surrogacy 380
Ghetto/s 216f., 231f., 234, 239f., 245–248, 253, 255, 259, 261f., 312, 319, 393
GI Bill of Rights / Servicemen's Readjustment Act 156, 216
Good housekeeping 159, 170, 182
Governmentality 30
Governor 135, 324, 336, 363
Grassroots Movement 34, 275, 305, 308, 330, 391
Great Society 230, 358, 399
Griswold vs. Connecticut 278
Guttmacher Institute 283

Harvard University 84, 118, 227, 243, 255, 259, 261, 408
Heartbeat bills 2
Historically black colleges and universities (HBCUs) 231

History
- Contemporary history 15, 17, 20, 407
- Discursive history 21
- History of mentalities 21
- Media history 21
- Social/economic history 15, 28, 92, 155, 333f., 352, 407f.
Homosexuality 158, 332
Housewife/wives 117, 166, 169, 171, 173–175, 178, 180, 183, 190, 198, 200, 202–204, 206, 294, 327, 346, 350, 402
Housework 145, 160, 166f., 177, 190f., 193
Howard University 228, 231, 233, 250, 254
Human genetics 310f.
Human Life Review 364
Human sciences 27, 44, 257
Human scientists 26, 316
Hyde Amendment 321f., 368

Illegitimacy 218, 220, 224, 234, 237, 247, 260, 274
Immigrant families 7, 14, 32, 100
Individual 4, 6, 11, 13, 16, 19, 27, 43, 57, 59, 69f., 78, 81, 84f., 88, 101, 110, 128, 130, 152, 158, 256, 321, 343, 355, 358, 373, 391
Individual rights / right of the individual 3, 33, 330, 332, 358, 387, 395, 400 / 43, 373
Industrial society 6, 8f., 17, 88, 155
Infertility 186
Intersectionality 22–24

Jet 159, 205, 249
Johnson era 229, 253
Joint Center for Urban Studies 243, 259
Journalist/s 1, 6, 12f., 76, 151, 157, 166–168, 174, 178f., 185, 195, 197, 233, 245f., 251, 300, 317f., 340, 397
Jurist/s / lawyer/s 12, 52, 59, 62, 73f., 75, 80f., 85, 89, 93, 134, 277, 292, 295, 321, 325f., 364, 379, 381, 383
Juvenile delinquency 14, 106f., 177, 181f., 185, 220, 238, 240, 252, 263, 318f.

Kitchen debate 173
Knowledge 14, 26f., 86, 91, 109–111, 114, 125, 141, 143f., 196, 257, 310f., 316, 331, 346f., 388, 391f., 395, 398

Ladies' Home Journal 289
Late-term abortion 364
Leave it to Beaver (sitcom) 156
Levittown 9, 217
LGBTQIA+ 4
Liberalism 30
Liberalization 10f., 20, 31, 33, 38, 51, 64f., 72, 274, 278, 350, 353, 386, 402f., 405,
- Liberalization of divorce law/s 51, 64
- Liberalization of sexual morality 10, 31
- Liberalization of West Germany 20

Magazine/s 12, 37, 44, 159, 170, 194, 197, 209, 378, 404
Male breadwinner 12, 30, 99, 163, 165, 246, 258, 317, 322, 333, 335, 339, 342, 353, 357, 386, 390, 398f., 401, 403
March for Life 298, 301
Market economy 30, 45, 357
Marriage
- Marriage 38, 43, 45–53, 56, 58–71, 73–77, 79–82, 84, 87, 89, 91, 93, 99, 113, 116f., 121, 131, 138–144, 146f., 151f., 171, 177, 179–181, 189–191, 193, 224, 279, 294, 297, 327, 335, 340, 400, 402
- Marriage counseling 71, 139, 141, 147, 169, 346, 396f., 402
- Marriage counselor 37, 96, 139, 142, 146, 151
Masculinity/ies
- Hypermasculinity 264, 270, 329, 402
- Hegemonic masculinity 12, 25, 208, 265, 403
- Masculinity ideal 25, 209, 265, 267, 398
Massachusetts Institute of Technology 259
Materialists/post-materialists 18
Matriarchy 175, 204, 247, 268f., 402
Media 5, 12f., 43, 157, 208f., 214, 302, 348, 397, 401
Medicaid 230, 322, 372
Medicare 230
Mexican American families/families of Mexicandescent 32, 104, 288, 317
Mexican American Women 164, 199, 275, 283, 323, 395
Middle class/es 11f., 14, 31f., 73, 78, 99, 100, 114, 117, 128, 144, 152, 156, 163, 178, 188, 190, 193, 202, 216, 220f., 235, 238, 245f., 252, 254, 258, 262, 288, 361, 400

Middletown 107f.
Migrants / Immigrants 12, 48, 78, 96–98, 103, 116, 217
Miltown 188
Modernity
- Entangled modernities 35
- Multiple modernities 35
- Highly modern / cutting-edge 152, 392
- Modern society 19, 40, 42, 66, 68, 73, 76, 85, 87, 89, 115, 150, 186, 220, 260, 313, 325, 331, 352, 362, 393, 395
- Postmodernity 20
Modernization
- Modernization of Western societies 20
- Modernization theory 35, 276
Momism 174–176, 178, 180, 185, 269
Mother/s, motherhood
- All-American Mom 175
- Moral motherhood 176
- Scientific motherhood 95, 109, 111, 115, 117, 151, 392, 398
- Mother/s / single mother 199, 211–213, 216, 234f., 240, 258, 263, 318, 322, 335f., 338, 340–242, 344f., 353, 355, 358, 377, 384, 386, 389f., 392
- Maternity 113, 141
- Mother role 158, 362, 381
- Mother's little helper 188
- Motherhood 13, 29f., 38, 60, 95f., 101, 108–117, 136, 138, 143, 145, 151, 154–156, 158f., 162, 170, 174, 176–178, 183, 185–189, 196, 198, 201, 206, 270, 340, 362, 384, 390, 392, 398, 407
Moynihan-Report 210–212, 225, 227f., 230, 233, 238f., 243, 245, 247, 249, 250, 252, 257f., 261, 263f., 268f., 312, 340, 357
#MeToo 4

NARAL MASS Choice 37, 333
Narcotics 188
Nation 6f., 11–13, 27, 30–33, 37f., 88, 95f., 106, 129, 140f., 150–152, 171, 175, 177, 185, 232, 248, 251, 266, 292, 313f., 317, 326, 328, 335, 338, 353, 362–364, 386–400
Nation of Islam 266, 314
National Abortion Rights Action League (NARAL) 37, 275, 302, 333, 366

National Adoption Week 375f.
National Association for the Advancement of colored people (NAACP) 129, 241, 314
National Birthparents Week 378
National Catholic Conference 272
National Catholic Conference of Bishops 300
National Committee for Adoption (NCFA) 385
National Conference on Families 39
National Conference on Family Life 345
National Fertility Study 281
National Organization of Women (NOW) 196, 275, 365, 395
- NOW Bill of Rights 286f.
- NOW Task Force on Family Life 287
- NOW Task Force on Marriage, Divorce, and Family Relations 327
- NOW Task Force on Reproduction and its Control 290, 296
National Sanctity of Human Life Day 365
National Urban League 249, 341
National Welfare Rights Organization (NWRO) 339
Negro Family in America, The (Moynihan-Report) 217
Neurosis 166f., 183, 185, 187, 206
Neurotic 166, 177, 185
New Christian Right 34, 332, 360
New Deal 100, 106, 151, 241, 399
New York Times (NYT) 1, 37, 101, 116f., 134, 159, 166, 168, 225, 229, 244, 252, 271, 273, 288, 296, 325, 375
Newsweek 244
No-Fault divorce 34, 49, 52, 324–326, 329, 360, 389, 390, 394, 402, 404f.
Norms
- Gender norms 6, 9–12, 16, 22–25, 29f., 32, 38, 108, 152, 172f., 178, 182, 191, 209, 269, 328f., 332, 345, 377, 382, 388f., 391, 395, 398f., 402f.
- Social norms 16, 194
Norplant 284, 321

Office of Economic Opportunity (OEO) 242
Operation Rescue 361
Our Bodies, Ourselves 297, 323
Ozzie and Harriet (sitcom) 156

Part-time work 38, 163, 181f., 207, 346, 390, 393, 396
Patchwork families 5, 7, 9, 31, 51
Pathology 210, 221, 223f., 228, 234, 239, 245f., 357, 396
Patriarchy 25, 292
People for the American Way (PFAW) 6, 294
Personal Responsibility and Work Opportunity Reconciliation Act (PRWORA) 334, 339
Planned Parenthood Federation of America (PPFA) 276, 279, 309, 367f., 370
Political Action Committee (PAC) 302
Poor People's Campaign 255f.
Population
– Population control 3, 149, 276, 281, 306, 308f.
– Population Control Movement 37, 276, 305f., 309
– Population Council (PC) 276, 281, 307, 309, 311, 321
– Population Crisis Committee 308, 312
– Population dispositive 315
– Population expert/s 305, 308f., 322, 329
– Population explosion 280
– Population growth 38, 46, 51, 102, 104, 108, 150, 276, 279, 280, 291, 305–308, 311–316, 398, 404
– Population Institute 307f., 316
– Population Oriented Organization People (POOP) 308
– Population policy 27, 184, 243, 275, 306, 310–312, 314, 316, 328, 397f., 404
– Population Reference Bureau (PRB) 307–312, 316
– Population scientist 148, 276
Processes
– Process/es of individualization 35, 65, 73, 85, 93
– Process/es of liberalization 11, 33, 65, 274, 353, 405
– Process/es of modernization 35
– Process/es of pluralization 11, 33, 93, 353
– Process/es of scientification 11, 26
Progressive Era 13, 40, 43, 46, 48, 65, 106, 206, 389, 394, 404
Pro-life movement 369, 377, 404
Protest movement 30f., 106, 157, 205, 275, 331
Proud Boys 4

Psyche
– Psyche 121, 183, 185, 205
– Psychoanalysis 188
– Psychoses 193
– Psychotropic drugs 188
Public debates 6f., 11–13, 32, 37, 52, 64, 101, 154f., 157, 278, 303, 329, 338, 388f.
Puerto Rico 279

Race
– Race riots 227, 244, 255, 319
– Race suicide 78, 96, 109, 151, 184, 306, 389, 399
Racial discrimination 3, 160, 165, 209, 221f., 227, 230, 239, 243, 283, 393, 394
Readers' letters 12, 157, 169, 180, 183, 204, 245, 271
Reagan Era 39, 360, 405
Redlining 216f.
Religious Coalition for Abortion Rights (RCAR) 308, 367
Representative of the (Catholic/Episcopal) Church 61, 82, 89
Reproduction / reproductive
– Reproduction (human) 3, 5–7, 12–15, 32f, 37–39, 75, 89, 91, 96, 102, 108f, 114f, 119, 121–124, 130–132, 136, 140f, 150–153, 157f, 183f, 201f, 205–207, 271, 275f, 278f, 285, 289–291, 296f, 300f, 305f, 310, 316f, 320f, 328–331, 350, 372, 387–392, 395–397, 400–404
– Reproductive biology 188, 277
– Reproductive choice 3, 38, 271, 285, 328, 367, 387, 395, 402, 404
– Reproductive control 270, 274f., 280, 290f., 294, 306, 322f., 328f., 346
– Reproductive Health Equity Act 368
– Reproductive justice 3, 324
– Reproductive medicine 186, 400
– Reproductive rights 3, 37–39, 96, 150, 271, 283, 285, 298, 307, 316f., 321f., 350, 365, 367, 375, 397
Resurrection City 255–257
Right
– Right to life of the fetus/embryo/unborn (child) 2, 33f., 304, 350, 361f., 363, 364f., 391, 400, 403
– Right to privacy 278, 295, 297

Rockefeller Foundation 309
Roe vs. Wade 2f., 274, 295–297, 307, 329, 353, 355, 364f., 367, 371

Same-sex couples 5, 7, 51
Scientification
- Scientification of child-rearing and motherhood 110
- Scientification of the social 26f., 42, 158, 210, 257–259, 391, 397
Second World War 155, 159, 316
Self-made men 209
Senate Subcommittee on Constitutional Amendments on Abortion 301
Servicemen's Readjustment Act/GI Bill of Rights 156, 216
Sex and the single girl (monograph) 278
Sexism 25, 265, 288
Sexual revolution/s 31, 204, 273, 276, 279, 287, 358
Sexuality 5, 16, 26, 144, 147, 179, 184, 270, 276, 278f., 328, 402
Silent majority 34
Silent No More (NARAL-Campaign) 369, 372, 374f.
Silent scream, The (film) 304, 369f.
Single-family home 216
Sitcom/s 156, 353, 399, 407
Sisterhood of Black Single Mothers 342
Slavery 60, 204, 218, 220, 223f., 228, 232, 234, 238
Social
- Social engineering 27, 42, 144, 158, 210, 222, 229, 251, 258, 260–262, 269, 343, 345, 397f.
- Social experts 7, 12f., 26f., 31, 37f., 44, 92, 95f., 104, 126f., 138, 150, 152, 157–159, 164, 167, 185, 193, 202, 210f., 225, 249, 251, 257f., 262, 269f., 275f., 315, 319, 326, 387–390, 392, 395–397, 401–404
- Social history 15, 28, 92, 155, 333f., 352, 407f.
- Social movement 9, 12, 34, 37, 330, 361, 377, 387, 392, 396f., 402
- Social politician/s 252f.
- Social reform 33, 106, 109, 151, 218, 251
- Social reformers 12, 42, 58, 89, 91, 104, 110, 124
- Social science research on value change 17
- Social scientists 6, 10, 12, 19, 21, 28, 38, 42f., 52, 63, 66, 69, 76, 81, 87f., 92f., 107, 109f., 157, 174, 196, 201, 206, 209f., 217, 221, 226, 232, 242, 253, 260f., 269, 328f., 392, 395f., 398, 401
- Social statistics 31, 51, 54f., 109, 128, 259, 386
- Social technologies 27, 398
Sociology 21, 40–42, 63, 66f., 69f., 130, 189, 218, 221f., 226, 242f., 250, 253, 261, 389, 394
Sociologist/s 10, 12, 19, 25, 40–44, 52, 63f., 66, 68f., 71, 73f., 88, 91, 93, 107f., 135, 191, 193, 210, 217–220, 222, 226, 235, 325f., 392
Southern Christian Leadership Conference (SCLC) 37, 247, 342
Soviet Union 172f.
Sterilization
- Sterilization 3, 38, 97, 101, 114, 119, 129, 131–140, 142, 151f., 274f., 280, 282f., 300, 306f., 316, 320f., 328–330, 392, 395–397, 400, 403–405
- Sterilization (eugenic) 97, 101, 129, 131f., 142
- Sterilization policy 114, 135
Stop ERA-movement 292, 294
Student movements 329
Student Non-Violent Coordinating Committee (SNCC) 314
Suburbia 31, 197, 217
Suffragettes 75, 291
Supreme Court 1f., 12, 34, 37, 51, 133, 135, 137, 152, 272f., 294–298, 300, 304, 308, 362, 364, 366f., 380f., 395f., 399
Surrogacy 380f.
Survey/s 18f., 20f., 41, 47, 107, 162, 174, 191, 222, 282, 336, 367f.

Tangle of Pathology 221, 228, 234, 239
Teenage mothers 340f., 387, 394
Temporary assistance for needy families (TANF) 334
To Fulfill These Rights (conference) 230, 249
Trad[itional] wives 4f.

Ultrasound images 369
Underclass 246, 317–319, 337
University
- University of Atlanta 217f.
- University of Kansas 126, 278

– Wesleyan University 243
Uplift ideology 202

Valium 188
Value(s)
– Historical research on value change 17, 21f., 26
– Traditional family values 13, 34, 128, 152, 267, 333, 335, 345, 352f., 361, 364, 392
– Value change 15–22, 171, 333, 391, 403–405
– Values, change in 11, 15, 17–20, 22, 63, 274, 325, 328, 330, 341, 388, 390, 392, 400, 404
Vanishing Family: Crisis in Black America, The (film) 340
Veteran 216, 308
Victorian domesticity 176
Vietnam War 30, 252, 393
Visualization 120, 273
Voting Rights Act 214, 231

Wage labor 76, 160, 163, 167, 178, 206, 359f., 390, 401
War on poverty 210, 240, 243, 259, 317, 339, 393
Washington Post (WP) 37, 101, 134, 136, 159, 168f., 177, 179–181, 195, 244, 251, 296, 311, 375
Washington Star 244f.
Watts, Los Angeles 227, 242, 244, 248f., 263
Welfare
– Welfare moms 319, 333
– Welfare program 100, 241, 322, 350, 360
– Welfare queen 320, 335f., 387, 391
– Welfare Rights Movement 339, 345, 401
West 19f., 36, 47, 125, 325
– Western Europe 36, 105
– Westernization 20
White House Conference on Families / National Conference on Families 39, 330f., 345, 348, 351, 358, 393

Wings of hope 342f.
Woman / Women
– Woman's Foundation, The 346
– Womanhood 72, 185, 188
– Women exploited by abortions (WEBA) 375
– Woman, healthy 68, 116
– Women work/Women's work 6, 12–15, 37f., 116, 171f., 176, 178, 168, 180–183, 185, 193–195, 201f., 205f.
– Women's Army Corps (WAC) 203
– Women's clubs / New York state federation of Women's clubs 75, 79, 110, 134, 175, 177
– Women's decision-making rights 2
– Women's education 96, 111, 159, 198
– Women's health movement 297, 392
– Women's liberation movement 268, 291f., 402
– Women's movement 3, 22, 38, 45, 74–76, 91, 150f., 153, 196, 205f., 268, 270, 273, 279, 285, 289–292, 296f., 305f., 323, 326, 328f., 357, 359f., 362f., 365f., 370, 374, 377, 386f., 390–392, 394f., 397, 400–402
– Women's National Abortion Action Coalition (WONAAC) 290
– Women's suffrage 42, 75, 90, 151, 157, 206, 402
– Working women 117, 154, 159, 163, 170, 172, 181, 183, 185, 193f., 201, 203, 205
Working-class / Working class 7, 32, 108, 111, 113, 117, 182, 199, 206, 249, 254, 262, 361, 390, 400

Young people 68f., 76, 84, 91, 99, 106, 142f., 195, 234, 239, 344

Zero Population Growth / Zero Population Growth Movement (ZPG) 38, 150, 276, 291, 305, 30

www.ingramcontent.com/pod-product-compliance
Lightning Source LLC
Chambersburg PA
CBHW031720230426
43669CB00007B/193